D1570025

WORD
BIBLICAL
COMMENTARY

WORD
BIBLICAL
COMMENTARY

VOLUME 27

Jeremiah 26–52

GERALD L. KEOWN

PAMELA J. SCALISE

THOMAS G. SMOTHERS

WORD BOOKS, PUBLISHER · DALLAS, TEXAS

Word Biblical Commentary
JEREMIAH 26–52
Copyright © 1995 by Word, Incorporated

Library of Congress Cataloging-in-Publication Data
Main entry under title:

Word biblical commentary.

    Includes bibliographies.
    1. Bible—Commentaries—Collected works.
BS491.2.W67   220.7'7   81-71768
ISBN 0–8499–0226–6 (vol. 27) AACR2

Printed in the United States of America

Scripture quotations in the body of the text are the authors' own unless otherwise designated. The authors' own translation of the text appears in italic type under the heading *Translation.*

56789 AGF 987654321

In memoriam
Peter C. Craigie
(1938–1988)

Contents

Foreword

Because of the tragic and untimely death of Peter Craigie in September 1988, the editors of the Word Biblical Commentary decided to use multiple authors to complete the work Craigie had begun on the commentary on the book of Jeremiah. Sections of Jeremiah not treated by Craigie were divided among five authors who, at the time, were colleagues in the Old Testament Department at The Southern Baptist Theological Seminary. The division of labor followed the discernible organization of the book of Jeremiah as closely as that could be determined, with the notable exception that all material completed by Craigie was used. The dividing line between the first and second volumes corresponds well to a recognizable break point between chaps. 25 and 26 in the book of Jeremiah itself.

The first volume of the commentary on Jeremiah (WBC 26) identified the book of Jeremiah as an "anthology of anthologies" that in many respects defies any attempt to reconstruct an organizing principle for the shaping of the book (xxxii). At the same time, some internal clues do exist that may aid in any attempt to develop an outline of the book. In the second volume, we have divided chaps. 26–52 into three sections on the basis of clues within the text.

For the second volume, Pamela Scalise prepared the material for Jer 26–34. The Jeremianic message of the new covenant and its accompanying texts are the focus of this segment of the book. Gerald Keown was responsible for Jer 35–45 and Jer 52. Thomas Smothers treated the oracles against the nations in Jer 46–51.

Specific information related to the organization of the book will be discussed under the *Form/Structure/Setting* headings of the appropriate sections of the commentary. The Introduction of the first volume contains a fuller treatment of the overall questions related to the book of Jeremiah.

JOHN D. W. WATTS
DAVID A. HUBBARD

Editorial Preface

The launching of the *Word Biblical Commentary* brings to fulfillment an enterprise of several years' planning. The publishers and the members of the editorial board met in 1977 to explore the possibility of a new commentary on the books of the Bible that would incorporate several distinctive features. Prospective readers of these volumes are entitled to know what such features were intended to be; whether the aims of the commentary have been fully achieved time alone will tell.

First, we have tried to cast a wide net to include as contributors a number of scholars from around the world who not only share our aims but are in the main engaged in the ministry of teaching in university, college, and seminary. They represent a rich diversity of denominational allegiance. The broad stance of our contributors can rightly be called evangelical, and this term is to be understood in its positive, historic sense of a commitment to Scripture as divine revelation, and to the truth and power of the Christian gospel.

Then, the commentaries in our series are all commissioned and written for the purpose of inclusion in the Word Biblical Commentary. Unlike several of our distinguished counterparts in the field of commentary writing, there are no translated works, originally written in a non-English language. Also, our commentators were asked to prepare their own rendering of the original biblical text and to use those languages as the basis of their own comments and exegesis. What may be claimed as distinctive with this series is that it is based on the biblical languages, yet it seeks to make the technical and scholarly approach to a theological understanding of Scripture understandable by—and useful to—the fledgling student, the working minister, and colleagues in the guild of professional scholars and teachers as well.

Finally, a word must be said about the format of the series. The layout, in clearly defined sections, has been consciously devised to assist readers at different levels. Those wishing to learn about the textual witnesses on which the translation is offered are invited to consult the section headed *Notes*. If the readers' concern is with the state of modern scholarship on any given portion of Scripture, they should turn to the sections of *Bibliography* and *Form/Structure/Setting*. For a clear exposition of the passage's meaning and its relevance to the ongoing biblical revelation, the *Comment* and concluding *Explanation* are designed expressly to meet that need. There is therefore something for everyone who may pick up and use these volumes.

If these aims come anywhere near realization, the intention of the editors will have been met, and the labor of our team of contributors rewarded.

General Editors: *David A. Hubbard*
Glenn W. Barker †
Old Testament: *John D. W. Watts*
New Testament: *Ralph P. Martin*

Abbreviations

PERIODICALS, SERIALS, AND REFERENCE WORKS

AAS	*Acta apostolicae sedis*
AASF	Annales Academic Scientarum Fennicae
AASOR	Annual of the American Schools of Oriental Research
AB	Anchor Bible
ABD	*Anchor Bible Dictionary*
AbrN	*Abr-Nahrain*
AcOr	*Acta orientalia*
ADAJ	Annual of the Department of Antiquities of Jordan
AfO	*Archiv für Orientforschung*
AGJU	Arbeiten zur Geschichte des antiken Judentums und des Urchristentums
AHW	W. von Soden, *Akkadisches Handwörterbuch*
AJA	*American Journal of Archaeology*
AJAS	*American Journal of Arabic Studies*
AJBA	*Australian Journal of Biblical Archaeology*
AJSL	*American Journal of Semitic Languages and Literature*
AJT	*American Journal of Theology*
ALBO	Analecta lovaniensia biblica et orientalia
ALUOS	Annual of Leeds University Oriental Society
AnBib	Analecta biblica
ANEP	J. B. Pritchard (ed.), *Ancient Near East in Pictures*
ANESTP	J. B. Pritchard (ed.), *Ancient Near East Supplementary Texts and Pictures*
ANET	J. B. Pritchard (ed.), *Ancient Near Eastern Texts*
AnOr	Analecta orientalia
AOAT	Alter Orient und Altes Testament
AOS	American Oriental Series
APOT	R. H. Charles (ed.), *Apocrypha and Pseudepigrapha of the Old Testament*
ARG	*Archiv für Reformationsgeschichte*
ARM	Archives royales de Mari
ArOr	*Archiv orientální*
ARW	*Archiv für Religionswissenschaft*
ASSR	*Archives des sciences sociales des religions*
ASTI	*Annual of the Swedish Theological Institute*
ATAbh	Alttestamentliche Abhandlungen
ATANT	Abhandlungen zur Theologie des Alten und Neuen Testaments
ATR	*Anglican Theological Review*
AusBR	*Australian Biblical Review*
AUSS	*Andrews University Seminary Studies*

BA	*Biblical Archaeologist*
BANE	G. E. Wright (ed.), *The Bible and the Ancient Near East*
BAR	*Biblical Archaeologist Reader*
BASOR	*Bulletin of the American Schools of Oriental Research*
BAT	Die Botschaft des Alten Testaments
BBB	Bonner biblische Beiträge
BCSR	*Bulletin of the Council on the Study of Religion*
BDB	F. Brown, S. R. Driver, and C. A. Briggs, *Hebrew and English Lexicon of the Old Testament*
BeO	*Bibbia e oriente*
BETL	Bibliotheca ephemeridum theologicarum lovaniensium
BEvT	Beiträge zur evangelischen Theologie
BFCT	Beiträge zur Förderung christlicher Theologie
BGBE	Beiträge zur Geschichte der biblischen Exegese
BHH	B. Reicke and L. Rost (eds.), *Biblisch-historisches Handwörterbuch*
BHK	R. Kittel, *Biblia hebraica*
BHS	*Biblia hebraica stuttgartensia*
BHT	Beiträge zur historischen Theologie
Bib	*Biblica*
BibB	Biblische Beiträge
BibLeb	*Bibel und Leben*
BibOr	Biblica et orientalia
BibS(F)	Biblische Studien (Freiburg, 1895–)
BibS(N)	Biblische Studien (Neukirchen, 1951–)
BIES	*Bulletin of the Israel Exploration Society*
BIFAO	*Bulletin de l'institut français d'archéologie orientale*
BJRL	*Bulletin of the John Rylands University Library of Manchester*
BK	*Bibel und Kirche*
BKAT	Biblischer Kommentar: Altes Testament
BLit	*Bibel und Liturgie*
BMik	*Beth Mikra*
BN	*Biblische Notizen*
BO	*Bibliotheca orientalis*
BR	*Biblical Research*
BSac	*Bibliotheca Sacra*
BSO(A)S	*Bulletin of the School of Oriental (and African) Studies*
BSS	*Bibliotheca Sanctorum*
BSt	Biblische Studien
BT	*The Bible Translator*
BTB	*Biblical Theology Bulletin*
BTS	*Bible et terre sainte*
BVC	*Bible et vie chrétienne*
BWANT	Beiträge zur Wissenschaft vom Alten und Neuen Testament
BZ	*Biblische Zeitschrift*
BZAW	Beihefte zur *ZAW*
CAD	*The Assyrian Dictionary of the Oriental Institute of the University of Chicago*

CAH	*Cambridge Ancient History*
CAT	Commentaire de l'Ancien Testament
CB	*Cultura bíblica*
CBQ	*Catholic Biblical Quarterly*
CBQMS	Catholic Biblical Quarterly—Monograph Series
CCath	Corpus Catholicorum
CJT	*Canadian Journal of Theology*
CleM	*Clergy Monthly*
CML	G. R. Driver, *Canaanite Myths and Legends* (Edinburgh, 1956); rev. ed. J. C. L. Gibson (Edinburgh, 1978)
ConB	Coniectanea biblica
COT	Commentaar op het OT
CQ	*Church Quarterly*
CQR	*Church Quarterly Review*
CRAIBL	*Comptes rendus de l'Académie des inscriptions et belles-lettres*
CSCO	Corpus scriptorum christianorum orientalium
CTA	A. Herdner, *Corpus des tablettes en cunéiforms alphabétiques*
CTM	*Concordia Theological Monthly*
CurTM	*Currents in Theology and Mission*
DACL	*Dictionnaire d'archéologie chrétienne et de liturgie*
DBSup	*Dictionnaire de la Bible, Supplément*
DISO	C.-F. Jean and J. Hoftijzer, *Dictionnaire des inscriptions sémitiques de l'ouest*
Div	*Divinitas*
DJD	Discoveries in the Judaean Desert
DOTT	D. W. Thomas (ed.), *Documents from Old Testament Times*
DTT	*Dansk teologisk tidsskrift*
Ebib	Etudes bibliques
ECarm	*Ephemerides Carmeliticae*
EHAT	Exegetisches Handbuch zum Alten Testament
EHO	Cross and Freedman, *Early Hebrew Orthography*
EI	*Ereṣ Israel*
EnchBib	*Enchiridion biblicum*
EncJud	*Encyclopaedia judaica* (1971)
EstBib	*Estudios bíblicos*
ET	*Église et Théologie*
ETL	*Ephemerides theologicae lovanienses*
ETR	*Etudes théologiques et religieuses*
EvK	Evangelische Kommentare
EvQ	*Evangelical Quarterly*
EvT	*Evangelische Theologie (EvTh)*
Exp	*The Expositor*
ExpTim	*Expository Times*
FrancSt	*Franciscan Studies*

FRLANT	Forschungen zur Religion und Literatur des Alten und Neuen Testaments
GAG	W. von Soden, *Grundriss der akkadischen Grammatik*
GKB	Gesenius-Kautzsch-Bergsträsser, *Hebräische Grammatik*
GKC	*Gesenius' Hebrew Grammar*, ed. E. Kautzsch, tr. A. E. Cowley
GTJ	*Grace Theological Journal*
HALAT	W. Baumgartner et al., *Hebräisches und aramäisches Lexikon zum Alten Testament*
HAR	*Hebrew Annual Review*
HAT	Handbuch zum Alten Testament
HDR	Harvard Dissertations in Religion
Hen	*Henoch*
HeyJ	*Heythrop Journal*
HibJ	*Hibbert Journal*
HKAT	Handkommentar zum Alten Testament
HS	*Hebrew Studies*
HSAT	*Die Heilige Schrift des Alten Testament*, 2 vols.; ed. E. Kautzsch and A. Bertholet (Tübingen: ⁴1922–23)
HSM	Harvard Semitic Monographs
HTR	*Harvard Theological Review*
HTS	Harvard Theological Studies
HUCA	*Hebrew Union College Annual*
HUCM	Monographs of Hebrew Union College
IB	*Interpreter's Bible*
ICC	International Critical Commentary
IDB	G. A. Buttrick (ed.), *Interpreter's Dictionary of the Bible*
IDBSup	Supplementary volume to *IDB*
IEJ	*Israel Exploration Journal*
IndJTh	*Indian Journal of Theology*
Int	*Interpretation*
ISBE	G. W. Bromiley (ed.), *International Standard Bible Encyclopedia*, rev.
ITQ	*Irish Theological Quarterly*
ITS	*Innsbrucker theologische Studien*
JA	*Journal asiatique*
JAAR	*Journal of the American Academy of Religion*
JAC	Jahrbuch für Antike und Christentum
JANESCU	*Journal of the Ancient Near Eastern Society of Columbia University*
JAOS	*Journal of the American Oriental Society*
JAS	*Journal of Asian Studies*
JBC	R. E. Brown et al. (eds.), *The Jerome Biblical Commentary*
JBL	*Journal of Biblical Literature*
JBR	*Journal of Bible and Religion*
JBS	Jerusalem Biblical Studies
JCS	*Journal of Cuneiform Studies*

JDS	Judean Desert Studies
JDT	*Jahrbücher für deutsche Theologie*
JEA	*Journal of Egyptian Archaeology*
JEOL	*Jaarbericht . . . ex oriente lux*
JETS	*Journal of the Evangelical Theological Society*
JJS	*Journal of Jewish Studies*
JMES	*Journal of Middle Eastern Studies*
JNES	*Journal of Near Eastern Studies*
JNSL	*Journal of Northwest Semitic Languages*
JPOS	*Journal of the Palestine Oriental Society*
JPSV	Jewish Publication Society Version
JQR	*Jewish Quarterly Review*
JQRMS	Jewish Quarterly Review Monograph Series
JR	*Journal of Religion*
JRAS	*Journal of the Royal Asiatic Society*
JRelS	*Journal of Religious Studies*
JSOT	*Journal for the Study of the Old Testament*
JSOTSup	Supplement to *JSOT*
JSS	*Journal of Semitic Studies*
JSSR	*Journal for the Scientific Study of Religion*
JTC	*Journal for Theology and the Church*
JTS	*Journal of Theological Studies*
Judaica	*Judaica: Beiträge zum Verständnis . . .*
KAI	H. Donner and W. Röllig, *Kanaanäische und aramäische Inschriften*
KAT	E. Sellin (ed.), Kommentar zum Alten Testament
KB	L. Koehler and W. Baumgartner, *Lexicon in Veteris Testamenti libros*
KD	*Kerygma und Dogma*
KlT	Kleine Texte
KTU	*Die Keilalphabetischen Texte aus Ugarit*, vol. 1, ed. M. Dietrich, O. Loretz, and J. Sammartin, AOAT 24 (1976)
LCC	Library of Christian Classics
LCL	Loeb Classical Library
LD	Lectio divina
Leš	*Lešonénu*
LLAVT	E. Vogt, *Lexicon linguae aramaicae Veteris Testamenti*
LQ	*Lutheran Quarterly*
LR	*Lutherische Rundschau*
LSJ	Liddell-Scott-Jones, *Greek-English Lexicon*
LTK	*Lexicon für Theologie und Kirche*
LumVit	*Lumen Vitae*
LUÅ	Lunds universitets årsskrift
MBA	Y. Aharoni and M. Avi-Yonah, *Macmillan Bible Atlas,* rev. ed. (New York: Macmillan, 1977)
McCQ	*McCormick Quarterly*
MDB	*Mercer Dictionary of the Bible*, ed. W. Mills (Macon, GA: Mercer UP, 1990)
MDOG	Mitteilungen der deutschen Orient-Gesellschaft

MelT	*Melita Theologica*
MGWJ	*Monatsschrift für Geschichte und Wissenschaft des Judentums*
MScRel	*Mélanges de science religieuse*
MTZ	*Münchener theologische Zeitschrift*
MVAG	Mitteilungen der vorder-asiatisch-ägyptischen Gesellschaft
NedTTs	*Nederlands theologish tijdschrift*
NGTT	*Nederduits Gereformeerde Teologiese Tydskrif*
NHS	Nag Hammadi Studies
NICOT	New International Commentary on the Old Testament
NKZ	*Neue kirchliche Zeitschrift*
NorTT	*Norsk Teologisk Tidsskrift*
NovT	*Novum Testamentum*
NRT	*La nouvelle revue théologique*
OBO	Orbis biblicus et orientalis
OIP	Oriental Institute Publications
OLP	Orientalia lovaniensia periodica
OLZ	*Orientalische Literaturzeitung*
Or	*Orientalia* (Rome)
OrAnt	*Oriens antiquus*
OrChr	*Oriens christianus*
OrSyr	*L'orient syrien*
OTL	Old Testament Library
OTS	*Oudtestamentische Studiën*
OTWSA	Die Outestamentiese Werkgemeenskap in Suid-Afrika
PAAJR	*Proceedings of the American Academy of Jewish Research*
PCB	M. Black and H. H. Rowley (eds.), *Peake's Commentary on the Bible* (London: Thomas Nelson and Sons, 1963)
PEFQS	*Palestine Exploration Fund, Quarterly Statement*
PEQ	*Palestine Exploration Quarterly*
PG	J. Migne, *Patrologia graeca*
PJ	*Palästina-Jahrbuch*
PL	J. Migne, *Patrologia latina*
PRU	*Le Palais royal d'Ugarit*
PSTJ	*Perkins (School of Theology) Journal*
PW	Pauly-Wissowa, *Real-Encyclopädie der classischen Altertumswissenschaft*
PWSup	Supplement to PW
QDAP	*Quarterly of the Department of Antiquities in Palestine*
RA	*Revue d'assyriologie et d'archéologie orientale*
RAC	*Reallexikon für Antike und Christentum*
RArch	*Revue archéologique*
RB	*Revue biblique*
RCB	*Revista de cultura biblica*
RE	*Realencyklopädie für protestantische Theologie und Kirche*

RechBib	Recherches bibliques
REJ	*Revue des études juives*
RelS	*Religious Studies*
RelSRev	*Religious Studies Review*
RES	*Répertoire d'épigraphie sémitique*
ResQ	*Restoration Quarterly*
RevExp	*Review and Expositor*
RevistB	*Revista biblica*
RevQ	*Revue de Qumran*
RevScRel	*Revue des sciences religieuses*
RevSém	*Revue sémitique*
RGG	*Religion in Geschichte und Gegenwart*
RHPR	*Revue d'histoire et de philosophie religieuses*
RHR	*Revue de l'histoire des religions*
RivB	*Rivista biblica*
RLA	*Reallexikon der Assyriologie*
RR	*Review of Religion*
RSO	*Revista degli studi orientali*
RSP	*Ras Shamra Parallels*, ed. L. R. Fisher, AnOr 49 (Rome: Pontifical Biblical Institute, 1972)
RSPT	*Revue des sciences philosophiques et théologiques*
RSR	*Recherches de science religieuse*
RTL	*Revue théologique de Louvain*
RTP	*Revue de théologie et de philosophie*
RUO	*Revue de l'université d'Ottawa*
SANT	Studien zum Alten und Neuen Testament
SAOC	Studies in Ancient Oriental Civilization
SAT	Die Schriften des Alten Testaments in Auswahl übersetzt und erklärt, ed. Herman Gunkel
SAYP	Cross and Freedman, *Studies in Ancient Yahwistic Poetry*
SB	Sources bibliques
SBA	Studies in Biblical Archaeology
SBB	Stuttgarter biblische Beiträge
SBFLA	*Studii biblici franciscani liber annuus*
SBLASP	Society of Biblical Literature Abstracts and Seminar Papers
SBLDS	SBL Dissertation Series
SBLMasS	SBL Masoretic Studies
SBLMS	SBL Monograph Series
SBLSBS	SBL Sources for Biblical Study
SBLSCS	SBL Septuagint and Cognate Studies
SBLTT	SBL Texts and Translations
SBM	Stuttgarter biblische Monographien
SBS	Stuttgarter Bibelstudien
SBT	Studies in Biblical Theology
ScEs	*Science et esprit*
Scr	*Scripture*
ScrB	*Scripture Bulletin*

SD	Studies and Documents
SEÅ	*Svensk exegetisk årsbok*
Sef	*Sefarad*
SEHM	Stuart, *Studies in Early Hebrew Meter*
Sem	*Semitica*
SJOT	*Scandinavian Journal of the Old Testament*
SJT	*Scottish Journal of Theology*
SOTP	H. H. Rowley (ed.), *Studies in Old Testament Prophecy*
SOTSMS	Society for Old Testament Study Monograph Series
SPAW	Sitzungsberichte der preussischen Akademie der Wissenschaften
SR	*Studies in Religion / Sciences religieuses*
SSS	Semitic Study Series
ST	*Studia theologica*
STÅ	*Svensk teologisk årsskrift*
STK	*Svensk teologisk kvartalskrift*
StudOr	Studia orientalia
SVTP	Studia in Veteris Testamenti pseudepigrapha
SWJT	*Southwestern Journal of Theology*
TBl	*Theologische Blätter*
TBT	*The Bible Today*
TBü	Theologische Bücherei
TD	*Theology Digest*
TDOT	G. J. Botterweck and H. Ringgren (eds.), *Theological Dictionary of the Old Testament* (Grand Rapids, MI: Eerdmans, 1974–)
TextsS	Texts and Studies
TF	*Theologische Forschung*
TGl	*Theologie und Glaube*
TGUOS	*Transactions: Glasgow University Oriental Society*
ThEv	*Theologia Evangelica* (Pretoria)
ThLife	*Theology and Life*
ThV	*Theologische Versuche* (Berlin)
TLZ	*Theologische Literaturzeitung*
TP	*Theologie und Philosophie*
TQ	*Theologische Quartalschrift*
TRev	*Theologische Revue*
TRu	*Theologische Rundschau*
TS	*Theological Studies*
TSK	*Theologische Studien und Kritiken*
TT	*Teologisk Tidsskrift*
TTKi	*Tidsskrift for Teologi og Kirke*
TToday	*Theology Today*
TTZ	*Trierer theologische Zeitschrift*
TU	Texte und Untersuchungen
TV	*Theologia Viatorum*
TWAT	G. J. Botterweck and H. Ringgren (eds.), *Theologisches Wörterbuch zum Alten Testament*

TWOT	R. L. Harris et al. (eds.), *Theological Wordbook of the Old Testament* (Chicago: Moody Press, 1980)
TynBul	*Tyndale Bulletin*
TZ	*Theologische Zeitschrift*
UF	*Ugarit-Forschungen*
USQR	*Union Seminary Quarterly Review*
UT	C. H. Gordon, *Ugaritic Textbook*
UUÅ	Uppsala universitetsårsskrift
VC	*Vigilae christianae*
VD	*Verbum domini*
VF	*Verkündigung und Forschung*
VSpir	*Vie spirituelle*
VT	*Vetus Testamentum*
VTSup	Vetus Testamentum, Supplements
WBC	Word Biblical Commentary
WDB	*Westminster Dictionary of the Bible*
WHAB	*Westminster Historical Atlas of the Bible*
WMANT	Wissenschaftliche Monographien zum Alten und Neuen Testament
WO	*Die Welt des Orients*
WTJ	*Westminster Theological Journal*
WuD	*Wort und Dienst*
WUNT	Wissenschaftliche Untersuchungen zum Neuen Testament
WZKM	*Wiener Zeitschrift für die Kunde des Morgenlandes*
WZKSO	*Wiener Zeitschrift für die Kunde Süd- und Ostasiens*
ZA	*Zeitschrift für Assyriologie*
ZAW	*Zeitschrift für die alttestamentliche Wissenschaft*
ZDMG	*Zeitschrift der deutschen morgenländischen Gesellschaft*
ZDPV	*Zeitschrift des deutschen Palästina-Vereins*
ZEE	*Zeitschrift für evangelische Ethik*
ZKG	*Zeitschrift für Kirchengeschichte*
ZKT	*Zeitschrift für katholische Theologie*
ZNW	*Zeitschrift für die neutestamentliche Wissenschaft*
ZRGG	*Zeitschrift für Religions- und Geistesgeschichte*
ZTK	*Zeitschrift für Theologie und Kirche*
ZWT	*Zeitschrift für wissenschaftliche Theologie*

HEBREW GRAMMAR

abs	absolute	adj	adjective/adjectival
acc	accusative	adv	adverb/adverbial
act	active	aor	aorist

apoc	apocopated	juss	jussive
c	common	masc, m	masculine
coh	cohortative	niph	niphal
conj	conjunction	obj	object
consec	consecutive	pass	passive
const	construct	pf	perfect
conv	converted	pl	plural
dittogr	dittography	poss	possessive
fem, f	feminine	prep	preposition
fut	future	pronom	pronominal
gen	genitive	ptcp	participle
haplogr	haplography	sg, s	singular
hiph	hiphil	stat	stative
hithp	hithpael	subj	subject/subjective
hoph	hophal	suff	suffix
impf	imperfect	voc	vocative
impv	imperative	1	first person
ind	indicative	2	second person
inf	infinitive	3	third person

TEXTUAL NOTES

Akk.	Akkadian	Q	Qere (Masoretic suggested reading)
Arab.	Arabic		
Aram.	Aramaic	2Q Jer	Jeremiah from Qumran Cave 2
C	Codex of the Prophets from Cairo	4Q Jer	Jeremiah from Qumran Cave 4
Eg.	Egyptian		
Eng	English versions	Syr	Syriac Peshitta
Eng.	English language	Syrh	Syrohexapla
Eth.	Ethiopic	Tg	Targum
Gk.	Greek	*tiq. soph.*	"*tiqqune sopherim,*" corrections of the Scribes
Heb.	Hebrew		
Hex.	Hexapla		
K	Kethib (consonantal text)	Ug.	Ugaritic
		Vg	Vulgate
L	Leningrad Codex	a'	Aquila
LXX	The Septuagint	θ'	Theodotion
LXX^A (etc.)	Alexandrinus Codex of the Septuagint (etc.)	σ'	Symmachus
		>	mutated/transformed to
MT	Masoretic Text		
OG	Old Greek	<	from
OL	Old Latin		

BIBLICAL AND APOCRYPHAL BOOKS

Gen	Genesis	Dan	Daniel
Exod	Exodus	Hos	Hosea
Lev	Leviticus	Joel	Joel
Num	Numbers	Amos	Amos
Deut	Deuteronomy	Obad	Obadiah
Josh	Joshua	Jonah	Jonah
Judg	Judges	Mic	Micah
Ruth	Ruth	Nah	Nahum
1–2 Sam	1–2 Samuel	Hab	Habakkuk
1–2 Kgs	1–2 Kings	Zeph	Zephaniah
1–2 Chr	1–2 Chronicles	Hag	Haggai
Ezra	Ezra	Zech	Zechariah
Neh	Nehemiah	Mal	Malachi
Esth	Esther	Sir	Ecclesiasticus or The
Job	Job		Wisdom of Jesus Son
Ps(s)	Psalm(s)		of Sirach
Prov	Proverbs		
Eccl	Ecclesiastes	Matt	Matthew
Cant	Canticles, Song of	John	John
	Solomon	Acts	Acts
Isa	Isaiah	Rom	Romans
Jer	Jeremiah	Phil	Philippians
Lam	Lamentations	Heb	Hebrews
Ezek	Ezekiel	Rev	Revelation

MISCELLANEOUS

ANE	Ancient Near East	ET	English translation
ASV	American Standard Version, American Revised Version (1901)	FS	Festschrift
		GN	geographical name
		hap. leg.	*hapax legomenon,* sole occurrence
AV	Authorized Version = KJV	J	Yahwist (supposed biblical literary source)
b.	*breve* (metrically short poetic line)		
B.C.	Before Christ	JB	Jerusalem Bible
c.	circa	KJV	King James Version
chap(s).	chapter(s)	l	*longum* (metrically long poetic line)
cols.	columns		
diss.	dissertation	lit.	literally
E	Elohist (supposed biblical literary source)	MS(S)	manuscript(s)
		n.	note
		NAB	New American Bible
ed(s).	edition; edited by; editor(s)	NASB	New American Standard Bible
esp.	especially	NEB	New English Bible

NIV	New International Version	p.	page
NJV	New Jewish Version	Pers.	Persian
NRSV	New Revised Standard Version	pl.	plate
		PN	personal name
n.s.	new series	rev.	reverse
NT	New Testament	RSV	Revised Standard Version
OAN	oracles against foreign nations	tr.	translated; translator
		UP	University Press
obv.	obverse	v(v)	verse(s)
OT	Old Testament	viz.	by alteration

General Bibliography

In the bibliography that follows, there have been listed (i) commentaries, both general and technical, on the book of Jeremiah, (ii) other studies pertaining, for the most part, to the book as a whole or general issues related to the book, and (iii) reviews of current scholarship. As there is a vast body of secondary literature associated with the book of Jeremiah, the bibliography is limited to fairly recent works on the book; a few older and classical works have been included. The bibliography has excluded particular items pertaining to the detailed study of a chapter or verse; these items are all listed separately in the detailed bibliographies that precede each section of the commentary.

Commentaries
(referred to in the text by authors' names only)

CHURCH FATHERS

Origen. *Homilias in Jeremiam.* Origenis opera omnia, III. *PG* 13. Paris: 1857. Col. 256–534. [Greek. Third century. Only covers Jer 1–20.] **Chrysostom.** *Commentarium in Jeremiam prophetam.* S. P. N. Joannis Chrysostomi opera omnia quae extant, xiii. *PG* 64. 1860. Col. 739–1038. [Greek. Fourth century.] **Ephraim of Syria.** *Commentarium in Jeremiam.* Opera Syriaca et Latina, 2. Rome: 1740. Col. 98–162. [Fourth century.] **Cyril of Alexandria.** *Fragmenta ex Catenus in Jeremiam.* S. P. N. Cyrilli opera quae reperiri potuerunt omnia, III. *PG* 70. 1859. Col. 1451–58. [Greek. Fifth century. Very short and fragmented.] **Theodoret of Cyrene.** *Beati Theodoreti, in divini Jeremiae prophetam interpretatio.* Theodoreti opera omnia, III. *PG* 81. 1859. Col. 495–760. [Greek. Fifth century.] **Jerome.** *S. Eusebii Hieronymi, Commentarium in Jeremiam prophetam libri sex.* Sancti Eusebii Hieronymi opera omnia, IV. *PL* 24. Col. 706–936. [Latin. Fifth century. Only covers Jer 1–32.]

MEDIEVAL CHURCHMEN

Maurus. *Beati Rabani Mauri, Expositionis super Jeremiam prophetam libri viginti.* B. Rabani Mauri opera omnia, V. *PL* 111. 1852. Col. 793–1182. [Latin. Ninth century.] **Rupert of Deutz.** *In Jeremiam prophetam commentarium liber unus.* R. D. D. Ruperti opera omnia, I. *PL* 167. 1854. Col. 1363–1420. [Latin. Twelfth century.] **Thomas Aquinas.** *In Jeremiam prophetam expositio.* Opera, 13. Rome: 1570. Venice: 1594. Antwerp: 1612. [Latin. Thirteenth century. Only covers Jer 1–42.]

MEDIEVAL JEWISH COMMENTATORS

Rashi (Solomon ben Isaac). *Commentary on the Latter Prophets.* Venice: 1608. [A Latin version edited by Johann Fr. Breihaupt, Gotha: 1713. Rashi lived 1040–1105.] **David Kimchi.** *Commentary on the Latter Prophets.* Pesaro: 1515. Paris: 1556. [Also included in Moses Frankfurter's larger Bible, Amsterdam: 1724–1727. Kimchi's dates: 1160?–1235?.] **Arama** (Meir ben Isaac). *Urim ve-Tummim.* Venice: 1603. [A commentary on Isaiah and Jeremiah.

Included in Moses Frankfurter's larger Bible, Amsterdam, 1724–1727. Arama lived in Spain, 1460?–1545?]

REFORMATION AND COUNTER-REFORMATION

Calvin, J. *Commentaries on the Book of the Prophet Jeremiah and Lamentations.* Trans. and ed. J. Owen. 5 vols. Grand Rapids, MI: Eerdmans, 1950. [Originally Latin. 1589. Can be found in Latin as vols. 37–39 of the Opera omnia, Corpus reformatorum, 65–67.] **Zwingli, U. D.** *Huldrichi Zwingli, annotationes in Genesim, Exodum, Esaiam & Jeremiam Prophetas.* Zurich: 1581. [Also in Opera omnia, 14. Corpus reformatorum, 101.] **Melanchthon, P.** *Argumentam in Jeremiam Prophetam.* Opera omnia, 13. Corpus reformatorum, 13. Col. 804–14. [Very short and fragmentary. Not really commentary.] **Capella, A.** *Commentaria in Jeremiam prophetam, in cartusia Scalae Dei.* Rome: 1586. [Latin. Roman Catholic.] **Christoph a Castro.** Paris: 1609. [Latin. Jeremiah, Lamentations, Baruch.] **Maldonatus, J.** Lyon: 1611. [Latin. Jeremiah, Baruch.] **Sanctius (Sanchez), G.** Antwerp: 1611. Lyon: 1618. [Latin.] **Ghislerius, M.** Lyon: 1623. [Latin.]

ENLIGHTENMENT THROUGH NINETEENTH CENTURY

Lowth, W. *Commentary upon the Prophecy and Lamentations of Jeremiah.* London: 1718. **Michaelis, J. D.** *Observationes philologicae et criticae in Jeremiae vaticinia.* Göttingen: 1743. **Cheyne, J. K.** *Jeremiah.* The Pulpit Commentary. London: 1883. **Keil, C. F.** *Biblischer Commentar über den Propheten Jeremia.* Leipzig: 1872. ———. *Jeremiah.* Biblical Commentary. Edinburgh, 1880. **Naegelsbach, C. W. E.** *The Book of the Prophet Jeremiah, Theologically and Homiletically Expounded.* New York: Scribner's, 1886.

TWENTIETH CENTURY

Achtemeier, E. *Deuteronomy, Jeremiah.* Proclamation Commentaries. Philadelphia: Fortress, 1978. **Aeschimann, A.** *Le prophète Jérémie: Commentaire.* Neuchâtel: Delachaux and Niestlé, 1959. **Blackwood, A. W.** *Commentary on Jeremiah.* Waco, TX: Word Books, 1977. **Boadt, L.** *Jeremiah 1–25.* Old Testament Message 9. Wilmington: Glazier, 1982. ———. *Jeremiah 26–52.* Old Testament Message 10. Wilmington: Glazier, 1983. **Bright, J.** *Jeremiah.* AB. Garden City, NY: Doubleday, 1965. **Brueggemann, W.** *A Commentary on the Book of Jeremiah 1–25: To Pluck Up, to Tear Down.* International Theological Commentary. Grand Rapids, MI: Eerdmans, 1988. **Carroll, R. P.** *Jeremiah.* OTL. Philadelphia: Westminster, 1986. **Clements, R. E.** *Jeremiah.* Interpretation. Atlanta: John Knox, 1988. **Condamin, A.** *Le Livre de Jérémie.* Ebib. Paris: Gabalda, 1936. **Cornill, C. H.** *Das Buch Jeremia.* Leipzig: Tauchnitz, 1905. **Craigie, P. C.** *The Book of Deuteronomy.* The New International Commentary on the Old Testament. Grand Rapids, MI: Eerdmans, 1976. ———. *Psalms 1–50.* WBC 19. Waco, TX: Word Books, 1983. **Cunliffe-Jones, H.** *The Book of Jeremiah: Introduction and Commentary.* The Torch Bible Commentaries. London: SCM, 1960. **Dalglish, E. R.** *Jeremiah, Lamentations.* Layman's Bible Book Commentary 2. Nashville: Broadman, 1983. **Davidson, R.** *Jeremiah, Volume I.* The Daily Study Bible. Philadelphia: Westminster Press, 1983. ———. *Jeremiah, Volume II.* The Daily Study Bible. Philadelphia: Westminster, 1985. **Driver, S. R.** *The Book of the Prophet Jeremiah.* London: Hodder & Stoughton, 1906. **Duhm, B.** *Das Buch Jeremia.* Kurzer Hand-Commentar zum Alten Testament. Tübingen/Leipzig: Mohr (Siebeck), 1901. **Feinberg, C. L.** *Jeremiah: A Commentary.* Grand Rapids, MI: Zondervan, 1982. **Fohrer, G.** *Die propheten des Alten Testament 3. Die Propheten des Frühen 6 Jahrhunderts.* 1975. ———. *Die symbolischen Handlungen der Propheten.* 2nd ed. ATANT 4. Zürich: Zwingli, 1968. **Freedman, H.** *Jeremiah: Hebrew Text and English Translation with an Introduction and Commentary.* London: Soncino, 1949. **Freehof, S. B.** *Book of Jeremiah: A Commentary.* The Jewish Commentary for Bible Readers. New York: Union of American Hebrew Congregations, 1977. **Giesebrecht, F.** *Das Buch Jeremia.* HKAT 3/2. Göttingen: Vandenhoeck & Ruprecht, 1907. **Green, J. L.** "Jeremiah." In *The Broadman*

Bible Commentary. Nashville: Broadman, 1971. 6:1–202. **Haag, E.** *Das Buch Jeremia.* Vols. 1 and 2. Geistliche Schriftlesung 5/1 & 2. Düsseldorf: Patmos, 1971, 1977. **Harrison, R. K.** *Jeremiah and Lamentations: An Introduction and Commentary.* Tyndale Old Testament Commentaries. London: Tyndale, 1973. **Heschel, A. J.** *The Prophets.* New York: Harper, 1962. **Holladay, W. L.** *Jeremiah 1.* Hermeneia. Philadelphia/Minneapolis: Augsburg Fortress, 1986. ———. *Jeremiah 2.* Hermeneia. Philadelphia/Minneapolis: Augsburg Fortress, 1989. **Hyatt, J. P.** "Introduction and Exegesis, Jeremiah." In *IB.* Nashville: Abingdon, 1956. 5:775–1142. **Kuist, H. T.** *Jeremiah.* Layman's Bible Commentaries. London: SCM, 1961. **Lamparter, H.** *Prophet wider Willen: der Prophet Jeremia.* BAT 20. Stuttgart: Calwer, 1964. **Leslie, E. A.** *Jeremiah: Chronologically Arranged, Translated, and Interpreted.* New York: Abingdon, 1954. **Martens, E. A.** *Jeremiah.* Believers Church Bible Commentary. Scottdale, PA: Herald, 1986. **McKane, W. A.** *Critical and Exegetical Commentary on Jeremiah, I.* ICC. Edinburgh: T. & T. Clark, 1986. **Neil, W.** *Prophets of Israel (2): Jeremiah and Ezekiel.* Bible Guides 8. Nashville: Abingdon, 1964. **Nicholson, E. W.** *The Book of the Prophet Jeremiah.* The Cambridge Bible Commentary on the New English Bible. 2 vols. Cambridge: Cambridge UP, 1973, 1975. **Nötscher, F.** *Das Buch Jeremias.* Die Heilige Schrift des Alten Testaments 7/2. Bonn: Hanstein, 1934. *Peake's Commentary on the Bible,* ed. H. H. Rowley. London/New York: Nelson, 1962. **Rudolph, W.** *Jeremia.* HAT. Tübingen: Mohr (Siebeck), 1968. **Schreiner, J.** *Jeremia 1–25:14.* Die Neue Echter Bibel. Würzburg: Echter, 1981. **Sekine, M.** *Eremiya-sho chūkai Joū* ("A Commentary on the Book of Jeremiah"). The Works of M. Sekine, vol. 14. 1962. Reprint. Tokyo: Sinchi-Shobo, 1981. **Selms, A. van.** *Jeremia.* Deel 1 (Jer. 1–25). De Predeking van het Oude Testament. Nijkerk: G. F. Callenbach, 1972. *Starý zákon: překlad s výkladem: 12. Jeremjáš- Pláč.* Prague: Kalich, 1983. [A commentary in modern Czech on Jeremiah and Lamentations.] **Strobel, A.** *Trauer um Jerusalem: Jeremia-Klagelieder-Baruch.* Stuttgarter Kleiner Kommentar AT 11. Stuttgart: KBW, 1973. **Thompson, J. A.** *The Book of Jeremiah.* NICOT. Grand Rapids, MI: Eerdmans, 1980. **Volz, P.** *Der Prophet Jeremia.* KAT. Leipzig: Deichert, 1928. **Wambacq, B. N.** *Jeremias, Klaagliederen/Baruch, Brief van Jeremias vit de grondtekst vertaald en uitgelegd.* De Boeken van het Oude Testament. Roermond: Romen and Zonen, 1957. **Weiser, A.** *Das Buch des Propheten Jeremia.* Das Alte Testament Deutsche. Göttingen: Vandenhoeck & Ruprecht, 1969. **Wildberger, H.** *Jesaja.* 3 vols. Kommentar alttestament 10/2. Neukirchen: Neukirchener, 1978. **Woods, J.** *Jeremiah.* Epworth Preacher's Commentaries. London: Epworth, 1964.

Monographs and Other Books
(referred to in the text by authors' names and shortened titles)

Ackroyd, P. *Exile and Restoration: A Study of Hebrew Thought of the Sixth Century B.C.* Philadelphia: Westminster, 1968. **Andersen, F. I.,** and **Forbes, A. D.** *A Linguistic Concordance of Jeremiah: Hebrew Vocabulary and Idiom.* 2 volumes. The Computer Bible, 14 and 14a. Wooster, OH: Biblical Research Associates, 1978. **André, G.** *Determining the Destiny: PQD in the Old Testament.* ConBOT 16. Lund: Gleerup, 1980. **Avigad, N.** *Discovering Jerusalem.* Nashville: Thomas Nelson, 1983. ———. *Hebrew Bullae from the Time of Jeremiah: Remnants from a Burnt Archive.* Jerusalem: Israel Exploration Society, 1986. **Baumgartner, W.** *Die Klagegedichte de Jeremia.* BZAW 32. Giessen: Töpelmann, 1917. ———. *Jeremiah's Poems of Lament.* Trans. D. E. Orton. Sheffield: Almond, 1988. **Berridge, J. M.** *Prophet, People and the Word of Yahweh: An Examination of Form and Content in the Proclamation of the Prophet Jeremiah.* Zürich: EVZ-Verlag, 1970. **Blank, S. H.** *Jeremiah: Man and Prophet.* Cincinnati: HUC, 1961. **Bogaert, P. M.,** ed. *Le Livre de Jérémie: Le prophète et son milieu, les oracles et leur transmission.* BETL 54. Leuven: Leuven UP, 1981. **Bonnard, P. E.** *Le Psautier selon Jérémie.* LD 26. Paris: Cerf, 1960. **La Bonnardière, A.-M.** *Le Livre de Jérémie.* Biblia Augustiniania. Paris: Études Augustiniennes, 1972. **Bozak, B.** *Life 'Anew': A Literary-Theological Study of Jer. 30–31.* AnBib 122. Rome: Pontifical Biblical Institute, 1991. **Briend, J.** *Le Livre de Jérémie.* Cahiers Evangile 40. Paris: Cerf,

1982. **Bright, J.** *Covenant and Promise: The Future in the Preaching of the Pre-exilic Prophets.* London: SCM, 1977. ———. *A History of Israel.* 3rd ed. Philadelphia: Westminster, 1981. **Carroll, R. P.** *From Chaos to Covenant: Prophecy in the Book of Jeremiah.* New York: Crossroad, 1981. ———. *When Prophecy Failed: Cognitive Dissonance in the Prophetic Traditions of the Old Testament.* New York: Seabury, 1979. **Childs, B.** *Introduction to the Old Testament as Scripture.* Philadelphia: Fortress, 1979. **Davis, E.** *Swallowing the Scroll: Textuality and the Dynamics of Discourse in Ezekiel's Prophecy.* JSOTSup 78. Sheffield: Almond, 1987. **Diamond, A. R.** *The Confessions of Jeremiah in Context: Scenes of Prophetic Drama.* JSOTSup 45. Sheffield: JSOT Press, 1986. **Durham, J. I.,** and **Porter, J. R.,** eds. *Proclamation and Presence: Old Testament Essays in Honour of Gwynne Henton Davies.* Richmond: John Knox Press, 1970. **Efird, J. M.** *Jeremiah: Prophet under Siege.* Valley Forge: Judson, 1979. **Eissfeldt, O.** *The Old Testament: An Introduction.* Tr. P. R. Ackroyd. New York/Evanston: Harper & Row, 1965. **Finkelstein, I.** *The Archaeology of the Israelite Settlement.* Jerusalem: Israel Exploration Society, 1988. **Fishbane, M.** *Biblical Interpretation in Ancient Israel.* Oxford: Clarendon, 1985. **Fohrer, G.** *Die Propheten des Alten Testaments: Band 7. Prophetenerzählungen.* Gütersloh: Mohn, 1977. **Hayes, J.,** and **Hooker, P.** *A New Chronology for the Kings of Israel and Judah and Its Implications for Biblical History and Literature.* Atlanta: John Knox, 1988. **Hillers, D. R.** *Treaty-Curses and the Old Testament Prophets.* BibOr 11. Rome: Pontifical Biblical Institute, 1964. **Holladay, W. L.** *Jeremiah: Spokesman Out of Time.* New York: Pilgrim, 1974. ———. *The Architecture of Jeremiah 1–20.* London: Associated University Presses, 1976. **Hyatt, J. P.** *Jeremiah: Prophet of Courage and Hope.* Nashville: Abingdon, 1958. **Janzen, J. G.** *Studies in the Text of Jeremiah.* Cambridge, MA: Harvard UP, 1973. **Johnson, A. R.** *The Vitality of the Individual in the Thought of Ancient Israel.* Cardiff: University of Wales, 1949. **Kessler, M.** "A Prophetic Biography: A Form Critical Study of Jeremiah, Chapters 26–29, 32–45." Diss., Brandeis, 1965. **König, E.** *Historisch-Comparative Syntax der hebräischen Sprache.* Leipzig: Hinrichs, 1897. **Kraus, H.-J.** *Prophetie in der Krisis: Studien zu Texten aus dem Buche Jeremia.* Neukirchen-Vluyn: Erziehungsverein, 1964. **Levenson, J.** *Sinai and Zion: An Entry into the Jewish Bible.* Minneapolis: Winston, 1985. **Lundbom, J. R.** *Jeremiah: A Study of Ancient Hebrew Rhetoric.* SBLDS 18. Missoula, MT: Scholars, 1975. **McKane, W.** *Prophets and Wise Men.* SBT 44. Naperville, IL: Allenson, 1965. **Meier, S.** *The Messenger in the Ancient Semitic World.* HSM 45. Atlanta: Scholars, 1988. **Melchert, J.** *Jeremia als Nachricht: Prophetische Texte im Religions-unterricht-Reflexionen und Unterrichtsplanungen.* Düsseldorf: Patmos, 1977. **Meyer, I.** *Jeremia und die falschen Propheten.* OBO 13. Göttingen: Vandenhoeck & Ruprecht; Fribourg: Universitätsverlag, 1977. **Miller, J. W.** *Das Verhältnis Jeremias und Hesekiels sprachlich und theologisch untersucht, mit besonderer Berücksichtigung der Prosareden Jeremias.* Assen: Van Gorcum, 1955. **Mowinckel, S.** *Zur Komposition des Buches Jeremia.* Oslo: Dibwad, 1914. **Neher, A.** *Jérémie.* Paris: Librairie Plon, 1960. **Nicholson, E. W.** *Preaching to the Exiles: A Study of the Prose Tradition in the Book of Jeremiah.* New York: Schocken Books, 1970. **O'Connor, K. M.** *The Confessions of Jeremiah: Their Interpretation and Role in Chapters 1–25.* SBLDS 94. Atlanta: Scholars, 1988. **Overholt, T. W.** *The Threat of Falsehood: A Study in the Theology of the Book of Jeremiah.* SBT 2nd ser. 16. Naperville, IL: Allenson, 1970. **Parrot, A.** *The Temple of Jerusalem.* Tr. B. E. Hooke. Studies in Biblical Archaeology 5. London: SCM Press, 1957. **Perdue, L. G.,** and **Kovacs, B. W.,** eds. *A Prophet to the Nations: Essays in Jeremiah Studies.* Winona Lake, IN: Eisenbrauns, 1984. **Pohlmann, K.-F.** *Studien zum Jeremiabuch.* Göttingen: Vandenhoeck & Ruprecht, 1978. **Polk, T.** *The Prophetic Persona: Jeremiah and the Language of the Self.* JSOTSup 32. Sheffield, 1984. **Raitt, T. M.** *A Theology of Exile: Judgment/Deliverance in Jeremiah and Ezekiel.* Philadelphia: Fortress, 1977. **Reventlow, H. G.** *Liturgie und prophetisches Ich bei Jeremia.* Gütersloh: Mohn, 1963. **Ridouard, A.** *Jérémie, l'épreuve de la foi.* Paris: Cerf, 1983. **Rietzschel, C.** *Das Problem der Urrolle: Ein Beitrag zur Redaktionsgeschichte des Jeremiahbuches.* Gütersloh: Gütersloher (Mohn), 1966. **Savran, J.** *Telling and Retelling: Quotation in Biblical Narrative.* Bloomington, IN: Indiana UP, 1988. **Schneider, D.** *Der Prophet Jeremia.* Wuppertaler Studienbibel. Wuppertal: Brockhaus, 1977. **Schultes, J. L.** *Umkehre ist immer moglich: Ein Arbeitsheft zum Buch Jeremia.* Gespräche zur Bibel 6. Klosterneuburg: Österreichisches Katholisches Bibelwerk, 1978.

Seidl, T. *Texte und Einheiten in Jeremia 27–29.* Literaturwissenschaftliche Studien 2. Teil, Arbeite zu Text and Sprache im Alten Testament 5. Munich: Eos, 1978. **Seierstad, I. P.** *Die Offenbarungserlebnisse der Propheten Amos, Jesaja und Jeremia.* 2nd ed. Norwegian Research Council: Universitetsvorlaget, 1965. **Seitz, C. R.** *Theology in Conflict: Reactions to the Exile in the Book of Jeremiah.* BZAW 176. New York: de Gruyter, 1989. **Seow, C.** *Myth, Drama and the Politics of David's Dance.* HSM 44. Atlanta: Scholars, 1989. **Skinner, J.** *Prophecy and Religion: Studies in the Life of Jeremiah.* Cambridge: Cambridge UP, 1922. **Smith, D. L.** *The Religion of the Landless: The Social Context of the Babylonian Exile.* Bloomington, IN: Meyer-Stone, 1989. **Smith, M. S.** *The Laments of Jeremiah and Their Contexts: A Literary and Redactional Study of Jeremiah 11–20.* SBLMS 42. Atlanta: Scholars, 1990. **Stulman, L.** *The Other Text of Jeremiah.* New York: Lanham, 1985. ———. *The Prose Sermons of the Book of Jeremiah: A Redescription of the Correspondences with the Deuteronomistic Literature in the Light of Recent Text Critical Research.* SBLDS 83. Atlanta: Scholars, 1986. **Thiel, W.** *Die deuteronomistische Redaktion von Jeremia 1–25.* WMANT 41. Neukirchen: Neukirchener, 1973. ———. *Die deuteronomistische Redaktion von Jeremia 26–45: Mit einer Gesamtbeurteilung der deuteronomistischen Redaktion des Buches Jeremias.* WMANT 52. Neukirchen: Neukirchener, 1981. **Thompson, J. G. S. S.** *The Word of the Lord in Jeremiah.* Tyndale Old Testament Lecture. London: Tyndale Press, 1959. **Waltke, B.,** and **O'Connor, M.** *Hebrew Syntax.* Winona Lake, IN: Eisenbrauns, 1990. **Wanke, G.** *Untersuchungen zur sogenannten Baruchschrift.* BZAW 122. Berlin: de Gruyter, 1971. **Weinfeld, M.** *Deuteronomy and the Deuteronomic School.* Oxford: Clarendon, 1972. **Weippert, H.** *Die Prosareden des Jeremiabuches.* BZAW 132. Berlin: de Gruyter, 1973. ———. *Schöpfer des Himmels und der Erde: Ein Beitrag zur Theologie des Jeremiabuches.* SBS 102. Stuttgart: Katholisches Bibelwerk, 1981. **Westermann, C.** *Basic Forms of Prophetic Speech.* Philadelphia: Westminster, 1967. **Wilson, R. R.** *Prophecy and Society in Ancient Israel.* Philadelphia: Fortress, 1980. **Wiseman, D. J.** *Chronicles of Chaldean Kings (626–556 B.C.) in the British Museum.* London: British Museum, 1956. ———. *Nebuchadrezzar and Babylon.* Oxford: Oxford UP, 1985. **Wisser, L.** *Jérémie, critique de la vie sociale: justice sociale et connaisance de Dieu dans la livre de Jérémie.* Geneva: Labor et Fides, 1982. **Wolff, C.** *Jeremia in Frühjudentum und Urchristentum.* Texte und Untersuchungen zur Geschichte der Altchristlichen Literatur 118. Berlin: Akademie, 1976. **Wolff, H. W.** *Anthropology of the Old Testament.* Philadelphia: Westminster, 1974.

Articles
(referred to in the text by authors' names and journal citations)

Ackroyd, P. R. "Aspects of the Jeremiah Tradition." *IndJTh* 20 (1971) 1–12. ———. "Biblical Classics, I: John Skinner: Prophecy and Religion." *ExpTim* 89 (1978) 356–58. **Augustin, F.** "Baruch und das Jeremia." *ZAW* 67 (1955) 50–56. **Avigad, N.** "Jerahmeel and Baruch: King's Son and Scribe." *BA* 42 (1979) 114–18. **Barker, K. L.** "Jeremiah's Ministry and Ours." *BSac* 127 (1970) 223–31. **Berger, K.** "Hartherzigkeit und Gottes Gesetz: die Vorgeschichte des antijüdischen Vorwurfs in Mc 10:5." *ZNW* 61 (1970) 1–47. **Berridge, J. M.** "Jeremia und die Prophetie des Amos." *TZ* 35 (1979) 321–41. **Blank, S. H.** "The Confessions of Jeremiah, and the Meaning of Prayer." *HUCA* 21 (1948) 331–54. **Briggs, C. R.** "Prophets and Traditions: The Relations between Jeremiah and the Traditions of Northern Israel." *AusBR* 20 (1972) 1–15. **Bright, J.** "Book of Jeremiah: Its Structure, Its Problems, and Their Significance for the Interpreter." *Int* 9 (1955) 259–78. ———. "The Date of the Prose Sermons in Jeremiah." *JBL* 70 (1951) 15–35. ———. "The Prophetic Reminiscence: Its Place and Function in the Book of Jeremiah." In *Biblical Essays, Proceedings: Die Ou Testamentiese Werkgemeenskap* (1966) 11–30. ———. "Jeremiah's Complaints." In *Proclamation and Presence.* FS G. H. Davies, ed. J. I. Durham and J. R. Porter. Richmond: John Knox, 1970. 189–214. **Broughton, P. E.** "The Call of Jeremiah: The Relation of Dt. 18:9–22 to the Call and Life of Jeremiah." *AusBR* 6 (1958) 39–46. **Brueggemann, W.** "Intense Criticism/ Thin Interpretation." *Int* 42 (1988) 268–80. ———. "Jeremiah's Use of Rhetorical Questions." *JBL* 92 (1973) 358–74. **Buchanan, G. W.** "The Word of God and the Apocalyptic

Vision." SBLASP 14 (1978) 183–92. **Busch, R. J. Vanden.** "Jeremiah: A Spiritual Metamorphosis." *BTB* 10 (1980) 17–24. **Carlson, E. L.** "The World of Jeremiah." *SWJT* 4 (1961) 57–68. **Cassuto, U.** "The Prophecies of Jeremiah concerning the Gentiles." In *Biblical and Oriental Studies, I: The Bible,* tr. I. Abrahams. Jerusalem: Magnes, 1973. 178–226. **Childs, B. S.** "The Enemy from the North and the Chaos Tradition." *JBL* 78 (1959) 187–98. **Corré, A. D.** "ʿelle, hēmma = sic" [pronouns in Jeremiah]. *Bib* 54 (1973) 263–64. **Crenshaw, J. L.** "YHWH Ṣᵉbaʾot Šhᵉmo: A Form-critical Analysis." *ZAW* 81 (1969) 156–75. **Cummins, P.** "Jeremias Orator." *CBQ* 11 (1949) 191–201. **Dahood, M. J.** "Two Textual Notes on Jeremia." *CBQ* 23 (1961) 462–64. **Davidson, R.** "Orthodoxy and the Prophetic Word: A Study in the Relationship between Jeremiah and Deuteronomy." *VT* 14 (1964) 407–16. **Dobbie, R.** "Jeremiah and the Preacher." *CJT* 4 (1958) 37–45. **Driver, S. R.** "Linguistic and Textual Problems: Jeremiah." *JQR* 28 (1937–38) 97–129. **Eichler, U.** "Der Klagende Jeremia: Eine Untersuchung zu den Klagen Jeremia und ihrer Bedeutung zum Verstehen seines Leidens." *TLZ* 103 (1978) 918–19. [Summary of 1968 Heidelberg dissertation.] **Eissfeldt, O.** "Voraussage-Empfang, Offenbarungsgewissheit und Gebetskraft-Erfahrung bei Jeremia." *NovT* 5 (1962) 77–81. **Ellison, H. L.** "Prophecy of Jeremiah." *EvQ* 31 (1959) 143–51, 205–17; 32 (1960) 3–14, 107–13, 212–23; 33 (1961) 27–35, 148–56, 220–27; 34 (1962) 16–28, 96–102, 154–162; 35 (1963) 4–14, 160–67, 196–205; 36 (1964) 3–11, 92–99, 148–56; 37 (1965) 21–28, 100–109, 147–54, 232–41; 38 (1966) 40–51, 158–68, 233–40; 39 (1967) 40–47, 165–72, 216–24. **Elliot, R. H.** "Old Testament Prophecy." *RevExp* 58 (1961) 407–16. **France, R. T.** "Herod and the Children of Bethlehem." *NovT* 21 (1979) 98–120. **Frank, R. M.** "Jeremias of Pethion ibn Ayyub al-Sahhar" [with Arabic text of chaps. 1–6]. *CBQ* 21 (1959) 136–70. ———. "'Citation' from the Prophet Jeremias in Ibn Qutaiba and Tabari" [with Arabic texts and ET]. *CBQ* 17 (1955) 379–402. **Gerstenberger, E.** "Jeremiah's Complaints." *JBL* 82 (1963) 393–408. **Gordon, T. C.** "A New Date for Jeremiah." *ExpTim* 44 (1932–33) 562–65. **Granild, S.** "Jeremia und das Deuteronomium." *ST* 16 (1962) 135–54. **Grelot, P.** "Soixante-dix Semaines d'Annees." *Bib* 50 (1969) 186. **Habel, N. C.** "Appeal to Ancient Tradition as a Literary Form." *ZAW* 88 (1976) 25–72. ———. "The Form and Significance of the Call Narratives." *ZAW* 77 (1965) 297–323. **Herrmann, S.** "Forschung am Jeremiabuch: Probleme und Tendenzen ihrer neueren Entwicklung." *TLZ* 102 (1977) 481–90. **Hobbs, T. R.** "Some Proverbial Reflections in the Book of Jeremiah." *ZAW* 91 (1979) 62–72. ———. "Some Remarks on the Structure and Composition of the Book of Jeremiah." *CBQ* 34 (1972) 257–75. **Hoffken, P.** "Zu den Heilszusatzen in der Volkerorakelsammlung des Jeremiabuches." *VT* 27 (1977) 398–412. **Holladay, W. L.** "The Background of Jeremiah's Self-Understanding." *JBL* 83 (1964) 153–64. ———. "The Book of Jeremiah." *IDBSup,* 470–72. ———. "A Fresh Look at 'Source B' and 'Source C' in Jeremiah." *VT* 25 (1975) 394–412. ———. "Jeremiah and Women's Liberation." *ANQ* 12 (1972) 213–23. ———. "Jeremiah in Judah's Eyes and Ours: Musing on Some Issues in Old Testament Hermeneutics." *ANQ* 13 (1972) 115–32. ———. "Jeremiah's Lawsuit with God: A Study in Suffering and Meaning." *Int* 17 (1963) 280–87. ———. "Prototype and Copies: A New Approach to the Poetry-Prose Problem in the Book of Jeremiah." *JBL* 79 (1960) 351–67. ———. "Recovery of Poetic Passages of Jeremiah." *JBL* 85 (1966) 401–35. ———. "Style, Irony, and Authenticity in the Book of Jeremiah." *JBL* 81 (1962) 44–54. **Honeycutt, R. L.** "Jeremiah and the Cult." *RevExp* 58 (1961) 464–73. **Horwitz, W. J.** "Audience Reaction to Jeremiah." *CBQ* 32 (1970) 555–64. **Hyatt, J. P.** "The Beginnings of Jeremiah's Prophecy." *ZAW* 78 (1966) 204–14. ———. "The Deuteronomic Edition of Jeremiah." *Vanderbilt Studies in the Humanities* 1 (1951) 71–95. ———. "Jeremiah and Deuteronomy." *JNES* 1 (1942) 156–73. ———. "Torah in the Book of Jeremiah." *JBL* 60 (1941) 381–96. **Janzen, J. G.** "Double Readings in the Text of Jeremiah." *HTR* 60 (1967) 433–47. **Jeremias, J.** "Die Vollmacht des Propheten im Alten Testament." *EvT* 31 (1971) 305–22. **Jobling, D. K.** "The Quest of the Historical Jeremiah: Hermeneutical Implications of Recent Literature." *USQR* 34 (1978) 3–12. **Kapelrud, A. S.** "Jeremia—en landsskiver?" *Kirke og Kultur* 83 (1978) 28–39. **Keller, B.** "Langage de Jérémie." *ETR* (1978)

53, 360–65. **Kelley, P. H.** "Jeremiah's Concept of Individual Religion." *RevExp* 58 (1961) 452–63. **Kessler, M.** "Jeremiah Chapters 26–45 Reconsidered." *JNES* 27 (1968) 81–88. **Klein, W. C.** "Commentary on Jeremiah." *ATR* 55 (1963) 121–58, 284–309. **Kuist, H. T.** "Book of Jeremiah." *Int* 4 (1950) 322–41. **Kurichianil, J.** "Jeremiah, the Prophet of Prayer." *ITS* 18 (1981) 34–46. **Kutsch, E.** "Das Jahr der Katastrophe: 587 V Chr. Kritische Erwägungen zu Neueren Chronologischen Versuchen." *Bib* 55 (1974) 520–45. **Laberge, L.** "Le drame de la fidélité chez Jérémie." *ET* 11 (1980) 9–31. **Long, B. O.** "Prophetic Authority as Social Reality." In *Canon and Authority*, ed. G. W. Coats and B. O. Long. Philadelphia: Fortress, 1977. 3–20. **Lörcher, H.** "Das Verhältnis der Prosareden zu Erzählungen im Jeremiabuch." *TLZ* 102 (1977) 395–396. [Summary of 1974 Tübingen dissertation.] **Ludwig, T. M.** "Law-gospel Tension in Jeremiah." *CTM* 36 (1965) 70–79. **Malamat, A.** "Jeremiah and the Last Two Kings of Judah." *PEQ* 83 (1951) 81–87. **Manahan, R. E.** "An Interpretive Survey: Audience Reaction Quotations in Jeremiah." *GTJ* 1 (1980) 163–83. ———. "A Theology of Pseudoprophets: A Study in Jeremiah." *GTJ* 1 (1980) 77–96. **Marböck, J.** "Jeremia." *BLit* 50 (1977) 85–95. **Martin-Achard, R.** "Esaie et Jérémie aux prises avec les problèmes politiques." *RHPR* 47 (1967) 208–24. **May, H. G.** "The Chronology of Jeremiah's Oracles." *JNES* 4 (1945) 217–27. ———. "Jeremiah's Biographer." *JBR* 10 (1942) 195–201. ———. "Towards an Objective Approach to the Book Jeremiah: The Biographer." *JBL* 61 (1942) 139–55. **Milgrom, J.** "Concerning Jeremiah's Repudiation of Sacrifice." *ZAW* 89 (1977) 273–75. **Muilenburg, J.** "The Terminology of Adversity in Jeremiah." In *Translating and Understanding the Old Testament*, ed. H. T. Frank and W. L. Reed. Nashville: Abingdon, 1970. 42–63. **Orlinsky, H. M.** "Nationalism-Universalism in the Book of Jeremiah." In *Understanding the Sacred Text*, ed. J. Reumann. Valley Forge: Judson, 1972. 61–84. **Overholt, T. W.** "Jeremiah and the Nature of the Prophetic Process." In *Scripture in History and Theology: Essays in Honor of J. Coert Rylaarsdam*, ed. A. Merrill and T. Overholt. Pittsburgh: Pickwick, 1977. 129–50. ———. "Remarks on the Continuity of the Jeremiah Tradition." *JBL* 91 (1972) 457–62. ———. "Some Reflections on the Date of Jeremiah's Call." *CBQ* 33 (1971) 165–84. **Pilch, J. J.** "Jeremiah and Symbolism." *TBT* 19 (1981) 105–11. **Reid, D. P.** "Prophet Wanted—No Coward Need Apply." *TBT* 18 (1980) 11–16. **Roche, M. de.** "Contra Creation, Covenant and Conquest (Jer. viii 13)." *VT* 30 (1980) 280–90. **Rowley, H. H.** "The Early Prophecies of Jeremiah in Their Setting." *BJRL* 45 (1962) 198–234. **Schehr, T.** "Jeremiah: The Power of God's Word." *TBT* 19 (1981) 87–92. **Schreiner, J.** "Ja sagen zu Gott—Der Prophet Jeremia." *TLZ* 90 (1981) 29–40. **Schutzinger, H.** "Die arabische Jeremia-Erzählungen und ihre Beziehungen zur jüdischen religiosen Überlieferung." *ZRGG* 25 (1973) 1–19. **Sturdy, J. V. M.** "The Authorship of the 'Prose Sermons' of Jeremiah." In *Prophecy*, ed. J. A. Emerton. BZAW 150. Berlin: de Gruyter, 1980. 143–50. **Tambasco, A.** "Jeremiah and the Law of the Heart." *TBT* 19 (1981) 100–104. **Telcs, G.** "Jeremiah and Nebuchadnezzar, King of Justice." *CJT* 15 (1969) 122–30. **Tov, E.** "Some Aspects of the Textual and Literary History of the Book of Jeremiah." In *Le Livre de Jérémie: Le prophète et son milieu, les oracles et leur transmission*, ed. P.-M. Bogaert. BETL 54. Leuven: Leuven UP, 1981. 145–67. **Urbock, W. J.** "Jeremiah: A Man for Our Seasoning." *CurTM* 5 (1978) 144–57. **Vermeylen, J.** "Jérémie: le prophète et le livre." *ETL* 58 (1982) 140–44. **Weinfeld, M.** "Jeremiah and the Spiritual Metamorphosis of Israel." *ZAW* 88 (1976) 17–56. **Weisman, Z.** "Stylistic Parallels in Amos and Jeremiah: Their Implications for the Composition of Amos." *Shnaton* 1 (1975) 129–49. **Weften, P.** "Leiden und Leidenserfahrung im Buch Jeremia." *ZTK* 74 (1977) 123–50. **Whitley, C. F.** "The Date of Jeremiah's Call." *VT* 14 (1964) 467–83.

WORD
BIBLICAL
COMMENTARY

XV. Three Prophets, One Message
(26:1–24[LXX 33:1–24])

Bibliography

Boecker, H. J. *Redeformen des Rechtslebens im Alten Testament.* WMANT 14. 2nd ed. Neukirchen: Neukirchener, 1970. **Broshi, M.** "The Expansion of Jerusalem in the Reigns of Hezekiah and Manasseh." *IEJ* 24 (1974) 21–23. **Busink, T.** *Der Tempel von Jerusalem von Salomo bis Herodes: 1. Der Tempel Salomos.* Leiden: Brill, 1970. **Carroll, R.** "Prophecy, Dissonance, and Jeremiah xxvi." *TGUOS* 25 (1976) 12–23. Repr. in *A Prophet to the Nations: Essays in Jeremiah Studies,* ed. L. Perdue and B. Kovacs. Winona Lake, IN: Eisenbrauns, 1984. 381–91. **Clark, W. M.** "Law." In *Old Testament Form Criticism,* ed. J. H. Hayes. San Antonio: Trinity UP, 1974. **Driver, G. R.** "Abbreviations in the Massoretic Text." *Textus* 1 (1960) 112–31. ———. "Hebrew Notes." *VT* 1 (1951) 241–50. **Fishbane, M.** "Varia Deuteronomica." *ZAW* 84 (1972) 349–52. **Geva, H.** "The Western Boundary of Jerusalem at the End of the Monarchy." *IEJ* 29 (1979) 84–91. **Hadey, J.** "Jérémie 7 et 26." *ETR* 54 (1979) 438–43. **Haran, M.** *Temples and Temple Service in Ancient Israel: An Inquiry into the Character of Cult Phenomena and the Historical Setting of the Priestly School.* Oxford: Clarendon, 1978. **Holt, E. K.** "Jeremiah's Temple Sermon and the Deuteronomists: An Investigation of the Redactional Relationship between Jer 7 and 26." *JSOT* 36 (1986) 73–87. **Hossfeld, F. L.,** and **Meyer, I.** "Der Prophet vor dem Tribunal: Neuer Auslegungsversuch von Jeremia 26." *ZAW* 86 (1974) 30–50. **Janzen, W.** "Withholding the Word." In *Traditions in Transformation: Turning Points in Biblical Faith,* ed. B. Halpern and J. D. Levenson. Winona Lake, IN: Eisenbrauns, 1981. **Koch, K.** "Der Spruch 'Sein Blut bleibe auf seinem Haupt' und die israelitische Auffassung vom vergossenen Blut." *VT* 12 (1962) 396–416. **North, F. S.** "Textual Variants in the Hebrew Bible Significant for Critical Analysis." *JQR* 47 (1956/57) 77–80. **O'Connor, K. M.** "'Do Not Trim a Word': The Contributions of Chapter 26 to the Book of Jeremiah." *CBQ* 51 (1989) 617–30. **Ollenburger, B. C.** *Zion, the City of the Great King.* JSOTSup 41. Sheffield: JSOT, 1987. **Ramsey, G. W.** "Speech–Forms in Hebrew Law and Prophetic Oracles." *JBL* 96 (1977) 45–58. **Reventlow, H. G.** "Gattung und Überlieferung in der 'Tempelrede Jeremias': Jer. 7 und 26." *ZAW* 81 (1969) 315–52. **Schottroff, W.** *Der altisraelitische Fluchspruch.* WMANT 30. Neukirchen: Neukirchener, 1969. **Schulz, H.** *Das Todesrecht im Alten Testament: Studien zur Rechtsform der Mot–Jumat–Sätze.* BZAW 114. Berlin: de Gruyter, 1969. **Seidl, T.** "Datierung und Wortereignis: Beobachten zum Horizont von 27:1." *BZ* 21 (1977) 23–44, 184–99. **Steck, O. H.** *Israel und das Gewaltsame Geschick der Propheten.* WMANT 22. Neukirchen: Neukirchener, 1967. **Thomas, W.** "Again 'The Prophet' in the Lachish Ostraca." In *Von Ugarit nach Qumran,* ed. J. Hempel and L. Rost. BZAW 77. Berlin: de Gruyter, 1958. 244–49.

Translation

[1] *In the accession year*[a] *of Jehoiakim, the son of Josiah, the king of Judah, there was this word*[b] *from*[c] *the* LORD:
[2] *"Thus says the* LORD: *Stand in the court of the* LORD'*s house and speak against*[a] *all the cities of Judah who are coming to worship at*[b] *the* LORD'*s house all the words which I command you to speak to them. Do not hold back a word.* [3]*Perhaps they will listen and turn back, each one from his [or her]*[a] *evil*[b] *way, so that I will repent of*[c] *the evil*[b] *which*

I am planning to do to them because of the evil[b] *of their doings.* [4]*So say to them, 'Thus says the LORD: If you do not listen to me by walking in my Law, which I have set before you,* [5]*by listening to the words of my servants the prophets whom I send to you — sending*[a] *persistently, but you did not listen—* [6]*then I will make this house like Shiloh while I make this*[a] *city a curse*[b] *for all the nations of the earth.'"*

[7]*The priests, the prophets, and all the people heard Jeremiah speaking these words in the house of the LORD.*

[8]*As soon as*[a] *Jeremiah finished speaking all that the LORD had commanded (him)*[b] *to speak to*[c] *all the people, the priests, the prophets, and* [d]*all the people*[d] *seized him, saying, "You must die!* [9]*Why do you prophesy*[a] *in the name of the LORD, saying, 'Like Shiloh will be this house, and this city will be desolate, without an inhabitant'?" Then all the people assembled around*[b] *Jeremiah in the house of the LORD.*

[10]*The royal officials of Judah heard these words and went up from the king's house to the house of the LORD and sat down at the entrance of the new gate of the LORD('s house).*[a]

[11]*Then the priests and the prophets said to the officials and to all the people, "The death sentence for this man! For he has prophesied against*[a] *this city as you have heard with your own ears."*

[12]*Jeremiah said to all*[a] *the royal officials and to all the people, "The LORD sent me to prophesy to this house and to this city all the words which you have heard.* [13]*So now make your ways and your works good and obey the LORD your God so that the LORD will repent of*[a] *the evil which he has spoken against you.* [14]*As for me, I am in your power, so do to me what you consider good and fair.* [15]*Only you must know that if you put me to death you are certainly going to put innocent blood on yourselves and onto this city and its inhabitants, because the LORD truly has sent me to you to speak all these words in your ears."*

[16]*Then the royal officials and all the people said to the priests and the prophets, "No death sentence for this man! For he has spoken to us in the name of the LORD our God."*

[17]*Men of the elders of the land rose and said to the whole assembly of the people:* [18]*"When Micah*[a] *the Moreshetite was prophesying*[b] *in the time of Hezekiah, the king of Judah, he said to the whole people of Judah, 'Thus says the LORD* [c]*of Hosts:*[c]

'Zion as a field[d] *shall be ploughed,*
and Jerusalem shall be ruins,[e]
and the mountain of the house, wooded heights.' [f]

[19]*Did Hezekiah, the king of Judah, and all Judah put*[a] *him to death? Didn't he fear*[b] *the LORD and*[c] *pray for the favor of*[c] *the LORD? Didn't the LORD repent of the evil which he had spoken against them? We are about to do a great evil against our very lives!"*

[20]*A man was also prophesying in the name of the LORD, Uriah the son of Shemaiah from Kiriat Jearim.*[a] *He prophesied* [b]*against this city and*[b] *against this land in accordance with all the words of Jeremiah.* [21]*The king, Jehoiakim,* [a]*all his mighty men,*[a] *and all the royal officials heard his words, and the king*[b] *sought*[c] *his execution. Uriah heard;* [d]*so he was afraid and fled*[d] *and went to Egypt.* [22]*Then the king, Jehoiakim, sent*[a]*men to Egypt,*[a] [b]*Elnathan the son of Achbor and other men with him.*[b] [23]*They brought Uriah out of Egypt, took him to the king, Jehoiakim, and he killed him with the sword. He*[a] *sent his corpse to the graves*[b] *of the sons of the people.*[c]

[24]*But the hand of Ahikam, the son of Shaphan, was with Jeremiah so as not to give him into the hand of the people to put him to death.*

Notes

1.a. The abstract noun ממלכות in the sense of "reign" is unique in Jeremiah. There is no evidence, however, to support emendation to the more common spelling ממלכת, "reign" (27:1; 28:1), or מלכות, "reign." The equivalent Akk. phrase, *reš šarruti*, "accession year," uses a noncognate word. The inconsistent Heb. usage probably results from the newness of the expression. A standardized form had not yet been achieved.

1.b. Syr (and OL) add "to Jeremiah." Beginning with 25:1, the headings of the major units in this section of the book all introduce Jeremiah either by name (25:1; 27:1; 29:1; 30:1; 32:1; 33:1; 34:1; 35:1; 36:1) or with the first person pronoun (28:1 and, in LXX, 35:12; 36:1). The heading of the Temple Sermon in 7:1 also names Jeremiah. Since 26:1 begins a major division of the book, and, since it is otherwise nearly identical to 27:1, the pressure to insert the prophet's name in this heading must have been acute. Therefore, the verse should be left as in MT.

1.c. מאת, "from," appears frequently in headings of major units in this section of the book (27:1; 30:1; 32:1; 34:1; 34:8; 35:1; 36:1), indicating the origin of the word.

2.a. The hostile intent expressed by this prep fits the content of v 6 (GKC § 119dd).

2.b. The deity being worshiped is not specified, and the place of worship is indicated by an adv acc (GKC 118 § d–g). Compare Exod 33:10; Ezek 46:3.

3.a. Women may have been among Jeremiah's hearers.

3.b. The same Heb. word is used in each case.

3.c. אל הרעה. The usual combination is על הרעה, and many MSS support that reading. אל replaces על in this chapter (26:3, 13, 19) and once in 2 Sam 24:16, without any change in meaning.

5.a. Lit. "getting up early and sending," interpreted as hendiadys, "persistently."

6.a. The unusual K form of the demonstrative adj with final ה leads Janzen to conclude that the demonstrative הזאתה originated in a MS tradition in which this spelling is usual (*Studies*, 45). The Q calls for the standard spelling. The word is absent from LXX. In divine speeches in Jeremiah prose, the usual designation for Jerusalem is העיר הזאת, "this city."

6.b. The prep ל marks the product of the divine activity אתן, "I make."

8.a. The prep כ has a temporal function.

8.b. The ancient versions all have the obj pronoun, "him." In Heb. the person(s) receiving the command may be omitted, as it is here (e.g., Exod 16:16).

8.c. *BHS* suggests substituting על, "against, about," for אל, "to." LXX translates אל as "against" in v 11b, but *BHS* proposes no emendation there. The interchange of these two preps is so frequent in Jeremiah that one is deterred from attempting to bring them into conformity with earlier usage.

8.d-d. *BHS* judges כל־העם, "all the people," to be an addition from v 7a. See the *Comment* on v 8.

9.a. Some MSS correct the spelling to נבאת by reinstating the א.

9.b. Several MSS and versions substitute the more threatening על, "against," for אל, "to." על, "against," does occur with קהל, "assemble, congregate," in circumstances where a threat is clearly present (Exod 32:1; Num 16:3; 17:7; 20:2). The prep אל, "to," however, may also occur with this verb, as in Lev 8:4, Aaron's ordination, and 1 Kgs 8:2, the dedication of the temple. Furthermore, אל, "to," frequently occurs in the book of Jeremiah where one would otherwise expect על, "against." Emendation of the text is not warranted.

10.a. LXX^Q, Arab, Syr, Tg, and Vg insert בית, "house of." "The new gate of the house of the LORD" is known from Jer 36:10. It is clear from the context that the royal officials go to the temple courtyard to participate in the trial. There is no significant difference in meaning between "the New Gate of the LORD" and "the New Gate of the LORD's house."

11.a. LXX translates κατά, "against," suggesting Heb., על, "against." In the book of Jeremiah, אל, "to," frequently occurs where one would expect על, "against." No emendation is warranted.

12.a. LXX omits "all." Its presence in MT can be explained as dittogr from the following phrase, "all the people," either accidental or intentional, or as another example of the longer Heb. text behind MT.

13.a. Several MSS substitute על, "against," for אל, "to." נחם על, "repent of," is the more common form of this expression in the OT. However, נחם אל, "repent of," is also found (e.g., 2 Sam 24:16//1 Chr 21:15). נחם אל, "repent of," is used regularly in chap. 26 (vv 3, 13, 19; and in 42:10). No emendation is warranted.

18.a. The Q, supported by many MSS, is the short form מיכה, "Micah," as in Mic 1:1. The K is

מִיכָיָה, "Micaiah," as in 2 Kgs 22:12 and Neh 12:35, 41. The K ending corresponds to the alternate form of Jeremiah's and others' names in chaps. 27–29 (יִרְמְיָה, "Jeremiah").

18.b. LXX omits the ptcp "prophesying" in this verse but not in v 20. Pf of הִיה plus ptcp is an unusual construction (GKC § 116r) but not impossible. The simpler syntax in LXX does not significantly alter the meaning of the sentence.

18.c-c. LXX lacks "of Hosts." The longer form of the divine name is more common in MT than in LXX (Janzen, *Studies*, 79–80).

18.d. Adv acc, "fieldlike."

18.e. In Mic 3:12 this word is spelled עִיִּין. Fishbane suggests that עִיִּין is a northern dialect form (*Interpretation*, 459). One MS of LXX reads ὡς ἄβατον, "as a desolation," substituting a relative adj for the article. Another LXX MS has ὡς ὀπωροφυλάκιον, "as a watchman's hut in a garden," a description of Zion found in Isa 1:8 that forms a fine parallel to the preceding colon.

18.f. The verb from the preceding colon, תִהְיה, "will be," indicates the relationship between subj and predicate in this colon also. The prep ל indicates product.

BHS notes a proposal that בָמוֹת is a variant of בְהֵמוֹת, "beasts, animals." This reading would maintain the agricultural imagery of the rest of the verse. Occupation of a ruined city by animals is a motif found in judgment oracles (e.g., Ezek 25:5), but בְהֵמוֹת, "beasts, animals," is never used in this way in the rest of the OT. The phrase בְהֵמוֹת יַעַר, "beasts of the forest," occurs once, in Mic 5:7[Eng 8], but בָמוֹת יַעַר, "wooded heights," is unique to Jer 26:18 and Mic 3:12. Fishbane accounts for בָמוֹת as a northern dialect version of בְהֵמוֹת, "beasts, animals," in which intervocalic ה has been elided (*Interpretation*, 459). There is, however, no support in the ancient versions for this reading. LXX interprets בָמוֹת יַעַר and corrects it to the sg ἄλσος δρυμοῦ, "grove of trees." In the OT בָמוֹת, "high places," were worship sites, regularly associated with trees (e.g., 2 Kgs 16:4), so the translators of LXX understood בָמוֹת as "high places," not as a variant spelling of בְהֵמוֹת, "beasts, animals." Syr reads *lbjt*, "to a house," copying the previous word. Lacking overwhelming evidence for Fishbane's hypothesis, it seems best to go on reading בָמוֹת as "high places, heights" as it has been for at least two millennia.

19.a. LXX, Vg, Syr all have a sg verb. Since Heb. style permits an initial masc sg verb before a compound subj (GKC § 146F), the versions may have translated according to that pattern.

19.b. LXX, Vg, Syr translate these verbs as pl. Hezekiah and all Judah are the subjs. By including "all Judah," these two rhetorical questions are even more effective in reaching the elders' audience by comparing them not just with the king but with their counterparts a century earlier. The pl forms also agree with the pl suff of עֲלֵיהֶם, "against them," at the end of the sentence. The MT is retained in the translation for two reasons: (1) It is the more difficult reading, because the sg subj does not agree with the pl pronom suff. (2) 2 Kgs 19, to which this verse apparently refers, is only about Hezekiah's repentance and prayer. The people's response is not reported, although the threat endangered all of them.

19.c-c. Lit. "soften" or "smooth the face," or perhaps "stroke the cheek," a gesture intended to have a calming effect.

20.a. The second word in this name has the definite article, a form unique to this verse.

20.b-b. LXX lacks "against this city and." The phrase may have been lost from LXX or its *Vorlage* by haplogr, or MT may be a conflate text (so Janzen, *Studies*, 21, 199). The city has been the subject of prophecy in the rest of the chapter (vv 6, 9, 12), so its mention here confirms the similarity of Uriah's prophesying to Jeremiah's.

21.a-a. "All his warriors" is lacking in LXX. The term is not part of the stereotyped pairing of the king and the royal officials. All three appear together in at least one other place, 2 Chr 32:3, where King Hezekiah makes plans with his royal officials and warriors to prepare Jerusalem for the Assyrian siege. The inclusion of "all his warriors" subtly advances the comparison between Hezekiah and Jehoiakim.

21.b. Not in LXX. King, warriors, and officials together are the subj of "sought," which is pl in LXX. In v 23 it is the king's men who bring Uriah back from Egypt, but the king puts him to death. LXX fits the context, but there is no compelling reason to favor it over MT.

21.c. LXX has the pl. See *Note* 21.b.

21.d-d. Lacking in LXX. MT provides the obvious motivation for Uriah's flight to Egypt. Janzen considers this a conflate text: "heard" and "fled"//"feared" and "went" (*Studies*, 21).

22.a-a. Syr smooths out the Heb. syntax by a small change. "Men to Egypt" becomes "an Egyptian man," which identifies Elnathan, son of Achbor. This eliminates the repetition of "to Egypt," but Elnathan was not Egyptian. He was a member of a prominent Judean family. The syntax of MT is awkward, because of the repetition of "men to Egypt," but not impossible.

22.b-b. Not in LXX. MT provides the detail of Elnathan's participation, which was probably not in LXX's *Vorlage.* Janzen (*Studies,* 14, 100–101) and Holladay (2:101) describe MT as conflate. Holladay brackets the first occurrence of "men to Egypt."

23.a. The king.

23.b. Sg in LXX: "the grave of his people," namely his family tomb. See *Note* 23.c.

23.c. LXX has υἱὸν λαοῦ αὐτοῦ, "of the sons of his people," belonging to his family. Uriah was from Kiriat-Jearim. Why would his family have a tomb in the vicinity of Jerusalem?

Form/Structure/Setting

Chap. 26 is a new unit, clearly distinguished from the poetry at the end of chap. 25 by the compound heading in v 1. The almost identical heading in 27:1 sets the end boundary for this set of narratives. The lack of a connecting verb at the beginning of the chapter also suggests the relative independence of this unit. (Compare the use of ויהי, "and it came to pass," in 28:1 and 33:1 to establish a connection with the preceding chapter.)

Vv 1–6 constitute a report of revelation to a prophet. This genre provides a narrative setting for private oracles and words of instruction, but it may also have the effect of transforming an oracle addressed to Israel into a private revelation to the prophet. In chap. 26 the divine word addressed to the prophet has three parts: (1) a commission to prophesy to a particular audience at a specific location; (2) a description of the hoped-for response; and (3) the oracle itself. Similar reports are found throughout the book of Jeremiah (7:1–8:4; 16; 17:19–27; 18:1–12; 19; 21; 22:1–9; 24; 27–28; 29:29–32; 32–36). Although these reports often include a divine command to speak or act, they only occasionally recount the fulfillment of the command or the response by the people to the prophet's ministry.

The three-part introduction to chap. 26 (date formula, word-event formula, and messenger formula) marks this chapter in its present form as a composition of the traditionists who preserved the Jeremiah materials in a book. The section ruled by this heading is only this chapter. (See *Excursus: Introductory Formulas.*)

לאמר, "saying," at the end of 26:1 marks the beginning of a direct quotation of God's speech in vv 2–6. It seems odd that God's private words of instruction to Jeremiah should begin with the messenger formula, כה אמר יהוה, "thus says the LORD." This formula originally was not employed by the one sending the message. The messenger would prefix the formula to the message when delivering it.

The unit 26:2–7 reports the LORD's command to prophesy. It follows the literary pattern found throughout the books of Jeremiah and Ezekiel. The narrator's voice does not report the command and its execution in retrospect. Instead, the narrator quotes God's speech, which relates the events in prospect, in a series of commands to the prophet. Even the oracle meant to be delivered to the people is quoted in God's commands to Jeremiah. E. Davis attributes this form to the particular needs of written discourse. Writing everything as God's speech enhances the text's claim to authority. Portraying the prophet as a listener puts him in a position like that of the text's reader, who also hears God's word, so that he shows how a listener should respond (*Swallowing the Scroll,* 83). The narrator's voice is heard again in the last verse of the unit, which emphasizes the audience's hearing rather than Jeremiah's speaking in order to lead into the trial report in vv 8–16.

The oracle itself is a conditional sentence. Other reports of commands to prophesy include longer and more complex conditional messages (cf. 17:19–27; 18:1–11; 22:1–5). 26:4–5 also shares with these passages the motifs of adherence to the law and persistent rejection of the divine word. The distinctive reference to Shiloh in v 6 cues the reader to recognize vv 4–6 as an abridgment and interpretation of the Temple Sermon of 7:1–15.

The language of accusation in vv 8b–9a and 11 belongs to a trial and indicates the genre of the next part of the chapter. The report of the trial begins in v 8, but the end point is in dispute. Three possibilities have been advanced: (1) The trial lasts to the end of the chapter (Fishbane, *Interpretation*, 246). The royal officials proposed a "not guilty" verdict (v 16), which, however, was not accepted. The fact that v 16 refers to Jeremiah in the third person rather than addressing him in the second person is taken as evidence that it was not the official or final verdict. Two contradictory precedents are reported, the actions of King Hezekiah and Micah (vv 17–19) and those of King Jehoiakim and Uriah (vv 20–23), and the people decide to execute Jeremiah (implied in v 24). Only Ahikam's intervention rescues the prophet (v 24). (2) The precedent cited by the elders (vv 17–19) served as a defense speech, which preceded the verdict (v 16). Rudolph (156–57) proposes understanding v 17 in the pluperfect, "had risen and said." Calvin (3:331) raised the possibility of moving vv 17–19 before v 16. According to this interpretation, the elders' speech was part of the trial, which concluded with the verdict in v 16. (3) The trial ends in v 16 with the "not guilty" verdict, but opposition to Jeremiah's ministry, and others like it, continued (vv 20–24), in spite of the acquittal and the elders' speech.

The differences in these three analyses depend upon the interpretation of v 16 and vv 17–19. The major objection to accepting v 16 as the conclusion of the trial is that the verdict is expressed in the third person. In OT accounts of trials before a king (e.g., 1 Sam 14:44) or Joshua (Josh 7:25), the verdict is stated in the second person, but chap. 26 recounts a different sort of trial, a trial for a capital crime before the people. There is no other OT narrative of such a trial, but the law in Num 35 and Deut 19:1–13 gives instructions for handling fugitives accused of murder. The accused is referred to in the third person in the sentencing formulas, "the murderer shall be put to death" (Num 35:16–21) and "no death sentence for him" (Deut 19:6). A murderer was executed by the avenger of blood, and in some other capital cases the men of the city carried out the sentence by stoning the guilty party (Deut 21:21). It is reasonable that the verdict would be addressed to those who must perform the execution, so it is possible that the third-person form of the verdict is normal in this kind of trial. The official charges against Jeremiah in v 11 are also expressed in the third person and are addressed to the very judges who render the verdict in v 16, the royal officials and all the people.

Hossfeld and Meyer give three reasons for understanding v 16 in its present position as the concluding verdict in the trial (*ZAW* 86 [1974] 38). (1) The ones who speak the verdict are the very persons to whom the accusation and defense speeches have been addressed (vv 11 and 12). "The royal officials and all the people," therefore, speak here as judges. (2) V 17 begins with a new verb, קום,

"arise," as opposed to אָמַר, "say," and introduces new speakers, the elders, and hearers, קָהָל, "the assembly." (3) The verdict stated here neatly concludes the trial by rejecting the plaintiffs' proposed verdict and accepting the argument for the defense.

Nevertheless, v 24 implies that v 16 was not the final decision about Jeremiah's case, since the people want to put him to death (hiphil of מוּת, "die"). V 24, however, is closely connected by the conjunction אַךְ, "but," to the account in vv 20–23 of events that did not necessarily occur before Jeremiah's trial (cf. 26:1). The verdict in chap. 26 is never mentioned in the rest of the book, and it does not prevent further action against Jeremiah by the priests, the prophets, the royal officials, and the king (chaps. 29, 36, 37).

Jer 26:8–16 is the only complete trial account in the OT, so it serves as Boecker's chief model of the genre (*Redeformen*, 59–79, 94–120, 133–34, 180). He labels the parts of the trial account as follows:

(1) Proposed verdict and complaint, vv 8–9a. The priests, prophets, and all the people address Jeremiah, quoting a paraphrase of part of his oracle as proof of the charge. The complaint is made in the form of a reproachful question. Boecker believes that the reproachful question usually came first, opening the opportunity for a pretrial settlement (*Redeformen*, 67).

(2) The introduction of a proposed verdict (v 9) initiates a move from pretrial discussions to the assembly of the court. The people (v 9b) and the royal officials (v 10) gather to form the court.

(3) The accusation speech by the plaintiffs, the priests, and the prophets to the judges, the royal officials, and the people (v 11) refers to the accused in the third person. The first sentence of this speech is another statement of the proposed verdict, "The death sentence for this man." This formula is not used in any other narrative context in the OT, but it corresponds to the formula in Deut 19:6. An abridged version of the oracle is presented as evidence of the charge.

(4) The defense speech by the accused follows in vv 12–15. Jeremiah speaks to the judges, the royal officials, and the people. The speech begins and ends with a direct answer to the charges (vv 12b, 15). Jeremiah admits to the charge, emphasizing that truly the LORD had sent him to prophesy the words they had heard. He offers no evidence other than his own claim. He does not mention the precedent of the prophets whom the LORD had sent persistently in the past (v 5). Boecker calls v 13 a settlement proposal, as indicated by the imperative verbs (*Redeformen*, 117; see *Comment* on v 13).

The final two verses of the defense speech seem to have a strong emotional tone, but they are actually based on legal formulas. In v 14 Jeremiah acknowledges and does not dispute the court's jurisdiction in his case, but in v 15 he articulates the weighty legal responsibility of which they were already aware. Putting an innocent man to death would endanger the judges and their whole community, Jerusalem and all the other cities of Judah.

(5) The judges state the verdict (v 16). They simply negate the accusers' proposed verdict in a statement like Deut 19:6. The judges address their decision to the accusers, not to Jeremiah. They accept Jeremiah's argument in his own defense, "He has spoken to us in the name of the LORD our God."

The report of one final speech completes the account of Jeremiah's prophesying and trial in the temple. Instead of the expected word of acquittal addressed to Jeremiah, a previously unmentioned group speaks to the assembled people. Their perspective on the oracle they quote from Mic 3:12 is like that of the canonical book of Micah. The oracle is identified as the word of a particular person from the past whose name and home town are given and whose ministry is dated according to the reigns of particular kings (cf. Mic 1:1). Although the verse is from an oracle addressed to "rulers" and "chiefs" (Mic 3:9), the elders interpret it as a divine word for all the people of Judah, just as the book of Micah addresses the whole people of God. Finally, the elders add the messenger formula as an introduction to the verse they quote, testifying that they believe that Micah had truly spoken a word from the LORD.

The elders begin to tell a short, simple story in v 18, and then, by means of a series of rhetorical questions, they draw upon their audience's knowledge to complete it. In the course of acknowledging the answers to their questions, the elders' hearers compare themselves to Hezekiah and are reminded of the divine offer they have heard by way of Jeremiah (v 13). The elders conclude their speech with an unconditional word of warning, but the story of Hezekiah offers a way to imagine a different ending for their community. Hezekiah's response to Micah is a model of human repentance that leads God to repent.

The story of Jeremiah's prophesying in the temple ends inconclusively with v 19, but the chapter continues with two connected reports of the persecution of prophets. This final unit lacks an introduction. These verses are either a continuation of the elders' speech (vv 18–19) or a report by the narrator of the chapter. Although the first verse matches v 18 in syntax and diction and vv 20–23 mirror the content of vv 18–19, the style of this unit is quite different, indicating a narrator other than the elders. (Note the style of 36:20–26 in comparison to the rest of chap. 36.) These verses narrate several actions, but they quote no direct speech. The story, which spans the space and time of a round trip to Egypt, is told quickly, without any words of evaluation. The critique is to be provided by the reader after considering these verses in their context. The sparse details of the account give a glimpse of the relentless pursuit of a desperate fugitive, a violent death, and an ignominious burial, but the only mention of emotion is that of Uriah's fear.

The word נֵם, "also, another," in v 20, together with the similarities in form and content between vv 18–29 and vv 20–23, invite comparison between Micah and Hezekiah on the one hand and Uriah and Jehoiakim on the other. Hezekiah repented, but Jehoiakim killed the prophet. The similar content of Jeremiah's message (v 6) and Micah's oracle (v 18) has already been observed. Now the narrator reports that Uriah prophesied "according to all the words of Jeremiah," his contemporary. One must conclude from the context that Jehoiakim has shed innocent blood by killing God's prophet Uriah and has refused the opportunity to repent and avert the judgment.

The cases of Micah and Uriah have other functions in the chapter. They illustrate God's persistence in sending prophets (v 5). The plural noun in this stereotyped expression is illustrated by these stories of two other prophets. The LORD addresses the generation of Jeremiah, and the audience of the book, through prophets from the past as well as a prophet sent in the present.

The report of Uriah's death at the hand of King Jehoiakim also serves as evidence of continuing danger to Jeremiah, despite his acquittal by the court at the gate. In its context its function is similar to the reminder in 1 Kgs 18:3b–4, 13 of the way the royal official Obadiah had hidden one hundred prophets in a cave to save them from Queen Jezebel. The threat to Elijah's life was genuine (1 Kgs 19:2). Ahikam, a latter-day counterpart of Obadiah, saves Jeremiah from the people in the very brief report in v 24. The conjunction אַךְ, "but," indicates that the people's move against Jeremiah should be seen as related in some way to the execution of Uriah (contrary to Bright, 169, who moves v 24 after v 19).

This final unit, vv 20–24, is sometimes identified as a subsequent addition to the chapter (e.g., Carroll, 519, 522), but it is better to observe how it fits in the context of the chapter and of the book. Holladay (2:110) draws attention to the repetition of "cast his corpse" in 26:23, in the report of what King Jehoiakim did to Uriah, and in 22:19 and 36:30, in oracles against Jehoiakim. V 24 also offers the only available explanation for Jeremiah's inability to go to the temple in 36:5.

Jer 26:1–24 may be outlined as follows:

I. Jeremiah's prophesying in the temple (vv 1–19)
   A. Introduction (v 1)
   B. The command to prophesy (vv 2–7)
      1. The command to prophesy in the temple (vv 2–3)
      2. The oracle (vv 4–6)
      3. Report of Jeremiah's prophesying (v 7)
   C. The trial (vv 8–16)
      1. Pretrial accusation (vv 8–9a)
      2. Formation of the court (vv 9b–10)
      3. Formal indictment (v 11)
      4. Defense speech (vv 12–15)
      5. Verdict (v 16)
   D. The elders' speech (vv 17–19)
      1. Introduction (v 17)
      2. Report of Micah's prophesying (v 18)
      3. The lesson from Hezekiah (v 19)
II. Uriah's execution by Jehoiakim (vv 20–24)
   A. Report of Uriah's prophesying (v 20)
   B. Report of extradition and execution (vv 21–23)
   C. Report of Jeremiah's rescue by Ahikam (v 24)

Comment

1 בְּרֵאשִׁית מַמְלְכוּת, "at the beginning of the reign of" or "in the accession year of," is probably a technical term, parallel to the Akkadian *reš šarruti*, "accession year," which refers to the period between the death of the former king and the official enthronement of the new monarch at the new year. The first full year of the king's reign was reckoned as his first year. If the Hebrew term is being used in this technical sense, and if the new year was celebrated in the spring in Judah, as Hayes and Hooker propose, then the accession year of Jehoiakim would be calculated as Elul (August/September) 609 B.C. to the coronation in Nisan 608 (*Chronology*, 90). They propose that the occasion of the sermon was the fall pilgrimage festival in Tishri 609. The OT gives us no direct evidence about the enthronement of Judean kings in this period or the means of calculating dates according to their reigns.

The narrator composed this chapter within a Babylonian setting, so it seems likely that Babylonian terminology would have been employed, regardless of the customs of Jehoiakim's time. Elsewhere in the book, in 32:1 and 52:12, dates are given in terms of the regnal years of Nebuchadrezzar as well as of the Judean king. Both practices demonstrate a desire to coordinate the account of Jeremiah's ministry in the last years of the kingdom of Judah with the chronology of the Neo-Babylonian Empire.

Jehoiakim, son of Josiah, king of Judah, was made king in Jerusalem by Pharaoh Neco II. Following his victory over Josiah at Megiddo (2 Kgs 23:29) and an inconclusive battle with the Babylonians at Carchemish (both in 609 B.C.), Neco laid claim to Syria-Palestine. The pharaoh took prisoner the newly crowned Jehoahaz, installed Jehoiakim as his vassal, and collected a heavy tribute from Judah (2 Kgs 23:33–35). Jehoiakim, also called Eliakim, was the older half brother of Jehoahaz, also called Shallum (2 Kgs 23:31, 36). According to 1 Chr 3:15, Josiah had two other sons: Johanan, the firstborn, and Zedekiah, the third.

The death of Josiah, the imprisonment of Jehoahaz, and the appointment of Jehoiakim by Pharaoh Neco II ended the last period of Judean independence from the superpowers of the first millennium B.C. The planting and flowering of a faithful kingdom under Josiah never had a chance to produce fruit. Except for the date of the beginning of Jeremiah's ministry (or his birth, according to Holladay, 2:25) in the thirteenth year of Josiah (1:2; 25:3), the date in 26:1 is the earliest in the book. This incident from the beginning of Jehoiakim's reign cuts off the reader from speculation about what might have been if Josiah had not been killed and renders the question of Jeremiah's participation in the Josianic reform moot. From now on, one must respond to God's word through Jeremiah in a setting of the foreign domination of God's people.

Excursus: Introductory Formulas

Bibliography

Althann, R. "*berēʾšit* in Jer 26:1; 27:1; 28:1; 49:34." *JNSL* 14 (1988) 1–7. **Neumann, P. K. D.** "Das Wort, das geschehen ist." *VT* 23 (1973) 171–217. **Seidl, T.** "Die Wortereignisformel in Jeremia: Beobachtung zu den Formen Redeeröffnung in Jeremia, im Anschluss an Jer 27:1,2." *BZ* 23 (1979) 20–47.

The prose portions of the first half of the book (chaps. 1–25) use both the messenger formula and the word-event formula to introduce divine words within a narrative. In chap. 13, for example, three commands to perform symbolic acts are introduced by different formulas, the messenger formula in v 1, the word-event formula in v 3, and ויאמר . . . אלי, "said to me," in v 6. The oracle that interprets the actions is introduced by the word-event formula (v 8) and begins with the messenger formula (v 9). In 24:4–5 the word-event formula and the messenger formula together introduce a private oracle explaining the vision of good and bad figs.

The earliest function of the messenger formula, according to Westermann (*Basic Forms*, 131), was within a judgment oracle, following the reasons for judgment and introducing the announcement of judgment, as in Jer 11:11; 14:15. Already in the book of Amos, however, the messenger formula appears at the beginning of oracles (chaps. 1–2). The messenger formula may also appear at the beginning or in the middle of a private message to a prophet, which he is not commanded to repeat to others (e.g., 13:1, 9; 16:3, 5, 9; 32:28). Neumann judges this practice to have begun after Jeremiah's ministry (*VT* 23 [1973] 180). In 13:1; 17:19; 25:15; 27:2 the addition of אֵלַי, "to me," turns the messenger formula into a narrative introduction. The insertion of לֵאמֹר, "saying," after the messenger formula in 30:2 has the same effect. The divine name יהוה, "the LORD," in the messenger formulas in 33:2; 34:2; 35:12; 37:7 has been lengthened by descriptive phrases. These trends may give a hint of the reason for the existence of this pattern. Additional titles magnify the authority of the sender and the urgency of the commands. Notice the extended description of God before the oracle assigned to the foreign envoys in 27:4–5, which also begins with the messenger formula. When spoken, the messenger formula authenticates the oracle by naming its source. As part of the heading of a written report, it validates the divine origins of the prophet's actions as well as his or her words. All traditions connected with the prophet should be seen as the LORD's words (Neumann *VT* 23 [1973] 180). This development is evident in the headings of whole books that are titled "the word [sg] of the LORD" (Hos 1:1; Joel 1:1; Mic 1:1; Zeph 1:1).

The word-event formula typically concludes with לֵאמֹר, "saying," the term that signals the beginning of a direct quotation. When a temporal clause is added after the word-event formula, לֵאמֹר, "saying," moves to the end of the sentence, as in 25:1–2. When the description of the circumstances is long enough, the word-event formula may have to be repeated before the quotation begins, as in 32:1–6 and 34:8–12. The function of the word-event formula as a stereotyped heading for prophetic narratives is even more evident in 40:1 and 42:7. לֵאמֹר, "saying," is missing from the end of 42:7, since a third-person narrative about Jeremiah follows; God does not command him to speak. The unit introduced by the word-event formula in 40:1 contains no oracle at all. Does the captain of the guard speak the word of the LORD? This formula has come to function as a structuring element that stands at some distance from the content of the unit it heads.

The detailed form-critical studies of Neumann, on the word-event formula, in chaps. 1–25 (*VT* 23 [1973] 171–217), and Seidl, on the formulas found in 27:1–2 (*BZ* 23 [1979] 20–47), each propose a hierarchical as well as a chronological order of the function and forms of the word-event formula and other introductory formulas used in the book of Jeremiah. Neumann concludes that the variants of the word-event formula, as an incomplete sentence or title, head seven complexes of related material in Jer 1–25, chaps. 1–6, 7–10, 11–13, 14–17, 18–20, 21–24, and 25:1–13a (*VT* 23 [1973] 210). These divisions are the same as Rudolph's (1). Only the first and the seventh are dated. Within these large complexes, the word-event formula with imperfect verb, along with various other formulas, introduces the individual pericopes. Neumann attributes the seven-part arrangement marked by the word-event formula to a post–exilic redactor with a developed theology of the "word" of the LORD. McKane, on the other hand, treats this phenomenon as editorial touching up (lxxxv, 1). Seidl pursues this development further by identifying the combination of a date formula and the word-event formula in chaps. 1, 25–45 as a characteristic of the later stages of the book's development (*BZ* 21 [1977] 198), dated sometime in the late exilic or post-exilic period.

Chap. 26 begins a major division of the book. Its heading includes all three formulas discussed above, the date, word-event, and messenger formulas. The date formula that begins 26:1 is unusual because of its content and its initial position in the verse. The rare technical term בְּרֵאשִׁית מַמְלְכוּת, "in the accession year of," is the counterpart in form and specificity of the much more common date formula beginning בִּשְׁנַת, "in the year," and continuing with the number of the year and the name of the king. The latter formula is used in 1–2 Kings to state the synchronism of the reigns of the kings of Judah and Israel (e.g., 1 Kgs 15:1, 9, 33). 1–2 Kings and 1–2 Chronicles also use it to introduce reports of a king's activities (e.g., 2 Kgs 17:6; 1 Chr 26:31). In every occurrence in Kings and Chronicles, this date formula begins the sentence and the main clause has a verb in the perfect state (cf. 26:1, היה, "was"). Seidl (*BZ* 21 [1977] 191) locates the origin of the בשנת, "in the . . . year," date formula in the annals kept at the royal court. The accession-year formula has the same source, even though it happens to occur in the OT only in the book of Jeremiah (26:1; 27:1; 28:1; 49:34). Date formulas giving specific regnal years are concentrated in the second half of Jeremiah (26:1; 27:1; 28:1; 32:1; 36:1, 9; 39:1; 45:1; 49:34; 51:59; 52:4), but they also occur in the framing chapters of the first half (1:2–3 and 25:1). The regnal-year date formula is in initial position in its sentence only in 26:1; 27:1; 39:1. (Only ויהי, "and it came to pass," precedes it in 28:1; 36:1; 52:4.)

The second element in this complex heading is the word-event formula. This formula is very common in the deuteronomistic history as well as in the prophetic books, and it exists in several variations (Neumann, *VT* 23 [1973] 171–217). The characteristic vocabulary of this formula includes (1) the verb היה, "be," (2) its subject דבר, "word," (3) modified by the divine name יהוה, "the LORD," usually in the construct relationship דבר יהוה, "the word of the LORD," and (4) the person addressed, introduced by the preposition אל, "to." The formula may be a complete sentence that is part of the ongoing narrative or an incomplete sentence resembling a title. The most frequent variation is the sentence, "The word of the LORD came to me/to PN, (saying)." By Neumann's count this variation occurs eighty-five times in the OT, including twenty-one times in Jeremiah (*VT* 23 [1973] 174). The formula introduces a private word of divine instruction given to a prophet or a king (twice, in 1 Kgs 6:11; 1 Chr 22:8). The formula may signal an occurrence of revelation in the midst of a longer account of prophetic activity, or it may introduce a unit that contains both divine words and the prophet's own speech. In Ezekiel, the first-person version of the word-event formula marks the major divisions in the book (Neumann, *VT* 23 [1973] 191).

The word-event formula in 26:1 is also a complete sentence, but the verb היה, "be," is in the perfect state rather than in the narrative tense (waw consecutive plus imperfect). There are several other occurrences of this formula with perfect state היה, "there was," in initial position (Gen 15:1; 2 Chr 12:7; Jer 25:3; 27:1; 32:6; 36:1; Hag 1:1; 2:1, 10). The word-event formula in 26:1 exhibits two features distinctive to Jeremiah. The word was מאת יהוה, "from the LORD." With one exception, Ezek 33:30, this prepositional phrase modifies דבר, "word," only in the book of Jeremiah (7:1; 11:1; 18:1; 21:1; 26:1; 27:1; 30:1; 34:1, 8, 12; 35:1; 36:1; 37:17; 40:1). The word-event formulas in Jer 26:1; 27:1; 36:1 also have in common the phrase הדבר הזה, "this word." This phrase is used elsewhere in the OT to refer to a short saying, command, oracle, or report. It is most frequent in the book of Jeremiah, where elsewhere it specifies a single unit of speech, from a phrase in 23:38 to a whole "sermon" in 7:2. In the headings of chaps. 26, 27, and 36, "this word" refers to God's commands to the prophet regarding the circumstances for delivering the message as well as to the message itself.

2   The divine command is to stand in the court of the LORD's house (compare Jer 19:14). (Jeremiah's standing place in 7:2 is the gate of the LORD's house.) Like the palace and the homes of common folk, the LORD's house included a roofed structure (the temple proper), open courtyards, and outbuildings (1 Chr 28:11–12). The temple courts probably surrounded the building on at least three sides, and the whole area was rimmed by a wall with several gates. There are many references in the OT to "courts" and names of distinct courtyards or parts of the whole. 1 Kgs 7:12 distinguishes inner court and great court, which may correspond to the priests' court and great court in 2 Chr 4:9. 2 Chr 20:5 mentions a new court in the reign of Jehoshaphat, and Jer 36:10 locates the entry of the New Gate (26:10) in the upper court.

The courts of the temple were the public areas, open to all worshipers. Only priestly personnel entered the temple building or its porch (2 Chr 23:4–5). The Psalms speak often of the blessedness of time spent in worship in the courts of the LORD (Pss 65:5; 84:3, 11; 92:14; 100:4; 116:18–19; 135:2). This motivation brought Jeremiah's audience to the temple. The text mentions no particular feast, fast, or holiday.

"The cities of Judah" refers to their inhabitants, as in Jer 11:12, where this phrase is parallel to "the inhabitants of Jerusalem." Jer 36:6, 9 give the fuller expression "all the people who came from the cities of Judah." It seems likely that this congregation was not limited to city dwellers but included the rural population dependent upon each of the fortified cities.

God's command to speak "all the words which I command you" or "which I have commanded you," omitting nothing, could be heard as an introduction to a collection of all of Jeremiah's prophecies (Meyer, *Jeremia und die falschen Propheten,* 19). The goal of the preaching (26:3) is like the purpose of the scroll in 36:3: repentance by the people and forgiveness by God. The following vv 4–6 offer an abridgement of the Temple Sermon in Jer 7:1–15 as an indication of the specific content of the message on this occasion. The command not to withhold a word, therefore, must have to do with the authenticity of the message rather than its comprehensiveness. The message Jeremiah delivers is "the whole word of the LORD and nothing but the LORD's word." If the goal of repentance is to be achieved, the full message in all its harshness must be heard. V 8 reports that Jeremiah did speak every word that the LORD had commanded.

It is not unknown in the OT for a prophet to withhold the divine word, at least for a time. Samuel was reluctant to repeat a devastating message to Eli (1 Sam 3:15–18). Micaiah ben Imlah gave the expected favorable word first and only delivered the true message of doom when the king insisted (1 Kgs 22:13–28). W. Janzen ("Withholding the Word," 106–9) lists several reasons that a prophet might withhold the word; he finds examples of all but one of these in the book of Jeremiah: (1) fear of reprisal, Jer 11:21; 26:20–24; 38:15; (2) ill will toward personal enemies, Jer 43:2–3; (3) lying in God's service, 2 Sam 17:14; (4) commanded silence, Jer 23:33–40; and (5) a sense of futility, Jer 38:15. God commands neither lying nor silence in this case, and there is no indication that Jeremiah's emotional state prompted this divine instruction. In Jer 26 there is no suspense over Jeremiah's obedience. As an honest messenger, he delivers the authentic word of the LORD. By the standards of Ezek 3:16–21, Jeremiah is a faithful watchman.

K. M. O'Connor (*CBQ* 51 [1989] 627–28) translates אל־תגרע, "do not trim a word." She likens the Jeremiah tradition to a beard that must be allowed to grow. Cutting the beard is a sign of mourning over defeat, but a beard allowed to grow signals hope. Unlike the commands to Moses in Deut 4:2 and 13:1, Jeremiah is not commanded "Do not add." In chap. 36, the second, replacement scroll contains additional words (36:32).

3 The first half of v 3 is a shortened form of Jer 36:3a; it shares the key words "listen," "turn," and "from his evil way." Jer 36:7a is also very close in form and content to 26:3a. Jer 25:5 and 35:15 use the same terms to summarize the message of the LORD's servants the prophets, sent persistently in the past, to whom the people have refused to listen, "Turn now, every one of you, from your evil way." This is the LORD's message through Jeremiah in 18:11 and 25:5 also. In Ezekiel, too, the function of a true prophet is "to warn the wicked to turn from their ways" (Ezek 3:18, 19; 13:22; 33:8, 9, 11).

נחם, "repent," expresses an emotion-laden change of heart by which grief over one's actions or plans is assuaged. In the OT, human persons repent of something they have done or said that hurts God, others, or themselves (Exod 13:17; Job 42:6; Jer 31:19). God also may repent of a deed or, more often, of an announced plan and then act to undo the deed or cancel the plan. For example, the LORD repented of the creation of human beings and brought the flood (Gen 6:6, 7). Samuel's rhetorical insistence in 1 Sam 15:29 should not be taken as a statement of principle, "The Glory of Israel . . . will not repent, for he is not a human that he should repent," because just a few verses later, in 1 Sam 15:35, the narrator concludes, "for the LORD had repented that he had made Saul king over Israel."

On a few other occasions, the LORD does rule out the possibility of a change of heart (Ps 110:4; Jer 4:28; Ezek 24:14; Zech 8:14), but elsewhere the willingness to repent is presented as an integral part of divine dealings with humanity. The LORD responds to intercession by Moses (Exod 32–33) and Amos (Amos 7) by repenting of the disaster he intends to bring upon Israel. In Jer 18 and 26 the prophet is sent with a warning in the hope that the people will choose to turn from their evil in order that God may repent of and cancel the announced punishment. The LORD's willingness to repent of such plans is related to חסד, "steadfast love," or covenant loyalty, according to Ps 106:45; Joel 2:13; Jonah 4:2. The latter two verses echo the classic statement of God's mercy in Exod 34:6–7a except that "forgiving iniquity and transgression and sin" has been replaced by "repents from punishing." Given the relational, even passionate sense of the term, it is better to translate נחם by "repent" than to resort to the cooler alternatives "change his mind" or "relent."

4–5 The divine threat uses familiar terminology but somewhat surprising logic. The main clause of the protasis, "If you do not listen to me," is followed by two dependent clauses, each beginning with an infinitive construct with ל preposition, "by walking" and "by listening." The absence of waw conjunction at the beginning of v 5 indicates that the second dependent clause modifies the first. The logic goes like this: How does one listen to (i.e., obey) God? By walking in God's law. How does one walk in God's law? By listening to (i.e., obeying) God's servants the prophets. Refusing to listen to God is defined as failure to keep or walk in the law in Jer 6:19; 9:12; 16:11–12; 32:23; 44:10, 23. The full expression "my law . . . which I set before them/you" appears in 9:12; 44:10 as well as in 26:4. Jer 32:23; 44:10 offer reminders that the law had been given to the ancestors, who had also been disobedient. "Statutes" and "decrees" are listed with the law in 44:10, 23, but nowhere in Jeremiah is the law defined by a summary of its contents or a statement of its origin from Moses (contrast Neh 10:30). The implied audience of the book knows what the LORD's law entails and is accustomed to receiving this instruction from priests (Jer 18:18) or scribes (Jer 8:8).

5 Rudolph (154) and Holladay (2:104) identify this verse as a secondary addition because it overloads the protasis of the conditional sentence in vv 4–6. Vv

4 and 6 do make sense together in terms of grammar and content, but v 5 intervenes and introduces a crucial Jeremianic theme, God's persistent sending of the prophets, whose word the people continually reject. This theme occurs in five other passages in Jeremiah (7:25; 25:4; 29:19; 35:15; 44:4). In every one of these passages, plus the summary in 2 Chr 36:15, the indictment extends beyond the present generation to include their ancestors as well. Jer 25:3 uses the same adverb, "persistently," to characterize the twenty-three years of Jeremiah's speaking ministry. Add to these the passages in which God is said to have spoken or warned persistently (7:13; 11:7; 32:33; 35:14), and one has a depressing picture of continual rejection by Israel of the divine word, even though it was offered urgently and faithfully throughout her generations.

When the content of the prophets' words is indicated in these passages, their messages are similar: (1) turn back from your evil ways (25:5; 35:15; [44:5]); (2) do not worship other gods (25:6; 35:15; 44:5); (3) so that you may remain in the land (25:5; 35:15; 44:6). Jer 35:15 also has the command (4) "amend your doings" (compare 7:5–7). Three of these four motifs are found in Jer 26: (1) the LORD's goal in sending Jeremiah, v 3, is that the people may "turn back from their evil way"; (3) the threatened punishment includes the loss of Jerusalem, vv 6, 9; (4) Jeremiah's defense speech includes an exhortation to "amend your ways and your doings," v 13. There is no mention in chap. 26 of worshiping other gods. Jer 26:5 provides a link to other passages where the theme of prophets sent persistently and rejected consistently is expressed more fully. V 5 indicates that the threats against Jeremiah's life and the killing of Uriah in chap. 26 illustrate the theme and are part of the pattern. (See also Jer 44:4–14; 2 Kgs 17:13; Dan 9:10.)

6 The apodosis of the conditional sentence that begins in v 4 expresses the threatened judgment in two parallel statements. The second is a circumstantial clause syntactically subordinate to the first. The fates of city and temple are bound together, as they usually are in the book of Jeremiah.

The mention of Shiloh calls up the memory of Jer 7:1–15 and reveals the function of Jer 26 as an interpretive narrative contextualization of the longer sermon in the earlier chapter. Only Jer 7:12; 26:6; Ps 78:60–69 in the OT compare the fate of the house of the LORD in Jerusalem to that of Shiloh.

The occasion of the destruction of Shiloh remains in dispute, but the rhetorical effect of this comparison does not depend upon the resolution of the historical questions. (See *Excursus: Shiloh.*) By the time of Jeremiah's ministry, there was no place to worship the LORD in Shiloh. Jeremiah's audience and the audience of the book are presumed to know that Shiloh had once been an important cultic site, where the LORD had dealt with the whole people of Israel and where crucial events had taken place before the establishment of the monarchy (Josh 18–22; Judg 21; 1 Sam 1–4). They also knew or could see for themselves that Shiloh had been destroyed; no sanctuary existed there anymore. Jer 7:12 invites, "Go to my place which was in Shiloh and see what I did to it." It is impossible to know what remains a visitor in the sixth century B.C. would have seen there. Modern archeological investigations have found no ruins identifiable as a temple. Indeed, the summit of the tell was bare of architectural remains (I. Finkelstein, *The Archaeology of the Israelite Settlement* [Jerusalem: Israel Exploration Society, 1988] 205). One can be sure, however, that they would not have found a sanctuary where the legitimate worship of the LORD was conducted and that they would not have found the Ark.

To be made like Shiloh, therefore, involves at least three things: (1) demolition or delegitimation of the sanctuary; (2) removal of cultic implements, especially the Ark; and (3) withdrawal of God's name (Jer 7:12; Ps 78:61). These punishments are found elsewhere in Jeremiah's preaching, and all of them did happen to Jerusalem and the temple: (1) Jer 52:13; (2) 52:17–23; (3) Lam 2:7.

The threat that the city would be made a curse for the nations is a more common idea and involves a broader range of disasters (cf. 25:18). The nations would curse their enemies by saying, "May you be made like Jerusalem." An example of this kind of curse can be found in Jer 29:22, in which the false prophets Zedekiah and Ahab become a curse among the exiles, "The LORD make you like Zedekiah and Ahab, whom the king of Babylon roasted in the fire." This is the opposite of being made a blessing, as Abram is in Gen 12:2–3.

Being made a curse for other nations results in international celebrity as an example of horrible suffering. The punishments in store for Jerusalem, according to Jeremiah's preaching in the rest of the book, were severe. The echo of 26:6 by Jeremiah's accusers in v 9 names desolation or depopulation. 7:15, 20 name exile and destruction by fire. The poetry of Jer 9:10, 16–21[Eng 11, 17–22] laments Jerusalem's losses even more vividly, "Death has come up to our windows" (9:20[Eng 21]). It would be "made like Topheth," a city as defiled as a cemetery and overflowing with corpses according to chap. 19. Humiliation increases as the infamy of Zion's desolation spreads.

Excursus: Shiloh

Bibliography

Buhl, M. L., Holm–Nielson, S., and **Riis, P. J.** *Shiloh: The Danish Excavations at Tell Sailun, Palestine, in 1926, 1929, 1932, and 1963: The Pre-Hellenistic Remains.* Archaeological-Historical Series 1/12. Copenhagen: National Museum, 1969. **Day, J.** "The Destruction of the Shiloh Sanctuary and Jeremiah VII 12, 14." In *Studies in the Historical Books of the Old Testament.* VTSup 30. Leiden: Brill, 1979. 87–94. **Eissfeldt, O.** "Silo und Jerusalem." *Volume du Congres, Strasbourg 1956.* VTSup 4. Leiden: Brill, 1957. 138–47. **Finkelstein, I.** *The Archaeology of the Israelite Settlement.* Jerusalem: Israel Exploration Society, 1988. ———, **Bunimovitz, S.,** and **Lederman, Z.** "Excavations at Shiloh 1981–84: Preliminary Report." *Tel Aviv* 12 (1985) 123–80. **Pearce, R. A.** "Shiloh and Jer. VII 12, 14 & 15." *VT* 23 (1973) 105–8. **Schley, D. G.** *Shiloh, a Biblical City in Tradition and History.* JSOTSup 63. Sheffield: JSOT Press, 1989. **Seow, C. L.** *Myth, Drama, and the Politics of David's Dance.* HSM 44. Atlanta: Scholars, 1989.

Shiloh was an object lesson offered to the worshipers in the Jerusalem temple. For the ancient audiences, a multitude of implications and allusions were compressed in the short saying "this house shall be like Shiloh." Modern interpreters must address several historical and exegetical questions in order to tap the significance of this analogy.

Shiloh's rise to prominence in premonarchic Israel is cloaked in obscurity. It is not mentioned in Genesis, except for the poetic 49:10, nor does the OT describe the acquisition of Shiloh by the tribes. Nevertheless, in Joshua, Judges, and 1 Samuel, Shiloh is the place where the tent of meeting or tabernacle was pitched (Josh 18:1; 19:51; 22:12, 19, 29), the Ark was kept (1 Sam 3:3), sacrifices were burned on an altar (1 Sam 2:12–17, 28), and the family of Eli served as priests (1 Sam 1:3). It is also the site of the allotment of land to seven tribes (Josh 18–19). The occasions of the girls' dancing in the vineyard (Judg 21:19–21) and the sacrifice to which Elqanah brought his family annually (1 Sam 1:3) remain in dispute.

The complicated question of the nature of worship in Israel's earliest times cannot be resolved here. It is, however, essential not to lose sight of the canonical portrayal of Shiloh, according to which it bears several significant points of resemblance to Jerusalem: (1) The Ark, tent, and ephod were located in both cities. (2) Both cities possessed a house of the LORD. (3) Priests officiating at the altars in Shiloh and Jerusalem claimed descent from Aaron. (4) Shiloh was related to Israel's first kings, Saul and David, through the prophet Samuel and the Ark, although it never became a royal capital like Jerusalem. Even after Jerusalem became preeminent, the prophet Ahijah from Shiloh continued Samuel's role as divinely commissioned kingdom-taker and king-maker in his dealings with Jeroboam I (1 Kgs 11). (5) Shiloh was the site of decision making affecting all of Israel on two occasions: Joshua's allotment of land to the tribes (Josh 19:51) and the action taken with regard to the Transjordanian tribes and the altar they had built on the banks of the river (Josh 22). (In addition, Josh 24:1, 25 in LXX have "Shiloh" instead of "Shechem.") (6) The epithets "the LORD of hosts" and "the LORD of hosts who is enthroned on the cherubim" belong particularly to the worship of the LORD at Shiloh and Jerusalem (Seow, *Politics*, 10). (7) The most striking statement about the likeness of Shiloh to Jerusalem is made in Jer 7:12: the LORD's name had dwelt there before it was made to dwell in Jerusalem. The possibility of succession, which is implied in Deuteronomy's formula "the place where I will cause my name to dwell," has been realized in the OT only in the case of Shiloh and Jerusalem. (The Samaritan Pentateuch claims Mount Gerazim as the exclusive dwelling place of the divine name.) This claim is the most effective means of establishing the high status of Shiloh, a status equal to that of Jerusalem.

Furthermore, the OT never identifies the altar and sanctuary at Shiloh as rivals to the Jerusalem temple. Shiloh is absent, for example, from Amos 5:5. Other ancient holy places continued to attract worshipers, but Shiloh is not listed among them. Jeroboam I chose Bethel rather than Shiloh for the site of one of his official shrines, so, from the perspective of the deuteronomistic history, Shiloh escaped the taint of illegitimacy. The name of the LORD had once dwelt at Shiloh, but it had been withdrawn from there and settled in Jerusalem instead.

Judg 18:30–31 raises the possibility that a temple remained in Shiloh until the Assyrian conquest. According to v 30, the priests at Dan served until "the captivity of the land," in the eighth century B.C. The next verse says that the idols made by Micah were used in Dan as long as "the house of God was in Shiloh." Do vv 30 and 31 equate the two time measurements? Pearce concludes that these verses "attest to Shiloh's continued existence and function as a shrine until at least 732 B.C. and more probably 722 B.C." (*VT* 23 [1973] 107). It seems possible that the tenure of the priests was different from the period of use of the idols and that this difference was expressed by the two chronological comparisons. The date meant by v 31, then, would remain unknown and could be much earlier than the eighth century.

The canonical portrayal of Shiloh establishes its superiority to all other places of worship of the LORD before the temple was built in Jerusalem but then proclaims Shiloh's rejection in Jerusalem's favor. Descriptions of Shiloh's fall focus upon rejection and abandonment rather than destruction. In 1 Sam 4:21 Ichabod's name interprets the capture of the Ark that had been housed in Shiloh and the death of the priests who had officiated there. These losses meant that "the glory has departed from Israel."

"Glory" refers to the LORD's presence, not to fame or honor. Notice also that, according to this saying, Israel as a whole had been abandoned, not just Shiloh. The preceding narrative deals specifically with the punishment of the priestly line of Eli (1 Sam 2:27–36; 3:11–14), but Ichabod's mother articulates the full cost of their corruption when she names her son.

Ps 78:60–61 also uses the language of abandonment rather than annihilation. Shiloh and its tent are forsaken when the Ark and, with it, the divine splendor are exiled among God's enemies. The following verses (62–64) describe how the people were killed, and v 59 speaks of the complete rejection of Israel. Both "my people" and "Israel" are terms that encompass many more than the inhabitants of Shiloh. As in 1 Sam 4:21, when the LORD's presence forsakes Shiloh, the whole nation suffers the consequences.

Hannah's prayer or thanksgiving song in 1 Sam 2 does not mention the abandonment of Shiloh, but its theme of divine judgment and reversal of status fits the other descriptions of Shiloh's fate. The LORD kills and makes alive, humbles and exalts. While celebrating her own reversal from barren wife to happy mother of a son, the prayer anticipates the other reversals and replacements in the books of Samuel: Eli and his sons die, and then the Zadokites become priests in Jerusalem; the LORD rejects Saul and chooses David as king; the LORD abandons Shiloh and elects Jerusalem.

In Jer 7 and 26, the result of the LORD's rejection of Shiloh and, by analogy, Jerusalem, is first of all expulsion of the people. "What I did to Shiloh" in 7:14 is not explained in terms of ruins but in terms of exile: "I will thrust you out from my presence" (7:15) or "this city will be desolate, without an inhabitant" (26:9).

In spite of the emphasis upon rejection and abandonment in the passages about Shiloh's decline, recent exegesis has focused its efforts upon determining the date(s) when the shrine and settlement were destroyed. Because Jeremiah prophesies the military defeat and subsequent destruction of Jerusalem, it seems logical that the analogy with Shiloh has to do with the ruins to be found there.

The site of ancient Shiloh is generally agreed to be Seilun, located about thirty miles north of Jerusalem in the territory of the tribe of Ephraim. Three expeditions have carried out excavations at the tell, but varying interpretations of the archeological evidence have prevented the achievement of consensus about the history of the settlement. Buhl and Holm-Nielsen concluded from the findings of the Danish excavations in the 1920s and 1963 that the site had been occupied continuously from the second millennium until the end of the eighth century B.C., when it was destroyed by the Assyrians (Schley, *Shiloh*, 70). I. Finkelstein interprets the remains examined by the recent Israeli excavations (1981–84) as evidence of a destruction by fire c. 1050 B.C., which he associates with the Philistine defeat of the Israelites at Aphek (*Archaeology*, 225–26). The date of the destruction of Iron Age Shiloh remains in dispute because it depends upon the relative chronology of pottery types (Schley, *Shiloh*, 78). No dated artifacts were discovered that could help to fix the precise date of the destruction layer. It is still impossible to know what ruins were to be seen in Shiloh in Jeremiah's time at the end of the seventh century or what had caused the city's destruction.

Another question also remains unresolved: Was a temple ever built at Shiloh? Jer 26 mentions only the city's name, not the structure within it, and 7:12 calls it "my place" (מקומי). "Place" specifies neither building nor tent. Several passages refer to the tabernacle (Ps 78:60) or tent of meeting (Josh 18:1; 19:51) at Shiloh. 2 Sam 7:6 states that the LORD had never lived in a "house" before the temple was built in Jerusalem. The story of Samuel and Eli in the early chapters of 1 Samuel, however, refers to the בית, "house" (1:24), and even the היכל, "palace," of the Lord (1:9; 3:3). Although there is at least one reference to the making of בתים, "houses," for a cultic setting that seems to be about the weaving of cloth for draperies or a canopy (2 Kgs 23:7), היכל, "palace," is always a building. The detail that the temple at Shiloh had a doorpost (1:9) confirms this interpretation. Haran proposes that the author has projected features of the temple he knew later in Jerusalem onto his description of the structure in Shiloh (*Temples*, 202). Schley proposes both a temple, probably surviving from an earlier period, and the tent on the same site (*Shiloh*, 141). The Talmud suggests a hybrid structure, built "of stones below and curtains above" (*b. Zebah.* 112b, 118a and *y. Meg* 1.14, cited by Haran, *Temples*, 202). No one knows what Jeremiah's audience would have seen in Shiloh, except that they would not have seen a temple. Perhaps Mic 3:12, quoted in Jer 26:18, describes the usual appearance of abandoned cities.

7 Hossfeld and Meyer (*ZAW* 86 [1974] 36) propose to translate v 7 as a dependent temporal clause, "When the priests, the prophets, and all the people heard . . ." They connect v 7 to vv 4–6, and v 8a, which is also a temporal clause, to v 2. Even if two parallel reports have been combined in these verses, the function of v 7 in the present form of the narrative is not to make a distinction between the oracle in vv 4–6 and "all the words which I command you to speak" in v 2. There is no syntactical marker to indicate a subordinate, temporal function for v 7. (The verse begins with waw consecutive.)

This report, therefore, completes the chain of evidence and makes the transition to the trial scene. Jeremiah did, indeed, speak "these words," just given to him in vv 4–6. He spoke in the house of the LORD, as he had been instructed (v 2). The priests, prophets, and all the people even heard (שׁמע), but not as God had hoped. They "heard" Jeremiah speaking, but they did not "hear" in the sense of heeding and obeying. The following trial scene, as well as the report in v 24, demonstrates their failure to turn back from their evil ways (compare v 3). V 7 completes the first episode of the chapter.

8 A new unit, recounting Jeremiah's trial in the temple courtyard, begins with a recapitulation in the form of a temporal clause. It is not surprising that the narrative reports again that Jeremiah had spoken "all that the LORD had commanded" (v 2), since this claim is the point at issue in Jeremiah's trial. The narrator's verdict is stated at the beginning of the report, but the trial scene proceeds in a straightforward manner using direct quotes and lacking negative comments about Jeremiah's accusers and judges. The main verb, תפשׂ, "seize," also occurs in 37:14 in the sense of "arrest, take into custody."

"All the people" is a somewhat fluid designation in these verses. This group hears the preaching (v 8a), participates in the arrest (v 8b), and shares with the royal officials the duty of deciding the case (vv 9b, 11, 16). Only in v 8b do "all the people" act with the priests and prophets. Rudolph (170) deletes the phrase from v 8b to eliminate the apparent confusion. Nicholson (*Preaching to the Exiles*, 53) does not find it necessary to alter the text. Instead, he interprets "all the people" in v 8b as a "mob," distinct from the people who formed the court in vv 11, 16. Going further, he equates "all the people" in vv 11, 16 with "the elders of the land" in v 17. Both of these solutions presume that the judges must exhibit pretrial impartiality. Not enough is known about Israelite court procedure to support this assumption. In this case, there is certainly no indication that the judges were screened before taking their places. Accusers and defendant had to argue their case before whoever happened to be present. The effect of the shifting role of "all the people" in this chapter is to portray them as a changeable crowd, not as a group divided into pro- and anti-Jeremiah parties. At one moment they share the outrage of the priests and prophets and call for a trial (vv 8–9). When they hear Jeremiah's defense, however, they decide to acquit him (v 16). Even so, they reject the divine word and want to assassinate the LORD's prophet (v 24).

The very first words of the accusers, "You must die!" are not just a cry of rage. They are a second-person active form of the death sentence. A third-person passive form, מות יָמוּת, "he shall be put to death," is found in several places in the Pentateuch, including three lists of capital crimes in Exod 21, Lev 20, and Num 35. Many of these occurrences are apodictic, taking the form "whoever does X" (expressed by a participle in Hebrew) or "the one who does X" (expressed by a relative clause). They are categorical, expressing legal penalties applicable at all times. Only three times in the OT is this apodictic form used to formulate a prohibition of limited duration: Gen 26:11; Exod 19:12; Judg 21:5. Active forms of the same clause, in first, second, and third person are found in direct address, in which a sentence of death is threatened or announced for a particular individual or group within specific circumstances. (An exception is the first-person expression in 2 Sam 14:14, which acknowledges general human mortality rather than a sentence of death for a particular offense.) God or a king gives a command or imposes an oath, warning of the death penalty for violators, or pronounces the death sentence personally. 1 Sam 14:26–46; 1 Kgs 2:36–46 tell of oaths imposed by kings upon subject persons under the threat of death. When they are violated, the king declares, "You must die." God gives personal commands to the humans in Gen 2:17 and to Abimelech in Gen 20:7 that carry the death penalty. Prophets reveal the divine sentence of death against the child of David and Bathsheba (2 Sam 12:14), King Ahaziah of Israel (2 Kgs 1:4, 6, 16), and King Ben-Hadad in Damascus (2 Kgs 8:10). In Ezekiel 3, 18, 33, this death sentence appears as part of case law defining the responsibilities of a prophet. If the LORD announces the judgment "You must die" upon a wicked person, who is defined in 18:13 as a violator of law, the prophet must communicate that warning or be guilty of a capital crime himself. The possibility of turning from evil and receiving a promise of life is also laid out in these chapters.

"You must die," the proposed verdict, appears first, before the accusation in v 8. According to Boecker (*Redeformen*, 59), the order of these formulas has been reversed because of the plaintiffs' excitement. Normally the pretrial discussion begins with an accusation in the form of a reproachful question, leaving open the possibility that the defendant's answer will settle the matter, as in Exod 1:18 (*Redeformen*, 67). Elsewhere the defendant's answer does no good. In 1 Sam 14:24–46; 22:6–19; 1 Kgs 2:36–46, the accusation is made in question form. The accused answers, but the sentence, "You must die," is declared by the king and executed. What right did priests and prophets have to impose such a penalty? Elsewhere in the book of Jeremiah the priests' authority over false prophets is limited to incarceration in the stocks (20:2; 29:26). Because they lacked the authority to have someone executed, they had to call for a trial on a capital charge. Prophets were sometimes sent to deliver this sentence as a divine word of judgment, but Jeremiah's accusers do not claim to be speaking as divine messengers here. In fact, Jer 26:8 is the only place in the OT where the sentence מות תמות, "You must die," is pronounced without the direct authorization of God or the king.

9 The priests, the prophets, and all the people make their accusation in the form of a reproachful question addressed to Jeremiah, following a standard formula for pretrial speech (Boecker, *Redeformen*, 66). When the accusers are witnesses to the alleged crime, the initial accusation is couched as a question (see 1 Sam 22:13; 2 Sam 12:9; 1 Kgs 2:43). When the accused has been identified by casting lots, he is asked to tell what he has done (Josh 7:19; 1 Sam 14:43).

On what basis do Jeremiah's accusers bring a capital charge against him? There are at least four possibilities: (1) Jeremiah has violated an oath or command imposed upon him by the priests. The proposed verdict, "You must die," is found in narratives of broken oaths or personal commands (1 Sam 14:24–46; 1 Kgs 2:36–46). No such oath or command is mentioned in the accusation, however. (2) The plaintiffs assume that prophecy against the temple and city constitutes treason. In 1 Sam 22:6–19, "You must die" is the verdict of Saul upon the priest whom he judges to be guilty of treason. Elsewhere in the book, Jeremiah is accused of deserting to the Babylonians (37:13) or acting on their behalf (38:4). Foreign conquerors would profane or pollute the temple (Ps 74:7; Ezek 7:21–22; 23:39; 24:21; 44:7; Dan 11:31), the holiness of which the priests were responsible to protect and maintain (Lev 21:23). Such a charge is not articulated in chap. 26, however. (3) Jeremiah has violated the law against blasphemy (Schulz, *Das Todesrecht*, 120). In Exod 22:27[Eng 28] and Lev 24:16, cursing or reviling the LORD or the LORD's name is punishable by death. (In 1 Kgs 21 Naboth is prosecuted on a trumped-up charge of cursing the LORD's name.) It is difficult to see how the oracle in vv 4–6 would constitute cursing the LORD's name unless the temple is understood as a substitute for the name. Jer 7:11, 14 speak of "this house, which is called by my name." Jer 7:12 uses the deuteronomic language of the LORD's name dwelling in a holy place (Deut 12:5–14). Temple, altar, and holy objects appeared in oaths in NT times in place of the divine name (Matt 5:34–35; 23:16, 21), but Jeremiah's message is not in the form of a curse or an oath. There is no indication that either of these laws is behind the accusation because the key verbs are not used (קלל, "curse, revile," and נקב, "curse"). Schulz suggests that the threat of doom against the temple was potent enough to be equated with a curse against the deity resident there (*Das Todesrecht*, 120). (4) Jeremiah has prophesied presumptuously, violating Deut 18:20. The priests and the prophets accuse Jeremiah of prophesying a particular message in the name of the LORD. If they assumed that such a word could not have come from the LORD, as Jeremiah claimed it did, then what would have been for them an irreconcilable conflict between the message and its claimed source would have led them to conclude that Jeremiah had lied about God's word. Persons who had devoted their lives to promises and beliefs like those found in Ps 132:13–18 would understandably hear the threat in v 6 as falsehood. The LORD, who had promised security in Zion for the temple, priesthood, people, and Davidic king, could not now say just the opposite. Furthermore, the miraculous preservation of Jerusalem in the days of Hezekiah had proved that the LORD's promises were true (2 Kgs 19). Therefore, according to this reasoning, Jeremiah must be lying about the LORD's word. This line of thought is not articulated in chap. 26, but just such belief in the security of the temple in Jerusalem is precisely what Jeremiah's Temple Sermon in chap. 7 attacked. The reader of chap. 26 is cued by the oracle comparing the temple in Jerusalem to Shiloh that chap. 26 provides a narrative context for the sermon in

chap. 7. Conversely, chap. 7 fills in the gaps in the portrayal of the priests, prophets, and people in chap. 26 by suggesting a probable basis for their desire to have
Jeremiah condemned to death. The comparison to Shiloh was especially devastating for those who believed that Solomon's temple superseded Shiloh's
sanctuary and did not simply succeed it. Ps 78:56–72 expresses this belief. Vv 68–
69 underline the permanence of the temple in Zion, which had been "founded
forever."

The accusation against Jeremiah in v 9 cites only the apodosis of his conditional message in vv 4–6 and does not repeat even that part exactly. The
comparison with Shiloh is only slightly different, substituting one verb for another without changing the meaning. The second clause of v 6, the prophecy
against the city, is completely restated. The plaintiffs interpret being made a curse
as a threat of desolation, the death or exile of the city's population. This is a
reasonable interpretation. Jer 44:22, a prophecy against the land of Judah, combines the terms found in 26:6, 9, "curse," "desolation," and "without inhabitant."
(Compare Jer 29:21–22; Zedekiah and Ahab would become a curse after being
executed by Nebuchadrezzar.) The final two words, מֵאֵין יוֹשֵׁב, "without inhabitant," are typical of the book of Jeremiah. This phrase, or its synonym, בְּלִי יוֹשֵׁב,
"without inhabitant," occurs eleven times in the book, most often with reference
to the cities of Judah. It is common in the OT for quoted statements to be refor-
mulated rather than repeated word for word (Savran, *Telling and Retelling*, 109).
The plaintiffs have not altered the meaning of v 6.

It is significant, however, that Jeremiah's accusers do not repeat the first two
verses of his oracle. They ignore the invitation to hear and obey God's law and
prophetic word and focus instead upon the threat against the city and temple.
The trial is about the truth of this threat. Does Jeremiah speak with the LORD's
authority as he claims, or is he speaking falsely, out of his own mind? Has he
presumed to speak a word in the LORD's name that the LORD had not commanded
him to speak (Deut 18:20)? This is the legal question at issue in Jeremiah's trial.
His defense speech addresses this question first (26:12), and the verdict of acquittal answers it (26:16). Jeremiah's accusers do not cite Deut 18:20, nor do they
use its distinctive term, אֲשֶׁר יָזִיד לְדַבֵּר, "who presumes to speak." Nevertheless, this
law prompts their charges and their call for the death penalty (Fishbane, *Interpretation*, 246).

The end of the verse reports the gathering of the people as judges by using a
potent term, קהל niphal, "assemble, congregate." This verb is used of preparation for concerted action. The Israelites assemble themselves together in order
to lay their joint complaints before Moses and Aaron (Exod 32:1; Num 16:3; 17:7;
20:2) or to go to war (Josh 22:12; Judg 20:1; 2 Sam 20:14). The Jews of Persia
congregate for self-defense in the book of Esther (8:11; 9:16). This verb also has
religious connotations, as when the tribes assemble themselves for Aaron's ordination (Lev 8:4), to set up the tent of meeting (Josh 18:1), or to dedicate the
temple (1 Kgs 8:2). The cognate noun קָהָל, "congregation, assembly," refers most
often to the people as a worshiping community. This verb, therefore, conveys
both the solemnity and the potential threat inherent in a trial.

10 The royal officials of Judah join the court, taking their places as judges.
These men appear frequently in the book of Jeremiah, always as a group of in-

determinate size, and usually associated closely with the king. The most common translations of שָׂרִים are "princes" (NRSV) and "officials" (NIV). These leaders might have included, but were not limited to, sons of the king. (Zeph 1:8 lists the two groups separately; Jer 36:12 names royal officials who had fathers other than the king.) To the modern reader, the title "prince" suggests blood kinship to the king. Since that relationship cannot be verified, it is best to avoid that term. The term "officials" indicates their leadership and authority but does not convey the close connection between these men and the king. In lists of leaders of the people, the royal officials regularly come second, after the king (as in 1:18; 2:26; 4:9; 8:1; and others.) Jer 24:8; 34:21 list Zedekiah and *his* royal officials. 1 Kgs 4:2–6 names Solomon's royal officials, who held positions such as priest, secretary, and commander of the army. In the book of Jeremiah, the royal officials act as advisers to the king. In chap. 36 they listen to Jeremiah's scroll being read and report it to the king. In chaps. 37–38 they beat and imprison Jeremiah and petition the king to put him to death. In Jer 34:19, 21 the royal officials appear in two parallel oracles, implying some distinction between "the royal officials of Judah" and "the royal officials of Jerusalem" in v 19 and "his [Zedekiah's] royal officials" in v 21. In Jer 26, however, "the royal officials of Judah" in v 10 are the same group as "the royal officials" in vv 11, 12, 16.

The king's house and the LORD's house were situated next to each other, so that the temple courtyard in which Jeremiah preached overlooked the palace courtyard to the south (Busink, *Der Tempel*, 160). They must have been connected since, in 2 Kgs 11:13, Athaliah was able to pass unhindered from palace to temple when she heard the sounds of Joash's coronation. After the ceremony the new monarch was brought down directly to the king's house by way of the Bodyguards' Gate (2 Kgs 11:19//2 Chr 23:20, "Upper Gate"). This gate may have existed already in the time of Rehoboam, who would go back and forth to the temple accompanied by bodyguards carrying bronze shields (1 Kgs 14:27–28). Nowhere is a gate between temple and palace called the New Gate.

According to Jer 36:10 the New Gate was located in the upper court of the temple, the open area nearest the temple building. Gemariah had a room in the upper court by the New Gate. Busink identifies the New Gate with the Bodyguards' Gate, which he locates in the east wall of the temple court. The temple was built on an east-west axis, with the entrance on the east. It is hard to imagine why the gate opposite the temple doorway, on the main approach, would have been "new" or would have been named "Bodyguards' Gate."

Gates served as courtrooms in ancient Israel (Deut 21:19; Ruth 4:1–12; 2 Sam 15:2; Amos 5:10–12). An ancient gate could be a structure containing rooms, often with benches along the walls. The entrances on either side would have been closed with doors. Perhaps the royal officials took their seats at the "entrance" of the New Gate because all the people were in the courtyard, there being too many of them to fit into a room in the gate.

The OT does not report the construction of the New Gate. Its name does not necessarily mean that it had been built recently. (Compare New College, Oxford, founded in the fourteenth century.) 2 Kgs 15:35//2 Chr 27:3 credit Jotham with building the Upper Gate of the LORD's house. 2 Chr 23:20 gives this name to the Bodyguards' Gate (2 Kgs 11:19), which already existed in the time of Athaliah, a century earlier. Recent excavations on the western hill of Jerusalem have uncovered parts of a broad wall that may have enclosed most of the hill. It was built at the end of the eighth century, when refugees displaced by the Assyrians settled in Jerusalem (Avigad, *Discovering*, 49, 55). 2 Chr 32:2–5 reports that Hezekiah built a wall at this time. Perhaps the New Gate was located on the western side of the temple court and provided access to the temple from the recently fortified western neighborhoods.

11 The priests and prophets repeat the charge against Jeremiah, but this time they address the judges, the royal officials, and the people. The shift to third-person reference to Jeremiah marks the beginning of the trial proper (Boecker, *Redeformen,* 71). This accusation speech has the same two parts as the earlier speech in vv 8–9, but they are worded differently. The proposed verdict is expressed in a verbless sentence, "The death sentence for this man!" (The actual verdict in v 16, an acquittal, simply negates this sentence with אֵין, "no.") Their description of Jeremiah's alleged crime has been pared down to one verb and one prepositional phrase, "he has prophesied against this city." His actual words are not quoted, nor is his claim to speak in the LORD's name. It seems surprising that the priests and prophets should omit mention of the temple when summarizing Jeremiah's message. (Perhaps the fates of the city and the temple were so closely linked that the destruction of one was equivalent to the loss of the other.) Furthermore, if, as proposed above, Deut 18:20 provides the basis for their charge, then some allusion to it would be expected in this verse. These expectations demand too much of this brief narrative, however. It is not a court reporter's transcript. The end of the verse answers the objections; the people and the royal officials have heard Jeremiah speaking. They are "ear-witnesses" who do not need to have the whole case described to them. The people had been present for the sermon (v 8), and the proximity of the palace to the temple courtyard could have put the royal officials within earshot. In any case, the narrative does not allow this to become an issue. The purpose of the accusation speech to the judges was to persuade them to support the plaintiffs' case. Mentioning only the city underscored the threat to everyone's home, not just to the domain of the priests and prophets.

12 Jeremiah's defense speech to the judges begins by denying the implied charge that he has spoken presumptuously (Deut 18:20). His statement gives his first-person account of the assignment described in 26:2. According to both verses, "all the words" that Jeremiah spoke were from the LORD. God's command to Jeremiah in 26:2 used key words from Deut 18:15–22; the prophet was to speak (דבר) what the LORD commanded (צוה). Jeremiah's own description of the contested clauses of his oracle (26:5) restores mention of the temple, "to prophesy against this house and this city." (Compare v 11.)

The verse ends with the clause "which you have heard." This clause functions on more than one level in this passage because of the various nuances and allusions associated with the verb שׁמע, "hear." (1) It echoes the end of v 11, acknowledging that the royal officials and the people were "ear-witnesses" who possessed personal knowledge of the case. (2) It alludes to God's hope expressed in v 3, "Perhaps they will listen [שׁמע] and turn back." Will the people who have heard (שׁמע) Jeremiah's oracle listen (שׁמע) to God's word? (3) It lays the groundwork for further charges against the people by reminding them, and the reader, of their responsibility to obey (שׁמע) God's word given through Jeremiah and the other prophets (26:4–5; Deut 18:18–19). Jeremiah begins here to turn the tables on his judges.

13 Boecker (*Redeformen*, 118–19) identifies this verse as a "settlement proposal" but fails to explain why it is addressed to the judges and not to Jeremiah's accusers (Hossfeld and Meyer, *ZAW* 86 [1974] 38). The imperative verbs are characteristic of this form. A proposed settlement was supposed to satisfy the accusers' complaints and end the trial. It seems doubtful, therefore, that a settlement proposal from the defendant would have any place in a death-penalty case. One case in the OT where something like this does happen is 1 Sam 14:45, when the people ransom Jonathan and overrule Saul after he had announced the sentence, but the settlement proposal does not come from the defendant. Boecker (*Redeformen*, 117) compares v 13 to Hos 4:15, but that settlement proposal is offered by God as the plaintiff to Israel, the accused.

Jeremiah's speech in this verse does not have to do with this case; it has to do with the reason the LORD sent him to preach in the temple in the first place. His judges must make a decision about their own lives, which is more important than Jeremiah's case; they had to choose whether to obey God's word. The defense speech gave Jeremiah an opportunity to draw his audience's attention back to the rest of the message God had given them (26:4–6), to *all* the words that they had heard him speak.

The exhortation or command that begins v 13, "make your ways and your works good," comes from Jer 7:3, 5. In 7:5 this amendment of life is described in terms of a short summary of righteous behavior: "enact justice," do not "oppress a sojourner, an orphan, or a widow," "do not shed innocent blood," and "do not go after pagan gods."

The rest of v 13 reveals God's intent, as in v 3. "Obey [שׁמע] the LORD" (v 13) echoes "Perhaps they will listen [שׁמע] to me" (v 3). The promised result is the same, "so that I will repent of the evil which I am planning to do to them" (v 3) and "so that the LORD will repent of the evil which he has spoken against you" (v 13). V 13 is a settlement proposal after all; God, the plaintiff and judge, invites the accused people to turn back from their wickedness and be saved.

14 Jeremiah formally acknowledges the judges' authority to decide his case and, if he is found guilty, to hand him over for the execution of the sentence. This statement is a formula, which is also found in Gen 16:6; Josh 9:25; Jer 38:5. Therefore, it is not an emotional or rhetorical appeal to the consciences or sympathies of the judges.

15 Jeremiah acknowledged the court's authority in v 14, but in v 15 he reminds them of the danger of condemning an innocent person to death. The oracles in the first half of the book of Jeremiah had accused the people of causing the undeserved deaths of the innocent poor (2:34; 22:17). Innocent blood calls out for vindication by God (Gen 4:10) and endangers the whole community (Num 35:33; Deut 21:8–9). This danger was sufficient to deter Joseph's brothers from killing him (Gen 37:21–22). Did it also give the royal officials pause in Jer 38:4–8, so that they put Jeremiah into the cistern rather than killing him on the spot? In the law, Deut 19:10–13 makes the community, led by the elders, responsible for the life of an accused murderer. If he has not committed premeditated murder, the community must not allow the avenger of blood to kill him. If guilty, he must be handed over for execution. Jeremiah was not threatening his judges with some form of personal revenge, a haunting from his grave, or a curse laid upon them; he was reminding them of an accepted principle of justice: the death of innocent persons (i.e., those who have done nothing deserving of death) must be avenged or atoned (Gen 9:5–6; Deut 19:13). Vindication could even be accomplished by exacting retribution from the culprit's descendants (2 Sam 3:28–29; 21:1; 1 Kgs 21:29; 2 Kgs 24:3–4).

W. Janzen ("Withholding," 97–114) proposes that the priests, prophets, and all the people had made an agreement with Jeremiah to hear everything the LORD had given him to say, like the agreement made by King Zedekiah in Jer 38:14–16. By bringing capital charges against him on account of the very message they had agreed to hear in its entirety, they had violated their oath. Janzen's hypothesis seems far-fetched. It is the LORD who requires Jeremiah not to withhold a word (v 2). There is no hint of an agreement with the audience to grant Jeremiah immunity from prosecution for his preaching.

Jeremiah concludes his defense by repeating his claim to have been sent by the LORD and to have delivered the complete divine message (v 12). He boldly echoes the plaintiffs' formal indictment (v 11), באזניכם, "with/in your ears." Whereas v 14 seemed to be addressed specifically to the judges, in v 15 Jeremiah redefines the court as the audience of the LORD's word.

16 The royal officials and all the people render the verdict by speaking to the priests and prophets who were Jeremiah's accusers. The third-person reference to Jeremiah is notable. Other acquittals, in 2 Sam 12:13 and 19:24 (Eng 23), address the accused in language resembling 26:8b. On those occasions, however, there was no court; God or the king was both plaintiff and judge. The third-person form of the verdict in v 16 is the same as the formula used in Deut 19:6. It consists of the proposed verdict from v 11 negated by אין, "no." The judgment of the court was that the accusers had failed to prove that Jeremiah had done or said something deserving of death.

The judges cite Jeremiah's own defense, with themselves as witnesses, as the reason for the verdict, "he has spoken to us in the name of the LORD our God." The reason is introduced by the particle כי, "for," which is the typical form (Boecker, *Redeformen*, 133). The verdict answers the charge by the priests, prophets, and all the people that began the case in vv 8b–9, referring only to the source of Jeremiah's message, not to its content. The address of v 16 to the accusers rather than to Jeremiah functions as part of the canonical shaping of the chapter. The final disposition of the matter raised by Jeremiah's oracle depends upon the people's response to the divine word. Instead of addressing the LORD or the prophet, however, the people address each other in v 16; the LORD's intention for Jeremiah's preaching (v 3) remains unfulfilled.

How the royal officials and the people made their decision is not explained. They do not mention the threat of being stained by innocent blood, perhaps because that was a constant element of jurisprudence, not a special factor in this case. The test for prophets prescribed in Deut 18:22 was not applied. The judges did not wait to see the destruction of the city before they acknowledged that

Jeremiah had spoken a genuine word from the LORD. A situation such as this one exposes the limitations of the test in Deut 18:22. How long must they wait before they know that Jeremiah has prophesied falsely? Will he be allowed to go on preaching in the interim? If this is a word from the LORD, their lives are at stake. To wait for empirical confirmation for the threatening word is to miss the chance to be saved.

17 "The elders of the land" is a rare term in the OT. It can be found again in Prov 31:23, which tells how the husband of the woman of valor takes his place in the city gate among the elders of the land. "Elders," "elders of the people," and "elders of Israel" are much more common titles in the OT. There is no information in the OT beyond Prov 31:23 about how one became an elder, nor is there a complete description of their authority and responsibilities. They receive God's law and instruction as representatives of the people in Exod 24:1; Deut 31:9, 28; 2 Kgs 23:1. In Deut 19:12; 21:3, 4, 6, 19, 20; 22:15–17; 25:7–9; Ruth 4:9, 11, the elders of the city act as judges. Elsewhere, elders serve as advisers to kings (1 Kgs 12:6, 8, 13; 20:8; Ezek 7:26), but they also exercise independent political power (2 Sam 3:17–18; 5:3; 2 Kgs 6:32; 10:1, 5). The office of elder survived the exile (Jer 29:1; Ezek 8:1; 14:1; 20:3; Ezra 10:8). The elders of the people appear in Jeremiah's audience in chap. 19, the sermon at the Potsherd Gate, and in chap. 29, the letter to the exiles. In both of these chapters, a priest or prophet takes action to punish Jeremiah for his message (20:1–2; 29:24–32), but the elders are not mentioned again. In chap. 26, the elders are not mentioned in the report of the trial in vv 8–16. They appear suddenly in v 17 as a voice from the past (Brueggemann, "Intense Criticism/Thin Interpretation," *Int* 42 [1988] 270).

All the people (כל־העם) who had congregated (קהל) in v 9 to form the court are addressed here as כל קהל העם, "the whole assembly of the people." This subtle transformation of terminology serves to identify the elders' audience as the people who had heard and tried Jeremiah. The term קהל, "assembly," also maintains the archaic flavor of the verse. The people of Israel appear in the OT as an "assembly" in passages set in the period before the divided monarchy.

Interpreters who include vv 17–19 in the trial report (see *Form/Structure/Setting*) identify the elders in various ways. (1) The elders are the same as the royal officials (Fishbane, *Interpretation*, 246). The two groups are distinct, however, in Deut 29:9(Eng 10). (2) All the people did not act as judges; only the elders among them did (Nicholson, *Preaching to the Exiles*, 53). The elders and the royal officials represented, respectively, the people and the king as judges in the case. The royal officials rendered their verdict in v 16, and the elders gave theirs in vv 17–19. Notice, however, that "all the people" join in giving the verdict in v 16. (3) The elders appear as witnesses on Jeremiah's behalf. Either v 16 was not the final verdict of the court (Fishbane, *Interpretation*, 246), or v 17 should be understood in the pluperfect tense, "the elders of the land *had* spoken" before the verdict in v 16 was decided (Rudolph, 154).

18–19 The elders' speech cites part of an oracle by the prophet Micah (Mic 3:12), places it in its historical context, and uses rhetorical questions to lead the audience to make a decision. The information in v 18a is found in Mic 1:1. This superscription is the only place in the book of Micah where the prophet is named, and where the period of his ministry is identified. Mic 1:1 lists three kings of

Judah, Jotham, Ahaz, and Hezekiah, but the elders in chap. 26 place this particular word in the time of Hezekiah. Jer 26:18–19 is, in fact, the only biblical narrative about Micah's ministry. He is not mentioned in 2 Kings or 2 Chronicles. King Hezekiah ruled from Jerusalem a century earlier than Jehoiakim, when the Assyrian empire was expanding into Syria-Palestine.

The elders identify Micah's audience as "all the people of Judah," the same group that listened to Jeremiah and then arrested and tried him in Jer 26. Mic 3:12, however, ends a unit, vv 9–12, addressed to "you rulers of the house of Jacob, and chiefs of the house of Israel" (two groups not mentioned in Jer 26). The rest of the oracle indicts judges, priests, and prophets (v 11). Like the audience of Jer 7:1–15, Micah's addressees believe that God will go on protecting them in spite of their corruption. The elders cite the introductory messenger formula, "Thus says the LORD of Hosts," which is quite common in the book of Jeremiah but does not occur in the quoted verse from Micah or elsewhere in that book. It takes the place of the connecting clause, "Therefore, because of you," at the beginning of Mic 3:12. The messenger formula makes the point that Micah, like Jeremiah, prophesied in the name of the LORD.

Just as Jeremiah's accusers cite only the threat portion of his oracle, so the elders quote only the threat from Mic 3:9–12. The quotation of the final three cola of the verse is precise. (Slight differences in spelling are discussed above under *Notes*.) The elders do not indicate in what form they know the Micah tradition, oral or written. (Clements, 156, thinks they had it in writing.) Their interpretation is a canonical one, however. It exemplifies how setting a prophetic word within the OT's account of Israel's history can enable it to address a later generation.

2 Kgs 19:1 reports King Hezekiah's repentant actions. The Assyrians had conquered all the other fortified cities of Judah, and the Rabshakeh had delivered a threatening and disheartening speech about Jerusalem (2 Kgs 18). Hezekiah's acts of mourning and repentance (19:1) were in response to that speech. The elders' speech in Jer 26 maintains that Micah's preaching had prompted the king's reaction, even though Mic 3:9–12 is unconditional in form. Such prayers of repentance are invited by the canonical shape of the book of Micah, in which oracles of doom alternate with promises of salvation and which concludes with a liturgy of personal repentance and prayer for forgiveness (Childs, *Introduction*, 437). In 1 Kgs 19:15–19 Hezekiah prays for deliverance from the Assyrians, after which the prophet Isaiah brings the divine word of salvation. By the end of the chapter the Assyrian army has withdrawn. This preservation of Jerusalem at the end of the eighth century was a matter of wonder and gratitude. The elders in Jer 26 contribute to the growing interpretation of this series of events by relating them to the ministry of Micah.

The series of rhetorical questions in v 19 does not have the expected tone of a report of legal precedent. There is a surplus of content and of emotional intensity that exceeds the bounds of the legal question at stake in Jeremiah's trial. The questions assume that the audience can recognize the similarities in Micah's and Jeremiah's messages and their contexts of ministry without being told (compare 26:20). The first question uses an argument from silence. There is no information in the OT about Micah's death; neither King Hezekiah nor the people executed him for his prophecy against Jerusalem. This point would have been sufficient if defending Jeremiah were the only interest of the elders. As vv 17–19 stand in the final form of the chapter, however, they reveal that there is more at stake than the capital charge against Jeremiah. The questions continue, raising Hezekiah as an example of one who listened to the LORD's word and turned back (cf. vv 3, 12). Hezekiah feared the LORD and prayed for grace. God had hoped for this kind of response from Jeremiah's audience (v 3). The third question is a reminder that the LORD, in turn, had repented of the disaster that had been announced to Judah. The Assyrian withdrawal in 701 B.C. is made a specific illustration of what the LORD's offer in v 13 could mean: The elders' audience stands in the temple in Jerusalem because Hezekiah feared the LORD and the LORD answered his prayer; the object lesson of living Jerusalem stands in contrast to empty Shiloh. The second and third questions have the same interest as the original divine command to deliver an oracle (vv 3–4) and Jeremiah's urging in v 13. All three of these brief passages go beyond the case against Jeremiah, as stated by his accusers in vv 9 and 11. They turn the attention of the people assembled in the temple to the rest of the message that Jeremiah had brought them from the LORD. Having formally acknowledged that Jeremiah is a true prophet, will they believe in the divine word he has spoken and respond to it?

The elders' final sentence is not a question but a warning. In its present place in the chapter, this warning cannot have anything to do with v 15. The leaders and the people have avoided the danger of shedding innocent blood because they acquitted Jeremiah in v 16. However, the people are about to do evil to themselves by rejecting God's offer. If they do not repent and amend their ways, then they will bring the threatened evil of vv 3 and 6 upon themselves and their country. The elders' speech receives no answer. Their warning stands poised on the edge of decision.

20–23 The next unit introduces new subject matter, a report about King Jehoiakim and the prophet Uriah. The sections vv 18–19 and vv 20–23 resemble each other in several ways. The contents are similar: a king's response to the LORD's prophet. Like Micah, Uriah comes from a town outside of Jerusalem. The grammatical structure of the first sentence of each account is also similar: subject + perfect of היה, "was," + participle. Furthermore, v 20 begins with a connecting adverb, גם, "also, another." These similarities, however, could have been the work of the narrator of the chapter, who placed vv 20–23 after vv 18–19. Indeed, several significant differences between vv 18–19 and vv 20–23 indicate a different narrative voice for the second unit: (1) The verb נבא, "prophesy," appears in niphal participial form in v 18 but in the hithpael participle in v 20. Nothing else in the passage supports Holladay's interpretation of the hithpael form as an indication that Uriah was prophesying falsely. In fact, the niphal of the same verbal root is used in the second half of the verse. R. Wilson's explanation of the hithpael of נבא as "act the way prophets act" is appropriate here (R. Wilson, *Prophecy*, 335–36). (2) No oracle of Uriah's is quoted. The narrator informs the reader that Uriah's prophesying agreed with Jeremiah's. The readers are not allowed to make the comparison themselves. (3) There are no rhetorical questions or warnings that press the hearer or reader to make a decision. The bare facts are presented without evaluation. (4) The events of vv 20–23 apparently took place sometime

after Jeremiah's trial in the temple court. V 1 places the trial at or near the beginning of Jehoiakim's reign. Vv 20–23 mention no date, but Jehoiakim is the king.
(5) The home town of Uriah is indicated by a prepositional phrase with מִן, "from,"
but Micah's origin is expressed by means of a gentilic adjective, "the Moreshetite"
(v 17), as in Mic 1:1.

20 Uriah the son of Shemaiah is not known from any other source. His home
town, Kiriat Jearim, was probably located in the Judean hills a few miles west of
Jerusalem. Modern Abu Gosh (Holladay, 2:109) and Nebi Samwil (J. M. Miller,
private communication) have been proposed as its site. The Ark had rested at
Kiriat Jearim after the Philistines returned it (1 Sam 6:21–7:2), until David
brought it into Jerusalem (2 Sam 6). The mention of its name is another reminder
of the loss of the Shiloh sanctuary.

Uriah's prophesying in the LORD's name (v 20a) is summarized by likening it
to Jeremiah's. This is not a case of one prophet stealing another's words (Jer
23:30). Uriah is presented as another in the line of prophets whom the LORD
had sent persistently (v 5). Uriah's oracles had to do with city and land. Within
chap. 26 Jeremiah's quoted words are against the temple and the city, but in the
following chapters he has much more to say about the land. Oracles "against this
city and this land" may be found in Jer 2–25. Uriah's prophesying, therefore, was
in accordance with Jeremiah's whole prophetic ministry, not just an echo of the
Temple Sermon.

21 King Jehoiakim, in council with his royal officials and his military officers, heard Uriah's words. It is not clear how they heard. Was Uriah's message
overheard (cf. 26:10), reported orally (cf. Amos 7:10–11), or read from a scroll
(cf. 36)? No answer is given. In any case, Uriah was not in the king's presence
when the decision was made to kill him.

The royal officials most often appear in the OT with the king. (See the *Comment* on v 10.) Here the mighty men or warriors are also present, but not the
priests or the prophets. Kings needed mighty men for war (e.g., 2 Sam 23:8–9)
and for planning fortifications (2 Chr 32:3). Warriors were among the leaders
exiled with King Jehoiachin (2 Kgs 24:14). It is not clear whether any of them
take part in the forcible return of Uriah in vv 22–23.

The king sought Uriah's execution (וַיְבַקֵּשׁ הַמֶּלֶךְ הֲמִיתוֹ). The desire and plan to
kill someone is usually expressed in the OT by בקשׁ נפשׁ, "seek the life (of someone)" (e.g., Exod 4:19; 2 Sam 4:8). In the prose of the book of Jeremiah, the
phrase "those who seek his/their life" frequently parallels "enemies" (19:7; 21:7;
22:25; 34:20, 21; 44:30; 46:26; 49:37). The particular phrase in this verse, the verb
בקשׁ, "seek," with the object הֲמִיתוֹ, "his execution," is unique in the OT. The other
occurrences of the hiphil infinitive construct of this root following בקשׁ, "seek,"
have the preposition לְ, "to" (2 Sam 20:19; 1 Kgs 11:40; Ps 37:32). The hiphil of
מות, "die," often has the specific meaning "execute, carry out capital punishment,"
just as it does in 26:15. It denotes killing done by someone in authority, very often the king (cf. 2 Sam 14:7, 32; 1 Kgs 2:26; 19:17; Jer 38:15–16).

How Uriah heard of the king's plan is not reported. Perhaps, like Jeremiah,
he had a supporter among the royal officials (see 26:24). Fear motivated flight,
and his flight took him to Egypt. Jehoiakim had been placed on his throne by
Pharaoh Neco II to be an Egyptian vassal, and he remained one until 604–603

B.C. It may seem foolish for Uriah to have sought refuge in Egypt, yet Jeroboam had found safety there when Solomon, Pharaoh's son-in-law and vassal, wanted to kill him (1 Kgs 11:40). Uriah's flight to Egypt also has symbolic significance. Jeremiah, too, was forced to go to Egypt (43:4–7), where, according to legend, he died. Being brought up out of Egypt had meant land and nationhood for Israel and a kingdom for Jeroboam, but, because of King Jehoiakim's wickedness, it meant death for Uriah.

22–23 Elnathan the son of Achbor leads the men sent to Egypt to get Uriah. Elnathan's father was probably the Achbor son of Micaiah who was sent with four others to the prophet Huldah to inquire of the LORD regarding the law book found in the temple (2 Kgs 22:12, 14). In 36:12 Elnathan is listed among the royal officials who listen to Baruch read Jeremiah's scroll and advise King Jehoiakim to hear it, too. He then dares with two others to urge the king to stop burning the scroll (36:25). His change of position is not explained. The royal officials as a group also shift position vis-à-vis the prophets. In chap. 26 they acquit Jeremiah but abet Uriah's execution. In chap. 36 they give a hearing to Jeremiah's scroll, but in chap. 38 they want to put him to death. While these changes may be generally illustrative of the turmoil of Judah's last decades, the book is not concerned to explain the motivation for each shift of opinion.

No further details are known of the pursuit, capture, and return of Uriah. If Jehoiakim was still Pharaoh's vassal, the treaty between them may have included protocols for the extradition of fugitives. No such official negotiations are included in this report, however. The account presses quickly to the climax in v 23. The first two verbs of v 23 match the stereotyped description of the exodus and the taking of the land of Canaan (e.g., Deut 26:8–9): יצא hiphil, "bring out," and בוא hiphil, "bring in." Instead of life and offspring in a land of plenty, however, Uriah receives death and burial in a common grave. Executions performed on the king's authority were usually done by the sword (as in 1 Sam 22:18–19; 1 Kgs 1:51; 2:8; 2 Kgs 10:25; 11:20). Uriah's corpse was spared the ignominy of display on a pole (Deut 21:22–23) and given a grave among the common people. Some well-to-do people in this period were buried in rock-cut tombs outside the city walls (Isa 22:16), but the form of cemeteries for the common folk is unknown. 2 Kgs 23:6 implies that the burial ground for the common people was located in or near the Kidron Valley, which runs along the eastern side of Jerusalem and then turns southeast toward the Dead Sea.

בני העם, "common people," is a rare term. בני, "children of," in construct with the name of a group has the sense "members of" (cf. בני ישראל, "Israelites"). In chap. 26, העם, "the people," may be understood to refer to all the people who do not belong to any of the various categories of leaders mentioned in the chapter, namely the "commoners."

24 The final verse of the chapter begins with אך, "but," a conjunction that connects and contrasts this verse with the preceding unit. Syntactically, v 24 follows logically from vv 20–23, but the contents do not match. King Jehoiakim executed Uriah, but Jeremiah's danger comes from the people, as in vv 8–16. Why did King Jehoiakim not go after Jeremiah, too? Why did the people want to put Jeremiah to death after Jehoiakim executed Uriah? These difficulties would be eliminated if v 24 recorded the outcome of Jeremiah's trial. The king was not involved in Jeremiah's trial, but the precedent established by his execution of Uriah freed the people to reject the verdict of acquittal and to try to put Jeremiah to death (Fishbane, *Interpretation*, 246). If we follow the interpretation of vv 20–23 offered above, however, then v 24 is far removed from Jeremiah's trial in the temple. According to this interpretation, vv 20–24 report two episodes that took place apart from and probably after the trial in the temple. The one who composed chap. 26 included this passage to illustrate the failure of king and people to repent in response to Jeremiah's prophecy and the elders' speech.

Jeremiah and King Jehoiakim never have a face-to-face encounter in the book of Jeremiah. The king takes no part in the trial in chap. 26. In chap. 36 Jehoiakim burns Jeremiah's scroll but cannot lay hands on the prophet because "the LORD hid him" (36:26). Perhaps v 24 is meant to explain in part why, in the fourth year of Jehoiakim, Jeremiah described himself as "prevented from entering the house of the LORD" (36:5). The chapters between 26 and 36 are either undated or assigned to the reign of Zedekiah, so the writing and reading of the scroll (chap. 36) are the next events from Jehoiakim's reign that are reported in the book.

Under King Josiah, Shaphan was "the secretary," a high official who read the law scroll found in the temple to the king, and was among the emissaries sent to the prophet Huldah to authenticate it (2 Kgs 22:8–20). This same Shaphan may have been the father of Ahikam (26:24) and Gemariah (36:12). Ahikam the son of Shaphan is also listed among the delegation sent by Josiah (2 Kgs 22:12, 14), before Shaphan the secretary. Since Ahikam's father is never called "the secretary," it is possible that there were two Shaphans. Ahikam's son Gedaliah was appointed governor of the cities of Judah by King Nebuchadrezzar in 586 B.C. (40:5).

Explanation

Chap. 26 provides a specific setting for Jeremiah's Temple Sermon (cf. 7:1–8:3) in order to enable the message of that sermon to address subsequent generations of hearers and readers. The elders' interpretation of Mic 3:12 (vv 17–19) shows how to understand chap. 26. The way that the elders' speech applies ancient prophetic tradition to their audience in the temple parallels the way that chap. 26 can affect its readers.

The elders do not speak as prophets themselves; they report a prophetic word, place it in the context of a dated period in the past, report the response of the prophet's audience, and make an appeal to their listeners to respond as God would have them do. Their speech does not spell out the similarities between Micah and Jeremiah or Hezekiah's Judah and Jehoiakim's, but they are readily apparent. For readers of the book, Jeremiah is a prophet from the past whose ministry in the time of Jehoiakim met with resistance and rejection. They know from the book of Jeremiah that his audience did not repent and that God did not turn back the threatened punishment. Vv 17–19 function as an example within an example. Just as the elders place Micah's oracle within the context of the traditions about Hezekiah in order to invite their audience to repent, so the author of chap. 26 has placed the Temple Sermon within the story of Jeremiah's ministry. Both the positive example of Hezekiah and the negative example of all the people and Jehoiakim are used to call for a decision in favor of God.

Chap. 26 as a whole is a more complex composition than vv 17–19 and uses different literary techniques to make its appeal to the reader. Like vv 17–19, the whole of chap. 26 assumes that its audience acknowledges that the prophet has brought a true word from God, and it relies on its readers to compare themselves to Jeremiah's audience. Several features of the chapter communicate the appeal for a change of heart: (1) The oracle is repeated in abridged and revised form by Jeremiah's accusers, and its content is echoed in the verse from Micah. Jeremiah and the elders call for the proper response to the divine word. In this way the content of vv 3–5 is repeatedly brought to the reader's attention in the form of second-person address. (2) No one speaks to Jeremiah at the conclusion of the trial. One expects an announcement of acquittal or even an answer to the settlement proposal in v 13, but the elders' speech intervenes. In this position, after the verdict, their speech leads the reader back to the call for repentance, which was the announced purpose of Jeremiah's prophesying (v 3). The validation of Jeremiah as a true prophet by a court is not an adequate response to the divine word. Having ruled that the LORD truly sent Jeremiah to deliver this message, logic, loyalty, and integrity demand that the judges heed it. It is a life-and-death issue for each reader also. (3) The trial takes place at the beginning of Jehoiakim's reign, the earliest date in the book, except for Jeremiah's call (1:2). Therefore, every subsequent account of Jeremiah's ministry and the resistance he encounters has this trial and its "not guilty" verdict in its background. The reader of the completed book of Jeremiah knows that the events of 587/6 B.C. had proven Jeremiah a true prophet according to the legal standard in Deut 18:20. The trial makes Jeremiah's contemporaries responsible for the same knowledge. (4) V 19 ends abruptly without any response to the elders' speech from the assembled congregation. In the following verses, Jehoiakim kills Uriah, whereas Ahikam saves Jeremiah. One knows from the rest of the book that Jeremiah's audience refused to turn; they were engulfed by the great evil they did to themselves. The open-endedness of v 19 confronts the reader with the same life-and-death question: If this word is from God, how will you respond?

Jeremiah's trial and Uriah's execution can serve as a backdrop for the Gospel accounts of the arrest and trial of Jesus. Jer 26 enriches the reading of these accounts in at least two ways. First, the matches and mismatches between Jesus' experiences and those of Jeremiah and Uriah sharpen the portrayal of Jesus' suffering by means of the phenomenon of intensification of the antitype over its type. Jeremiah calls for obedience to God's law (26:4), but Jesus forces compliance to law and prophecy by driving the commercial enterprises out of the temple (Matt 21:12–13; Mark 11:15–18; Luke 19:45–48). Jesus, like Jeremiah, is brought to trial as a prophet by the priests of Jerusalem and charged with preaching the destruction of the temple (Matt 26:57–68; 24:2; Mark 14:58). Yet the charge against Jesus goes further. According to witnesses, he had said that he would destroy the temple personally and construct a replacement for it in three days (Matt 26:61; Mark 14:58; John 2:19). Acquitted by the civil authorities (Jer 26:16; Luke 23:13–22), the people still seek their deaths (Jer 26:24; Luke 23:23–25). Jeremiah is rescued by Ahikam (26:24), but Jesus had been deserted by all his disciples and goes to his crucifixion alone (Matt 26:56, 74–75). Jeremiah warns his audience of the danger of incurring bloodguilt by executing an innocent person (26:15). Judas acknowledges his guiltiness (Matt 27:3–4), Pilate tries to wash his off (Matt 27:24), but the people take Jesus' blood upon themselves without hesitation (Matt 27:25).

Second, these points of comparison support the explicit teaching in the Gospels that Jesus went to this death as one in the long line of prophets persistently sent by God but rejected by the people and killed (Jer 26:5, 20–23; Luke 13:33–34; Matt 23:29–32). These prophets bear a common message, that unrepentant sinners are never safe, even in the temple of the LORD (Jer 26:4–6, 18, 20; Matt 24; Mark 13; Luke 21). God's people cannot create security for themselves by technology or strategies, theology or liturgies. They will find life and hope only at the intersection of human repentance and divine mercy (Jer 26:3). Jesus' lament over Jerusalem in Matt 23:37–39//Luke 13:34–35 reflects the content of Jer 26. The people of Jerusalem kill God's prophets (26:20–24), yet God persistently sends more, desiring the people's restoration (26:4–5, 13). The alternative is desolation of the temple and the city (26:5–6, 9, 18). But the people must recognize and listen to the one who comes and speaks in the name of the LORD (26:15–16).

O Jerusalem, Jerusalem, you who kill the prophets and stone to death the ones sent to you: How often have I longed to gather your children together like a hen gathers her chicks under her wings, but you were not willing! See, your house is left to you, desolate. For I tell you, you will not see me again until you say, "Blessed is the one who comes in the name of the Lord." (Matt 23:37–39)

XVI. True and False Prophecy (27:1–29:32 [LXX 34:1–36:32])

Bibliography

Avigad, N. *Hebrew Bullae from the Time of Jeremiah: Remnants from a Burnt Archive.* Jerusalem: Israel Exploration Society, 1986. **Janzen, J. G.** *Studies in the Text of Jeremiah.* Cambridge, MA: Harvard UP, 1973. **Kessler, M.** "Jeremiah Chapters 26–45 Reconsidered." *JNES* 27 (1968) 81–88. **Nicholson, E. W.** *Preaching to the Exiles: A Study of the Prose Tradition in the Book of Jeremiah.* New York: Schocken Books, 1970. **Seidl, T.** *Texte und Einheiten in Jeremia 27–29.* Literaturwissenschaftliche Studie 2. Teil, Arbeite zu Text und Sprache im Alten Testament 5. Munich: Eos, 1978. **Seitz, C. R.** *Theology in Conflict: Reactions to the Exile in the Book of Jeremiah.* BZAW 176. New York: de Gruyter, 1989. **Stulman, L.** *The Prose Sermons of the Book of Jeremiah.* SBLDS 83. Atlanta: Scholars, 1986. **Thiel, W.** *Die deuteronomistische Redaktion von Jeremia 26–45.* WMANT 52. Neukirchen: Neukirchener, 1981. **Tov, E.** "Some Aspects of the Textual and Literary History of the Book of Jeremiah." In *Le Livre de Jérémie: Le prophète et son milieu, les oracles et leur transmission,* ed. P.-M. Bogaert. BETL 54. Leuven: Leuven UP, 1981. 145–67. **Wanke, G.** *Untersuchungen zur sogenannten Baruchschrift.* BZAW 122. Berlin: de Gruyter, 1971. **Wiseman, D. J.** *Nebuchadrezzar and Babylon.* Oxford: Oxford UP, 1985.

Certain distinctive features of chaps. 27–29 set them apart from the rest of the book of Jeremiah and suggest a period of independent transmission and status as a "collection" before being incorporated into the book as a whole. The stylistic peculiarities shared by these chapters, including especially the spelling of names, are supported by the common themes and historical setting. Rudolph's list of these peculiarities is basic to the discussion (157–58): (1) Nebuchadnezzar is spelled with נ, *n.* 29:21, however, has the spelling with *r,* as found in the rest of the book of Jeremiah, which is closer to the Babylonian name *Nabû-kudurri-uṣur.* (The name probably means "O Nabu, protect my offspring"; Wiseman, *Nebuchadrezzar,* 3.) Wiseman cites a tablet in Aramaic from Nebuchadrezzar's thirty-fourth year that spells the name נבוכדנצר, with *n* (*Nebuchadrezzar,* 2). The *n* spelling is also used in 2 Kings, 1–2 Chronicles, Ezra, Nehemiah, Esther, and Daniel, while Ezekiel uses *r.* In the LXX of chaps. 27–29, the personal name of the Babylonian king appears only in 27:6, where it is transliterated with ν, *n.*

(2) Personal names with Yahwistic theophoric endings are usually spelled יָה, *-yah,* instead of יָהוּ, *-yahu,* as in the rest of the book. Jeremiah's name, for example, is יִרְמְיָה, without final waw, only in chaps. 27–29. The longer spelling, with waw, appears in several names in 29:21–32 (Zedekiah, Shemaiah, and Jeremiah), but short spellings of Kolaiah, Maaseiah, Zephaniah, and Shemaiah are found in the same verses. (The long spelling of Josiah appears in the textually problematic 27:1.) The book of Daniel also employs the short theophoric ending on the names Jeremiah and Hananiah. The more than two hundred clay bullae from the time of Jeremiah published by Avigad contain no clear examples of the shorter *-yah* ending but eighty names spelled *-yahu* (*Hebrew Bullae,* 116). Avigad comments

that the Hebrew letters from Lachish and Arad also employ the longer form, with waw, exclusively (*Hebrew Bullae*, 116). Judean scribal practice (or dialect?) clearly preferred *-yahu*.

(3) The title "the prophet" is attached to Jeremiah's name with remarkable frequency in these chapters (seven out of eleven occurrences). There is a general tendency in the MT of Jeremiah to add titles to names and names to titles (Janzen, *Studies*, Appendix A), but Jeremiah is not labeled "the prophet" with such consistency elsewhere in the book. The reason for this practice in chaps. 27–29 is the subject matter, conflict with false prophets. Hananiah is also given the title "the prophet" in chap. 28 (six out of eight occurrences).

The MT of Jeremiah is longer than the LXX. It includes words, phrases, sentences, and paragraphs not represented in the ancient Greek translation. Chaps. 27–29 are prime illustrations of this phenomenon. (For example, by Stulman's reckoning, MT of chap. 27 is 170 words or 42 percent longer than the Hebrew *Vorlage* of OG, and MT of chap. 29 is 192 words or 37 percent longer; *Prose Sermons*, 86, 90.) Tov's description of the original form of MT (his "Edition II") as compared with the first edition of the book ("Edition I"), which was the ancestor of the Hebrew source of LXX ("Some Aspects," 218–33), illustrates four of his six categories of differences with material from chaps. 27–29. They include (1) "addition of headings," 27:1; (2) "addition of new verses and sections," 27:7, 13–14a, 17; 29:16–20; (3) "addition of new details," as in 27:19–22; and (4) "changes in content," as in 29:25, including clarifications (27:1, 7; 28:1; 29:16–20), the filling in of details to make explicit certain matters that are implicit in LXX (e.g., names and titles, as in 28:4, 5; clarifications, as in 27:5, 8, 16–17; 28:3, 15; 29:6; and the formula "oracle of the LORD").

These three chapters make sense as a collection because they share common themes and a historical setting during the reign of Zedekiah. (For a discussion of dates, see chaps. 27–28 and 29, *Form/Structure/Setting*.) The chapters assume a time when it was possible to hope and plan that Judah and the neighboring kingdoms would soon break free from vassalage to Nebuchadnezzar and that the exiles in Babylon would return home. These dreams were supported by the ministry of false prophets. God's purpose through Jeremiah and in these three chapters was to counteract the effect of the false prophets' words and to lead Judah, her neighbors, and the exiles in Babylon to submit to Nebuchadnezzar's divinely delegated authority until Babylon's appointed time to rule was over. The emphasis of the material is "to Babylon." (The phrase occurs ten times in the three chapters.) Subsidiary themes include intercessory prayer, a more positive attitude toward other nations, especially Babylon (Carroll, 531, 533), and the unity of God's people Israel in spite of their dispersion in Judah and in the exile (Seitz, *Theology*, 82).

This century has produced numerous theories about the place of this collection in the history of the arrangement and development of the book. (See Seidl, *Texte*, 21–22, n. 5, for a survey of proposals.) Only a few views can be described here. Rudolph (157–58) found the origin of chap. 27 in Mowinckel's A source, while chaps. 28 and 29 (minus small additions) came from source B, Baruch's book. They were put together because of their common theme and setting in order to function as a sort of tract against false prophets among the exiles. The stylistic peculiarities acquired because of their independent existence were not eliminated when chaps. 27–29 were incorporated into the Jeremiah book, nor was the collection broken up. Because of the hopeful elements in 27:22 and 29:10–14, 32, these three chapters were placed before the salvation promises in chaps. 30–31. Thiel's reconstruction (*Redaktion*, 5–19, 100) differs in the first stage. He credits a deuteronomistic redactor with the composition of the collection 27–29. Nicholson also finds evidence of substantial deuteronomistic supplementation but places the initial formation of this unit of tradition earlier, "in the course of the transmission and development of the original Jeremianic material" (*Preaching to the Exiles*, 93). Carroll (523–24) describes these chapters as a "literary creation," as opposed to a historical record, in which Jeremiah has a "legendary role." He suggests a date in the fifth century B.C. or later for its composition. The purpose of this composition, later modified by a Judean redactor, was to argue that Babylon had become the legitimate center of life for the LORD's people. Carroll implies that the placement of chaps. 30–31 after 27–29 was meant to balance this perspective.

Kessler (*JNES* 27 [1968] 83–84) and Wanke (*Untersuchungen*, 144) each propose that chaps. 27–29 make up the core of a narrative cycle or complex within the present book. Wanke's "cycle" is composed of 19:1–20:6 and chaps. 26–29, 36, which are concerned with "the truth of the proclamation of the prophet Jeremiah." Kessler proposes a multi-stage development of chaps. 26–36 and arrangement according to content rather than chronology, which was apparently carried out primarily among the exiles. Chaps. 26 and 36 provide a frame for the narrative, which moves from a contingent announcement of doom in 26:3 to inevitable judgment in chap. 36, because of the people's failure to respond to the LORD's word given through Jeremiah. According to Kessler, chap. 26 was prefaced to chaps. 27–29; then 30–31 and 32–33 were added. Chaps. 34 and 35 prepared for the climax in 36.

Seitz (*Theology*, 241) analyzes 27:1–18; 28; 29:1–9, 15, 20–32 as the original introduction to his proposed Scribal Chronicle (chaps. 37–43, plus parts of 32 and 34; 283), a book produced in Mizpah after 587 B.C. (285), which advocated the possibility of continued life in the land and survival in the exile by submitting to Babylon. A later Exilic Redactor, according to this theory, supplemented and rearranged the Scribal Chronicle and other Jeremiah materials, interspersing pre- and post-597 passages (chaps. 21, 24, 27–29, 32–34, 37–39 from Zedekiah's time; 25, 26, 35, 36 from Jehoiakim's; 30–31 from before 597), in order to demonstrate the uniformity of the LORD's message given through Jeremiah in both periods and to show that the fall of Jerusalem in 586 B.C. followed from Jeremiah's preaching before 597 (227–28).

Another feature of the collection of chaps. 27–29 is the large number of points of contact with the book of Daniel. They have in common the spelling of Nebuchadnezzar with *n* and Jeremiah and Hananiah with the short *-yah* ending. They share motifs such as execution by fire (Jer 29:22; Dan 3), the articles taken from the temple in Jerusalem (Jer 27:16–28:9; Dan 5:1–4), the practice of prayer among the exiles in Babylon (Jer 29:7, 10–14; Dan 6, 9), and even a diet of vegetables (Jer 29:5; Dan 1:8–16). The book of Daniel also addresses the theological questions raised by the LORD's appointment of Nebuchadnezzar as ruler over human and animal kingdoms (Jer 27:6; 28:14; cf. Dan 2:21) by reporting Nebuchadnezzar's acknowledgment of the LORD's authority and power (Dan

3:28–29; 4:34–37). The story of Nebuchadnezzar's humiliation, during which he lived among the wild animals and "ate grass like cattle," ends with his confession of God's justice (Dan 4:37). Daniel and his three friends not only survive but are promoted by Nebuchadnezzar when they speak and act out of faithfulness to the LORD (Dan 1–3). Most explicitly, Dan 9 reports a heavenly interpretation of Jeremiah's seventy-years prophecy (29:10) in response to Daniel's prayer on behalf of desolate Jerusalem (cf. Jer 27:17). His prayer in chap. 9 exemplifies the attitude of repentance appropriate for God's people at any time and in any place.

A. The Yoke of Nebuchadnezzar   (27:1–28:17 [LXX 34:1–35:17])

Bibliography

Ackroyd, P. "The Temple Vessels, a Continuing Theme." *Studies in the Religion of Ancient Israel.* VT Sup 23. Leiden: Brill, 1972. 166–81. **Ben-Barak, Z.** "The Status and Right of the Gebira." *JBL* 110 (1991) 23–34. **Brueggemann, W.** "At the Mercy of Babylon: A Subversive Rereading of the Empire." *JBL* 110 (1991) 3–22. **Campbell, A.** *Of Prophets and Kings: A Late 9th Century Document (1 Sam 1–2 Kg 10).* CBQMS 17. Washington, DC: Catholic Biblical Society of America, 1986. **Childs, B.** *Old Testament Theology in a Canonical Context.* Philadelphia: Fortress, 1985. **Driver, G.** "Once Again Abbreviations." *Textus* 4 (1964) 76–94. **Fensham, F.** "Nebuchadrezzar in the Book of Jeremiah." *JNSL* 10 (1982) 53–65. **Fohrer, G.** "Die Gattung der Berichte über symbolische Handlungen der Propheten." In *Studien zur alttestamentlichen Prophetie.* BZAW 99. Berlin: de Gruyter, 1967. 92–112. **Haran, M.** "The Disappearance of the Ark." *IEJ* 13 (1963) 46–58. **Lemke, W.** "'Nebuchadrezzar, my Servant'." *CBQ* 28 (1966) 45–50. **Lust, J.** "'Gathering and Return' in Jeremiah and Ezekiel." In *Le Livre de Jérémie: Le prophète et son milieu, les oracles et leur transmission,* ed. P. M. Bogaert. BETL 54. Leuven: Leuven UP, 1981. 119–42. **Lys, D.** "Jérémie 28 et le problème du faux prophète ou la circulation du sens dans le diagnostic prophétique." *RHPR* 59 (1979) 453–82. **Malamat, A.** "The Last Kings of Judah and the Fall of Jerusalem: An Historical-Chronological Study." *IEJ* 18/1 (1968) 137–56. ———. "The Last Wars of the Kingdom of Judah." *JNES* 9 (Jan.–Oct. 1950) 218–27. **McBride, S. D.** "The Yoke of the Kingdom." *Int* 27 (1973) 273–306. **McKane, W.** "Jeremiah 27,5–8, especially 'Nebuchadnezzar, my servant'." In *Prophet und Prophetenbuch.* FS O. Kaiser. BZAW 185. Berlin: de Gruyter, 1989. 98–109. **Meier, S.** *The Messenger in the Ancient Semitic World.* HSM 45. Atlanta: Scholars, 1988. **Mottu, H.** "Jeremiah vs. Hananiah: Ideology and Truth in Old Testament Prophecy." In *The Bible and Liberation,* ed. N. Gottwald. New York: Orbis Books, 1983. 235–51. **Overholt, T.** "King Nebuchadnezzar in the Jeremiah Tradition." *CBQ* 30 (1968) 39–48. **Quell, G.** *Wahre und falsche Propheten: Versuch einer Interpretation.* BFCT 46.1, ed. P. Althaus, H. Dörries, and J. Jeremias. Gütersloh: Bertelsmann, 1952. **Sarna, N.** "The Abortive Insurrection in Zedekiah's Day." *EI* 14 (1978) 89–96. **Schmidt, H.** "Das Datum der Ereignisse von Jer 27 und 28." *ZAW* 39 (1931) 138–44. **Schreiner, J.** "Tempeltheologie im Streit der Propheten: Zu Jer 27 und 28." *BZ* 31 (1987) 1–14. **Seebass, H.** "Jeremia's Konflikt mit Chanania: Bemerkungen zu Jer 27 und 28." *ZAW* 82 (1970) 449–52. **Sheppard, G.** "True and False

Prophecy within Scripture." In *Canon, Theology, and Old Testament Interpretation,* ed. G. Tucker, D. Peterson, and R. Wilson. Philadelphia: Fortress, 1988. 262–82. **Starkey, P.** *Animal-Drawn Wheeled Toolcarriers: Perfected Yet Rejected, A Cautionary Tale of Development.* Braunschweig/Wiesbaden: Vieweg and Son, 1988. **Tov, E.** "Exegetical Notes on the Hebrew Vorlage of the LXX of Jeremiah 27 (34)." *ZAW* 91 (1979) 73–93. **Weinfeld, M.** "The Loyalty Oath in the Ancient Near East." *UF* 8 (1976) 379–414. **Wolff, H.** "Hauptprobleme alttestamentlicher Prophetie." *EvT* 15 (1955) 116–68 = *Gesammelte Studien zum Alten Testament.* Munich: Chr. Kaiser, 1964. 206–31. **Zevit, Z.** "The Use of עָבַד as a Diplomatic Term in Jeremiah." *JBL* 88 (1969) 74–77.

Translation

[1ab] *[In the accession year of [b] Jehoiakim[c] son of Josiah, the king of Judah,] this word came to Jeremiah from the LORD:* [2] *"Thus says the LORD (to me):[a] Make for yourself[b] yoke[c] bonds and bars and put them[d] on your neck.* [3] *Then send them[a] to the king of Edom, the king of Moab, the king of the Ammonites, the king of Tyre, and the king of Sidon by way of the[b] messengers who have come[c] to Jerusalem to Zedekiah the king of Judah.* [4a] *Give them a charge to say[a] to their lords, 'Thus says the LORD of hosts,[b] the God of Israel, (thus you shall say to your lords):* [5] *I alone made the earth, [a]the humans and the animals which are on the earth,[a] by my great power and by my outstretched arm, and I give it [b] to the one who seems right to me.* [6] *Now[a] I[b] have given [c]all these lands[c] to the control of Nebuchadnezzar, the king of Babylon, my servant, [d] and [e]I have also given him[e] the field animals to serve him.* [7a] *All of the nations shall serve him, his son, and his grandson until the appointed time for his own land comes too; then many nations and great kings shall use him[b] as a slave.* [8a] *It shall come to pass that[a] the nation and the kingdom which does not [b]serve him, Nebuchadnezzar, the king of Babylon, [c]and which[c] does not[b] [d]put its neck[d] in the yoke of the king of Babylon—I will deal with [e]that nation[e] with sword, famine, and pestilence[f] [gh]until I have consumed them[h] by his hand.* [9] *As for you, don't listen to your prophets, your diviners, your dreams,[a] your soothsayers,[b] or your sorcerers[c] who are saying [d]to you,[d] "You will not[e] serve the king of Babylon."* [10] *For they are prophesying falsehood to you in order to remove you from your land. [a]I shall banish[b] you, and you will die.[a]* [11] *But the nation which will put its neck in the yoke of the king of Babylon and serve him, I shall leave that nation in its land—[a]oracle of the LORD[a]— and they[b] will till it and dwell in it.'"*

[12] *To Zedekiah the king of Judah I spoke according to all these words, saying, "Put your neck in [a]the yoke of the king of Babylon;[a] serve[b]him and his people and live.* [13a] *Why should you and your people die by sword, famine, [b] and pestilence, as the LORD has spoken concerning the nation that will not serve the king of Babylon?* [14] *Stop listening to the words of the prophets who are saying to you, 'You will not serve[b] the king of Babylon,' for they are prophesying falsehood to you.* [15] *Indeed, I did not send them—oracle of the LORD —and they are prophesying falsely in my name with the result that I[a] shall banish you, and you will perish, you and the [b]prophets who are prophesying to you."[c]*

[16ab] *To the priests and to all these people[b] I spoke, saying, "Thus says the LORD: Stop listening to the words of your prophets who are prophesying to you, saying, 'Behold, the furnishings of the LORD's house are going to be brought back from Babylon [c]very soon now,'[c] for they are prophesying falsehood to you.[d]* [17a] *Stop listening to them. Serve the king of Babylon and live. Why should this city become a ruin?[b]* [18] *If they are prophets and if the word of the LORD is indeed with them, then let them entreat [a]the LORD of*

hosts[a][b] *so that the furnishings remaining in the* LORD'*s house and the house of the king of Judah will not go*[c] *to Babylon.*[b] [19]*Indeed, thus says the* LORD [a]*of Hosts about the pillars, the sea, the stands,*[ab] [c]*and the rest of the furnishings* [d]*remaining in this city,*[d] [20]*which Nebuchadnezzar,*[a] *the king of Babylon, did not take*[b] *when he exiled Jeconiah*[c] [d]*the son of Jehoiakim, the king of Judah,*[d] *from Jerusalem to Babylon,*[e] [f]*along with all the nobles of Judah and Jerusalem.*[f] [21a]*For thus says the* LORD *of hosts, the God of Israel, concerning the furnishings remaining in*[b] *the house of the* LORD *and the house of the king of Judah and* [c]*Jerusalem:* [22]*To Babylon*[a] *they shall be brought* [b]*and there they shall be until the day I deal with them*[b]—[c]*oracle of the* LORD[c]—[b]*then I shall bring them up and return them to this place."*[b]

[28:1]*So it happened [*[a]*in that year,* [a] [b]*in the accession year of Zedekiah the king of Judah, in the fourth year*[cb]*] in the fifth month, that Hananiah son of Azur, the prophet who was from Gibeon, spoke to me*[d] *in the house of the* LORD *in the sight of the priests and all the people, saying,* [2]*"Thus says the* LORD [a]*of Hosts, the God of Israel:*[a] *I will break the yoke of the king of Babylon.* [3]*Within two years*[a] *I will bring back to this place all*[b] *the furnishings of the house of the* LORD[c]*which Nebuchadnezzar*[d] *the king of Babylon took from this place and brought to Babylon,*[c] [4]*and Jeconiah* [a]*son of Jehoiakim, the king of Judah,*[a] *and all* [b]*the exiles of Judah* [c]*who are going to Babylon I am about to return to this place—oracle of the* LORD[f]*—for I shall break the yoke of the king of Babylon."*

[5]*Then Jeremiah the prophet said to Hananiah the prophet in the sight of* [a]*the priests and in the sight of all of the people*[a] *standing in the house of the* LORD, [6]*Jeremiah the prophet said, "Amen, may the* LORD *do so, may the* LORD *establish your words*[a] *which you have prophesied by bringing back the furnishings of the house of the* LORD *and all the exiles from Babylon to this place.* [7]*Only please listen to*[a]*this word*[a] *which I am speaking in your hearing and in the hearing of all the people:* [8]*As for the prophets who were before me and before you from time immemorial, they prophesied of* [a]*war, calamity,*[b] *and pestilence*[a] *to many nations and against great kingdoms.* [9]*As for the prophet who prophesies peace, when the word of that prophet comes, then the prophet whom the* LORD *truly has sent will be known."*

[10]*Then Hananiah the prophet took*[a] *the bar*[b] *off the neck of Jeremiah the prophet and broke it*[c] *to pieces.* [11]*Then Hananiah said in the sight of all the people, "Thus says the* LORD*: Thus I will break the yoke of Nebuchadnezzar*[a] *the king of Babylon off the neck of all the nations*[b]*within two years."*[b] *Then Jeremiah the prophet went his way.*

[12]*The word of the* LORD *came to Jeremiah after Hananiah the prophet had broken the yoke-bar*[a] *off the neck of Jeremiah the prophet, saying,* [13]*"Go and speak to Hananiah, saying, 'Thus says the* LORD*: Wooden yoke-bars*[a] *you have broken, but you*[b] *will make in place of them yoke-bars of iron.* [14]*For thus says the* LORD [a]*of hosts, the God of Israel:*[a] *I have put an iron yoke on the neck of all these*[b] *nations so that they will serve Nebuchadnezzar,*[c] *the king of Babylon,* [d]*and they will serve him. I have also given the animals of the field to him.'"*[d]

[15]*Jeremiah* [a]*the prophet*[a] *said to Hananiah* [b]*the prophet, "Listen, Hananiah,*[b] *the* LORD *did not send you, and you have caused this people to put their trust in falsehood.* [16]*Therefore, thus says the* LORD*: Now I am about to drive you off the face of the ground; this year you will die,* [a]*because you have spoken apostasy against the* LORD*."*[a]

[17]*So* [a]*Hananiah the prophet*[a] *died* [b]*that year,* [b] *in the seventh month.*

Notes

1.a. Entire verse not in LXX. The word-event formula would be adequate to head a chapter, but the connections that exist between chaps. 27 and 28 call for a date in 27:1. The date formula in v 1a MT (which is translated above) is a copy of 26:1 (with a variant spelling of "reign"). The chapter is about Zedekiah, however, so at least the name "Jehoiakim" is wrong in v 1 (see 27:3, 12). The rest of v 1a is probably also copied by mistake from chap. 26. The synchronism in 28:1, "in that year" (not in LXX) invites the reader to find the date for chap. 27 in 28:1, but there are two different dates in MT, "in the accession year of" and "in the fourth year." These dates are both absent from LXX, which has only "in the fifth month." "In the accession year of" could have been added to 28:1 in harmony with 27:1 after the current, incorrect, heading was affixed, which would point to "in the fourth year" as the original date of the unit (Rudolph, Holladay, and most commentators). Driver proposes that "in the fourth year" is a misreading of the abbreviation for בשנה הראשנה, "in the first year" (*Textus* 4 [1964] 86). See *Form/Structure/Setting* for historical considerations supporting this reading.

1.b-b, c. *BHS* recommends "in the fourth year" and "Zedekiah." See *Note* 1.a.

2.a. Not in LXX, Tg^Ms. Jer 13:1; 17:19; 25:15 MT share the same plus over LXX. Tov (*ZAW* 91 [1979] 81) thinks it was added to intensify the conflict. Driver (*Textus* 4 [1964] 79) reads it as an abbreviation for אל ירמיה, "to Jeremiah."

2.b. Not in LXX, which translates לך/לכם, "for yourself/yourselves," only part of the time.

2.c. על, "yoke," not in this verse, but context indicates that "bonds and bars" are part of a yoke. See *Comment*.

2.d. Pronom suff not in LXX.

3.a. *BHS* recommends reading qal 2ms pf (waw consec) without suffix, "send," with LXX^L.

3.b. LXX has poss "their," which makes the relationship between the kings and the messengers explicit.

3.c. LXX has εἰς ἀπάντησιν αὐτῶν, "to meet them."

4.a-a. Idiom for commissioning a messenger, as in Deut 1:3.

4.b. Not in LXX. צבאות, "Hosts," lacking in LXX fifteen of nineteen occurrences of "LORD of Hosts" in Jeremiah.

5.a-a. Not in LXX. Either lost from LXX by homoioteleuton (הארץ, "the land," so Janzen, *Studies*, 118) or added to proto-MT for clarification (McKane, "Jeremiah 27, 5–8," 98). Tov (*ZAW* 91 [1979] 82) notes that the plus in MT interrupts a stereotyped expression also found in 32:17; 10:12; 51:15.

5.b. Sg suff refers to "the earth" (and its inhabitants).

6.a. Not in LXX in this verse, but occurs several other places in Jeremiah in both LXX and MT.

6.b. No independent pronoun in LXX.

6.c-c. LXX has τὴν γῆν, "the earth," as in v 5. MT, however, refers to v 3. Bright (200) suggests that MT has a clarifying expansion of an original הארץ, "the land," to distinguish it from its frequent meaning "the land (of Judah)."

6.d. LXX has δουλεύειν αὐτῷ, "to serve him," either by corruption in its Heb. *Vorlage*, influenced by the end of the verse (Tov, *ZAW* [1979] 84), or to eliminate an offensive saying (Rudolph, 161). McKane ("Jeremiah 27, 5–8," 99–101) concludes that LXX is conflate. He argues that δουλεύειν αὐτῷ, "to serve him (as a slave)," preserves a misplaced variant of ἐργάζεσθαι αὐτῷ, "to work for him," and concludes that there was no form of עבד, "serve," in v 6a of LXX's Heb. *Vorlage* and עברי, "my servant," is a secondary addition to MT.

6.e-e. Not in LXX. Probably a stylistic expansion using the beginning of the verse (Tov, *ZAW* 91 [1979] 84).

7.a. Entire verse not in LXX. Resembles 25:14, also not in LXX.

7.b. Rudolph (161) emends to בה, "her," i.e., Nebuchadnezzar's land, which is the topic of the verse.

8.a-a. Not in LXX, Vg. (Compare 25:10.) Serves to connect v 8 to the fut tense narrative of v 7.

8.b-b. Not in LXX. Uses v 6 to explain the yoke metaphor.

8.c-c. *BHS* recommends correcting by removal of direct obj marker.

8.d-d. LXX switches to pl in conformity with the compound subj.

8.e-e. Not in LXX. Added to clarify the obj of the verb.

8.f. Not in LXX. Addition in MT to complete the full formula.

8.g. LXX has εἶπεν κύριος, "the LORD says," which usually translates נאם יהוה, "oracle of the LORD."

8.h-h. LXX has pass verb; MT has act verb.

9.a. LXX has τῶν ἐνυπνιαζομένων ὑμῖν, "your dreamers," to conform with the rest of the items on the list. MT is closer to 29:8.

9.b. Poᶜal ptcp but without ם.

9.c. *Hap. leg.*

9.d-d. Not in LXX. Perhaps an expansion in MT based on 27:14.

9.e. LXX uses the strongest negation, οὐ μή, "by no means."

10.a-a. Not in LXX. Clarifying addition in MT based on v 15.

10.b. In Vg, 3 sg "king of Babylon" in v 9 is implied subj.

11.a-a. Not in LXX. Formula is more common in MT than in LXX.

11.b. Lit. "he," i.e., "that nation."

12–14.a-a., b-b. Not in LXX, which does not make sense as it stands, "Put your neck in . . . and serve the king of Babylon . . . for they are prophesying falsehood to you." The missing pieces of vv 12 and 14 can be filled in from vv 8–10. Homoioteleuton ("serve" to "serve") could explain the loss of b-b.

13.a. The whole verse is lacking in LXX. (See *Note* on 12–14.a-a., b-b.) Holladay (2:116) argues for its authenticity on rhetorical grounds. It completes the chiasm in vv 12–14 and 16–17.

13.b. Several MSS and versions add the conjunction in conformity with the usual form of lists.

14.b. See *Note* 12–14.a-a., b-b. The section lacking in LXX ends here.

15.a. LXX and Vg lack the pronom suff on the inf const. Therefore, the subj is not indicated.

15.b. LXX has ὑμῶν, "your." This verse has four 2 pl pronouns in LXX, acc, nom, gen, and dat.

15.c. LXX adds ἐπ' ἀδίκῳ ψευδῆ, "unrighteously, lies." A clarifying addition, using terms found in these chapters to describe the other prophets (vv 10, 14, 15, 17). Tov (*ZAW* 91 [1979] 88) includes ὑμῖν, "to you," from the beginning of v 16 and finds a doublet preserved in LXX ὑμῖν ἐπ' αδίκῳ/ ψευδῆ ὑμῖν = שקר לכם/לכם לשקר, "to you falsely/lies to you."

16.a. LXX begins with ὑμῖν καί, "to you and." See *Note* 15.c.

16.b-b. LXX reverses the order.

16.c-c. Not in LXX. Probably based on 28:3 (cf. 28:11).

16.d. LXX adds οὐκ ἀπέστειλα αὐτούς, "I did not send them," as in v 15.

17.a. Entire verse not in LXX. Holladay (2:116) argues for authenticity on the basis of chiastic structure of vv 12–14 and 16–17. (See *Note* 13.a.)

17.b. Some MSS MT vocalize as adj, חָרְבָּה, "desolate."

18.a-a. LXX μοι, "me," from בי, "me." First and third person references to God alternate in the chapter, so these variants are not unusual. It is possible that בי, "me," originated as an abbreviation for ביהוה, "the LORD" (Driver, *Textus* 4 [1964] 79).

18.b-b. The rest of the verse is missing from LXX. Clarifying expansion from vv 21–22 (Janzen, *Studies*, 46).

18.c. *BHS* recommends emending to impf, and Holladay chooses the inf const with support from a few MSS. The pf is not suitable (GKC §§ 114s; 152x).

19.a-a. Not in LXX, which often lacks the divine epithet ("of Hosts"). The items in MT are also listed in Jer 52:17 = 2 Kgs 25:13.

19.b. Bases of lavers, as in 1 Kgs 7:27.

19.c. LXX begins a new sentence, which continues in vv 20 and 22. It does not mention the return of the furnishings.

19.d-d. Not in LXX. Refers to list (*Note* 19.a-a.), which is also not in LXX.

20.a. Name not in LXX. MT frequently fills out name or title.

20.b. Resumptive pronom obj suff with לקחם, "take them," not in LXX or in the *Translation*, to avoid redundancy.

20.c. Spelling in Q is also found in 28:4; 29:2. The name means "may the LORD endure."

20.d-d. As in 28:4, MT includes patronymic and title where LXX does not.

20.e. Not in LXX. Throughout chaps. 27–29, MT emphasizes movement "to Babylon."

20.f-f. Not in LXX. החרי, "the nobles," are listed in 2 Kgs 24:14.

21.a. Entire verse not in LXX. Serves to return attention to the furnishings specified in vv 18–19, which are the subject of the following oracle.

21.b. Many MSS and versions supply the prep ב, "in."

21.c. "and [in] Jerusalem," as in v 18. Not an expanded title for the king.

22.a. See *Note* 20.e.

22.b-b., b-b. LXX lacks all the hopeful elements in MT.

22.c-c. This formula concludes the verse in LXX.

28:1.a-a. Not in LXX. Serves to link chaps. 27 and 28.

1.b-b. LXX has "in the fourth year of Zedekiah." The accession-year formula contradicts "fourth year," and it probably came from the present heading of chap. 27. See *Note* 27:1.a. Hayes and Hooker interpret the double date using two calendars. The accession year of Zedekiah, ending 15 Nisan 596, overlapped with the fourth year of the sabbatical cycle. The sabbatical cycles had an autumn new year, so the fifth month was Shebat, January/February (*New Chronology*, 95–96).

1.c. K has the const form.

1.d. *BHS* suggests reading אֵלַי as an abbreviation for אֶל יִרְמִיָה, "to Jeremiah."

2.a-a. Not in LXX. MT typically fills out names and titles.

3.a. Lit., "a pair of days," but יָמִים, "days," means "year" in this context (compare 1 Sam 27:7; 2 Chr 21:19).

3.b. Not in LXX. Haplogr because of similarity of כֹּל, "all," and כְּלִי, "furnishings."

3.c-c. Not in LXX. Clarifies identity of the furnishings.

3.d. Many MSS add the syllable divider missing from ד in L.

4.a–a., b., c–c. Not in LXX. Clarifications and repetition of promise (from v 3). LXX simply continues the list begun in v 3.

5.a-a. LXX reverses the order, as in 27:16.

6.a. LXX, Tg read the sg, "your word," as in v 7.

7.a-a. LXX makes the divine source explicit, λόγον κυρίου, "the word of the LORD."

8.a-a., b. The stereotyped expression "sword, famine, and pestilence" is common in Jeremiah and Ezekiel. This variation suits the context. "War," which stands alone in LXX, is a suitable contrast to "peace" in v 9. The next item, רָעָה, "calamity," in MT only, refers back to 26:3 and forward to 29:11. דֶּבֶר, "pestilence," is the only item from the stereotyped list. Its presence may account for the appearance of רָעָב, "famine," in some MSS (8.b.).

10.a. LXX has, additionally, ἐν ὀφθαλμοῖς παντὸς τοῦ λαοῦ, "in the sight of all the people."

10.b. LXX, Syr have pl, as in v 13. Sg also in v 12.

10.c. *BHS* recommends emending to a fem sg suff to agree with the fem gender of מוֹטָה, "bar." Carroll (539) offers two explanations of MT: (1) dittogr of waw conj at beginning of v 11; (2) writer had עֹל, "yoke," masc, in mind as antecedent of the suff.

11.a. Not in LXX. MT often has full name and title.

11.b-b. Not in LXX. Clarification from v 3.

12.a. Sg, as in v 10. Pl reappears in v 13.

13.a. LXX has 1 sg, based on v 14; God puts an iron yoke on the nations. MT's 2 sg corresponds to 27:2, the command to Jeremiah to make the wooden yoke-bars.

13.b. LXX has 1 sg.

14.a-a. Not in LXX. MT often has full name and title.

14.b., c. Not in LXX. MT often has additional modifiers and names. "These nations" are the ones named in 27:3.

14.d-d. Not in LXX. The explanation in MT repeats material from 27:6.

15.a-a. Not in LXX. MT often has the title where LXX does not.

15.b-b. Not in LXX. Might have been lost by homoioteleuton, but the title, "the prophet," is a plus typical of MT.

16.a-a. Not in LXX. MT includes an additional reason for the judgment, based on Deut 13:6; 18:20.

17.a-a., b-b. Not in LXX. LXX has a much shorter sentence, analogous to the end of v 11. The additional material in MT underscores Hananiah's death as the fulfillment of Jeremiah's prophecy in v 16.

Form/Structure/Setting

Chaps. 27–28 must be read together in order to be understood properly in their present shape. Certain features, which may indicate independent origins for the two chapters, tend to separate them: (1) Chap. 27 is a first-person account by Jeremiah, but chap. 28 is in the third person after v 1. (2) The heading of chap. 28 with its date formula looks like the beginning of a new unit. (3) Each of the two chapters has a different "cast of characters." (Seidl offers a detailed survey of all the evidence and of others' analyses and concludes that chap. 28 remains a self-contained, discrete unit within the complex, chaps. 27–29. See *Texte*, especially 59–61, 85–87.) Nevertheless, four main features of the present shape of these chapters indicate that they now form a unit: (1) the story told or implied in the arrangement of the oracles and other materials; (2) the common formal pattern found in the oracles in both chapters; (3) intertextual connections by means of quotation, repetition, or allusion; (4) shared historical setting. The first, second, and fourth features will be addressed in this section. The *Comment* on individual verses will call attention to examples of the third feature.

Nine prophetic sayings compose these two chapters. Two of them interpret sign-acts, and all but one take the form of divine words, introduced by the messenger formula. The sign-acts, the introductions to each saying, the brief narrative sentences (28:11b, 17), and the "conversational" arrangement of chap. 28 all imply the "plot" of a story. (Compare the "plot" of the story implied by the exchange of letters in chap. 29.) Descriptions of personal motivation and responses are absent, however, and actions are reported in the barest terms, if at all. Even the narrative movement from the report of divine commissioning to an account of the prophet's obedience is missing; in each section only one of these elements is present, never both. These chapters place their emphasis on the signs and words, therefore—not on the actions or relationships between the parties involved. Nevertheless, the order of events apparent in or implied by the arrangement of these chapters can be told.

In obedience to the LORD's command, Jeremiah fashions a yoke or yoke-collar, which he puts on his own neck. He gains access to the envoys from the five neighboring kingdoms and commissions them to take yokes or parts of them to the kings who have sent them to Jerusalem and to deliver the LORD's word, which interprets this symbol: Submit to the king of Babylon and stop listening to the intermediaries who say that you will escape his rule. Jeremiah himself delivers similar oracles to Zedekiah and to the priests and people present, probably at the temple.

No report is given of a response to the LORD's word by any of these addressees. The third oracle, however, takes up the disputed topic of the temple furnishings and lays down a challenge to the other prophets who have not been interceding on behalf of the remaining furnishings, that they might be spared from deportation. Some time later, the prophet Hananiah from Gibeon answers this challenge with a salvation oracle for temple furnishings, the king, and the exiles, promising their restoration within two years. Jeremiah responds with a prayer of support but also an expression of doubt. Hananiah then breaks the yoke from Jeremiah's neck and interprets the act with an oracle: the LORD will bring Nebuchadnezzar's rule to an end. Thus stripped of his message and its symbol, Jeremiah departs. No one else's response to Hananiah's words or actions is reported.

Finally, a new word from the LORD comes to Jeremiah, which he delivers to Hananiah: Nebuchadnezzar's rule has not been shattered. Indeed, it is like an unbreakable iron yoke on the necks of Judah and her neighbors. Furthermore, Hananiah himself will die shortly because he has caused God's people to put their trust in a lie. Less than two months later, Hananiah dies. This last episode resolves all three strands of the story. Hananiah's death is the most direct and obvious, but the responses of the three audiences in chap. 27 are also indicated in the final unit (28:12–16). God will now impose Nebuchadnezzar's rule like an iron yoke on the six nations, implying that they had refused to submit to him (cf. 27:8). The people in Jerusalem had put their trust in Hananiah's lie and thereby had chosen death (cf. 27:17).

Continuity between chaps. 27 and 28 is also indicated by the similarities in form and vocabulary among the four oracles spoken by Jeremiah. Childs (*OT Theology*, 138–39) describes their common pattern, consisting of four main points: (a) serve Nebuchadnezzar (27:5–8//12//17//28:14); (b) don't listen to the prophets (27:9//14//16, missing in 28:14–16 because this is addressed to Hananiah); (c) they prophesy falsehood (27:10//14//16//28:15); (d) if you disobey, you or the temple furnishings will be removed from the land (27:11//15//22//28:16). (See also the comparison by Wanke of the three oracles in chap. 27; *Untersuchungen*, 26.) Since the oracle spoken by Jeremiah to Hananiah conforms so closely to the oracles he delivers in chap. 27, Childs concludes that the confrontation in chap. 28 now "functions to provide a concrete illustration of the one message against false prophets" (*OT Theology*, 138).

The following outline shows the similarities between Jeremiah's oracles and also the way that the theme of warning against false prophets waxes while the command to submit to Nebuchadnezzar wanes. 27:5–11 enfolds the warning against false prophets between the two alternatives offered to the nations with respect to Nebuchadnezzar's rule. In 27:12–15 the command to submit to the king of Babylon stands alongside the warning about prophets and their false message. The command to stop listening to the prophets and the challenge to the prophets to intercede enclose the command to submit to Nebuchadnezzar in 27:16–18. When Hananiah apparently cancels Jeremiah's message of submission to Nebuchadnezzar in chap. 28 (vv 1–4, 10–11), Jeremiah's arguments (28:7–9) and a new word from the LORD (28:12–16) overcome the false prophet and clear the way for a sharper restatement of God's plan to subjugate the nations to Nebuchadnezzar (28:14).

    I. Superscription (27:1)
       A. Date (v 1a)
       B. Word-event formula (v 1b)
    II. Divine commissioning of a sign-act and oracle, for the neighboring kings
       (vv 2–11)
       A. Sign-act (vv 2–4)
          1. Command to make yoke-bonds and bars (v 2)
          2. Command to send them to neighboring kings (v 3)
          3. Command to commission messengers (v 4)
       B. Oracle, for the five kings (vv 5–11)
          1. The Creator's self-introduction (v 5)
          2. Proclamation of Nebuchadnezzar as suzerain (vv 6–7)
          3. Negative alternative (v 8)
          4. Warning against false prophets (vv 9–10)
          5. Positive alternative (v 11)
    III. Oracle report, for Zedekiah (vv 12–15)
       A. Introduction, first person (v 12a)
       B. Command to submit to the king of Babylon (vv 12b–13)

1. Three imperatives implying a promise (v 12b)
2. Motivation for obedience, a rhetorical question (v 13)
C. Warning against false prophecy (vv 14–15)
IV. Oracle report, for priests and people (vv 16–22)
A. Introduction, first person (v 16a)
B. Warning against false prophecy (vv 16b–18)
1. Stop listening to prophets (vv 16b–17a)
2. Command to submit to the king of Babylon (v 17b)
a. Two imperatives implying a promise (v 17bα)
b. Motivation for obedience, a rhetorical question (v 17bβ)
3. Challenge to prophets, intercede for the temple furnishings (v 18)
C. Oracle about temple furnishings (vv 19–22)
1. Identification of furnishings (vv 19–21)
2. God's plan for furnishings (v 22)
a. Brought to Babylon
b. Wait for divine action
c. Returned to the temple
V. Oracle report, Hananiah to Jeremiah (28:1–4)
A. Introduction, first person (v 1)
1. Date (v 1a)
2. Report of delivery (v 1b)
B. Salvation oracle, for Judah (vv 2–4)
1. Doom for the king of Babylon (v 2)
2. Restoration promises (vv 3–4a)
a. Temple furnishings (v 3)
b. Exiles (v 4a)
3. Doom for the king of Babylon (v 4b)
VI. Speech report, Jeremiah to Hananiah (vv 5–9)
A. Introduction, third person (v 5)
B. Prayer for the restoration of exiles and furnishings (v 6)
C. Appeal to listen (v 7)
D. Criterion for war prophets (v 8)
E. Criterion for peace prophets (v 9)
VII. Sign-act and oracle report, by Hananiah (vv 10–11)
A. Report of sign-act (v 10)
B. Salvation oracle (v 11a)
C. Report of Jeremiah's response (v 11b)
VIII. Divine commission to prophesy (vv 12–14)
A. Introduction, third person (v 12)
B. Command to speak (v 13a)
C. Oracle, to Hananiah (vv 13b–14)
1. Command to make iron bars (v 13b)
2. Explanation of sign-act (v 14)
IX. Oracle report, to Hananiah (vv 15–17)
A. Introduction, third person (v 15a)
B. Accusation (v 15b)
C. Threat (v 16)
D. Report of Hananiah's death (v 17)

The shape of these chapters undoubtedly presents Hananiah as a false prophet and Jeremiah as true. Structure and content, as well as more subtle means, accomplish this effect. For example, no divine commissioning is reported for

Hananiah, whereas Jeremiah is commissioned twice (27:2; 28:13a). Nevertheless, the reader is able to see some of the ambiguity experienced by the ancient audience, for Hananiah acts like Jeremiah and speaks like him, using the messenger formula. Jeremiah himself seems open to the possibility that God has spoken a true word through the false prophet (28:6).

Short notes in 28:1, "in that year," and v 17, "that year," set the words and deeds of chaps. 27–28 within a single year's time. (Both phrases are lacking in LXX; see the *Notes*.) Difficulties with the text of 27:1 and 28:1 and with the reconstruction of Near Eastern history during Zedekiah's reign obscure the precise date. Internal evidence suggests a date after the conquest of Jerusalem in 597 B.C. and before the Babylonian siege, which began in 588 (27:18–20; 28:2–4). The headings in 27:3, 12; 28:1 also indicate the reign of Zedekiah. There is no extrabiblical reference to an alliance between Judah and the five neighboring kingdoms or to their plans for revolt against Nebuchadnezzar. Chap. 27 never says why the messengers from the kings of Edom, Moab, the Ammonites, Tyre, and Sidon had come to Jerusalem. Their resistance to Babylonian rule is implied, however, by the content of Jeremiah's prophecy. According to the present shape of the book, Jeremiah was preaching the conquest by Nebuchadnezzar at least by the fourth year of Jehoiakim, which was Nebuchadnezzar's first (25:1), and he continued to advocate submission to Babylon after the destruction of the temple in 586 B.C. (chap. 42). This consistency in Jeremiah's message means that chaps. 27–28 do not require any more chronological precision than they actually possess. Nevertheless, numerous attempts have been made to calculate precise dates for the events in chaps. 27–28 by making use of the Babylonian Chronicle (edited by D. J. Wiseman).

Driver (*Textus* 4 [1964] 86–88) proposes that the diplomatic mission from the five neighboring kings came during Zedekiah's first year, in the month of Shebat, 596 B.C. ("Fourth year" in 28:1 is a mistaken reading of the abbreviation for "first year"; see *Notes*.) The beginning of his reign seems to Driver to be the natural time for such an embassy. Meier (*Messenger*, 248) confirms this practice. The Chronicle reports serious difficulties for Nebuchadnezzar in Babylon and the east during the next two years. Hayes and Hooker (*New Chronology*, 95–96) also set these events near the start of Zedekiah's reign, and do so by reading the two dates in 28:1 as belonging to different calendars. Zedekiah's accession year, by their reckoning, ended 15 Nisan 596 and overlapped with the fourth year of the sabbatical cycle, which used the autumn new year. The fifth month was Shebat, January/February 596. They read Hananiah's two-year prophecy as specifically related to the rebellion that occurred in Babylon in Nebuchadnezzar's tenth year (595–94).

The more commonly held dating is represented by Malamat ("The Twilight of Judah: In the Egyptian-Babylonian Maelstrom," in *Edinburgh Congress Volume*, VTSup 28 [Leiden: Brill, 1975] 135–38). According to the Chronicle, in 596/95 Elam attempted to attack Babylon but was repelled (cf. 49:34–39). The following year, Nebuchadnezzar's tenth, he quickly put down a rebellion in Babylon itself. These evidences of the Babylonian king's potential vulnerability, together with the accession of Psammetichus II in Egypt, are thought to have stimulated aspirations for independence among Babylon's vassal states in Syria-Palestine. Malamat places the "conference" in Jerusalem in this setting, in Zedekiah's fourth year, Tishri 594–Tishri 593, and dates the confrontation with Hananiah to the month of Ab 593.

Chap. 29 shares the implied date of chaps. 27–28 plus several other features. See the *Introduction* to chaps. 27–29 for a description of this collection and its setting in the book of Jeremiah.

Comment

1–2 The chapter begins, like chap. 26, with a quadruple-formula introduction, including date, word-event, and messenger formulas followed by a command. (See the three articles by Seidl in *BZ* 21 [1977] 23–44, 184–99; 23 [1979] 20–47 for an intensely detailed study of these formulas.) The odd result of this combination is that God's private communication to Jeremiah begins with a messenger formula.

The context of the chapter makes clear that the terms "bonds" and "bars" refer to parts of a yoke (עֹל) such as was used to hitch oxen to a plow. Uncertainty remains, however, as to which parts of a yoke are meant. The design of the ox yoke has not changed significantly over the millennia. It consists of at least two parts: (1) the crossbar, which lies across the necks of the oxen, in front of the shoulder hump; and (2) thinner, bent bars or pairs of parallel wooden pegs, which go around the neck and brace the yoke against the animals' shoulders. The purpose of a yoke is to enable the draught animals to pull a plow. The tongue of the plow is fixed to the center of the crossbar. Holladay adds a third part, (3) straps to tie together the bottom ends of the pegs (2:120; based on G. Schumacher's description of Palestinian plows in "Der arabische Pflug," *ZDPV* 12 [1889] 157–66). He interprets the מֹטוֹת as the pegs (2) and the מוֹסֵרוֹת as the straps (3). Cf. Isa 58:6. Jeremiah, therefore, carried no crossbar but wore a collar made out of the other parts of a yoke. Wearing such a "collar" would have been easier on Jeremiah's back and would have resembled the collars worn by prisoners of war in some Assyrian reliefs. The more common understanding is that the מוֹסֵרוֹת are the bars or cords that go around the animal's neck and that מֹטוֹת refers to the crossbar. Several times in the OT מוֹסֵרוֹת, "bonds," appears in poetic parallelism with עֹל, "yoke" (Jer 2:20; 5:5; 30:8; Nah 1:13). The mental picture of Jeremiah going about with his lopsided burden, a half-filled yoke, is a vivid illustration of his message. He invited each hearer to occupy the empty place on the other side of the yoke.

3–4 The five kings in v 3 appear in the same order in 25:21–22, where they are part of a longer list of nations about to drink from the cup of God's wrath. Here, only Judah's immediate neighbors are named. The order moves from southeast to northwest. The Philistines are missing, perhaps because they had already been subjugated. The allusion to chap. 25 serves as a reminder that these nations stand with Judah under God's judgment. The gap where the Philistines would have been serves to underscore the point.

The five kingdoms had all been vassals or treaty partners of David. Furthermore, all of them but Sidon had provided furnishings for the temple in one way or another. David had dedicated to the LORD silver and gold articles taken from

Edom, Moab, and the Ammonites (2 Sam 8:11–12), which Solomon put in the temple treasuries (1 Kgs 7:51). A trade agreement with Hiram of Tyre provided Solomon with building materials for the temple and with skilled craftsmen to produce the bronze furnishings for the temple courts (1 Kgs 5; 7:13–47).

Zedekiah suffers silently throughout these two chapters. Here, the messengers sent to negotiate with him are intercepted by Jeremiah, who gives them yokes or yoke pieces as well as a message from the LORD to carry back to their masters. (According to Meier, messengers regularly carried goods as well as words; *Messenger*, 75.) As royal messengers, they were trusted representatives who had to answer questions about the messages they delivered and may even have engaged in negotiations. Part of their job was to report to the ones who sent them about the reception that they and the messages received (Meier, *Messenger*, 206, 232). They wouldn't have been available for Jeremiah to hire, but his prophesying could have been included in their reports as part of the description of the political climate in Jerusalem. Jeremiah's treatment of the royal messengers would have been an embarrassment to Zedekiah (Calvin, 3:350).

Concentric quotations enclose this unit, as introduced in v 4. God speaks to Jeremiah, telling him what to tell the five kings' messengers to say. Jeremiah cannot go to the kings, so he delegates delivery of the LORD's word as in chaps. 29; 36; 51:59–64.

5 Marduk of Babylon might claim authority over nations by right of conquest, but the LORD claims the right to rule as creator. The three parts of this verse bring together creation, power, and authority. The combination of God's power and outstretched arm is a familiar motif from descriptions of the Exodus (Deut 4:34; Jer 32:21). As used here (and in 32:17), it implies that the LORD's creating is an act of salvation. The modifying phrase "every human and animal on the face of the earth" focuses the creation claim and personalizes it. The בהמה, "animals," may mean all living creatures other than human beings (as in Ps 36:7[Eng 6]) or the cattle that work for and live with human families. (Jonah 4:11 and Zech 2:4 remind us that even cities were inhabited by cattle.) Both senses have connections within the chapter. God, the creator of all living creatures, can even make the wild animals serve Nebuchadnezzar (v 6). The sign-act of the yoke parts has its greatest effect among people who live and work with draught animals.

The final clause makes use of phraseology found in 1 and 2 Kings with respect to the kings of Israel. For example, the phrase "what is right in my eyes; what seems right to me" describes David's deeds in 1 Kgs 14:8, in contrast to Jeroboam's. In 27:5, however, it refers to the person chosen by God, not to his actions. The verb נתן, "give," also occurs in both verses, and in 27:6 it is used in describing God's action to grant authority on the earth to a chosen individual.

6–7 The principle having been established in v 5, the LORD makes the announcement in v 6. Nebuchadnezzar is granted royal authority over "all these lands." In the OT, prophets regularly participate in the transfer of kingship by announcing the removal of the old monarch and declaring the LORD's choice of the new. Chaps. 21–22 serve as background for the announcement of Nebuchadnezzar's rule. Judah's kings lose the throne because of their oppressive, unjust, and greedy administration (22:17). Chap. 27 needs this background lest the reader lose sight of the divine justice at work within the storm of political controversy.

ארצות, "lands," echoes ארץ, "earth," in v 5 but has the effect of limiting the domain to the kingdoms named in v 3. (Contrast LXX, which has "the earth" in v 6 also.) The LORD, creator of all living things, can also grant to Nebuchadnezzar the service of wild animals. Attacks by wild animals are among the dangers of war and its aftermath (Deut 7:22; Ezek 39:4), and it may be in this sense that the wild animals are to serve Nebuchadnezzar, by completing the work of his army.

Difficulties with the text (see the *Notes*) and offended theological sensibilities have raised questions regarding the place of the description "my servant" in this passage. (The designation is also used of Nebuchadnezzar in 25:9 and 43:10.) Nothing known about the historical Nebuchadnezzar makes him seem worthy to share this title with Moses, David, or the Servant of the LORD in Isaiah. Furthermore, Jer 50:17; 51:34 describe his actions against Judah in chilling terms. Interpreters have offered various proposals for countering this objection. Overholt (*CBQ* 30 [1968] 45–46) defines a servant according to his task: he performs a service. Nebuchadnezzar is used by God as an instrument for achieving the divine purpose, and in this sense he is the LORD's servant. Zevit (*JBL* 88 [1969] 74–77) cites ancient Near Eastern documents and selected biblical texts (1 Sam 27:12; 2 Kgs 16:7) where, עבד, "servant," is a diplomatic term meaning "vassal." A vassal was obligated to provide an army for his overlord's use, and this is what the LORD asks Nebuchadnezzar to do in Jer 25:8–11; 43:8–44:14. Zevit has offered extrabiblical evidence for a secularized interpretation of "my servant."

The OT itself, however, does not dispose of the theological problem of Nebuchadnezzar quite so easily. One response is found in the next verse. God has set a limit on the length of Babylonian rule, after which Babylon will suffer her just punishment. In 29:10 the length is set at seventy years, which would correspond to the three generations in v 7. (See the *Excursus: Seventy Years* under chap. 29.) 25:12–14 promises that Babylon will suffer enslavement herself because of her deeds and refers the reader to chaps. 50–51. The other biblical solution is found in the book of Daniel, in which Nebuchadnezzar acknowledges the superiority of Daniel's God (e.g., Dan. 2:46–47; 3:28–29). Dan 4 can be read as a reflection upon Jer 27:6. After claiming absolute sovereignty for himself, Nebuchadnezzar immediately suffers the punishment already revealed to him in a dream. Driven away from people, he must live with the wild animals and eat grass like the cattle. When the time is up, his sanity and his throne are restored and he gives praise and glory to the LORD in a speech worthy of God's servant (4:34b–35).

Wiseman (*Nebuchadrezzar*, 99) quotes an inscription by Nebuchadnezzar addressed to Babylon's patron deity, Marduk. He says, in part, "I am the prince who obeys you, the creation of your hand. You begot me and entrusted me with the rule over all peoples."

The Nebuchadnezzar dynasty outlined in v 7 does not match what is known about Babylon's kings from ancient sources. Nebuchadnezzar's grandson apparently never occupied the throne. After his son, Awel-Marduk (Evil Merodach in the OT), had ruled for only two years, he was succeeded by the general Neriglissar. Neriglissar's son, in turn, was murdered, and Nabonidus became king (Smith, *Religion*, 22).

8 Two alternatives are offered to the nations in vv 8 and 11. The choice not to serve Nebuchadnezzar will result in being destroyed. The threefold threat of "sword, famine, and pestilence" ending in destruction is also found in 27:13; 24:10; 29:17 (plus six other times in Jeremiah), addressed to the inhabitants of Jerusalem. 27:8 fits its context by mentioning again the role of Nebuchadnezzar in finishing off rebellious nations ("by his hand"), while maintaining God as the principal agent. Although the form of this sentence is that of a general principle, its context provides a more particular setting.

"The yoke of Nebuchadnezzar" makes use of a common ancient Near Eastern expression for authority or rule. Seow (*Myth,* 199) lists several expressions in which the Akkadian word *niru,* "yoke," has this sense, including "yoke of the king" and "yoke of the deity." In the OT, the yoke is used as an image for the dominance of Jacob over Esau (Gen 27:40) and Solomon over the northern tribes (1 Kgs 12:4), for slavery in Egypt (Lev 26:13), and for oppression by Assyria (Isa 9:3; 10:27; 14:25) and Babylon (Isa 47:6; Jer 30:8; Ezek 34:27). In the book of Jeremiah, the yoke image is also used of service to God, from which the people had revolted long before (2:20). The parallelism in 5:5 suggests that bearing the LORD's yoke involves walking in the LORD's way and living according to God's justice. This interpretation is not far removed from the rabbis' expression, "taking upon oneself the yoke of the Kingdom of Heaven," which they used to indicate the significance of reciting the *Šĕma͑* (Deut 6:4–9; Weinfeld, *UF* 8 [1976] 406, citing *m. Ber.* 2:2). Jesus' invitation to "take my yoke upon you" (Matt 11:28–30) is spoken against the background of these biblical and Jewish uses.

The expression קְשֵׁה־עֹרֶף, "stiff-necked," surely relates to the yoke image by describing persons who refuse to bend their neck under the yoke. (When the yoke is removed, a person can walk upright again, Lev 26:13.) Israel is repeatedly called "stiff-necked" following their apostasy with the golden calf (Exod 32:9; 33:3, 5; 34:9; Deut 9:6, 13), and Jer 19:15 also uses this description.

9–10 Three variants of this warning command appear in the chapter, one for each of Jeremiah's three audiences (vv 9–10, 14–15, 16b–17; cf. 28:15; 29:8–9). The second-person address is striking, coming as it does between the impersonal third-person conditional statements of vv 8 and 11. The stereotyped expression "they are prophesying falsehood" (v 9a) has its specific interpretation in v 9b, but the connection between their lie, "You will not serve the king of Babylon," and banishment from the land is less obvious. It depends on vv 8 and 11 for its explication. If the nations believe their intermediaries, then they will refuse to submit to Nebuchadnezzar, and the threat in v 8 will overtake them. V 10 makes clear that this punishment begins with deportation, the opposite of the assurance offered in v 11. Vv 9–10 both heighten the rhetorical effect of this speech and identify the major impediment to obedience and salvation. The danger of false prophets is that they prevent people and nations from responding to God's word. The consequences here are exile and death. The identical warning command stands at the beginning of the oracle in 23:16–22, which articulates the same reasoning. Prophets sent from God proclaim words that result in repentance (v 22).

11 The positive alternative closes the message. It is presented in the same impersonal third-person form as v 8, but two wordplays enliven the effect of the sentence. Assonance between הִדַּחְתִּי, "I shall banish" (v 10), and הִנַּחְתִּי, "I shall leave, cause to rest," emphasizes the contrast between the verses. Act and consequence are linked by the repetition of one verb with different objects. The nation that will "serve him (Nebuchadnezzar)" (ועבדו) will, as a result, be able to "till it (its land)" (ועבדה).

12–13 The three imperatives at the beginning of this saying have a logical connection. The first command, "put your neck in the yoke," is a link to Jeremiah's sign-act (v 2) and alludes to v 8, where the expression appears for the first time. The second imperative interprets the first and is equivalent to it, "serve him." The third imperative, "live," actually communicates assurance or promise of what will happen if the first commands are obeyed (GKC § 110f). This pattern is seen again in 27:17 and 29:5–6. The question that follows, beginning with למה, "why," introduces the undesirable alternative that will ensue if the commands are not obeyed. It has the sense "otherwise you and your people will die." Death by "sword, famine, and pestilence" for refusal to serve the king of Babylon has just been decreed in the message to the neighboring kings, and v 13b refers specifically to v 8. The oracle to Zedekiah applies the threat stated in the earlier verse.

14–15 These verses are nearly identical to v 9. The major difference is the additional charge against the prophets, "I did not send them." The neighboring nations had no reason to think that their prophets and intermediaries had been sent by Israel's God in the first place, so the absence of this denunciation from vv 5–11 is not surprising. The final phrase in v 15 explicitly includes the prophets in the death sentence. The judgments on Hananiah in 28:15–16 and Shemaiah in 29:31–32, whom the LORD had not sent, fulfill the threat in v 15.

16–17 Articles from the temple were the particular concern of the priests and the worshipers, and a promise of their return was an especially appealing lie. The conqueror carried off such articles not only because of their intrinsic value but because they were evidence of the defeat of the deity in whose cult they had been used. Conversely, the return of these things would be a sure proof that Babylon's power had been broken.

According to 2 Kgs 24:11–17, all the treasures of the temple and palace were taken away by Nebuchadrezzar in 597 B.C., yet Jer 27:18–22 indicate that some articles did remain in Jerusalem. 2 Kgs 25:13–17 = Jer 52:17–23 list the same large bronze items mentioned in v 19 as the articles broken up and carried away by Nebuzaradan in 586. 2 Chr 36:7, 10, 18 also report the removal of temple furnishings on both occasions. Haran (*IEJ* 13 [1963] 46–58) attempts to sort out the apparent contradictions by identifying three sources and types of temple furnishings: (1) bronze articles from the temple court, (2) gold and gold-plated furnishings from the holy place and holy of holies, and (3) gold and silver dedicated items from the temple treasuries, including things taken as booty in war by Judah's kings. On numerous occasions booty had been taken or tribute had been paid from the treasuries of temple and palace (e.g., 2 Kgs 14:14; 16:8; 18:14–15). According to Haran's reconstruction, Nebuchadrezzar plundered the treasuries (3) in 597 and also stripped the gold plating off the furnishings in the holy place and the holy of holies (2). In 586 the Babylonian conquerors broke up the large bronze pieces in the court (1) and carried off the scrap metal. Only the articles from (3) would have been intact and available to be returned to Jerusalem. The items in the inventory of returned goods in Ezra 1:5–11 are of the sort presumably found in the treasuries (3).

The ruin or desolation of Jerusalem is threatened in 25:18 and reported in 44:2, 6. (The same term is used in the book of Jeremiah of the land, 7:34; 25:11; 44:22, the nations, 25:9, the palace, 22:5, and the temple, 33:10, 12.) It epitomizes the devastation wrought by the conquering Babylonians, for Jerusalem was the last to fall.

18–22 Jeremiah assumes that intercession is a responsibility of true prophets, so the challenge he sets for the ones prophesying the return of the temple vessels is to pray that the remaining treasures would not be captured. To enter into this intercession, however, would indicate acceptance of Jeremiah's prophecy that the Babylonian army would sack the city and temple again. Since Jeremiah himself had been forbidden to intercede (11:14; 14:11–12), the tone of this verse should not be read as sarcastic. He invites the other prophets to believe the word of God given through him and to intercede for that which he has been forbidden to pray. The possibility that the LORD might relent is implicit in this challenge. The hope for the furnishings to remain in their place parallels the positive alternative offered to the nations in v 11: submit to the king of Babylon and be permitted to remain in your land.

The subjects of the proposed intercession in v 18 correspond to the subjects of the divine plan described in vv 21–22. They are, according to Haran's reconstruction (see above, *Comment* on vv 16–17), items from the temple and palace treasuries that could be transported intact to and from Babylon. 2 Kgs 25:14–15 = Jer 52:18–19 lists a number of smaller articles from the temple that were taken in 586 B.C. Jer 52 does not mention anything taken from the palace, but, since both palace and temple were burned (52:13), it is not unlikely that the king's house was plundered also. The large bronze fixtures listed in v 19, the pillars, sea, and stands, were cut to pieces by the Babylonians for ease of transport, according to 2 Kgs 25:13 = Jer 52:17. (See 1 Kgs 7:13–47 for a description of their size and construction.) The book of Ezra does not mention these large items or any scrap bronze among the 5400 silver and gold vessels brought back to Jerusalem by Sheshbazzar (chap. 1). The pillars, sea, and stands had been made by Phoenician craftsmen (1 Kgs 7:13–14) and had several features in common with Canaanite iconography (e.g., bulls, pomegranates; see J. Levenson, *Sinai and Zion: An Entry into the Jewish Bible* [Minneapolis: Winston, 1985], 138–39).

The divine plan for the temple furnishings encompasses judgment and salvation, with a wait of unspecified length in between. V 22 parallels the promise to the exiles in 29:10. The LORD will deal with (פקד) them and return (שוב) them to this place (אל־המקום הזה). Carroll (537) notes the unusual term אלה (hiphil), "bring up," which he identifies as a term appropriate for a sacred procession.

28:1 The complex date formula has two functions within the larger context. First, it synchronizes the events in chaps. 27 and 28. (See *Form/Structure/Setting* and *Notes* on 27:1 and 28:1 for discussions of the textual and historical problems.) The verb at the beginning of the verse, imperfect with waw consecutive, supports this connection between the chapters. Second, the fifth month is named in order to show the speedy fulfillment of Jeremiah's prophecy of Hananiah's death. He died, according to v 17, in the seventh month.

Hananiah is not mentioned anywhere else in the OT. Like Jeremiah, he is from a town in Benjamin not far from Jerusalem and he speaks as a prophet in the temple. He and Jeremiah are both given the title "prophet" in this chapter (vv 1,

5, 10, 15, 17). The addressee of his oracle is Jeremiah, but the priests and all the people are present to hear it and Jeremiah's response in vv 5–9. These same two groups are the addressees of Jeremiah's oracle about the temple furnishings in 27:16–22.

2–4 The first and last sentences of Hananiah's oracle announce Nebuchadnezzar's defeat by means of the yoke metaphor introduced in chap. 27 and illustrated by Jeremiah's sign-act. One expects Hananiah's own symbolic action to occur before he delivers this oracle, since sign-acts generally precede their interpretive sayings (cf. 1 Kgs 11:29–31; Jer 27), but he does not break Jeremiah's yoke until v 10, after which Hananiah speaks another, similar oracle about Nebuchadnezzar's end. Jer 19 has a structure that resembles chap. 28, however. Jeremiah is commanded to deliver a judgment oracle in the place where some of the culpable behavior has occurred (19:3–9); then he is to smash the jar as a sign-act of the way the LORD will smash the nation and the city, described in a second oracle (vv 10–13).

It is appropriate to compare the divine first-person statement that introduces Hananiah's oracle, "I break the yoke of the king of Babylon" (v 2), with the LORD's first statement in 27:5, "I alone made the earth . . ." Authentic divine words need not always begin with such a statement, but this is another subtle way in which the shape of these two chapters points to the truth of Jeremiah's message.

Hananiah's oracle is attractive in form as well as content. In the chiastic structure of vv 2–4, the two categories of exiles in Babylon, temple furnishings and people (vv 3–4a), are framed by the promise "I will bring back to this place" (vv 3aβ and 4ba) and the declaration "I break/will break the yoke of the king of Babylon" (vv 2b and 4bβ).

Note that Hananiah was, in effect, prophesying the end of Zedekiah's reign when he promised the return of Jeconiah = Jehoiachin. Carroll calls attention to the courage exhibited by Hananiah here as he risks his life by speaking against "the present state of power politics in Jerusalem" (543).

It is quite possible to speak of the return of furnishings and exiles without mentioning the end of Babylon's power (cf. 27:19–22). This oracle, however, brings together three main themes of chaps. 27–29: (1) the limit of Babylonian hegemony, (2) the fate of the temple furnishings, the king, and the other exiles, and (3) the LORD's intention eventually to return them all to Judah and Jerusalem. All of these elements are also part of God's word through Jeremiah. There is a decisive difference between the messages of these two prophets, however, and it is more than a matter of timing, Hananiah's two years to Jeremiah's seventy (29:10). The difference is the LORD's command to serve Nebuchadnezzar (27:11–12).

5–9 Jeremiah's reply to Hananiah's oracle is his own word. There is no messenger formula or other indication of prophetic speech. "Amen" is a relatively rare word in the OT, occurring in only two dozen verses. On several occasions it is the official response indicating acceptance of the terms of God's law or covenant (Num 5:22; Deut 27:15–26; Neh 5:13; Jer 11:5). It is never an Israelite equivalent of "Bravo" for a stirring performance by a prophet. The one passage that most closely resembles v 6 is 1 Kgs 1:36. David has given orders to anoint Solomon king; Benaiah responds "Amen! May the LORD declare it" and continues with a prayer on behalf of Solomon. The grammatical pattern, "Amen" followed by a jussive verb with the LORD as subject, is the same in both verses. As

Benaiah's support of Solomon was sincere, Jeremiah's response to Hananiah was probably not sarcastic. The verb used here, קום hiphil, "establish, fulfill," is the same verb used in the LORD's promise in 29:10. It is certainly significant that Jeremiah's reply does not include any mention of the breaking of Nebuchadnezzar's yoke. Vv 10–11 indicate that this omission was noticed by Hananiah. Contrary to Carroll's charge (540), Jeremiah has not disobeyed his own warning by listening to Hananiah. He has not advocated rebellion against Nebuchadnezzar.

The teaching that follows is for the benefit of Hananiah and all the people listening to them (v 7). Vv 8–9, however, are much more useful for readers of the book of Jeremiah than for the crowd in the temple. Several recent interpreters have recognized that these verses do not offer practical criteria that could have helped ancient hearers to distinguish true divine words from false (e.g., Carroll, *Chaos*, 192). Quell (*Wahre*, 61) comments that even Jeremiah does not know enough from these verses to make a determination about Hananiah. Carroll's analysis (544) is to the point: war oracles and peace oracles are treated separately, as each type is provided with a different means of validation, and the result is a "stalemate." The lack of a conjunction at the beginning of v 9 enforces this abrupt contrast (M. Kessler, "A Prophetic Biography: A Form-Critical Study of Jeremiah, Chapters 26–29, 32–45," Diss., Brandeis, 1965, 25).

At first glance, v 8 resembles the motif of God's persistent sending and the people's consistent rejection of prophets in the past, seen most recently in 26:5. The sending and rejecting may be assumed, but the accent in this verse falls upon the consistent character of their message. It is reminiscent of the king of Israel's description of Micaiah son of Imlah in 1 Kgs 22:8: "he never prophesies anything good about me." Jeremiah's description of these prophets as "before me and before you" does not exclude Hananiah or himself from this succession.

A certain ambiguity lingers in v 8. Although Jeremiah has prophesied to "many lands" (including Judah, 27:6–7), Hananiah has uttered a word against the "great kingdom," Babylon (28:2, 4), which is comparable to Isaiah's oracle against Assyria (Isa 10:12–19; Carroll, 544). The content of the past prophets' message, "war, calamity, and pestilence," is closer to Jeremiah's diction than to Hananiah's, although it has only one of three elements in common with the formula in 27:8, 13; 29:17 ("sword, famine, and pestilence"). "War" (מלחמה) is actually quite rare in Jeremiah (4:19; 6:4, 23; 21:4). It is more prosaic and has a broader meaning than "sword," which is used in the more common threefold expression. There are, after all, many kinds of weapons and strategies of war (21:4). The second term, רעה, "evil, wickedness, calamity," is also a much more inclusive term than its sound-alike counterpart, רעב, "famine." The same word can name both the offense and the punishment, and this feature is used to good rhetorical effect in 1:14, 16; 18:8, 10, 11; 23:10, 12, 14, 17.

The third word, דבר, "plague, pestilence," occurs nine out of twelve times in Jeremiah as part of the list of three threats. Its presence in this verse serves to indicate that Jeremiah's characteristic formula, "sword, famine, and pestilence," should be viewed as a particular way of expressing the message summarized in v 8. The only two times that "pestilence" stands alone in the book of Jeremiah are found in chap. 21 (vv 6, 7), a passage that also includes "war" (v 3) and "calamity" (v 10) in the LORD's actions against Jerusalem, as well as the list, "sword, famine, and pestilence" (v 9, and, in reverse order, v 7). Other points of contact with chaps. 27–28 are in 21:5, "outstretched hand and mighty arm" (cf. 27:5), in 21:6, "inhabitants of the city, human and animal" (cf. 27:5), and in 21:8–10, the opportunity to choose between rescue and death (cf. 27:8–11). Chap. 21 reports Zedekiah's request for a word from the LORD during the siege of Jerusalem and the divine response. The poetry at the end of the chapter (vv 12–14) provides a reminder of the reasons for the "war, calamity, and pestilence" that were about to overwhelm Zedekiah and Jerusalem: The royal house of Judah had failed to administer justice daily and to rescue the oppressed and exploited.

War prophets stand in a long succession in Israel, but one prophesying peace stands alone. Note the singular noun נָבִיא, "prophet," in v 9. A new word that stands outside the tradition must be put to the test of fulfillment. V 9 makes use of Deut 18:21–22. Two key terms occur in both passages. True prophets are "known" (ידע) when their words "come" (בוא). This test would surely have been inadequate in the situation of contradiction between Hananiah's message and Jeremiah's. Waiting two years for the return of the king, exiles, and temple articles would have meant giving up the opportunity to respond properly to Jeremiah's message. Yet the fulfillment criterion was certainly at work in the collection and preservation of Jeremiah's oracles. When God's judgment fell on Judah and Jerusalem, Jeremiah was shown to be a true prophet (Childs, *OT Theology*, 140). The fulfillment criterion also implicitly leaves open the possibility that God's plan will change. Jeremiah could not reject Hananiah's word out of hand because he recognized this possibility. The positive alternative offered to the nations in 27:11 and the challenge to intercede in 27:18 are also compatible with the belief that God may repent and change the plan. These two criteria may have originated as the beliefs of a particular group or groups of prophets and their supporters, but they now validate the canonical shape of the book of Jeremiah, which includes oracles of war and of peace (see Sheppard, "True," 271).

10–11 The drama of this incident is unprecedented. One prophet vandalizes another prophet's sign-act. To Hananiah, at least, Jeremiah had succeeded in communicating the meaning of the contraption he wore on his neck. The word here is מוֹטָה, "yoke-bar," the singular of the word in 27:2, not עֹל, "yoke," as in 30:8. If Holladay is right and this term signifies the pegs forming a collar (2:120), then Hananiah would have found it easier to break than the main crossbar of a yoke.

In the context of these chapters, Hananiah's act receives two interpretations. The first is his own oracle, in v 11, which closely resembles what Jeremiah is told to say in 19:11. Both sayings begin with the messenger formula and the words כָּכָה אֶשְׁבֹּר, "In this way I shall break." (The structure of chap. 19 also resembles that of 28:1–4, 10–11. The sign-act falls between two explanatory oracles.) This verse is a direct contradiction of 27:6–11, which employs the same terminology, "all nations" under "the yoke [עֹל] of Nebuchadnezzar." Even the verb forms serve to undermine Jeremiah's earlier word, which uses the imperfect to express the future or potential subjugation of the nations. What Nebuchadnezzar had done so far to gain control over the region was not yet the servitude envisioned in Jeremiah's prophecy. Hananiah's word subtly contradicts this stance by treating the release as future or potential and implying that in the current situation the nations are already "under the yoke." The oppression will not get any worse; it will end within two years. V 11 is, in effect, a critique of 27:1–11 in terms of 28:2–4. This observation leads to the second interpretation of Hananiah's sign-act, which is implied by its context in chaps. 27–28. By means of this act and its interpretive word (vv 10–11), Hananiah personally rejects the LORD's word and disobeys the commands "bring your neck under the yoke of Nebuchadnezzar" and "serve the king of Babylon and live" (vv 12, 17).

The single sentence of narrative that concludes the verse has been subjected to a steady flow of speculation regarding Jeremiah's spiritual, emotional, and vocational state. It cannot and need not bear that weight. This sentence serves to conclude an episode, vv 1–11, in which Jeremiah occupies the role of audience to Hananiah the prophet. His only speech in this passage is not a prophetic oracle; it functions as a dispute or objection to Hananiah's message. This passage, as shaped by the heading in v 1 and the short narratives in vv 5 and 11b, demonstrates by its form and structure the possibility that the LORD had changed the plan and that a word from the LORD might be spoken by a prophet otherwise thought to be false. As the audience of the prophetic word, Jeremiah demonstrates respect for this possibility. The divine source of the word, not the status of the human messenger, is the ultimate concern.

12–14 The word-event formula in v 12 and the messenger formula in v 13 indicate that Jeremiah has resumed the role of prophet. Jeremiah did not simply produce another oracle of the sort he described in v 8. He spoke again only after having received a fresh revelation of the LORD's word. In v 12, then, the word-event formula and the temporal clause do not appear simply pro forma; they serve an important narrative function. Even though the oracle in vv 13–14 closely resembles 27:5–11, it is not just a restatement of the earlier word. The heading in v 12 identifies it as a new word from the LORD, addressed to a different audience (Hananiah) with the specific purpose of showing that neither Hananiah's oracles nor his sign-act (28:1–11) had canceled or revoked the message given through Jeremiah in chap. 27.

An accusation is found in v 13, introduced, as so often in Jeremiah, by the messenger formula. When Hananiah broke the yoke-bar, it was a physical act with a rhetorical and metaphorical function. This shift is indicated by the change from the singular מוֹטָה, "yoke-bar," in v 12 to the plural in v 13. His hands broke Jeremiah's yoke, but his words had declared an end of service to Nebuchadnezzar for all the nations (v 11) to whom Jeremiah had sent yokes and God's command to submit (27:5–9). The last clause in v 13 remains metaphorical. The stronger iron is unbreakable. "Can anyone break iron?" asks Jer 15:12. No; nor can Hananiah's prophesying shatter God's plan for Babylonian rule over the nations and the wild animals (27:6; 28:14). The logic of the yoke image is spelled out in v 14. As animals are yoked in order to work, so the nations will be put under the yoke in order to serve Nebuchadnezzar.

15–17 The final word to Hananiah follows the classic form of the judgment oracle to an individual (Westermann, *Basic Forms*, 142), in which the accusation or diatribe is the prophet's composition. V 15 fits this description because there is no messenger formula and the initial "listen" echoes Jeremiah's nonoracular speech in 28:7. The announcement of judgment is linked to the accusation by לָכֵן, "therefore," and the messenger formula indicates its divine origin. An additional accusation comes at the end of v 16.

The accusations against Hananiah in vv 15–16 are composed of several generalizing statements that have the effect of identifying Hananiah as a particular example of the prophets about whom the various audiences are warned in chap. 27 (and 29): "Stop listening [שמע] to your prophets." Jeremiah invites Hananiah's attention with the same verb, "listen" (שמע). It is said of the unnamed Jerusalem prophets in 27:15, of the prophets and diviners among the exiles in 29:9, of Shemaiah in 29:31, and of Hananiah, "the LORD did not send [שלה] them/him/you." The LORD had sent Jeremiah (26:15) and many prophets before him (26:5). The prophets not sent by God were prophesying lies, according to 27:10, 14, 16 (and 29:9). Hananiah (and Shemaiah, 29:31) had gone one step further and succeeded in making the people put their trust in the lie. (28:16 and 29:31 are the only places where the causative form is used.) Jer 13:25 connects "trusting the lie" to forgetting the LORD, and this reasoning may explain why Hananiah could be charged with preaching apostasy even though he had spoken in the LORD's name. According to Deut 13, prophets who say "Let us follow other gods" are guilty of the capital crime of fomenting apostasy. Hananiah is sentenced to death on the same charge even though he has not said these plain words. To believe that a lie is a word from the LORD is equivalent to following other gods. V 15 implies the outcome of chap. 27. If the people (in Judah and Jerusalem) have indeed put their trust in Hananiah's lie, then the LORD will exile them and they will perish (27:15).

The first part of the sentence imposed upon Hananiah is a rather poetic saying involving an effective play on words. The LORD had not sent (שלח qal, v 9) Hananiah as a prophet but will send him off (שלח piel) "from the face of the earth," which is the habitation of humankind (Exod 33:16; Deut 7:6; Jer 25:26). With various other verbs, this phrase makes a formula for divine judgment on Cain (Gen 4:14), Israel (Exod 32:12; Amos 9:8), and humankind (Gen 6:1, 7; Zeph 1:3). The next sentence states the matter more plainly, and, in keeping with the style of chaps. 28–29, sets a date; Hananiah will die "this year." V 17 reports his death, "that year, in the seventh month," within two months of his first oracle.

A single verse of narrative ends the episode in which Hananiah is the audience. It parallels v 11b and invites comparison. In chaps. 26–29 the deaths of four prophets are predicted and/or reported. Of the prophets named in these chapters, only Jeremiah survives to see the fulfillment of the prophecies given to him by the LORD.

Explanation

The reader of chaps. 27–28 finds no uncertainty about the location of truth in the ancient situation. In the end, Jeremiah survives, and the divine word given through him is intact and strengthened (wooden yoke-bars are replaced by iron). The actions of God, reported in chap. 52, validate the message about another attack, victory, and deportation by the power of Nebuchadnezzar and Babylon. The profound appeal of Hananiah's message, however, continues to disturb confidence about the reader's own present. Hananiah and the anonymous prophets in chap. 27 give voice to the enduring temptation to claim the LORD's promises, to trust in God's choice and protection, to hope in the face of terrifying upheaval that everything will be put back the way it used to be, that the old king and the furnishings will be returned to their places in the palace and temple. It is the temptation to use God's own promises to resist the change that a true encounter with God requires of every person. Jeremiah's repeated command, "Stop listening" to the prophets, is a clear allusion to 23:16–22. When one truly listens to a prophet who has stood in the LORD's council, the response ought to be repentance and reformation of life (23:22). The storm and anger of the LORD in 23:16–22 reintroduce an awareness of God's justice in chaps. 27–28. The conquest of Judah and Jerusalem is not an arbitrary outburst of divine wrath or abandonment; it is a long-delayed but just judgment on wickedness. By denying the coming judgment, the false prophets also deny the people an opportunity to "turn from their evil way and from the evil of their deeds" (23:22).

Perhaps the greatest theological challenge of these chapters is the command to submit to the superpower, to serve Nebuchadnezzar. Voluntary submission is offered as a way to avoid conquest and death. But how can surrender be a mark of faithfulness? These chapters point to at least four ways to begin to answer these concerns. First, the assignment of authority to Nebuchadnezzar is an exercise of the Creator's rule, not an abdication. Second, "submit to the king of Babylon" is a historically conditioned command. The explanatory addition of Nebuchadnezzar's name and the date formulas define the particular circumstances in which the command is in effect. Third, the period of submission is also of limited duration (27:7). No eternal principle of "the divine right of emperors" is at work. One cannot conclude from this command that the LORD sides with the winners. Neither submission nor resistance to the despot is taught as an exclusive, eternal principle. Nebuchadnezzar is victor only because he acts as the LORD's vassal, supplying troops in service of his suzerain's purposes. Fourth, the greatest threat to God's people was not the loss of independent statehood but the decay of national and personal integrity of faith and service to the LORD. It was the ministry of God's servants the prophets to warn them against their true peril and to invite them to return to the LORD.

B. Correspondence with the Exiles (29:1–32 [LXX 36:1–32])

Bibliography

Begg, C. "The Non-mention of Ezekiel in the Book of Jeremiah." *ETL* 65/1 (1989) 94–95. **Berlin, A.** "Jeremiah 29:5–7: A Deuteronomic Allusion." *HAR* 8 (1984) 3–11. **Casson, L.** *Travel in the Ancient World.* London: Allen and Unwin, 1974. **Dietrich, E. L.** *šwb šbwt: Die endzeitliche Wiederherstellung bei den Propheten.* BZAW 40. Giessen: Töpelmann, 1925. **Dijkstra, M.** "Prophecy by Letter (Jeremiah xxix 24–32)." *VT* 33 (1983) 319–22. **Driver, G. R.** "Once Again Abbreviations." *Textus* 4 (1964) 76–94. **Eph'al, I.** "The Western Minorities in

Babylonia in the 6th–5th Centuries BC: Maintenance and Cohesion." *Or* n.s. 47 (1978) 74–90. **Fohrer, G.** *Die Propheten des Alten Testaments: Band 7. Prophetenerzählungen.* Gütersloh: Mohn, 1977. **Gevaryahu, H.** "Various Observations on Scribes and Books in the Biblical Period." (Heb.) *BMik* 43 (1970) 368–74. **Haran, M.** "Book-Scrolls in Israel in Pre-Exilic Times. *JJS* 33 (1982) 161–73. **Kilpp, N.** *Niederreissen und aufbauen: Das Verhältnis von Heilsverheissung und Unheilsverkündigung bei Jeremia und im Jeremiabuch.* Neukirchen: Neukirchener, 1990. **Lust, J.** "'Gathering and Return' in Jeremiah and Ezekiel." In *Le Livre de Jérémie.* BETL 54. Louvain: Louvain UP, 1981. 119–42. **Macholz, G.** "Jeremia in der Kontinuität der Prophetie." In *Probleme biblischer Theologie*, ed. H. Wolff. Munich: Kaiser, 1971. 306–34. **Malamat, A.** "The Last Wars of the Kingdom of Judah." *JNES* 9 (1950) 218–27. **Meier, S. A.** *The Messenger in the Ancient Semitic World.* HSM 45. Atlanta: Scholars, 1988. **Mettinger, T.** *King and Messiah: The Civil and Sacral Legitimation of the Israelite Kings.* Lund: Liber Läromedel, 1976. **North, R.** "Palestine, Administration of (Postexilic Judean Officials)." *ABD* 5:87. **Pardee, D.** *Handbook of Ancient Hebrew Letters.* Chico, CA.: Scholars, 1982. ———. "An Overview of Ancient Hebrew Epistolography." *JBL* 97 (1978) 321–46. **Porten, B.** "A New Look: Aramaic Papyri and Parchments." *BA* 42 (1979) 74–104. **Savran, G.** *Telling and Retelling: Quotation in Biblical Narrative.* Bloomington: Indiana UP, 1988. **Schmidt, W., and Becker, J.** *Zukunft und Hoffnung.* Stuttgart: Kohlhammer, 1981. **Schreiner, J.** "'Durch die Propheten gelehrt, das Heil zu erwarten': Erwägungen im Anschluss an Jeremia 29." In *Segen für die Völker*, ed. E. Zenger. Düsseldorf: Patmos, 1987. 153–65. **Smith, D.** *The Religion of the Landless: The Social Context of the Babylonian Exile.* Bloomington: Meyer-Stone, 1989. **Yaure, L.** "Elymas—Nehelemite—Pethor." *JBL* 79 (1960) 297–314.

Translation

¹ *These are the words of the document which Jeremiah* ª *the prophet* ª *sent from Jerusalem to the remnant* ᵇ *of the exiles' elders, to the priests, to the prophets, and to all the people* ᶜ *whom Nebuchadnezzar had exiled from Jerusalem to Babylon* ᶜ ²ª *(after the departure of Jeconiah the king, the queen mother, the palace officials,* ᵇ *royal officials* ᶜ *of Judah and Jerusalem,* ᵇ *the craftsmen and the smiths from Jerusalem)* ³ *by the hand of Elasah son of Shaphan and Gemariah son of Hilkiah whom Zedekiah, king of Judah, sent to Nebuchadnezzar,* ª *king of Babylon, to Babylon, saying:*

⁴ *"Thus says the* LORD *of Hosts,* ª *God of Israel, to all* ᵇ *the exiles whom I have exiled* ᶜ *from Jerusalem to Babylon,* ᵈ ⁵ *'Build houses and settle down. Plant gardens and eat their fruit.* ⁶ *Get married and have sons and daughters, and take wives for your sons and give your daughters to husbands* ª *so that they will give birth to sons and daughters.* ª *Multiply there* ᵇ *and do not decrease.* ⁷ *Seek the peace of the city* ª *where I have exiled you and pray on her behalf to the* LORD, *for in her peace shall be peace for you.'*

⁸ª *"Indeed, thus says the* LORD ᵇ *of Hosts, the God of Israel,* ᵇ *'Stop deceiving yourselves by* ᶜ *your prophets* ᶜ *who are in your midst and your diviners, and stop listening to your dreams* ᵈ *which* ᵉ *you are dreaming,* ᵉ ⁹ *for they are prophesying to you falsely* ª *in my name. I did not send them—* ᵇ *oracle of the* LORD. ᵇ

¹⁰ *"For thus says the* LORD, *'Only when seventy years are filled up for Babylon shall I deal with you and fulfill for you my pledge* ª *by returning you to this place.* ¹¹ *For I* ª *know the plans which I* ª *am planning for you—* ᵇ *oracle of the* LORD ᵇ *—plans for peace, not for calamity, in order to give you* ᶜ *a future and a hope.* ᶜ ¹²ª *You will call upon me and come* ᵇª *and pray to me,* ᶜ *and I shall listen to you.* ᶜ ¹³ *When you seek me* ª *you will find (me) if you seek me* ª *with your whole heart.* ¹⁴ *I will be found* ª *by you* ᵇ *—* ᶜ *oracle of the* LORD ᶜ *—and I will bring about your restoration,* ᵈ *and gather you from all the nations and from all the*

places where I have driven you—oracle of the LORD—I will bring you back to the place from which I have exiled you.' [b]

[15] *"Because you have said, 'The LORD has raised up prophets for us in Babylon.'* [a] [16a] *Indeed, thus says the LORD to the king who sits upon the throne of David and to all the people who dwell in that city, your kindred who did not go out with you into the exile:* [17] *Thus says the LORD of Hosts: I am about to send upon them sword,* [a] *famine, and pestilence, and I shall make them like the disgusting* [b] *figs which are too rotten to be eaten.* [18] *I shall pursue them with sword, with famine,* [a] *and with pestilence, and I shall make them a reason for trembling* [b] *to all the kingdoms of the earth, an execration and a horror and a hissing* [c] *and a reproach in all the nations where I banish them,* [19] *because they have not listened to my words—oracle of the LORD—in that I sent them* [a] *my servants the prophets persistently, but you* [b] *did not listen—oracle of the LORD.*

[20] *"Now, as for you, hear the word of the LORD, all you exiles whom I sent from Jerusalem to Babylon:* [21] *Thus says the LORD* [a] *of Hosts, the God of Israel,* [a] *to Ahab* [b] *son of Kolaiah* [b] *and to Zedekiah* [c] *son of Maaseiah, who are prophesying to you falsely in my name:* [c] *I am about to give them into the hand of Nebuchadrezzar,* [d] *the king of Babylon, and he will smite them in your sight.* [22] *A curse formula shall be derived from them for all the Judean exiles who are in Babylon, as follows, 'May the LORD make you like Zedekiah and like Ahab* [a] *whom the king of Babylon roasted in the fire,'* [23] *because they have committed shameful folly in Israel and committed adultery with their neighbors' wives and have spoken a word in my name falsely* [a] *which I had not commanded them. I am* [b] *the one who knows* [c] *and* [b] *the witness—oracle of the LORD.*

[24a] *"To Shemaiah the Nehelamite you shall say:* [b] [25] *Thus says the LORD of Hosts, the God of Israel:* [a] [b] *Because you have sent letters* [c] *in your name* [b] [d] *to the whole nation which is in Jerusalem and* [d] *to Zephaniah son of Maaseiah the priest* [e] *and to all the priests,* [e] *saying,* [26] *'The LORD made you priest in place of Jehoida the priest in order to act as overseer* [a] *in the house* [b] *of the LORD against any* [c] *prophesying madman* [c] *so that you would put him in the stocks* [d] *and the pillory.* [27] *Now, why haven't you rebuked* [a] *Jeremiah the Anathothite* [b] *who is prophesying* [c] *to you?* [28] *Because thus he has sent to us in Babylon,* [a] *saying, 'It will be long. Build houses and settle down, plant gardens and eat their fruit.'"*

[29] *(Zephaniah* [a] *the priest* [a] *read aloud this* [b] *letter in the hearing of Jeremiah* [c] *the prophet.* [c]*)* [30] *Then the word of the LORD came to Jeremiah:* [31] *"Send to all* [a] *the exiles, saying, 'Thus says the LORD to Shemaiah the Nehelamite: Because Shemaiah is prophesying to you, although I have not sent him, with the result that he has caused you to trust in a lie,* [32] *therefore, thus says the LORD: I am about to deal with Shemaiah* [a] *the Nehelamite* [a] *and his descendants. He shall not have a single person dwelling* [b] *in the midst of* [c] *this people* [c] [d] *and they shall not see* [d] *the good which I am about to do for my people* [c] —[f] *oracle of the LORD—for he has advocated apostasy against the LORD.'"* [f]

Notes

1.a-a. Not in LXX. MT typically has titles where LXX lacks them.

1.b. Not in LXX. In Gen 49:3 יתר means "excelling" or "foremost." Since the context is the exilic community, the more common meaning seems preferable.

1.c-c. Not in LXX. MT typically has modifiers lacking in LXX.

2.a. *BHS* questions whether this whole verse might be an addition in light of 24:1. See the *Comment*.

2.b-b. LXX has only καὶ παντὸς ἐλευθέρου, "and all nobles."

2.c. Some MSS, Syr, and Vg include the conj before "officials," in conformity with the usual form of lists. MT might be read as an explanation of the unusual term סָרִיס, "palace official."

3.a. Not in LXX.

4.a. Not in LXX.

4.b. Not in LXX.

4.c. *BHS* suggests emendation to hoph, הָגְלְתָה, "have been exiled," following Syr, to eliminate the inconsistency between third person "the LORD" at the beginning of the verse and first person verb with "God" as subj. According to Pardee, this is not the address of the letter but a prophetic form (*JBL* 97 [78] 331), so the change of person is not out of place. Cf. v 20.

4.d. "To Babylon" is not in LXX.

6.a-a. Not in LXX. This clause extends the family to the third generation (cf. 27:7) and completes the seventy years (v 11) in the life of a family.

6.b. Not in LXX. "There" emphasizes their location in Babylon. See the Introduction to chaps. 27–29, "True and False Prophecy."

7.a. LXX has τῆς γῆς, "the country." "City" remains preferable, since the contrasting pair of cities, Jerusalem and Babylon, is found throughout the book. Seven times in Jeremiah LXX translates Heb. עִיר, "city," or עָרִים, "cities," as γῆς, "land": 29[LXX 36]:7; 31[38]:24; 32[39]:29; 34[41]:22; 37[44]:2; 39[46]:16; 40[47]:5. Elsewhere the subject is Jerusalem or the cities of Judah. Perhaps this is evidence of an irregular practice of the translator to interpret the full effect of royal or divine action.

8.a. *BHS* suggests moving vv 8–9 after v 15. See *Form/Structure/Setting.*

8.b-b. Not in LXX. See the Introduction to chaps. 27–29, "True and False Prophecy."

8.c-c. LXX interprets the word in light of the rest of the chapter as ψευδοπροφῆται, "false prophets."

8.d. LXX also has μὴ ἀναπειθέτωσαν ὑμᾶς, "stop deceiving yourself by," echoing the earlier clause.

8.e-e. MT מַחְלְמִים, "are dreaming," is the only occurrence of חלם, "dream," in the hiph. BDB (321) suggests that initial מ arose by dittogr. With this emendation, *BHS*'s recommended reading, "their dreams which they are dreaming," following LXX[26], is not necessary. Third-person forms in LXX[26] could have arisen from Jer 23:25. Holladay retains the causative sense, "set to dream."

9.a. A few MSS of LXX, Syr, Tg lack the prep; "falsehood" could still be read as an adv acc, "falsely."

9.b-b. Not in LXX.

10.a. Not in LXX. הַדָּבָר הַטּוֹב, "the good word," usually has a more legal-contractual sense in OT and in other ancient Near Eastern sources, thus, "pledge" (Fishbane, *Biblical Interpretation,* 473 n. 37; Mettinger, *King,* 147).

11.a-a. Not in LXX. Lost by haplogr (Janzen, *Studies,* 118).

11.b-b. Not in LXX. This formula is typically more frequent in MT.

11.c-c. LXX has ταῦτα, "these [things]," perhaps a shortened version of LXX[OL] τὰ μετὰ ταῦτα, "what is after this," which probably renders MT אַחֲרִית, "what comes after." Holladay omits "and a hope" as a gloss or conflation of variants.

12.a-a. Not in LXX. LXX reads "You will pray to me and I will listen to you."

12.b. Not in Syr. *BHS* recommends deleting וַהֲלַכְתֶּם, "and come," as dittogr, but the source of the duplication is not apparent.

12.c-c. The promise does not appear in Syr until v 13. (Syr v 12: "You will call upon me and pray to me.")

13.a-a. Not in LXX[S] or Arab. The promise clause appears in v 14 instead. MT nearly duplicates Deut 4:29.

14.a. *BHS* recommends reading נִרְאֵיתִי, "I shall be seen," following LXX ἐπιφανοῦμαι, "and I shall be seen." This change would introduce some variety, since מצא, "find," occurs in the preceding verse, but the pair בקש/מצא, "seek/find," is very common in OT. Furthermore, the style of the immediate context is characterized by repetition of verbal roots.

14.b-b. In LXX the verse ends after "for you."

14.c-c. Not in LXX.

14.d. The K, שְׁבִיתְכֶם, indicates a derivation from the root שבה, "take captive." The Q reads שְׁבוּתְכֶם, from the root שוב, "return." The K represents a variant shaped by the later application of the formula primarily to the return from exile (Dietrich, *šwb šbwt,* 34). The idiom is a cognate acc.

15.a. *BHS* recommends moving vv 8–9 after 15 in order to restore the hypothetical original order of LXX, which lacks vv 16–20 of MT. See *Form/Structure/Setting.*

16.a. Vv 16–20 are lacking in LXX. See *Form/Structure/Setting.*

17.a. Several MSS of LXX^OL, Syr, Tg^f,Ms, Vg add the conj, bringing this item into conformity with the other members of the list.

17.b. *Hap. leg.*

18.a. Some MSS of θ', Syr, and Vg add the conj, making this item consistent with the following item in the list.

18.b. *BHS* recommends reading with the K, לזועה, "a trembling," from the root זוע, "tremble."

18.c. A few MSS have the more common expression לקללה, "a curse."

19.a. A few MSS have 2 pl, consistent with the following verb and v 20, although the context is 3 pl.

19.b. LXX^OL and Syr maintain 3 pl. MT's shift to 2 pl addresses the exiles. See the *Comment.*

21.a-a. Not in LXX. See Introduction to chaps. 27–29, "True and False Prophecy."

21.b-b., c-c., d. Not in LXX, which gives only personal names of the prophets and title of the king. The pun on "Kolaiah" (see *Comment*) would not have been apparent in translation. MT's spelling of Nebuchadrezzar with ר is unusual in chaps. 27–29. (See Introduction to chaps. 27–29, "True and False Prophecy.")

22.a. *BHS* recommends emending to the longer spelling, כאחאב, as in v 21 and Q^OR. This is the only occurrence of the short spelling in OT.

23.a. Not in LXX. The following clause makes it superfluous, but שקר, "falsehood," is part of the standard charge against such prophets in MT. Cf. 29:9, 31.

23.b-b. Not in LXX.

23.c. Three ways to deal with the difficult form הוידע: (1) Emend to היודע qal act ptcp, "the one who knows." (2) Emend, by adding one consonant, to הוא ידע, "he who knows." (3) Delete the word, lacking in LXX, and emend to העד, "the witness." Option (3) is consistent with the formula used elsewhere in OT (Gen 31:50; Mic 1:2; Job 16:19). MT may be a conflate text (Janzen, *Studies,* 22). Nevertheless, it has been interpreted in MT as a meaningful, though expansive, expression. The phrase might even be understood as a hendiadys, "the expert witness."

24.a.-25.a. Syr implies a missing oracle, spoken by Shemaiah: 24"Shemaiah the Nehelemite said, 25'Thus says the LORD of Hosts, God of Israel: [missing oracle] . . .' and sent in his name . . ." Holladay (2: 9) evaluates the reading of Syr as superior to MT or LXX. LXX's version of these verses is close to MT, but shorter: "24And to Shemaiah the Nehelemite say: 25'I did not send you in my name.' And to Zephaniah son of Maaseiah the priest say:" See *Form/Structure/Setting.*

24.b. לאמר, "saying," not in LXX, Syr, Vg. Its absence does not change the sense of the sentence.

25.a. Not in LXX. See *Note* 24.a.-25.a.

25.b-b. *BHS* proposes restoring LXX to "You sent in your name," as in MT.

25.c. Not in LXX, since the direct obj of "send" is "you." 2 Kgs 10:1; 19:14 also use the pl for a single letter, perhaps reflecting the practice of sending open and sealed copies.

25.d-d., e-e. LXX lacks these additional addressees. Compare v 1.

26.a. MT reads pl פקדים. LXX (θ', Syr, Vg) has the sg, in conformity with the sg address at the beginning of the verse. Perhaps the prep ב, "in," prefixed to the following word was misread as מ and metathesis occurred between ד and י. The original Heb. text would have been פקיד בית, "overseer in the house."

26.b. Read with many MSS LXX, Syr, Tg^Mss, Vg בבית, "in the house/temple." See *Note* 26.a.

26.c-c. MT איש משגע ומתנבא. LXX reverses the order. Another possible hendiadys: "prophesying maniac." Hithp of נבא, "prophesy," connotes the full range of behavior, not just inspired speech.

26.d. LXX ἀπόκλεισμα, "place of incarceration," but the same word is translated καταρράκτην, "dungeon" or "stocks," in 20:2 of LXX. καταρράκτην appears in this verse as the translation of *hap. leg.* צינק, "restraining device, pillory(?)." Perhaps the two Heb. words occurred in reverse order in LXX's Heb. text.

27.a. LXX has 2 pl because it addresses both Shemaiah and Zephaniah.

27.b. *BHS* compares the half vowel of the ע in L with the full vowel in many other MSS and eds.

27.c. Hithp as in v 26.

28.a. LXX^VCal διὰ τοῦ μηνὸς τούτου, "in the course of this month." MT is somewhat awkward, but LXX's information about the timing of Shemaiah's response has no counterpart in MT.

29.a-a., b., c-c. MT typically includes modifiers and titles that do not appear in LXX.

31.a. Not in a few MSS of LXX. MT typically includes modifiers that do not appear in LXX.

32.a-a. Not in LXX.

32.b. Not in LXX. The root ישב, "dwell, settle," occurs in v 5 also, inviting comparison of the two passages.

32.c-c. LXX has ὑμῶν, "of you [pl]," i.e., the exiles, to whom the oracle is addressed, v 31.

32.d-d. LXX has τοῦ ἰδεῖν, "to see," making it less ambiguous than MT. His descendants will not see the good.

32.e. LXX has ὑμῖν, "to you [pl]," i.e., the exiles.

32.f-f. Not in LXX. MT reflects legal terminology from Deut 13:6 (cf. 28:16). LXX has οὐκ ὄψονται, "they shall not see."

Form/Structure/Setting

This chapter is introduced as the text of a written document (סֵפֶר) that Jeremiah sent from Jerusalem to Babylon. The text includes a series of oracles with various subjects, but all are formally addressed to the Judean exiles in Babylon. The content of these messages requires two separate sendings by Jeremiah, however, with a letter sent from Babylon to Jerusalem in between. Jeremiah's second communication is not introduced as a סֵפֶר, "written document," but with the command to Jeremiah to "say."

The chapter heading identifies the recipients of these documents as the 597 B.C. exiles. They were joined all too soon, however, by the 586 B.C. exiles. This "letter" for the 597 deportees is now part of a book shaped to address the post-586 situation. Some subsequent interpretation within chap. 29 is to be expected.

Most scholarly attention has been directed toward identifying an original core of the chapter and the interpretive redactional additions. Since there is no poetry in this passage, decisions about secondary material are based largely upon the identification of distinctive vocabulary and formulaic expressions. The following list shows the range of conclusions regarding the original content of Jeremiah's letter in chap. 29:

(1) letter: vv 5–7 (Nicholson, *Preaching*, 98)

(2) introduction: vv 1, 3; letter: vv 4a, 5–7; subsequent history: vv 25, 26–30, 31a, 32a (Thiel, *Redaktion*, 19)

(3) letter: vv 5–7, 12b–14a (G. Fohrer, *Prophetenerzählung*, 149)

(4) introduction: vv 1, 3; letter: vv 4–13, 14 (as in LXX), 15, 21–23 (Bright)

(5) vv 1, 3–11, 12b, 14a, 16, 17ab, 18ab, 19ab, 20, 15, 21–23 (minus some short expansions; Holladay)

There is no space to describe all the efforts to discern the order of subsequent interpretive additions in chap. 29. Wanke, for example, postulates a series of expansions (*Untersuchungen*, 36–59), whereas Thiel thinks the additions were made all at once (*Redaktion*, 19).

The growth of the individual chapter is related to the composition of smaller collections and the formation of the book as a whole. Hypotheses about these processes fill many volumes. At this point one can only mention where chap. 29 falls in a selection of these reconstructions. Mowinckel (*Zur Komposition*) assigned chap. 29 to his source or tradition complex B, composed in Egypt around the turn of the fifth century B.C. Rudolph and Wanke maintain the B designation, and Rudolph attributes the work to Baruch. Wanke (*Untersuchungen*), however, discovers three cycles of tradition within the B material, none of which were composed by Baruch. Chap. 29 belongs to the cycle 19:1–20:6; 26–29; 36. Both Holladay and Seitz (*Theology*), who attribute much of the chapter to Jeremiah, propose early collections that include chap. 29. Holladay thinks that Jeremiah instructed Baruch to prefix chap. 29 to a "hopeful scroll" containing parts of chaps. 30–31, probably shortly after the events of chap. 32 (588 B.C.). Baruch (and others?) added the rest of the chapters in the section 26–36 in two or three more stages. Seitz's proposed "Scribal Chronicle," composed in Judah close to the the the time of its fall, includes 27–29; 20:1–6; 37:11–15; 38:1–6. The subsequent "Exilic Redaction" supplemented chap. 29 with vv 16–20. Nicholson concludes that the expansion and shaping of chap. 29 and the growth of the tradition complex in chaps. 26–36 were accomplished in the context of preaching and teaching by deuteronomistic traditionists among the post-586 exiles in Babylon (*Preaching*, 130–31). Thiel (*Redaktion*, 19) finds extensive deuteronomistic redaction also but locates the work in Jerusalem. According to his reconstruction, the D redactor inserted vv 15, 8–9 to connect the chapter to chap. 28, vv 10–14 to link it to chaps. 30–32, and vv 16–20, which correspond closely to chap. 24. The extent of the redactors' work and the labeling of their vocabulary, style, and theology as deuteronomistic remain issues of intense study and dispute (e.g., the books by Weippert, *Prosareden*, and Stulman, *Prose Sermons*).

The reader of the present, final form of this chapter needs to understand the form of the individual units, how they are connected to each other, and how they fit into the exchange of documents between Jeremiah and the exilic community that provides the framework for this chapter. The sequence of events implied by the present shape of chap. 29 is as follows: The king's messengers carry Jeremiah's document to the exiles in Babylon. Shemaiah, one of the exiles, sends a letter to Zephaniah the priest, in Jerusalem, in which he summarizes Jeremiah's letter and asks Zephaniah to rebuke Jeremiah and put him in the stocks. Zephaniah reads Shemaiah's letter to Jeremiah but takes no other action against him. The LORD then commands Jeremiah to deliver an oracle against Shemaiah. The text of Shemaiah's letter and the account of Zephaniah's reading to Jeremiah have been incorporated into the message that Jeremiah is ordered to "say" to Shemaiah as part of the accusation against him.

English translators usually call Jeremiah's documents "letters." Comparison with the Aramaic letters in Ezra and the extrabiblical Hebrew letters analyzed by D. Pardee (*JBL* 97 [1978] 321–46; *Handbook*) shows that Jeremiah's documents do not display the characteristic epistolary formulas, with the possible exception of the mention of a witness and an oath (v 23; Pardee, *Handbook*, 177–78). On three other occasions in the book, Jeremiah prepares a document containing his prophecies. In chap. 36 the writing and reading of the scroll are narrated, but its contents are not quoted. 30:2 reports the command to prepare a book but does not mention anything about delivery, reading, or storage. The book itself follows in chaps. 30–31, under the superscription "These are the words which the LORD spoke" (v 4). 51:59–64 describes how a scroll containing oracles against Babylon was sent there to be read and then sunk in the Euphrates river as a sign-act of Babylon's impending doom.

Perhaps it is better to characterize the documents in chap. 29 as composing another such prophetic "booklet," which contains a collection of prophecies. (Pardee, *Handbook*, 177, calls 29:4–23 "a series of prophetic oracles stated . . . to have been sent as a letter.") The messenger formula typical of prophetic speech begins every unit addressed to the exiles (vv 4, 8, 10, 16, 17, 21, 25, 31, 32). Even the letter from Shemaiah to Zephaniah the priest has been subsumed under an oracular heading. A command to prophesy (v 24), the messenger formula, and the conjunction כִּי, "because" (v 25), turn Shemaiah's letter in vv 25–28 into an extension of the diatribe in v 31. Shemaiah's letter had been an act of opposition and persecution from a distance (cf. Pashhur in chap. 20). Vv 24–32 illustrate the tension between the logic of the implied story about the correspondence, which is told by means of the letters themselves, and the expectations that guide the reading of a collection of oracles (e.g., the speaker is assumed to be God, through the true prophet). In a collection the connections between oracles may be quite loose; audience and circumstances may change from one prophecy to the next. In a letter, however, the addressee is expected to remain the same, and the parts are supposed to make sense together. Perhaps the apparently excessive use of the conjunction כִּי, "because, for, indeed" (six times in vv 8–16), results from an attempt to bind these oracles more closely to each other.

The structure of the chapter may be outlined as follows:

I. Jeremiah's first communication with the Judean exiles in Babylon (vv 1–23)
    A. Superscription: address, date, and couriers (vv 1–3)
    B. Text of the document (vv 4–23)
        1. Command to build houses and families and to pray for Babylon's peace (vv 4–7)
        2. Warning against false prophets (vv 8–9)
        3. Promises of restoration and answered prayer (vv 10–14)
        4. Disputation (vv 15–19)
            a. The people's claim to have true prophets (v 15)
            b. Judgment oracle against king and people in Jerusalem (vv 16–19)
                i. Address to king and people (v 16)
                ii. Judgment announcement (vv 17–18)
                iii. Accusation (v 19)
        5. Judgment oracle against Ahab and Zedekiah (vv 20–23)
            a. Address to exilic community (v 20)
            b. Judgment announcement (vv 21–22)
            c. Accusation (v 23)
II. Jeremiah's second communication to the Judean exiles in Babylon (vv 24–32)
    A. Command to speak to Shemaiah (v 24)
    B. Accusation against Shemaiah (vv 25–30)
        1. Narration: Shemaiah sent a letter to Jeremiah (v 25)
        2. Shemaiah's letter to Zephaniah (vv 26–28)
            a. Command to restrain and rebuke Jeremiah (vv 26–27)
            b. Summary quotation of Jeremiah's letter (v 28)
        3. Narration: Zephaniah read the letter, and God commanded Jeremiah to send a response (vv 29–30)
    C. Judgment against Shemaiah (vv 31–32)
        1. Command to send to exilic community (v 31a)
        2. Accusation (v 31b)
        3. Judgment announcement (v 32)

Jeremiah's first communication includes two promise oracles. The form of vv 4–7 can be described as commands with an implied promise of success (GKC § 110c: imperative expresses assurance). The first divine word to humanity in Gen 1:28 is in this form, and it is also found in prophetic speech (e.g., 1 Kgs 22:12, 15; 2 Kgs 5:10, 13; Jer 27:12, 17).

Holladay labels vv 10–14 an announcement of future salvation since there is no "fear not" or other reassurance for the present (2:138). Part of this unit, however, is the assurance of a divine answer in vv 12–14. Carroll calls vv 12–14 a later redactional development that adds the idea that crying out to God must precede deliverance (558). After removing interpretive additions in vv 13 and 14aβ, Wanke sees the remainder of the unit (vv 10–14) as a unified interpretation of vv 5–7 that was composed in the exilic or early post-exilic period on the basis of Jer 25:9–12 and Isa 55:6–11 (*Untersuchungen*, 50). Most modern commentators share Wanke's analysis of vv 10–14 as secondary, but Thompson and Fishbane do not. Fishbane, in fact, finds vv 10–15 at the center of the chiastic arrangement of vv 4–28 (*Interpretation*, 479 n. 55).

Between the promises in vv 4–7 and 10–14 stands a warning, vv 8–9. Two negative commands followed by a motivation clause function parenetically.

Chap. 29 includes three judgment oracles: vv 16–19 against the king and people in Jerusalem, vv 21–23 against Ahab and Zedekiah, and vv 31–32 against Shemaiah. All three refer to their subjects in the third person, like the oracles against Judean kings in chap. 22. Other words of threat against false prophets in Jeremiah are in the second person, 20:3–6 against Pashhur and 28:15–16 against Hananiah (plus the accusation against Shemaiah in 29:25–28). The words of judgment in chap. 29 are each headed by a second-person address to the whole exilic audience (vv 15, 19b; 20; 31a), which maintains the form of the document as a letter sent to the Judeans in Babylon.

The most awkward of these introductions is v 15. Vv 16–19 appear to have nothing to do with v 15. Therefore, most commentators would move them to another position in the chapter. There are three possibilities: (1) Move v 15 before vv 8–9. Thiel (*Redaktion*, 14) argues that v 15 was accidentally omitted, but retained in the margin, and then reinserted in its present position. (2) Move vv 8–9 after v 15 (Rudolph). This rearrangement allows vv 10–14 to follow immediately after vv 5–7. (3) Move vv 16–20 between vv 14 and 15 (Holladay, 2:135; Janzen, *Studies*, 118). The Lucianic rescension of LXX has this order. This rearrangement allows v 15 to form a unit with vv 21–23 and clarifies the parallel between 24:4–7, 8–10 and 29:4–14, 16–20.

Even if v 15 arrived at its present position because of a copyist's error, it has a meaningful function in the present shape of the chapter. The hypothetical original sayings vv 15, 8–9 and vv 15, 21–23 would have been disputations about prophets in Babylon ("you said . . . ," but "thus says the LORD"). With vv 16–20 included, chap. 29 mirrors chap. 24. Both offer hope to the exiles (24:4–7; 29:4–14) and announce doom to Jerusalem (24:8–10; 29:16–19). V 15 seems to interfere with this parallel, but its effect is to tie vv 16–20 more closely to the rest of the chapter. The second-person verb, "you did not listen" (v 19), secures the other end of the unit. Chap. 29 lacks the unifying vision of figs in chap. 24, but v 15 presents vv 16–19 as God's response to the exiles' own statement. It serves as a warning by example. Having true prophets in a community does no good if no one listens to their words. The picture of the exiles' future in chap. 29 is more complex than the simple "good" versus "bad" distinction in chap. 24 between the deportees and those who were left behind.

V 24 in MT is an incomplete introduction to vv 25–32. It does serve to identify the author of vv 26–28 and the addressee of v 25, but the speaker and the audience (second person masculine singular) remain ambiguous. The messenger formula at the beginning of v 25 calls for the word-event formula before v 24, as in 28:12–14, but there is no textual evidence to support such an addition. If this second document had a superscription like the one in v 1, then v 24 could be the address of the following letter, but again there is no support for reconstructing such a heading. Dijkstra interprets v 24 as the address of a letter written on Jeremiah's behalf and comprising vv 25–32 (*VT* 33 [1983] 319–20). His theory does account for the third-person narrative about Jeremiah in vv 29–30, but he must eliminate the messenger formula in v 25 and assume that readers will recognize without being told that vv 24–32 have a different author.

The difficulty of understanding vv 24–25 is evident from the distinctively different versions in LXX and Syr. Holladay concludes that Syr offers the best solution (2:136); v 24 was a narrative, "and Shemaiah the Nehelemite said," and the messenger formula in v 25 introduced an oracle by Shemaiah that has now been lost. Without that missing saying, however, Holladay's reconstruction does not help the reader of the present form of the text.

At the juncture between the two documents that now form the framework of chap. 29, there is no narrative bridge to clarify the plot of the story and no new superscription to mark the beginning of the second communication from Jeremiah to the exiles. The reader is left to figure out the unspecified relationship between the two parts of the chapter. One clue is that v 24 is the first command from God to Jeremiah in the chapter, so it suggests a new action.

The conjunction יַעַן אֲשֶׁר, "because, on account of the fact that," in v 25 marks off vv 25b–28 as an accusation that motivates the following announcement of judgment. The accusations in vv 19, 23, 31b are all in the third person, but this diatribe addresses its subject in the second person. Accusations frequently include quotations of the subject's words (as in 26:9), but this quotation is longer than usual. It includes two other accusations: v 27 against Zephaniah, in the form of a question, and v 28 against Jeremiah, by a quotation.

Vv 29–30 read like part of a narrative about the prophet's dealings with his audience. The pattern is as follows: (1) someone (third person) speaks or does something to Jeremiah; (2) word-event formula; (3) God commands Jeremiah to "say"; (4) oracle addressed (second person) to the subject of (1), introduced by the messenger formula. Several passages in the book of Jeremiah conform to this pattern: 20:1–6 (lacking [2]); 28:10–16; 34:1–3; 37:1–10; and chap. 42 (lacking [3]). The other examples of the pattern suggest that vv 29–30 are parts (1) and (2) of the framing narrative for vv 24–32, but there is no such frame. Shemaiah, not Zephaniah, would have to be the subject of both (1) and (4). V 25b does not qualify as (1) in the pattern either because it is a second-person accusation against Shemaiah, not a third-person narrative about him.

The three judgment oracles in chap. 29 are all concerned with false prophets who speak lies and people who do not listen to the prophets whom God has sent. This is also the subject of chaps. 27–28. Various thematic, literary, and textual features join these three chapters and suggest a common date for the events of chaps. 27–28 and Jeremiah's correspondence with the exiles. (See the Introduction to chaps. 27–29, "True and False Prophecy.")

The implied date of Jeremiah's correspondence falls between 597 and 588 B.C. According to v 2, it took place after the deportation of Jehoiachin in 597 but while a Davidic king still occupied the throne (v 16) and the temple was still standing (v 26), in other words, before 586 when the Babylonians captured Jerusalem, and probably before the siege began in 588. Either the opposition encountered by Nebuchadrezzar in Babylon in January–February 596 (so Driver, *Textus* 4 [1964] 84) or the attempted coup in December 595–January 594 (Holladay, 2:31, and many others) raised hopes among the Judeans in Jerusalem and in Babylon that their subjugation to Nebuchadrezzar would soon be over. The accession of Psammetichus II in Egypt in 594 may have fueled their expectation. God's word through Jeremiah, however, was to submit to Nebuchadrezzar's rule at home, by dropping plans for rebellion (chaps. 27–28), or in exile, by settling down there (chap. 29). King Zedekiah himself (51:59MT; but in LXX only his messengers) went to Babylon in his fourth year, 594–93 B.C., perhaps to reaffirm his loyalty oath.

Elements of chap. 29 expand its relevance beyond 594 B.C. The command to build a Jewish community in the diaspora would be valid for Babylon's seventy years (v 11), and beyond, according to the book of Daniel (chap. 9). The temptations of disobedience and misplaced trust would continue to endanger God's people. Nevertheless, chap. 29 offers a bridge to hope by its own promises and by its connections to chaps. 30–31 (e.g., 29:11 and 31:16–17).

Comment

1 No date, no word-event formula, and no divine instructions begin this chapter. As in 51:59, the reader is a step removed from Jeremiah's reception of revelation. This distancing of the reader parallels the separation of the audience in Babylon from Jeremiah's preaching ministry. A written document could go where the prophet could not. God's word was still valid when read from a scroll. (Compare chap. 36.)

Jeremiah's document was most likely written on papyrus (Haran, *JJS* 33 [1982] 168). Sheets of papyrus were glued together to form a long strip from which a piece of appropriate length for each document could be cut. Even documents only one sheet long were probably rolled, folded, tied, and sealed for storage or sending (Porten, *BA* 42 [1979] 90).

The community of exiles in Babylon to whom this document is addressed mirrors the prophet's audience in Jerusalem. The groups listed here, elders, priests, prophets, and all the people, are the same as the groups encountered by Jeremiah in chap. 26. (Only the royal officials are missing, and they appear in 29:2.) These are also the groups who would be part of the restoration community. The courtiers listed in v 2 would not.

2 This parenthesis dates the chapter and identifies the exiles in v 1 as persons deported in 597 B.C. with Jeconiah (= Jehoiachin) and his court (2 Kgs 24:12–15). Jer 24 shares the same date formula (v 1), minus the queen mother and palace officials, and similar content. This verse cues the reader to read chap. 29 against the background of chap. 24.

According to 2 Kgs 24:8, Jehoiachin's mother was Nehushta, daughter of Elnathan, from Jerusalem. The סריסים, "palace officials," are always associated with the king, often in military contexts. Isa 56:3 is the only exception. It is also the only verse where a סריס is necessarily to be understood as a castrated man.

The king's palace officials are never connected with a family. Perhaps they gave up their own families in order to become members of the king's household and to devote themselves to his service. Note the name of the סרים, Ebed-melech, "servant of the king," in Jer 38:7 (North, *ABD* 5:87).

The office(s?) and duties of the שׂרי, "officials, princes," of Judah and Jerusalem are never described. They usually appear as a group, but 1 Kgs 22:26 and 2 Kgs 23:8 speak of the שׂר, "ruler," of the city. 1 Kgs 22:26 and Zeph 1:8 differentiate the שׂרים, "officials," from the king's sons. Malamat translates the last two groups as "armorers and sappers" ("The Twilight of Judah," in *Edinburgh Congress Volume*, VTSup 28 [Leiden: Brill, 1975] 134). They would have been military engineers essential to the city's defense.

3 It is likely, if not certain, that Elasah, Ahikam (26:24), and Gemariah (36:10, 12, 25) were sons of the same Shaphan who was one of Josiah's officials and participated in the verification of the book of the law (2 Kgs 22:3–20). With Gemariah's son Micaiah added (36:11–14), three generations of the same family would have been instrumental in bringing God's word as written in a book to its audience. The father of the other messenger, also named Gemariah, may have been the Hilkiah who was high priest under Josiah when the book of the law was found in the temple (2 Kgs 22:3–23:4). The names of these messengers, together with the superscription of the chapter, "these are the words" (cf. Deut 1:1), lend weight to the authority of Jeremiah's short document.

Elasah and Gemariah traveled to Babylon as Zedekiah's messengers. Meier's study of ancient Near Eastern messengers offers a fuller understanding of their responsibilities. Vassals were expected to communicate steadily with the overlord (Meier, *Messenger*, 131), so this delegation and the one in 51:59 could have been sent during the same year (as Holladay suggests, 2:140). The overlord also expected his vassals to send messengers in response to crises in his life (Meier, *Messenger*, 31–32). This diplomatic mission may have been undertaken in response to the failed rebellion against Nebuchadrezzar in Babylon in 595/4 B.C., or to make peace after Zedekiah and the neighboring kings had met to plan revolt in the same year (chap. 27). High-ranking officials such as Elasah and Gemariah would have been sent in such circumstances. That Zedekiah sent two messengers when one was the norm may also indicate that their mission was especially dangerous (Meier, *Messenger*, 116–18, 194). They may have carried a letter from Zedekiah to Nebuchadrezzar, which would have been read aloud by a scribe, but they would have been expected to answer questions and otherwise represent Zedekiah's interests before the Babylonian king (Meier, *Messenger*, 206–7, 250). Messengers waited for permission from the overlord to return home. A messenger's task was not finished until he had been returned to the one who sent him (Meier, *Messenger*, 230, 245; perhaps Elasah and Gemariah carried Shemaiah's letter to Zephaniah, v 28). The messengers' report of how they had been received indicated the overlord's disposition toward the vassal's message.

Elasah and Gemariah probably traveled on roads built originally by the Assyrians. Although not paved, the surfaces were adequate for chariots. Guard posts approximately every six miles and wells in the desert protected travelers (Casson, *Travel*, 50). A messenger's pouch surviving from the fifth century (Meier, *Messenger*, 60) has a single strap to be worn over the shoulder or around the neck. It has no lock, but the documents inside were most likely sealed individually. Elasah and Gemariah did not necessarily read Jeremiah's document to the exilic audience. A scribe among the exiles could have done so. (Baruch the scribe was the reader in 36:8, 15.)

4 The body of the document begins here with the typical messenger formula of prophetic speech (Pardee, *JBL* 97 [1978] 331). Notice the significant change in the way the audience is described. The LORD, not Nebuchadrezzar (v 1), took them into exile.

5 "Build" and "plant" echo Jeremiah's call, 1:10. This modest domestic scene is a small beginning of God's plan to build and plant nations and kingdoms. Contrast the description of settlement in Canaan in Josh 24:13. Cultivated land, cities, vineyards, and olive groves, all of which were technical and cultural achievements representing generations of work, were given to the Israelite settlers. In Babylonian exile, however, they had to begin with the basics, family homes for shelter and kitchen gardens for sustenance.

Since newly built houses were customarily dedicated (Deut 20:5) and the firstfruits of the soil were presented to God (Deut 26:2), the commands to settle and eat implied either that these ceremonies could take place even in a foreign land or that such rituals were no longer necessary. Rudolph (167) opts for the latter possibility, seeing it as an example of prophetic piety that opened the way for the mission to the Gentiles announced by Deutero-Isaiah. In either case, these commands lay the foundation for survival in the Jewish diaspora.

Babylonian documents as well as biblical evidence (Ezek 3:15) suggest that many of the Judean exiles were settled in the region of the city of Nippur, through which ran the Kabaru-canal (biblical River Chebar), along with other conquered and exiled groups, in order to rebuild a region devastated by the wars between Assyria and Babylon in the previous century (Eph'al, *Or* 47 [1978] 81–82). Each group of exiles was able to live together and maintain their community identity. Settling the land was actually a concrete way of working for the שלום, "wholeness" or "peace," of Babylon (v 7).

In chap. 35 the LORD commends the Rechabites for their obedience to their ancestor's command not to drink wine, build houses, or have vineyards, fields, or crops. Their unsettled life was a model of obedience in Judah. The example of the Rechabites sharpens the contrast between God's plans for the people left in Judah and the commands to the exiles to build and plant.

6 Marriage and children complete the picture of "life as usual" as it had been lived by the majority of Judah's rural population. This command is directed to men, although the participation of daughters and daughters-in-law in giving birth to the third generation is acknowledged. The wording of this verse suits the exilic circumstances in which parents were not necessarily available to arrange marriages for their children. (Compare Jacob, who made his own marriage arrangements in his "exile," Gen 29:15–30.) The command to "multiply" (רבה) echoes the creation imperative (Gen 1:28) and the description of Jacob's descendants in Egypt (Exod 1:7). Jer 30:19 uses the same verbs in God's promise, "I will increase [רבה] them; they will not decrease [מעט]."

7 Would such a prayer be like the prayer for Jerusalem in Ps 122:6–9? It begins with the command "Pray [שאל, 'ask'] for the peace of Jerusalem" (v 6a).

Macholz ("Jeremiah," 317–18) specifies the meaning of דרש, "seek," and פלל, "pray for," as a request for a salvation oracle from the LORD, as in Jer 37:3, 7. Jeremiah had been forbidden to pray for a salvation oracle for Jerusalem (14:11–

12). The prophets who announced "Peace, peace" to her (שלום, as in v 7) had not been sent by the LORD (6:14, 8:11). This transfer of blessing and protection from Jerusalem (26:6) to Babylon (29:7) parallels the transfer of royal authority from the kings of Judah and her neighboring states to Nebuchadrezzar (27:6–7).

5–7 A. Berlin (*HAR* 8 [1984] 3–6) and D. Smith (*Religion,* 133–37) compare these verses to Deut 20:5–10; 28:30–32; Isa 65:21–23. All four passages include the elements "build," "plant," and "marry." In addition, Jer 29:7 and Deut 20:10 share the phrase "peace of [the city]." The context of the Deuteronomy and Isaiah passages is warfare; Deut 20:5–10 lists the exemptions from military service in holy war. By means of this allusion to Deut 20, Jer 29:5–7 warns the exilic community to refrain from revolt against Babylon (Berlin, *HAR* 8 [1984] 4; Smith, *Religion,* 135). Thus, the LORD's word through Jeremiah to the Judean exiles was the same as the divine message to Zedekiah and the others remaining in Jerusalem after 597, "Serve the king of Babylon and you will live" (27:17; also 27:11; 28:14). Jeremiah's audience is invited to abandon hope in a "holy revolt" against Babylon, which had been inspired by the false prophets' promises that God would bring the exiles back in a short time, and to place their hope instead in the LORD and a new way of life. Smith describes the strategy in 29:5–7 as "nonviolent social resistance" (*Religion,* 137).

Comparison with Deut 28:30–32 and Isa 65:21–23 reveals the hope in these verses. Deut 28:30–32 contains futility curses threatened against Israel for her disobedience. Under these curses, they would not enjoy the fruit of their labor or their marriages. Jer 5:15–17 and 6:12 describe the subjugation of Judah in similar terms. In addition, aspects of Jeremiah's personal life function as a sign-act to communicate the threat of childlessness (16:1–4). Jer 29:4–7, however, indicates that God has removed those curses from the exiles (Kilpp, *Niederreissen,* 57). The salvation oracle about the new heavens and the new earth in Isa 65:21–23 promises that the curses will be effective "no longer."

Pairs of logically connected imperatives are found in prophetic speech in 1 Kgs 22:12, 15; 2 Kgs 5:10, 13; Jer 27:12, 17 as well as here in 29:5–6. They imply a promise of success. God ensures the existence of the extended family by reestablishing the condition of blessing and protection from the danger of death, slavery, or exile (Kilpp, *Niederreissen,* 57). The uprooted and orphaned exiles are invited to invest their lives in this new realm of divine blessing.

8–9 Illegitimate sources of revelation were available to the exiles in Babylon. Prophets and dreams were not false in themselves, and divining had been practiced by at least one of Israel's ancestors (Joseph; Gen 44:5). The messages obtained by these methods were false and deceptive because the LORD did not send the intermediaries. This charge against false prophets is frequent in the book of Jeremiah (23:21, 32; 27:15; 28:15; 43:2). It has its roots in Deut 18:14–22. "Your dreams" could have been the prophets' or any of the people's. The exiles may have consulted dream interpreters or prayed for a dream like Jacob's (Gen 31:13), which would tell them that it was time to return home.

The content of the lies they were tempted to believe is not specified. The context of these verses, following v 7, implies that the answers given by their prophets, diviners, and dreams were the reverse of the "peace of Babylon" for which they had been commanded to pray in v 7. The parallel verse in 27:9 quotes the lie, "You will not serve the king of Babylon." Hananiah foretold the end of

Nebuchadrezzar's rule "within two years" (28:11) and was condemned for making "this nation trust in a lie." Chap. 29 names Ahab, Zedekiah, and Shemaiah as persons who had spoken lies to the exiles but does not report their words. Putting trust in these intermediaries would prevent the exiles from obeying God's commands in vv 5–7.

10–11 The first promise in this chapter stakes out a middle ground between the imperatives in vv 5–7 and the admonition in vv 8–9. From the perspective of the stated audience, the 597 B.C. deportees (vv 1–2), the exile would still be permanent, as vv 5–7 imply. They would have benefited from a return in the near future, as promised by the false intermediaries (vv 8–9), but none of them would expect to be alive or healthy enough to enjoy the restoration at the end of the seventy years. Their grandchildren and great-grandchildren could take part in that return only if the deportees and their children would obey God's commands and heed God's warnings. (Observe the judgment on Shemaiah, vv 31–32.) They had to relinquish their own schemes for escape from Babylonian rule and accept the authority of God's plan so that their future (i.e., their descendants) could have hope.

Life for the exiles is not devoid of hope, because of the LORD's presence in blessing and prayer (see *Comment* on vv 5–7). God carries out the plan to give them "a future and a hope" by granting them the blessing of fruitfulness, protection from calamity, and answer to prayer. (The next three verses underscore the last point.)

Jer 31:16–17 offers a poetic parallel to 29:5–7, 10–14. Weeping Rachel is promised "reward for your work" (i.e., the lifting of the futility curses) and her children's return home. The key terms of 29:11 occur in 31:17, "there is hope for your future."

The references to God's "pledge" (v 10; lit. "good word") and "plans" (v 11) point outside the chapter to other statements of God's intentions regarding Babylon and the Judean exiles. They are words that call for a background. The seventy-years prophecy appears first in 25:11–14, a chapter dated 605 B.C. (v 1). The order of the book places Jeremiah's vision of the figs before this, in chap. 24. It includes a promise to the exiles (24:4–7) and is logically placed prior to chap. 29. (29:17 also requires chap. 24 as background.)

In these verses the divine word puts a limit on Babylon's power, in accordance with the witness of the book as a whole (25:11; 27:7; chaps. 50–51). The seventy-years prophecy differs from Hananiah's forecast of two years (28:2–4), not only in duration but in content. An individual who hears "within two years" can think, "I can wait that long," but seventy years evokes the response, "I'll be dead before then." (See *Excursus: Seventy Years*.) Furthermore, Hananiah's two-year timetable is predicated upon the success of rebellions, while the seventy years are to be lived in submission and loyalty to the LORD's newly appointed king, Nebuchadrezzar, and his successors (27:5–7).

Excursus: Seventy Years

Bibliography

Ackroyd, P. "Two Old Testament Historical Problems of the Early Persian Period: B. The 'Seventy Year' Period." *JNES* 17 (1958) 23–27. **Borger, R.** *Die Inschriften Asarhaddons Königs von Assyrien*. AfO Beiheft 9. Graz, 1956. **Grabbe, L.** "'The End of the Desolations of Jerusalem': From Jeremiah's 70 Years to Daniel's 70 Weeks of Years." In *Early Jewish and Christian Exegesis*. FS W. H. Brownlee, ed. C. A. Evans and W. F. Stinespring. Atlanta: Scholars, 1987. 67–72. **Orr, A.** "The Seventy Years of Babylon." *VT* 6 (1956) 304–6. **Plöger, O.** "Siebzig Jahre." In *FS Friedrich Baumgärtel zum 70. Geburtstag*, ed. J. Hermann. Erlangen: Universitätsbund Erlangen, 1959. 124–30 (Repr. in *Aus der Spätzeit des Alten Testament*. Göttingen: Vandenhoeck, 1970. 67–73). **Vogt, E.** "70 anni exsilii." *Bib* 38 (1957) 236. **Whitley, C. F.** "The Term Seventy Years Captivity." *VT* 4 (1954) 60–72. ———. "The Term Seventy Years—a Rejoinder." *VT* 7 (1957) 416–18.

The concept of seventy years as the measure of Israel's subjugation under Babylonian rule occurs six times in the OT: Jer 25:11–12; 29:10; Zech 1:12; 7:5; Dan 9:2; 2 Chr 36:21. In addition, Isa 23:15, 17 promises that the LORD will deal with Tyre at the end of seventy years, a period equivalent to a king's lifetime. Ps 90:10 gives seventy years as the typical human lifespan, filled with suffering, but passing quickly. The number seventy, the product of the symbolic numbers seven and ten, is the measure of completeness in Gen 46:27; Deut 10:22; Gen 50:3; Judg 1:7; 1 Sam 6:19; 2 Sam 24:15.

Seventy years also appears in an inscription of Esarhaddon that states that Marduk declared seventy years of punishment against Babylon. This extrabiblical use may be coincidental, or it may be evidence of a scribal convention (so Weinfeld, *Deuteronomy*, 143–46). Possibly a conventional number of years for a human lifetime—a long, but not unimaginable period (Ps 90:10, Isa 23:15)—was used in the ancient Near East to express the typical duration of divine punishment (Esarhaddon inscription; Isa 23:15). This conventional time period turned out to correspond closely to the actual length of Babylonian domination or the temple's desolation, so the motif became an important part of biblical descriptions of those events. None of the OT occurrences, however, designates the precise dates (i.e., regnal years) for the beginning or ending of the seventy-year span. 2 Chr 36 comes closest by naming the first year of Cyrus in v 22, following the mention of seventy years in v 21. Cyrus's occupation of Babylon marked the terminus of Babylonian rule over the Jews. The complete context implies, however, that Chronicles is counting the years of the temple's desolation, which did not end with Cyrus's edict in 538 B.C. Whitley is correct, therefore, in seeing the seventy years in 2 Chr 36 as the period from the temple's destruction in 586 to the completion of the second temple in 515 B.C. (Whitley says 516; *VT* 4 [1954] 68–69.) Whitley concludes that 586–16 is the specific time indicated by "seventy years" in Jeremiah, Zechariah, and Daniel also, even though the period is described as pertaining to Babylonian rule in Jer 25 and 29.

Other terminal dates have been proposed. Nebuchadrezzar's victory at Carchemish and accession to the throne in 605 B.C. marked the beginning of Babylonian hegemony in Syria-Palestine. Cyrus's occupation of Babylon in 539 brought it to an end. These dates, a span of sixty-six years, fit the descriptions in Jer 25:11 (seventy years' service to the king of Babylon), 25:12 (Babylon punished after seventy years), and 29:10 (seventy years completed for Babylon). Thompson (547) observes that seventy-three years passed from the fall of Nineveh (612) to the fall of Babylon (539). It is also interesting to note that 609 was precisely seventy years prior to 539. In 609 Josiah died, and Jerusalem was made to accept her first foreign-appointed king, Jehoiakim, who eventually switched his allegiance from Pharaoh to Nebuchadrezzar.

Zechariah looks back on the past seventy years, which had been filled with God's anger (1:12) and with mourning and fasting by the people (7:5), and asks if the end is near. The verses appear in oracles dated, respectively, in 522 and 520 B.C. They focus upon the period of the temple's desolation, which was a major concern of Zechariah's ministry. The results of Babylonian conquest had endured longer than Babylon herself. Although there is no mention of a divine promise, these passages imply the expectation of an end to Jerusalem's suffering after seventy years.

Both 2 Chr 36 and Dan 9 engage in further interpretation and calculation with the number seventy. Gabriel informs Daniel (9:24) that the seventy-years prophecy read in the scroll of Jeremiah really means seventy weeks of years, seventy times seven or 490 years. Furthermore, Dan 9:25 places the beginning of the second week of years in 539 or 538, at the issuance of the decree to restore and rebuild Jerusalem (Fishbane, *Interpretation*, 483). These 490 years would be for the Jews and Jerusalem "to finish transgression, to put an end to sin." It appears that the exilic age, according to Daniel, will last until the age to come (P. Ackroyd, *Exile and Restoration: A Study of Hebrew Thought of the Sixth Century B.C.* [Philadelphia: Westminster, 1968] 242). The Chronicler offers another theological interpretation of the seventy years, this time by counting backward. The seventy years make up for seventy sabbatical years that were never observed (Lev 25:1–7; 26:27–35). Seventy seven-year periods, 490 years, had passed without the required observance. The beginning of this period would have coincided with the initiation of the Israelite monarchy in the eleventh century, which is where the Chronicler's narrative history begins (1 Chr 10).

Babylon's seventy years in Jer 29:10 should be interpreted both politically and personally. The political interpretation gives to the number seventy a meaning within international history as a more or less precise count of the time elapsed between two significant political events. Subsequent interpretation, beginning with 2 Chr 36 and Dan 9, has given attention to the coherence of the seventy-years prophecy with the known events of history. 2 Chr 36 reports its fulfillment. According to the test set forth in Deut 18:22, Jeremiah was a true prophet. The Daniel passage seems to be concerned with a delay in fulfillment. The seventy-years prophecy was true, but its full meaning had to be learned from further revelation (9:25).

Many contemporary commentators attribute 29:10 to the subsequent interpretation of Jeremiah's letter in vv 4–7, which gives no hint of an eventual return from exile. Some interpreters conclude that the seventy-years prophecy was added only after it was fulfilled (e.g., Nicholson, *Preaching*, 98). Why was a round number used, then, if the exact length of time was known? Orr attributes it to the "power of the mystical seven" (*VT* 6 [1956] 304). Another solution, put forward by Thiel (*Redaktion*, 17), dates 29:10 to a time around 550, when the eventual demise of Babylon was certain but had not yet occurred. Whitley believes that an optimistic supplement such as vv 10–14 would not increase the actual number of years until the time of salvation by rounding up sixty-six years to seventy. He argues for a precise period of seventy actual years, 586–516 (*VT* 7 [1957] 417).

Within the context of chap. 29, seventy years must also be understood as a number with meaning in personal and family history. Jer 27:7 describes the length of Babylonian rule in terms of three generations of kings, Nebuchadrezzar and his two successors. In chap. 29, three generations of Judean exiles span the seventy years. In the present shape of the chapter, the commands to beget children who will, in turn, have children of their own (vv 4–7) point to a family perspective on the seventy years. Adults hearing the seventy-year prophecy could calculate that they and most of their children could not live to enjoy the promise but that their grandchildren and great-grandchildren could expect to participate in the deliverance. The connection of "fathers" to "the third and fourth generations" is a common concept in the OT (e.g., Exod 34:7). Time can be measured there by the stages of personal and family life: Isa 8:4, "before the child knows how to say . . ."; Gen 15:16, "In the fourth generation your descendants will come back here . . ."; and the genealogies in Gen 5 and 11 with the form "When PN had lived X years, he begat . . ." Seventy years was a lifetime (Ps 90:10), and adult listeners would touch the promise only through the grandchildren and great-grandchildren born in their households.

12–14   The shorter Greek and Syriac versions of these verses are discussed in the *Notes*. The long and somewhat repetitive series of four pairs of verbs ("call"/ "come," "pray"/"hear," "seek"/"find," "seek"/"be found") encloses in v 13 a paraphrase of Deut 4:29, "If from there you seek the LORD your God, you will find him if you seek him with all your heart and all your soul." (The same verbs occur in the same order in both verses, and "there" in Deut 4:29 refers to the place of exile.) Deut 4:30–31 mentions the distress of the ones who would pray in this way as well as their subsequent deliverance. Jer 29:13 announces the fulfillment of the promise in Deut 4:29.

This assurance of the LORD's presence and response to prayer expands upon the command to seek and pray for the peace of Babylon in v 7. Since the exiles' peace is part of the divine plan (v 11), they may confidently call upon God for their own needs. In the time of salvation, they will not suffer as Job did (Job 30:20). Their cries will be heard as their ancestors' were (Pss 22:6; 107:13, 19; Exod 2:23–25; Jonah 2:3). These verses offer specific promises to the exiles rather than universal principles (Schmidt and Becker, *Zukunft*, 29). They are not platitudes thrown into the abyss of need but divine pledges anchored in the traditions of God's people and firmly connected to God's gracious presence with them.

The stereotyped expressions in v 14 (cf. 16:15; 32:37) expand the theme set forth in v 10. The last verb in v 14, "I will bring you back" (hiphil of שוב) forms an inclusio with v 10, "by bringing you back." This unit announces and expounds upon the salvation promised to the descendants of the 597 B.C. exiles. In this context, the second person plural verbs underscore the ideas that the deportees' identity will be perpetuated by their offspring and that only through them will they receive "a future and a hope."

15   (See *Form/Structure/Setting* for a discussion of proposals for moving v 15 to another place in the chapter.)

Deut 18:15, 18 are the only other occurrences of קום hiphil, "raise up," with "prophet(s)" as the object. This allusion to the LORD's promise to raise up a prophet like Moses makes the exiles' claim to have legitimate prophets among them sound even stronger. This statement is also an expression of rejection or doubt regarding their need for Jeremiah's document containing divine words. The responding oracle in vv 16–19 questions whether they would recognize a true prophet if they heard one.

16   The unusual features of this verse suit its purpose of introducing a judgment oracle against the king and people of Jerusalem that was written down "in this city," Jerusalem, and sent to an audience in Babylon. The subjects of the oracle are related to the exilic addressees, "your kindred, brothers," but they are separated by both distance and experience, because they "did not go out with you into exile."

17–19   The reader has the sense of having seen this oracle before. Most of the expressions in these verses are common in the prose of the book of Jeremiah, including, especially, chap. 24. Rudolph (170) notes the following parallels: 17a and 18a//24:10; 17b//24:2; 18b//24:9. The most colorful sentence in this unit, v 17b, requires the reader to know about Jeremiah's vision of good and bad figs in chap. 24.

The shape of chap. 29 calls for a similar sense of familiarity on the part of the exilic audience. This oracle should sound like others they had heard but not heeded in Jerusalem ("this city," v 16) before Nebuchadrezzar conquered it and they were banished. The fact that the Judean king is not named in v 16 contributes to this effect.

The threefold sufferings of warfare ("sword") and its effects ("famine and pestilence") occur thirteen times in the book of Jeremiah as a prose formula for divine judgment. C. Meyers' explanation of דבר, "pestilence, plague," is helpful. She defines it specifically as "endemic parasitic disease" ("The Roots of Restriction," *BA* 41 [1978] 95). The loss of shelter and the disruption of hygiene and nutrition caused by war weakens people and makes them vulnerable to organisms to which their bodies would normally have been resistant, as well as to infectious disease brought by the conquering army. The frequency and fixity of the "war, famine, pestilence" formula may dull its impact upon the reader. The book of Lamentations, especially passages such as 2:19–21 and 4:9–10, can serve as a sharp reminder of the horrors of human suffering behind these three words.

The metaphor of inedible figs in v 17b derives from Jeremiah's vision in chap. 24. This allusion to the earlier chapter invites the reader to return there, not only to discover the significance of figs but also to renew the comparison between the exiles and their kindred in Jerusalem. 29:18b explains the metaphor in much the same way as 24:9, with a long list of phrases describing the repulsiveness and humiliation of Zedekiah and the inhabitants of Jerusalem among the nations. The list in 29:18 has only two words in common with the list in 24:9, the first, "trembling, object of terror," and the last, "reproach." The first clause in both verses, "I shall make them an object of terror," quotes Deut 28:25. The second, third, and fifth items in 29:18 also appear together in Jer 42:18 and 44:12. The second item, אלה, "execration," is used this way only one other time in the OT. In Num 5:27 a woman found guilty of adultery becomes an "execration." The third and fourth items appear together in Jer 25:9 and 51:37. "The nations where I banish them" echoes v 14b and underscores the comparison between the exiles and the ones left behind in Jerusalem.

The charge in v 19 that they had not listened to the prophets whom the LORD had sent persistently appears frequently in the prose of Jeremiah (7:25–27; 26:4–5; 35:13–15; 36:1–26; 44:4–5). These passages are based on the belief that obeying these prophets is equivalent to obeying the LORD, as stated in Deut 18:9–22.

20 The verse serves as a reminder of the audience of this chapter and as a bridge to the next unit, a third-person judgment oracle against Ahab and Zedekiah. The imperative "hear" often marks the beginning of a new unit.

21–22 Ahab and Zedekiah are not mentioned elsewhere in the OT. The stereotyped clause, v 21, identifies them as false prophets, anticipating v 23, and refers the reader to 23:16–22 and chap. 28 for a description of such persons.

By handing them over to Nebuchadrezzar for punishment, the LORD demonstrates that Nebuchadrezzar has God-given authority over the exilic community and that he continues to be God's instrument for the execution of judgment on Israel. The unusual term קלה, "roasted," together with קללה, "curse," work a double pun on Ahab's family name, קוליה, "Koliyah." Execution by fire had been practiced in Babylon (Codex Hammurabi, laws 25, 110, 157; Pritchard, *ANET*, 167, 170, 172; cf. Dan 3:6), but fire was used especially to destroy cities (e.g., Josh 6:24; Isa 1:7; Amos 1:4, 7, 10). The LORD threatens Jerusalem with fire in Jer 17:27. When Ahab and Zedekiah perish in Nebuchadrezzar's fire, their death will be an illustration to the exiles in Babylon of what will happen to Jerusalem. According to Jer 52:13 and 2 Kgs 25:9, Nebuzaradan, commander of Nebuchadrezzar's guard, burned the temple, palace, and houses of the conquered city in 586. When their names are made into a curse, Ahab and Zedekiah suffer another one of the judgments in store for Jerusalem (v 18; 26:6; Lam 2:15–17; 3:45–46).

23 "Shameful folly in Israel" is a sexual crime that breaks the peace of a family or community (Gen 34:7; Deut 22:21; Judg 19:23–24; 20:6, 10; 2 Sam 13:12). Ahab and Zedekiah's folly is adultery with their neighbors' wives, a violation (Exod 20:14) that was punishable by death (Deut 22:22). Their crime undermined the foundation for the community of exiled Judeans laid by God's command in v 6, "take wives" (see also 23:14).

Ahab and Zedekiah are also specific examples of the prophets about whom the exiles are warned in vv 8–9. Their sayings are lies because they are not from God. This indictment is shaped to match Deut 18:20a. The LORD, the expert witness in this matter, testifies against them.

Many commentators find these charges inadequate to bring about action by Nebuchadrezzar against Ahab and Zedekiah. They propose that the two prophets supported the attempted coup against Nebuchadrezzar in Babylon in his tenth year (595–94) and were executed with the other conspirators (e.g., Rudolph, 169; Holladay, 2:143). Nebuchadrezzar's political or personal motives are not of any theological importance in the book of Jeremiah, however. It is the LORD's indictment that counts, not Nebuchadrezzar's, in the case of Ahab and Zedekiah just as in the case of Judah and Jerusalem.

24 This passage is Shemaiah's only appearance in the OT. No place or tribe named Nehelam is known. The name does share the consonants of the root חלם, "dream," making it a pun on the lying dreams of v 8. (Yaure's analysis of נחלמי, "Nehelemite," as a niphal participle of this root with the gentilic suffix indicating membership in a group is neither convincing nor necessary [*JBL* 79 (1960) 309]. Paranomasia makes the connection.) The rest of the passage, however, makes no mention of dreams or dreamers.

25 The accusation against Shemaiah, another 597 B.C. exile, has to do with a letter he sent to Jerusalem. The contents quoted in vv 26–28 are specifically directed to the priest Zephaniah, but this introductory verse grants him a larger audience. Jeremiah, however, is conspicuously absent (cf. v 29). The verse does not accuse Shemaiah of writing falsely in God's name; he has written in his own name. His offense is opposing Jeremiah and attempting to silence him.

In 21:1 and 37:3, King Zedekiah sends the priest Zephaniah to Jeremiah to inquire of the LORD through him. Pashhur, who is "overseer of the temple" in 20:1, accompanies him the first time. Zephaniah's father's name is Maaseiah, the same as the father of Zedekiah the prophet (vv 21–22). There is no way to know whether the two men were brothers.

26–27 These verses give the fullest description in the OT of the duties of the "overseer in the LORD's house [the temple]." Pashhur, an earlier holder of this position, had once put Jeremiah in the stocks overnight after hearing him preach about the destruction of Judah and Jerusalem (20:1–3). There are "overseers" of other groups in the OT, but no one else has the same title and responsibilities.

1 Sam 21:15 (Eng 14) describes the behavior of אִישׁ מִשְׁתַּגֵּעַ, a "madman" or "maniac," as David acted the part. He defaced the doors of the gates and drooled into

his beard. No such rude behavior is attributed to the prophet who anointed Jehu, yet one of the other military officers calls him הַמְשֻׁגָּע, "the madman" (2 Kgs 9:11). In Hos 9:7 Israel's sinfulness brings about a state of heart in which "the prophet is thought to be a fool, the man of the spirit, a maniac [מְשֻׁגָּע]." Shemaiah rejects Jeremiah and attempts to discredit him by this charge, but he only demonstrates his own hostility toward God. This word is also an allusion to yet another verse in Deut 28. Immediately following the futility curses in vv 30–33, which appear to be the background of 29:5–7, v 34 continues the threat, "You will become a madman from the sights which you will see." The irony is that Zephaniah would, according to Deut 28:34, become a madman himself when he witnessed the judgment coming upon Jerusalem. Jeremiah had already seen these horrors in God's plan, and his "Confessions" (11:18–12:6; 15:10–21; 17:12–18; 18:18–23; 20:7–13; 20:14–18) voice his despair.

The construction of the מַהְפֶּכֶת, "stocks," and צִינֹק, "pillory," is not known. Pashhur puts Jeremiah in the "stocks" in 20:2–3, but צִינֹק, "pillory," is a *hap. leg.* LXX translates the two words as "the dungeon" and "(place of) confinement." The MT in 37:16 and 38:6 uses the term בּוֹר, "pit, cistern," to indicate dungeons, however. Perhaps more abstract terms would serve: "confinement and restraints."

28 Shemaiah's summary of vv 5–7 focuses upon the commands that imply a long stay in Babylon. He bluntly spells out the implication, "It will be long," but does not mention the seventy-years prophecy. Paraphrase and shortening are characteristics of the majority of quotations within the OT (Savran, *Telling and Retelling*, 29–35). Compare the focused summary of Jeremiah's Temple Sermon in 26:9.

29–30 Zephaniah's position is ambiguous. He does not attempt to put Jeremiah in restraints, but he does cooperate with Shemaiah's effort to discredit Jeremiah by reading his letter aloud in Jerusalem. Shemaiah, assisted by Zephaniah, becomes an opponent of Jeremiah who, like the anonymous prophets in 26:8 and Hananiah in chap. 28, reject God's word given through him. Shemaiah's letter does not contain any oracle of his own, but his request in writing to punish Jeremiah is treated as evidence of false prophecy. (Compare 20:1–6, where Pashhur is accused of prophesying lies after he had held Jeremiah in restraints overnight.) His opposition to Jeremiah renders him guilty of "advocating apostasy against the LORD" (v 32). The narrative connection provided by these verses reminds the reader that the charges in vv 31–32 are based at least in part upon the letter in vv 25–28, as "because" in v 25 has already indicated.

31–32 Here we have competing written words. Shemaiah opposes Jeremiah's written document, and Shemaiah's letter becomes grounds for his punishment. The reader concludes from the context that Shemaiah believed, like Hananiah, that the exile would end soon. There is even a bit of irony in the comparison of Shemaiah and Hananiah; Hananiah broke the yoke-bar on Jeremiah's neck, but Shemaiah wants him put in the stocks. Both prophets are accused of causing the people to trust falsehood (28:15; 29:31) and of advocating apostasy (28:16; 29:32), which was a capital crime (Deut 13:6–10).

What is the unseen "good" in v 32b? The catchword connection suggests that the answer be found in the unit containing vv 10–11. None of Shemaiah's generation would live to see the restoration after seventy years, so to be excluded from that "good" would not make him worse off than his contemporaries. The "good" for Shemaiah's generation would include the blessings of fertility and answered prayer even in Babylon. The death of his offspring meant that he, like Ahaz and Zedekiah, would suffer under a judgment like that about to fall on the people remaining in Judah and Jerusalem. Without children or grandchildren, Shemaiah would have no connection to the "good" coming at the end of seventy years. Because of his opposition to God's word through Jeremiah, Shemaiah had been cut off from the gift of "a future and a hope."

Explanation

> . . . arriving on a nightmare
> Praying for a dream.
>
> Maya Angelou, *On the Pulse of Morning*
> (New York: Random House, 1993)

Suffering the loss of home, family, and freedom, removed from their king, temple, and homeland, exiles are vulnerable to dreams conjured out of denial and promises manufactured by human plots. When reality overtakes these first false hopes of a short-term stay, chap. 29 offers spiritual resources for the long haul. These resources remain powerful no matter how many generations one has lived in exile. The complexity of this chapter mirrors the continuing complexity of the exilic communities. They are not all automatically "good" figs, ready to receive God's salvation simply because they are exiles. The LORD's promises are like seeds of hope that are planted and grow into fulfillment in gardens, in families, and in the course of human history (cf. Isa 55:10–13). Exiles still have the freedom to choose to live according to God's plan, as vv 5–7 command, or to cut themselves off from hope by disobedience or apostasy, as did Ahab, Zedekiah, and Shemaiah. Exiles know, too, that their kindred back home face the same choices (vv 16–19).

The resources offered by this chapter begin with an assurance of the divine blessing, which makes human life possible (vv 5–6)—houses stand, crops grow, children are born and grow up, work has tangible results. The external circumstances are far removed from humanity's first home in a fruitful garden, but the divine blessing and human task are remarkably similar (compare Gen 1:28–29; 2:8–9, 15–16). The offer of a lively relationship with God through prayer is the second resource (vv 7–14). Prayers can be made and will be heard, even in exile, where they do not rise with the smoke of sacrifices and incense (compare Ps 141:1–2). Confidence in the LORD's reign, even when it is exercised through the foreign king instead of a descendant of David, is also a resource for exiles. According to 27:5–6, Nebuchadrezzar is the LORD's servant, the legitimate ruler. His actions can be God's doing (29:1, 4, 21), but the LORD has set a limit on the foreigner's reign (v 10). The place of exile can even substitute for Jerusalem as a locus of temporal security (v 7), according to God's plan.

Finally, all of these resources are available to exiles when they believe that the LORD's word is present with them and active among them even if it is written on a scroll. The very form of this chapter demonstrates the point. The written word goes where the prophet cannot go so that the LORD's word is still heard. Chap. 29 also shows how exiles are to read other parts of the book of Jeremiah. The way the "generic" judgment oracle against the king and people in Jerusalem (vv 16–19) has been incorporated into this chapter shows that God still speaks to exiles through words addressed to their kindred left behind, to their ancestors, and to their former selves. "You did not listen," v 19b, indicates how such judgment oracles account for their deportation. With vv 16–19 arranged as a disputation response to the exiles' statement in v 15, this oracle also becomes a warning to the exiles. They must hear and obey only the word God sends through the prophets. The judgments announced against Ahab, Zedekiah, and Shemaiah are chilling examples of what happens to exiles who reject the LORD's word or fraudulently claim to preach it themselves.

This chapter also instructs exiles how to read and understand oracles of salvation. Exiles know that God sets a limit on the foreign ruler's power (v 10), and they live under God's authority first of all (note the imperative verbs in vv 5–7). In spite of the divine gifts that make life in exile possible and even good, exiles know that returning home is even better. The LORD's promises of restoration (v 14) inspire desire for the God-given land of promise and keep alive the meaning of their traditions and their longing for God. Hope that seems beyond reach may be abandoned in despair and apostasy, or it may grasp and be grasped in the presence of the One who gives the blessings of life, answered prayer, and a future even to exiles—especially to exiles.

XVII. The Book of Consolation (30:1–31:40 [LXX 37:1–38:40])

Bibliography

Anderson, B. "The New Covenant and the Old." In *The Old Testament and Christian Faith*, ed. B. Anderson. New York: Herder and Herder, 1964. 225–42. **Becking, B.** "'I Will Break His Yoke from off Your Neck': Remarks on Jer xxx 4–11." In *Oudtestamentische Studien*, ed. A. van der Woude. Leiden: Brill, 1989. 63–76. **Biddle, M.** "The Literary Frame surrounding Jeremiah 30,1–33,26." *ZAW* 100 (1988) 409–13. **Böhmer, S.** *Heimkehr und neuer Bund: Studien zu Jeremia 30–31.* Göttinger theologische Arbeiten 5. Göttingen: Vandenhoeck & Ruprecht, 1976. **Bozak, B.** *Life 'Anew': A Literary-Theological Study of Jer. 30–31.* AnBib 122. Rome: Pontifical Biblical Institute, 1991. **Childs, B. S.** *Introduction to the Old Testament as Scripture.* Philadelphia: Fortress, 1979. **Clements, R.** "Jeremiah, Prophet of Hope." *RevExp* 78 (1981) 345–64. ———. "Patterns in the Prophetic Canon." In *Canon and Authority: Essays in Old Testament Religion and Theology*, ed. G. W. Coats and B. O. Long. Philadelphia: Fortress, 1977. **Eskenazi, T. C.** "Exile and the Dreams of Return." *CurTM* 17 (1990) 192–200. **Fackenheim, E. L.** "The Lament of Rachel and the New Covenant." *Cross Current* 40 (1990) 341–49. **Fischer, G.** *Das Trostbüchlein: Text, Komposition und Theologie von Jer 30–31*, ed. H. Frankemölle and F.–L. Hossfeld. SBB 26. Stuttgart: Katholisches Bibelwerk, 1993. **Fohrer, G.** "Der Israel-Prophet in Jeremia 30–31." In *Studien zum alten Testament (1966–1988)*. BZAW 196. Berlin: de Gruyter, 1991. 56–69. **Garnett, R.** "Jeremiah 30–33: Heart of Jeremiah's Covenantal Message." *Biblical Viewpoint* 25 (1991) 89–96. **Gerlach, M.** "Zur chronologischen Struktur von Jer 30,12–17: Reflexion auf die involvierten grammatischen Ebenen." *BN* 33 (1986) 34–52. **Golebiewski, M.** "L'alliance éternelle en Is 54–55 en comparaison avec d'autres textes prophetiques." *Collectanea Theologica* 50 (1980) 89–102. **Gosse, B.** "La nouvelle alliance et les promesses d'avenir se référant à David dans les livres de Jérémie, Ezéchiel et Isaïe." *VT* 41 (1991) 419–28. ———. "L'ouverture de la nouvelle alliance aux nations en Jérémie iii 14–18." *VT* 39 (1989) 385–92. **Gross, H.** "Der Mensch als neues Geschöpf (Jer 31; Ezk 36; Ps 51)." In *Der Weg zum Menschen.* FS A. Deissler, ed. R. Mosis and L. Ruppert. Freiburg: Herder, 1989. 98–109. **Hals, R. M.** "Some Aspects of the Exegesis of Jeremiah 31:31–34." In *When Jews and Christians Meet*, ed. J. Petuchowski. Albany, NY: State Univ. of NY Press, 1988. 87–97. **Jacob, E.** "Féminisme ou Messianisme? A propos de Jérémie 31,22." In *Beiträge zur alttestamentliche Theologie.* FS W. Zimmerli, ed. H. Donner, R. Hanhart, and R. Smend. Göttingen: Vandenhoeck & Ruprecht, 1977. 179–84. **Kegler, J.** "Beobachten zur Körperfahrung in der hebräischen Bibel." In *Was ist der Mensch? Beiträge zur Anthropologie des Alten Testaments.* FS W. Wolff, ed. F. Crusemann et al. Munich: Kaiser, 1992. 28–41. **Kilpp, N.** *Niederreissen und aufbauen: Das Verhältnis von Heilsverheissung und Unheilsverkündigung bei Jeremia und im Jeremiabuch.* Neukirchen: Neukirchener, 1990. **Kraus, H. J.** "Das Telos der Tora: Biblisch-theologische Meditationen." In *Zum Problem des biblischen Kanons*, ed. I. Baldermann et al. Neukirchen: Neukirchener, 1988. 55–82. **Lemke, W.** "Jeremiah 31:31–34." *Int* 37 (1983) 183–87. **Lindars, B.** "'Rachel weeping for her children': Jeremiah 31:15–22." *JSOT* 12 (1979) 47–62. **Lohfink, N.** "Der junge Jeremia als Propagandist und Poet: Zum Grundstock von Jeremia 30–31." In *Le Livre de Jérémie*, ed. P. Bogaert. Leuven: Leuven UP 1981. 351–68. ———. "Die Gotteswortverschachtelung in Jer 30–31." In *Künder des Wortes: Beiträge zur Theologie der Propheten.* FS J. Schreiner, ed. L.

Ruppert, P. Weimar, and E. Zenger. Würzburg: Echter, 1982. 105–19. **Lundbom, J.** *Jeremiah: A Study in Ancient Hebrew Rhetoric.* SBLDS 18. Missoula, MT: Scholars, 1975. **Nicholson, E. W.** *God and His People: Covenant Theology in the Old Testament.* Oxford: Oxford UP, 1986. **Odashima, T.** "Zu einem verborgenen 'Weltblick' im Jeremiabuch: Beobachtungen zu Jer 4,5a." In *Prophetie und geschichtliche Wirklichkeit im alten Israel.* FS S. Herrmann, ed. R. Liwak and S. Wagner. Stuttgart: Kohlhammer, 1991. 270–89. **Potter, H. D.** "The New Covenant in Jeremiah XXXI 31–34." *VT* 33 (1983) 347–57. **Quesnel, M.** "Les citations de Jérémie dans l'Evangile selon Saint Matthieu." *EstBib* 47 (1989) 513–27. **Renaud, B.** "L'alliance éternelle d'Ez 16,59–63 et l'alliance nouvelle de Jér 31,31–34." In *Ezekiel and His Book,* ed. J. Lust. Leuven: Leuven UP, 1986. 335–39. **Rendtorff, R.** "What Is New in the New Covenant?" In *Canon and Theology: Overtures to an Old Testament Theology,* trans. and ed. M. Kohl. Minneapolis: Fortress, 1993. 196–206. **Römer, T.** "Les 'ancien' pères (Jér 11,10) et la 'nouvelle' alliance (Jér 31,31)." *BN* 59 (1991) 23–27. **Schedl, C.** "'Femina circumdavit virum' oder 'via salutis'?" *ZKT* 83 (1961) 431–42. **Schenker, A.** "Die Tafel des Herzens: Eine Studie über Anthropologie und Gnade im Denken des Propheten Jeremia im Zusammenhang mit Jer 31, 31–34." In *Text und Sinn im Alten Testament.* OBO 103. Freiburg, Switzerland: Universitätsverlag, 1991. 68–82. ———. "Unwiderrufliche Umkehr und neuer Bund: Vergleich zwischen der Wiederherstellung Israels in Dt 4, 25–31; 30, 1–14 und dem neuen Bund in Jer 31, 31–34." In *Text und Sinn im Alten Testament.* OBO 103. Freiburg, Switzerland: Universitätsverlag, 1991. 83–96. **Schmidt, W.,** and **Becker, J.** *Zukunft und Hoffnung.* Stuttgart: Kohlhammer, 1981. **Schmitt, J. J.** "The Virgin of Israel: Referent and Use of the Phrase in Amos and Jeremiah." *CBQ* 53 (1991) 365–87. **Schröter, U.** "Jeremias Botschaft für das Nordreich: Zu N. Lohfinks Überlegungen zum Grundbestand von Jeremia XXX–XXXI." *VT* 35 (1985) 312–29. **Steele, D.** "Jeremiah's Little Book of Comfort." *TToday* 42 (1986) 471–77. **Stoebe, H. J.** "Schicksal Erkennen—Schuld Bekennen: Gedanken im Anschluss an Lev 5,17–19." In *Prophetie und geschichtliche Wirklichkeit im alten Israel.* FS S. Herrmann, ed. R. Liwak and S. Wagner. Stuttgart: Kohlhammer, 1991. 385–97. **Talbert, C. H.** "Paul on the Covenant." *RevExp* 84 (1987) 299–313. **Tov, E.** "4QJer (4072)." In *Tradition of the Text.* FS D. Barthélemy, ed. G. Norton and S. Pisano. Freiburg, Switzerland: Universitätsverlag, 1991. 249–76. **Vieweger, D.** "Die Arbeit des jeremianischen Schülerkreises am Jeremiabuch und deren Rezeption in der literarischen Überlieferung der Prophetenschrift Ezechiels." *BZ* 32 (1988) 15–34. **Weippert, H.** "Das Wort vom neuen Bund in Jeremia XXXI 31–34." *VT* 29 (1979) 336–51. **Westermann, C.** "Zur Erforschung und zum Verständnis der prophetischen Heilsworte." *ZAW* 98 (1986) 1–13. **Wiebe, J. M.** "The Jeremian Core of the Book of Consolation and the Redaction of the Poetic Oracles in Jeremiah 30–31." *Studia Biblica et Theologica* 15 (1987) 137–61. **Zatelli, I.** "The Rachel's Lament in the Targum and Other Ancient Jewish Interpretations." *RevistB* 39 (1991) 477–90.

The Book of Consolation stands as a refuge amid the storm of divine wrath that blows through the rest of the book of Jeremiah. Yet these two chapters are thoroughly integrated with the message and ministry of the book in its canonical form. The content of the Book of Consolation repeatedly deals with the relationship between present suffering, further danger, and future salvation. For example, childbirth imagery provides a picture of a process in which great pain, strenuous effort, and even bloodshed have a joyful outcome. The connection is also made liturgically, by evoking the situation of the lament psalms in which current distress and eventual deliverance are closely connected to faith in God. The theological conundrum of how God could announce both judgment and salvation for Israel and Judah is addressed in terms of covenant, election, and God's everlasting love. These chapters repeatedly acknowledge and describe their audience's grief and despair, but they offer comfort by showing in various ways how their hurt and their healing, their past and their posterity, are all bound up in God's holy and merciful will.

The main critical issues in dealing with this complex collection of sayings have been: (1) identifying the material from Jeremiah's preaching ministry; (2) describing the process by which these early oracles were collected, arranged, and supplemented; (3) accounting for its placement within the book of Jeremiah; and (4) analyzing the literary structure of the two chapters in their present form. Only a brief overview of study can be offered here.

Many interpreters agree that the following passages come from Jeremiah's own preaching: 30:5–7, 12–15; 31:2–6, 15–20 or 15–22 (e.g., Hyatt, 1022–23). Others would add 30:16–17 (Brueggemann, *JBL* 104 [1985] 427), 30:23–24 (Böhmer, *Heimkehr,* 81), 30:18–21 (Lohfink, "Der junge Jeremia," 351–68), 30:22–24 (Clements, *RevExp* 78 [1981] 359), or 30:10–11; 31:31–34, and possibly 30:12–17 and 31:35–37 (Bright, 285). Weiser (265–89) judges all to be authentic except 30:1–4 and 31:38–40, and Thompson (551–53) treats all the oracles in chaps. 30–31 as Jeremiah's but allows for some possible editorial activity. Some recent works have limited the Jeremiah core more severely, for example, to 30:5–6, 12–15; 31:4–5a, 15–16a, 18–20 (Kilpp, *Niederreissen,* 103) or 30:12–14, 16–17; 31:2–6, 9b, 15–22 (Wiebe, *Studia Biblica et Theologica,* 15 [1987] 157). These "core" materials share an orientation toward the Northern Kingdom exiles, addressed as Jacob and Ephraim. Their suffering had come from the LORD as a result of their sin (30:14–15), but with their repentance and out of the LORD's mercy and compassion (31:20) comes a promise of restoration to the land (31:17). These verses have several features in common with the book of Hosea (see Holladay, 2:45–47; Fischer, *Das Trostbüchlein,* 186–204). Three different periods have been proposed as the date when these oracles were first delivered, none of which can be established with any certainty: (1) the reign of Josiah, between 621 and 609 B.C., when hopes were high for the restoration of the Davidic-Solomonic empire and survivors in Samaria were invited to join themselves to the king and temple in Jerusalem, as in 3:22–24 (e.g., Rudolph, 172–29; Thompson, 551–53); (2) during the reign of Jehoiakim or Zedekiah, after Nebuchadrezzar had finally defeated Assyria and pacified the region, making the return of the Northern Kingdom exiles plausible; and (3) during the administration of Gedaliah at Mizpah in Benjamin (Clements, *RevExp* 78 [1981] 351).

The time and place of origin for these oracles is not as significant to their interpretation as their place within the Book of Consolation and within the book of Jeremiah. As in the book of Hosea, words addressed to the Northern Kingdom in the first instance stand alongside oracles about the Southern Kingdom, Judah, and the book is directed toward the future of God's people Israel as a whole. The names Jacob, Rachel, and Ephraim, along with references to the Exodus and wilderness wanderings, point to the common ancestry and origins of Israel and Judah, reminding them of the promises of land and offspring that the LORD had made to their forebears and kept. Furthermore, the earlier addressees, the northerners, have not been obscured, replaced, or converted to mere symbols (note the mention of Samaria). They are still included in the promises (30:3; 31:1, 27, 31, 37). Indeed, their inclusion proves God's faithfulness and implicitly gives encouragement. The Northern Kingdom exiles were carried off more than a century before the Southern Kingdom exiles, yet they remained part of God's plan.

The command to Jeremiah in 30:2 is to write down the words the LORD had already spoken (כל־הדברים אשר־דברתי אליך, "all the words which I have spoken to you"). The identical command also appears in 36:2, a chapter that reports the preparation, reading, and burning of a written collection of oracles preached in the past and the writing of a second, expanded version (36:32). Readers of the book of Jeremiah are aware of prophetic activity that involves writing down earlier preaching for a new audience, and also rewriting and supplementation. (See Davis, *Swallowing the Scroll,* especially chaps. 2 and 3, on prophets as makers of books.) Holladay's reconstruction of two recensions of the Book of Consolation will doubtless remain an influential hypothesis about the literary history of chaps. 30–31. According to his hypothesis, which relies on the work of Lohfink ("Der junge Jeremia"), Jeremiah himself composed a seven-strophe recension for an audience in the former Northern Kingdom, possibly at the time of Josiah's expedition to regain control of that territory (2 Kgs 23:15–22; Holladay, 2:156–59). Many years later, before the fall of Jerusalem (between summer 588 and summer 587), Jeremiah expanded his earlier composition to address his audience in that city, adding 30:10–11, 16–17; 31:7–9a (Holladay, 2:160–61). Because he was in custody, Jeremiah recorded his composition in a scroll, adding the framing passages 30:1–3 and 31:27–28 (2:162–63). Subsequent interpretive editorial work on Jeremiah's recension to the south plus his authentic word in 31:31–34 continued into the fifth century B.C., bringing chaps. 30–31 to their present form (Holladay, 2:163–67). Whatever the details of the history of redaction of these chapters, however, in their final form the contents have been "loosened from their original historical moorings" (Childs, *Introduction,* 351). All of Israel and Judah, whether exiled in the eighth century B.C., the sixth century, or not at all, and all of their descendants, hope in God through these promises. The distinctions present in chaps. 3, 24, and 29 will have no significance in their future.

The Book of Consolation stands between letters that promise a hopeful future to the exiles taken to Babylon in 597 B.C. (chap. 29) and a sign-act in which the deed for Jeremiah's newly purchased field is sealed and stored as a guarantee of the people's restoration to the land (chap. 32). Chap. 33 interprets the significance of the purchase in terms of chaps. 30–31 (see the *Comment* on chap. 33). The promises in chap. 29 of a limit to Nebuchadnezzar's suzerainty (29:10) and restoration from "all the nations and all the places" where the exiles had been sent (29:14) imply a wider range of beneficiaries than just the deportees of 597 B.C. Thus there are three written documents (ספר) grouped together in the middle of the book of Jeremiah that serve as a promissory note and a guide for living in hope under the authority of the foreign king (e.g., Dan 9). Together, under the leadership of the Book of Consolation, the three documents address all of God's people after the crisis of 586 B.C.

Chap. 29 is from the middle of Zedekiah's reign, and chap. 32 is set very near the end. Chaps. 30–31, however, have no date, like the material in Jer 2–24. Some interpreters take this as one indication that the Book of Consolation is a late insertion into its context (e.g., Fischer, *Das Trostbüchlein,* 179). Holladay, on the other hand, theorizes that the Book of Consolation was the core around which chaps. 26–36 were organized (2:22–23). Childs offers the most helpful assessment of this ordering of the material. The placement of this major collection of promises in Zedekiah's reign and before the description of Jerusalem's desolation in chaps. 39–40 reminds the reader of the book's claim that restoration had been part of the LORD's plan all along (Childs, *Introduction,* 351). It is not an afterthought or the result of Jeremiah's intercession (cf. 11:14; 37:3–10). Jeremiah's dual ministry of prophesying judgment and prophesying restoration is announced in the call account (1:10), echoed in 18:5–11; 24:6; 42:10; 45:4, and cited in the Book of Consolation (31:28). Furthermore, these promises stand at a place in the book analogous to the situation of the implied audience who continue to suffer the effects of the judgment that has not yet run its course (30:12–17, 24; 31:27–28). In the Masoretic text of Jeremiah, the oracles against the nations come at the end of the book (chaps. 46–51), where they function as an explication of the promises regarding enemies in 30:8, 11, 16, 20; 31:10, 16. The LORD's defeat of the enemies, especially Babylon, is prerequisite to restoration of Israel and Judah to their land (cf. 50:33, "all their captors have held on to them and refuse to release them").

The Book of Consolation is also connected to the preceding chapters of the book of Jeremiah by a web of verbal links. Many of them can be organized under four categories listed by Fischer (*Das Trostbüchlein,* 155–69). The Book of Consolation relates to earlier passages by (1) answering questions; e.g., 30:12–17 answers 15:18, and 31:6; 31:38–40 answers 8:19; (2) fulfilling requests; e.g., 30:11 fulfills 6:8; 10:24, and 31:20 fulfills 14:21; 15:15; (3) reversing former conditions or judgments; e.g., 30:9 reverses 22:9, 30:9, 21 reverse 22:30, and 30:18 reverses 9:18(Eng 19); 10:20; and (4) developing ideas by the technique of combining verses from two different contexts; e.g., 30:8 combines Jer 2:20 and Isa 10:27; 30:14–15 combines Jer 5:6 and 25; and 30:5–7 develops in each colon a different word from 6:24 in combination with words from other contexts. Other examples are noted in the *Comment.*

The fourth critical issue regarding the Book of Consolation, the literary structure of chaps. 30–31, is resolved in the commentary below by following the division of the text proposed by B. Bozak (*Life 'Anew',* 18–25). She identifies the Book of Consolation as a cycle of six poems with a short introduction and substantial conclusion in prose. The introduction begins with the formula that marks major divisions in the book of Jeremiah, "The word which came to Jeremiah from the LORD, saying" (cf. *Excursus: Introductory Formulas,* chap. 26). V 2 of the introduction and each one of the subsequent units begin with the messenger formula, "Thus says the LORD." This is a very common formula in prophetic books, but it only occurs two other times in chaps. 30–31. The six poetic units marked by the messenger formula exhibit an alternating pattern of masculine and feminine address (*Life 'Anew',* 20): (1) 30:5–11, masculine; (2) 30:12–17, feminine; (3) 30:18–31:1, masculine; (4) 31:2–6, feminine; (5) 31:7–14, masculine; and (6) 31:15–22, feminine-masculine-feminine. The prose conclusion could also be identified as having a masculine addressee. The audience is the same throughout, namely, God's people Israel, but the poetic images and, therefore, the grammatical forms alternate. The appropriateness of this division is confirmed by the discovery of two main subdivisions in each unit except the sixth, which has three. This analysis differs from the divisions followed by Brueggemann, Clements, and Thompson only in treating 30:18–31:1 and 31:23–40 as compositional units.

Bozak's formal, structural analysis is attractive and useful for three main reasons. First, the alternating masculine and feminine address is not only aesthetically interesting but also theologically significant. In these poems the two most devastating and demeaning images for Israel's sinfulness, both of which had been drawn from the intimate life of the family, are redeemed and transformed. The rebellious son becomes the beloved child, and the adulterous wife becomes a virgin, a bride, and a mother of many children. The inclusive imagery, male and female, young and old, also coincides with the extent of the community under the new covenant (31:34). Second, the compositional units she has identified each contain a contrast that is theologically significant in the book as a whole, so these "poems" can give guidance for understanding the rest of the book of Jeremiah. For example, 30:12–17 deals with the relationship between Israel's deserved punishment and the defeat of her enemies, which will be part of her healing. Finally, Bozak's literary analysis, most of which is not reported here, supports the designation of these two chapters as a unified composition, a "book," which is a significant aspect of their canonical shape and function.

The prophetic speech in these two chapters is introduced as the content of a book, written in obedience to the LORD's command. The salvation oracle in v 3 interprets the writing of the book as a sign of God's intention to restore the exiles of Judah and Israel. It will function as a sort of letter of intent to fill the gap between the broken covenant and the new covenant (31:31–34). The book of Jeremiah teaches its audience that the LORD's word through the prophet continues to be authoritative when written in a book. Their response to such a book is a matter of life and death (cf. chap. 36). The response that leads to life is repentance and submission to the LORD's plan. The book of Deuteronomy has provided the interpretive framework for the canonical form of Jeremiah (Childs, *Introduction*, 346–48). Within this framework, the logic of the covenant is operative in chaps. 30–31. The implied audience of the Book of the Consolation still experiences suffering and oppression in the land of the enemy, which is interpreted as just judgment for their sin and appropriate discipline (30:11; 31:18). To acknowledge the truth of this assessment and to repent are the responses that follow the logic of the covenant. This logic also affirms that the law (or "instruction," תורה) and covenant were given in order to fulfill the promises of land and descendents to the ancestors (Deut 8:1; Jer 11:3–5). To heed the words of this book, chaps. 30–31, is to believe God, who renews the promises of offspring and land, and to submit to the LORD's exclusive authority while waiting in hope. The grace and love by which the LORD first drew Israel into covenant and the faithfulness that maintained it for so many generations, are still present in all their power (30:18; 31:2–3, 9, 20, 35–37). Reminders of answered prayer and the goodness of God experienced on pilgrimage to the temple encourage the people to return to the LORD and sustain their loyalty and their longing for the righteousness and holiness of the LORD's presence. The ministry of the Book of Consolation is to keep God's people ready for the fulfillment of the promise of the new covenant.

A. Write These Words   (30:1–4[LXX 37:1–4])

Bibliography

See *Bibliography* for 30:1–31:40.

Translation

[1] *The word which came to Jeremiah from the LORD, saying,* [2] *"Thus says the LORD, the God of Israel: Write down all the words which I have spoken to you in a book.* [3] *For behold, days are coming—oracle of the LORD—when I will bring about the restoration of my people Israel and Judah,"* [a] *the LORD says. "I will cause them to return to the land which I gave to their ancestors so that they took* [b] *possession of it."* [4] *These are the words which the LORD had spoken to Israel* [a] *and to Judah:* [a]

Notes

3.a. *BHS* suggests that "and Judah" is an addition. There is no textual evidence for the omission.
3.b. The subj of the verb is ambiguous. The translation makes it part of the relative clause, with "their ancestors" as the subj. "My people" could also be the subj: "and they will take possession of it."
4.a-a. As in v 3, *BHS* suggests that the reference to Judah is an addition, although it is present in the MSS and versions.

Form/Structure/Setting

A word-event formula (v 1) is followed by a report of the commissioning of a sign-act. The command to write the LORD's words in a book as a sign-act (v 2) lacks the detailed instructions found in other sign-act reports. The explanatory oracle (v 3) is introduced by the conjunction כִּי, "for." The connection between the sign-act itself and the divine message is considerably more obscure than smashing the bottle in chap. 19 or wearing yoke-bars in chaps. 27–28. Other written collections mentioned in the book of Jeremiah are produced so that God's word can go where the prophet cannot go, to Babylon (chaps. 29 and 51) or to the temple (chap. 36). Since v 3 promises a return to the land, exiles constitute the audience for this document, as for the letters in chap. 29. The purpose for writing chaps. 30–31 was to go into the future, where Jeremiah could not go himself. The social disruptions, which required a written, signed, sealed, and preserved deed (chap. 32) rather than just an oral transaction before witnesses (compare Ruth 4), also called for a written scroll of prophecies that could survive to prove God's pledge of restoration even if the chain of transmission from mouth to ear were broken.

This narrative introduction lacks a date and any description of the circumstances in which the command was given. The implied audience for the new book is exiles (v 3), but the original addressees for the various earlier prophecies included in it are identified in the most general terms as the prophet ("to you," v 2) and "Israel and Judah" (v 4).

Comment

2 A divine command to write a "document" (ספר) occurs three other times in the book of Jeremiah: a letter to the exiles in chap. 29, a scroll to be read in the temple in chap. 36, and a scroll of oracles against Babylon in chap. 51. The wording of the relative clause matches 36:2 (אשר דברתי, "which I have spoken"), where the following temporal clause clearly indicates that the scroll was to contain oracles already delivered on previous occasions. The command in 30:2 should be understood in the same way.

3 This salvation announcement interprets the writing of the book as a sign of God's intention to bring back the exiles of Judah and Israel. There is no mention that repentance by the people, as in 36:3, is the desired effect. The causal clause resembles 32:15, where the preservation of the deed signals that such transactions will be made again in the land.

The opening formula, "behold, days are coming," recurs in 31:27, 31, 38, where it introduces more detailed depictions of the promised restoration, including fertility for humans and animals, a new covenant with the LORD, and the rebuilding of Jerusalem.

"Their ancestors," to whom the land had been given, were the ones with whom the LORD had made a covenant after bringing them out of Egypt, a covenant that they broke (31:32). ירש, "take possession," is a key word in the book of Joshua for Israel's conquest and settlement of the land God had sworn to give them. Therefore, the final verb in the verse could have the ancestors as its subject. The recipients of the restoration promised in v 3 could also be the ones who "take possession" after their return to the land. This ambiguity is not easily retained in English translation.

The land given to the ancestors included not only the land of Judah but also the territory of the northern tribes of Israel (cf. Num 34; Josh 13–19). According to this promise, the whole of God's people, Judah and Israel, united by their common ancestry, will again possess the whole land, which is their joint inheritance. (32:44 has a less expansive "map.") There is room in this picture for descendants of the deportees taken from the defeated Northern Kingdom in the eighth century B.C., although there is no evidence that they retained their Israelite identity in dispersion. Ezra and Nehemiah do not mention the participation of Northern Kingdom exiles in the return to and rebuilding of Jerusalem in the sixth and fifth centuries.

4 The shift to third person marks this verse as the title of the document commissioned in v 2. (The "title" of the book of Deuteronomy also begins "these are the words which . . . spoke.") The following words are the ones the LORD had already spoken. These divine words have two addressees: first the prophet (v 2) and then his audience. Israel and Judah in exile are the audience for this written collection because they are the recipients of the promised restoration (v 3).

Explanation

The prose introduction to the Book of Consolation assigns a new audience and a new function to this collection of oracles that had already been delivered on various occasions in the past. The production of the book as a written document is in itself a sign pointing to the LORD's promise to return the whole nation, both Judah and Israel, to their ancestral land. It is a sort of promissory note or written guarantee of the survival of God's people into the future. A shadow lies over the sign, however, because in the book of Jeremiah prophecies are written down only in times of distress, when communication of the divine word is impeded in some way. The written form of the promises simultaneously indicates that their fulfillment is assured but that it will be delayed.

B. From Panic to Peace   (30:5–11[LXX 37:5–9])

Bibliography

Conrad, E. W. *Fear Not Warrior: A Study of ʾal tiraʾ Pericopes in the Hebrew Scriptures.* Brown Judaica Studies 75. Chico, CA: Scholars, 1985. 108–15.

Translation

> [5] "[a]*For thus says the LORD:*[a]
>   '*We*[b] *have heard a voice of panic,*   (3+3)
>   *"Dread" and "No peace."*'
> [6] *Ask now and see if a male bears a child.*
>   [a]*Why do I see every he-man*   (4+3+3)
>   *with his hands on his loins*[a]
>   [b]*like a woman giving birth*[b]
>   *and every face turned an unhealthy color?*
> [7] *Alas,*[a]   (1+4+2+3+2)
>   *for that day is greater*
>   *than any like it*
>   *and it is a time of distress for Jacob,*
>   *but he will be delivered from it.*
> [8] *It shall come to pass on that day*   (3+3+4+2)
>   *—oracle of the LORD of Hosts—*
>   *that I shall shatter the yoke from off your*[a] *neck*
>   *and your*[b] *yoke-straps I shall burst,*
>   *so that strangers will not subjugate him*[c] *again.*   (3+4+3+3)
> [9]   *But they shall serve the LORD their God*
>   *and David their king,*
>   *whom I shall establish for them.*
> [10] [a]*As for you, my servant Jacob, do not fear*   (4+1+2)
>   *—*[b]*oracle of the LORD*[b]*—*
>   *and do not be dismayed, Israel.*
>   *For I am about to save you from afar*   (4+3)
>   *and your offspring from the land of their captivity.*

> *Then Jacob will return and be quiet* (3+3)
> *and be at ease and no one will panic him.*
> [11] [a]*For I am with you—*[b]*oracle of the Lord*[b]*—to save you.* (4+4+3)
> *For I shall make an end of all the nations where I scattered*[c] *you,*
> *But I shall not make an end of you.*
> *I shall discipline you justly,* (4+5)
> *and I shall certainly not withhold punishment from you.*

Notes

5.a-a. *BHS*, without any textual support, labels the messenger formula an addition.

5.b. LXX has 2 pl. *BHS* recommends reading 1 sg. MT's 1 pl is inconsistent with the speaker of the rest of the verse (the LORD) and with v 6, "I see." The MT, however, can be read as a quotation in which the people address God (or the prophet).

6.a-a. LXX includes two variants of this clause, with different translations of "loins." It interprets the gesture as an expression of fear by someone looking for safety (σωτηρίαν).

6.b-b. Not in LXX. See *Note* 6.a-a.

7.a. MT הוי. LXX has ἐγενήθη, "For they will be." *BHS* suggests that this word be read as היו, "they were," which requires only the inversion of two letters, and be included at the end of v 6, ירקון היו, "have become an unhealthy color." This change would repair the uneven meter in both verses and would eliminate the dangling "alas." The MT is not impossible, however, and this translation retains it.

8.a., b. MT's 2 m sg suffixes are not expected in this context. LXX has "their" in both places, and *BHS* recommends emending accordingly.

8.c. LXX has αὐτοί, "them," in conformity with the 3 pl of v 9. MT's 3 sg refers to "Jacob" in vv 7 and 10.

10.a. Vv 10–11 are virtually duplicated in 46:27–28 (LXX 26:27–28). They are lacking in LXX chap. 37, in accordance with the usual LXX practice of omitting the second occurrence of a duplicate passage.

10.b-b. Lacking in 46:27.

11.a. Holladay restores the first colon of 46:28, which is a duplicate of the beginning of 30:10, minus the conj.

11.b-b. In the parallel, 46:28, this formula is part of the first line, which is lacking in 30:11, "As for you, do not fear, my servant Jacob—oracle of the LORD."

11.c. 46:28 has הדחתיך, "I have driven you," as in 8:3; 23:3, 8; 27:10; 29:14, 18; 32:37.

Form/Structure/Setting

This mixed composition of poetry (vv 5–7, 10–11) and rhythmic prose (vv 8–9) is bounded by the messenger formulas in vv 5 and 12. The second-person addressee is masculine gender throughout vv 5–11, but feminine forms appear in v 12. Several verbal links also hold the passage together: חרד, "panic," in vv 5, 10; היום ההוא, "that day," in vv 7, 8; יעקב, "Jacob," in vv 7, 10; עבד, "serve, servant," in vv 8, 9, 10; and ישע, "save," in vv 7, 10, 11.

The near chaos of voices and addressees in vv 5–7 portrays the confusion that is part of Jacob's distress. A group (Israel? the enemies?) reports hearing cries of fear (v 5). An individual (God? the prophet?) responds with a series of questions that taunt and mock the supposed heroes, who are incapacitated like women in labor (v 6). Finally, woe is pronounced but without naming its object (v 7a). This omission happens only one other time in a woe oracle, in Isa 1:24. The "summary appraisal" form (Holladay, 2:167, using B. Childs' term) in v 7b*a* finally names Jacob as the sufferer. This order reverses the usual woe-oracle form, which has its roots in the funeral lament, "Alas, [name of deceased]" (e.g., 1 Kgs 13:30; Jer 22:18): (1) הוֹי, "alas"; (2) name and/or description of the recipient of judgment, often using participles; (3) an announcement of judgment, often in the form of taunting rhetorical questions that expose guilt or reveal punishment. (Hab 2:6 calls these questions taunts and riddles.) Several holy war motifs appear in this inverted woe oracle: panic, dread, and no peace (v 5), warriors who have become like women (v 6), and the expectation of "that day" (v 7).

Two salvation oracles (vv 8–9 and 10–11) describe how Jacob will be delivered from his distress. The contents of these promises imply that the time of distress involves dispersion (vv 10–11) and subjugation by foreign powers (vv 8–9). The panic and fear of the incapacitated warriors on the day of their defeat in battle now characterize the experience of exile.

Many commentators treat vv 8–9 as a late insertion that breaks the continuity between vv 5–7 and 10–11, which had been established at an earlier stage in the formation of chaps. 30–31 (e.g., Rudolph, 190; Carroll, 575; Holladay, 2:173). Literarily and thematically these verses may be experienced as an interruption in their immediate context, but they serve important functions in the canonical shape of the book. First, they confirm that this passage addresses the people of Israel living under foreign rule, at a time when there was no Davidic king. The promised establishment of "David their king" remains in the future (v 9). Second, this oracle relates the contents of chaps. 30–31 to chaps. 27–29. Submission to Nebuchadrezzar's yoke, as commanded in chap. 27, was to be of limited duration, according to 29:10. V 9 promises that the LORD will restore to David's line the sovereignty that had once been transferred to Nebuchadrezzar. V 8 resembles Hananiah's false prophecy in 28:2, but here it has a different audience: namely, God's people scattered among many nations where they serve "foreigners" (v 11). Nevertheless, they remain the LORD's servant (v 10).

The salvation-oracle form found in vv 10–11 is especially prominent in the latter part of the book of Isaiah. Its distinctive features include the words of exhortation, "do not fear" and "do not be dismayed" (v 10); substantiation, "I will save you" (v 10) and "I am with you . . . to save you" (v 11); and result, "Jacob will return and be quiet" (v 10). This example of the genre is modified by a warning (v 11b) concluded by a citation from Exod 34:7, "I shall certainly not withhold punishment from you." The expectation of a future deliverance, in which "all the nations" are brought to an end and Israel suffers "corrective discipline" but survives, corresponds to the post-586 B.C. prophecies in Ezekiel (e.g., chaps. 38–39).

Comment

5 The poem begins with a report from an unidentified plural subject, a sort of chorus, which announces the words they have heard spoken by a fearful voice. Holladay thinks that the LORD is the subject of the first-person plural verb (2:171). Martens notes that a quotation of the people's speech initiates a salvation oracle in 31:17b–21 and in Ezek 37:11–14 (187). They hear the sounds before they see their source, which is identified in v 6. Crying out is part of the childbirth image in Jer 4:31 and Isa 42:14, but the specific words, חרדה, "panic," פחד, "dread," and אֵין שָׁלוֹם, "no peace," belong to the vocabulary of holy war (e.g., Deut 2:25; 11:25; 1 Sam 14:15; Isa 19:16; Jer 6:24–5) and the day of the LORD (Isa 2:10–17).

6 The LORD's response invites those who have heard the cry to "ask" and "see" (plural imperatives) its source. The rhetorical question underlines the unnatural and incredible conditions that the LORD sees in v 6b–c. Of course a "male" (זכר, as in Gen 1:26) cannot give birth to a child. Nevertheless, "every he-man" (כל גבר, a term that stresses virility) has assumed the position of a woman in labor and their faces have turned "greenish" (לְיֵרָקוֹן). This word is used elsewhere in the OT only of unhealthy growths on plants (Holladay, 2:172). LXX and Vg translate it "jaundiced." Whether it means "pale" or sickly "yellow-green," this word may indicate the opposite of "ruddy," the healthy complexion that David displayed (1 Sam 16:12). This depiction of childbirth views it as an experience of vulnerability and terror rather than power and productivity, because the pain of labor comes on without warning and it cannot be postponed or avoided. It is an example of the curse of warriors who become like women (Isa 19:16; Jer 50:37; 51:30).

B. Bozak draws attention to the fact that the qal of ילד can also mean "beget." There would be two answers to the rhetorical question, then, both "no" and "yes," depending on how the verb is understood. She suggests that this pun holds in tension the promise of restoration in v 3 and the panic in v 5 (*Life 'Anew'*, 36–37). One might then read v 6 this way: Can a male beget a child? Yes, of course he can, and that is the basis of hope for the people's survival. Why then does every he-man look like a woman in labor? A male cannot give birth to a child! Their efforts are absurd and will be fruitless.

Carroll observes (574) that elsewhere in the book of Jeremiah this image is a simile for pain or anguish, "like that of/as a woman in labor" (4:31; 13:21; 49:24; 50:43). In 30:6, however, the simile describes the posture and complexion of the men, their external appearance rather than their internal disposition. Carroll concludes that this inversion, or "transmogrification, of the normal patterns of life" is "preternatural" and that it refers to the future day of the LORD, not to 587/6 B.C. The vocabulary of this verse is related to 31:22. Both verses use גֶּבֶר, "he-man." In addition, two terms that are rare in the prophetic literature, זָכָר, "male," and נְקֵבָה, "female," appear in 30:6 and 31:22, respectively. Carroll (602–3) suggests that the "new thing" in 31:22 is actually the restoration of the childbearing function to women so that the land will be repopulated. He does not work out the implications of this interpretation for 30:6, however. Males cannot bear children, but if males are the only ones "with their hands on their loins" in labor, then no children will be born and the nation will be desolate. The cry of woe in v 7 is an appropriate response. (Compare 30:15, where Rachel mourns for her children because they "are no more.")

7 This verse confirms that the day of the LORD is in view in this inverted woe oracle (see *Form/Structure/Setting*). That day is so great that no other day can compare with it. The surprise turn toward salvation in the final colon, "but he will be delivered," corresponds to the end of v 11, where disciplinary correction and punishment are part of Jacob's promised salvation.

8–9 The promise to remove "his yoke from off your neck" is also found in Isa 10:27, where it refers to the end of Assyrian domination of Judah. In this context,

however, the yoke is Nebuchadrezzar's (27:12), to which the LORD had commanded Judah and her neighbors to submit. Nebuchadrezzar is not "my servant"
here, as in 27:6. He has become one of the "strangers" who have subjugated God's
people and is not even mentioned by name. עוד, "again," at the end of v 8 ar-
ranges this promise in sequence with the command in chap. 27 to submit to
Nebuchadrezzar and the subsequent conquest of Judah. In isolation, the promise of the shattered yoke would sound just like Hananiah's false prophecy in 28:2.
The present context indicates, however, that this promise of deliverance comes
after Jacob had been carried "far away" into captivity (v 10) and after further
action against the nations (v 11). V 8 promises the end of foreign rule (cf. v 11)
over the people of Israel so that they are free to serve the LORD and their own
divinely appointed king. There is a subtle allusion to the exodus from Egypt, when
the LORD commanded the pharaoh who had subjugated Israel "Let my people
go that they may serve me" (Exod 7:16). The establishment (קום hiphil, as in
23:5) of David as their king completes the reversal of the judgment (27:7, 12; cf.
Jer 33:26).

   10   The stereotypical language of this assurance of salvation addresses the anguish and terror portrayed in vv 5–7. V 8 has identified the cause of this panic as
the "strangers" who had subjugated Jacob/Israel. After rescuing them and returning them to the land, the LORD will not allow anyone to make them panic
again. Subsequent generations are included in this promise.

   11   In order to shatter the yoke of servitude (v 8), to deliver the people from
their distant captivity (v 10), and to guarantee that they will be able to live undis-
turbed (v 10c), the LORD promises to make an end of all the nations among which
they have been scattered. The dispersion, therefore, is broader than Babylon.
The people's well-being will no longer be bound up with the well-being of their
exilic home, as in 29:7, and they will escape the destruction that will fall upon
those nations, just as they were spared from the plagues in Egypt.

   "But of you I will not make an end" occurs elsewhere in the book of Jeremiah
in the midst of judgment oracles, in 4:27; 5:10, 18. It is a notice of mere survival,
which is not developed into a promise of salvation in any of these contexts. Only
30:11 gives some indication of how those who escape the judgment are to interpret their survival. Their tribulations under judgment are "corrective discipline"
(מוסר) that is supposed to result in a changed life. Correction done "in just measure" (למשפט) contrasts with "in anger" in 10:24. The latter may bring a person to
nothingness, but the restraint implied by the former gives one a chance to live.
The preposition in 30:11 is different from that in 10:24, ל rather than ב, and the
noun is definite, giving the sense "according to the standards of justice." If correction fails, judgment follows, as in 2:30; 5:3; 7:28; 15:7; 31:18; 32:33. The citation
from Exod 34:7 communicates the necessity of bearing the penalty for sin, while
leading the reader to think about 34:6–7a also, "a God, merciful and gracious . . . , forgiving iniquity, transgression, and sin."

Explanation

   The reader of this poem visualizes two tableaux portraying the condition of
God's people Israel and Judah in their captivity. In the first, her warriors are incapacitated, having assumed the posture of a woman in labor, and cry out in panic

and dread (vv 5–7). In the second scene, God's people are bent under the yoke of servitude to strangers (vv 8–9). Both pictures reveal the inability of the people to save themselves. The strength and effort required for childbirth or for pulling the plow produce no benefit for Jacob in these scenes of futility and humiliation. The divine word promises them release from oppression and terrorizing by strangers and restoration to their own land, which will be made secure by the LORD's presence. Their life there will not be the bucolic retirement of oxen put out to pasture, however. Jacob will be saved in order to serve the LORD. Even when they are saved from external threats and harassment, God's people can still be endangered by their own sin.

C. Healing for an Incurable Wound (30:12–17 [LXX 37:12–17])

Bibliography

Brueggemann, W. "The 'Uncared For' Now Cared For (Jer 30:12–17): A Methodological Consideration." *JBL* 104 (1985) 419–28. **Dahood, M.** "The Word–Pair ʾakal//kalah in Jeremiah xxx 16." *VT* 27 (1977) 482. **Gerlach, M.** "Zur chronologischen Struktur von Jer 30,12–17: Reflexion auf die involvierten grammatischen Ebenen." *BN* 33 (1986) 34–52.

Translation

¹²*For thus says the LORD:*
   ^a*"Incurable is your [f sg] shatteredness;*^{ba}   (2+2)
      debilitating is your wound.
  ¹³ *There is no one* ^a*judging your case*^a *concerning a running sore.*^b   (3+4)
      There is no healing^c *of new flesh for you.*
  ¹⁴ *All your lovers have forgotten you.*   (2+3)
      They will not take care of you.
    Indeed, with an enemy's blow I have struck you,   (2+3)
      with a cruel one's^a *discipline,*
  ^b*Because of the abundance of your iniquity,*   (3+2)
    (Because)^c *your sins are so numerous.*^b
  ¹⁵ *Why do you*^a *[m sg] cry out about your [f sg] shatteredness?*   (2+2)
      An incurable wound^b *is your anguish.*
    Because of the abundance of your iniquity,   (3+2+3)
      (because) your sins are so numerous,
      I have done^c *these things to you.*
  ¹⁶ ^a*Therefore all*^a *the ones eating you will be eaten,*   (3+4+3+3)
    and all your adversaries, ^b*all of them,*^c *shall go into captivity;*^b
    and all your plunderers^d *shall become plunder,*
    and all your despoilers I will make spoil.

17 ^a*For I will bring healing over you,*   (4+2)
    and from your wounds^b I will heal you
           —oracle of the LORD—
  For they have called you "Banished: (4+2+3)
    She is Zion;^c
    no one cares for her."

Notes

12.a-a. LXX ἀνέστησα σύντριμμα, "I have brought destruction."

12.b. MT לְשִׁבְרֵךְ. *BHS* suggests rearranging the consonants to בְרָךְ לָךְ , "for you is your shatteredness." The prefixed ל in MT is most likely emphatic (GKC § 143e).

13.a-a. The mixed metaphor prompts a suggestion by *BHS* and various commentators to read רְכָּכִים, "soothings, alleviation" (cf. Isa 1:6). Carroll and NRSV rearrange the verse into three cola. See the *Comment.*

13.b. *BHS* proposes adding the definite art, but there is no textual support for the change.

13.c. *BHS* calls רפאות, "healings," a gloss on תעלה, "new skin." The "healings" are the new tissue growing over the wound (Carroll, 580).

14.a. *BHS* suggests reading the absolute state (מוּסָר, "discipline"). MT parallels "an enemy's blow" in the preceding colon, however.

14.b-b. *BHS* calls this an addition from v 15b. Such a judgment is based on the desire to eliminate duplications.

14.c. "Because" fills out the ellipsis.

15.a. This verse is either missing entirely from LXX, or v 15b appears in the middle of v 16.

15.b. *BHS* proposes that כִּי, "because, for," has been lost as a result of haplogr.

15.c. LXX^{OL} has 3 pl, as in 4:18.

16.a-a. *BHS* suggests emending to וכל, "and all of," because לכן, "therefore," does not fit the context (also Carroll, 581). לְכֵן could have arisen by dittogr from לָךְ in v 15 (so *BHS*).

16.b-b. LXX κρέας αὐτῶν πᾶν ἔδονται (< יאכלו בשרם כלה), "shall all eat their own flesh."

16.c. Holladay revocalizes כֻּלָם, "all of them," to כֻּלָם, "are consumed," following Dahood in *VT* 27 (1977) 482. The word is lacking in one MS of LXX, Syr, and Vg.

16.d. Reading the Q שֹׁסַיִךְ , "your plunderers," from the root שׁסס, "plunder."

17.a. *BHS*, without textual support, suggests moving v 17a after v 17b, since v 17b continues the description of the enemies in v 16.

17.b. LXX has ἀπὸ πληγῆς ὀδυνηρᾶς, "from your grievous wound."

17.c. LXX has θήρευμα ὑμῶν, "our prey," which suggests Heb. צֵידֵנוּ, "our prey." "Zion" in MT identifies the addressees more precisely within the OT tradition.

Form/Structure/Setting

This poem announces salvation in the form of divine healing for the people personified as Zion. The speaker throughout is the LORD, and the addressee is second person feminine singular. V 17 identifies her as Zion. The beginning of the unit, however, is devoted to a description of the people's hopeless condition (vv 12–14a) and the reasons for it (vv 14b–15). The salvation promise includes destruction of the enemies (v 16) and healing for Zion (v 17a). Following the oracle formula (נְאֻם יְהוָה, "oracle of the LORD"), a report of the enemies' taunt against Zion (v 17c) functions as an explanation for the LORD's promise to bring healing.

The vocabulary, motifs, and order of this poem mirror the lament psalm form. Shatteredness, wounds, pain, abandonment, enemies, and taunts are all features compatible with a lamenter's complaint. Yet in this passage it is the LORD who describes the suffering, not the human victim. This change of voice continues in vv 14–15, where the LORD acknowledges, "I have done these things to you." Lament psalms sometimes charge the LORD with being the source of suffering (e.g., Pss 44:10–15, 23[Eng 9–14, 22]; 60:5[Eng 3]), as does Jeremiah's "confession" in 15:17–18. Here the truth of the charge is acknowledged. The wound inflicted by the enemy came from the LORD by reason of the people's guilt. A few lament psalms do include the psalmist's confession of sin (Pss 32, 38, 41, 51, 102, 130, 143). Pss 38:4[Eng 3]; 41:4 make the connection between loss of health and sin. According to Jer 30:15, the cause of the shatteredness that the people lament (צַעַק, "cry out") is their vast evil and sinfulness.

The word לָכֵן, "therefore," at the beginning of v 16 typically signals the beginning of a judgment announcement following an indictment. In this passage, however, it introduces judgment on the enemies, which, by implication, means deliverance for Zion. The salvation announcement in vv 16–17 promises answers to two typical categories of lament petitions by removing the enemies (v 16) and healing injuries (v 17a). As a result, there will be no more taunts like the ones cited in v 17c. Such an oracle given in answer to a psalmist's complaint is implied by many psalms, but it is rarely included in the text (e.g., Ps 12).

Contemporary analyses of this poem typically divide it into an early or original part, vv 12–15, and a later addition, vv 16–17. Holladay, for example, gives the setting of vv 12–15 in Jeremiah's preaching to the survivors of the Northern Kingdom in the period 615–609 B.C. (2:158), and he assigns vv 16–17 to a much later Judean edition prepared just prior to the fall of Jerusalem (2:160). The literary features that establish the unity of the poem in its present form do not confirm in themselves whether the unit was composed in a single stage or in two or more. The imagery suits the condition of Judah and Jerusalem resulting from conquest by the Babylonians, but the personal connotations of the motifs typical of the individual lament genre free this poem to address readers long after the sixth century B.C.

Words repeated in different parts of the poem form the links in its unified structure. The diseased wound (v 12) was from the LORD's hand (v 14), but the LORD will heal their wounds (v 17). No healing (v 13) will be replaced by healing (v 17). The people's former lovers do not "seek" or "care for" them (v 14), but when the enemies taunt them with their abandonment ("No one cares for her," v 17c), the LORD takes action against the taunters (v 16). This structure corresponds to the theological logic of the lament, discussed above, and with the canonical shape of the book of Jeremiah. According to Jer 1:10, Jeremiah's ministry was "to pluck up and tear down . . . to build and to plant." "Wound" and "heal" in 30:12–17 make an analogous pair. Furthermore, the destruction of the Babylonians in chaps. 50–51 is based upon what they had done to Israel, Judah, and Jerusalem, as promised in v 17.

This unit ends with the citation of the enemies' taunts, which serves to prepare for the next unit by calling attention to the people's location in exile. 30:18–31:1 begins with a promise of restoration and rebuilding for Jerusalem.

Comment

12 This verse combines the language of judgment prophecy with the vocabulary of lament. The noun שֶׁבֶר, "fracture, shatteredness," frequently indicates the

destruction of a nation by its enemies (e.g., Nah 3:19; Jer 48:3; 50:22) or of the
wicked by God (e.g., Isa 1:28; 65:14). Jer 4:2 and 6:1 use the term to describe the
destruction to be wrought by the enemy from the north. This destruction of God's
people is a reason for mourning and lament (as in Jer 8:21; 14:17; cf. Lam 2:11,
13; 3:19, 48). In the context of the book of Jeremiah, therefore, the term שֶׁבֶר,
"shatteredness," immediately identifies the people's broken condition as the result of the divine judgment they had suffered at the hand of the Babylonians.
This verse mirrors Mother Zion's lament in 10:19a, "Woe is me because of my
shatteredness; my wound is grievous," adding only the term אָנוּשׁ, "fatal, incurable," from Jeremiah's "Confessions" (15:18; 17:16). This remarkable change of
voice from first to second person results in the LORD's uttering the lament on
behalf of the people. Vv 12–15 constitute the description of distress, or the complaint proper. They describe existing conditions, not punishment to come.

13   The mixed metaphor in this verse has called forth various proposals for
rearranging or emending the text. "Judging your case" (13a) seems at first to
have nothing to do with a sore that will not heal. Therefore, Rudolph (175) replaces the phrase with רְבָכִים, "soothing things," as in Isa 1:6. Carroll (580) and
NRSV set aside the Masoretic accents and divide the verse into three cola:

> "There is no one judging your case.
> (You don't have) remedies for your open wound;
> You don't have new skin."

(In Jer 46:11 רְפֻאוֹת, "remedies," and תְּעָלָה, "new skin," in its only other occurrence, appear in successive cola.) This rearrangement at least assigns the
apparently conflicting images to separate sentences. (Note that the metaphor
changes again in v 14.) Bozak likes the mixed metaphor, however, finding in the
tension a stimulus to reflection and increased understanding (*Life 'Anew'*, 49–
50). She concludes that the presence of the courtroom image indicates that the
wound is spiritual.

The lack of one to judge might also be understood as a form of the lament
and thanksgiving motif of sufferers who need someone to vindicate them (e.g.,
Pss 9:5, 9[Eng 4, 8]; 54:3[Eng 1]). According to *lex talionis* in Lev 24:20, the punishment for a שֶׁבֶר, "fracture" (v 12), was a fracture. (Compare 30:16.) The wounded
wanted justice as well as healing. The cognate accusative construction in v 13
occurs only two other times, both in the book of Jeremiah (5:28, concerning orphans, and 22:16, concerning the poor and needy). Jer 22:16 describes Josiah, so
30:13 could allude to the absence of a just king or ruler, like the one promised in
v 21. On another level, however, such a ruler is lacking because no human could
sit in judgment on a case against the LORD, who is the one who has wounded
Zion (vv 14–15).

The clinical details of a wound that does not heal (v 13a) include the lack of
new skin to cover and close it (v 13b).

14   This verse also combines the vocabulary of prophecy with the language
of lament. "Lovers" is a metaphor for foreign allies. The connection with the medi-
cal image in v 13 may have been prompted by reflection upon Hos 5:13, in which
Ephraim has sent to Assyria and her emperor for help, but he was not able to
heal their מָזוֹר, "open wound." (Hos 5:13 and Jer 30:13 are the only occurrences

of this word in the OT.) The particular nations referred to as "lovers" may have been the ones listed in 27:3, or the Egyptians, who caused a temporary interruption of the final siege of Jerusalem (37:5), or some other alliance not mentioned in the OT. In Ezek 23:5, 9, the "lovers" are also the Assyrians, but elsewhere in Hosea and Ezekiel the term stands for foreign deities. Israel's "lovers" are to abandon her, according to Hos 2:9a(Eng 7a), and in Jer 30:14 they have forgotten her. The final colon converts the complaint heard in Ps 142:5(Eng 4) from first to second person, "No one cares for you." דרש, "care for," includes the senses of care for the sick as well as searching for one who is lost (Brueggemann, *JBL* 104 [1985] 421).

The "lovers" have deserted Israel, but the LORD has attacked her. An enemy's blows are intended to be mortal, as in Jer 15:9; 19:7; 20:4; 44:30. (Lam 2:5, "like an enemy" the LORD has destroyed the people, and Isa 63:10, the LORD "became their enemy," go even further than the analogy in Jer 30:14.) מוסר, "discipline," on the other hand, is meant to correct or train the people so that they can escape destruction (Jer 2:30a; 5:3; 7:28; 17:23). This correction, however, is administered by a cruel person (אכזרי), a term for enemy soldiers in Jer 6:23; 50:42. The order still seems to be reversed, since people who have been struck a fatal blow are no longer in need of discipline. Bozak (*Life 'Anew'*) suggests that v 14b cites the people's understanding of the cause of their suffering, with the terms "enemy" and "cruel one" sharpening the tone of complaint. The significance of this observation is that the LORD accepts the charge by stating it in the first person. There is, however, a prior cause, namely, the people's iniquities and sins (v 14c).

15 The question "why?" is a typical feature of laments. A different word is used here (מה as opposed to למה or מדוע), and, more importantly, the LORD asks the question rather than being its addressee. The LORD has heard the people cry out (זעק) in their pain and has articulated their complaint. Crying out (זעק) often preceded deliverance in Israel's past (e.g., Ps 107:13, 19), and it was part of the process of lament (Ps 142:2, 6[Eng 1, 5]), but the LORD had determined not to hear it (Jer 11:11–12). Does the question "why?" indicate the futility of crying out (in light of 11:11) over an incurable wound? Brueggemann accepts this reading (*JBL* 104 [1985] 422), which is consistent with the usual connotation of this interrogative particle. מה, "why?" has a nuance of disapproval, implying that one ought not to be doing whatever is questioned. Exod 14:15 also asks, "Why [מה] do you cry out . . . ?" not because the cry is futile but because the LORD is already determined and at work to deliver them. This allusion subtly prepares the way for vv 16–17.

Two cola from v 14c are repeated in v 15b, and the final line of v 15 parallels v 14b, which contains the antecedents of "these things." These elements form a chiasm with the question at the center. The B elements, "your iniquity," are surrounded by the A elements, which claim divine origin, "I have done these things."

¹⁴Indeed, with an enemy's blow I have struck you, With a cruel one's discipline,	A
Because of the abundance of your iniquity, (Because) your sins are so numerous.	B

15Why do you cry out about your shatteredness?   C
   An incurable wound is your anguish.
   Because of the abundance of your iniquity,   B′
   (Because) your sins are so numerous,
   I have done these things to you.   A′

This structure reminds the reader of God's sovereignty and freedom to choose to save rather than to destroy.

16 "Therefore" (לכן) at the beginning of this verse is surprising logic. Brueggemann lists eight other passages where לכן, "therefore," introduces an announcement of hope following a description of judgment: Isa 30:18; Jer 15:19; 16:14; Ezek 36:2–7, 13–15; 37:11–12; Hos 2:16; Mic 5:2 (*JBL* 104 [1985] 422). The LORD's acknowledgment that "I have done these things" at the end of v 15 is the basis for the promise of vindication. God, who had used their enemies to discipline Israel, will now judge the case of Israel's wound (v 13) and will give those same enemies punishments that correspond to their actions of eating, being adversaries, plundering, and despoiling. The foe from the north is described in 5:17–18 as eating every plant, animal, and person in the nation. Perhaps this metaphor derives from the imagery of the locust plague (e.g., Joel 1).

17 Healing accompanies vindication for Israel, because the wounded one receives justice, restored health, and forgiveness of sins (cf. Ps 41:5[Eng 4]). Taunting by enemies is typically one aspect of a lamenter's sufferings. Jeremiah prays in 18:19, "listen to what my adversaries say," and lament psalms like Ps 35:24–26 pray that the LORD will silence the enemies who congratulate themselves, saying things like, "We have swallowed you up." Hearing such taunting is what motivates God's decision to heal and vindicate Israel (כי, "because," v 17a), even though the enemies are saying just what God has already said, "There is no one caring for you" (v 14). The shift in this passage from distress to deliverance is as dramatic as in the psalms of lament. The brief explanation of motivation in v 17b hints that God does listen to the needy person's prayer and is moved by his or her suffering. God hears when the people cry out (v 15) and when their enemies mock them (v 17) and responds with a promise.

Explanation

In these verses the LORD addresses people in a hopeless situation, suffering from a fatal injury but abandoned by the friends and allies from whom they expected to receive help. The divine word contains a paradoxical message of explanation and hope in terms of the LORD's own actions. Their abundant sins had resulted in the disciplining blow and grievous wound, which had come ultimately from the LORD. This suffering was also from the hand of human enemies who then taunt Zion because of her abandonment. In response, the LORD promises to act in mercy to deal with the enemies in the ways they had dealt with Zion and to heal her incurable wounds. The poem offers no explicit explanation to resolve this paradox. The larger context mentions the people's repentance (31:19) and the LORD's forgiveness of sin (31:34) as bases for restoration. The climactic location of the enemies' taunt suggests the sort of reasoning found in

Ezek 36:22–32, where the LORD rescues and renews Israel so that the LORD's name will be sanctified among the nations. The best preparation for comprehending this word from the LORD is training in the spiritual discipline of the lament, by which one learns to accept the LORD's surprising grace and mercy.

D. Restoration of the Covenant Community (30:18–31:1[LXX 37:18–38:1])

Bibliography

Kselman, J. S. "rb//kbd: A New Hebrew-Akkadian Formulaic Pair." *VT* 29 (1979) 110–13. **Trible, P.** "The Journey of a Metaphor." In *God and the Rhetoric of Sexuality*. Philadelphia: Fortress, 1978. 31–59.

See also *Bibliography* for 30:1–31:40.

Translation

¹⁸ *Thus says the LORD:*

Behold, I am bringing about the restoration of the tents ᵃ *of Jacob,* (4+2)
ᵇand on his dwellings ᵇ *I will have compassion.*
City shall be rebuilt on its mound (3+3)
and citadel shall occupy its rightful site.
¹⁹ *A thank offering shall come forth* ᵃ*from them* ᵃ (3 + 2)
and a sound ᵇ *of merrymakers.*
I will multiply them, and they shall not decrease. (3+3)
ᶜ*I will make them imposing and they shall not be insignificant.*ᶜ
²⁰ *His children* ᵃ *shall be as of old,* (3+3+3)
and his congregation shall be established before me.
ᶜ*I will punish all* ᵇ *his oppressors.*ᶜ
²¹ ᵃ*His noble one shall be from him,*ᵃ (3+3+3)
and his ruler shall come forth from his midst.
ᵇ*I will bring him near, and he shall approach me.*ᵇ
ᶜ*For who is he who would give his heart in pledge to approach me?*
oracle of the LORD. ᶜ
²² ᵃ*You shall be my people,* (3+4)
and I will be your God.
²³ ᵃ*Behold, the storm of the LORD!* (3+2+2+4)
Wrath ᵇ *has gone forth,*
a sweeping ᶜ *tempest.*
It will burst on the head of the wicked.
²⁴ *But the blazing* ᵃ *anger of the LORD will not turn back* (4+4)

until he has executed and accomplished the purposes of his heart. In the latter days you shall understand it. [b] [31:1] *At that time—oracle of the LORD—I will be God* [a] *of all* [b] *the families of* [a] *Israel and they shall be my people.*

Notes

18.a. Not in LXX, but it should be retained in MT because of the parallel with "dwellings" in the next colon, where LXX has "prisoners."

18.b-b. LXX has καὶ αἰχμαλωσίαν αὐτοῦ, "and upon his prisoners." LXX focuses directly upon the people instead of using the metonymy found in MT.

19.a-a. Noting that the gender of the verb (m) does not match the subj (f), Holladay (2:151, 177) emends מהם, "from them," to מבא, "he who brings," making this ptcp the subj of the verb. MT continues the metonymy of v 18, and m sg verbs with f sg subjs are common enough in the OT to allow MT to stand.

19.b. Holladay (2:177) reads קול as "frivolity," from קלל, "be slight," citing the pairing of קלל, "bring into contempt," and כבד, "make glorious," in Isa 8:23 (Eng 9:1). The usual understanding of קול as "voice" is more consistent, however, with the similar promise in 33:10–11.

19.c-c. Not in LXX. These two closely parallel cola may appear conflate, but their form is consistent with similar pairs in the book (e.g., 5:21b, 22b).

20.a. LXX εἰσελεύσονται, "shall go in," an allusion to entering the land or the sanctuary.

20.b. Not in LXX. Janzen (66) omits. MT typically has additional modifiers.

20.c-c. Noting the lack of a parallel to "oppressors," Holladay (2:178–79) proposes an original version of this colon without "all" and with sg "oppressor," which meant "I will appoint [פקד] (him) over his oppressor [i.e., Assyria]," which is parallel to the first colon of v 21. (See *Note* 21.a-a.)

21.a-a. Holladay (2:178–79), following Volz, proposes dropping the pronom suffix from אדיר, "mighty, noble one"; thus Holladay recognizes two meanings for the same sentence: (1) "and he (Jacob) shall be mightier than he (Jacob's oppressor)," parallel to the last colon in v 20; (2) "and his prince shall be from him," parallel to the second colon of v 21.

21.b-b. In LXX the remainder of the verse applies to the people rather than to a ruler, "and I will gather them and they shall return to me . . . ."

21.c-c. Holladay (2:152), following Volz, suggests omitting this colon because the interrogative does not fit the style of the context. כי, "for," would be moved to the beginning of 31:1. The style of the poem is not sufficiently uniform, however, to justify omitting this colon on the basis of style alone. It makes an important comment on the relationship of this ruler to God.

22.a. The entire verse is not in LXX. The 2nd person pl form of the covenant promise is also found in Jer 7:23; 11:4, but it does not fit the predominantly 3rd person pl context here. (The last colon of v 24 is also 2nd person pl.) The verse serves an important function in the structure of this unit, however.

23.a. Vv 23–24 are almost identical to 23:19–20. Unlike most other duplicate sayings in the book of Jeremiah, vv 23–24 do appear in LXX.

23.b. Here and in 23:19 *BHS* labels חמה, "wrath," an addition. Without it, the figurative "storm of the LORD" would be the subj of the verb. The explanatory noun, "wrath," makes explicit the usual meaning of סערה, "storm," as the instrument of divine wrath. LXX speaks only of "wrath" (ὀργή) and not of the storm.

23.c. Jer 23:19 has מתחולל, "whirling," instead, which creates assonance with יחול, "burst," in the next colon. Rudolph (192) cites G. R. Driver's thesis that מתגורר, "sweeping," is an intentional change from the verb in 23:19.

24.a. *BHS* recommends omitting this word because it is not in the parallel verse, 23:20. The combination, חרון אף, "blazing anger," occurs seven other times in Jeremiah and a total of thirty-two times in the OT.

24.b. σ' adds συνέσει, "with understanding," translating בינה, "understanding," which stands at the end of the parallel verse in 23:20.

31:1.a-a. LXX has the sg τῷ γένει, "the family," but the pl is found in 1:15; 2:4; 3:14. MT's pl balances 30:18.

1.b. Not in LXX. MT frequently has this modifier where LXX lacks it.

Form/Structure/Setting

Salvation and judgment stand in juxtaposition in this unit, as in 30:12–17. The LORD, speaking in the first person, promises restoration of Jacob's rural, urban, and political life and of the covenant relationship (vv 18–22). In penultimate position in the composition, however, vv 23–24a describe the LORD's wrath in action against the wicked. These verses are a virtual copy of Jer 23:19–20. (See the *Notes* for a description of the differences.) Salvation is announced in the midst of judgment. The two parts of this composition each begin with a form of "behold" (vv 18, 23) and conclude with a variation of the covenant formula (vv 22, 24). The verbs שׁוב, "return" (vv 18, 24), and יצא, "go forth" (vv 19, 21, 23) link the salvation and judgment announcements. Comments that stand outside the poetry and that invite reflection upon it follow each oracle in vv 21c and 24c. Two references to time connect the concluding promise to the judgment announcement ("in the latter days," 30:24, and "at that time," 31:1).

Holladay assigns 30:18–21 and 31:1a, b to his proposed "Northern Recension" (2:168). According to his reconstruction, the oracle promised the survivors of the Northern Kingdom that the Assyrian oppressor would be removed and invited them to accept Josiah as their legitimate king and the Jerusalem temple as their center of worship. Jer 3, which has much in common with chap. 31, points to an appropriate setting in Jeremiah's ministry for Holladay's reconstruction, but this composition must be interpreted in its present form within the Book of Consolation.

Comment

18 The familiar restoration formula is interpreted by the promise "I will have compassion [רחם]." Jer 33:26b holds the same combination. The LORD's actions described in the following verses specify the effects of this compassionate restoration, but one must look to 31:20 for a portrayal of the divine passions that motivate it. The etymology of רחם, "have compassion," from the same root as רחם, "womb," suggests the interpretation "motherly love" (P. Trible, "The Journey of a Metaphor," 31–59). This fierce attachment to the beloved child is articulated in 31:20. (Compare Isa 49:15.)

The structures in this promise are characteristic of rural life (tents and dwellings) and royal (city and citadel). The first two terms appear in the same order in Num 24:5, where they also function as a double metonymy for the people Israel. The second pair may have a similar function with respect to the king. (Rudolph, however, reads these indefinite singular nouns as collectives [175].) The vocabulary of the final colon is particularly suggestive. Both the verb ישׁב, "sit, be enthroned," and the adverbial phrase על משׁפטו, "on its rightful site/his legitimacy," can refer to the king (1 Sam 10:25; cf. Holladay's translation [2:177], "a citadel shall be enthroned on [the basis of] its legitimacy"). This prepositional phrase echoes descriptions of the construction of both the tabernacle and the temple "according to [all] its plans and specifications" (כמשפטו, Exod 26:30; לכל משפטו, 1 Kgs 6:38). ארמון, "citadel," however, refers to the palace rather than the temple. It is a fortification of some sort, and in Samaria one was part of the king's house (1 Kgs 16:18; 2 Kgs 15:25). Vv 20–21 promise the restoration of people and ruler explicitly, following the same order.

19–20   Metonymy is found again in v 19a, where "thank offering" and "sound" stand for the people who offer these things in worship. The thank offering was made voluntarily in response to answered prayer for deliverance (e.g., Ps 116). It could include various fruits of the people's labor and the LORD's blessing on the land. In it the reader sees evidence of the people's return, both spiritually and physically. Jer 33:11 cites Ps 136:1 as a thanksgiving psalm to be sung by Israelites bringing their thank offerings to the temple and so provides a specifically cultic text for the merrymakers' song. These sounds may have a broader referent, however. This promise implicitly reverses the judgment that silenced "the sound of mirth and the sound of gladness, the voice of the bridegroom and the voice of the bride" (Jer 7:34; 16:9; 25:10), and 33:10–11 does so explicitly.

The assurance of human fertility by which families and the nation will flourish uses the same terminology as the command to the Judean exiles in 29:6, "multiply" (רבה) and "not decrease" (לא מעט). In v 19b, however, the LORD promises direct action, "I will multiply them." Furthermore, the purpose of this population growth is not merely survival, as in chap. 29, but honor and fame (cf. 33:9). Holladay (2:177–78) refers to the discovery of the fixed pair *rb*//*kbd* in Akkadian, which are cognates of Hebrew רבה, "multiply," and כבד, "honor" (J. S. Kselman, *VT* 29 [1979] 110–13). This evidence suggests that v 19bβ also has to do with great size. Israel will increase to an imposing number, a nation that cannot be overlooked. This allusion to the promise to Abraham, Isaac, and Jacob is confirmed by the next colon, v 20a, "[Jacob's] children shall be as of old." Exod 1:7, 9, 10 describe their former strength. They "multiplied" (רבה) and filled the land so that the king of Egypt feared their power.

The final colon in v 20 sounds a somber note in this portrayal of salvation. Oppressors will still arise to exploit God's people, as they had in a long line from Pharaoh through Nebuchadrezzar.

21   The noble ruler promised here is not called "king." He is Israelite, as required in Deut 17:15, but not specifically Davidic. (Note the contrast between v 21b and the promises in 2 Sam 7:12 and Isa 11:1.) The oracle concentrates on his mediatorial function, coming from the people and brought near by God. The verb "I will bring him near" (קרב hiphil) refers to Levites in Num 16:5 and 10. Priests also "approach" (נגש niphal) the LORD (Exod 19:22). But at the crucial occasion of covenant making at Sinai, only Moses was allowed to do so (Exod 20:21; 24:2). The rhetorical question in v 21c serves as a reminder of the grave danger to any human who would initiate or presume this approach to God. The expression "pledge the heart" is unique. In Neh 5:3 people give fields, houses, and vineyards in pledge in order to get the grain they need. Here not property but life itself is put at risk. The לב, "heart," can stand for the person as a whole, as in Ps 22:26 (Wolff, *Anthropology*, 54).

23–24 This "storm warning" gives assurance of God's justice. The same two verses appear in 23:19–20 as an epitome of the divine word of judgment, which was heard by those who stood in the LORD's council. It was the opposite of the false prophets' message. God's true word had this purpose, to turn the LORD's people from their wicked way (23:22). The wicked who are the objects of the divine anger must be identified from the context. רשעים, "the wicked," may refer to oppressors, as in Isa 14:5, but it is often a term for those who have been proclaimed guilty by God (e.g., Jer 5:26, and frequently in Psalms, Proverbs, and Job). In the rest of the Book of Consolation, the people of Israel are the object of just punishment (30:11) for their guilt and sins (30:14–15). Israel's enemies and oppressors, however, are not identified as "the wicked" (רשעים, v 23), nor as sinful, guilty, or evil. 31:18–19 offers an appropriate response of repentance for Israel, followed by the assurance of divine mercy. In both of its contexts, chaps. 23 and 30, this short saying serves as a stern reminder of the continuing function of judgment oracles in the book of Jeremiah to call Israel to turn away from sin and return to the LORD.

31:1 The unique form of this covenant formula specifies "all the families of Israel" as the LORD's covenant partners. The designation has an archaic flavor, reminiscent of pre-state Israel, like "Jacob's children" in v 20. Together with 30:3–4; 31:31, this verse makes clear that the contents of the Book of Consolation are addressed to the whole nation of Israel. (Compare the indictment in 2:4–37 addressed to "all the families of the house of Israel.")

Explanation

The barren landscape and ruined cities of the plundered and depopulated land (30:16) will be filled again. The reader sees the buildings first, and then the thanksgiving offerings, accompanied by the noise of pilgrims. The scene is animated by Jacob's numerous children, multiplied by the LORD's blessing to their ancient strength. This picture of coming salvation and blessing contrasts with the ongoing storm of judgment against the wicked among them. Understanding of this tension is promised for "the latter days," but the context supplies some explanation. The extent of God's wrath against them is limited, according to 30:11, 15, to the just punishment for sin, and by God's love and compassion for them (31:3, 20). The tension is resolved in the LORD's heart (v 24). God's commitment to Israel is sealed not once but twice by the covenant formula (30:22; 31:1).

E. Israel Lovingly Rebuilt and Planted   (31:2–6 [LXX 38:2–6])

Bibliography

Jones, I. H. "Music and Musical Instruments." *ABD* 4:936. **Meyers, C.** "Of Drums and Damsels: Women's Performance in Ancient Israel." *BA* 54 (1991) 16–27. **Schmitt, J.** "The Virgin of Israel: Referent and Use of the Phrase in Amos and Jeremiah." *CBQ* 53 (1991) 365–87.

Translation

^{2}*Thus says the LORD:*
> ^{a}*He^b found favor ^{c}in the wilderness,^{c}*   (3+3+3)
> *a nation^d of survivors of the sword,^{ea}*
> ^{f}*going^g to his rest—Israel.^{f}*

^{3} *From afar the LORD appeared to him:^{a}*   (3+3+3)
> *"^{b}I have loved you [f sg] with an everlasting love;*
> *therefore I extended^c lovingkindness to you.*

^{4} *"Again I will build you and you shall be built,*   (3+2)
> *O virgin Israel.*
> *Again you shall ornament yourself with your timbrels*   (3+3)
> *and go forth ^{a}in a dance of merrymakers.^{a}*

^{5} *"Again you shall plant vineyards*   (3+2+3)
> *on the mountains of Samaria.*
> ^{a}*The planters shall plant and put it to profane use.^{ab}*

^{6} *"For there will be a day when ^{a}guards call out^a*   (4+2)
> *on Mount Ephraim,*
> *'Arise, let us go up to Zion*   (3+2)
> *to the LORD our God.'"*

Notes

2.a-a. LXX has Εὗρον θερμὸν ἐν ἐρήμῳ μετὰ ὀλωλότων ἐν μαχαίρᾳ, "I found him warm in the desert with them that were slain by the sword," reading חם, "warm," rather than חן, "favor."

2.b. LXX and σ′ have the 1st person, "I found."

2.c-c. *BHS* recommends changing the prep to כמדבר, "as in the wilderness."

2.d. LXX and α′ have μετά, "with," from Heb. עם, "with," which differs from MT's עם, "nation," by only a single vowel.

2.e. Holladay (2:152) revocalizes as חֹרֵב, which can mean "Horeb" or the ptcp "sword–wielder." This change is not necessary unless one adopts Holladay's rewritten version of the verse, which includes moving the first four words of v 3 to a position immediately after the messenger formula in v 2 (2:152).

2.f-f. LXX has two imperatives, βαδίσατε καὶ μὴ ὀλέσητε τὸν Ισραηλ, "Go ye and destroy not Israel," which nevertheless does not clarify the meaning of the verse (MT's inf abs can be read as an impv).

2.g. *BHS* recommends emending to the qal act ptcp הֹלֵךְ, "going," following α' and σ'. The inf abs can function like a ptcp, however, so emendation is not necessary (Waltke and O'Connor, *Hebrew Syntax*, 597). Holladay (2:152) makes it a hiph ptcp, הוֹלִיךְ, "bringing."

3.a. MT's 1st person לִי, "to me," would work in a narrative introduction to a new unit, but it does not fit well following v 2. *BHS* recommends emending to לוֹ, "to him," i.e., "Israel," of v 2, following LXX, which has αὐτῷ, "to him." Holladay (2:180) suggests that MT resulted from an adaptation to Exod 3:16. Bozak rejects emendation but reads לִי as "to him," citing a few other occurrences of yod as 3 m sg suff (*Life 'Anew'*, 75). M. Dahood (*Psalms III*, AB [Garden City, New York: 1970] 376) lists more than two dozen examples from the Psalms where yod functions as 3 m sg pronom suff.

3.b. Several MSS and LXX lack the conj.

3.c. In LXX the prep εἰς, "in," precedes the noun. MT חֶסֶד, "lovingkindness," is translated here as a direct obj, but it could also be understood as an adv acc, "I drew you with lovingkindness" (Bozak, *Life 'Anew'*, 76).

4.a-a. LXX has μετὰ συναγωγῆς, "with a congregation," which would translate Heb. בקהל, "with a congregation." MT's במחול, "in a dance," shares three letters, so a misunderstanding or a copying error is possible. Syr, Tg translate the same word as LXX.

5.a-a. *BHS* and some commentators think this sentence might be a gloss derived from Deut 28:30. It proposes an emendation, נטעי נטעים יחללו, "planters of plantings shall profane by use," to improve the syntax.

5.b. LXX has καὶ αἰνέσατε, "and praise," from הלל, "praise," rather than MT's חלל, "treat something as profane by using it." Syr is similar to LXX.

6.a-a. LXX has κλήσεως ἀπολογουμένων, "those who plead in defense cry out." MT's "guards" fits the unit's vineyard theme better (cf. Job 27:18; Isa 27:3).

Form/Structure/Setting

The messenger formula introduces this composition as it does the other units in 30:5–31:26. Direct speech does not begin, however, until v 3b. (The unit 31:15–22 also begins with third-person narrative in v 15.) Following the messenger formula, four cola describe Israel's survival, by God's grace, in the wilderness. The fourth introduces the LORD's words. This speech invites Israel to recall her history of blessing by a series of three promises beginning with עוד, "again." These blessings of landedness include being built, merrymaking, and enjoying the produce of vineyard and field. The "again" promises are framed by God's reminder of love and compassion in v 3b and a promise of the people's return to worship in v 6.

In the narrative introduction, God is referred to in the third person and Israel in the third person masculine singular. But the LORD then speaks in the first person, addressing Israel in the second person feminine singular. She is called "Virgin Israel." The promises are consistent with this form of address. For example, adornment and timbrels are usually associated with females in the OT (e.g., Exod 15:20). This unit continues the alternating pattern of masculine and feminine forms of address for Israel that is characteristic of chaps. 30–31.

The northern place names, "mountains of Samaria" (v 5) and "Mount Ephraim" (v 6), and the invitation to their inhabitants to go on pilgrimage to Jerusalem may point to survivors from the Northern Kingdom as the original addressees. Jer 3:6–14 gives Jeremiah a message for "the north" during Josiah's reign, and the king's religious reforms laid claim to the loyalty of the northern territory (2 Kgs 23). Holladay assigns 31:2–6, 9b to his theoretical "Northern Recension" (2:179). In the context of the Book of Consolation, however, this oracle is for all of God's people. Names associated with the northern tribes evoke memories of the premonarchical period and the days before the kingdom was divided, when all the families of Israel shared the land and worshiped the LORD together. Furthermore, the return of both the Northern Kingdom and Judah and the restoration of the Jerusalem temple cult fit the picture of post-exilic promises common to OT prophecy, which portrays the whole covenant people Israel worshiping the LORD in Zion (e.g., Hos 2:1–2[Eng 1:10–11]; Amos 9:7–15; Isa 11:12–16; Jer 3:18; Ezek 40–48). This oracle is for Israel as she stands under judgment. These promises are for the people who have lost homes and families, kings and temple, and for their desolate land.

Comment

2–3 The survivors in vv 2–3 are first of all the Israelites in the wilderness between Egypt and the land of Canaan. The LORD rescued them from the sword of the Egyptians (Exod 15) and of the Amalekites (Exod 17) and appeared to them at Sinai (Exod 19–24). Jer 2:2 describes Israel's love and devotion to the LORD in the wilderness. The temporal translation of מרחוק, "long ago," suits this historical interpretation, which is also found in the Targum. The description of the wilderness generation is expressed in words appropriate to the survivors of the Babylonian sword also, whether in exile or left in the desolate land. The audience for the oracle could see the similarity between themselves and early Israel and could hope, like them, to find favor and rest. (Compare Exod 33:12–23, where finding favor, rest, and the LORD's presence are also at issue.) To them, the LORD must come "from afar" (מרחוק). The following verses (vv 4–5) confirm this comparison by presenting the promised future as a return to former conditions in a series of lines beginning עוד, "again."

להרגיעו, "to his rest," is from a rare root that also occurs in Deut 28:65, one of the futility curses of exile, "Among those nations you shall find no rest [לא תרגיע], no resting place [מנוח] for the sole of your foot." God had given Israel "rest" (נוח, hiphil) by giving her the land (Exod 33:14; Deut 3:20; Josh 1:13, 15; 22:4; Isa 63:14).

The appeal to the LORD not to remain "far off" but to come "from afar" to save is language from the Psalms (e.g., 22:12[Eng 11], 20[Eng 19]; 35:22; 71:12), which is appropriate to the ethos of the Book of Consolation. The LORD's appearing happens at crucial junctures in Exodus (3:16; 24:17), signaling a new stage in Israel's deliverance.

God's love (אהבה) for Israel motivated the election of the people and their deliverance from Egypt, and lovingkindness (חסד) "for a thousand generations" measures the LORD's commitment to the covenant (Deut 7:9). The unique description of the divine love as עולם, "everlasting" moves beyond the conditional promise in Deut 7:9, no longer counting generations or sins. It is the LORD's constant commitment to Israel that bridges the generations and makes restoration possible.

4 The vocabulary of v 4 has numerous intertextual connections. To "build" (בנה) is part of Jeremiah's assignment at his call, "to build and to plant" (1:10). It is also a characteristic description of God's restoration of Israel after the Babylonian conquest (Jer 24:6; 30:18; 31:38; 33:7; 42:10). Since this promise is addressed to "Virgin Israel," other uses of the term may also be appropriate. God "built" (בנה) the woman from part of the man in Gen 2:22. Creation or recreation is part of the larger context (31:22). A woman "built" a family or household by bearing children (Ruth 4:11) and was herself "built" by becoming a mother (Gen 16:2; 30:3). The promise of children to Israel is made explicit in 31:16 and 27.

עדה, "putting on ornaments," is part of a bride's preparation (Isa 61:10; Ezek 16:13) or a seductress's (Jer 4:30; Ezek 23:40; Hos 2:15[Eng 13]). The desolate one, who had vainly tried to attract her lovers (Jer 4:30), now appears as Virgin Israel ready to go up to the LORD. Women playing tambourines, dancing, and singing went out to meet the victors in battle (Exod 15:20; Judg 11:34; 1 Sam 18:6). Worshipers could be merrymakers (Jer 30:17), and dancing to the accompaniment of tambourines could express praise to the LORD (Ps 149:3). This joyous dance reverses the silencing of joy in Jer 7:34; 16:9; 25:10. The future of Virgin Israel (בתולת ישראל) stands in sharp contrast with the tragic death of Jephthah's daughter. She, too, went forth dancing (במחלות) with her tambourines (תופים, Judg 11:34), but, as victim of her father's vow, she could only mourn her virginity (בתוליתיה) on the mountains (Judg 11:37–38; compare Jer 31:5), because she would not be built up by having children of her own.

5 נטע, "plant," is another key word from Jeremiah's call (1:10) that also serves as an image for God's original gift of the land to Israel (2:21; 11:17) and her future restoration to it (18:9; 24:6; 31:28; 32:41; 42:10). Here Israel does the planting. She does not find mature vines, as she had when she first entered the land (Num 13:23; Deut 8:8), but God's blessing is at work. Between planting vineyards and enjoying the fruit extend several seasons of careful tending, as described in Isa 5:2. Furthermore, the technical term חלל, "treat something as common by putting it to ordinary use," refers to the end of a period of ritual abstinence from the produce of new plantings. For fruit trees, the rule in Lev 19:23–25 forbade putting the harvest to ordinary use until the fifth year, after the fourth year's yield had been set apart "for rejoicing in the LORD." In Deuteronomy even holy war does not keep a man from enjoying in due time the fruit of his vinicultural labors (Deut 20:5–6), but the activation of the covenant curses could separate the people from their crops (Deut 28:30). This verse, like Isa 65:21, announces the removal of this futility curse and the gift of a stable, prosperous existence.

6 Guards watched the vineyards to keep marauders from the harvest, but these "watchers" (נצרים) utter the pilgrims' cry. Here is another reversal of judgment. In Jer 4:16 Jerusalem is warned of foreign נצרים, "besiegers," who shout against Judah's cities. Holladay cites 6:4–5 as an example of such a verbal assault (2:184). The guards in 31:6 call for pilgrimage rather than conquest. Ps 122:2 (Eng 1) exemplifies a worshiper's glad response to such an invitation.

Explanation

This poem of restoration recapitulates God's provision for ancient Israel in the wilderness, the settlement of the land, and the choice of Zion as the place of worship in a portrayal of the promised future. This restoration reverses at least six aspects of the judgment suffered by Israel and Judah: no resting place in exile, a nation torn down, celebrations silenced, vines and plants uprooted, watchmen announcing the invading conqueror, and the temple destroyed. The poem also introduces an Israel transformed from a desperate adulteress (4:30) to a joyful maiden on her way back to God. The overwhelming witness of the rest of the book of Jeremiah to the people's rejection of their God raises this question: Why would the LORD choose to start over again with them? This passage answers with the divine declaration "I have loved you with an everlasting love." This love, which preceded covenant making, extends God's covenant חסד, "loyalty," even beyond Israel's covenant breaking into their needy present to guarantee a hopeful future. The poem demonstrates the proper joyful response, "Arise, let us go . . . to the LORD our God."

F. Return from Exile to Enjoy the LORD's Goodness (31:7–14[LXX 38:7–14])

Bibliography

Mendecki, N. "Jer 31,7–9—Berührungen mit der Botschaft Deuterojesajas?" *Collectanea Theologica* 57/Fasc. specialis (1987) 45–55. ———. "Stammt Jer 31,10–14 aus der Schule Deuterojesajas?" In *Beiträge zur Erforschung des Alten Testaments und des antiken Judentums.* Frankfurt am Main: Lang, 1992. 20:57–67.

Translation

[7]*For thus says the LORD:*	
Sing out for Jacob gladly[a]	(3+3)
and shout for the chief of the nations.[b]	
Proclaim, praise, and say,	ʹ (3+3+3)
"O LORD save[c] *your*[d] *people,*	
[e]*the remnant of Israel.*[e]*"*	
[8] *I am about to bring them*	(3+2+2)
from the north country	
and I will gather them from the ends of the earth.	
[a]*Among them will be blind and lame,*[a]	(3+3+4)
[b]*pregnant woman and one giving birth together.*	
As a great company[b] *they shall return here.*[c]	
[9] *Weeping they shall come,*[a]	(2+2)
but with consolations[b] *I will lead them.*	
I will make them walk by rivers of water	(3+5)
in a straight way in which they will not stumble.	
For I have become Israel's father;	(3+3)
Ephraim is my firstborn.	

10	*Hear the word of the LORD, O nations,*	(3+3+1)
	and recount it on the distant coasts,	
	and say, [a]	
	"The one who scattered Israel will gather him	(3+3)
	and will keep him as a shepherd keeps his flock."	
11	*For the LORD has ransomed Jacob*	(3+4)
	and has redeemed him from a hand too strong for him.	
12	*They shall come and sing out* [a] *on the height of Zion,* [a]	(3+3+3+2)
	and they shall be radiant [b] *over the LORD's goodness,*	
	[cd] *over the grain,* [d] *the wine, and the oil,*	
	and over the young of flock and herd. [c]	
	Their life shall be [e] *like a well-watered garden,* [e]	(4+3)
	and they shall not languish anymore.	
13	*Then virgins shall rejoice* [a] *in a dance,*	(4+3)
	and young men [a] *and elders together.* [b]	
	I will turn their mourning into joy;	(3+3)
	[c] *I will comfort them* [c] *and gladden them* [d] *from their sorrows.* [d]	
14	[a] *I will drench the appetite of the priests* [b] *with fatness,* [b]	(4+3)
	and my people shall be satisfied by my goodness	
	—*oracle of the LORD.*	

Notes

7.a. LXX makes Jacob the addressee and omits "gladly": τῷ Ιακωβ Εὐφράνθητε καὶ χρεμετίσατε ἐπὶ κεφαλὴν ἐθνῶν, "to Jacob, 'Rejoice and exult over the head of the nations.'"

7.b. *BHS*, without supporting evidence, suggests emending הגוים, "the nations," to הרים, "hills, mountains."

7.c. LXX ἔσωσεν, "saved," and Tg are past tense. Therefore, *BHS* recommends revocalizing to the pf הושׁע, "saved." The five preceding impvs call for praise and thanksgiving rather than petition. The impv does fit with the following verses as the prayer to which the LORD's promises give an answer.

7.d. *BHS* follows LXX and Tg again, recommending עמו, "his people," as the obj of the pf verb.

7.e-e. *BHS* speculates that this colon is a later addition but offers no evidence. The assonance of ראשׁ, "chief," and שׁארית, "remnant," argues against the proposal.

8.a-a. LXX has ἐν ἑορτῇ φασεκ, "to the Passover feast," which would be from Heb. במועד פסח, differing by only two letters and word division from MT's consonantal text. The proposed emendation fits the context of v 8a. MT, however, is a closer counterpart to the next colon.

8.b-b. LXX condenses this to καὶ τεκνοποιήσῃ, "and they shall beget," and makes "a great crowd" the direct obj.

8.c. *BHS* revocalizes as הנה, "behold," and connects it to the beginning of v 9. This change would balance the length of each member of the tricolon, but it would deprive this verse of any indication of the destination of the returnees.

9.a. LXX ἐξῆλθον, "went forth," implies a Heb. original יצאו. Having gone out (into exile) weeping, their return is "with consolations," in a nice poetic reversal. MT is more difficult and should be retained.

9.b. LXX ἐν παρακλήσει = ובתנחונים, "with consolations," as in Jer 16:7. MT follows 3:21, ובתחנונים, "with supplications." The two Heb. words differ only in the reversal of two consonants.

10.a. Rudolph (178) and *BHS* would omit this verb as an addition superfluous to the meaning and the meter, but there is no evidence to support the change.

12.a-a. *BHS* recommends emending במרום, "on the height," to בהרים, "on the mountains," and deleting "of Zion," which Rudolph labels a "Judean correction" (179). LXX uses the more familiar designation, ἐν τῷ ὄρει Σιων, "in the mount of Zion" (similarly, Vg).

12.b. The verb may mean "flow like a river" or "be radiant." LXX translates prosaically καὶ ἥξουσιν, "and they shall come."

12.c-c. Holladay, following Volz, omits this list as a "prosaic gloss" (2:153).

12.d-d. LXX has ἐπὶ γῆν σίτου, "to a land of grain," which modifies ἥξουσιν, "they shall come," in the preceding line.

12.e-e. LXX has a different image: ὥσπερ ξύλον ἔγκαρπον, "like a fruitful tree."

13.a-a. LXX ἐν συναγωγῇ νεανίσκων, "in the assembly of youth," parallels v 4b, μετὰ συναγωγῆς παιζόντων, "in the company of merrymakers." MT parallels v 4b in MT.

13.b. LXX χαρήσονται, "they shall rejoice," translates a different vocalization of the same consonants, יְחְדּוּ (< חֶדְהּ), "they shall be merry."

13.c-c. Not in LXX. MT may be conflate (Holladay, 2:153).

13.d-d. Not in LXX.

14.a. LXX has μεγαλυνῶ, "I will enlarge," at the beginning. An original רביתי, "I will enlarge," could have dropped out of MT because of similarity to the next verb, רויתי, "drench."

14.b-b. LXX has υἱῶν Λευι, "the sons of Levi," instead of "with fatness," which does not fit with the verb in LXX, μεθύσω, "cheer with wine."

Form/Structure/Setting

The messenger formula that introduces this section varies slightly from the others in 30:5, 18; 31:2, 15, for it begins with the conjunction כִּי, "for." There is a particularly close connection between the pilgrim call of the watchers in 31:6, "Arise, let us go up to Zion," and the promises that the LORD will bring the exiles back to Zion (31:12) from the ends of the earth (31:8). The preceding unit, 31:2–6, portrays the people established in the land, so this composition, 31:7–14, describes how they will get there. The conjunction כִּי, "for," suits this logical connection.

This salvation oracle is divided into four parts. The first (v 7) and third (vv 10–11) parts give commands to speak. The first speech asks for salvation from the LORD, and the next one announces its coming. The summons to praise in v 7 is at home in the context of worship, but "proclaim" and "say" are commands like those given to watchmen or messengers. As in Jer 4:5; 5:20; Amos 3:9, they have no specified addressee. They are directed by implication to the reader of the Book of Consolation. V 10 calls on the nations to hear and then "recount" (נגד hiphil) and "say" (אמר) to the distant coastlands a message (vv 10b–11), which reports how God (third person) has saved Israel (third person).

The second (vv 8–9) and fourth (vv 12–14) parts have the LORD, speaking in the first person, promising to regather Israel (third person plural) and provide for them a joyful and bountiful life. The alternating pattern of masculine and feminine figures for God's people continues here with v 9. The LORD calls Ephraim בכרי, "my firstborn." This identification forms a link with the following unit, 31:15–22, in which God calls Ephraim "my precious son" and "my darling child" (v 20). The safe travel promised to women who are pregnant or giving birth (v 8) contrasts with the memory of Rachel (v 15), who died in childbirth while on a similar journey from Mesopotamia to the sworn land (Gen 35:16–19). The promise to Rachel in 31:16–17 summarizes 31:7–14, "your children shall come back."

Comment

7 The petition, "Save, O LORD," fits the lament genre, not the thanksgiving or hymns commanded by the imperatives "proclaim" and "praise." Yet the implied audience of the Book of Consolation remains in a situation in which lament is the appropriate form for prayer (see 30:12–17). The designation "remnant of Israel" encapsulates past suffering and current need. Indeed, the people will continue to weep on their way home from exile, according to v 8. The verb רנן, "sing out," refers to desperate cries of need in Lam 2:19, and Jer 5:8; 13:27 use צהל, "shout," for the neighing of a horse. There is no ethereal sacred music in these words. The painful tension between Israel "the chief of the nations" and Israel the "remnant" will only be resolved by the fulfillment of God's promises in the verses that follow. Israel is the "chief" only because of God's choice (Deut 7:7–8; 32:8–9).

8 B. Bozak calls attention to the step pattern in the first four words, making up the initial colon (*Life 'Anew'*, 83). Each successive word begins with the consonant that ended the previous word. In order to articulate each word fully, the reader must slow down and pause between each one. This effect serves to underscore the basic promise of this unit (cf. 30:10; 31:17).

The invading army, a "great nation" (גוי גדול), comes from the north and the ends of the earth, according to Jer 6:22. (The terms are identical to the words in v 8.) The exiles will return, however, as a "great company" (קהל גדול), not as a military force. Their company includes even the most vulnerable travelers, the persons needing the most assistance on the journey, who could never serve in any army. The blind and lame are not able to fight because they need help even to walk (cf. 2 Sam 5:5, 8). In Jer 30:6, and elsewhere, the suffering of a woman in labor serves as a simile for a warrior incapacitated by terror. These points of contrast with 6:22 underscore the returnees' utter dependence on the LORD. They cannot return home on their own strength. (1 Esdr 5:2; 8:61 give some hint of the dangers returning exiles encountered along the way.)

Blind and lame priests were excluded from service (Lev 21:18), and postpartum women were ceremonially unclean (Lev 12:1–8). They are unlikely pilgrims to Zion (v 12). Mothers would be essential for repopulating the land, but the LORD's mercy and faithfulness are surely demonstrated by the inclusion of the blind and lame in the acts of redemption and guidance. If even these will be brought back, then certainly everyone can be included. Other passages promise healing for the blind and lame when they reach Zion (e.g., Isa 35:5–6), but this verse does not.

9 In the context of the Book of Consolation, returning exiles would weep because they repent (31:18–19). The identification of Israel as God's son, Ephraim, in v 9c suggests a connection with Ephraim's prayer of repentance in vv 18–19. Although divine consolations accompany them on their journey, joy and gladness will replace sorrow only when they reach their destination (v 13).

The LORD's provisions for the journey in the second bicolon function poetically in several ways. It is a realistic description of how travelers, especially those listed in v 8, should be cared for on a long trip, with good roads and ample supplies. This promise calls to mind how God preserved Israel in the wilderness (Exod 17:1–7; Isa 48:21) and the divine provisions for Zion-bound pilgrims (Pss 23; 84:5–7). If weeping indicates repentance, then the "straight path" must be understood figuratively as well as concretely. The faithful walk in the LORD's דרך, "way," which is ישר, "straight" (Hos 14:10[Eng 9]), and do not כשל, "stumble," as sinners do (Hos 14:10; Jer 6:15; 8:12; 20:11).

The reason for this careful tending is God's special relationship with Israel, who is בכרי, "my firstborn" (v 9) and ראש הגוים, "chief of the nations" (v 7). The language of v 9c points to adoption, a kinship by choice, as the LORD promised to adopt David's son (2 Sam 7:14) and as Jacob put Ephraim ahead of his older brother Manasseh when he took them as his own (Gen 48:5, 14, 17–20). The syntax of v 9c resembles that of the covenant formula (e.g., 31:1). The naming of Israel as the LORD's בכרי, "firstborn," in Exod 4:22 sets the tone for the contest with Pharaoh, making clear what was at stake from God's perspective. Israel, in turn, ought to respond faithfully to God as their "father" (Deut 32:6; Jer 3:19). The family relationship serves as the foundation for "redemption" (גאל, v 11), "ransom" (פדה, v 11), and "motherly love" (רחם, v 20).

10   A nation had come from "the distant coastlands" to conquer Zion (6:22). Now the nations are assigned the task of announcing in the conquerors' home territory that the LORD has delivered Israel from them. God, and not the victorious enemy, was "the one who had scattered Israel." Part of Israel's suffering was her shame in the sight of the nations, as in Jer 30:17. Their derisive comment, "no one cares for her," is to be replaced by an acknowledgment of the Good Shepherd's guardianship. God's promises in v 9b are the actions of a shepherd on behalf of the flock (compare Ps 23:2–3).

11   V 11 offers an explanation, introduced by כי, "for," by using the only perfect-aspect verbs in the unit. Persons who had been sold as slaves (Exod 21:8; Lev 19:20) or the first-born sons who were consecrated to the LORD could be ransomed (פדה) by a prescribed payment or substitute (Exod 34:20; Lev 27:27; Num 3:46–51; 18:15–17). According to Exod 13:14–16, ransom of the firstborn (בכור) of human families serves as a sign that בְּחֹזֶק יָד, "by strength of hand" (compare מִיַּד חָזָק מִמֶּנּוּ, "a hand too strong for him"), the LORD had brought Israel out of Egypt. "Ransom" is a typical term in Deuteronomy for the deliverance of Israel from slavery in Egypt (Deut 7:8; 9:26; 13:6[Eng 5]; 15:15; 21:8; 24:18). It occurs only one other time in Jeremiah, in 15:21. גאל, "redeem," is a legal term for a person's obligation to buy back family land that a close relative had sold to pay debts (Lev 25:25; Jer 32:7, 8). But Exod 6:6; 15:15 use the same verb to describe how the LORD rescued Israel from Egypt. Isaiah also applies it to the exodus from captivity in Babylon (43:1; 44:22, 23; 48:20) and calls God "Redeemer" (59:20). Jacob may be "chief of the nations" by virture of election, but he remains the weaker party under the domination of the prevailing world empire until the LORD ransoms and redeems him. Isa 35:8–10 also describes the protected pilgrimage of the redeemed and ransomed ones to Zion.

12–14   The LORD will prepare a great banquet for the redeemed who are brought back to Zion. The description in these three verses alternates between rejoicing (vv 12a, 13) and feasting (vv 12b–c, 14) and shares many details with other portrayals of pilgrimage feasts at the temple (e.g., Ps 84) and the eschatological banquet (e.g., Isa 25:6–10). This text must be read against the background of sorrow and starvation expressed in Lamentations (e.g., 2:19–20; 4:10; 5:9, 15). The remnant of Israel had seen pilgrimage cease (Lam 1:4; Jer 41:4–8).

Shouting, as commanded in v 7, and radiant, like the one in Ps 34:6(Eng 5) who has been saved, God's people will join the festivities on Mount Zion. Maidens, strong young men, and the elders will join together in the dance (cf. 31:4). (Are adult women excluded by custom, or because Rachel is weeping in v 15?)

Jer 6:26 had called for mourning (אבל, as here) when the enemy approaching from the north was announced (6:22), so this promise is a reversal of the earlier judgment oracle. Mourning someone's death was not just an emotion; it involved customary or ritual behavior over a specific period of time (e.g., Gen 27:41; 50:10–11; Deut 34:8; Esth 4:3; Ezek 24:17). Jeremiah had been told to withdraw from such observances as a sign-act to demonstrate the horror of the time of conquest when the dead would not even be buried or lamented (16:1–9). The physical signs of mourning will be set aside by God and replaced by manifestations of joy such as the dance at the beginning of v 13 (cf. Ps 30:12[Eng 11]). God's comforting will enable those who sorrow over Israel's death-ridden condition to be glad again. The prophet and even God had experienced such sorrow (Jer 20:18; 8:18).

Food and water in bountiful quantities complete the picture. The foodstuffs listed in v 12b include basic necessities of life (Hos 2:8[Eng 10]) or the menu for worshipers' feasts within the temple precincts. God had promised to bless the production of grain, wine, oil, herds, and flocks when they first entered the land, if Israel would be diligently obedient (Deut 7:12–14). The priests will not eat or drink the fatty ashes of the sacrifices (דשׁן; cf. Lev 1:16), but an abundance of ashes is evidence of an abundance of sacrifices, from which the priests will receive their provisions (Lev 7:28–36). The water in the temple complex (Ps 46:5[Eng 4]; cf. Ezek 47:1–12) helped to make it like the garden of Eden, out of which four rivers flowed (Gen 2:10–14). This allusion to Eden in v 12c expands the bounty of the promise to include the blessing of God's presence. At the temple one might see the טוב, "goodness," of the LORD (Ps 27:4; cf. Pss 36:7–9; 63:2–5 [Eng 1–4]). M. Smith calls the experience of feasting and seeing the LORD in the temple "paradise regained" ("The Psalms as a Book for Pilgrims," *Int* 46/2 [April 1992] 161).

The final colon in v 12 returns to the people's needy condition. God promises that they will no longer faint from hunger or weaken from malnutrition (דאבה, "languish," from a rare root appearing only five times in the OT), reversing a covenant curse from Deut 28:65 (דאבון, "languishing"). The composition concludes with a summary promise, "my people will be satisfied by my goodness." Physical satiety will come from the bounty (טוב) of food and drink (v 12), and spiritual fulfillment will come from the goodness (טוב; see Exod 33:19) of the LORD's presence.

Explanation

By God's grace, the route of the enemy advance will become the road for the exiles' return, and their path will merge with the pilgrim "highways to Zion" (Ps 84:5, NRSV). No one will be left behind or fall by the wayside because of physical disability. God, as father, will bring home his firstborn son, ransomed and redeemed as he once had been from Egypt. Even the nations that despise the people of Israel in their weakness will have to broadcast the news that the LORD has saved them and will lead them safely back. Their period of mourning will be brought to an end by their encounter with the LORD's goodness. While feasting on the abundance of Zion and drinking from the river of divine "delights" (Ps 36:9–10 [Eng 8–9]), the people of Israel will know God as father, shepherd, redeemer, and king. They will experience the joyful abundant life of the eschatological banquet (cf. Isa 25:6–10). In the meantime, God's people can say in the words of the psalm (Ps 27:13–14, tr. P. Craigie, *Psalms 1–50*, WBC 19 [Dallas: Word, 1991] 229):

> I believe that I will see the goodness of the LORD
>   in the land of the living.
> Wait for the LORD! Be strong,
>   and let your heart be bold.
> Yes, wait for the LORD!

G. Rachel's Repentant Children Invited to Return (31:15–22[LXX 38:15–22])

Bibliography

Anderson, B. "The LORD Has Created Something New: A Stylistic Study of Jeremiah 31:15–22." *CBQ* 40 (1978) 463–77 (Repr. in *A Prophet to the Nations*, ed. L. Perdue and B. Kovacs. Winona Lake: Eisenbrauns, 1984. 367–80). **Dresner, S.** *Rachel.* Minneapolis: Fortress, 1994. **Holladay, W.** "Jer. xxxi 22b Reconsidered: 'The Woman Encompasses the Man.'" *VT* 16 (1966) 236–39. **Trible, P.** "Journey of a Metaphor." In *God and the Rhetoric of Sexuality*. Philadelphia: Fortress, 1978. 31–59.

Translation

¹⁵*Thus says the LORD:*
A voice is heard in Ramah,[a] *wailing,*   (4+2)
    bitter weeping,
Rachel, weeping for her children,   (3+2+4)
    refusing to be comforted
    concerning her children, for[b]*they are not.*[b]
¹⁶*Thus says the LORD:*
Hold back your [f sg] voice from weeping   (3+2)
    and your eyes from tears,
for there is reward for your work: (4+2+3)
            [a] *oracle of the LORD*[a]—
    they shall return from enemy territory.
17   [a]*And there is hope for your posterity:*   (2+2+3)
            oracle of the LORD[a]—
    [b]*offspring shall return to their borders.*[b]

¹⁸ *I have surely heard*   (2+2)
   Ephraim swaying with sorrow.
   "You have disciplined me, and I have been disciplined   (2+3)
    like an untrained calf.
   Return me so^a *I can return*   (2+4)
    because you are the LORD my God.

¹⁹ *For after I turned away*^a   (3+1)
   I repented,
   and after I came to know   (2+2)
    ^b*I slapped my thigh.*
   I was ashamed and even humiliated,   (2+4)
    for^b *I bore the disgrace of my youth."*

²⁰ *Is*^a *Ephraim my precious son,*   (4+3)
    ^b*my darling child?*
   For as often as I speak^c *of him*   (3+3)
   I surely remember him again.
   Therefore my inmost being^d *stirs for him;*   (4+2+2)
   I surely have compassion for him
         —*oracle of the LORD.*

²¹ ^a*Erect markers for yourself [f sg],*^a   (3+3)
   set up signposts^b *for yourself;*
   pay attention to the highway,^c   (3+2)
    ^d*the road you walked.*^d
   Return, Virgin Israel,   (3+3)
   return to these^e *cities of yours.*

²² *How long will you turn this way and that,*^a   (3+2)
   O daughter who turns^b *away?*
For the LORD has created^c*something new in the land:* ^d*Female encircles he-man.*^{cd}

Notes

15.a. *BHS* suggests revocalizing to include the definite article, as in Josh 18:25. LXX and Syr translate the place name. Vg and Tg have the common noun.

15.b-b. MT is sg, and the ancient versions have the pl, so *BHS* proposes an emendation. Trible translates the clause as a speech beginning with emphatic כִּי, "Oh, not one here!" ("Journey," 40).

16.a-a. Not in LXX (cf. 17.a-a.).

17.a-a. Not in LXX, which connects v 17b to v 16.

17.b-b. LXX is elliptical, μόνιμον τοῖς σοῖς τέκνοις, "[There shall be] a lasting (place) for your children."

18.a. Reading וְאָשׁוּבָה as coh dependent clause of purpose; see Waltke and O'Connor, *Hebrew Syntax*, 575.

19.a. LXX has αἰχμαλωσίας, "my captivity," so Rudolph (178), Holladay (2:153), and *BHS* emend to שִׁבְיִי, "my captivity," and add שַׁבְתִּי (< שׁוּב), "again." MT can stand, but it does not account for LXX.

19.b-b. LXX, ἐστέναξα ἐφ᾽ ἡμέρας αἰσχύνης καὶ ὑπέδειξά σοι, "I groaned for the day of shame, and showed you," is a paraphrase of MT, unlike Syr "I found rest."

20.a. No interrogative in LXX, Syr.

20.b. No interrogative in LXX, Syr.

20.c. *BHS* would emend to הַנָּכְרִי, "I estrange myself against him." The sense of rejection can come from the prep בְּ in MT, "against" (RSV) without emendation, "speak against him."

20.d. The מֵעַי, "internal organs, belly, viscera," used for the organs of digestion or generation. Figuratively, the seat of emotions.

21.a-a. LXX Στῆσον σεαυτήν, Σιων, "set yourself, O Zion," perhaps a misreading of the the rare Heb. noun צִיֻּנִים, "markers." The sg noun has the same consonants as "Zion."

21.b. *BHS* suggests emending to an otherwise unknown noun, תִּימֹרִים, on the basis of the apparent transliteration in LXX, τιμωρίαν. The Heb. word would mean "columns, signposts," like the noun תִּימֹרָה, "palm-like column" (< תֹּמֶר). This would be the second of three words in vv 20–22 that also occur in Cant 3, a pattern that lends support to the emendation. MT may have been influenced by 31:15, תַּמְרוּרִים, "bitterness." LXX may be understood as "vengeance, punishment."

21.c. LXX εἰς τοὺς ὤμους, reading οἴμους, "to the path."

21.d-d. LXX subordinates this phrase to the following verb. K is an archaic 2 f sg, as in 2:20.

21.e. The demonstrative adj אֵלֶּה, "these," lacks the expected definite article, and LXX has πενθοῦσα, "mourning," corresponding to Heb. אֲבֵלָה (so *BHS*) or אֵל הָ (Holladay, 2:193). Holladay is dissatisfied with the demonstrative because it "adds nothing" and rejects the reading "mourning" because it does not fit the context (2:193). He suggests בְּעֻלָה, "with mastery," in part on the basis of the semantic association and assonance of the the the pair בְּעוּלָה, "married woman," and בְּתוּלָה, "virgin," in the preceding colon. The proposal is clever but would eliminate mention of the returnees' destination (compare 31:8).

22.a. Unique occurrence of hithp of חמק, "turn away from side to side, waver."

22.b. *BHS* suggests a vowel change that does not alter the meaning of the word.

22.c-c. LXX σωτηρίαν εἰς κατα φύτευσιν καινήν, ἐν σωτηρίᾳ περιελεύσονται ἄνθρωποι, "safety for new plantings; men shall walk about in safety."

22.d-d. *BHS*'s emendation seeks to interpret the cryptic sentence as "the cursed one is changed into a lady."

Form/Structure/Setting

A messenger formula marks the beginning of this poem as it did in the preceding pericope. The extended messenger formula in v 23 begins the next main redactional unit, but "thus says the LORD" in v 16 functions within the composition to introduce the LORD's speech to Rachel. Although three separate representative figures appear in the poem, Rachel, Ephraim, and Virgin Israel, and the speaker alternates between God, Ephraim, and the prophet, this composition is held together by a "plot" of sorts and by repetition of key words. For example, the root שׁוב, "turn," occurs in every verse except vv 15 and 20, for a total of nine times in eight verses. "Children" (בנים / בניה) in vv 15–17 are present as בֵן, "son," in v 20 and as בת, "daughter," in v 22. תַּמְרוּרִים, "bitterness" (v 15), appears again with the meaning "signposts" in v 21. The beginning, "a voice is heard . . . crying" (v 15), and end, "return . . . daughter who turns away" (v 21), correspond to the beginning and end of the short poem in 3:21–22a. (Several connections between chap. 31 and chap. 3 are cited in the *Comment* on 31:15–22.) Bright (275–76), Anderson (*CBQ* 40 [1978] 468), Trible ("Journey," 40–50), Bozak (*Life 'Anew'*, 92–105), and Brueggemann (64–65) all treat 31:15–22 as a compositional unit.

The unit consists of three parts, each with a different speaker or addressee. A brief judgment portrayal, in v 15, serves as a narrative introduction, similar to 31:2–3a, that identifies the addressee of the LORD's speech in vv 16–17. Rachel is the female ancestor of Israel who corresponds to Jacob in 30:10. She was the grandmother of Ephraim, who stands for the nation in this chapter (31:9, 18–20). Her mourning returns the reader to the setting of the implied audience of the Book of Consolation, who are not yet enjoying the eschatological pilgrim banquet of vv 12–14. A messenger formula marks the beginning of God's words of comfort to Rachel. This salvation oracle, vv 16–17, is punctuated by two oracle formulas, "oracle of the LORD."

The LORD's speech continues in v 18 in a report about Ephraim's repentance. The content has shifted from the ancient mother, mourning the loss of her children, to the children, personified in Ephraim. The report describes Ephraim's posture of remorse, quotes his prayer of repentance, and vividly portrays God's determination to show mercy.

The third and final section gives God's answer to the people's prayer to be brought home but addresses it to "Virgin Israel," the "daughter who turns away." At the end, in v 22b, is a mysterious prose comment in the form of a salvation oracle. In it, the LORD is referred to in the third person. (Cf. the reflective prose comments in 30:21bβ–22; 24bβ–31:1.) The announced salvation is expressed in the terse style of a proverb.

This composition completes the reverse chronology found in 31:2–22. The first section, 31:2–6, portrays Israel settled into life in the land and enjoying its fruits. The next unit, 31:7–14, describes the return from exile to Zion, and this poem, 31:15–22, shows the land empty of its people, whom God invites to begin their journey home. The invitation fulfills the promise made to Jacob in 30:10 and to Rachel in 31:16–17.

Feminine singular addressees dominate this composition (31:15–17, 21–22) and continue the alternating pattern in the preceding five redactional units. Within this poem, gender alternates feminine-masculine-feminine among the three representative figures, Rachel (vv 15–17), Ephraim (vv 18–20), and Virgin Israel (vv 21–22).

Comment

15 Ramah in Benjamin is named in Jer 40:1 as a stopping-off point for the captives from Judah and Jerusalem on their way to exile in Babylon. It is an appropriate site at which to picture Rachel mourning for her offspring because they have been killed or carried off. Both the NT (Matt 2:18) and Jewish tradition (e.g., *Zohar* 2.29b, cited by Dresner, *Rachel,* 152) see Rachel weeping for subsequent generations of Israelites who are killed or banished. Holladay presents two arguments against reading בְּרָמָה as the place name, "in Ramah" (2:186–87): (1) The proper name "Ramah" usually takes the definite article, but there is no article here in MT. (2) Neither of the references to Rachel's burial place, Gen 35:19–20; 1 Sam 10:2, locates her tomb at Ramah, although the latter verse does place it in the territory of Benjamin. It does not matter, however, where she was buried. Rachel's weeping does not have to be placed at her gravesite unless one is bound by a presupposition that 31:15 describes a "haunting" by Rachel's ghost. The common noun רמה, "height," appears only as a technical term for the site of illicit worship (Ezek 16:25, 31, 39; 1 Sam 22:6), not as a generic word for a hill.

Rachel's life story sets her apart from the other Israelite ancestors. She alone had only a grave and never a home in the promised land (Jer 30:3). She died "on the way" (Gen 35:19), and her last words express her sorrow (Gen 35:18). Not every mother will give up her own life for her child's (e.g., Jer 19:9; Lam 2:20; 4:10; 2 Kgs 6:28–29). Rachel's death in childbirth makes her deeply credible as an example of the profound extent of a mother's love. Rachel is a mother who does not forget her children (cf. Isa 49:15).

16–17 The LORD's comfort for Rachel represents a fulfillment of the promise in 31:13, "I will turn their mourning into joy." Since Rachel mourns in v 15 for her missing children (בניה), the answering promise has to do with the return of "children" or "offspring" (בנים) from the enemy's land to their own. This return is called a reward or payment for her פְּעֻלָּה, "work." The same word is used for God's deeds on behalf of Israel's salvation (Ps 28:5) and a laborer's work (Jer 22:13) or wages (Lev 19:13). Rachel's most recent work has been as a mourner, a job done by women in ancient Israel (Jer 9:16[Eng 17]). Rudolph (188) says that Rachel's work was rearing children, but she did not live to see her sons Joseph and Benjamin mature. (This word is not used in the OT for the labor of childbirth.) The "reward" or "payment" is שָׂכָר, a key word in Gen 30. Leah "hired" (שׂכר) Jacob for a night by giving Rachel some mandrakes in return. Leah described Issachar, her next son, as her שְׂכָר, "payment," from God (Gen 30:18) for giving her maid to Jacob as a secondary wife (30:9–11). Jacob himself received livestock as his "wages" from Laban (Gen 30:25–43). In Gen 30, Rachel received only mandrakes, which did not heal her barrenness. The use of שָׂכָר, "reward," in this promise suggests that children are the "reward" or "wages" she did not receive in Gen 30:14–21. Within this context אַחֲרִית, "what comes after, future," means specifically "posterity." Rachel's descendants have hope because of the LORD's promise given in response to her mourning.

18–20 The verbal construction, infinite absolute plus perfect, occurs once in v 18a and twice in v 20b–c, in the LORD's speech that frames Ephraim's prayer. Both syntax and diction emphasize the intensity of the LORD's response. The three verbs שמע, "hear," זכר, "remember," and רחם, "have mercy," appear in prayers for divine salvation (e.g., Pss 27:7; 64:2; 106:45; Jer 14:21; 18:20; Hab 3:2), but these customary terms are absent from Ephraim's prayer of repentance. God's answer exceeds the request and puts it in its proper context.

Rhetorical questions without לא, "not," can have a positive sense (cf. Gen 27:36), and the context of this poem (and 31:9) calls for answers in the affirmative. The two modifiers are unique in Jeremiah. שעשעים, "darling," describes the people of Judah in Isa 5:7 and personified wisdom in Prov 8:31 as objects of God's devoted care. Divine speech about Israel in this book is neither neutral nor indifferent, and translators disagree regarding whether the prepositional phrase בו should be rendered "against him" or "about him." Holladay's decision to retain both meanings is most attractive (2:191–92). To be spoken of by God, whether for good or ill, is to be preferred over silence (cf. Amos 8:12).

The LORD's actions in this verse are motivated by powerful emotions expressed in metaphors derived from women's bodies and experiences. מעי, "my inward parts," and the verb המה, "stir," with "heart" as its subject appear in Jer 4:19 to communicate the distress felt by Jeremiah (and by God). The expression in 31:20 is repeated only two other times in the OT, in Isa 16:11 and Cant 5:4. In the latter verse, the woman gives her reaction to seeing her lover's hand thrust into the opening in her door. The "inward parts" may be the internal organs in general, but several times the word refers specifically to the generative organs of the male (Gen 15:4; 2 Sam 7:12) or female (e.g., Gen 25:23; Ruth 1:11; Ps 71:6; Isa 49:1). The verb רָחַם, "have compassion," comes from the same root as the noun רֶחֶם, "womb." On the basis of these two allusions to the womb, and other evidence,

Trible hears the voice of God speaking as mother in v 20 ("Journey," 45). In the context of this poem, a mother's devotion to her children points to the nature of God's everlasting love (31:3) for Israel. Hos 11:8–9 uses similarly vivid anthropomorphic language. Both women and men can understand these metaphors because of their own experiences within families.

Ephraim describes himself as "an untrained calf," a reversal of the metaphor "a trained heifer" in Hos 10:11. He had not learned to serve under the yoke of divine sovereignty (cf. 2:20; 5:5). Throughout the book of Jeremiah, Israel is accused of rebellion and rejection of the LORD's word through the prophets with the charge that they did not לקח מוסר, "accept correction" (2:30; 5:3; 7:28; 17:23; 32:33). In the Book of Consolation, the punishment suffered by Israel at the hands of her enemies is God's just "discipline" (יסר or מוסר) for their sin (30:11, 14). Ephraim has accepted this correction. By means of the formula in v 18ba, he acknowledges his guilt and the effectiveness of the LORD's punishment, and in v 18cβ, he submits to the LORD of the covenant (compare 3:22b).

The two expressions of submission surround the only request in this prayer, "Return [שׁוב] me so I can return [שׁוב]." The LORD's initiative will make Ephraim's action possible. Confession continues in v 19. A few brief lines set forth the course from apostasy to contrition: turning away, remorse, recognition, humiliation, and disgrace. Not knowing (ידע) is a charge brought against Israel in Jer 4:22 and several times in Hosea (e.g., 4:1), but Ephraim has come to know (ידע) in the midst of his remorse. (Compare the prodigal son in Luke 15:11–32.) Slapping the thigh (ספקתי על־ירך) is an onomatopoeic expression found only one other place in the OT, in Ezek 21:17, where it is also a gesture of sorrow. "I was humiliated" (כלם) follows in the next colon. Together, the two cola form a contrast with 3:3, which charges the people with not being humiliated (כלם) and with displaying "the forehead of a whore" (NRSV). Body language expresses a spiritual or emotional condition. The mention of נעורי, "youth," is not an excuse for sin but a confession of how long ago Ephraim had turned away from the LORD (cf. 3:24–25).

21–22 The LORD answers Ephraim's prayer with a call to return (שׁוב). The road once taken, interpreted metaphorically, could be the ancient path, "the good way" (Jer 6:16) or the "highway" (סלולה, 18:15) where they had found peace with God. Concretely, it is the route taken into exile, which becomes the pilgrim highway back to the land and to Zion (cf. 31:7–14). "Straight way" in 31:9 had the same potential for double meaning (see the *Comment*). Israel must decide to stop turning from side to side and take up the challenge of marking the way with stone monuments and signposts. The LORD invites, even pleads, but does not capture or coerce. The תמרורים, "bitterness," of Rachel's weeping (v 15) appears as תמרורים, "signposts," erected by Virgin Israel, and the ציּנים, "markers," can indicate the position of graves as well as highways (e.g., 2 Kgs 23:17).

The answer to Ephraim's prayer is addressed to Virgin Israel. As in 31:2–6, where "Virgin Israel" first appears, there is no mention of Israel's previous identification as a faithless wife (cf. 3:1–2, 20). Yet the numerous allusions to chap. 3 in this unit (noted in the *Comment*) serve as cross references that tie the two passages together and reveal the LORD's grace. "Daughter who turns away [השׁובבה]," v 22, establishes continuity with "faithless [שׁובבים] children" in 3:14, but "faithless [מְשֻׁבָה] Israel," who committed adultery under every tree (3:12–13), has been transformed into Virgin Israel.

The salvation oracle in v 22b offers a reason for Israel as "daughter" to stop vacillating and return to the LORD and to the land. (Note the conjunction כִּי, "for.") The "new thing" created by God should be understood as something attractive and reassuring to the people in the guise of Virgin Israel. Although consensus on the meaning of this enigmatic saying is unlikely, its context puts boundaries around the range of possibilities.

The verb בּרא, "create," is used only once in Jeremiah. The LORD is its only subject in the OT. It is used most often for the first creation, as in Genesis, and for recreation or new creation in eschatological contexts. Isa 65:17–18 promises, "I am about to create a new heaven and a new earth [אָרֶץ חֲדָשָׁה]" and "Jerusalem as a joy and her people a delight." The rest of the oracle promises no more weeping, long life for all, successful pregnancies, and the enjoyment of houses and crops. This content is similar to the promises in Jer 31. Num 16:30, "If the LORD creates a new creation [בְּרִיאָה, hap. leg.]," refers to a divine act of judgment in contrast to natural death. In Exod 34:10 the LORD promises to "create" marvels for Israel that will set them apart from all other nations. Thus, there is a broad range of possible objects for בּרא, "create." The promised "new thing" will be בָּאָרֶץ, "in the land," a word that points back to the introduction in 30:3. The Book of Consolation is about the restoration by God of Israel and Judah to the land once given to their ancestors.

The three-word saying at the end of v 22 also uses vocabulary not found elsewhere in the Book of Consolation. Three relatively rare words appear in a unique collocation. נְקֵבָה, "female," is a legal category used of both humans and animals. Every use with respect to humans is paired with זָכָר, "male," except Num 31:5 (female captives in war) and Jer 31:22. נְקֵבָה, "female," is never the subject of an active verb except in this verse in Jeremiah. It is an anonymous designation for a category. Only in this verse does an individual representative emerge from the category and act, yet she remains anonymous. "Female" is the object of "create" in Gen 1:27 (and 5:2) and the recipient of blessing and command in 1:28. Together, female and male human beings are to reproduce and rule the earth (הָאָרֶץ). "Female will encircle he-man" is more likely about giving birth than about finding a husband, since being without a husband is not a problem raised in chaps. 30–31. (Compare Carroll, 602.) The blessing that enables offspring to be born and survive to adulthood (גֶּבֶר, "he-man") comes only from God (P. Scalise, "'I Have Produced a Man with the LORD': God as Provider of Offspring in Old Testament Theology," *RevExp* 91 [1994] 581–86). A noun referring to an adult is not out of place in an OT "birth announcement." Compare Gen 4:1, אִישׁ, "man," and Job 3:3, גֶּבֶר, "he-man." Within the context of this poem, the salvation oracle promises the renewal of fertility, the return of sons to their mothers' arms.

The verb סבב may mean "surround" in the sense of "protect," as in Deut 32:10; Ps 32:10. The promise would transform the situation of defeat in Jer 30:6, where warriors act like women in labor because they are too terrified to fight. Calvin understands v 22b as an announcement that Israel's forces, who had been like women in 30:6, will be stronger than their enemies (4:114–15). Holladay accepts this interpretation plus one other, which he considers to be more important

(2:195): in the future that God will create, the female will assume the initiative and dominance that had been the male role. (Compare the woman אֹסוֹבְבָה, "going around," the city, searching for her lover, in Cant 3:2.) Thompson calls her "something of an Amazon" (576). Carroll also sees in this colon an inclusio with 30:6 but reads it as a removal of the curse "warriors shall become women" rather than a reversal of roles. The "new" thing is that women will return to their roles as mothers and will give birth to more warriors (602–3). Bozak (*Life 'Anew'*, 104), too, finds the reversal of a curse, but she points to Gen 3:16, "your husband shall rule over you." Such a reversal and transformation would mean that there will be no more wives, like Leah, who desire their husbands but are not loved by them (Gen 30:15–16).

Wordplay connects the current situation, represented by the daughter הַשּׁוֹבֵבָה, "who turns away," and the new thing created by God, a female who תְּסוֹבֵב, "encircles." The pun suggests that the "female" corresponds to the "daughter," who is Virgin Israel, and that this salvation oracle announces the reversal of her situation of need. God creates for Virgin Israel the capacity to stop vacillating and return to God. The people will "assemble around" (סבב) God in worship (cf. Ps 26:6). גבר, "he–man," would refer to God in this reading. Comparable titles for God are אִישׁ מלחמה, "man of war," Exod 15:3, and הגבור, "the valiant One," Jer 32:18. The advantage of this interpretation is its compatibility with the new covenant (ברית חדשה) promised in 31:31–34 (E. Martens, *Jeremiah*, Believers Church Bible Commentary [Scottdale, PA: Herald Press, 1986] 194). God's new work makes possible the spiritual return (31:22) and continuing faithfulness (31:34) of Israel.

Within chap. 31 Virgin Israel also needs to be rebuilt (בנה), v 4, both in terms of houses, walls, and terraced fields, and in terms of children (cf. בנה, "build, have children," in Gen 30:3). The LORD has promised to build her (v 4) and to restore Rachel's children (v 15).

The enigmatic saying at the end of v 22 need not be made to bear the weight of summarizing the entire Book of Consolation. If the pun in v 22 is the key to interpreting the saying within its context, then its meaning has to do with Virgin Israel's most important problems, namely, her estrangement from God and her childlessness. In this chapter she is promised spiritual and geographical return to the LORD and the blessing of offspring. These two promises are "something new" because, in the world of Israel's experience, a husband cannot remarry his adulterous wife (3:1–2) and mothers and fathers do not always see their children grow to maturity (31:15, 20).

Explanation

The salvation announced in the Book of Consolation involves the concrete necessities of human existence (cf. Isa 65:17–25). Two things are "new," which have not been seen before in the land: (1) Faithless Israel, who is called a whore in chap. 3, will be taken back by God, even though such a thing is never done (3:1–2). (2) Mourning will be turned to joy. This composition, 31:15–22, shows the depths of divine love out of which the new creation springs. The creation of new identities for God and for Israel opens up new possibilities for their relationship. The LORD steps out of the role of deserted husband (3:20) and is revealed in the role of parent. Israel, adulteress and prostitute, is recreated as virgin daughter. God had wanted to be like a father to the people of Israel (3:19), but they had proved themselves unfaithful (3:21). In 31:15–22 the LORD, like Rachel the bereaved matriarch, yearns to bring back precious son Ephraim and beloved daughter Israel. God's love and mercy, deeper even than that of a mother who dies giving life to her child, brings forth reconciliation, in spite of sin, and victory over death.

H. The New Covenant and Other Promises (31:23–40[LXX 38:23–40])

Bibliography

Baltzer, K. *The Covenant Formulary in Old Testament, Jewish, and Early Christian Writings.* Tr. D. Green. Philadelphia: Fortress, 1971. **Brueggemann, W.** "A Shattered Transcendence? Exile and Restoration." In *Old Testament Theology: Essays on Structure, Theme, and Text,* ed. P. Miller. Minneapolis: Fortress, 1992. 183–203. **Childs, B. S.** *Old Testament Theology in a Canonical Context.* Philadelphia: Fortress, 1985. **Crenshaw, J.** "YHWH Ṣᵉbaʾot Šᵉmo: A Form-Critical Analysis." *ZAW* 81 (1969) 156–75. **Eskenazi, T.** "Hananel, Tower of." *ABD* 3:45. **Fishbane, M.** "Accusations of Adultery: A Study of Law and Scribal Practice in Numbers 5:11–31." *HUCA* 45 (1974) 25–43. **Geva, H.** "The Western Boundary of Jerusalem at the End of the Monarchy." *IEJ* 29 (1979) 84–91. **Hauge, M. R.** "Some Aspects of the Motif 'The City Facing Death' of Ps 68,21." *SJOT* 1 (1988) 1–29. **Herion, G.** "Gareb." *ABD* 2:907. ———. "Goah." *ABD* 2:1040. **Hillers, D.** *Covenant: The History of a Biblical Idea.* Baltimore: The Johns Hopkins UP, 1969. **King, P.** *Jeremiah: An Archaeological Companion.* Louisville: Westminster/John Knox, 1993. ———. "Jerusalem." *ABD* 3:747–66. **McAlpine, T.** *Sleep, Divine and Human, in the Old Testament.* JSOTSup 38. Sheffield: JSOT Press, 1987. **Mettinger, T.** *In Search of God: The Meaning and Message of the Everlasting Names.* Tr. F. Cryer. Philadelphia: Fortress, 1988. **Simons, J.** *Jerusalem in the Old Testament.* Leiden: Brill, 1952. **Smith, E. J.** "The Decalogue in the Preaching of Jeremiah." *CBQ* 4 (1942) 197–209. **Weinfeld, M.** "Jeremiah and the Spiritual Metamorphosis of Israel." *ZAW* 88 (1976) 17–56.

Translation

[23] *Thus says the LORD of hosts, the God of Israel: This word will be said again in the land of Judah and in her cities when I bring about their restoration,* [a]*"May the LORD bless you, dwelling of righteousness, O mountain of holiness."*[a] [24]*Judah and all its cities will dwell in it together, farmers and* [a]*the ones who travel*[a] [b]*with a flock.*[b] [25]*For I will make the weary drink their fill, and every languishing*[a] *person I will replenish.* [26]*"Thereupon I awoke and looked,*[a] *and my sleep was pleasant to me."*

[27]*Behold, days are coming—oracle of the LORD—when I will sow the house of Israel*

and the house of Judah with human seed and with animal seed. [28]*Just as I have watched over them* [a]*to pluck up, to break down, to overthrow, to destroy, and to bring evil,*[a] *so shall I watch over them to build and to plant.* [29]*In those days it will no longer be said, "Parents have eaten sour grapes and children's teeth are numb."* [a] [30]*But each person shall die for his or her own sin. Every person who eats the sour grapes, that one's teeth shall be numb.*[a]

[31]*Behold, days are coming—oracle of the LORD—when I will make with the house of Israel* [a]*and with the house of Judah*[a] *a new covenant,* [32]*not like the covenant which I made with their ancestors*[a] *on the day when I grasped them by their hand to bring them out from the land of Egypt. It was they who broke my covenant,* [b]*although I was master over them like a husband*[b]*—oracle of the LORD.* [33]*But this is the covenant which I will make with the house*[a] *of Israel after those days—oracle of the LORD:* [b]*I will put my instruction in the midst of them, and upon their heart I will write it. I will be their God, and they shall be my people.* [34]*They shall not teach their neighbor or their kin anymore, saying, "Know [pl] the LORD," because all of them shall already know me, from the least to the greatest of them—oracle of the LORD—for I will forgive their iniquity, and their sin I will not remember anymore.*

[35a]*Thus says the LORD,*
    the one who sets the sun to light the day,   (4+3+2+4+3)
    [b]*the one who establishes*[b] *the moon and stars*
        to light the night,
    [c]*the one who stirs up the sea*[c] *so its waves roar,*
    the LORD of hosts is his name:

[36]*If these statutes were to depart from before me—oracle of the LORD—then the offspring of Israel would cease from being a nation before me for all time.* [37a]*Thus says the LORD:*[a] *If the heavens could be measured*[b] *above*[c] *and the foundations of the earth could be explored*[d] *below, then I would cast off all*[e] *the offspring of Israel*[f] *because of everything they have done—oracle of the LORD.*

[38a]*Behold, days are coming*[a]*—oracle of the LORD—when the city of*[b] *the LORD shall be rebuilt, from the tower of Hananel to*[c] *the Corner Gate.* [39]*The measuring line*[a] *shall go forth again opposite it*[b] *on*[c] *Gareb Hill and turn around toward Goah,*[d] [40a]*and the whole*[b] *valley,*[c] *the corpses and the ashes,*[a] *and all the terraces*[d] *as far as*[e] *the brook Kidron, as far as the corner of the Horse Gate eastward, shall be holy to the LORD. It shall not be uprooted or overthrown again forever.*

Notes

23.a-a. LXX blesses God rather than Zion, Εὐλογημένος κύριος ἐπὶ δίκαιον ὄρος τὸ ἅγιον αὐτοῦ, "Blessed be the LORD on his righteous, holy mountain."

24.a-a. MT "and they shall travel" does not fit the list of nouns, and the same may be said of LXX καὶ ἀρθήσεται, "and they shall go forth." *BHS* suggests reading the const ptcp וְנֹסֵעַ, "and those who travel," as in α', σ', Tg, Vg.

24.b-b. Several MSS indicate the definite article: בָּעֵדֶר, "with the flock."

25.a. MT's pf דָּאֲבָה, "languishes" (3 f sg), does not easily fit the syntax. Either add אֲשֶׁר, "who" (Carroll, 605), or revocalize as the adj דָּאֵבָה, "languishing."

26.a. *BHS* suggests emending to וָאֶרְוֶה, "and I was refreshed," but has no evidence to support the change.

28.a-a. In place of the five infs in MT, LXX has only two, καθαιρεῖν καὶ κακοῦν, "to destroy and to bring evil." MT's list echoes 1:10.

29.a. Holladay's translation, following Vg *obstipuerunt,* "become numb."

30.a. See *Note* 29.a.

31.a-a. *BHS* and Rudolph (201) would remove this phrase as an addition, citing its absence from v 33.

32.a. The same word is translated "parents" in v 29.

32.b-b. LXX καὶ ἐγὼ ἠμέλησα αὐτῶν, "and I loathed them," from Heb. נעלתי, "I loathed," as in Heb 8:9. *a'* and Vg support MT, which should be retained.

33.a. A few MSS read בני, "sons/children of." MT's "house of" follows the diction of v 31.

33.b. Several MSS add waw consec to MT's pf, ונתתי, "then I will put." The pf could stand alone in its prophetic sense, GKC § 106n.

35.a. V 37 in LXX, which positions MT's vv 35–36 between v 37 and v 38.

35.b-b. Lacking in LXX. Janzen (*Studies,* 49) and Holladay (2:155) would delete it as an intrusion from v 36. *BHS* recommends emending to חֹקֵק, "one who orders," in order to parallel נֹתֵן, "one who sets."

35.c-c. LXX has καὶ κραυγὴν ἐν θαλάσσῃ, "and makes a roaring in the sea," a less anthropomorphic expression than MT.

37.a-a. Not in LXX, where this verse follows v 34.

37.b. LXX ὑψωθῇ, "could be raised," from Heb. יֵרֹמּוּ, "could be raised," which could have resulted from miscopying MT ימדו, "could be measured."

37.c. LXX has φησὶν κύριος, "oracle of the LORD," balancing the same formula between the final two clauses in the verse. (See *Note* 37.f.)

37.d. LXX ταπεινωθῇ, "could be sunk," is the opposite of "could be raised" in the first half of the verse.

37.e. LXX lacks "all."

37.f. LXX has φησὶν κύριος, "oracle of the LORD," here instead of at the end of the verse.

38.a-a. Translating the Q of many MSS and versions. *BHS* suggests that באים, "coming," was lost because of its resemblance to the following word, נאם, "oracle."

38.b. See the *Comment* and cf. 31:4.

38.c. The prep is lacking in MT. It may have been lost through haplogr (so *BHS*), since the previous word ends in the letter ל. LXX reads ἕως, "as far as."

39.a. Q and K are variants of the const. (Cf. 1 Kgs 7:23.)

39.b. LXX has αὐτῶν, "of them," referring to the two places mentioned in v 38. *BHS* proposes emending to "toward the south."

39.c. Some MSS of LXX and Tg suggest an original עד, "to, unto."

39.d. The versions have widely varying designations for this site: LXX κύκλῳ ἐξ ἐκλεκτῶν λίθων, "a wall of choice stones"; *a', σ'* Γαβαθα, "Gabatha," a location in Jerusalem; Syr, Tg *lbrjkt ʿglʾ,* "to the pool of precious stones." (Cf. Isa 54:11–12 for precious stones in Jerusalem.)

40.a-a. Not in LXX. Holladay (2:155) calls it a gloss.

40.b. *BHS* proposes adding נכה, "in front of," but gives no evidence or explanation.

40.c. *BHS* suggests that וּמְקֹם, "and the place of," was lost by haplogr and should be reinserted. Waltke and O'Connor (*Hebrew Syntax,* 231) label the following phrase an appositive of material, "the whole valley, where dead bodies and ashes are thrown."

40.d. Many MSS follow Q השדמות, "the terraces" (Holladay, 2:200; King, *Jeremiah,* 157–59). LXX transliterates the K, which is an otherwise unknown term. The word is lacking in Syr. Tg has *ʾadjʾ,* perhaps "watery field." Vg has *regionem mortis,* "region of death," from שדה מות, "field of death," which is graphically similar to Q and a logical parallel to "valley, corpses and ashes," at the beginning of the verse.

40.e. *BHS* recommends correcting to על, "upon, by," with one MS.

Form/Structure/Setting

The Book of Consolation concludes with a series of five short salvation oracles. The five oracles form a chiasm centered on 31:31–34, the promise of the new covenant. The first (vv 23–26) and fifth (vv 38–40) oracles are about Jerusalem. The second (vv 27–30) and fourth (vv 35–37) form a contrasting pair. The responsibility of each person for sin contrasts with God's enduring commitment to the survival of Israel as a nation. The logical tension between these two affirmations will be resolved by the initiation of the new covenant, which includes forgiveness of sin (v 34) and transformation of the human party to the relationship (v 32).

These oracles also supplement, explain, and draw out the implications of the primarily poetic compositions that precede them in chaps. 30–31. They are more consistently future oriented than the rest of the Book of Consolation, and they refer to the recipients of the promises in the third person throughout (Bozak, *Life 'Anew'*, 110). Each of the first three units includes a change-of-speech-pattern promise. The five oracles also forge a link with chaps. 32–33, which provide a context in Jeremiah's ministry for the announcement of the restoration promises. Biddle locates a redactional structure connecting chaps. 30–33 and created by the repetition of "promises assured by ordinances of nature" in 31:35–37: 33:19–26. The conclusion of chap. 31, vv 38–40, is the beginning of the second half, "promises to the city," of this four-chapter composition (Biddle, *ZAW* 100 [1988] 411). Chap. 33 expounds on the sign-act in chap. 32 in terms of chaps. 30–31. (See the *Comment* on 33:1–26.)

A messenger formula with an extended divine name begins the final section of the Book of Consolation and introduces a proclamation of salvation for Judah and its cities. The LORD, speaking in the first person, promises a restoration of urban and rural life in the land that will be focused on worship in Jerusalem. A prayer for the temple city is quoted in v 23c as an indication of what will be said עוֹד, "again" (salvation indicated by a change of speech pattern). V 25 promises the blessings experienced by God's servant people at the temple (cf. רָוָה, "satisfy," 31:14, and לֹא דָאַב, "they shall not languish," 31:12). The passage concludes with a sentence spoken by a different, unidentified voice, which testifies to the fulfillment of the promise in v 25.

An eschatological formula, "the days are surely coming," begins the second section, vv 27–30, as well as the third (vv 31–34) and fifth (vv 38–40; cf. 30:3). This salvation proclamation promises the end of the sufferings of judgment in the broadest terms (vv 27–28) and then spells out one particular consequence (vv 29–30). The coming time of salvation will silence the recitation of a proverbial expression of complaint against injustice, quoted in v 29. The previous passage cites a blessing that will be spoken once "again" (עוֹד), but this unit articulates a complaint which will be uttered "no longer" (לֹא עוֹד). Salvation is portrayed as the removal of complaint and the renewal of praise (cf. 30:12–17, 19).

The third and central unit in the concluding collection also begins with the eschatological formula "the days are surely coming." In this proclamation of salvation, the LORD, speaking in the first person, promises to make a new covenant with Israel and Judah and to forgive their sin. A change in speech pattern will also be a consequence of the fulfillment of this promise. They will "no longer" (לֹא עוֹד) catechize one another saying, "Know the LORD" (v 34). The covenant formula also appears within the promise (v 33; cf. 30:22; 31:1, 9b).

The messenger formula that marks the beginning of the fourth unit (vv 35–37) is extended by a hymn, describing the LORD in participial phrases and concluding "the LORD of hosts is his name." V 36 and v 37, which begins with another messenger formula, are separate but parallel words of assurance. Both use the rhetorical device of a protasis that provides negative reinforcement to the statement in the apodasis. The "if" clause states a situation that the audience recognizes as inconceivable in order to convince the hearer that the second, "then," clause is also impossible.

A proclamation of salvation introduced by the "days are coming" formula ends the section. It illustrates the promise that Jerusalem will be rebuilt by mapping the line of the new boundary wall, citing particular place names and directions. In form and style, it resembles the map of the boundaries of Judah's tribal allotment in Josh 15:1–12.

Comment

23 The messenger formula includes the extended divine name and title "the LORD of hosts, the God of Israel," which is particularly associated with the worship of the LORD as king in Jerusalem (Mettinger, *In Search*, 126–33). The oracle that follows portrays salvation in the form of the restoration of prayer for Zion (cf. Isa 27:13; Zech 8:3). "Dwelling of righteousness" appears as a title for the LORD in Jer 50:7, and the Masoretic accents support this reading in 31:23 also (Bozak, *Life 'Anew'*, 111; cf. NJV). The specification of Judah and her cities as the object of the LORD's deeds of restoration removes any doubt about their participation in the promised salvation. This short oracle parallels 31:7–14, explaining that Judah will be included in those promises to Jacob.

24–25 The place where the restored Judeans will dwell is identified simply as בה (feminine singular), "there." Since all segments of the population, townsfolk, farmers, and wandering shepherds, are included, "the land of Judah" in v 23 is the appropriate antecedent. (The אֶרֶץ, "land," is feminine singular, but הַר, "mountain," is not.) The promise in v 25 includes blessings that are associated with worship on Zion in Jer 31:12 (דאב, "languish") and 31:14 (רוה, "satisfy"). The experience of God's presence is like water to a person fainting from thirst (עיפה, v 25) in Pss 63:2, 6(Eng 1, 5); 143:6. Filling those who "languish" also reverses the covenant curse of Deut 28:65.

26 The next verse announces no change of speaker, so Bozak proposes to interpret this statement as a continuation of the LORD's speech. "My sleep had overtaken [עדבה] me," expresses regret for inaction, and "I awoke and saw" means that the LORD became aware of the people's need and took action to help, as in Pss 44:24(Eng 23); 78:65. This awakening to save should be at the beginning of the salvation oracle, however, not at the end, if the "I" who speaks is the LORD.

Another proposal identifies this verse as a concluding comment to an earlier version of the Book of Consolation, spoken or written by the prophet to mark the end of a message received from God during the night (cf. Job 35:10–11; Ps 16:7). The verb ואראה, "I saw," indicates receipt of the message introduced in 30:1–3 (Wiebe, *Studia Biblica et Theologica* 15 [1987] 151; Thompson, 577). Whether or not this verse ever had this concluding function, it does not now in the final form of the text.

Its position at the end of the oracle suggests that v 26 should be read as a new or restored speech pattern, like the blessing in v 23. Because the LORD will satisfy the weary (v 25), God's people will be able to give this testimony of "sweet" (ערבה)

sleep. McAlpine identifies the pair עָיֵף, "weary," and יָשֵׁן, "sleep," as a typical collocation of sleep-related words. Although "weariness" (עָיֵף) is not often remedied by sleep in the OT, it may be in this passage (McAlpine, *Sleep*, 49–50). Sleep is a time of vulnerability, but the security gained from wisdom ensures "sweet" (עָרְבָה) sleep, according to Prov 3:24 (similarly, 6:22). The LORD protects the psalmist during sleep (Pss 3:6[Eng 5]; 4:9[Eng 8]) and provides food for him or her (Ps 127:2, the opposite of Isa 29:8). Being able to sleep safely is evidence that the nation is at peace (Lev 26:6). The experience of exile described in Deut 28:65–67 is the opposite. To the exiles God gives a דַּאֲבוֹן נֶפֶשׁ, "languishing spirit," and they live in fear for their lives day and night. The promise in v 25 will reverse this curse, and, "thereupon," the people will be able to give the testimony in v 26. Similarly, the psalmist praying for deliverance in Ps 17:15 looks forward to awakening to see the LORD's face and being satisfied (שָׂבַע; cf. Jer 31:14). In the context of the Book of Consolation, a further implication may be derived from this saying. Sleep resembles and symbolizes death (Job 14:12). Judah, the sleeper who awakens (קִיץ) and speaks in 31:26, is not dead. Mourning will be turned to joy (cf. 31:13).

27–28 The next salvation oracle begins with a promise to reverse past judgments. Jer 7:20; 21:6 had announced judgment and death extending to humans and even animals, but both populations will be restored. The metaphor comes from Hos 2:25(Eng 23), in which the LORD's "sowing" is to repopulate the land (זָרַע, in a pun with יִזְרְעֶאל, "Jezreel"). זֶרַע, "seed," is also a key word in the pledge made to the Israelite ancestors that they would have innumerable descendants (Gen 12:7; 13:16; 22:17; 28:14; 35:12). Thus the implication points beyond the restoration generation alone. The future of the whole nation, Israel and Judah, will be assured because of the fertility of human families and of the animals on which they depend for work and food. The seven infinitives in v 28 summarize the message of the book by quoting from the call account in Jer 1:10. The LORD's "watching" (שָׁקַד) evokes the promise in 1:12, "I am watching [שֹׁקֵד] over my word to fulfill it." This repetition of verbs from chap. 1 shows that all of the destruction Jeremiah was called to bring into effect has been accomplished, as promised. All four verbs of judgment in 1:10 are repeated in 31:28 plus one additional, לְהָרַע, "to bring evil," from 1:14, "From the north disaster [הָרָעָה] shall break out" (cf. Jer 25:6, 29). Similarly, the rest of Jeremiah's ministry, as set forth in 1:10, will be accomplished under the LORD's hand. What has been broken down, uprooted, and annihilated will be built and planted. The latter verb establishes a connection with v 27 and interprets these verbs as applying to the people themselves, not just to their cities, homes, and farms. The audience of the Book of Consolation knows the thoroughness of the judgment, and they are invited to believe that the LORD's vigilance will also bring about the promised restoration. How can this about-face be understood? The following verses begin to provide an answer.

29–30 "Those days" at the beginning of v 29 refers to the coming days in v 27. In the future, when the LORD repopulates and rebuilds the land, the complaint quoted here will be silenced. This oracle is not of the disputation genre (cf. Ezek 18:25–29). Its form implies that the people's complaint is justified or at least understandable, because God promises to change the situation so that the reason for the complaint will be removed. (Calvin, on the other hand, sees the

proverb as an expression of perverseness and pride rather than despair 4:123].)
This speech pattern will change as a result of the LORD's actions to save and restore (compare Jer 3:16; 16:14–15; 23:7–8). In the context of the book of Jeremiah,
the complaint proverb does not refer explicitly to Exod 34:7b; Deut 5:9. Rather,
the background in the book is the recurring motif of the people's persistent rebellion against the LORD's word and their idolatry extending over many
generations (7:13–14, 25–26; 11:7–8; 32:31–34; 44:9–10; see the *Comment* on 26:5).
The generation that had suffered conquest and exile by the Babylonians had themselves committed wickedness, but their sinful ancestors had escaped this near
annihilation, even though they were responsible for it, too. The complaint is expressed indirectly by a proverb that implies that it is unnatural for one generation
to experience the direct consequences of the previous generation's actions. (Precisely what the consumption of sour grapes does to one's teeth remains unclear.)
The proverb form itself signals resignation or despair rather than a cry for vindication. Note the contrast with the charge "the way of the LORD is unfair" in the
disputation saying in Ezek 18:25–29. Lam 5:7 states this complaint directly, "Our
ancestors sinned; they are no more, and we bear their iniquities" (NRSV). In its
context, the last clause implies "we bear their iniquities as well as our own."

The Book of Consolation reminds its audience of their great guilt and many
sins (30:14–15) and assures them that their punishment will be "in just measure"
(30:11) and according to God's plan (30:24). The LORD answers their complaint
in v 30 with a promise to restore the just and consistent application of the law in
Deut 24:16 (cf. 2 Kgs 14:6). By translating the complaint from the inexplicable
realm of "the way things are," expressed by a proverb, into the language of the
law, the oracle brings the people's experience into the realm of divine justice.
The LORD who vindicates answers the complaint (cf. Jer 30:12–17). Where the
LORD is at work there is still hope for Israel, as a nation and as individuals. The
grace of divine justice expressed in this promise will make it possible for the people
who will be planted and built in the land (31:28) to be free from the burden of
their ancestors' guilt. It will not stand in the way of the future for the people
Israel (31:37). Ezek 18 explains how the LORD's justice will silence this proverb
by showing case by case that neither a person's own past sin nor his or her ancestors' sin can prevent that person from choosing to turn away from wickedness to
righteousness and life. The chapter concludes with a call for repentance and an
invitation to "get a new heart and a new spirit" (v 31). In Jeremiah, however,
another promise follows, but it also has to do with a changed heart.

31 Can anything new be said about 31:31–34? An attempt will be made in
what follows to comment on the meaning of these verses in the context of the
Book of Consolation and of the book of Jeremiah. NT commentators and theolo-
gians must deal with the way the promises given here were understood in the
light of Christ's ministry (Luke 22:20; 1 Cor 11:25; 2 Cor 3:1–14; Heb 8:8–12;
10:16–17). The "new covenant" promised in this verse is not a fixed theologu-
menon in the OT, which labels the future, changed relationship between God
and the people of God in many ways. In fact, the term "new covenant" occurs
only in this verse in the OT. What will make this covenant "new" is indicated in
the following verses. Discontinuity with the past is also emphasized by the ad-
verbs "not like" (v 32) and "not anymore" (twice in v 34; cf. 30:8; 31:12, 40).

To "make [literally, 'cut' (כרת)] a covenant" is an act accomplished at a particular point in history. As such, it is a divine deed that can be promised for some time in the future, like the repopulation and rebuilding of the land promised in vv 27–28. Other covenants in the OT are formalized following a brief period of preparation (e.g., Exod 19–24), but the date of this covenant making is unspecified and this passage gives no indication of how the people are to ready themselves for it. The parties to the covenant are not addressed in the second person but are identified in the third person as "the house of Israel" and "the house of Judah." These groups also appear in v 27 as the ones whom the LORD will save. The two names serve as a reminder of how God's people were affected by their history in the land. In the book of Jeremiah, the houses of Israel and Judah stand together under judgment (5:11; 11:10, 17) and promise (33:14). Indeed, the reunification of the two houses is part of the promised restoration (3:18). Jer 50:4–5 portrays the nations Israel and Judah returning together to Zion in tears in order to "join themselves to the LORD; the eternal covenant will not be forgotten."

The basic situation addressed by this oracle in the context of the Book of Consolation resembles the circumstances for covenant renewal outlined by K. Baltzer (*Covenant Formulary*, 51–60). God's people Israel have violated the substance of the covenant by their apostasy, and the curse has come into effect (30:12–15, 23–24). The LORD alone decides and makes known whether the covenant has been broken (31:32; 11:10). The people repent of their sin, and the LORD alone decides whether to forgive (סלח, 31:34; cf. Exod 34:9). The LORD indicates acceptance of the covenant renewal request with the statement אנכי כרת ברית, "I make a covenant" (Exod 34:10). Jer 31:31–34 begins with an analogous statement. The LORD initiates this covenant making by promising it far ahead of time. No one like Moses (Exod 34:1–28) or the king (2 Kgs 23; Jer 34:8–22) leads the people in seeking it. All of the people, from least to greatest, participate in the renewal ceremony (31:34; cf. 2 Kgs 23:2). The goal of covenant renewal had been to avoid total destruction under the effects of the curse, but in Jer 31:28 the end of the destruction has already been announced. Just as the LORD had voiced the people's lament for them and then answered it in 30:12–17, here the LORD initiates the covenant renewal and then promises a new covenant in its stead.

32 The new covenant will not be like the covenant that the LORD made with Israel's and Judah's ancestors of the exodus generation. The new covenant will be cut with a later generation who will have undergone spiritual return and geographical removal from a different place of captivity (31:15–22; 50:4–5). The former covenant had been broken (פרר hiphil) by the exodus ancestors, by Jeremiah's audience, and by all the generations in between. For the reader of the book of Jeremiah, this verse finds its primary background in chap. 11. This passage (11:1–17) interprets the indictments against the people in the rest of the book as evidence of covenant breaking (פרר hiphil) and the disaster they suffer as the judgment that results from it (11:11). Jer 7:21–34 makes the same argument. The frequent allusions in the book of Jeremiah to the covenant curses in Deut 28 provide further support for this interpretation. Moses had interceded successfully for the exodus generation (Exod 32–33), but Jeremiah was forbidden to pray for his community (11:14). This command ruled out the possibility of covenant renewal. The people's penitential lament in 14:19–22, asking the LORD to "remember, do not break your covenant with us" would not be heard, accord-

ing to 11:11b, 14b. The generation of Israelites to whom Jeremiah ministered
and the implied post-586 B.C. audience of the book are among the ancestors of
the future "house of Israel" and "house of Jacob" in 31:32, the ancestors who
broke the covenant (11:10).

In light of chap. 11, the double significance of the verb in the concessive clause,
"although I had mastered them as a husband [בעלתי]," becomes clear. The verb
means to "marry," with an emphasis on the rights and authority the husband exercised over his wife or concubine (e.g., Gen 20:3; Deut 21:13; 22:22; 24:1). The
intimacy and affection of the marriage relationship analogy are evident in 11:15–
16, where the LORD calls the people יְדִידִי, "my beloved," but bars them from the
temple and marks them for destruction. There is also a pun with the name Baal
(בעל), the strange god to whom the people were making offerings (11:13, 17).
To serve בעל, "Baal," was to abandon the LORD who had mastered them as a בעל,
"husband." By this verb the LORD states the prior claim to the worship they had
offered to Baal (cf. Isa 54:5). Covenant breaking in the form of apostasy is likened to adultery, making the separation irreparable in human terms (Jer 3:1;
Deut 24:1–4). The Sinai/Horeb covenant had been brought to an end. Both the
analogy to a broken marriage and the promise of a "new" covenant make this
point clear. Only a powerful act of divine mercy could make them God and people
for each other again.

33   The promise unites the two houses of v 31 into the one "house of Israel."
The reading of some manuscripts, בני, "children of," Israel, makes this interpretation explicit by adopting the old pentateuchal term for the covenant people as a
whole (e.g., Exod 19:3–6). Clements (191) finds "house of Israel" significant as a
new title for the people scattered in diaspora. The nonspecific dating formula,
"after those days," is curious following "the days are surely coming" in v 31. A
date formula also occurs in the middle of the previous oracle. "In those days," v
29, establishes simultaneity with the coming "days" in v 27. "After those days" in v
33 indicates sequence, a later time, but does not specify the antecedent. It cannot be a time after the covenant making in v 31, unless there are two such occasions
envisioned. That the new covenant will be made after the breaking of the old is
self-evident, but the date formula in v 33 may serve as a reminder that the breaking of the covenant resulted from the iniquity of many generations of ancestors,
from the day (v 32) the LORD brought Israel out of Egypt down to the present
day of the book's audience. The shift from the second-person invitation to return in 31:21–22 to the third-person promises in 31:23–40 contributes to this
sequencing effect. The Israelites who will receive these promises are the descendants of the implied audience. The promise in 31:1 also fits this chronological
scheme by setting the coming into effect of the covenant formula in the future,
and by referring to the human partner in the third person. Rudolph (188) identifies "those days," v 33, as the time of the promised return of Ephraim. In the
present context of the Book of Consolation, "those days" could mean the days
described in 31:27–30 when the judgment will be complete and God will begin
planting, building, and repopulating the land.

The new covenant will establish the relationship between the same parties, the
LORD and Israel. The familiar covenant formula at the end of the verse succinctly
communicates this continuity. It summarizes the substance of the relationship

(Baltzer, *Covenant Formulary,* 102) and reassures the people that the LORD will not start over again with another. (Compare the offer to Moses in Exod 32:10.) The formula has already appeared twice in the Book of the Covenant as a promise (30:22; 31:1; cf. Zech 8:8), and it occurs four other times in the book of Jeremiah, twice with reference to the Sinai/Horeb covenant (7:23; 11:4) and two more times as a promise for the future (24:7; 32:38). Hosea was the first prophet to formulate the promise of reconciliation in terms of this formula, and he portrays it as a mutual commitment, "You are my people" and "You are my God" (Hos 2:25[Eng 23]). Exod 6:7 connects the formula to knowledge of the LORD, who freed Israel from service to the Egyptians, while Deut 26:16–19; 29:10–13 emphasize the obligation enjoined upon the people who are God's by covenant to obey the commandments. In Ezekiel the covenant formula summarizes the relationship promised after the judgment, return to the land, cleansing, and a transformation of heart and spirit have been wrought by God (Ezek 11:20; 14:11; 34:30–31; 36:28; 37:23, 27). If the sheer grace of God's election of Israel as covenant partner was apparent in the first covenant making, how much more so in this promise following their history of unfaithfulness and rebellion (v 32).

At the center of v 33 and at the heart of the oracle is the announcement of the new thing God will do. After the heading "this is the covenant," one expects a statement of its substance, as in the covenant formula just discussed, but the promise at the center is more like the "provision for deposit and reading" in the treaty form (Hillers, *Covenant,* 29). The first covenant document was written by God on two stone tablets and given to Moses for conveyance to the people (Exod 31:18; Deut 4:13; 5:22; 10:1–4). Exodus also speaks of the words of the covenant on tablets (34:27–29) and the book of the covenant (24:7) written by Moses. At the end of the book of Deuteronomy, just prior to his death, Moses writes הַתּוֹרָה הַזֹּאת, "this law" or "instruction," and gives it to the priests and elders with instructions to read it aloud to all the people every seven years (Deut 31:9–13). Holladay posits the observance of this practice during Jeremiah's ministry and dates the oracle in 31:31–34 to the reading in September/October 587 B.C., two months after the fall of Jerusalem (2:165). Whether or not this hypothesis is true, Deut 31 is essential background for Jer 31:31–34 within the final form of the OT. When God writes the *torah* ("law, instruction") on the people's heart, mediators are bypassed and the limitations of written documents are superseded. Jeremiah's audience knows that stone tablets can be broken (Exod 32:19; Deut 9:17) and that scrolls can be lost or ignored (2 Kgs 22:8), and burned (Jer 36:23) or drowned (Jer 51:63). Written documents are also limited to one location, and their availability is restricted. Deut 31:26 directs that the book of the law (תּוֹרָה, "instruction") be stored next to the Ark, but Jer 3:16 promises that, in the future, restored city of Jerusalem, the Ark will be obsolete. This promise of the LORD's instruction written on hearts fits the same picture. The promise made in Jer 31:33 overcomes the inherent tension in even so hopeful a passage as Deut 30, which is also a promise to the survivors of the covenant curses. In Deut 30:6–8, the LORD promises through Moses to circumcise the heart (singular) of every generation so that they will obey the commandment of Deut 6:5 to love the LORD by keeping the commandments and, therefore, will live. In spite of the assurances that "this commandment" is not hidden in heaven or in a distant country and that no messenger is needed to retrieve it because it is "in your [sg] mouth and in your heart" (30:11–14), it is still "written in this book of the law" (30:10). The metaphor of writing on the heart shows how the external limitations and vulnerability of the old system of written documents and human mediators will be eliminated.

The metaphor of the heart also shows how the internal impediment to the perfection of the covenant relationship will be overcome. The conviction that having the LORD's word in or on one's heart prevents sin and fosters obedience is found in various places in the OT (e.g., Pss 40:9[Eng 8]; 119:11; Deut 11:18). The heart stands for the mind, the organ of memory (Jer 3:16), of understanding (Deut 29:3[Eng 4]), of ideas (Jer 23:16), and, especially, of conscious decisions of the will (Jer 3:10; 29:13). Only God is able to discern what is in an individual's heart (Jer 17:9–10). The metaphor of writing on the heart is found one other place in Jeremiah, in 17:1. The hearts of the people of Judah are depicted as tablets that require the hardest writing instrument. The inscription on them is not the LORD's instruction but the people's sin, the commitment of their will against the LORD. The LORD was far from their hearts (12:2). Their שְׁרִרוּת לֵב, "hardness of heart," is also evident in Jer 13:10; 23:17. Such people can no more start doing good than a leopard can change its spots (13:23). In the context of Jeremiah, only the metaphors of surgery (4:4) and of writing by God's own hand (31:33) can overcome their stubbornness and prepare them for loyal obedience.

The content of the covenant agreement will be "my *torah* [instruction, law]" in v 33 and knowledge of the LORD in v 34. In the book of Jeremiah, תּוֹרָה, "instruction, law," usually refers to the revelation of God's will and way in the form of commandments, statutes, and words that must be heeded (6:19; 9:12–13[Eng 13–14]; 16:11; 26:4; 32:23; 44:10, 23). Going after the Baals has been the people's choice instead (9:12–13[Eng 13–14]; 16:11). Priests (2:8) and scribes (8:8) are accused of failing in their responsibility to uphold the law for the sake of the people. Deut 31:9 calls the covenant document written by Moses הַתּוֹרָה הַזֹּאת, "this instruction." Like other formulations of covenant and renewal in the OT, the book of Deuteronomy includes a recitation of the covenant partners' history, how the LORD had saved the people of Israel and entered into covenant with them in order to give them the land. In Jeremiah, the ability to recount how the LORD saved Israel (2:6–8) and obedience to divine commands (22:15–17) are aspects of knowing the LORD (Brueggemann, 71), so both of these things will be included in the instruction to be written on the heart. A new historical prologue for the covenant document is suggested by 16:14–15, substituting restoration from exile for exodus from Egypt. There is no indication, however, that the content of the law, God's will revealed in commandment, statute, and ordinance, will be altered in the new covenant.

34 A salvation oracle in the form of a change of speech pattern begins this verse and describes the consequences of having the LORD's instruction written on the heart. It expands upon the promise in Jer 24:7. The exhortation "know [pl] the LORD" will fall silent, because *torah* ("instruction, law") written on the heart means that the LORD is known already. This speech pattern is not described or commanded anywhere in the OT. In Deut 6 Moses receives the command to "teach" (לִמֵּד) the commandments to Israel (6:1), and parents are enjoined to recite them to their children on every possible occasion (6:7). Psalmists pass on knowledge of the covenant (Pss 40:6–11[Eng 5–10]; 78:1–7; 81:5–17[Eng 4–16]; 105:1–5; 111:4; 135:4–20; Baltzer, *Covenant Formulary*, 88). Hos 4:4–6 blames the priests and prophets for the loss of the knowledge of God in the land. The closest formulation to "know the LORD" is found in Prov 3:6, "in all your ways know him," the words of a wisdom teacher to a pupil. Jer 34:17 has a similar formulation with a different verb; the people are charged with disobedience under the covenant for failing "to proclaim release to their kin or neighbor" (לקראו דרור איש לאחיו ואיש לרעהו). The teaching "know the LORD" sounds like a good thing, a transformation of the situation described in Jer 9:3–8(Eng 4–9) where neighbor and kin "have taught [למד] their tongue to speak falsehood" and have refused to know (ידע) the LORD. Yet the fulfillment of this promise will create an even better time, when knowledge of the LORD cannot be perverted by false teaching or rivalry between teachers (Martens, 196), because all will know the LORD without needing to learn from human instructors (cf. Isa 54:13).

Knowledge of God will extend to all ages and classes (Holladay, 2:198–99). The phrase "from the least to the greatest of them" sums up a list of people from children to the very aged in Jer 6:11–13. Although it lacks this phrase, Jer 5:1–5 serves as background because it describes a situation that will be eradicated by this promise: neither poor nor rich "know the way of the LORD or the law of their God." The same phrase, but without pronominal suffixes, describes the lay participants in the covenant renewal led by Josiah in 2 Kgs 23:2 (cf. the list in Deut 29:9–10[Eng 10–11]). Both Martens (196) and Brueggemann (71) call attention to the absence of a religiously privileged elite.

According to Hos 8:1–2, the opposite of knowing the LORD is breaking the covenant and transgressing the law (תורה; cf. Jer 4:22). Israel knows only the LORD as savior; she has no shared history with Baal (Hos 13:4; 2:10[Eng 8]; cf. Exod 20:2). In Jeremiah, knowing God includes an awareness of God's character and the nature of divine actions (9:23[Eng 24]), the memory of what God has done for Israel (2:6–8), and the acceptance of God's rule by obeying the commands (9:3[Eng 2]; 22:15–16; 24:7). Childs' definition is appropriate, "Israel does not first know God, then later discover what God wants. Knowledge of his person and will are identical, and both are grounded in his self-revelation" (B. Childs, *Old Testament Theology*, 51). In the promised new covenant each person's desires and decisions will embrace, without reservation, God's self-revelation.

Israel had survived because of the LORD's willingness to pardon (סלח) her sin (Exod 34:9; Num 14:19–20). Through Jeremiah's ministry, the LORD had invited Israel to repent and be forgiven (5:1; 36:3), but his contemporaries had refused the pardon. The final promise in this verse will put an end to the threat in Jer 14:10: when the LORD remembers sin, punishment follows (cf. 44:21). But the LORD's promise not to remember their sins anymore means an end to divine wrath (31:23, 28). The people of the new covenant will not bear the guilt of their ancestors' sin or their own. They will be free to make a fresh start, under no lingering threats (compare Num 14:20–23), because of God's gracious gift of pardon. The LORD will write the *torah* ("instruction, law") on a heart polished smooth by forgiveness (cf. Jer 50:20). The heart and mind inscribed with the revelation of God cannot turn to sin again (Rudolph, 185; Brueggemann, 71). Therefore, faithfulness to the new covenant will be a gift of divine mercy, not a human achievement.

35–36 A brief hymn identifies the LORD who speaks in v 36 as the creator of sun, moon, and stars. The participial form ("the one who") portrays the acts of creation as matters of ongoing divine maintenance. V 36 pictures the words of creation as "statutes" that keep the heavenly bodies in their places and functioning on schedule. (Jer 33:20 calls this astral obligation a covenant.) This thought is in line with the promise given to humans and animals through Noah in Gen 8:22 that "day and night shall not cease" (שבת, as in 31:36). Their subsequent permanence results from the LORD's faithfulness to this post-deluvian pledge (*contra* Brueggemann, *Old Testment Theology*, 197–98). The stability of times and seasons, guaranteed by the LORD's word, makes life on earth possible. The irregular, mysterious behavior of the sea is also the LORD's doing (cf. Isa 51:15; Amos 5:8–9). If the sea is a symbol of the primordial chaos here, then this clause is also about the LORD who creates and preserves the dry land (cf. Pss 74:12–17; 89:10–12[Eng 9–11]; Isa 51:9–16). The sea has no power even to make its own waves. It is entirely under the LORD's control, as the covenant with Noah promises (Gen 9:8–17). The connection with the Noah covenant is explicit in Isa 54:9–10, a promise that follows a line of reasoning similar to that in Jer 31:35–37.

After the defeat of Israel, and then Judah, and the destruction of the temple, the ministry of the prophets included reminders of the LORD's identity as creator, which could not be disproved by the conquest of Samaria or Jerusalem. The despairing question "Is the LORD powerless to help?" is answered by theological reflection on the created order and the identification of the LORD as its maker. Jer 32:17 states the reasoning clearly, "O Lord GOD, since you have made the heavens and the earth by your great might and your outstretched arm, nothing is too difficult for you." This is not a new revelation but an appeal to an ancient belief. "The LORD of Hosts" had been worshiped as king in Israel, and especially at the temple in Jerusalem (Isa 6:5; Pss 24:10; 46:5–8[Eng 4–7]; 48:8; Mettinger, *In Search of God*, 124–33). In Jeremiah, God is called "the king, the LORD of Hosts is his name" when acting as judge of the nations (46:18; 48:15; 51:57). The creator of time (days, seasons, years) continues to reign over the nations in order to bring about a particular plan in history (Jer 31:36; cf. Isa 14:24, 26–27). This same God, the LORD of Hosts, will preserve Israel's continuing existence as a nation.

Taken alone, these two verses read like an unambiguous statement of a Zion theology that guarantees the inviolability of the nation. In their context in the Book of Consolation, however, they give assurance of the permanence of Israel's future relationship with the LORD. The offspring (זרע, "seed") of Israel are the result of God's sowing the land with human "seed" (זרע), promised in 31:27, after bringing them back from the land of exile (31:10). These verses restate the promise of 30:10–11 in a more forceful way while subtly directing the promise to the future. It is no longer about "you," the implied audience of the book, but about the offspring of Israel who will perdure in the LORD's presence under the terms of the new covenant (31:31–34), just as day and night have continued after the flood because of God's promise. They will have not only a spiritual identity as the LORD's people (עם, v 33) but a national existence also (גוי, v 36).

37 A second impossible condition indicates the permanence of the LORD's choice of Israel's offspring. Only God can measure the heavens (Isa 40:12), and humans cannot explore the foundations of the earth (Job 38:4–7). The impossibility of these achievements may not seem as obvious to modern readers as it was to the ancient audience, but the theological point must still be granted. Within the context of the book of Jeremiah, this assurance that the LORD will not "cast off" or "reject" (מאס) the offspring of Israel functions as a reversal of judgment. The people had rejected (מאס) the divine word and instruction (Jer 6:19; 8:9), and God had rejected them (מאס; 6:30; 7:29; 33:24). Jer 33:24–26 interprets 31:35–37, making clear that מאס, "reject," is the opposite of בחר, "choose, elect." The possible reason, "for all they have done," for their impossible rejection must be understood from the contents of the rest of the book, which devotes considerable space to detailing the sins of Israel and Judah (e.g., 7:8–15, "because you have done all these things," v 13). The anouncement of rejection in Jer 7:29 follows the charge that the "nation" (גוי, as in v 36) had not obeyed the LORD's voice or accepted discipline (cf. 31:18). The verses immediately after this, 7:30–31, recount the abominations committed in Topheth (cf. 31:38–40, *Comment*). The penitential lament of the community in Jer 14:19–22 begins with the question, "Have you completely rejected [מאס] Judah?" Jer 31:37 offers an assurance of preservation in answer to their prayer (Fischer, *Das Trostbüchlein*, 155–56). Furthermore, the sins of the ancestors will not destroy the future generations, as promised in 31:30 (cf. Ezek 18:20). They will remain faithful and escape punishment because the LORD will write the *torah* ("instruction, law") on their hearts (31:31–34).

38 A passive verb describes the rebuilding of Jerusalem, and it is modified by the prepositional phrase ליהוה, which may mean "for," "of," or "by the LORD." Since the LORD is subject of the active verb "build" in 31:4 and 28, the passive verb plus ל preposition construction may embrace all three possibilities. The LORD will build this city (cf. Rudolph, 188), but it will be built in the LORD's honor (NEB), and it will continue to belong to the LORD (Hauge, *SJOT* 1 [1988] 9). All of these forms of relationship are compatible with Jerusalem's status in v 40, קדש ליהוה, "holy to the LORD." According to the syntax of the verse, the actual building could be limited to the area between the Tower of Hananel and the Corner Gate. Note that Nehemiah's work crews בנה, "built," structures along the north wall, including the Tower of Hananel (Neh 3:1–3), but "made repairs" (חזק hiphil) on most of the rest of the wall (Neh 3:4–32). The sites and directions named in Jer 31:39–40, however, outline the perimeter of a larger area enclosing the older city boundaries. The movement is counterclockwise, as in Neh 3. The summary in v 40 implies that the whole area mapped in vv 38–40 will be built up and preserved.

This map begins at a well-known site on the north wall. According to Neh 3:1; 12:39; Zech 14:10, the Tower of Hananel was on the north side of the temple mount. The Corner Gate is also mentioned in 2 Kgs 14:13(//2 Chr 25:23), which locates it at the northwest corner, and 2 Chr 26:9, which tells how Uzziah fortified it with a tower. "Gate of the Corners" in Zech 14:10 is probably the same structure. The northern wall was the most vulnerable to attack since steep valleys surrounded the other three sides of the city. King Jehoash of Israel breached the northern wall near the Corner Gate (2 Kgs 14:13). The Babylonians probably entered from the north also. (Malamat, "The Last Kings of Judah and the Fall of Jerusalem: An Historical-Chronological Study," *IEJ* 18 [1968] 155, presents the evidence, including Jer 39:3.)

39   The image of a measuring line evokes the allotment of the land to the Israelite settlers (Jer 13:25; Isa 34:17) as well as the marking out of persons and places for destruction (2 Sam 8:2; 2 Kgs 21:13; Lam 2:8). Measuring precedes building (Job 38:5; Neh 3:11). Zechariah and Ezekiel report visions in which a man with a measuring line measures Jerusalem (Zech 2:5[Eng 1]) or the temple area (Ezek 40:3, 5; 42:16, 19). Jer 31:39 shares the vocabulary of the eschatological visions and the report of the rebuilding and repair of Jerusalem's walls under Nehemiah. Both the visionary guide and the human workers are missing, however, and the line itself יצא, "goes forth" (compare Ezek 47:3). The measuring line suggests the course of a wall that has not yet been built (Rudolph, 187).

The two place names are unknown. "Gareb" is the name of one of David's mighty men (2 Sam 23:38). Assonance with גָּרָב, "itch, scab," suggests an unclean site. Priests suffering from this condition were excluded from service at the altar (Lev 21:20). Gareb's location is "opposite it [m sg]." The closest antecedent for the pronominal suffix is the Corner Gate in v 38. During the eighth century B.C. the ridge west of the temple mount had been settled and then encircled with a defensive wall that was still standing at the time of the Babylonian conquest (Avigad, *Discovering*, 54). Gareb Hill may be a rise on the western ridge along the line of the eighth-century wall. (Simons, *Jerusalem*, 232, says it was the whole western boundary.) V 40 implies that the Valley of ben-Hinnom, which borders the western ridge to the west and south, will be inside the new perimeter. Gareb Hill would then have to be located even farther west or southwest, across the Hinnom Valley from the western ridge. (Herion, *ABD* 2:907, advances the same possibility.) The mountain west of the Hinnom Valley in Josh 15:8 may be a candidate. The location of Goah is also unknown. Since the measuring line will make a turn (סבב niphal) to get there, it may be near the southwest corner of the area being defined, southwest or south of the Hinnom Valley. The wall built under Nehemiah's leadership did not include the Hinnom Valley or even the western ridge, which is called Mount Zion today (King, *ABD*, 3:757).

40   The Valley of ben-Hinnom is infamous in the book of Jeremiah as the site of Topheth, where children were "passed through the fire" to strange gods. (See the *Comment* on 32:35.) The הַדֶּשֶׁן, "fatty ashes," of the sacrificial victim (Lev 6:3 [Eng 10]) would refer to their remains. Jer 19:6–13 warns that Topheth will be filled with dead bodies and graves as a judgment upon the city's false worship. Recent archeological investigation in the valley has brought to light several tombs from the seventh and sixth centuries B.C. (King, *Jeremiah*, 134–36). The place represents the epitome of the people's unholiness.

The Valley of ben-Hinnom joins the Kidron Valley southeast of Jerusalem. North of this intersection, the Kidron lies just outside the eastern wall of the city and the temple. The Horse Gate was located in that wall, somewhere south of the temple mount (Neh 3:28). The name קדרון, "Kidron," sounds like the verb קדר, "be dark, mourn." The Kidron Valley was a garbage dump (1 Kgs 15:13; 2 Kgs 23:6) and the location of the graves of the common people, which Josiah defiled with the dust and ashes of the image he removed from the temple and destroyed (2 Kgs 23:6). Monumental tombs from the eighth and seventh centuries B.C. have been found on the east side of the Kidron Valley, while on the west slope, below the city walls, there were terraces for the cultivation of vineyards and orchards (King, *Jeremiah*, 130–34, 158–60). The best news of this salvation oracle is not the enlargement of the city but the sanctification of the most polluted and defiled regions. The people will stop defiling it, and the LORD will declare it holy. This is essential preparation for a city that will be called "the LORD's throne" (Jer 3:17) and "holy hill" (31:23). The city made holy to the LORD symbolizes the same spiritual transformation for its people.

Although no new fortifications are mentioned, the LORD guarantees Jerusalem's inviolability. The boundary sketched in vv 38–40 would be a poor location for a defensive wall because the strategic valleys would be inside the city instead of outside the walls. This map illustrates that Jerusalem will not need defenses made of stone. It will be safe because it will be holy. Its people will not continue in the sin and apostasy that led to its destruction. The LORD's new building, v 38, will be protected by the promise not to uproot or overthrow (cf. 31:28).

Explanation

The conclusion to the Book of Consolation uses the more concrete, prosaic language of justice, covenant, oath, and topography to offer assurance and hope to the people who hear the urgent invitation to return to the LORD in chaps. 30–31. Those hearers know what it means to bear the burden of the nation's guilt. The five oracles in this section offer them the best possible news about what the LORD will do for their descendants, who are referred to in the third person throughout vv 23–40. Their posterity or lineage, the houses of Israel and Judah, will one day see the final end of the judgment that has engulfed the lives of those readers and hearers (v 28). Their descendants will be spared from the suffering that results from sin for four reasons: (1) Their ancestors' sins will not be held against them (v 30). (2) The city and land polluted by their ancestors' idolatry will be made holy to the LORD (v 40). (3) Their sin will be forgiven and forgotten (v 34). (4) Their memories, desires, and decisions will be brought into conformity with God's self-revelation to Israel (vv 33–34). The LORD will do all of this under the new covenant in order to secure the future of the people the LORD loves. Rachel's weeping will end (31:15). After these promises are fulfilled, joyful worshipers will again bless the LORD's city, Zion, and marvel at the power of forgiveness and the strength of holiness.

XVIII. A Promise, Signed and Sealed
(32:1–44[LXX 39:1–44])

Bibliography

André, G. *Determining the Destiny: PQD in the Old Testament.* ConBOT 16. Lund: Gleerup, 1980. **Avigad, N.** *Hebrew Bullae from the Time of Jeremiah: Remnants of a Burnt Archive.* Jerusalem: Israel Exploration Society, 1986. **Begg, C.** "Yahweh's 'Visitation' of Zedekiah (Jer 32,5)." *ETL* 63 (1987) 113–17. **Brueggemann, W.** "The Book of Jeremiah, Portrait of the Prophet." *Int* 37 (1983) 130–45. ———. "Israel's Sense of Place in Jeremiah." In *Rhetorical Criticism.* FS J. Muilenburg, ed. J. Jackson and M. Kessler. Pittsburgh: Pickwick, 1974. 149–65. ———. *The Land: Place as Gift, Promise, and Challenge in Biblical Faith.* Philadelphia: Fortress 1977. 107–29. **Chang, P.** "Jeremiah's Hope in Action: An Exposition of Jeremiah 32:1–15." *The East Asia Journal of Theology* 2 (1984) 244–50. **Clements, R.** "Jeremiah, Prophet of Hope." *RevExp* 78 (1981) 345–63. **Crenshaw, J.** "YHWH Ṣᵉbaʾot Šᵉmo: A Form-Critical Analysis." *ZAW* 81 (1969) 156–75. **Davies, E.** "Land: Its Rights and Privileges." In *The World of Ancient Israel, Sociological, Anthropological and Political Perspectives,* ed. R. Clements. Cambridge: Cambridge UP, 1989. 349–70. **Day, J.** *Molech, A God of Human Sacrifice in the Old Testament.* Cambridge: Cambridge UP, 1989. **Eissfeldt, O.** *Molk als Opferbegriff im Punischen und Hebräischen und das Ende des Gottes Moloch.* Halle, 1935. **Fischer, L.** "Die Urkunden im Jer 32,11–14 nach der Ausgrabung und dem Talmud." *ZAW* 30 (1910) 136–42. **Gevaryahu, H.** "Biblical Colophons: A Source for the 'Biography' of Authors, Texts and Books." In *Edinburgh Congress Volume.* VTSup 28. Leiden: Brill, 1975. 42–59. **Greenberg, M.** *Biblical Prose Prayer as a Window to the Popular Religion of Israel.* Berkeley: University of California Press, 1983. **Gunneweg, A.** "Heil im Gericht, Zur Interpretation von Jeremias später Verkündigung." In *Traditio-Krisis-Renovatio aus theologischer Sicht.* FS. W. Zeller, ed. B. Jaspert and R. Mohr. Marburg: N. G. Elvert, 1976. 1–8. **Haran, M.** "Book–Scrolls in Israel in Pre-Exilic Times." *JJS* 33 (1982) 161–73. ———. "Temples and Cultic Open Areas as Reflected in the Bible." In *Temples and High Places in Biblical Times,* ed. A. Biran. Jerusalem: Nelson Glueck School of Biblical Archaeology of Hebrew Union College-Jewish Institute of Religion, 1981. 31–37. ———. *Temples and Temple-Service in Ancient Israel: An Inquiry into the Character of Cult Phenomena and the Historical Setting of the Priestly School.* Oxford: Clarendon, 1978. 20–25. **Kilpp, N.** *Neiderreissen und aufbauen.* Biblisch-theologische Studien 13. Neukirchen: Neukirchener, 1990. 68–85. **Lang, B.** "The Social Organization of Peasant Poverty in Biblical Israel." In *Anthropological Approaches to the Old Testament,* ed. B. Lang. Philadelphia: Fortress 1985. 83–99. **Lundbom, J.** "Baruch, Seraiah, and Expanded Colophons in the Book of Jeremiah." *JSOT* 36 (1986) 89–114. **Macholz, G. C.** "Jeremia in der Kontinuität der Prophetie." In *Probleme biblischer Theologie,* ed. H. W. Wolff. Munich: Chr. Kaiser, 1971. 306–34. **Malamat, A.** "The Last Kings of Judah and the Fall of Jerusalem: An Historical-Chronological Study." *IEJ* 18 (1968) 137–56. **Migsch, H.** *Gottes Wort über das Ende Jerusalems: Eine literarstil- und gattungskritische Untersuchung des Berichtes Jeremia 34,1–7; 32,2–5; 37,3–38,28.* Österreichische Biblische Studien 2. Klosterneuburg: Österreichisches Katholisches Bibelwerk, 1981. **Oppenheim, A.** "'Siege–Documents' from Nippur." *Iraq* 17 (1955) 69–89. **Patrick, D.** *Old Testament Law.* Atlanta: John Knox, 1985. 181–85. **Porten, B.** "A New Look at Aramaic Papyri and Parchments." *BA* 42 (1979) 74–104. **Rubinger, N.** "Jeremiah's Epistle to the Exiles and the Field in Anathoth." *Judaism* 26 (1977) 84–91. **Smith, M.** *The Early History of God.* San Francisco: Harper and Row, 1990. 132–38. **Thiel, W.** *Die deuteronomistische Redaktion von Jeremia 26–45.* WMANT 52. Neukirchen: Neukirchener,

1981. 29–37. **Untermann, J.** *From Repentance to Redemption: Jeremiah's Thought in Transition.* JSOTSup 54. Sheffield: JSOT Press, 1987. 111–40. **Wanke, G.** "Jeremias Ackerkauf: Heil im Gericht?" In *Prophet und Prophetenbuch.* FS O. Kaiser, ed. V. Fritz, K.-F. Pohlmann, and H.-C. Schmitt. BZAW 185. Berlin: de Gruyter, 1989. 265–76. **Weinfeld, M.** "Jeremiah and the Spiritual Metamorphosis of Israel." *ZAW* 88 (1976) 17–56.

Translation

[1] *The word which came to Jeremiah from the* LORD *in the tenth year*[a] *of Zedekiah,* [b] *the king of Judah* [b] *(that was the eighteenth year of Nebuchadrezzar* [c] *):*
[2] *At that time the army* [a] *of the king of Babylon was besieging Jerusalem and Jeremiah* [b] *the prophet* [b] *was confined in the court of the guard which was at the house of the king* [c] *of Judah,* [c] [3] *because Zedekiah, the king* [a] *of Judah,* [a] *had confined him, saying, "Why do you prophesy, 'Thus says the* LORD: *Behold, I am about to give this city into the control of the king of Babylon and he will capture it,* [4] *so that Zedekiah,* [a] *the king of Judah,* [a] *will not escape from the control of the Chaldeans,* [b] *for he will surely be given into the control of the king of Babylon. He will speak with him mouth-to-mouth and see him* [c] *eye-to-eye.* [cd] [5] *Then he will make Zedekiah go to Babylon, and there he will remain* [a] [b] *until I decide his fate—oracle of the* LORD. *If you go on fighting the Chaldeans, you will not succeed* [b] *'?"*
[6a] *Then Jeremiah said, "The word of the* LORD *came to me, saying,* [7] *'See here, Hanamel, son of Shallum your uncle, will come to you, saying, "Buy for yourself my field which is in Anathoth, for yours is the right of redemption by purchase."'* [8] *Then Hanamel, my uncle's son, came to me,* [a] *in accordance with the* LORD'S *word,* [a] *to the court of the guard, and said to me, 'Please buy my field which is in Anathoth,* [b] *which is in the land of Benjamin,* [b] *for yours is the right of possession* [c] *and yours is (the right) of redemption.* [d] *Buy [it] for yourself.'* [cd] *Then I knew that it was the word of the* LORD. [9] *So I bought the field from Hanamel, my uncle's son,* [a] *which was in Anathoth.* [a] *I weighed* [b] *the money for him,* [b] *the seven shekels and ten of silver.*
[10] *"I wrote in the deed, sealed it,* [a] *had it witnessed, and weighed out the money on the scales.* [11] *Then I took the deed of purchase, the sealed one—* [a] *the commandment and the statutes* [a] *—and the open copy,* [12] *and I gave* [a] *the deed of purchase* [a] *to Baruch son of Neriah, the son of Mahseiah, in the sight of Hanamel* [b] *my uncle and the witnesses* [c] [d] *who wrote in* [d] *the deed of purchase,* [e] *in the sight of all* [f] *the Judeans sitting* [g] *in the court of the guard.* [13] *I commanded* [a] *Baruch in their sight, saying,* [14] *'Thus says the* LORD *of hosts,* [a] *the God of Israel:* [a] *Take* [b] *these documents,* [b] *this deed of purchase,* [c] *and the sealed one* [c] [d] *and this open document* [d] *and put them* [e] *in a clay jar so that they* [f] *will survive for a long time.* [15] *For thus says the* LORD [a] *of hosts, the God of Israel:* [a] *Houses, fields, and vineyards will again be bought in this land.'*
[16] *"Then I prayed to the* LORD, *after I gave the deed of purchase to Baruch son of Neriah,* [17] *'O Lord* [a] GOD, *since you have made the heavens and the earth by your great might and your outstretched arm, nothing is too difficult for you.* [18] *One who does mercy to thousands and recompenses the parents' iniquity to the bosom of their children after them, the great God, the valiant One, the* LORD [a] *of Hosts is his name.* [a] [19] *Great the counsel and many the deed* [a] *of you whose eyes are open toward all* [b] *the ways of human beings, to give to each according to his or her ways* [c] *and according to the fruit of his or her deeds,* [c] [20] *who worked signs and wonders in the land of Egypt* [a] *until today, and also in Israel and with humankind, and made for yourself a name as at this day.* [21] *You brought out your people, Israel, from the land of Egypt by signs and wonders and with a strong hand and an outstretched arm and* [a] *with great fear.* [a]

²²*You gave them this land which you had sworn to their fathers* ᵃ*to give to them,*ᵃ *a land flowing with milk and honey.* ²³*They came and took possession of it, but they did not listen to your voice and they did not walk in your law; all that you had commanded them* ᵃ*to do*ᵃ *they did not do, so all this calamity happened to them.* ²⁴*Behold the siege ramps*ᵃ *are coming to the city to destroy it, since the city is given into the control of the Chaldeans who are fighting against it by sword, famine, and pestilence,*ᵇ *and what you have spoken is happening.* ᶜ*Look, you can see.*ᶜ ²⁵*You said to me,* ᵃ*O Lord GOD,*ᵃ *"Buy for yourself the field with silver,*ᵇ *and have it witnessed," while the city is given into the control of the Chaldeans.'"*

²⁶*The word of the LORD came* ᵃ*to Jeremiah,*ᵃ *saying,* ²⁷*"Behold, I am the LORD, the God of all flesh. Is anything too difficult*ᵃ *for me?* ²⁸*Therefore, thus says the LORD:* ᵃ*Look at me,*ᵃ *I am about to give this city* ᵇ*into the control of the Chaldeans and*ᵇ *into the control of Nebuchadrezzar*ᶜ *the king of Babylon, and he will conquer it.* ²⁹*The Chaldeans who are fighting against this city will come, and they will kindle this city with fire and burn it and the houses where incense has been burned upon the roofs to the Baal and libations have been poured out to other gods in order to provoke me to anger.* ³⁰*For the Israelites and the Judeans have surely been doing evil since their youth;* ᵃ*for* ᵇ*the Israelites are surely provoking me to anger by the works of their hands—oracle of the LORD.*ᵃ ³¹*Because this city has been mine, to my anger and my rage, from the day she was built until this day, I will remove it from before my face,* ³²*because of all the evil of the Israelites and the Judeans which they have done to provoke me, they, their kings, their royal officials, their priests, and their prophets, even*ᵃ *every Judean and the inhabitants of Jerusalem.* ³³*They turned their back to me and not their face.* ᵃ*I taught*ᵃ *them, teaching persistently, but none of them listened to take correction.* ³⁴*They put*ᵃ *their abominations in the house upon which my name is called in order to pollute it,* ³⁵*and they built the high places* ᵃ*of the Baal*ᵃ *which are in the Valley of ben-Hinnom to cause their sons and daughters to pass through to 'the Molech'* ᵇ *(which I had not commanded them, and to do this abomination had never arisen upon my heart), in order to make Judah sin.*ᶜ

³⁶*"Now, therefore,*ᵃ *thus says the LORD, the God of Israel unto this*ᵇ *city, of which* ᶜ*you are saying,*ᶜ *'It has been given into the control of the king of Babylon by sword, famine, and pestilence*ᵈ*':* ³⁷*Look at me, I am about to gather them* ᵃ*from all the lands*ᵃ *to which I have banished them in my anger, in my rage, and in great wrath, and I am about to return them to this place and make them dwell securely.* ³⁸*They will be my people, while I will be their God.* ³⁹*I will give them* ᵃ*one heart and one way*ᵃ *to fear me always, for their good and for the good of their descendants after them.* ⁴⁰*I will make an eternal covenant with them to the effect that I will not turn from going after them* ᵃ*so that I can do them good;*ᵃ *I will put fear of me in their hearts so that they will not turn aside from me.* ⁴¹ᵃ*I will rejoice over them*ᵃ *to do them good, and I will plant them in this land faithfully with all my heart and with all my self.* ⁴²*For thus says the LORD: When I have brought all this great calamity upon this people, then I will bring upon them all the good which I am promising concerning them.* ⁴³*Fields*ᵃ *will be purchased in this land of which* ᵇ*you are saying,* ᵇ *'It is desolate, without human being or animal. It has been given into the control of the Chaldeans.'* ⁴⁴*They will buy fields with silver and will write in the deed, seal it, and have it witnessed in the land of Benjamin, in the environs of Jerusalem, in the cities of Judah, in the cities of the mountain, in the cities of the Shefelah, and in the cities of the Negeb, for I will bring about their restoration—* ᵃ*oracle of the LORD."*ᵃ

Notes

1.a. K בִשְׁנַת, according to GKC §§ 128k, 134p, is a merely formal genitive, epexegetical, an appositive, like the Q בִּשְׁנֵה.
1.b-b. Not in LXX. MT frequently expands titles.
1.c. LXX has βασιλεῖ Ναβουχοδονοσορ βασιλεῖ Βαβυλῶνος, "King Nebuchadrezzar, king of Babylon," an unusual form of the title in LXX.
2.a. Collective noun with pl verb, as in Jer 34:7; 39:5; 52:8, 14; 2 Kgs 25:5, 10.
2.b-b., c-c. Not in LXX. MT typically adds or expands titles.
3.a-a. LXX has "the king, Zedekiah."
4.a-a. LXX has only "Zedekiah," as in v 5.
4.b. Nebuchadrezzar's dynasty.
4.c-c. Heb. idiom, lit. "his eyes with his eyes."
4.d. MT עֵינוֹ, a defective spelling of עֵינָיו; cf. the preceding עֵינֵי.
5.a. LXX^{A,Cmin} have ἀποθανεῖ ται, "die," as in 22:12, 26, which would not fit with the following clause in MT.
5.b-b. Not in LXX. MT clarifies the implications of the Zedekiah oracle for the current military situation.
6.a. LXX has another title, καὶ λόγος κυρίου ἐγενήθη πρὸς Ιερεμιαν, "And the word of the LORD came to Jeremiah," as in MT 28:12; 29:30; 32:26; 33:1, 19; 34:12; 35:12; 36:27; 37:6; 42:7; 43:8. MT suggests that the rest of the chapter serves as response to Zedekiah's question in vv 3–5.
8.a-a. Not in LXX. MT emphasizes fulfillment of God's word in v 7.
8.b-b. LXX has the clause after "my field."
8.c-c. LXX has ὅτι σοὶ κρίμα κτήσασθαι καὶ σὺ πρεσβύτερος, "for you have a right to buy it and you are elder," perhaps another reversal of clause order.
8.d-d. Not in LXX.
9.a-a. Not in LXX. MT adds a clarification derived from v 8.
9.b-b. Not in LXX. Cf. the similar clause in v 10. MT has two phrases in apposition, for clarification. The second phrase is unusual: "seventeen" is not usually expressed as a sum, and the unit, "shekels," does not appear when the substance, "silver," is definite.
10.a. *BHS* suggests appending עַל הַמִּצְוָה וְהַחֻקִּים, "according to the commandment and the conditions," from v 11, where the phrase seems out of place.
11.a-a. Not in LXX. *BHS* recommends adding עַל, "according to," and moving to the end of v 10. Cf. *Note* 10.a. Prefixing עַל, "according to," would also improve the sense in v 11.
12.a-a. LXX "it." Q^{Or} has the const, "the deed of purchase," as in v 11. MT has appositives, with the second indicating a subcategory of the first.
12.b. *BHS* recommends prefixing בֶּן, "the son of," with some MSS, LXX, Syr, Tg, and v 8.
12.c. LXX has τῶν ἑστηκότων, "the ones standing," suggesting an original Heb. הָעֹמְדִים, "the ones standing," which differs by only one letter from MT הָעֵדִים, "the witnesses."
12.d-d. Several MSS of LXX, α'σ', Syr, Tg, Vg translate the pass הַכְּתוּבִים, "who were written," i.e., their names.
12.e. *BHS* recommends adding the conj with several MSS of LXX, Syr, Vg.
12.f. Not in LXX. MT frequently has an additional כֹּל, "all."
12.g. Not in LXX.
13.a. L erroneously omits maqqeph.
14.a-a. Not in LXX. MT frequently expands titles.
14.b-b. Not in LXX. Clarifying addition in MT.
14.c-c. Not in LXX. Clarifying addition in MT, from v 11.
14.d-d. *BHS* recommends shortening to וְאֵת הַגָּלוּי, "and the open one," as in v 11. LXX translates καὶ τὸ βιβλίον τὸ ἀνεγνωσμένον, "and the document which had been read (aloud)," perhaps because the scribal practice of the unsealed copy was not known to the translators.
14.e., f. LXX has sg, "it."
15.a-a. Not in LXX. MT typically adds titles.
17.a. Not in LXX. MT typically expands titles.
18.a-a. LXX omits and moves "the LORD" to the beginning of v 19.
19.a. LXX adds ὁ θεὸς ὁ μέγας ὁ παντοκράτωρ καὶ μεγαλώνυμος κύριος, "the great, almighty God, and Lord of great name."

19.b. Not in LXX. MT typically adds כל, "all."

19.c-c. Not in LXX. MT echoes 17:10.

20.a. *BHS* recommends adding the conj, as in LXX[L], so that the following phrase does not refer to Egypt alone.

21.a-a. Syr (Tg) *wbhzw'*, suggesting Heb. ובמראה, "vision, spectacle."

22.a-a. Not in LXX. MT adds a clarification.

23.a-a. Not in LXX. MT adds a clarification.

24.a. LXX has ὄχλος, "crowd," which *BHS* suggests is a misreading of ὁ χοῦς, "the soil, dust put on the head when mourning," or LXX may be trying to make sense of a difficult Heb. description.

24.b. Not in LXX. MT has the full stereotyped expression.

24.c-c. Not in LXX. MT reinforces the prediction.

25.a-a. Not in LXX. MT clarifies the identity of the addressee.

25.b. LXX adds καὶ ἔγραψα βιβλίον καὶ ἐσφραγισάμην, "and I wrote a document and sealed (it)," and the following verb is also 1st person, as in v 10, "and I had it witnessed."

26.a-a. LXX has πρός με, "to me." Perhaps MT read אלי, "to me," as an abbreviation (Driver, *Textus* 1 [1960] 121).

27.a. LXX has κρυβήσεται, "be hidden," as in v 17. Syr and Tg follow.

28.a-a. LXX lacks הנני, "Look at me," and continues in the 3rd person.

28.b-b. Not in LXX. MT clarifies that Nebuchadrezzar will not take the city without the help of his army; cf. v 43.

28.c. Not in LXX. MT frequently adds names to titles.

30.a-a. Not in LXX. MT adds a clarifying expansion, using the charge from vv 29, 32 and introducing "the works of their hands" described in the following verses.

30.b. Rudolph recommends reading כל, "all," so that "Israelites" in v 30b combines "Israelites" and "Judeans" in v 30a. Such an equation can be assumed without the emendation.

32.a. Not in LXX.

33.a-a. MT has the inf abs where a finite verb is needed. *BHS* recommends emendation to ואלמד, "I taught," following LXX, Syr, Vg. The inf abs could have been miscopied from later in the verse.

34.a. K[Or] has pf with waw conj. The last clause of v 33 has interrupted the consecutive sequence.

35.a-a. Syr *btpt* = בתפת, "in Topheth," a place equated with the Valley of ben-Hinnom in 19:6, and a word that shares the same vowel pattern as בושת, "shame," a circumlocution for "baal" in some personal names (e.g., Mephibosheth = Meribbaal).

35.b. LXX adds the title βασιλεῖ, "king."

35.c. MT יחטי, with final א accidentally omitted from K. Driver calls it an abbreviation (*Textus* 1 [1960] 118).

36.a. Not in LXX, Syr. MT adds clarification.

36.b. Not in LXX.

36.c-c. MT is pl; LXX is sg, addressed to Jeremiah, as in v 43.

36.d. LXX has καὶ ἐν ἀποστολῇ, "and by banishment," for MT's ובדבר, "by pestilence." Cf. v 24, where LXX lacks the third part of the stereotyped expression.

37.a-a. LXX has the sg, ἐκ πάσης τῆς γῆς, "from the whole earth," a somewhat more expansive term than MT's "all the lands."

39.a-a. LXX reverses the order, ὁδὸν ἑτέραν καὶ καρδίαν ἑτέραν, "another way and another heart."

40.a-a. Not in LXX. MT explains the preceding clause, using material from v 41.

41.a-a. LXX has καὶ ἐπισκέψομαι . . . αὐτούς, "and I will visit them," a more common expression, consistent with the following clause.

43.a. LXX is pl. MT definite sg noun השדה, "field(s)," is generic.

43.b-b. LXX is sg, as in v 36, which is appropriate to the context addressed to Jeremiah.

44.a-a. Not in LXX. MT frequently adds this formula.

Form/Structure/Setting

Chap. 32 is marked off from the preceding chapter by its superscription (v 1) and from the following chapter by the heading in 33:1. The wording of a superscription appears in 32:26 (cf. 16:1), but there it serves to link the LORD's answer (vv 27–44) to Jeremiah's prayer (vv 17–25). Under the initial superscription stand passages representing at least four distinct types of prose literature, but their contents and order in this chapter connect them as the presentation of a single episode in Jeremiah's ministry. The connections may be awkward, especially between vv 5 and 6, but the chapter as it stands effectively communicates a coherent message, consistent with the book of Jeremiah as a whole, which addresses subsequent generations of God's people. The chapter may be outlined as follows:

I. Superscription (v 1)
II. Setting and background (3rd person; vv 2–5)
  A. Jeremiah confined during siege (v 2)
  B. Prophecy about Zedekiah (vv 3–5)
III. Report of buying the field (1st person; vv 6–9)
  A. Word-event formula (v 6)
  B. The LORD discloses what Hanamel will do (v 7)
  C. Hanamel's proposal (v 8)
  D. Report of the purchase (v 9)
IV. Report of the sign-act: preserving the deed (vv 10–15)
  A. Report of the preparation of the deed (vv 10–12)
  B. Command to Baruch (vv 13–14)
  C. Interpretation: salvation announcement (v 15)
V. Jeremiah's prayer (vv 16–25)
  A. Narrative introduction (v 16)
  B. Praise description (vv 17–22)
  C. Israel's distress (vv 23–24)
  D. Complaint (v 25)
VI. The LORD's answer (vv 26–44)
  A. Narrative introduction (v 26)
  B. Self-description (v 27)
  C. Doom oracle against Jerusalem (vv 28–35)
    1. Judgment (vv 28–29a)
    2. Indictment (vv 29b–35)
  D. Salvation oracles for Jerusalem (vv 36–44)
    1. Restoration (vv 36–37)
    2. Eternal covenant (vv 38–41)
    3. Ownership of land (vv 42–44)

The core of the chapter is the first-person report of Jeremiah's redemption purchase of a field in his home town of Anathoth and the subsequent sign-act in which the deed was preserved in a pottery vessel (vv 6–15). Other first-person accounts in the book of Jeremiah include chap. 11; 13:1–14; 14:11–16; 16:1–18; 17:19–27; chap. 27. Three of these passages also contain God's disclosure to Jeremiah of the present or future speech or actions of other persons (11:18–23; 13:12–13; 16:10), as in 32:7. This phenomenon is also a feature of the book of Ezekiel (e.g., 12; 14:1–11; 33:23–33). A divine command usually follows the disclosure. 32:7, however, lacks such a command, unless the emendation advocated by Holladay (2: 203) is accepted. He moves "buy it for yourself" from Hanamel's speech in v 8 to the end of the LORD's speech in v 7. The unusual confirmation statement at the end of v 8 addresses the same concern. It seems to imply that, since the LORD had foretold what Hanamel would do, Hanamel's request should be fulfilled. V 25 concurs. The first command from the LORD comes in v 14, and it is addressed by Jeremiah to Baruch.

The purchase, which is described in detail in vv 9–12, is preparation for the sign-act commanded in vv 13–14, preserving the deed in a jar, and its interpretation, v 15. (Compare the form of 28:2–4.) The effect of this arrangement is to emphasize the time that will elapse ("a long time") before houses, fields, and vineyards will "once again" be bought in the land. It does not seem likely that the present form of the passage would support hope for the uninterrupted continuation or the imminent restoration of normal life in the territory of Benjamin or anywhere else in the land.

J. R. Lundbom (*JSOT* 36 [1986] 89–114), following H. M. I. Gevaryahu ("Biblical Colophons," 42–59), identifies in 32:6–15 an "expanded colophon," which contains five of the standard colophon elements: (1) name and genealogy of the scribe; (2) reason for writing the document; (3) blessing; (4) date, now in v 1; and (5) disposition of documents. Colophons could be written as narratives, describing how the scribe performed the necessary duties. The main texts of some contracts from the ancient Near East were also written as narrative or dialogue, as in vv 6–15. One such document, quoted by Oppenheim (*Iraq* 17 [1955] 71), has several features in common with our passage. During a siege of Nippur in the seventh century B.C., parents sold their daughter as a slave in order to assure that she would be fed and to raise cash (silver) to buy food for themselves, "Take my daughter and keep her alive! She shall be your (slave)girl . . ." Note the imperative verbs in this contract, as in 32:7. Other documents found in the same person's family archives included five purchase deeds for real estate (Oppenheim, *Iraq* 17 [1955] 70). While these scribal genres may have left their mark on 32:6–15, other forms have also helped to shape its wording and structure, such as the command to perform a sign-act (vv 13–15).

Wanke ("Jeremias Ackerkauf," 265–76) finds the earliest version of the account in vv 6–14, minus some expansions in v 8, and dates its composition before the fall of Jerusalem. Like 27:2–3, 12b; 29:4–7, this passage warned the people of further judgment and suffering and called upon them to acknowledge their guilt. The subsequent addition of v 15 as a second interpretation of the sign-act added the hopeful element. Holladay (2: 203–12), similarly, finds the core of the chapter in vv 6–15, but he also includes vv 17, 21–25 from the prayer and vv 26–27, 36–37, 41–44 from the LORD's response. According to his view, the sign-act has two interpretations. The first, in v 14, is primarily for Jeremiah, indicating that this proof of "modest reconciliation" (212) with his family would be known for a long time. The second divine word, in v 15, reveals the significance of the land transaction for the whole people and becomes the turning point in Jeremiah's understanding of God's plan.

References to Jeremiah's confinement in the court of the guard (vv 8, 12) invite an explanation, which is provided by a third-person account in vv 2–5. Zedekiah had imprisoned Jeremiah because he had prophesied the defeat of Jerusalem and the capture and deportation of Zedekiah. The reason for his incarceration is couched as a question, "Why do you prophesy?" followed by a précis of the oracles given to Zedekiah through Jeremiah in chap. 21, 34:1–8, and chap. 37. The strange effects of this interrogative are to make Zedekiah refer to himself in the third person in vv 3–5 and to render the first-person account (vv 6b–25) a response to Zedekiah's accusation. V 6a, "Jeremiah said," makes this connection by introducing vv 6b–25 as Jeremiah's answer to Zedekiah's question. To be completely consistent, v 26 should have been in first person also, so that the LORD's answer to Jeremiah's prayer would have been included explicitly in Jeremiah's response. LXX does have "to me" in v 26, and Holladay advocates adopting this reading (2:205). Vv 27–35 reconfirm the first and last statements of vv 3b–5, against the city and its resistance to the Babylonians, but do not mention Zedekiah.

Two other impediments exist to reading vv 6–44 as Jeremiah's response to Zedekiah, however. First, the answer does not fit the question. Not only does Zedekiah not appear in these verses (6–44), but they also promise restoration of the exiles instead of expanding the judgment theme. Second, Jeremiah has already been confined in the court of the guard when the matters recounted in vv 6–44 begin. In chap. 26 the question-accusation (26:9) accompanies Jeremiah's arrest. He does not give a defense speech until later, after the trial begins. There is no trial in chap. 32, and vv 6–44 need not be read as a speech by a defendant. The king's question is rhetorical, introducing a quotation of 34:2b–3. The purpose of vv 2–5 is not only to explain Jeremiah's confinement and to set the time for the episode in vv 6–15; the passage also provides background for the prayer, especially vv 24–25. Jeremiah is confined inside a besieged city, about to be overrun by the Babylonians, and God's will for Jeremiah is to redeem a piece of land that he cannot visit, much less use. This tension is heightened by the information in vv 2–5. The juxtaposition of vv 2–5 and 6–44 as implied accusation and response contributes to the picture of Zedekiah as a ruler who is concerned primarily with his personal fate. The LORD, on the other hand, cares for all the people and the whole land (vv 42–44).

The prayer and God's answer, vv 16–44, seem to come too late, however, because Jeremiah brings before the LORD his confusion over the meaning of the purchase of land in his current circumstances (vv 24–25) only after he has completed the transaction. The whole passage of prayer and answer would seem to fit logically immediately after Hanamel's speech in v 8. Having asked for and heard the explanation, Jeremiah would acknowledge that the LORD was behind it (v 8b) and would carry out the command. Interpreters have explained the current arrangement of the chapter in terms of Jeremiah's spirituality or his psychology and by theories of composition and redaction. Calvin (4:183–84) teaches that Jeremiah obeyed first, because he was convinced of God's truth, and then "bridled" his petulance with praise (vv 17–22) before bringing his complaint. Rudolph (193), who includes only vv 17aα, 24–29a, 42–44 in the original text of the prayer, proposes that Jeremiah acts as a prophet in vv 6–15 and then succumbs to typical human doubts. Nicholson (2:79) and Thiel (*Redaktion*, 32) find nothing from Jeremiah himself in vv 16–44 and assign the whole passage to a deuteronomistic author or authors who supplemented and explained the chapter's core for the edification of the exilic community (a process that continued in chap. 33). These later hands did not break up the original passage, however.

The order of material in chap. 32, the account of a ministry incident followed by the text of a prayer, is also found in chap. 20. The juxtaposition of 20:1–6 and 7–18 implies that Jeremiah's suffering at Pashhur's hands prompted the lament, even after Jeremiah had delivered a judgment oracle against him. The parallel between chaps. 20 and 32 is not exact, however. There is no divine response to Jeremiah's prayer in chap. 20, and 32:17–25 are not poetry.

The form of the prayer in chap. 32 resembles the lengthy prose prayers in

Neh 9:6–37 and Dan 9:4–19. All three prose prayers include these three elements, in varying proportions: (1) praise describing the LORD's character and deeds, especially those things done on Israel's behalf; (2) confession of the people's sin; and (3) lament over the current situation of distress. Daniel's prayer, like Jeremiah's, is prompted by perplexity over the tension between God's word through Jeremiah (9:2) and his own present circumstances. Daniel also receives a divine word of explanation and promise as an answer to his prayer (9:20–27).

Weinfeld (*Deuteronomy*, 42) calls vv 17–23 a "liturgical oration" in a prayer by a national leader, comparable to Deut 3:23–25; 2 Sam 7:22–24; 1 Kgs 8:23–53; 2 Kgs 19:15–19; Neh 9:6–37. These orations open with a statement about the LORD's uniqueness and the theme of world creation. Macholz ("Jeremia in der Kontinuität," 317) suggests the label "judgment doxology" for vv 17–24. Crenshaw's form-critical study (*ZAW* 81 [1969] 156–75) of the sentence יהוה צבאות שמו, "The LORD of Hosts is his name" (v 18), offers even more precision on vv 16–25. He concludes that Jewish worshipers in the exile used this sentence in penitence and fasting (173) to confess faith in their God, "who appeared to be impotent because of the defeat of his people and destruction of his temple" (168), but whom they believed in as creator and judge (174). Jeremiah's faith contrasts with the people's, who perform acts of devotion to Baal and Molech (vv 29, 34–35).

The verb in v 16, ואתפלל, "and I prayed," introduces vv 16–25 as a prayer. This verb often has the specific sense of "intercede for" or "inquire of the LORD for a salvation oracle." Like other prose prayers in the OT, this one maintains a consistent second-person address to God throughout. It begins with a formula, "Alas," found sometimes in the speech of one person to another (Judg 11:35; 2 Kgs 6:5) but more often in prayers to God in times of deep distress and danger (Josh 7:7; Judg 6:22), including especially the prayers of Ezekiel (4:14; 9:8; 11:13; 21:5[Eng 20:49]) and Jeremiah himself (1:6; 4:10). In v 24 הנה, "see," calls attention to the circumstances in which the prayer is uttered and in which the answer is expected (cf. Gen 24:13). The final formula, "but you have said," is found in prayers of Jacob (Gen 32:12) and Moses (Exod 33:12; Num 11:21). In Gen 32:12 the formula introduces a citation of the LORD's promise of prosperity and descendants, which is offered to God as a motivation for granting Jacob's petition. The danger facing Jacob stands in tension with the promise. Similarly, Moses quotes the LORD's words in two prayers where a mismatch exists between the LORD's assurance or promise and the help that has been provided for him up to that point (Exod 33:12; Num 11:21). Num 11:21 resembles the prayer in Jer 32:16–25 because it includes no petition. Moses expresses his perplexity by juxtaposing a description of his current situation of distress and the LORD's assurance (compare Jer 32:25). Moses' prayer continues (11:22) with questions about the source of the promised food. Questions regarding the LORD's actions in the past or future frequently follow the formula "Alas, Lord GOD," as in Josh 7:7; 2 Kgs 3:10; Ezek 9:8; 11:13. Jer 32:16–25, however, does not articulate Jeremiah's apparent perplexity in the form of questions. This prayer, therefore, is truncated. It does not do the things that a prayer like this is expected to do. Israel's sin is confessed (v 23), but there is no request for forgiveness. Instead, the justice of the judgment being endured by the people at that very moment (see v 1) is acknowledged (v 23). The situation of distress in the midst of which Jeremiah and his people live is described (v 24), but there is no petition for deliverance (contrast Hezekiah's prayer, 2 Kgs

19:15b–19). Their end is inevitable because God had said it would happen. Jeremiah expresses perplexity about the contradiction between what he had been commanded to do in buying the field and the current circumstances, which make the purchase seem foolish, but he asks no questions seeking an explanation of the LORD's plans. Nevertheless, all three unspoken aspects of this incomplete prayer receive answers in the verses that follow.

The LORD's response in vv 27–44 is composed largely of material also found elsewhere in the book: a judgment oracle resembling 32:3; 34:2, several familiar descriptions of Israel's sin, from Jeremiah as well as Deuteronomy and 1–2 Kings, and salvation promises from 24:7; 31:31–34; 32:15. God's response is introduced in MT by the narrator of the chapter, who refers to Jeremiah in the third person. LXX, however, uses the first person. V 42 initiates a series of prose oracles, each introduced by the messenger formula, which continues through chap. 33, interrupted only by the superscriptions in 33:1, 19, 23. Holladay (2:209) calls attention to the parallels between Jeremiah's prayer and the LORD's response (vv 17//27, 24//36).

The setting of chap. 32 in the book of Jeremiah makes it an extension of the Book of Consolation in chaps. 30–31. Those chapters are primarily poetry, but the prose passages (30:8–9; 31:1, 26–40) bear some resemblance to the oracles in 32:36–44 (and chap. 33). Furthermore, in chaps. 30–31 salvation is declared in the shadow of continuing and worsening suffering (30:5–7, 12–15), just as in 32:2–5, 24–25, 28–35. The land purchase and sign-act in 32:6–15, as interpreted in vv 36–44, underscore and expand upon the salvation announcement in 30:3 that the LORD will restore Israel and Judah to the land sometime in the future. Carroll (622) comments that in chap. 32 the LORD makes good on the promises in chaps. 30–31. The preservation of the "deed" (ספר) "for a long time" (32:14) seems to imply that the function of the "book" (ספר) in 30:2 is also to guarantee the promises it holds until those coming days. In other words, chaps. 30–31 give further interpretation for the sign-act in chap. 32, and the sign-act demonstrates the truth of the broader promises that the people of Israel will once again possess the land that God had given to their ancestors (cf. 31:23). The law that provided for redemption of fields and houses (Lev 25:25), which Jeremiah follows in vv 6–15, was designed to perpetuate the people's possession of the land given to their ancestors by God and apportioned among the tribes, clans, and families. The literary alliance between chaps. 30–31 and 32 is a fruitful one.

Recently, Seitz (*Theology*, 244) has proposed that 32:2, 6–15 were part of another collection of Jeremiah traditions first and were moved later to their present position. He observes that the style and form of vv 2–5, 6–15 are different from any passage in chaps. 30–31, that the setting described in vv 2–5 corresponds to the situation in chaps. 37–38, and that the detail-laden style also suits these later chapters. Seitz concludes that the original position of 32:2, 6–15 in his proposed Scribal Chronicle was between 37:20–21 and 38:1–6 (*Theology*, 283). This arrangement fills in some gaps in the account as it now stands in chaps. 37–38 (*Theology*, 243–45). In 37:11–15 Jeremiah attempts to leave Jerusalem during a temporary lifting of the siege in order to acquire land in Anathoth. He is stopped at the gate and handed over to the royal officials for punishment, but Zedekiah moves Jeremiah to the court of the guard to protect him from them (37:20–21). This courtyard is Jeremiah's location in 32:6–15. Seitz thinks that 32:6–15 provides a better explanation for the renewed opposition from the royal officials and their call for the death penalty in 38:1–4, although he cites no clear verbal connections between the two passages. Finally, Seitz would include something like v 2 to report that the Babylonians had resumed the siege, information that is now missing from chap. 38 but is implied in it.

Subsequently, according to Seitz's reconstruction, an Exilic Redactor moved 32:2, 6–15, and other pieces of the Scribal Chronicle, to their present positions "in order to serve as pretexts for redactional elaboration" (*Theology*, 224–25). The account of the land purchase was provided with background information (vv 3–5) derived from 34:1–5, which, according to Seitz's theory, originally stood after 37:3. (Contrast Holladay's proposal in 2:34 that the command to prepare the Book of Consolation scroll followed closely the purchase of the field.) The theological reflection and exposition of Jeremiah material that was carried out in the exile after 597 B.C. developed the conviction that further disobedience and another judgment by the LORD were inevitable, but that there would be a future for God's people, led by the return of the exiles from Babylon (Seitz, *Theology*, 224–25). The rearrangement of Zedekiah material among Jehoiakim chapters expresses an awareness of the essential similarity and unity of the judgments carried out in 597 and 587–86 B.C.

The events of chap. 21; 32:1–6; 34:1–7; chaps. 37–38 are all set during the lengthy final siege of Jerusalem by the Babylonians, which began in Zedekiah's tenth year. The walls were breached on the ninth of Tammuz in Zedekiah's eleventh year, and on the fifth or tenth of Ab in Nebuchadrezzar's nineteenth year, the Babylonians burned the city and the temple. The exact reckoning of these regnal years is disputed. Holladay (2:34) dates the siege from January 588 to July 587, whereas Hayes and Hooker (*New Chronology*, 97–98) put it one year later, from January 587 to July 586. Malamat ("The Twilight of Judah," in *Edinburgh Congress Volume*, VTSup 28 [Leiden: Brill, 1975] 145) calculates the length of the siege as thirty months, from January 588 to July 586. The Babylonians lifted the siege temporarily (37:5–11), apparently because of the threatening approach of an Egyptian army under Pharaoh Hophra (Holladay, 2:34, in the summer of 588; Malamat, *IEJ* 18 [1968] 152, in winter-spring 587). This provided a brief period of hope for the people in Jerusalem, which was followed by bitter disappointment when Egyptian help did not materialize (Lam 4:17). Most of the fortified cities of Judah had been conquered (34:7), but Malamat cites evidence that suggests that cities in Benjamin (including Mizpah and Ramah) were not destroyed, perhaps because Benjamin had already surrendered to Nebuchadrezzar ("The Last Wars of the Kingdom of Judah," *JNES* 9 [1950] 227). A complete account of these crucial months cannot be given because the book of Jeremiah is less concerned with a thorough depiction of political and military events than with evoking the atmosphere of crisis within which Zedekiah and the other leaders decided to reject the LORD's word given through Jeremiah.

Comment

1   The heading used here, "The word which came to Jeremiah from the LORD," also appears in 25:1; 30:1; 34:1, 8. In 25:1 it is also accompanied by a date for-

mula that includes the regnal year of the king of Judah and the regnal year of Nebuchadrezzar. Holladay considers the synchonisms in 25:1 (1:667–68) and 32:1 (2:213) to be erroneous, however, and suggests that they result from a corruption or misunderstanding in 25:1 of "accession year" as "first year." Nebuchadrezzar became king in the autumn of 605 B.C., and his first regnal year began March-April 604. Holladay concludes that the synchronism in 32:1 is one year off because of this error (1:668). According to Hayes and Hooker's new chronology (*New Chronology*, 94–95), however, there is no discrepancy in 32:1. They calculate Zedekiah's first year as 596–95, so his tenth year was the same as Nebuchadrezzar's eighteenth, Nisan (March-April) 597–Nisan 596. Malamat ("The Twilight of Judah," 144–45) dates Jeremiah's purchase to 29 April 587 B.C.E., which was at the beginning of Nebuchadrezzar's eighteenth year and just after the middle of Zedekiah's tenth year. Malamat reckons the regnal years of Judean kings from Tishri, the seventh month (September-October), instead of Nisan. Holladay, therefore, puts the events of chap. 32 in 588, while Malamat and Hayes and Hooker date them in 587.

The precise location of the court of the guard in the palace complex is unknown. According to A. Parrot's reconstruction (*The Temple of Jerusalem*, tr. B. E. Hooke, SBA 5 [London: SCM, 1957] 19–21), the various palace buildings were arranged around a large courtyard. Perhaps this courtyard gets its name from an adjacent guard post or house. The open-air setting, even if under the eyes of the guards, was preferable to the dungeon cell that Jeremiah had occupied in the house of Jonathan the secretary (37:15, 16, 20). A cistern belonging to Malkijah the king's son was located in (actually under) this courtyard (38:6). Like the city, Jeremiah was besieged.

3–5 If this confinement is the same as that described in 37:16–21, the reason given for it in chap. 32 is somewhat different. In chap. 32 it appears to be purely punitive, the consequence of giving the king an unfavorable oracle. In chap. 37, however, Zedekiah spares Jeremiah from a return to the dungeon in which the royal officials had put him. Holladay (2:213) calls it "protective custody." Six passages in the book of Jeremiah report a word from the LORD given through Jeremiah to Zedekiah (21:1–7; 32:1–5; 34:1–7; 37:1–10, 17; 38:14–28). The short sentence in 37:17b, "you [sg] will be handed over to the king of Babylon," is an accurate précis of 32:3–5. The other passages share common themes; 21:4–7; 34:2–3; 37:7–10, 17 all announce the certain conquest of Jerusalem by the Babylonians and Zedekiah's capture. This message is softened in various ways, however. The LORD promises Zedekiah a proper funeral in Babylon in 34:4–5 (contrast 16:5–7; 22:18–19). In 21:8–10; 38:2–3 the people are offered a way to escape with their lives if they leave the city and surrender. Only in 21:11–14; 38:17–18, which are addressed to the king, is the possibility raised of saving the city from destruction. The king must reestablish justice (21:12) and surrender to Nebuchadrezzar (38:17). The wording of 32:3b–5a closely resembles 34:2–3, except that the latter passage addresses Zedekiah in the second person. The expressions "speak mouth to mouth" and "see eyes to eyes" occur together only in these two passages. In chap. 32, however, Zedekiah's fate in Babylon is stated more ambiguously. He will "be" (היה) there until the LORD "decides [his] fate" (פקד; G. André, *Determining the Destiny*; J. D. W. Watts, *Isaiah 1–33*, WBC 24 [Waco: Word, 1985] 325–26).

The latter term may indicate judgment or deliverance. In 32:5 it might simply mean his death (Rudolph, 190). Considering what happened to Zedekiah, according to 39:5–7, death may have been a welcome visitation. Captured while trying to flee the country, Nebuchadrezzar took from him his freedom, the lives of his sons, and his sight. Nebuchadrezzar was one of the last people he ever saw "eyes to eyes." C. Begg, however, argues for a positive interpretation of פקד, "deal with," on the basis of the close similarity between 32:5a and 27:22a (*ETL* 63 [1987] 113–17).

The vocabulary of the final sentence in v 5, לחם, "fight," and צלח, "succeed," serves to remind the reader of the ancient origin of this scene (cf. 1 Kgs 22:15). The king in the midst of a military endeavor consults a prophet in order to hear a word from the LORD. Jeremiah's oracle for Zedekiah and the Jerusalemite forces is a promise of failure.

6–9 In 11:18–23 the LORD reveals to Jeremiah a plot against his life made by his own relatives in Anathoth. It is tempting to see in vv 7–8 a reconciliation of sorts (Holladay, 2:212). Jeremiah's prophetic ministry had cut him off from normal family activities and relationships (chaps. 11 and 16) in order to illustrate the suffering in store for the people of Judah and Jerusalem. If the redemption purchase of his cousin's field is seen as one step toward his restoration to normal family life, then Jeremiah is again "living ahead of time," experiencing in advance what is in store for God's people.

Neither Hanamel nor his name appear anywhere else in the OT. ("Hananel" in 31:38 comes close.) R. Wilson suggests (*Prophecy*, 223) that his father was the same Shallum who was married to the prophet Huldah (2 Kgs. 22:14). There is no way to prove or disprove this suggestion, but Holladay (2:213) notes that Huldah's husband seems to be from a Jerusalem family, whereas Jeremiah's uncle was a Benjaminite. The name was certainly used in Judah (cf. 22:11, Shallum = Jehoahaz). On the other hand, if Hanamel lived in Jerusalem, it would explain how he had access to Jeremiah during the siege. He could have settled in Jerusalem along with other refugees from the countryside (cf. 4:5–6; 35).

The legal terminology at the end of v 7, "for yours is the right or obligation [משפט] of redemption by purchase," raises the question of the laws that governed such a transaction. Lev 25:23–28 is the only passage in the OT law that can be applied to Hanamel's transaction, and it covers only some of the details. The principle that the land allotted by the LORD to the families of Israel cannot be sold in perpetuity is threatened by the fact that individual landholders do become impoverished and may have to sell their property in order to pay their debts. The text does not tell how or why Hanamel had become poor. It happened often enough in peacetime, but the demands of the Babylonian occupation forces no doubt increased the rate of bankruptcy. (See 33:10, 12 on the loss of livestock and Lang, "Social Organization," 83–99, for one theory of the causes of peasant poverty in Israel.) Legal documents dated during a siege of Nippur in the seventh century B.C. provide evidence that people sold real estate and even their children in order to raise cash, in the form of silver, to pay for food (Oppenheim, *Iraq* 17 [1955] 69–72).

Lev 25 provides three ways for the poor man to be restored to his patrimony: (1) His closest male relative may redeem it by buying it from the purchaser, to bring the land back into the extended family. (2) The seller may buy it back him-self. (3) At the jubilee year the land will return to the original owner. The transaction between Hanamel and Jeremiah does not fit any of these possibilities but comes closest to (1). The law does not tell how to identify the nearest rela-tive, and Jer 32 says only that Jeremiah and Hanamel were related through their fathers, who were brothers. There is no mention of an unrelated third party who had already bought the field. Instead, Hanamel offers the field for sale to Jeremiah, the kinsman redeemer (גֹּאֵל), first. D. Patrick (*OT Law*, 183) interprets Lev 25:25 as a moral obligation on the part of the next of kin not only to buy back the land but to return it, without payment, to the original owner. If Jeremiah had done this, there would have been no need for a deed, for the field would have become Hanamel's again.

Several other questions remain that are not explained by Lev 25. The other OT account of land redemption, in Ruth 4, does not add any clarification be-cause it raises very similar questions. How could Naomi, a widow, or Hanamel, from a priestly family, own a field in the first place? (Cf. Num 18:20–24; Josh 21:1–3.) Calvin (4:163) reasons that his field was a small suburban pasture such as the Levites were allowed to own (Num 35:5; but see Lev 25:34). How was the closest male relative identified? (The LXX of v 8 indicates one possible factor, "you are the oldest.") Why were the transactions completed in a public place? One cannot expect the legal material in the OT to explain every feature of narra-tives such as Ruth 4 and Jer 32. The purpose of the narratives is to show how the LORD is at work in particular circumstances, not to illustrate the general applica-tion of laws.

V 8 reports Hanamel's coming as a fulfillment of the LORD's word, "according to the word of the LORD," and his speech as its authentication, "Then I knew that it was the word of the LORD." By v 25 Hanamel's request has become the LORD's command. Hanamel's speech as reported in v 8 is almost identical to the predic-tion in v 7, but there are three significant differences. (1) The urgent request, "buy" (קְנֵה), is repeated at the end of the verse in the form found in vv 7 and 25 (with לְךָ, "for yourself"). It is appropriate to reiterate the main point of a persua-sive speech at the end (but see *Note* 8.d–d.). (2) V 8 adds the right or obligation of "possession" (יְרֻשָּׁה), a root used regularly in Deuteronomy and Joshua for re-ceiving land given to Israel and other nations by God (e.g., Josh 12:7). When Jeremiah redeems the field, he is not just doing a favor for his cousin; he is tak-ing possession of a piece of Israel's inheritance from the LORD (see vv 22–23, 41). (3) A clause locating Anathoth and the field in the land of Benjamin is another reminder of the allotment of the land of Canaan to the tribes in Joshua. It also implies that the restoration promised in v 15 will include Benjamin with Judah and Jerusalem (Wanke, "Jeremias Ackerkauf," 268; see v 44). The motif of all Israel in chaps. 30–31 is confirmed to this extent in chap. 32.

Chap. 32 does not say how the price was decided or how Jeremiah had this much silver. No coins were minted in the region until the Persian period, so the shekel was a measure of weight. (Note the scales in v 10.) Stone weights from ancient Palestine marked as shekels weigh 11.3–11.47 grams (Sellers, *IDB* 4:831–32), so Jeremiah paid just under 200 grams of silver for the field. Seventeen shekels is not expensive when compared with the fifty shekels David paid for Araunah's threshing floor and oxen (2 Sam 24:24) or the fifty-shekel tax imposed by Menahem on wealthy Israelites in order to raise the tribute due to Assyria (2 Kgs 15:20).

10–12 V 10 introduces the deed of purchase and reports its proper execution, with witnesses and seals. Lev 25:25 mentions no written record, but the circumstances of Jeremiah's transaction require one. The siege and subsequent capture and destruction of Jerusalem kept him from living on and working the land himself, so Jeremiah's ownership could only be proved by the written record of the transaction.

The order of actions in v 10, sealed and then witnessed, and the reference in v 11 to sealed and open copies make sense in light of legal documents, written in Aramaic, from the fifth through the third centuries B.C., which have been discovered in various places in the Near East. B. Porten describes the preparation of papyrus documents as follows (*BA* 42 [1979] 78–83). The scribe cut a piece of the proper length from a blank papyrus roll, turned it sideways, and laid the sheet out with the longest dimension on the vertical. This made the fibers run vertically on the right side of the sheet. The scribe wrote out the text of the contract or deed twice, leaving a space between the two copies, and then rolled up half of the sheet and pressed it flat. Small holes in the blank space between copies allowed the rolled copy to be tied with thread and sealed with one or more lumps of clay. A stamp seal pressed into the soft clay left an impression of the owner's name. The witnesses signed the outside of the rolled, tied, and sealed copy, and the scribe's name might be written there also. The copy of the document on the unsealed half of the sheet remained open for inspection.

There were no coins in use in Judah at this time, so the silver would have been measured in a balance scale with stone weights in the other pan. See *Comment* on vv 6–9.

The two words that intrude into the middle of v 11, "the commandment and the statutes," sound like an exclamation underscoring the idea that all proper legal formalities have been observed. Rudolph (190) adds a preposition and moves the phrase to the end of v 10, "according to the command and the statutes." Holladay (2:215) proposes two other possible explanations. The two words may have a more technical meaning here, indicating that the sealed copy includes stipulations or conditions not mentioned in the open copy. However, he tentatively adopts an explanation offered more than a century ago by J. Peters ("Notes on Some Difficult Passages in the Old Testament," *JBL* 11 [1892] 43), that these two words are a gloss, based on Isa 8:16, which explains "the sealed one."

12 Jeremiah entrusts written documents to others in 29:3 (Elasah and Gamariah); 36:6 (Baruch); 51:59 (Seraiah), to be read aloud by their bearers in places where Jeremiah himself could not go. King Jehoiakim burns the scroll in chap. 36, and Seraiah's instructions in chap. 51 are to drown the scroll in the Euphrates. Baruch's assignment, however, is to preserve the deed.

Baruch is not titled "the scribe" in this passage, but a longer genealogy is provided, naming both his father, Neriah, and his grandfather, Mahseiah. A group of more than two hundred bullae (lumps of clay with seal impressions) from Judah, described by Avigad, include at least one stamped with the name "Berekhyahu son of Neriyahu son of Mahseiah" (Avigad, *Hebrew*, 29). In spite of the longer forms of the first two names, the owner of the seal and the man named in 32:12 may be the same person. Elsewhere in the book Baruch serves as Jeremiah's scribe, messenger, and companion in suffering (36:4–8, 19, 26; 43:6). Mention of the Judeans or Jews "sitting" in the courtyard adds a final detail indicating that this was a formal legal procedure. (Compare Ruth 4:1–4, where all the parties sit down.)

14 The survival of some of the Dead Sea Scrolls stored in pottery vessels for two millenia proves the efficacy of this mode of preservation, at least in a desert climate. It is not known with any certainty whether the command to Baruch was the usual practice in that day or an extraordinary measure. There is no indication of where the jar was stored. Avigad speculates that public archives of deeds and contracts probably existed at that time (*Hebrew,* 121, 127) but that such documents may also have been stored at home (127). Within the book of Jeremiah the clay jar and the scroll are significant items. The sign-acts in 19:10; 51:63 destroy a jar and a scroll separately as signs of the coming destruction. Together, in chap. 32, they point to eventual restoration.

In the book of Jeremiah the messenger formula frequently introduces a word from the LORD addressed to the prophet, so it is not out of place in v 14. The narrative in v 13, however, makes Jeremiah the messenger and not the recipient of this command to perform a sign-act. Jeremiah and Baruch seem to have switched roles. Jeremiah writes the deed, and then Baruch performs the sign-act.

15 The sign-act involved the deed for a field, but the interpretation extends its meaning to include houses and vineyards. The redemption laws in Lev 25 deal with houses as well as fields (vv 29–33) but do not mention vineyards in particular. Fruitful vineyards and new wine are among the blessings for the restored community in chap. 31 (vv 5, 12), so this allusion serves as a reminder of the more bountiful gifts promised in the previous chapter. By contrast, v 15 is a very sobering promise. People sold their fields, houses, and vineyards to strangers only because they were impoverished. The redemption laws provide a "safety net" to keep people from being alienated permanently from their land. This promise of return to "normal" life, when property is bought and sold, implies, on the one hand, that indebtedness and poverty will also be present and, on the other, that Jews who returned from exile could redeem their own ancestral lands or would be able to purchase some other place to live and support their families. In this sense the verse gives a very practical word of assurance in the face of the massive dislocation resulting from conquest and exile. Like Abraham (Gen 23), some returning exiles would have to buy their first piece of the promised land.

16 The relative dating refers to v 12, giving the deed to Baruch, but not to the sign-act in v 14. Jeremiah is the subject of the verb פלל hithpael, "pray, intercede," only one other place in the book, 42:4.

17 God is addressed אדני יהוה, "Lord GOD," as in Gen 2:4–3:24 and the book of Ezekiel. The creation of the heavens and the earth (Gen 1:1) is presented as evidence of God's unlimited and incomprehensible strength and capacity to act. Nothing is beyond the power of the Creator. The LORD's answer begins in v 27 with the same affirmation, in the form of a rhetorical question (cf. Gen 18:14). The means or intruments of creation include the "outstretched arm" (cf. 27:5) usually associated with the deliverance from Egypt (e.g., Deut 26:8; Jer 32:21). In most of the book of Jeremiah, however, the power of Creator God is exercised in judgment. Compare 27:5, where the same prepositional phrase is used to describe creation, "by my great power and by my outstretched arm," but the Creator's action is to subjugate human and animal kingdoms to Nebuchadrezzar. If Jeremiah is wondering about the LORD's capacity to restore the people to the land, the answer is in his own prayer. The Creator has the power and freedom to punish and to save.

18–19 The address continues in v 18 with a short version of the divine description seen first in Exod 34:6–7. The LORD is merciful to multitudes but also lets the punishment for the parents' sin fall upon the next generation. The body metaphor, חיק, "bosom, lap," suggests a picture of this sin as a dangerous presence that threatens the vital organs (cf. Ps 79:12; Isa 65:6–7). This saying points to the awesome freedom of God, like that of a monarch who holds the power of life and death over every subject person. The following string of epithets, in vv 18b–19a, supports this image. God is the valiant commander of the heavenly armies who excels in both wisdom and action.

The tension and terror produced by the confession of God's freedom in v 18a is resolved by the affirmation of God's justice in v 19b. The LORD is able to see the way people live and the effect their lives have in the world ("the fruit of their deeds," as in 17:10 and 21:14) and will reward them accordingly (cf. 31:29–30; Ezek 18). In these verses, the LORD's insight, justice, and mercy are not limited to the people of Israel.

20 The hymnic style continues, using the language of Pss 78:43; 105:27 to describe the LORD's acts of deliverance, beginning in Egypt. "Make a name for yourself" is an expression rarely used of God. In Isa 63:12, 14 it is also associated with the Exodus. Neh 9:10 is a close counterpart of 32:20, mentioning "signs" and "wonders" in Egypt and repeating the final clause verbatim, "you made a name for yourself which continues today." V 20 looks beyond Israel in Egypt, however, to include humankind "until this day." The LORD's renown among the nations because of Israel's deliverance is a theme of the ancient victory song in Exod 15:14–16. It is also part of Moses' intercession in Num 14:13–16. If the LORD destroys Israel, the nations will conclude that the LORD "was not able" to bring them into the land. This verse, 32:20, seems to imply that other peoples have been more than mere observers of God's "signs and wonders" in Israel. The perspective of v 19 is reversed. God is known by God's deeds, just as people are known to God by theirs.

21–23 This brief summary of the LORD's dealings with Israel from Egypt to the present is composed of conventional expressions, familiar especially from the book of Deuteronomy. Vv 21–22 are nearly an exact quote of Deut 26:8–9. The frequent deuteronomic designation of the land "which the LORD swore to their ancestors to give to them" (cf. Deut 26:3) is included in v 22 in second-person form. "A land flowing with milk and honey" appears twenty times in the OT and lingers in the imagination. The "honey" (דבש) may have been a sort of molasses made from grapes (Anson Rainey, private communication). If so, the expression would incorporate the products of herding and horticulture. Bees' honey cannot be ruled out, however. It is part of the bounty of the land that one might discover and enjoy without any investment of labor. The story of God's gift of the land ends with the verb יָרַשׁ, "take possession, inherit," a term that emphasizes that the legal status of Israel's ownership of the land results from God's decision rather than from their own efforts.

Three nearly synonymous clauses, typical of Jeremiah prose (cf. 9:12[Eng 13]; 11:8; 44:10, 23), provide the motivation for the current judgment, "all this evil" (v 24). They span Israel's entire history in the land.

24–25 After praise of God, a summary of God's dealings with Israel, and a blanket indictment, Jeremiah's prayer returns to the setting introduced in vv 1–2. V 24 identifies "all this evil" in v 23 with the sufferings of Jerusalem during the final Babylonian siege. A single aspect of the Babylonian strategy, the siege ramps, is used to evoke a sense of the slow but inevitable progress of their assault upon Jerusalem. The ramps are personified in this verse; they are the subject of "come up . . . to destroy." They are the visible evidence that the LORD's words, as in v 3, are certainly being fulfilled. The contradiction or absurdity of God's command to buy the field while the Babylonians are conquering the city needs no explanation. It is sufficient to juxtapose the two sayings in v 25. The root question, unspoken in this prayer, is still asked: Can and will the LORD save?

26–27 The LORD's answer to Jeremiah's prayer begins with a unique self-introduction, "the God of all flesh." This title may be related to "God of the spirits of all flesh" in Num 16:22; 27:16. The shorter form, כָּל־בָּשָׂר, "all flesh," parallels and even rhymes with כָּל־דָּבָר, "anything," at the end of the verse. This epithet in effect summarizes the praise given to the LORD in Jeremiah's prayer, vv 17–20. The LORD's question, "Is anything too difficult for me?" ironically turns back Jeremiah's affirmation in v 17. Jeremiah already knows the words that will answer his questions because he has uttered them in prayer to God.

28–29 The announcement of judgment elaborates on v 25b by echoing other doom oracles in the book (cf. 32:24; 21:10b). According to 52:13, Nebuzaradan, the Babylonian commander, set fire to all important buildings (בַּיִת, "house") in Jerusalem and burned them down. Destruction by burning seems a fitting punishment for burning incense to other gods. Incense was burned and drink offerings were poured out to the LORD in the temple (בֵּית יְהוָה, "the house of the LORD") to accompany whole burnt offerings, animal sacrifices, and offerings of flour (Exod 29:38–41; 30:7–8; Num 15:1–16), but the people stand accused of making these offerings to Baal and other deities on the roofs of other "houses." (Jer 19:13 is a duplicate of this description except that "the host of heaven" replaces "Baal.")

30–32 The indictment, vv 30–35, follows the announcement of judgment, v 29. The Israelites and Judeans, v 30, and the city, v 31, have angered God since their earliest days. God's relationship to Jerusalem, "mine . . . from the day when she was built until this day" (v 31), resembles the extended allegory in Ezek 16, which depicts Jerusalem as an abandoned infant, the offspring of an Amorite and a Hittite, whom the LORD raises to adulthood and marries (16:8). (Note that Ezek 16:20–21 accuses Jerusalem of sacrificing her children to idols; cf. Jer 32:35.)

The syntax of v 31 is awkward (cf. 52:3). If the preposition עַל is understood to indicate a condition or attendant circumstance (BDB 754), then the sense is that God's possession of Jerusalem has always been accompanied by anger and wrath, with the result that the city will now be destroyed.

The list in v 32 specifies the subgroups among the offenders designated in v 30. Similar lists are found in 2:26; 8:1, and all of these groups have a role in chap. 26.

33–34   The next three verses specify "all the evil" (v 32) the Israelites and Judeans have done. Turning one's face toward another is an indication of favor and attention, but turning the back signals rejection. This general sense may be all that is meant by the opening clause, but it is also possible that this is an allusion to Ezek 8:16 and its depiction of false worship within the temple precincts. Twenty-five men face east with their backs to the temple and bow down to the sun. Pious Daniel, by contrast, prays facing in the direction of Jerusalem (Dan 6:10), as 1 Kgs 8:29–30 seems to stipulate.

The persistent sending of prophets to speak the LORD's word is a common motif in the book of Jeremiah (e.g., 26:5), but God's teaching (למד) occurs in 35:13 as well. In 17:23 the people are also accused of being unresponsive to discipline.

V 34 may have in view the abominations done by Manasseh, who built an asherah and altars for other gods in the temple (2 Kgs 21:4–5, 7), or the detestable practices during Jeremiah's lifetime that are described in Ezek 8. The verse duplicates 7:30b.

35   Two other verses in Jeremiah, 7:31; 19:5, are variations on this one. The people built the high places of Topheth (7:31) or of Baal (19:5; 32:35). The rite practiced there is called burning (שׂרף) their children (7:31; 19:5), which is defined further in 19:5 as "a whole burnt offering to Baal." Our verse uses distinct terminology, "they passed their sons and their daughters through for Molech." Both the verb, עבר hiphil, "cause to pass through," and the noun, "Molech," have been the subject of much discussion among interpreters since ancient times. Disagreement still exists over the meaning of "Molech." M. Smith (*Early History*, 132–38) maintains on the basis of Punic and Phoenician texts and artifacts that *mlk* was a type of sacrifice that involved offering up children. He suggests that the laws against this rite (Lev 18:21; 20:3) imply that some Israelites did offer this sacrifice in the LORD's name. He notes that child sacrifice is often practiced in besieged cities (138), an association that may explain the presence of this indictment in this chapter. Smith does not deny that *mlk* served as a divine name or epithet in the ancient Near East, but he does not think that the deity so named is ever associated with child sacrifice (137). J. Day argues that Molech names an underworld deity corresponding to Ugaritic *mlk* and Akkadian *Malik* (cf. Isa 57:9; *Molech*, 46–50). Later Jewish tradition named the underworld "Gehenna," the Greek version of the "Valley of ben-Hinnom," probably because of its association with dead bodies (Jer 7:32; 19:11), the slaughter of children, and burning. (The site's alternate name, "Topheth," means "fireplace.") If Molech is an underworld deity and if the sacrifices in question are made in a place perceived to be like "Sheol on earth," Day reasons, then it is likely that those sacrifices were performed in Molech's name and contributed to the development of the image of fiery, hellish Gehenna (*Molech*, 50–55).

J. Day's thorough investigation of the verb עבר hiphil, "cause to pass through," demonstrates that in the OT it means "slaughter as a sacrifice" (cf. Exod 13:12–15; Ezek 16:21; 23:37; *Molech*, 15–20). The parallel verses in Jer 7:31; 19:5 leave no doubt that the children offered in this rite did indeed die.

This rite took place at high places outside the city walls. According to M. Haran ("Temples," 33), a high place was an open-air altar for burnt offerings and sacrifices. M. Smith describes several scenes from ancient Near Eastern art that he interprets as depictions of child sacrifice (*Early History*, 134–36). In at least some of these pictures the child's limbs hang limp, suggesting that he or she has been put to death before being burned. A figure holding a sword appears in at least one picture. Perhaps the procedures followed to prepare this type of sacrifice were like Abraham's actions in Gen 22:9–10, in which he binds Isaac and prepares to slay him with a knife.

The LORD's absolute disclaimer in v 35b, "I had not commanded them," hints that some people claimed to be fulfilling God's law when they sacrificed their sons and daughters. Ezek 20:25–26 implies that people tried to fulfill the command to dedicate their firstborn to the LORD by passing their children through the fire. The victims of the rite in v 35, however, extend beyond the requirement of the firstborn male to include sons and daughters. According to 29:6, both sons and daughters are needed if the people of God are to survive and increase. By sacrificing their children, v 35, they are killing their future.

The LORD's answer to Jeremiah's prayer has so far only heightened the contradiction between the necessity of the judgment and the hope of salvation. The three charges against the people in v 23 of the prayer are so broadly formulated in familiar terms that the reader may be in danger of forgetting the depth of the perversion and the extent of the violence that result from turning away from God, but vv 33–35 surround the reader with smoke, blood, and the fires' heat, which force him or her to face the horrors of sin.

36–44 Second-person address (plural in MT, singular in LXX) appears for the first time in v 36. This part of the LORD's response is framed by the repetition of two sayings delivered originally by Jeremiah. V 36 cites v 24, which is itself a précis of several other oracles about besieged Jerusalem. The same announcement of doom begins the judgment oracle in vv 28–35. (V 43 gives a similar description of the land.) V 44 refers to the other side of the paradox by quoting in an expanded form the interpretation of the sign-act found in v 15. Jeremiah's prayer (v 25) expresses his perplexity over God's instructions to him to buy Hanamel's field just when the Babylonian conquest was almost complete. The subsequent interpretation in this chapter of Jeremiah's actions shifts attention to the divine word that interprets the actions. The frame around vv 36–44 invites the reader to look in this passage for some indication of how God's people can move from judgment at the hand of the Babylonians to restoration to their land.

36–37 Jeremiah's prophetic utterance (see 32:3, 24; 34:2; 38:18), repeated by the LORD in v 28, now functions in this verse as part of a disputation, in the form, "You say, '. . .' but this is what the LORD, the God of Israel says, '. . .' " The first saying is the LORD's word (v 28), but it is not the LORD's last word, and the new word, a salvation oracle, follows. "You are saying" is plural in MT, so the audience for this oracle is not Jeremiah alone. V 36 introduces the word as "about this city." The LORD's words that follow promise salvation to an unspecified "them," not to the "you [pl]" who are being addressed. The preceding judgment oracle (vv 27–35) also has the city (vv 29, and 31) and "them" as its subjects, and "they" are identified as "the people of Israel and Judah" (v 30). Jerusalem may also be "this place," the destination of the promised restoration, in v 37. (Compare vv 41, 44, in which the land is their destination.) The distinct futures of the 597 B.C. exiles and the people who remained in Judah and Jerusalem, as announced in 29:17–19, are joined here into a single promise. The "sword, famine, and pestilence" that threaten Judah and Jerusalem in 29:17–18 have come upon them in 32:36, and the promise given to the exiles of 597 B.C. in 29:14 is offered to the 586 exiles in 32:37. (Note the occurrence of key terms in both verses: "gather," "banish," "bring back," and "the place.") "Anger, rage, and great wrath" also accompany God's actions against Jerusalem in 21:5, in an oracle given to Zedekiah. The promise of ingathering and being brought back is expressed poetically in 31:8–10. (Vv 37–44 restate several motifs from chap. 31.) "Dwell securely" echoes 23:6, part of a promise of the beneficent reign of a new king.

38–40 These verses provide the heart of this chapter's explanation of how God's people could go from being handed over to the king of Babylon to being planted in the land, how they could be transformed from the objects of the LORD's "anger, rage, and great wrath" (v 37) to the ones to whom God delights to do good (v 41). The context will not allow a purely political answer, such as a promise that Babylon's power would fail. How could a people guilty of offering incense, libations, and even their own children to other gods (vv 32–35) become the LORD's people again? Even this is not beyond the LORD's power. Vv 38–40 answer with a distinct formulation of the promise of a new covenant (cf. 31:31–34).

38 The covenant formula duplicates 24:7 and 31:33bβ, except that in the latter case the order of the clauses is reversed. In these verses God speaks in the first person of Israel in the third person. The third-person form and the absence of the command to obey God distinguish these promises of covenanted relationship from the original offer of the covenant as it is reported in Jer 7:23, "Obey my voice, and I will become your God and you will become my people" (cf. Exod 19:5). Israel's repentance and obedience are not specified as prerequisites for the covenant relationship, which is to be sustained by divine initiative (vv 39–40).

39 Divine action upon the human heart, understood to be the corporal site of the mind in its capacity to reason, will, decide, make commitments, and control actions, enables people to fulfill God's call upon their lives (e.g., Saul in 1 Sam 10:9 and Solomon in 1 Kgs 3:9, 12; 10:24). There is no fixed formula for the way God prepares Israel's heart for participation in the promised covenant. It is described elsewhere as circumcision of the heart (Deut 30:6), giving a heart (Jer 24:7), writing the law upon it (Jer 31:33), and replacing the heart of stone with one of flesh (Ezek 36:26), with the result that Israel will love, fear, know, or obey God.

The LORD calls the people, in Jer 7:3, to "make good" their ways and, in 26:3, desires that they will "turn from their evil way." Both chapters offer more specific instructions for living God's way (7:5–7; 26:4–5). The promise of "one way" in v 39 can be understood as a sort of hendiadys with "one heart." Together they mean integrity, the complete compatibility of will and way of life. The gift of "one heart and one way," singular, to "them," plural, signifies unity and solidarity among God's people. The unity of the people supports and promotes the integrity of individuals, and vice versa. Furthermore, the specific content of this integrity and unity is the fear of the LORD, that commitment of life and thought commensurate with the respect, awe, worship, and love due to God alone. According to v 40b, fear of the LORD prevents apostasy.

God's gift of "one heart and one way" is for the good of this and each succeeding generation. Ways characterized by obedience to the law bring about good for the whole people in the form of justice, the elimination of oppression, the protection of life, and the blessings of God's presence (7:5–7; cf. Deut 5:29; 6:24). The LORD will also do them good by restoring them to the land (vv 41–44; 29:14; 7:7).

40 This verse expounds and expands the promises in vv 38–39. The covenant formula in v 38 finds its counterpart in v 40a, the promise to "cut" a covenant. Its duration ("eternal") comprehends the extent of the people's devotion ("always," v 39). The elegant structure of v 40b–c is worth noting. Syntactically the sentences are parallel, consisting of a main clause followed by a purpose clause. The motif of turning away in v 40bα and cβ forms an inclusio. The interplay of syntax and content emphasizes that Israel's loyalty to God is made possible by God's loyalty to them. This is the first and most important "good" that the LORD can do for them.

41 31:4, 7, 12, 13 promise that God's people will rejoice. Here, however, as in Zeph 3:17, the LORD's own joyful celebration of their restoration is announced. The rest of the verse suggests that it is like the farmer's rejoicing when planting is completed. In Ps 80:9–12(Eng 8–11); Isa 5:1–2, Israel's first settlement in the land is portrayed as a vine planted and tended by God but subsequently destroyed by enemies when divine protection is withdrawn. "To plant" is an aspect of Jeremiah's call (1:10) that reappears in promises in 31:28; 42:10. Hos 2:25(Eng 23); Amos 9:15, however, are the closest counterparts to v 41. The LORD's genuine and unreserved commitment to doing Israel good is characteristic of the eternal covenant (v 40). Calvin (4: 221–22) interprets the final three adverbial phrases in v 41, in the light of God's nature, as constant and enduring faithfulness, which makes the planting "solid and perpetual." The LORD's "anger, rage, and wrath" (vv 29–31) disappear from this covenant relationship along with the people's disobedience (Carroll, 629–30). The metaphor of planting introduces the land into this divine speech about the city (vv 26–41; cf. "land" in v 22) and leads into vv 42–44, which return to the interpretation of the sign-act.

42 The certainty that judgment had come serves as a guarantee that salvation will come, too (Kilpp, *Niederreissen*, 84). The extent of the calamity, which touched everyone, will be matched by the extent of the blessing.

43–44 Jerusalem (v 36) and the land (v 43) are said to be "desolate" and uninhabited, so the return of the exiles promised in vv 37–41 must precede the fulfillment of the promise in v 43 (cf. 30:1–2). What is said about the land in v 43 echoes the description of Jerusalem in v 36, the verse that introduces the unit vv 36–44. The effect of this order and repetition is to communicate that the future of the land can only be seen in connection with the future of the city (Kilpp, *Niederreissen*, 85) and the return of the exiles. Other cities in the land are included in the promise, too, implying their restoration as well. (See 34:7 on the conquest of Judah's fortified cities.) They are brought in by making them the sites of the future purchase transactions, just as Jeremiah has paid for the field and executed the deed in Jerusalem. Jeremiah's single purchase becomes the model for all future purchases. In this action Jeremiah is again living Israel's future in his present.

V 44 forms an inclusio with vv 11–12. It summarizes how the LORD's response in vv 27–44 interprets and applies the oracle in v 15 by indicating who will be buying fields (the exiles) and where they will buy them. The "map" names three political entities, Benjamin, the location of Hanamel's field, and Jerusalem and the other cities of Judah, where Jeremiah and his audience reside. The three topographical designations that follow indicate the geographic regions in which the various cities of Judah had been located, the hill country, where Jerusalem is found, the western foothills (Shefelah), and the southern semiarid wilderness (Negeb). The restoration formula, which is especially frequent in chaps. 30–33, concludes the promise.

Explanation

When Jeremiah completes his redemption purchase of his cousin's field, he is living in anticipation of the people's future in two ways. He had been prevented from participating in family and community life as a demonstration of the suffering in store for his audience (chap. 16), and he had been incarcerated within the city while it was under siege (32:2). By buying the field, however, he takes up again the responsibilities of family membership and signals the promise that God's people will be restored to their land to resume life in community (32:15).

The purchase and the deed stored in a jar seem such small and futile gestures in the face of the imminent conquest of Jerusalem. If Jeremiah were not known as "the weeping prophet," one might imagine him laughing like Sarah (Gen 18:12–15) at the LORD's impossible promise. Unlike Sarah, however, he says himself that "nothing is too difficult" for the LORD (32:17), nothing falls outside the realm of God's power to act. Nevertheless, the LORD's response must explain what this theological claim will mean for the future of the people.

The prayer in vv 17–24 is a combination of a number of stereotypical biblical confessions about God. The very conventionality of these expressions indicates that the function of this prayer is to articulate Jeremiah's question as one whose answer is desired by all of God's people living under the control of the Babylonians. These verses of praise are the fund of spiritual knowledge and biblical tradition out of which the LORD's response is constructed. The LORD as creator possesses unlimited power and authority (vv 17, 27). The statement that "nothing is too difficult" for the LORD in vv 17 and 27 alludes to the way that the LORD fulfilled the promise of a son for Sarah and Abraham (cf. Gen 18:14). The promise of the land to the ancestors is named explicitly in v 22 and corresponds to planting in "this land" in v 41. The future covenant in v 40 is "eternal," as was the LORD's covenant with Abraham (Gen 17:7).

The conditional nature of Israel's possession of the land, as taught especially in Deuteronomy (e.g., 28:64–67; 29:24–27[Eng 25–28]; 30:20; and also Lev 26:33–39) is the source of the acute theological dilemma faced in this chapter. God's justice (v 19) and the people's sin (vv 23, 30–35), not Babylonian might, made the promise of v 15 seem impossible of fulfillment. The paradox of banishment followed by gathering, which God promises in v 37 and 42, is an example of the paradoxical confession in v 18, which is a short form of Exod 34:6–7. The restoration to the land has its source in God's mercy. Life there will be possible and will endure because the obedience that the LORD requires will be given to them as a gift (vv 39–40).

XIX. More Promises of Compassionate Restoration (33:1–26[LXX 40:1–13])

Bibliography

Baldwin, J. "*Semah* as a Technical Term in the Prophets." *VT* 16 (1964) 93–97. **Biddle, M.** "The Literary Frame surrounding Jer 30:1–33:26." *ZAW* 100 (1988) 409–13. **Coppens, J.** "L'espérance messianique royale à la vielle et au lendemain de l'exil." In *Studia Biblica et Semitica.* FS T. C. Vriezen. Wageningen: H. Veenman en Zonen N.V., 1966. 46–61. **Gosse, B.** "La nouvelle alliance et les promesses d'avenir se référant à David dans les livres de Jérémie, Ezéchiel et Isaïe." *VT* 41 (1991) 419–28. **Grothe, J.** "An Argument for the Textual Genuineness of Jeremiah 33:14–26 (Massoretic Text)." *Concordia Journal* 7 (1981) 188–91. **Kenyon, K.** *Digging up Jerusalem.* New York: Praeger, 1974. 167–69. **Lipiński, E.** "Etudes sur des textes 'messianiques' de l'Ancien Testament." *Sem* 20 (1970) 41–57. **McConville, J.** *Judgment and Promise: An Interpretation of the Book of Jeremiah.* Winona Lake, IN: Eisenbrauns, 1993. 92–103. **Snaith, N.** "Jeremiah xxxiii 18." *VT* 21 (1971) 620–22. **Stuart, D.** "The Prophetic Ideal of Government in the Restoration Era." In *Israel's Apostasy and Restoration.* FS R. K. Harrison, ed. A. Gileadi. Grand Rapids, MI: Baker, 1988. 283–92. **Swetnam, J.** "Some Observations on the Background of צמח in Jeremias 23, 5a." *Bib* 46 (1965) 29–40. **Waltke, B.** "The Phenomenon of Conditionality within Unconditional Covenants." In *Israel's Apostasy and Restoration.* FS R. K. Harrison, ed. A. Gileadi. Grand Rapids, MI: Baker, 1988. 123–39. **Wambacq, B.** "Jérémie 33,4–5." *Bib* 54 (1973) 67–68. **Yadin, Y.** *The Art of Warfare in Biblical Lands.* New York: McGraw-Hill, 1963. 20.

Translation

[1] *The word of the LORD came to Jeremiah a second time, while he was still confined in the court of the guard, saying,* [2] *"Thus says the LORD* [a]*who makes it, the LORD* [ba] [c]*who forms it* [d] *to accomplish it, the LORD is his name:* [3] *Call to me and I will answer you, and I will recount to you great and inaccessible things,* [a] [b]*you do not know them.* [4] *For thus says the LORD, the God of Israel, about the houses of this city and the houses of the kings* [a] *of Judah which have been pulled down* [b]*near the siege mounds* [c] *and for the sword* [c] [5]*going* [a] *to engage in battle with* [b] *the Chaldeans,* [c] [d]*and to fill them* [d] *with human corpses that I smote in my anger and in my wrath, because* [e] *I had hidden my face* [f]*from this city* [f] *on account of all their evil:* [6] *I am about to bring upon it* [a] *restoration and healing,* [b]*and I will heal them.* [c] *I will reveal for them* [bd] *a fragrance,* [c] *namely peace and faithfulness.* [7] *I will bring about the restoration of Judah and the restoration of Israel,* [a] *and I will build them as at first.* [8] *I will purify them from all their iniquity which they have sinned against me, and I will pardon all* [a] *their iniquities which they have sinned against me and which they have transgressed against me.* [9] *It shall be* [a]*to me a name of rejoicing,* [a] *an object of praise, and a thing of beauty to all the nations of the earth that will hear all the good which I am about to do to them,* [b] *and will be in awe and will tremble in terror at all the good and all the peace which I am about to provide for it.* [c]

[10] *"Thus says the LORD: Once again in this place of which you are saying, 'It is a ruin, without human and without animal,' in the cities of Judah and in the devastated*

streets of Jerusalem, without human, ªwithout inhabitant,ª and without animal, will be heard ¹¹*a sound of rejoicing and a sound of gladness, a voice of a bridegroom and a voice of a bride, a sound of people saying,*

'*Give thanks to the Lord of Hosts,*
for good is the Lord,
whose loyal love is forever,'

*while bringing a thank offering*ª *to the house of the* LORD. *For I will bring about the restoration of the land as at first, says the* LORD.

¹² "*Thus says the* LORD *of Hosts: Once again there shall be in this ruined place, without either human or animal, and in all its cities, a habitation for shepherds resting flocks.* ¹³ *In the cities of the mountain, in the cities of the Shephelah, and in the cities of the Negeb, and in the land of Benjamin, in the environs of Jerusalem, and in the cities of Judah,* ª*the flocks will again pass by the hands of one who counts them,*ª *says the* LORD.

¹⁴ª "*Behold, the days are coming—oracle of the* LORD—*when I will fulfill the pledge which I made to the house of Israel and to the house of Judah:*

¹⁵   *In those days and at that time*
        I will cause to sprout for David
        *a righteous*ª *shoot,*ᵇ
        and he will do justice
        and righteousness in the land.
¹⁶   *In those days Judah will be saved,*
        and Jerusalem will settle down to live in safety,
        *and this*ª *is what* ᵇ*it will be called,*ᵇ
        '*The* LORD *is our righteousness.*'ᶜ

¹⁷*For thus says the* LORD: *There shall not fail for David a man sitting upon the throne of the house of Israel.* ¹⁸ *There shall not fail the* ª*levitical priests*ª *a man in my presence, burning whole burnt offerings, making offerings smoke, and performing sacrifices every day.*"

¹⁹ *The word of the* LORD *came to Jeremiah, saying,* ²⁰ "*Thus says the* LORD: *If* ª*you [pl] can break*ª *my covenant*ᵇ *with the day and my covenant with the night* ᶜ*so that daytime*ᵈ *and night are not at their proper time,* ²¹ *then even my covenant with David my servant may be broken so that he will not have a descendant reigning upon his throne, and (my covenant) with the Levites, the priests*ª *who are ministering to me.* ²²*Just as the host of the heavens cannot be counted and the sand of the sea cannot be measured, so I will multiply the seed of David my servant and the Levites* ª*ministering to me.*" ªᵇ

²³ *The word of the* LORD *came to Jeremiah, saying,* ²⁴ "*Have you not observed what the people are saying,* '*The two families which the* LORD *chose, he has rejected them*'? *So they spurn my people from still being a nation before them.*ª ²⁵ *Thus says the* LORD: *If I had not established my covenant*ª *with daytime*ᵇ *and night, and the statutes for the heavens and the earth,* ²⁶ *then the descendants of Jacob and David my servant I will also reject, by not taking from among his descendants rulers*ª *over the descendants of Abraham, Isaac, and Jacob. I shall certainly bring about* ᵇ *their restoration and have compassion on them.*"

Notes

2.a-a. LXX has ποιῶν γῆν, "who made the earth" (compare 32:17[LXX 39:17]). *BHS* recommends a slight emendation of the second word from יהוה, "the LORD," to יהיה, "and he will be." Rudolph makes the same emendation and translates *der macht, und es ist da*, "who makes, and it is there." An accidental reduplication of the divine name before the second ptcp could explain MT, but it is also possible that the parallel phrases are original.

2.b. Lacking in some MSS of MT, LXX, Syr, Vg, leaving two coordinated ptcps, "who makes" and "who forms." See *Note* 2.c.

2.c. LXX, Syr, Vg have the conj "and."

2.d. *BHS* tentatively proposes emending the 3rd person obj pronoun to אותיה, "a thing to come." The pl of this word appears in Isa 41:23; 44:7.

3.a. A few MSS, K^{Or}, Tg have another unusual word, ונצרות, "and guarded things," which involves changing only one consonant.

3.b. Many MSS add the conj ו, "and," and a few add אשר, "which," to smooth the syntax.

4.a. LXX, Vg have sg "king."

4.b.-5.c. *BHS*, without any textual evidence, suggests removing the most awkward section of these two difficult verses. Rudolph interprets these words as an addition that sought to secure the future sense of הנתצים, "which are about to be torn down." To accomplish this he interprets the first אל, "to," as the equivalent of על, "against," and emends אל החרב, "to the sword," to אל הנם, "in vain" (see *Note* 4.c-c.). He translates *gegen die Belagerungswälle wird man umsonst* [5] *angehen, um mit den Chaldäern zu kämpfen*, "they will go against the siegewalls in vain in order to fight with the Chaldeans."

4.c-c. LXX καὶ προμαχῶνας, "and ramparts," might reflect Heb. החל, "the rampart," which shares one letter with the MT, and which would be a fitting couterpart to "siege mounds." Holladay follows Volz's less drastic emendation to החרכים, "gaps" or "lattice" (in Cant 2:9), and translates the two nouns with the technical terms "merlons and crenels," which indicate the "teeth" and the gaps between them in a crenelated parapet, constructed with the materials from the demolished houses (Yadin, *Art of Warfare*, 20). This alternate meaning of סללות, "mounds," and the appearance of the root בוא, "come, go," create an ironic reversal of 32:24, in which the סללות, "siege mounds," of the Chaldeans are coming up to the city (Holladay, 2:23). Holladay does not, however, answer Rudolph's earlier objections to Volz's interpretation to the effect that סללות, "mounds," always refers to offensive structures and החרכים, "lattice," only means "dormer windows," never "gaps."

5.a. Lacking in LXX. Wambacq (*Bib* 54 [1973] 67–68) solves the numerous problems with this and the surrounding words by emending ואל החרב באים, "and to the sword coming," to ו(ה)חרבים (pl of חרב), "ruins," another description of the houses in v 4.

5.b. Some MSS have אל, "against," but את occurs frequently with לחם, "fight, do battle," so no change is necessary (cf. Jer 21:4; 32:5).

5.c. See *Note* 4.b.-5.c. above.

5.d-d. Rudolph and *BHS* follow Duhm in recommending an emendation of the inf const to the pl ptcp, which, following Rudolph's other proposed changes, modifies "houses" in v 4. The antecedent of the pronom suffix in MT is uncertain, but it should probably be the "houses." Burial outside the city walls was impossible during the siege, so corpses had to be disposed of on the sites of the demolished houses, rendering them doubly uninhabitable.

5.e. *BHS* recommends deleting the conjunction ו, "and," or reading באשר, "because," instead. Either of the resulting forms can introduce a causal clause.

5.f-f. LXX ἀπ᾽ αὐτῶν, "from them," is consistent with the 3rd person pl in the rest of the verse. (See *Note* 6.a.) "This city" and "they" (Israelites and Judeans) alternate as objects of divine activity in chap. 32 also.

6.a. *BHS* recommends emending לה, "to her, to it" (the city), to להם, "to them," following LXX^A, Tg, Vg, to match the 3rd person reference in the second half of the verse. (See *Note* 5.f-f.) The MT should be retained, however, since it refers to "this city" in v 5.

6.b-b. LXX reverses the order of the verbs, so that "peace and faithfulness" cannot be the objects of "reveal."

6.c. LXX has αὐτήν, "her."

6.d. LXX inserts εἰσακούειν, "to hear" (especially prayer).

6.e. Numerous emendations of the *hap. leg.* עתרת, "abundance," have been proposed. LXX has in its place the verb καὶ ποιήσω αὐτοῖς, "and I will make for them," with "peace and faithfulness" as its objects (see *Note* 6.b-b.). *BHS* proposes an Aramaism, ועבדתי, "I will make," as the background of LXX. LXX^{B 106} has only εἰσακούειν, "to hear," at this point (cf. *Note* 6.d.), and *BHS* postulates a form of the verb עתר, "pray, supplicate," like Vg's *deprecationem*, "entreaty." Syr seems to be translating נתבת, "paths of," which makes a smooth reading but is graphically quite unlike MT. *BHS* offers a new solution, reading רוח עת, "a time of refreshment." Holladay's emendation is simpler, calling for a different vocalization, עתרת, and a new interpretation of the word as "a feminine by-form" of "fragrance" (cf. Ezek 8:11), indicating the removal of the corpses' stench from the houses (2:222–23). Carroll's proposal is עֲטָרֹת, "crown."

7.a. Some MSS of LXX have Ιερουσαλημ, "Jerusalem," which is paired with Judah in vv 10, 16.

8.a. K לְכֹל, "all" cannot be read following maqqeph.

9.a-a. LXX has only εἰς εὐφροσύνην, "for joy." *BHS* reads יְרוּשָׁלַם, "Jerusalem," in place of לִי לְשֵׁם, "for me a name of." MT makes sense when שֵׁם, "name," is understood in the sense of "fame, reputation." (See the *Comment.*)

9.b. Lacking in some MSS of LXX. *BHS* recommends deleting or reading the sg אֹתָהּ, "to her, to it," in conformity with לָהּ, "for her, for it," at the end of the verse.

9.c. Other MSS of MT and the versions harmonize the pronouns by making this one pl.

10.a-a. Not in LXX. Perhaps it was included in MT on the basis of the similar expression in 26:9; 34:22, "without inhabitant."

11.a. LXX, θ' have δῶρα, "gifts."

13.a-a. Tg interprets as *jtnhwn ʿmʾ lptgmj msjhʾ*, "a people will join itself to the words of a messiah."

14.a. Vv 14–26 are not in LXX. Vv 15–16 are very similar to 23:5–6. See the *Comment.*

15.a. A few MSS of MT have the adj צַדִּיק, "righteous," instead of the noun in const, as do LXXO,L, θ'. The parallel in 23:5 has the adj.

15.b. ἀνατολήν, "rising," in LXXO,L, and θ' probably translates MT. Tg has *msjh*, "messiah." Many MSS also have וּמָלַךְ מֶלֶךְ וְהִשְׂכִּיל, "and a king will rule and act prudently/have success," as in 23:5.

16.a. A few MSS of MT plus Syr add שְׁמוֹ, "his name." *BHS* recommends inserting הַשֵּׁם, "the name," following LXXO,L, θ', Vg, or שְׁמָהּ, "her name," as in Tg.

16.b-b. A few MSS have יִקְרָאוּהוּ, "they shall call him/it, he/it shall be called," as do Syr, Vg, in agreement with שְׁמוֹ, "his name" (cf. *Note* 16.a.).

16.c. Vg has *iustus noster*, "our justice," as in 23:6.

18.a-a. LXX62, Syr, Vg insert the conj, "the priests and the Levites."

20.a-a. LXXL, Tg, Vg have sg, pass verbs, as in v 21.

20.b. For other examples of a noun with suffix in a const chain, see Lev 26:42; Num 25:12.

20.c. *BHS* recommends deleting the conj, following θ', Syr, Vg.

20.d. *BHS* reads יוֹם, "day," here and in v 25. יוֹמָם can be a noun, "daytime," as in Jer 15:9.

21.a. *BHS* recommends reversing the order of "Levites" and "priests," as in v 18, or deleting "priests," as in v 22.

22.a-a. The problem of a ptcp in const with an obj pronoun prompts *BHS* to propose a slight emendation to מְשָׁרְתַי אֹתוֹ, "my ministers with him."

22.b. Many MSS lack the final word. Deleting it and revocalizing the ptcp to match the form at the end of v 21 is another solution to the problem indicated in *Note* 22.a-a.

24.a. LXXL, θ', Syr have a 1st-person sg suff.

25.a. The first part of the protasis lacks a verb. *BHS* proposes emending בְּרִיתִי, "my covenant," to בָּרָאתִי, "I created," in order to supply one. This slight change would eliminate the echo of v 20, however.

25.b. See *Note* 20.c.

26.a. LXXO,L, θ', Syr have the sg.

26.b. Many MSS follow Q אָשִׁיב (hiph), "I will restore," which is transitive and, therefore, fits the context better.

Form/Structure/Setting

Chap. 33 serves as a continuation and further development of chap. 32. It makes use of material from that chapter, from other parts of the book of Jeremiah, and from the rest of the OT. The sense of continuation is clear from the heading in v 1, which locates the following revelation in the time during which Jeremiah was "still" (עוֹד) incarcerated in the court of the guard at the temple, as in 32:1, and which says that the LORD's word came "a second time" (שֵׁנִית). The second and third headings, in vv 19 and 23, give no date or location, but vv 19–26 form an inclusio with 31:31–36 (Biddle, *ZAW* 100 [1988] 411). Messenger formulas appear in 32:36, 42 and continue in 33:2, 10, 12, 17, 20, 25. This series of oracles takes up again God's response, which begins in 32:26, to Jeremiah's prayer (32:16–25). Formally, they are private revelations to the prophet, which are now reported to the larger audience in written form.

The proposed inclusio, formed by 33:19–26; 31:31–36 (Biddle, *ZAW 100* [1988] 411), has the effect of linking chaps. 32 and 33 to chaps. 30–31. Indeed, many interpreters treat chaps. 30–33 as a larger "Book of Consolation" because of the theme of hope and promise of restoration that runs through all four chapters (e.g., Brueggemann). Chap. 33 must be connected to chap. 32, and, together, they owe their position in the book of Jeremiah to the features they share with chaps. 30–31. As noted above (chap. 32, *Form/Structure/Setting*), 32:1–15 could belong with chaps. 37–38 because of their similar date and literary type. 32:16–33:26, however, fits best in this context, after chaps. 31–32.

The oracles in this chapter are written in prose, but they include two fragments of poetry. V 11 quotes part of a hymn as an illustration of the psalms that people will recite again in the temple. An earlier promise, in poetry, is cited, with modifications, in vv 15–16 in order to add an expansion to it in vv 17–18. Standard prophetic formulas mark off each section. Within some units a judgment announcement or description is followed by a salvation oracle. The words "nevertheless" or "yet" indicate the transition from one to the other. The chapter may be outlined as follows:

I. Introduction (vv 1–3)
   A. Heading (v 1)
      1. Setting (v 1a)
      2. Word-event formula (v 1b)
   B. Opening promise (vv 2–3)
      1. Self-introduction (v 2)
      2. Promise to answer (v 3)
II. Judgment and promise for Judah and Jerusalem (vv 4–9)
   A. Judgment on the houses (vv 4–5)
   B. Promise of restoration (vv 6–9)
      1. Jerusalem healed (v 6)
      2. Judah and Israel brought back and forgiven (vv 7–8)
      3. Jerusalem brings praise and renown (v 9)
III. Restoration for Jerusalem and the towns of Judah (vv 10–13)
   A. A home for people (vv 10–11)
      1. What is said about this place: a ruin (v 10a)
      2. Normal life restored to Jerusalem and the towns (vv 10b–11)
   B. A home for flocks (vv 12–13)
      1. What is said about this place: ruined (v 12a)
      2. Normal life for shepherds and flocks in the whole land (vv 12b–13)
IV. Promise about Davidides and Levites (vv 14–18)
   A. A former promise repeated (vv 14–16)
      1. Assurance of fulfillment (v 14)
      2. Former promise quoted (vv 15–16)
   B. The promise extended (vv 17–18)
      1. David's line will not fail (v 17)
      2. The priestly line will not fail (v 18)
V. The LORD's sworn covenant with David and the Levites (vv 19–22)
   A. Heading: word-event formula (v 19)

B. Enduring covenant with David and the Levites (vv 20–21)
C. Promise of innumerable descendants for David and the Levites (v 22)
VI. The restoration of Jacob as a nation under a Davidic king (vv 23–26)
  A. Heading: word-event formula (v 23)
  B. God's people despised among the nations (v 24)
  C. Davidic rule over Israel guaranteed by oath (vv 25–26a)
  D. Promise of restoration (v 26b)

This chapter is a development, elaboration, and explanation of earlier promise themes. The focus upon Jerusalem and the king and priests who will lead and serve there is especially appropriate to the concerns of the Judean exiles and the restoration community. (Compare the Zion-centeredness of other books with a similar audience or origin, such as 1–2 Chronicles, Ezra-Nehemiah, Ezekiel, Isaiah 40–66, Haggai, and Zechariah.) The form, style, and content of vv 1–13 have led to widely varying views of the time of composition. Holladay, for example, detects a core of material attributable to Jeremiah within vv 4–9 (2:222). Carroll, following Thiel (*Redaktion*, 37), labels the whole of vv 1–13 post-deuteronomistic (634). He assesses vv 14–26, which are entirely absent from LXX, as a "minority report" from the Persian period, perhaps as late as the Chronicler (639). Nicholson, on the other hand, thinks that vv 14–26 could have been composed late in the exilic period, after the edict by Cyrus (*Preaching*, 91–92). Absence from LXX does not necessarily prove a late origin for vv 14–26 since the *Vorlagen* of MT and LXX represent distinct text types (McConville, *Judgment*, 177; Tov, "Some Aspects," 178). The passage is well integrated into its context. (See *Comment* on vv 14–26.)

Within the context of the book of Jeremiah, chap. 33 continues the explanation of how the promises contained in chaps. 30–31 (and 32) can be fulfilled in the face of the dissolution of God's people, which most of the rest of the book describes so vividly.

Comment

1 The temporal notice indicates that Jeremiah was still being held in the court of the guard and the Babylonians were still besieging the city (32:2). Chap. 33 is linked thereby to chap. 32, which shares the same setting in Jeremiah's ministry. The prophet does not act or speak at all here, however, not even by praying in response to the LORD's invitation in v 3.

2 A hymnic fragment similar to Amos 4:13; 5:8–9; 9:5–6 supplements the messenger formula. All four passages consist of a series of participial phrases describing God as creator and conclude with "the LORD is his name" or "the LORD of Hosts is his name." The lack of specific antecedents for the feminine singular object pronouns make this verse more open-ended than the comparable passages in Amos. What does the LORD make, form, and establish? LXX has "who makes earth." *BHS* proposes an emendation of the independent object pronoun so the second phrase reads "the LORD who forms a thing to come, to establish it." The main feminine singular noun in the context is Jerusalem. "Great things" in v 3 is feminine plural. Isa 37:26 uses feminine singular object pronouns to point to something God ordained (עשׂה, "do, make"), planned long ago, and brought about, namely, Sennacharib's conquest of Judah's fortified cities. The most likely object of the participles in this verse is the phrase "great and inaccessible things" (v 3).

3 The invitation to call upon the LORD and the assurance of an answer probably have cultic roots (cf. Ps 91:15). The promised divine response is not presence and help in trouble, however, but the revelation of previously unknown things. These "great things" are also described, uniquely, as "fortified." While the fortifications of Jerusalem are about to fall at the hand of the Babylonian army, the "wall" around the unknown divine plan is opened for the benefit of Jeremiah and his audience.

4–5 These two verses present numerous textual difficulties that result in syntactic confusion. (See the *Notes.*) The beginning and end are fairly clear, however. The function of these two verses is to identify the addressees of the salvation announcement in v 6. The recipients of the promises in v 6 are "it" (feminine singular), referring to Jerusalem in v 5b, and "them" (masculine plural), referring to the compound subject of vv 4–5a, the houses of the city and of the kings. The people who have died in Jerusalem appear only as corpses in a dependent clause. By using only inanimate objects to describe the suffering of Jerusalem, these verses prepare for the description "without human and without animal" in vv 10 and 12.

The confusing central portion of vv 4–5 has to do with fighting (לחם) the Chaldeans. סללות, "mounds," and החרב, "the sword," are two items of military technology mentioned here. In 32:24, סללות, "mounds," are the siege ramps being built up ("coming") to the walls of Jerusalem in preparation for breaching the wall. If these ramps are meant in 33:4, also, then the houses being torn down might have been the ones built against the inside of the city wall. They would have been flammable and would have blocked efforts to reinforce the wall. The kings' houses probably were not built against the city wall, however, but they would have been an excellent source of stone. They may be included to indicate the fulfillment of the threat in 22:5. If the "mounds" are being built by the city's defenders (see the *Note*), then they and "the sword" might be the ones "going to do battle." Jer 21:3–7 is another oracle about the siege of Jerusalem, which bears some resemblance to 33:4–5 and provides a clearer picture. In this passage the implements of war used by the Jerusalemites to do "battle" (לחם) with the Babylonians will be turned against them, and the LORD will "smite" (נכה; cf. 33:6) the inhabitants. The king of Babylon will put them to the "sword" (החרב). One might speculate that 33:4–5 reports the fulfillment of 21:3–7 and that its confused state has something to do with the literary figuration of "turn the implements of war against them."

Despite the difficult syntax, three aspects of the experience of siege are evident in these verses: (1) the defensive action of demolishing houses in order to remove flammable material and to strengthen the wall at the point where the battering ram and other siege machines will attack; (2) the offensive activity of "the sword," which will fight against the Chaldeans; and (3) the victims of divine judgment who have already died inside the besieged city and who cannot be given a proper burial outside it. The second item may comprise the last word of v 4 and the first four words of v 5, but this presents several difficulties. First, a singular noun, "the sword," is modified by a plural participle, "going." הַחֶרֶב, "the sword," however, can refer to warfare or armed combat in general rather than to a specific weapon (e.g., Jer 5:17; 6:25; 31:2; Ezek 7:15). Second, the participle at the beginning of v 5 also lacks the relative, אֲשֶׁר, "which," or the definite article. Third, the role of this phrase in the syntax of the sentence is uncertain. The introductory וְאֶל might be understood as "and about," making "the sword" parallel to "the houses of this city" and "the houses of the kings of Judah," and the third subject of the oracle in v 6. V 6, however, does not seem to be about "the sword." If the phrase begins "and for," it is parallel to "near the siege mounds," and describes further the reasons for pulling down the houses. Strengthening the wall would also allow armed defenders a place to stand.

The remainder of v 5 makes more sense if the emendation proposed by *BHS* is followed, substituting a plural participle for the infinitive construct. In MT, וּלְמַלְּאָם, "and to fill them," parallels לְהִלָּחֵם, "to engage in battle," and is also dependent on בָּאִים, "going," but the rest of the verse says that the LORD, not the sword of the defenders, has smitten these bodies. The nearest possible antecedent of the pronoun "them" is "the Chaldeans," but it is the dismantled houses of Jerusalem, not the attackers, that are further defiled by the corpses disposed of in them. The emendation proposed by *BHS*, וְהַמְמֻלָּאִים, "and which are filled," is parallel to the description of the houses in v 4, הַנְּתֻצִים, "which have been torn down."

According to Num 19:11–20, uncleanness resulting from contact with a corpse lasts seven days, if the purification ritual is followed. If not, the person must be "cut off from Israel." The place of death also remains unclean for a week and renders unclean everyone who enters it.

6 The promise for the city that is torn apart from within, "smitten" (נכה) by God, and polluted with unburied corpses is literally "new flesh" (אֲרֻכָה as in 8:22), healing, and the balm of peace and faithfulness (or "true peace"). The healing sought in several verses in the first part of the book (6:14 = 8:11; 8:15 = 14:19b; 8:22; 15:18; 30:13) is promised here. This promise echoes 30:17, a word of comfort after a description of the incurable wounds caused by Israel's sin and unfaithfulness (30:12–15), and adds the key term from 8:15 = 14:19b, אֲרֻכָה, "restoration" (i.e., the new flesh that closes the wound). Two terms from 30:17a, רפא, "heal," and נכה, "smite," appear in 33:5–6. (30:17b deals with the same theme as the last oracle in chap. 33, vv 23–26, the nations' claim that the LORD has rejected Israel.) The language of divine wounding and healing apparently has its origin in the image of the LORD as a lion who tears the people to pieces (Hos 5:14–6:2). The lion is no longer present in Jer 30:15, but the divine word says of the people's wound and pain that "I have done these things to you" (cf. Deut 32:39). Wounds have also been inflicted by enemies (30:16), but only the LORD can heal (Hos 5:13). Spiritual waywardness can be "cured" (רפא; 3:22 = Hos 14:4), but 33:6 has in view the damage done to land and people by God's judgment at the hand of the Babylonians. The pronouns "it" (feminine singular) and "them" have their antecedents in vv 4–5, the ruined city and the destroyed houses.

7 The restoration formula includes both Israel and Judah, as in 30:3, and the promise to build them resembles 30:18; 31:4. בנה, "build," is the second verb from 1:10, describing Jeremiah's call, to appear in this chapter. In v 4 the houses of Jerusalem are being "torn down" (נתץ; cf. 1:10). The verb בנה, "build," fits the context as well as the allusion. The result of this rebuilding will not be some utopian state but simply "as at first," as it had been before.

8 The three most familiar Hebrew terms for sin occur in this verse. The verbs חטא, "sin" (twice), and פשע, "rebel," take singular and plural forms of the noun עון, "iniquity," as their objects (cf. Hos 12:9). Every indictment in the book of Jeremiah contributes to the description of Israel's and Judah's iniquity. 32:30–35 details "the wickedness" (הרע) by which the whole populace had provoked divine wrath (cf. 33:5) and would lead to their banishment. The promise of restoration to the land and to relationship with God, 32:37–41, which follows the judgment, 32:36, includes no mention of forgiveness or cleansing. 33:8 fills that gap.

The form of this verse is a promise of pardon, expressed by the verbs טהר, "purify, cleanse" (as in the restoration promise in Ezek 36:25), and סלח, "forgive, pardon" (as in Jer 31:34, preparation for the new covenant). The density of teminology in this verse, with no rhetorical flourishes beyond the repetition of עון and חטא, expresses the breathtaking thoroughness of God's forgiveness.

9 The LORD's plan for Israel and Judah to be "a name . . . praise . . . and beauty" (13:11; cf. Deut 26:19) is renewed in this salvation promise for Jerusalem. There are two dramatic reversals promised in this verse. The nations will no longer see Jerusalem as something to be despised and abhorred (as in 25:9b; 30:17b), and they will praise and honor the LORD for its restoration, because the city bears the LORD's name (25:29; cf. 33:16). Furthermore, when the nations respond "in awe" (פחד) and "tremble in terror" (רגז), it will not be because of the LORD's military victories, as in the past (Exod 15:14–16); it will be because of the good and the peace that God gives to Jerusalem (cf. 29:11).

10–11 A series of sayings continues here (vv 10–13) that are characterized by the word עוד, "once again," and the restoration formula "I will bring about the restoration of . . ." They follow the promise in 32:15, "once again fields will be bought." What is said about "this place" in v 10 also resembles what is said about "this land" in 32:43. Both are "without human and without animal" as a result of the Babylonian conquest.

The LORD promises to break the silence of the empty, ruined place with the sounds of celebration and thanksgiving (cf. 30:19a). The specific reasons for celebration are also occasions of solemn commitment to marriage and to worship. They picture in sound a time when normal life has been restored around the rebuilt temple. V 11a promises the reversal of the judgment announced in 7:34; 16:9; 25:10, using the exact terminology of the earlier verses. Marriages are a sign of hope for the future and a prerequisite for the survival of God's people (cf. 29:4–7). The song quoted is the beginning of the thanksgiving psalms, Pss 107; 136. Thank offerings were spontaneous expressions of gratitude and praise (Lev 7:12–18).

The concluding restoration formula is distinctive in that it promises the restoration of "the land" (ארץ), forming a link to the pastoral imagery of vv 12–13.

12–13 The series of "once again" oracles continues here. The pastoral imagery is instinctively appealing, but actual shepherds with flocks grazing in cities (five times in vv 12–13) is not a picture of restoration. The image makes sense if shepherds and flocks represent leaders and people, as they frequently do in the OT. Jer 23:1–2; Ezek 34:1–6 condemn the leaders, especially the kings, for destroying the very people whom they had the responsibility to tend and protect. This salvation promise echoes Jer 23:3 but describes the shepherding in vivid terms. The new shepherds will comfort the people by making them "lie down" or "stretch out" (רבץ), as the LORD who is shepherd does in Ps 23:2; Ezek 34:14–15. These shepherds will "count" (מנה) the sheep as they enter the fold for the night, just as the LORD "counts the stars and calls them each by name," Ps 147:4. The intimate knowledge and committed caring suggested by this image is illustrated in the parables of the good shepherd in Luke 15:3–7; John 10:1–18.

The sets of three topographical and three political designations for the parts of the land are in reverse order from 17:26; 32:44. This is a more restricted view of the territory included in the land of Israel than the one given, for example, in Ezek 47:15–20.

14–25 This passage is absent from LXX, but it is well integrated into MT. Like the rest of chap. 33, these verses restate and extend promises found elsewhere in the book. Vv 15–16 quote 23:5–6, and the larger context, beginning in v 12, reflects the content of 23:1–8. 33:12–13 reverses the woe saying about the destroying shepherds in 23:1–4, and 33:23–24; 23:7–8 are both concerned with public opinion about the LORD's dealings with Israel. Other hints in the preceding chapters prepare for the promises of an enduring Davidic dynasty and an unbroken line of levitical priests. If the palace is rebuilt (30:18; 33:4–6) and a ruler will arise from among them (30:21), who would this be other than a descendant of David (30:9)? Harmonization with other biblical traditions (2 Sam 7:11–16; 23:1–7; Jer 23:5–6) confirms this answer, given in 33:14–25. Joyful singing and dancing (30:19; 31:4, 13), and invitations to "go up to Zion, to the LORD" to sing and pray for the salvation of Israel (31:6–7), imply the restoration of the temple, and 32:11 assumes it explicitly when it speaks of "those who bring thank offerings to the house of the LORD." If sacrifices are to be made at a rebuilt temple, "as at first" (v 11), who will administer them? 33:18–22 gives the answer, the levitical priests. The promise of a new and eternal covenant with Israel (31:31–34; 32:36–41) raises the question of the status of the other covenanted institutions in the nation's life, the Davidic monarchy and the priesthood. The promise of a "righteous [צדקה] sprout" who will do "righteousness" (צדקה) provides a hopeful stance for the reader of the following chapters about the decline and fall of Zedekiah's (צדקיהו) monarchy.

14 This verse introduces vv 15–16 as the reiteration of an earlier promise, now found in 23:5–6. The initial clause duplicates the beginning of 23:5. This introduction is used a dozen times in the book of Jeremiah, most recently in a series of three oracles in chap. 31 (vv 27, 31, 38). The coming "days" of v 14 are "those days" of vv 15, 16. The "good word" or "promise" is 23:5–6. No addressee is specified in chap. 23, but 33:14 names "the house of Israel and the house of Judah." (Note another use of the term בית, "house"; cf. v 4. Later, in v 24, the two nations are called "families.") According to 30:3, the promises in the Book of Consolation are about "Israel and Judah."

15–16 The image of a new shoot, sprouting from the stump of an old tree, fits the situation of the truncated Davidic dynasty (cf. chap. 22, especially v 30). The phrase, צמח צדקה, "righteous shoot," is probably the Hebrew version of an ancient Near Eastern term meaning "legitimate scion" (Baldwin, *VT* 16 [1964]

93–97). The OT expectation regarding kings emphasizes the characteristics of righteousness and justice (1 Kgs 10:9; Ps 72:1–3; Isa 9:7). Jer 22:15–17 describes Josiah's reign in these terms. These virtues are demonstrated especially in defending the oppressed and saving the poor (Ps 72:4; Jer 22:16). The king is the LORD's agent, however. In v 16 the LORD receives the credit for the salvation of Judah and Jerusalem, expressed in a new name for the city ("she"), "the LORD is our righteousness." In 23:6 the new king bears this name, but in 33:16 it goes to Jerusalem. (Ezek 48:35 also gives Jerusalem a new name, "The LORD is there.")

Vv 15–16 make two significant changes in the oracle from 23:5–6. (1) Chap. 33 omits the clause "then a king will rule and act prudently" and does not use the term "king" anywhere else in the passage. (2) 23:6 assigns the name "The LORD is our righteousness" to the king, but 33:16 gives it to the city.

17 David, in 1 Kgs 2:4, and Solomon, in 1 Kgs 8:25; 9:5, cite the LORD's promise to David in these very words. (Compare Jer 35:19, the promise to Jonadab the Rechabite.) The righteousness and justice of the new rule (v 15) fulfill the conditions of the earlier promise, "If your descendants . . . walk faithfully before me . . ." (1 Kgs 2:4).

18 The language of the promise to David is taken over into this announcement of an unbroken line of levitical priests to perform the proper sacrifices. A lack of Levites and legitimate priests was a genuine problem in the early years of the restored temple (Ezra 8:15). This verse uses the deuteronomic terminology, הכהנים הלוים, "the levitical priests" (Deut 18:1).

Burning whole burnt offerings (עלה) and slaughtering sacrifices (זבח) were the exclusive responsibilities of the priests (Lev 1; 3:16; 6; Deut 12:8–14; 18:1–5). The second item on the list, מקטיר מנחה, "making offerings smoke," is an unusual expression. It may refer to the grain offering that was burned daily with a lamb, oil, and olives (Exod 29:38–46; Num 28:1–8). Snaith (VT 21 [1971] 620–22) supports another interpretation. He thinks it is the "priest's *minha*," which was part of the installation rite for priests (Lev 6:16[Eng 23]; 9:15–17). This reading creates a picture of a continual stream of new priests being initiated into the LORD's service.

19–21 The second version of the promise identifies it as the content of the LORD's covenant with David and the Levites. In Num 25:12–13 the LORD grants Phinehas and his descendants a covenant of "eternal" (עולם) priesthood. The covenant with David is also called "eternal" (עולם) in 1 Sam 23:3. The enduring nature of Davidic rule and the levitical priesthood is expressed here by likening their permanence to the constant alternation of day and night, which are also secured by divine promise (Gen 8:22).

David is called "my servant," a title used many times in Samuel, Kings, and Psalms, but only in 33:21, 22, 26 in the book of Jeremiah. (Compare 27:6.)

22 A third variation on the promise regarding the lines of David and the Levites echoes the promise of innumerable descendants made to the ancestors (Gen 13:16; 22:17). It uses a traditional expression to explicate the unlimited extent of its fulfillment. The rare term מדד niphal, "be measured," links this verse to Jer 31:37; Hos 2:1 (Eng 1:10). The promise to the ancestors still holds, but here is the assurance that there will be enough rulers and priests to take care of all of Abraham's seed.

23–24 The LORD invites Jeremiah to take notice of what "this people" (העם הזה), the Israelites, are saying in their despair about the two chosen "families" whom the LORD has rejected. Since Israelites are speaking, they could be talking about the family lines of David and Levi, which are the subject of vv 17–22. The response in v 26, however, names David but not the Levites. "The descendants of David" and "the descendants of Abraham, Isaac, and Jacob" are linked in v 26, and the symmetry of the two phrases suggests that they might be the two families of v 24. The last clause in v 24 serves to explain the people's saying, and it subsumes the two families under the term עמי, "my people." The one people of God made up of the two nations, Israel and Judah, is a more common prophetic concern, however (Jer 3:6–18; 33:14; Isa 8:14; Ezek 23; 35:10; 37:15–28). The two families are probably Israel and Judah, as in 30:3.

The people who are saying these despairing words have turned their backs on the possibility that the LORD's people will ever achieve the status of a "nation" (גוי) again. In their view, the LORD's rejection is final.

25–26 The LORD's covenant with day and night, which secures their regular alternation (v 20; cf., Gen 8:22), is joined by the much broader concept of divine statutes governing all of creation (cf. Gen 9:8–17; Jer 31:35–36) in the protasis of this unreal condition. The logic is like that of vv 20–21. The LORD, as creator, established the order governing the heavens and the earth. Therefore, the LORD will never reject Jacob's offspring or refuse to choose their ruler from among David's descendants.

Following the restoration formula stands a concluding word of mercy. The LORD's compassion prevents the abandonment of Israel and gives birth to her restoration (cf. Jer 30:18; 31:20; Hos 2:25[Eng 23]; 11:8–9).

Explanation

The salvation announcements in chap. 33 answer at least two questions left from chap. 32 (and 30–31): (1) How can people who persistently rebelled and even offered their children to Molech, become covenant partners with God? The LORD will heal, cleanse, and forgive them (vv 6–8) out of mercy for them (v 26). (2) What will life be like for the people whom God will plant in the land? Families will grow again (v 11), worship will resume at the temple (vv 11, 18), and God will always provide a legitimate and righteous ruler (vv 14–26), so that people can live in safety (v 16). All this will be accomplished by the Creator, for whom nothing is too difficult (32:17, 26) and whose willingness and power to do good inspires awe among the nations (33:9).

The invitation in v 3 is a fitting call to study this chapter, and the rest of biblical tradition, to discover how old promises are renewed and new experiences are interpreted in the light of older texts. "Call to me and I will answer you, and I will recount to you great and inaccessible things." William Carey preached from this text, saying, "Expect great things from God; attempt great things for God," and brought modern Christian missions to birth.

XX. Zedekiah's Choice   (34:1–7 [LXX 41:1–7])

Bibliography

Kilpp, N. *Niederreissen und aufbauen.* Biblisch-Theologische Studien 13. Neukirchen: Neukirchener, 1990. 90–93. **Lipiński, E.** "Prose ou poésie en Jér. xxxiv 1–7?" *VT* 24 (1974) 112–13. **Malamat, A.** "The Last Kings of Judah and the Fall of Jerusalem." *IEJ* 18 (1968) 137–56. **Martens, E.** "Narrative Parallelism and Message in Jeremiah 34–38." In *Early Jewish and Christian Exegesis.* FS W. H. Brownlee, ed. C. Evans and W. Stinespring. Chico, CA: Scholars, 1987. 33–49. **Migsch, H.** *Gottes Wort über das Ende Jerusalems.* Österreichische Biblische Studien 2. Klosterneuburg: Verlag Österreichisches Katholisches Bibelwerk, 1981. **Pardee, D.** *Handbook of Ancient Hebrew Letters.* Chico, CA: Scholars, 1982. 89–95.

Translation

¹*The word which came to Jeremiah from the LORD while Nebuchadrezzar, the king of Babylon, and his whole army and* ᵃ*all earthly kingdoms which his hand ruled and all the nations*ᵃ *were making war against Jerusalem and against all her cities,*ᵇ *saying,* ²*"Thus says the LORD,* ᵃ*the God of Israel:*ᵃ *Go* ᵇ*and speak*ᵇ *to Zedekiah, the king of Judah, and say to him, 'Thus says the LORD:* ᶜ*I am about to give*ᶜ *this city into the control of the king of Babylon,*ᵈ *and he will burn it with fire.* ³*You will not escape from his control for you will certainly be seized and will be given into his control. Your eyes will see* ᵃ*the eyes of the king of Babylon*ᵃ ᵇ*and his mouth will speak to your mouth,*ᵇ ᶜ*and you will go to Babylon.*ᶜ
⁴ᵃ*"Only listen to the word of the LORD, Zedekiah, king of Judah.* ᵃ*Thus says the LORD concerning you:*ᵃ ᵇ*You will not die by the sword.*ᵇ ⁵*You will die peacefully,*ᵃ *and like the burnings*ᵇ *for your fathers,* ᶜ*the former kings, who were before you,*ᶜ *so*ᵈ*they will burn*ᵉ (incense) for you and "Alas, Lord"* ᵈ *they will wail for you, for I have made a promise'—oracle of the LORD."*
⁶*So Jeremiah* ᵃ*the prophet*ᵃ *spoke all these words to Zedekiah, the king* ᵇ*of Judah,*ᵇ ᶜ*in Jerusalem,* ᶜ ⁷*while the army of the king of Babylon was waging war against Jerusalem and against all*ᵃ *the cities of Judah* ᵇ*which remained,*ᵇ *against Lachish and against Azekah, for they alone were left among the cities of Judah as fortified cities.*

Notes

1.a-a. LXX is shorter, καὶ πᾶσα ἡ γῆ ἀρχῆς αὐτοῦ, "and all the country of his rule." Holladay calls MT conflate. מַמְלְכוֹת, "kingdoms," and מֶמְשֶׁלֶת, "authority, rule," are synonyms.
1.b. LXX specifies τὰς πόλεις Ιουδα, "the cities of Judah," as in 32:44.
2.a-a. Not in LXX, which frequently lacks titles found in MT.
2.b-b. Not in LXX. MT appears redundant, but it is not unusual for a form of the root אמר, "say," to appear immediately before a direct quotation.
2.c-c. LXX uses the pass construction παραδόσει παραδοθήσεται, "shall surely be given," as in 32:28.

2.d. LXX has, in addition, καὶ συλλήμψεται αὐτὴν, "and he will take it." The same verb describes the king of Babylon's actions in 32:3, where it translates לכד, "capture, take."

3.a-a. LXX has simply τοὺς ὀφθαλμοὺς αὐτοῦ, "his eyes."

3.b-b. Present in Rahlfs' LXX, but *BHS* judges it to have been absent from the original Gk. version.

3.c-c. *BHS* suggests that this clause is an addition. Rudolph calls it a *vaticinium ex eventu*, which contradicts the original form of v 5.

4.a-a. Not in LXX. *BHS* suggests substituting the conj. attached to the following word, ולא, "not."

4.b-b. Not in LXX, perhaps lost by haplogr. It parallels v 5a, however.

5.a. Rudolph suggests that בירושלם, "in Jerusalem," belongs here instead of in v 6. It could have been omitted because of its similarity to בשלום, "in peace," preserved in the margin, and inserted again in the wrong verse. Holladay wonders if it was purposely moved when the prediction of burial in Jerusalem did not come true.

5.b. Many MSS of MT (and the versions) read the prep ב instead, with no significant difference in meaning. LXX has ἔκλαυσαν, "they wept," a free translation, according to *BHS*, and perhaps more intelligible to the LXX audience.

5.c-c. LXX, τοὺς βασιλεύσαντας πρότερόν σου, "who ruled before you," apparently read a ptcp rather than a noun, as in MT. Since πρότερόν, "former, before," is used elsewhere in LXX to translate both לפני, "before," and ראשנים, "former," Holladay suggests that MT is a conflation.

5.d-d. Not in Syr. Probably lost through homoioarchton.

5.e. LXX has κλαύσονται, "they will weep." See *Note* 5.b.

6.a-a., b-b. Not in LXX, which frequently lacks titles found in MT.

6.c-c. *BHS* recommends moving this word to v 5, where Rudolph thinks it makes more sense. It is not superfluous in v 6, however. (See the *Comment*.)

7.a. Not in LXX. MT echoes v 1, where LXX also has πάσας, "all."

7.b-b. Not in LXX. The clarification is necessary in MT in light of v 7b, but not in LXX, which lacks "all." (See *Note* 7.a.)

Form/Structure/Setting

This narrative resembles other reports of a divine commissioning of prophetic speech. It begins with a third-person word-event formula, a common feature of Jeremiah narratives (cf. *Excursus: Introductory Formulas*, chap. 26), and a description of historical circumstances, but no date. The messenger formula precedes the command to "go and speak" to Zedekiah. The text of the message is included in the LORD's command, as, for example, in chap. 26 (and throughout the book of Ezekiel), not in the report (vv 6–7) that Jeremiah spoke "all these words" to Zedekiah. V 8 initiates another unit with a different word from the LORD.

The passage may be outlined as follows:

I. Heading (v 1)
    A. Word-event formula (v 1a)
    B. Setting: the Babylonian invasion (v 1b)
II. Command to prophesy (v 2a)
    A. Messenger formula (v 2aα)
    B. Command to go and speak to Zedekiah (v 2aβ)
III. The LORD's message to Zedekiah (vv 2b–5)
    A. The judgment in force (vv 2b–3)
        1. Messenger formula (v 2bα)
        2. The city will be given to Nebuchadrezzar (v 2bβ)
        3. Zedekiah will be captured by Nebuchadrezzar (v 3)
    B. Another possibility (vv 4–5)
        1. Command to heed the LORD's word (v 4a)

    2. Promise of a peaceful death and a proper funeral (vv 4b–5)
      a. Messenger formula (v 4b*a*)
      b. A peaceful death (vv 4b*β*–5a*a*)
      c. A proper funeral (v 5a*β*–b*a*)
      d. The LORD's assurance (v 5b*β*)
  IV. Jeremiah fulfills the command (vv 6–7)
    A. Report of prophesying (v 6)
    B. Setting: the Babylonian invasion (v 7)

Thiel notes the unusual order of the parts of the heading (*Redaktion*, 38). Elsewhere the command formula דברת/ואמרת הלך, "go and speak," is fixed between the word-event formula and the messenger formula (2 Sam 24:12; Isa 38:5; Jer 28:13; 39:16). The messenger formula also precedes the command to speak in Jer 35:13 and the commands to symbolic action in 13:1; 19:1; 27:2; 30:2; 32:14. Thiel concludes from this observation that v 2a and v 6b, which is dependent upon it, are later revisions. He agrees with Rudolph (202) that v 1 is a redactor's composition that contradicts v 7. V 6a is then proposed as the original introduction, a report of Jeremiah's prophesying rather than a command to deliver an oracle. According to this reconstruction, only one messenger formula remains in v 2, introducing the oracle to Zedekiah.

Seitz (*Theology*, 250) offers a similar reconstruction and an explanation for it. He claims vv 6–7 as the original introduction to the message in vv 2b–5. His proposed original version also lacked the burning of Jerusalem (v 2b) and Zedekiah's deportation (v 3b). In this reading, the contrast indicated by אך, "yet" (v 4), remains, but there is no contradiction; Zedekiah would be captured by Nebuchadrezzar, but not killed, and would be mourned in a manner appropriate for Judean kings (contrast the word about Jehoiakim's death in 22:18–19; *Theology*, 251). This oracle would have been consistent with other messages to the effect that people who surrendered to Nebuchadrezzar would survive in Judah (21:8–10; 27:11; 38:17). Rudolph suggests that Jeremiah recalled how Jehoiakim had submitted to Nebuchadrezzar in 604/3 B.C. (with a speech preserved in 12:7–13) and was allowed to remain on the throne (203). Seitz proposes that the rearrangement of vv 6–7 and the provision of a new heading serve to connect, awkwardly, vv 1–7 to the rest of the chapter. The apparent contradiction between Jerusalem and "all her cities" (v 2) and Jerusalem, Lachish, and Azekah alone (v 7) serves, in his view, to imply the passage of time between the oracle in vv 2b–5 and the undated actions of Zedekiah in vv 8–22 (*Theology*, 249). This implication of two phases is, indeed, awkward, since v 7 is related syntactically to v 6 and not v 8.

The relationship of the present shape of vv 1–7 to vv 8–22 goes beyond chronology, however. The word-event formula in vv 1–2a provides an appropriate introduction to a major unit in the book. The command and fulfillment schema distinguishes this account of an oracle for Zedekiah from all other such accounts in the book. In the other accounts, Zedekiah "inquires" (דרש) of the LORD through Jeremiah (21:1–7; 37:3–10, 17–21; 38:14–28), but here the LORD initiates the encounter. The heading, the command-and-fulfillment pattern, plus the command to Zedekiah to "heed" (שמע; v 6) the LORD's word, shapes this unit in a manner reminiscent of other chapters in the book where the audience's response to a prophetic word or symbolic action is described (e.g., chaps. 19–20; 26; 27–

28). Further, the apparent contrast or contradiction between the two parts of the oracle (vv 2b–3 and 4–5) has led some commentators to interpret the second part as a conditional promise, "[if] you hear the word of the LORD . . . [then] you shall die in peace" (most recently, Brueggemann, 105). The juxtaposition of vv 8–22 with vv 1–7 tends to make that narrative an indication of whether Zedekiah "heeded" (שמע) the LORD's word. In 34:17 the LORD declares, "You have not obeyed [< שמע] me." The narrative in vv 8–22 is about heeding the word of the divine law, however, not the immediate issue of submission to Nebuchadrezzar.

E. Martens accounts for the present arrangement of 34:1–7 by proposing that it functions as the first member of an inclusio, with 38:14–23 as the closing section ("Narrative Parallelism," 38–39). The two passages share the following features: (1) Jeremiah alone with Zedekiah; (2) the message from the LORD that the city will be captured and burned, and Zedekiah will be caught; (3) a conditional promise to Zedekiah that his life will be spared if he obeys; and (4) the promise of public lament if Zedekiah obeys (34:5) is contrasted with the threat that women will taunt the king if he refuses to submit to Babylon (38:21–23). The function of this framing device is to direct the reader to understand the intervening material as two pairs of parallel but contrasting accounts. (See the *Comment* on 34:8–22 and chaps. 35–38 below.)

Seitz's treatment of 34:1–7 is part of his larger hypothesis regarding a Scribal Chronicle composed in Palestine to support the existence of the remnant who remained in the land. He proposes that 34:6–7, 2b–5 be substituted for 37:4–10, as the oracle given in response to Zedekiah's inquiry in 37:3. This reconstruction would indicate a setting for the oracle prior to the Egyptian advance that prompted the Babylonians to lift their siege of Jerusalem temporarily. (See chap. 32, *Form/Structure/Setting*, for discussion of possible dates.)

Migsch's hypothesis places 34:1–7 at the beginning of a proposed source document comprising 34:1–7; 32:2–5; 37:3–38:28a, which reported the events of the Babylonian conquest of Jerusalem in chronological order. In this hypothetical source, Jer 34:1b announced the beginning of the invasion of Judah by the Babylonian army, a function for which its universalizing style is appropriate. (Note the number of occurrences of כל, "all.") Jeremiah's imprisonment, 32:3, was the result of delivering the message in 34:2b–5 to Zedekiah.

The location of 34:1–7 in the book of Jeremiah and the details of vv 1 and 7 do not provide enough information to arrive at a precise date. The lack of any mention of the siege of Jerusalem suggests a time in the early months of the invasion, before the siege began in January 588. Lachish Letter IV depends on Jer 34:7 for its dating rather than vice versa. Malamat ("The Last Wars of the Kingdom of Judah," *JNES* 9 [1950] 225) argues on the basis of internal evidence that the Lachish Letters could not have been written at a late stage in the war. Malamat concurs with Seitz and Migsch and places all the events of chap. 34 before the Egyptians invaded and the Babylonians temporarily lifted the siege of Jerusalem ("The Last Kings of Judah and the Fall of Jerusalem," *IEJ* 18 [1968] 152).

Comment

1 Nowhere else in the book is there such a grandiose description of the invading host. The more common expression is simply "Nebuchadrezzar, the king of Babylon, and his whole army." 35:11 mentions the Aramean army alongside the Babylonians, and Ps 137:7 and the book of Obadiah condemn Edom for her participation. However, no troops of other subject nations are named with the Babylonians in the descriptions of the 589 B.C. invasion in Jeremiah and 2 Kings. In all likelihood Nebuchadrezzar's "whole army" included soldiers from other conquered lands, since ancient Near Eastern vassal oaths usually involved the obligation to act on the overlord's behalf against rebels (Weinfeld, "The Loyalty Oath in the ANE," *UF* 8 [1976] 380). The purpose of this verse, however, is not to provide additional details about military strategy. This verse underscores that the Nebuchadrezzar who now invades Judah is the same Nebuchadrezzar to whom the LORD, the creator, had granted authority over "all nations," and even the wild animals, for a time (27:6–7). These nations will, according to the promise in 33:9, eventually offer their praise and honor to the LORD, who will give Jerusalem abundant prosperity and peace.

2   The consistent threat against Jerusalem in the oracles given to and about Zedekiah is that Nebuchadrezzar will burn the city with fire (שְׂרָף בָּאֵשׁ; 21:10; 34:2–3, 21–22; 37:10; 38:18). The Babylonian conquerors did burn the city in 586 B.C. (52:13; 2 Kgs 25:9; 2 Chr 36:19), including especially the temple. Ashes, soot, and charred wood found together with Israelite and foreign arrowheads outside a tower in the Iron Age II city wall provide artifactual evidence of the burning of Jerusalem in 586 B.C., according to Avigad (*Discovering*, 52). These fires made the desolation of the city complete, in contrast to the conquest of Jerusalem in 597.

To label the final clause in this verse a *vaticinium ex eventu*, as Rudolph does (202), is not an adequate assessment of how this motif functions in the book of Jeremiah. The same phrase, שְׂרָף בָּאֵשׁ, "burn with fire," also describes the abominable deeds of Jehoiakim, who burned Jeremiah's scroll (36:32), and of the people who immolated their own children as offerings to Baal (7:31; 19:5). Therefore, it is a fitting punishment for the city.

3   A third-person version of this verse is to be found in 32:4–5aα. The description of an eyes-to-eyes and mouth-to-mouth meeting in v 4b occurs only these two times in the OT. It is reminiscent of Moses' speaking "mouth to mouth" (Num 12:8) or knowing the LORD "face to face" (Deut 34:10), experiences that indicate his unique status with God. As king, Zedekiah has the privilege of a personal audience with Nebuchadrezzar, but this promise functions in these circumstances as a threat (Holladay, 2:235). The report of Zedekiah's meeting with Nebuchadrezzar at Riblah (39:5–7) provides a poignant twist to this saying. Nebuchadrezzar kills Zedekiah's sons in his sight and then puts out his eyes, before taking him to Babylon in chains.

4–5   Strictly speaking, only v 4a is controlled by the restrictive adverb אַךְ, "only, however," with the sense "You will go to Babylon. (That being understood) just heed the word [דבר] of the LORD." The reference to God's "word" (דבר) at the end of v 5 suggests that vv 4b–5 contain a divine word that must be heard and heeded. The whole utterance (vv 4–5) restricts the meaning of v 3 by contradicting some of its implications. Holladay (2:234) and Brueggemann (105) refer to the choice offered explicitly to Zedekiah in 38:17–18 and find a choice implied in v 4 as well. The idea of contingency is suggested by the adverb אַךְ, "only," and by the imperative שְׁמַע, "hear, heed." Another strong reason for finding in these verses a conditional sentence is the widespread assumption that the promises in v

5 could not be fulfilled in Babylon, especially after the events foretold in v 3 (e.g., Carroll, 642). However, already in v 3bβ Zedekiah survives the conquest of the city in 586 B.C. and is taken to Babylon (cf. 38:17, and contrast 21:7). Although mourning rites fit for a king are promised in v 5, there is no promise that mourning would necessarily be limited to a location in Judah. The verse is silent about burial in the family tomb and resting with his ancestors.

"You shall die in peace" is such a familiar expression to modern ears that it tends to invite interpretations that reflect personal hopes and fears. It is a unique expression in the OT, however, and the definition offered by the immediate context is simply a death that is not "by the sword," in battle or its aftermath, one that can be mourned by the community. A nearly synonymous passage in Gen 15:15, "you shall go to your ancestors in peace," is defined by its context as death at a good old age and as a free person. The promise of lamentation for Zedekiah, "Alas, LORD," is the exact reversal of the judgment announced on Jehoiakim in 22:18. The "burning" probably refers to spices, as in 2 Chr 16:14. Josephus (*Ant.* 10.143–53) even reports that Nebuchadrezzar buried Zedekiah "royally." V 5 stands in clear contrast to the judgment oracles in Jer 16:5–7; 22:18–19. Its content may have as much to do with this function as with the actual possibilities for mourning rites among the Jewish exiles in Babylon.

6–7 This sober historical note shows the vulnerability of Jerusalem. Only two of the fortified cities ringing the capital continued to resist (cf. 2 Chr 11:5–11). Azekah is identified with Tell Zakariya, southwest of Jerusalem (Stern, *ABD* 1:538), and Lachish with a site farther south, Tell ed-Duweir (Laughlin, *MDB*, 495–96). Both cities are in the Shephelah (cf. 32:44), on the strategic route to Egypt. One of the letters found in the debris of Lachish's destruction in 587 B.C. apparently refers to the next stage of Babylonian conquest. The final sentence of Letter IV says, "we are watching for the signals of Lachish, . . . for we cannot see Azekah" (Pardee, *Handbook*).

Explanation

The Book of Consolation has ended, and 34:1 confronts its readers with the full force of the invading imperial army. The destruction of Jerusalem and the remainder of Judah seems inevitable (v 3) because the LORD has made Nebuchadrezzar ruler over all the nations and because burning with fire is a fitting consequence for their deeds. Nevertheless, Zedekiah still has an opportunity to heed the LORD's word and to receive his proper funeral as a "spoil of war."

This unit serves to direct the readers' attention to the issue of obedience to the LORD's word as it is explored in 34:8–22 and chaps. 35–36.

XXI. A Covenant of Release (34:8–22 [LXX 41:8–22])

Bibliography

Baltzer, K. *The Covenant Formulary in Old Testament, Jewish, and Early Christian Writings.* Tr. D. Green. Philadelphia: Fortress, 1971. 54–56. **Cardellini, I.** *Die biblischen "Sklaven"-Gesetze im Lichte des keilschriftlichen Sklavenrechts: Ein Beitrag zur Tradition, Überlieferung und Redaktion der alttestamentlichen Rechtstexte.* BBB 55. Bonn: Hanstein, 1981. 312–23. **David, M.** "The Manumission of Slaves under Zedekiah (A Contribution to the Laws about Hebrew Slaves)." *OTS* 5 (1948) 63–79. **Jackson, B.** "Ideas of Law and Legal Administration: A Semiotic Approach." In *The World of Ancient Israel: Sociological, Anthropological and Political Perspectives.* Cambridge/New York: Cambridge UP, 1991. 185–202. **Kapelrud, A.** "The Interpretation of Jeremiah 34,18ff." *JSOT* 22 (1982) 138–40. **Kessler, M.** "The Law of Manumission in Jer 34." *BZ* n.f. 15 (1971) 105–8. **Kraus, F.** "Ein Edikt des Königs Šamšu-Iluna von Babylon." *Assyriological Studies* 16 (1965) 225–31. **Lemche, N.** "The Manumission of Slaves—The Fallow Year—The Sabbatical Year—The Jobel Year." *VT* 26 (1976) 38–59. **Lewy, J.** "The Biblical Institution of D^{e}ror in the Light of Akkadian Documents." *EI* 5 (1958) 21–31. **McConville, J.** *Judgment and Promise.* Winona Lake, IN: Eisenbrauns, 1993. 103–9. **Martens, E.** "Narrative Parallelism and Message in Jeremiah 34–38." In *Early Jewish and Christian Exegesis.* FS W. H. Brownlee, ed. C. Evans and W. Stinespring. Chico, CA: Scholars, 1987. 33–50. **Miller, P.** "Sin and Judgment in Jeremiah 34:17–19." *JBL* 103 (1984) 611–13. **Oppenheim, A.** "'Siege-Documents' from Nippur." *Iraq* 17 (1955) 69–89. **Patrick, D.** *Old Testament Law.* Atlanta: John Knox, 1985. 69–72, 111–13, 133, 181–85. **Sarna, N.** "Zedekiah's Emancipation of Slaves and the Sabbatical Year." In *Orient and Occident.* FS C. H. Gordon, ed. H. A. Hoffner. AOAT 22. Neukirchen: Neukirchener, 1973. 143–49. **Schedl, C.** "Zur logotechnischen Struktur von Jeremia 34,18." *BZ* 26 (1982) 249–51. **Thiel, W.** *Die deuteronomistische Redaktion von Jeremia 26–45.* WMANT 52. Neukirchen: Neukirchener, 1981. 38–43. **Weippert, H.** *Die Prosareden des Jeremiabuches.* BZAW 132. Berlin: de Gruyter, 1973. 86–106, 148–91. **Williamson, H. G. M.** *Ezra, Nehemiah.* WBC 16. Waco, TX: Word Books, 1985. 231–46, 320–40.

Translation

[8] *The word which came to Jeremiah from the LORD after the king, Zedekiah, had made a covenant with all*[a] *the people* [b]*who were in Jerusalem*[b] *to make a proclamation of release*[c] *to them,*[c] [9] *so that each one would set free his Hebrew male slave and each one his Hebrew female slave, so that no Jew*[a] [b]*among them*[b] *would be a slave to his or her brother.* [10] *They obeyed*[a]*—all the royal officials and all the people who entered into the covenant to set free,*[b] *each one, his male slave and each one his female slave* [c]*so that they would not be slaves among them again—they obeyed and set free.*[c] [11a]*But they reneged after that and made the male slaves and the female slaves whom they had set free come back,*[a] *and they subjugated them*[b] *as male slaves and female slaves again.* [12] *The word of the LORD came to Jeremiah* [a]*from the LORD,*[a] *saying,* [13] *"Thus says the*

LORD, *the God of Israel: I made a covenant with your ancestors on the day that I brought them out of the land of Egypt, from the house of slaves, saying,* [14]*'At the end of seven*[a] *years you shall send out, each one, his brother the Hebrew who sells himself to you and serves you six years, you shall send him out from you free.' But your ancestors did not obey me, they did not incline their ear.* [15]*So you*[a] *repented*[b] *today and did what I consider just by proclaiming release from bondage, each one for his*[c] *neighbor, and you made*[b] *a covenant before me in the house over which my name is proclaimed.* [16]*But then you reneged and defiled my name, and you made, each one, his male slave and his female slave, whom you had set free according to their desire, turn back,* [a]*and you subjugated them to be*[a] *your male slaves and female slaves.*

[17] *"Therefore, thus says the LORD: You have not obeyed me by proclaiming release from bondage, each to his brother and each to his neighbor. I, then, proclaim release with respect to you—oracle of the LORD—to the sword,* [a]*to pestilence, and to famine, and I will make you* [b]*a source of terror*[b] *to all the kingdoms of the earth.* [18]*I will make the people who transgressed my covenant, who did not establish the words of the covenant which they made before me,* [a]*like the calf*[a] *which* [b]*they cut in two and passed between its pieces*[b] [19]*—the royal officials of Judah and* [a]*the royal officials of Jerusalem,*[a] *the palace officials, the priests,* [b]*and all the people of the land—everyone who passed between the pieces of the calf.*[b] [20]*I will give them into the control of their enemies* [a]*and into the control of the ones who are seeking their lives,*[a] *and their corpses will become food for the birds of the sky and for the animals of the earth.* [21]*Zedekiah, the king of Judah, and his royal officials I will give into the control of their enemies* [a]*and into the control of the ones who are seeking their lives,*[a][b] *and into the control of the army*[b] *of the king of Babylon which is withdrawing from you.* [22]*I am giving the command—oracle of the LORD—and I will bring them back* [a]*to this city,*[a] *and they will wage war against it and destroy it and burn it with fire, and the cities of Judah I will make desolate, without inhabitant."*

Notes

8.a. Not in LXX. MT frequently has an additional "all."

8.b-b. Not in LXX. MT frequently has additional modifiers.

8.c-c. Not in LXX or Syr. MT specifies the indirect obj.

9.a. The gentilic יהודי, "Jew, Judean," interprets "Hebrew." Thus it emphasizes ethnic identity rather than citizenship or geographic location.

9.b-b. Superfluous following יהודי, "Jew." Perhaps derived from v 10 (Rudolph, 204).

10.a. LXX has καὶ ἐπεστράφησαν, "and they returned" < וישובו, "and they returned," which appears as the first word of v 11 in MT.

10.b., c-c. Not in LXX, because the report of the people's renunciation of the covenant of release begins in this verse.

11.a-a. Not in LXX, which already reported their change of mind in v 10.

11.b. Q is qal, as in v 16 and 2 Chr 28:10; Neh 5:5. The hiph of K is *hap. leg.*

12.a-a. LXX, Syr, Tg[Ed] lack this redundant phrase.

14.a. ἕξ, "six," in LXX is an attempt to solve the mathematical contradiction between six years of service and release at the end of seven years. The same tension exists between Deut 15:1 and 12, but the latter ("in the seventh year") clearly interprets the former ("at the end of seven years"), so Rudolph translates "every seven years." Holladay (2:238) cites the conclusions of M. Wallenstein ("Some Lexical Material in the Judean Scrolls," *VT* 4 [1954] 213), based upon usage in the Dead Sea Scrolls, that מקץ means "at the beginning of."

15.a. Emphatic pronoun lacking in LXX, which has a 3rd-person verb, like the end of v 14, so the comparison between the ancestors and Jeremiah's audience is not introduced in this verse.

15.b. LXX continues, incorrectly, the sequence of 3rd pl verbs begun at the end of v 14.

15.c. Women probably did not personally or independently "own" debt slaves.

16.a-a. Not in LXX. MT harmonizes this verse with v 11.

17.a. Numerous MSS of LXX, Syr, Tg have the conj, following the usual Heb. pattern.

17.b-b. The K לזועה, "a horror, a source of terror," is preferable. The Q, לזעוה, results from an internal metathesis. The same variants are found in 15:4; 24:9; 29:18.

18.a-a. *BHS* proposes adding the prep כעגל, "like the calf," which sounds smoother but is not necessary.

18.b-b. LXX has instead ἐποίησαν ἐργάζεσθαι αὐτῷ, "(which) they made to serve it," a possible reference to the golden calf in Exod 32 that Moses ground to powder (32:20).

19.a-a. Not in LXX. MT fills a perceived gap.

19.b-b. LXX has simply καὶ τὸν λαόν, "and the people," not the specific group designated by the Heb. term.

20.a-a. Not in LXX. The phrase also occurs in 21:7, in reference to Jeremiah's enemies, and MT of 34:21.

21.a-a. Lacking in LXX, as in v 20.

21.b-b. LXX simply has καὶ δύναμις, "and the power of"; compare Eng. "forces."

22.a-a. LXX has "to this land" instead. (Several times in the book of Jeremiah LXX γῆ, "land," corresponds to MT עיר, "city.")

Form/Structure/Setting

This report of the divine word given to Jeremiah includes no command to act or speak, yet the oracle is not addressed to Jeremiah himself (as it is in 16:1–3; 32:1–15, 26–44; 33). The delivery of the message to King Zedekiah and the other slaveholders in Jerusalem is only implied. (Compare chap. 14, which has the same introductory formula in v 1.) An account of the behavior that provoked the oracle is incorporated in an awkward paragraph subordinated to the introductory formula by a temporal clause (v 8b, "after King Zedekiah . . ."). Vv 8bβ –9 are composed of infinitive phrases, but vv 10–11 have finite verbs, like v 8bα. This account of the covenant made and violated is less specific than the details contained in the oracle itself, and, therefore, it is in some tension with it (Rudolph, 203; Thiel, *Redaktion,* 39). Its syntactical subordination also gives the impression that it is a secondary addition, inserted to conform this chapter to its context (chaps. 32 and 35, see further below). Indeed, without vv 8b–11 the passage resembles chap. 14, a word-event formula followed by a judgment oracle. Thiel argues, however, that the unit in its original form, vv 8b, 9a, 10–13a, 18, was about the general release of all slaves. The specification of Hebrew slaves and Jewish brothers and the judgment sermon in vv 13b–22 are the work of the deuteronomistic editor who interpreted the earlier account in light of Deut 15 (*Redaktion,* 40–42). Nicholson charts the structure of 34:8–22 as matching the pattern of deuteronomistic prose sermons in the book of Jeremiah (*Preaching,* 34): introduction, vv 8–12; "Yahweh's command, call to obedience," vv 13–14; "description of Israel's apostasy and disobedience," vv 15–16; and "judgment announced," vv 17–22. He does not attempt to discover any actual words of Jeremiah in this deuteronomistic sermon, but he does not question the historicity of the events (*Preaching,* 64).

Carroll, however, labels the whole passage midrash, produced by exegetical activity during the Persian period, and not a report of any actual historical events (647–48). He observes that too many practical details of the situation go unexplained and that the reason for entering into this covenant to release slaves during the Babylonian siege of Jerusalem is never stated. Instead, attention is given to establishing a parallel between Zedekiah and Josiah, who each made a covenant with "all the people" (34:8; 2 Kgs 23:3), in order to underline the virtue of making such a commitment and the profound consequences of breaking it (compare Jer 17:19–27). Just as Zedekiah and the slaveholders had "brought" their former slaves "back" (שוב hiphil) into subjection, so the LORD would "bring back" (שוב hiphil) the Babylonian army to capture and destroy Jerusalem (Carroll, 650). Both the purpose and the method of this passage indicate its midrashic character. Carroll notes that the details of the release involve the reinterpretation of Exod 21:1–11; Deut 15:12–18 in light of Deut 15:1; Lev 25:39 as well as the combination of features of the covenant-making ceremonies in Gen 15; 2 Kgs 23 (648–49).

H. Weippert represents the opposite position regarding the authorship of 34:8–22. She reassesses the three main pieces of evidence used by others to support the hypothesis of deuteronomistic editing. (1) Weippert would resolve the apparent tension between the general liberation of slaves in vv 8b–11 and the release of debt slaves in vv 14–15 according to the law in Deut 15 by proposing that the sabbatical year of Deut 15:1–11 and the slave release after six years in 15:12–18 have been combined, so that all debt slaves were released in the same year, regardless of when they had entered service (*Prosareden*, 92). The sabbatical year, then, would have functioned like the jubilee year (Lev 25). Perhaps the use of the term דרור, "release," from Lev 25, instead of שמטה, "release," from Deut 15 hints at this analogy. (2) The numerous repetitions of terms in this passage are judged by Weippert to be an example of skillful technique rather than evidence of editorial expansion (93–94; it should be noted that the two possibilities are not mutually exclusive). (3) Weippert shows how the structure of the judgment speech conforms to the standard form in prophetic speech, not to the proposed pattern of deuteronomistic prose sermons (103). She concludes that Jeremiah composed the oracle itself (vv 13–18), while Baruch contributed the description of the setting (vv 8b–12). The deuteronomistic language in the passage results from its subject, the law in Deut 15.

Another possibility for reconciling the description of the setting with the specific references to Deut 15 in the judgment speech is based on a comparison with the ancient Near Eastern practice of *mesharum* acts. The king, usually on the occasion of his accession to the throne, would declare a temporary measure of debt relief. F. Kraus's study of Old Babylonian *mesharum* texts reveals that they were not enacted at fixed intervals of years but rather in response to specific needs (*Assyriological Studies* 16 [1965] 230). They provided a way to exalt the new king as protector of the weak by alleviating excessively oppressive debt loads resulting from wartime disturbances of the economy or poor harvests (231). Law codes published later in the reign usually included provisions for gaining release from debt slavery. If such regulations had been followed during the previous king's reign, the *mesharum* act would have been unnecessary. According to B. Jackson ("Ideas," 186), Jer 34 refers to both of these practices. When Zedekiah issues the proclamation of release, his action is like the Babylonian *mesharum* acts. Neglect of the customary means of limiting the servitude of debtors (Deut 15) had created a situation ripe for the king's proclamation (v 14b).

Neh 5 and 10 recount similar occasions in the life of the post-exilic community. In chap. 5, peasant farmers working to rebuild the wall of Jerusalem complain
that they are forced to mortgage their fields and sell their children in order to
buy food during the famine and pay their taxes. Nehemiah persuades the lend-
ers to cancel debts and "return" (שוב hiphil; 5:11) the property already accepted
in repayment. Part of his argument is that Jews ought not to be owned by other
Jews, their "brothers" (5:8; cf. Jer 34:17). To redeem fellow Jews from their gen-
tile owners only to hold them as slaves themselves was not an adequate solution
to the community's need (Williamson, *Ezra, Nehemiah*, 239). The people swear
(שבע; v 12b) to the measures adopted under Nehemiah's leadership, but the term
ברית, "covenant," is not used either in chap. 5 or in chap. 10, where the people
"enter [בוא; 10:30(Eng 29); cf. Jer 34:10] into a curse and an oath" to "obey"
(שמע) the LORD's commandments. The specific provisions that the people swear
to follow (Neh 10:31–40[Eng 30–39]) have been developed from pentateuchal
law but are not simply citations of it. Williamson (*Ezra, Nehemiah*, 333–35) lists
five types of legal development defined by D. Clines ("Nehemiah 10 as an Example of Early Jewish Biblical Exegesis," *JSOT* 21 [1981] 111–17). The fifth type,
"the integration of separate legal prescriptions," seems to fit Neh 10:32 (Eng 31),
where the release from debts is tied to the sabbatical fallow year for the land so
that both would be observed simultaneously throughout the whole country. Neh
5 regards the laws of Deut 15:1–18 as "cumulative rather than alternative"
(Williamson, *Ezra, Nehemiah*, 335). The same interpretation of Deut 15 seems to
be present in Jer 34 (Weippert, *Prosareden*, 92; Carroll, 648–49). Furthermore,
the covenant in Jer 34 under which the slaveholders of Jerusalem comply with
Zedekiah's proclamation of release resembles the occasions described in Neh 5
and 10, which also involve swearing oaths to obey a particular law or laws.

Jer 34:8–22, however, likens the covenant making under Zedekiah to two earlier covenant ceremonies. The oath-taking ceremony involves cutting up a calf,
as in Gen 15:7–21, the LORD's covenant with Abraham, and it takes place in the
temple, as did the the covenant-renewal ceremony under Josiah (2 Kgs 23:1–3).
These associations with the ancient, foundational covenants with Abraham and
with Israel at Sinai indicate the gravity of the offense when Zedekiah's subjects
renege on their own sworn promise.

The specific setting of Zedekiah's covenant making and his subjects' covenant
breaking is indicated in vv 21–22. Zedekiah proclaimed the release during the
initial siege of Jerusalem, and slaves were freed, but as soon as the siege was lifted
their former masters subjugated them again. The lengthy final siege of Jerusalem by the Babylonians began in Zedekiah's tenth year. The walls were breached
on the ninth of Tammuz in Zedekiah's eleventh year, and on the fifth or tenth of
Ab in Nebuchadrezzar's nineteenth year, the Babylonians burned the city and
the temple. The exact reckoning of these regnal years is disputed. Holladay (2:
34) dates the siege from January 588 to July 587 B.C., while Hayes and Hooker
(*New Chronology*, 97–98) put it one year later, from January 587 to July 586. Malamat
("The Twilight of Judah: In the Egyptian-Babylonian Maelstrom," in *Edinburgh
Congress Volume*, VTSup 28 [Leiden: Brill, 1975] 145) calculates the length of the
siege as thirty months, from January 588 to July 586. The Babylonians lifted the
siege temporarily (37:5), apparently because of the threatening approach of an

Egyptian army under Pharaoh Hophra (Holladay, 2:34, in the summer of 588; Malamat, *IEJ* 18 [1968] 152, in winter-spring 587). N. Sarna dates the release within the sabbatical year 588/87 B.C. ("Zedekiah's," 149). Holladay, however, calculates the beginning of that sabbatical year in September/October 587. Therefore, the feast of booths in that month, when the law (Deuteronomy) was read, could not have been the occasion for Zedekiah's proclamation. Noting that King Asa "entered into covenant" during the feast of weeks (2 Chr 15:10–14), Holladay proposes that the covenant to release slaves was made in the feast of weeks in late spring 588 (2:239). There is, however, no consensus about this date.

Most commentators speculate about the motivation for releasing slaves during a siege. Three possibilities are usually mentioned: (1) Economic—to reduce the number of mouths to feed. According to documents from the siege of Nippur, some people sold their children into slavery in part to ensure that they would be fed, believing that slaveholders would protect their investments by keeping their slaves alive (Oppenheim, *Iraq* 17 [1955] 69–72). Taking the slaves back as soon as the Babylonian forces withdrew makes less sense, as it presumes an extraordinary level of confidence about the future. (2) Military—to make more men available to defend the city. Why couldn't they fight while they were still slaves? The release of female slaves along with males is not explained by this hypothesis. (3) Religious—to gain the LORD's favor. The Babylonian withdrawal could have been interpreted as God's response to their act of obedience. Nevertheless, to subjugate their slaves again right away would have been remarkably cynical, showing profound disrespect for the king as well as God. The passage itself shows no interest in discussing such motivations, however. The only reason given is in v 9b, that no Jew should enslave another. It is much more concerned with evaluating theologically the people's temporary obedience and subsequent turning away in relation to the law and with setting the episode in comparison with others in the immediate context of the book of Jeremiah. It is the divine word, not Zedekiah or the people, that interprets the initial release as an attempt to act in accordance with the covenant made at Sinai and that views their subsequent reversal as a continuation of the covenant violations of their ancestors (vv 14–16; cf. Jer 31:32). Furthermore, they had broken their promise, which had been made with an oath sworn in the LORD's name, and in so doing had desecrated that name (Exod 20:7; Deut 5:11). Their cruel betrayal of the slaves who were released temporarily is revealed to be, in fact, a betrayal of their relationship with the LORD.

Integrity in the covenant relationship is the subject of both chap. 34 and chap. 35. E. Martens ("Narrative," 40) points out a shared sequence of component parts and formulaic expressions that may be the product of deliberate shaping, meant to direct the reader to compare the two passages. 35:12–17 makes this point explicitly when the people of Judah and Jerusalem are addressed and invited to compare their own faithlessness to the loyal obedience exhibited by the Rechabites.

Shared features of chaps. 32 and 34 also suggest comparison. They have a similar setting during the final months before Jerusalem fell to the Babylonians, while the city was besieged. Both chapters begin with a private oracle about Zedekiah that leaves room for hope that he might survive the conquest. The subjects of the two accounts are measures taken to help impoverished people who are oppressed by debt. Redemption of a relative's land (Jer 32) and release of Hebrew debt slaves (Jer 34) are both found in Lev 25 (vv 25–28, 39–43). Legitimizing legal actions that secure these transactions are found in both Jeremiah chapters but not in Lev 25. The purchase document of chap. 32 is sealed in a jar so that it will survive a long time, but the covenant made before the LORD in chap. 34 is broken almost immediately. The continuation of chap. 32 in chap. 33 ends with the LORD's promise never to break the covenant with David. The juxtaposition of chaps. 32–33 and 34, therefore, invites the comparison of Jeremiah's faithfulness to the law and to his extended family with the vacillation and treachery of Zedekiah and his slaveholding subjects in relation to the LORD and to their Jewish slaves. This contrasting pair provides a transition from the salvation message of the Book of Consolation to the depiction of Jerusalem's fall in the following chapters.

Comment

8–10   The picture of a ruler in Israel making a covenant with all the people should signal the beginning of a period of peace and commitment (Josh 24:25; 2 Kgs 23:3; 2 Chr 15:12; Isa 61:1). The purpose of Zedekiah's covenant is "release" (דרור) for Hebrew slaves. ("Hebrew" in v 9 clearly means "Jewish," regardless of what the term may have meant earlier, as is evident from v 9b.) דרור, "release, liberty," is the term used in Lev 25:10 for the various social transformations in the jubilee year, including manumission of slaves and cancellation of debt, which were designed to enable the poor to "return" (שוב) to their families and their inherited land (Lev 25:10), a restoration to conditions as God meant them to be, according to the book of Joshua. Like the jubilee year דרור, "release," Zedekiah's covenant was effective for everyone simultaneously, even for slaves who had not completed six years of service. (For an ancient Near Eastern parallel, the *mesharum* act, see *Form/Structure/Setting*.)

11   There is no explanation given of how the slaveholders were able to find and repossess their former slaves, but a very strong word, כבש, "subdue, overpower," is used to describe the process (cf. Gen 1:28; Zech 9:15; Neh 5:5; Esth 7:8). The creditors probably knew the location of their slaves' family lands, to which they would return upon their release.

12   The word-event formula is repeated in v 12 because the extensive description of setting in vv 8b–11 has broken the syntactic connection between v 8a and the oracle beginning in v 13.

13   The covenant making at Sinai is dated three months after the departure from Egypt (Exod 19:1). "In the day," therefore, should be understood less precisely as "at the time." Egypt is called "the house of slaves" frequently in accounts of the Exodus (Exod 13:3, 14; Deut 5:6; 6:12; 7:8; 8:14; 13:6, 11[Eng 5, 10]; Josh 24:17; Judg 6:8; Mic 6:4). The presence of this term here is a deliberate choice. V 14 cites the law regarding debt slavery from Exod 21; Deut 15 but omits the motivation, "Remember that you were a slave in Egypt" (Deut 15:15). V 13 provides this reminder of their status in Egypt instead. It also stands in contrast with the indictment in v 16, "you subjugated them to be your male slaves [עבדים] and female slaves [שפחות]."

14   The form of this law is not identical with either Exod 21:2–6 or Deut 15:12–17. The dating formula follows Deut 15:12, but it mentions only the male slave,

as in Exod 21. Regulations governing the slave's family and providing for gener-
ous gifts with which to set up housekeeping (Exod 21:3–4; Deut 15:14) are not
mentioned. The possibility that a slave would choose to remain in slavery permanently is not considered either (Exod 21:5–6; Deut 15:16–17). These other matters
were moot questions, however, if the law was never observed.

15–16 Here the LORD retells vv 9–10 with three significant variants. The
people's repentance preceded the release, the Hebrew slaves are called "neighbors, companions" rather than "slaves," and the people's violation of covenant is
identified as defiling the divine name.

These verses are linked by a play on words. "Repented" (v 15) and "reneged"
(v 16) are translations of identical verb forms, ותשבו, from the root שוב, "turn," a
term extremely common in the prose material in the book of Jeremiah.

17 The pair אחיו, "his brother," and רעהו, "his neighbor," do not correspond,
respectively, to עבדים, "male slaves," and שפחות, "female slaves." Together, "brother"
and "neighbor" indicate the relationship between the slaveholders and their slaves
that should take precedence over their economic relationship. This interpretation of the law shares the motivation of v 9. No Jew should subjugate another Jew
as a slave.

This verse includes the essential components of a judgment oracle. V 17a is
the indictment, and v 17b is the announcement of judgment, which, in this case,
is made up entirely of stereotypical expressions. The two parts are linked by the
passage's key wordplay. Because the people had failed to grant "release" (דרור)
to their Jewish debt slaves, the LORD would grant "release" (דרור) to sword, famine, and pestilence. They would no longer be restrained from destroying the ones
who had refused to obey.

18–19 The ceremony that accompanied the covenant making of v 8 is found
elsewhere in the OT only in Gen 15:7–21. V 18 indicates the function of the ceremony. The people who entered into the covenant accepted the threat of the
curse demonstrated by the cut-up calf. Whoever violated the terms of the covenant would be killed like the calf (Rudolph, 225).

MT lists the groups who entered into the covenant with Zedekiah with more
specificity than does the LXX. The difference between the royal officials of Judah
and those of Jerusalem is unknown, unless it was simply a matter of where they
were stationed. Notably absent from this list are the prophets and the royal family. The effect is to include everyone else in Judah who could have been in a
financial position to acquire debt slaves.

20–21 "Enemies" and "the ones who are seeking their lives" are the typical
vocabulary of lament psalms. The curse of having one's unburied corpse consumed as carrion by animals or birds is part of the stereotypical list of treaty curses
(Deut 28:26). The same threat appears in Jer 7:33; 16:4; 19:7b.

21–22 The final two verses provide the only information regarding the time
during Zedekiah's reign when the covenant was made and then broken. Judgment is pronounced when the Babylonian army is withdrawing from Jerusalem
(v 21b). The most logical implication is that the covenant was made while the city
was being besieged and that the people reneged and took back their slaves when
the siege was lifted. (See *Form/Structure/Setting* for possible dates.) V 22 announces
that the withdrawal of the Babylonian forces is only temporary. The LORD will

bring them back to conquer the city as punishment for covenant breaking. The purpose for indicating the setting is not to explain the political, economic, or even religious reasons for releasing the slaves in the first place (see *Form/Structure/Setting*), for these are never explained. Rather, the setting serves to interpret the final destruction of the city and temple in 587/6 B.C. as punishment for this covenant violation. Vv 21–22 connect the general threats in vv 18–20 to a specific historical setting. The lesson to be learned from this passage, according to R. Carroll (650), is that to violate even one stipulation of the Sinai covenant is to break the whole and to risk total destruction.

Explanation

The Judean upper classes betrayed Israel's deliverance from slavery in Egypt as well as their covenant with the LORD by their treacherous treatment of their debt slaves. The general release proclaimed by King Zedekiah, in which all Hebrew slaves went free, corresponds to the Exodus. When the slaveholders reneged and subjugated their former slaves again, they succeeded where Pharaoh had failed. The slaveholders and their slaves were actually brothers (and sisters) and neighbors, and it was not fitting for any Jew to hold another in bondage (v 9). The treachery of the leading Judeans took place within the context of the Babylonian invasion. The distinction between the wealthy, who had money to lend, and, therefore, could end up owning slaves, and the poor, who had to sell themselves or their children to pay their debts, was about to collapse when all of them became Nebuchadrezzar's slaves.

When Jeremiah redeems his cousin's land (chap. 32) and when the Rechabites refuse to drink wine (chap. 35), they act out of loyalty to ancient obligations in spite of the threatening circumstances of the Babylonian attack. When Judah's leading citizens take back their slaves, they not only violate covenants old and new; they deny the LORD's word through Jeremiah that their land had been assigned to Nebuchadrezzar's control, just as King Jehoiakim had denied it (chap. 36).

XXII. Jeremiah and the Rechabites   (35:1–19 [LXX 42:1–19])

Bibliography

Abramsky, S. "House of Rechab [in Hebrew, English summary, 76]." In *E. L. Sukenik Memorial Volume*, ed. N. Avigad. Jerusalem: Israel Exploration Society, 1976. 255–64. **Bosman, H. L.** "The Rechabites and 'Sippenethos' in Jeremiah 35." *ThEv* 16 (1983) 83–86. **Frick, F. S.** "Rechabites Reconsidered." *JBL* 90 (1971) 279–87. **Keukens, K. H.** "Die rekabitischen Haussklaven in Jeremia 35." *BZ* 27 (1983) 228–35. **Levenson, J. D.** "On the Promise to the Rechabites." *CBQ* 38 (1976) 508–14.

Translation

[1] *The word which came to Jeremiah from the LORD; in the days of Jehoiakim, the son of Josiah,*[a] *the king of Judah, saying:* [2] *"Go to the house of the Rechabites and speak with them,*[a] *and bring them to the house of the LORD, to one of the rooms, and offer them wine to drink."* [3] *And so I took Jaazaniah, the son of Jeremiah,*[a] *son of Habazziniah, and his brothers and all*[b] *his sons, and all of the house of the Rechabites.* [4] *And I brought them to the house of the LORD, to the room of the sons*[a] *of Hanan,*[b] *the son of Igdaliah,*[c] *the man of God, which was beside the room of the princes, which was above the room of Maaseiah, the son of Shallum the doorkeeper.* [5] *And I set before the sons of the Rechabites*[a] *bowls filled*[b] *with wine, and cups; and I said to them,*[c] *"Drink wine!"* [6] *But they said, "We will not drink wine; because Jonadab, the son of Rechab, our ancestor, commanded us, saying, 'You shall not drink wine, you or your children, forever.* [7] *And you shall not build a house, and you shall not sow a seed, and you shall not plant*[a] *or own a vineyard; but you shall dwell in tents all of your days, so that you may live many days upon the face of*[b] *the land where you sojourn.'* [8] *And we obeyed the voice of Jonadab, the son of Rechab,*[a] *our ancestor, all which he commanded us;*[b] *not to drink wine all of our days, (neither) we, (nor) our wives, our sons, nor our daughters.* [9] *And not to build houses for our dwellings; nor a vineyard, nor a field, nor seed; they are not for us.* [10] *And we have always lived in tents; and we have obeyed, we have done just as Jonadab our ancestor commanded us.* [11] *But when Nebuchadrezzar, the king of Babylon, came up against the land, then we said, 'Come, and let us go to Jerusalem from before the army of the Chaldeans, and from before the army of Syria';*[a] *and (that is why) we are dwelling in Jerusalem."*

[12] *And the word of the LORD came to Jeremiah,*[a] *saying:* [13] *"Thus says the LORD of Hosts, the God of Israel,*[a] *go and say to the men of Judah and to the inhabitants of Jerusalem: 'Will you not take instruction to listen to my words' —an oracle of the LORD.*[b] [14] *The words of Jonadab the son of Rechab have been kept, who commanded his sons not to drink wine, and they have not drunk (wine) unto this day, because they obeyed the commandment of their ancestors;*[a] *yet I have spoken to you persistently, and you do not listen to me.*[b] [15] *And I sent you all*[a] *my servants, the prophets, persistently,*[b] *saying, 'Turn now, each from his wicked way, and amend your ways, and do not go after other gods to*

serve them, and you will dwell in the land which I gave to you and to your fathers'; but you did not incline your ears, and you did not listen to me.[c] [16]For the sons of Jonadab the son of Rechab have kept the command of their ancestors which he gave them,[a] but this people has not obeyed me.

[17] "Therefore, thus says the LORD, the God of Hosts, the God of Israel,[a] 'Behold, I am bringing against Judah and against all the inhabitants of Jerusalem, every evil which I have spoken against them; because I spoke to them and they did not listen, and I called to them and they did not respond.' "[b] [18]But to the house of the Rechabites Jeremiah said,[a] "Thus says the LORD of Hosts, the God of Israel,[b] 'Because you[c] obeyed the command of Jonadab[d] your[e] ancestor, and you have kept all his commands,[f] and you have done[g] all that he[h] commanded you';[i] [19]Therefore, thus says the LORD of Hosts, the God of Israel,[a] 'there will never be lacking a descendant for Jonadab[b] standing before me all the days.' "[c]

Notes

1.a. MT בן־יאשיהו, "the son of Josiah," is absent in LXX.

2.a. MT ודברת אותם, "and speak with them," not present in LXX.

3.a. This is, of course, other than the prophet. See also 52:1. LXX reads Ιερεμιν.

3.b. LXX lacks "all."

4.a. Some versions have the sg here.

4.b. LXX[B] reads יחנן, "Jehanan."

4.c. LXX has "Gedaliah."

5.a. LXX has simply "set before."

5.b. LXX lacks "filled."

5.c. MT "to them" missing in LXX.

7.a. LXX lacks "you shall not plant."

7.b. "the face of" is not present in LXX.

8.a. Lacking in LXX, possibly an expansion in MT.

8.b. Phrase "according to all which he commanded us" is absent in LXX.

11.a. Syr has אדם, "Edom," the only difference being the easily confused Heb. ד for ר.

12.a. LXX has πρός με, "to me."

13.a. LXX lacks "of Hosts, the God of Israel."

13.b. LXX lacks נאם־יהוה, "an oracle of the LORD."

14.a. The lengthy phrase "unto this day, because they obeyed the commandment of their ancestors" is lacking in LXX.

14.b. LXX lacks אלי, "to me."

15.a. כל, "all," is lacking in LXX.

15.b. LXX lacks the verb in Heb., השכים, lit. "rising early and often," which gives the nuance of "persistently" in MT.

15.c. LXX lacks "to me."

16.a. MT אשר צום, "which he gave [lit. commanded] them," is lacking in LXX.

17.a. LXX lacks "the LORD of Hosts, the God of Israel."

17.b. The last phrase in MT, emphasizing the reason for judgment, is missing in LXX.

18.a. LXX has διὰ τοῦτο, "Because of this," or "For this reason," lacking the longer phrase of address.

18.b. LXX lacks the longer title of MT, צבאות אלהי ישראל, "of Hosts, the God of Israel."

18.c. LXX has the longer descriptive phrase υἱοὶ Ιωναδὰβ υἱοῦ Ρηχαβ, "sons of Jonadab son of Rechab."

18.d. Lacking in LXX.

18.e. LXX has "their" ancestor.

18.f. LXX lacks the phrase "and you have kept all his commands."

18.g. LXX has ποιεῖν, "doing."

18.h. "their" ancestor in LXX.

18.i. LXX has αὐτῶν, "them," for MT "you."

19.a. LXX lacks the entire phrase to this point.
19.b. LXX has "sons of Jonadab."
19.c. LXX adds τῆς γῆς, "of the earth."

Form/Structure/Setting

The faithlessness of Judah, highlighted in Jer 34, is even more graphically presented by means of the prophet's use of contrast in Jer 35. The emphasis in the message of Jeremiah to Zedekiah in Jer 34 is upon the crucial sin of covenant breaking. Jer 35, by introducing the strange story of the Rechabites, provides a sequel to the message of judgment in the preceding chapter. Not all scholars, however, are convinced that any connection exists between Jer 34 and 35.

Bright (lviii) does not consider Jer 35 to be a part of the three major "books" of which Jeremiah is composed (see Introduction to volume 1 of our commentary on Jeremiah, "The Form and Structure of the Book of Jeremiah"). Instead, he classifies it as biographical narrative and sets it aside with other such material in a chronologically arranged separate unit. The result is that Jer 35 is placed between Jer 45 and Jer 24, ignoring the fidelity/infidelity contrast evident in Jer 34 and 35. By removing Jer 35 from any contact with Jer 34, Bright has ignored what was likely an editorial decision on the part of the collectors of the Jeremiah text.

While no one would disagree with Bright's statements regarding the difficulties associated with the arrangement of the Jeremiah text, the correct response to that difficulty is not necessarily to replace its disorder with one proposed by a modern commentator. A more fruitful approach might well be to seek those possible links between passages that seem unconnected. Is there some discernible pattern beneath the surface to explain the arrangement of material as it stands? Even if such is not forthcoming, it is better to leave the text as it stands than to provide an arbitrary arrangement in its place.

In terms of arrangement, this chapter serves as another example of the lack of chronological order in Jeremiah. Quite obviously, some grouping of material by content or theme takes precedence over the chronology of events. Jer 35 is dated during the reign of Jehoiakim. Jer 34 is a message delivered to Zedekiah some years later. Nevertheless, in organization, the message of Jer 35 gives a fitting "closure" to the themes elaborated in Jer 34.

The chapter is divided into three narrative segments. The first unit is to be found in vv 1–11, intended to confirm the faithfulness of the Rechabite clan by means of the "test" at the temple.

The second section, vv 12–17, is a prose oracle directed to the faithless Judeans so prominent in Jer 34. The oracle explains the significance of the "test" administered to the Rechabites. The Judeans' faithlessness is contrasted pointedly to the "faithfulness" of the Rechabite clan. While the "faithfulness" of the Rechabites is not of exactly the same order as that lacking in Judah, it gives the prophet a suitable method of identifying the terrible nature of Judah's sin. It may be that the difference in pattern even adds to the weight of the prophet's message.

The chapter concludes with an oracle of promise from the LORD to the Rechabites as a result of their obedience to Jonadab. In wording reminiscent of other covenant promises in the OT (See Levenson, *CBQ* 38 [1976] 508–12), the Rechabites are assured an everlasting place among those who serve the LORD. The pattern of promise is noted by Carroll (655) as the same as that elsewhere granted to David and the levitical priests. Yet, in those cases, the promise comes in spite of failure, not at all in the manner of "reward," which is suggested here.

The historical setting of this event is a Babylonian incursion that took place during the last years of the reign of Jehoiakim as king of Judah. Jerusalem was not the victim of actual assault during these events, but virtually the whole surrounding countryside was enveloped by the invading Babylonians.

The Rechabites are central characters in the events of Jer 35. However they are defined or identified, their presence in Jerusalem provides the prophet Jeremiah with a fitting symbol to use in his message against Judah. The background of the entire chapter concerns the history of this group of people, their customs stemming from ancestral instruction, and their faithfulness to those customs as a paradigm of covenant fidelity. Consistent with the parallel that Jeremiah establishes by means of this group of people, the chapter concludes with a word of promise to them, the word of promise that Jeremiah has rejected as impossible for a faithless people such as Judah.

The chapter may be outlined as follows:

I. The test of the Rechabites (vv 1–11)
  A. The LORD's command (vv 1–2)
  B. Jeremiah's obedient response (vv 3–4)
  C. The test (v 5)
  D. The testimony of the Rechabite lifestyle (vv 6–10)
  E. The reason for the Rechabite presence in Jerusalem (v 11)
II. Prose oracle against the Judeans (vv 12–17)
  A. Contrast between the Rechabites and faithless Judah (vv 12–16)
  B. The word of judgment (v 17)
III. An oracle of promise for the Rechabites (vv 18–19)

Comment

1–2 Jeremiah is called to go to the group known as the Rechabites in order to involve them in a strange kind of "test," which provides a symbolic prophecy for Judah. The prophet is told to bring the Rechabites to a particular room in the temple precincts and to invite them to drink wine.

3–4 Jeremiah does as he was instructed and assembles the Rechabites in the room of the "sons of Hanan the son of Igdaliah the man of God." The identity of the sons of Hanan and their relationship to Jeremiah are not clear. Igdaliah, part of the named ancestry, is referred to as "the man of God" (Carroll, 652). This term may indicate a specialized prophetic role for Igdaliah and could identify Igdaliah and those with him as allies of Jeremiah.

5–10 Once in place, the invitation to drink wine is given to the assembled Rechabites, an invitation that is refused. The refusal is accompanied by an elaboration of the Rechabites' idiosyncratic lifestyle as a group, traced to the command of the ancestor Jonadab ben-Rechab. Prohibitions include the drinking of wine, building and dwelling in stone houses, and the planting of seeds and vineyards.

Excursus: The Identity of the Rechabites

Bibliography

Budde, K. "The Nomadic Ideal in the Old Testament." *The New World* 4 (1895) 726–45. **Frick, F. S.** "Rechabites Reconsidered." *JBL* 90 (1971) 279–87. **Keukens, K. H.** "Die rekabitischen Haussklaven in Jeremia 35." *BZ* 27 (1983) 228–35.

The elaborate response of the Rechabites to Jeremiah's invitation to drink wine brings to the fore the question of the precise identity of these persons known as Rechabites. What do such prohibitions represent in the larger cultural patterns of the ancient Near East? Is this a group of desert nomads practicing an ascetic way of life? What other explanations would fit? Much energy has been expended in an attempt to answer these and related questions.

The traditional understanding has been to identify the Rechabites as an ascetic throwback to desert nomadism once common to the Israelite experience. Bright (191), for example, describes them as part of a protest movement upholding the pristine traditions of old times against the decay illustrated by syncretistic lifestyles in monarchic Israel. Thompson (616–17), similarly, links the Rechabites with the Kenites, using the genealogical information of 1 Chr 2:55, identifying the Kenites as a clan of seminomads friendly with Israel since the days of the Exodus. Carroll (652-56) generally follows the same accepted pattern of interpretation, though recognizing the apparent contradiction inherent in the presence of such a group in the urban center of Jerusalem. These three modern scholars illustrate the traditional mode of interpretation applied to the Rechabites across the centuries. Their efforts continue approaches begun with Budde (*The New World* 4 [1895] 726–45) and followed by others since, all of which more or less treat the Rechabites as the representatives of a kind of "old time religion" in Israel.

As the incident in Jer 35 unfolds, it becomes clear that the drinking of wine is prohibited by the tradition of this clan, though the specific reason or reasons for the prohibition are not clear. Typically, interpreters of this passage have identified the Rechabites as an ascetic throwback to a desert nomadism once common to the Israelite people. Inevitable connections are made to the Nazirite pattern, even to suggesting that the Rechabites are the proto-Nazirites, who perpetually lived what later became a temporary ascetic ideal. Yet, none of this is directly suggested by any text related to the Rechabites in the OT. The group is assumed to be the successors of Jonadab ben-Rechab, who assisted Jehu in the destruction of the Omrides (2 Kgs 10).

There have been attempts to move a bit further into the shadows in order to learn more about these elusive figures. The impetus for most such inquiry is the paucity of information available about the Rechabites. A careful perusal reveals that much that has typically been assumed about them is based on very flimsy evidence, several layers of which eventually formed the established tradition. For example, the named ancestor, Jonadab ben-Rechab, has always been identified with the events of Jehu's purge of the Omrides in the ninth century B.C. Accounts of that episode do not mention anything at all about the lifestyle of Jonadab, nor is it certain that the Jonadab of the Jehu story should be seen as the ancestor in Jer 35.

Nowhere else in the OT is a particular way of life attributed to Jonadab. It has even been pointed out that every mention of the Rechabites in the OT occurs in an urban setting. The *only* support for a long-established tradition of asceticism comes from creating *ex nihilo* a geometric progression from the single reference in Jer 35 and speculating as to its linkage to other persons/events/times. It is not even certain that the lifestyle described by the Rechabites is intended to be an ascetic lifestyle. Two other explanations have been put forward that have at least as much merit.

The first is the proposal of F. S. Frick (*JBL* 90 [1971] 279–87). He argues that the group could just as easily be identified as a guild of artisans, specifically, chariot makers. The Heb. name רכב also can be the basis for the word "chariot." A guild of artisans would, of necessity, be somewhat nomadic in lifestyle, moving to ply their trade. The prohibition against wine becomes a possible caution against what Frick calls the "loose lips sink ships" syndrome in this munitions craft, for chariots were certainly major elements in defense arsenals of the day. As is evident, the support for Frick's case is not substantial. It is probably as firm as that for the traditional understanding.

The second optional proposal is not far from the first. Keukens (*BZ* 27 [1983] 228–35), rejecting the traditional hypothesis as well, proposes that the Rechabites be identified as a group of former household servants who have received specific instructions from the householder (Jonadab). Keukens is concerned to separate the traditions of the Rechabites from any linkage with the classical prophetic tradition. He notes the contradiction in patterns of life evident with Elisha in the early period, and such contradictions would also apply to the other major prophets in Israel's tradition. The rules, then, are uniquely to be applied to the Rechabites, not set up as any ideal for Israel or any portion thereof. Jonadab is not to be seen as the founder of any way of life, or as the ancestor of an ascetic group, but only as the legal master of a group of household servants. (Examples from Gen 15, Job 19, and others are used to show similar biblical parallels for this pattern.) Keukens' proposal goes on to suggest a reason for the inclusion of the Rechabite tradition in the message of Jeremiah. He postulates that the story provides a pre-exilic linkage to an important group in post-exilic Israel. The Rechabites are not as significant, then, because of what they once represented but because of the foundation they provide for another group more contemporary to the collection of Jeremiah's message.

Both nontraditional options sketched above develop understanding of the Rechabites using the information about the group available in the OT. Perhaps the most valuable contribution of these options is the realization that too scant information is available to draw many conclusions about the Rechabites. Some of the traditional approaches may have merit. The full identity of the Rechabites and their place in the cultural patterns of Israel cannot be determined. The clearest description of the group begins and ends with the passage in Jer 35. What is indicated is not a full-blown treatment of a historical group of people; rather, it is a powerful word of rebuke and challenge by means of a clear message about obedience. The Rechabites, whatever their specific identity or heritage, represent a symbol of faithfulness to prior commands that is not to be found in Judah and her relationship with the LORD.

11 The end of the narrative section describing the encounter of Jeremiah with the Rechabites seems to provide the reason for the group's presence in Jerusalem. That such an explanation is given may suggest that the Rechabites' tradition was somewhat compromised. The hostile incursion of the armies of Babylon and Syria apparently has forced upon the Rechabites action they would not otherwise have taken. The tone of the rest of the chapter suggests that the obedience of the Rechabites to their ancestor Jonadab is not seriously questioned, in spite of their presence in the city.

12–17 Vv 12–17 represent a prose oracle directed to the people of Jerusa-

lem and Judah. Jeremiah is instructed to announce the faithfulness of the
Rechabites to Jonadab's commands as a means of emphasizing the depth of
Judah's unfaithfulness to the LORD. The Rechabites become a kind of clinching
argument in a "trial" against Judah. In language somewhat similar to the formal controversy settings common in the prophetic tradition, the case is overwhelmingly
presented against Judah. As in 2:9–13, where the prophet contrasts the sin of
Judah to the relative fidelity of the "nations" to their gods, here the Rechabites
are the foil. They are obedient to a human ancestor, whose commands are not
substantially at issue. The Rechabites condemn the people of Judah by their obedience.

The oracle, which hits hard at the sin of Judah, is not without its element of
pleading. The call to repent, שׁוּב, one of Jeremiah's most often used pleas, is issued to faithless Judah. There is still time for repentance and renewal. There is
still the possibility that God's promise for Judah can be realized, but it can only
come through the faithfulness of a people.

The conclusion of this section is a harsh word of judgment. The key word in
this part of the oracle is לכֵן, "therefore." Any time this word appears in a prophetic oracle, what follows is the announcement of God's judgment. Judgment
comes because of a continued refusal to obey, in spite of God's repeated calls to
obedience.

18–19 The chapter ends with an oracle of promise directed at the
Rechabites. In the language of covenant promise, the LORD assures the Rechabites
of a continued role in service to him. There will always be a Rechabite, a descendant of Jonadab, serving the LORD.

This promise is the focus of attention for Keukens (see *Excursus* following *Comment* on vv 5–10). Certainly, this promise would provide a needed link between
any later Rechabite presence in the life of Israel and a supportable foundation
for that presence. Unlike other of the Kenite groups, who are not allowed to
enter fully into the life of the cult, these are special persons, made special by the
example of obedience presented in Jer 35. Whether Keukens' hypothesis can be
supported further is impossible to say, but it does offer an attractive option for
consideration.

Explanation

The word of judgment against Judah and Jerusalem is made more severe by
contrasting the faithlessness of Judah and Jerusalem to the faithfulness of the
clan of the Rechabites. Judah has consistently broken faith with God. For their
part, the Rechabites have been more faithful to their ancestor Jonadab than Judah
has been faithful to God. Though there is no intention of presenting an exact
parallel, the Rechabites, through their faithfulness to a human ancestor, emphasize the sin of the people of Judah, who have refused to keep faith with God.

The key to the entirety of Jer 35 is the theme of obedience, or perhaps better,
the contrast between unfaithfulness and faithfulness. Unfaithfulness is the pattern of life that has characterized the people of Israel and Judah for the whole of
their existence as a people. The prophets make clear that infidelity is the norm,
not the exception, for those who like to call themselves the people of God.

Jeremiah continues in the line of those prophets. Repeatedly, Jeremiah attempts to demonstrate the depths of Judah's faithlessness, only to have his messages ignored and his stance ridiculed.

Interpreters of this passage should carefully avoid the pitfalls presented by the mystery of the Rechabites. That mystery is not capable of solution, but the theme of obedience is not a part of the mystery. Jeremiah makes no attempt to hold up the lifestyle of the Rechabites as a model for Judah. He does not call for abstention from wine for the nation. He does not advocate a return to nomadic life. Instead, he presents a powerful contrast between a small group of people who have kept with determination the customs established centuries earlier by a human ancestor and the people of the nation of Judah, who seem unable to hear or keep the commands of the LORD of Hosts.

Other passages in Jeremiah (Jer 7, in particular) emphasize the danger of a religious faith that loses awareness of all but its ritualistic elements. Jer 35 adds to the words of challenge and condemnation issued throughout Jeremiah against religious ideas that lack the heart of religious faith: obedience to the LORD. As simple as it seems, the lesson of the Rechabites is one Judah never learned. One wonders whether it has yet been learned by those who bear the label of the people of God.

XXIII. The Scroll (36:1–32[LXX 43:1–32])

Bibliography

Baumann, A. "Urrolle und Fasttag: Zur Rekonstruktion der Urrolle des Jeremiabuches nach den Angaben in Jer 36." *ZAW* 80 (1968) 350–73. **Hicks, R. L.** *"Delet* and *M'gillah:* A Fresh Approach to Jeremiah xxxvi." *VT* 33 (1983) 46–66. **Holladay, W. L.** "A Fresh Look at 'Source B' and 'Source C'." *VT* 25 (1975) 394–412. ————. "The Identification of the Two Scrolls of Jeremiah." *VT* 30 (1983) 452–67. **Isbell, C. D.** "2 Kings 22:3–23:24 and Jeremiah 36: A Stylistic Comparison." *JSOT* 8 (1978) 33–45. **Kessler, M.** "Form Critical Suggestions on Jer 36." *CBQ* 28 (1966) 389–401. ————. "Jeremiah Chapters 26–45 Reconsidered." *JNES* 27 (1968) 81–88. ————. "The Significance of Jer 36." *ZAW* 81 (1969) 381–83. **Long, B. O.** "Social Dimensions of Prophetic Conflict." *Semeia* 21 (1981) 31–53. **Perdue, L. G.** "Jeremiah in Modern Research." In *A Prophet to the Nations,* ed. L. G. Perdue and B. W. Kovacs. Winona Lake, IN: Eisenbrauns, 1984. 1–32.

Translation

[1]*In the fourth year of Jehoiakim the son of Josiah, the king of Judah, this word*[a] *came to Jeremiah*[b] *from the LORD:* [2]*"Take a scroll*[a] *and write on it all the words which I have spoken to you concerning Israel*[b] *and Judah and all the nations, from the day I spoke to you, from the days of Josiah*[c] *until today.* [3]*Perhaps the house of Judah will hear all the evil which I intend to do to them, so that every one may turn from his evil way and I may pardon their iniquity and their sin."*

[4]*So Jeremiah called Baruch the son of Neriah, and Baruch*[a] *wrote upon a scroll at the dictation of Jeremiah all the words of the LORD which he had spoken to him.* [5]*And Jeremiah commanded Baruch, saying: "I am under restraint and I cannot go to the house of the LORD.* [6]*So you are to go*[a] *and, on a fast day in the hearing of the people in the house of the LORD, read from the scroll*[b] *the words of the LORD that you have written at my dictation; and also read them in the hearing of all the men of Judah who come out of their cities.* [7]*Perhaps their supplication will come before the LORD, and every one*[a] *will turn from his evil way; for great is the anger and the wrath*[b] *that the LORD*[c] *has pronounced against this people."* [8]*And Baruch the son of Neriah*[a] *did all that Jeremiah the prophet*[b] *commanded him about reading from the scroll the words of the LORD in the house of the LORD.*

[9]*And in the fifth*[a] *year of Jehoiakim the son of Josiah, the king of Judah, in the ninth month, they*[b] *proclaimed a fast before the LORD, (for) all the people in Jerusalem and all the people who came from the cities of Judah to Jerusalem.*[c] [10]*So from the room of Gemariah the son of Shaphan the scribe, in the upper court, at the entrance of the New Gate of the house of the LORD, in the hearing of all the people, Baruch read the words of Jeremiah from the scroll in the house of the LORD.*

[11]*When Micaiah the son of Gemariah the son of Shaphan heard all the words of the LORD from the scroll,* [12]*he went down to the house of the king to the room of the scribe, and all the princes were sitting there: Elishama the scribe, and Delaiah the son of Shemaiah,*[a] *and Elnathan*[b] *the son of Achbor, and Gemariah the son of Shaphan, and*

Zedekiah the son of Hananiah, and all the princes. [13]*And Micaiah told them all the words that he had heard, when Baruch read from the scroll*[a] *in the hearing of the people.*

[14]*Then all the princes sent to Baruch*[a] *Jehudi the son of Nethaniah the son of Shelemiah the son of Cushi, saying: "The scroll from which you read in the hearing of the people, bring it in your hand and come"; so Baruch the son of Neriah*[b] *took the scroll in his hand,*[c] *and he came*[d] *to them.* [15]*And they said to him, "Sit down and read it*[a] *to us"; so Baruch read it to them.* [b] [16]*And when they heard all the words, they turned one to another in fear; and they said to Baruch,*[a] *"We must report all these words to the king."* [17]*And they asked Baruch, "Tell us, how*[a] *did you write all these words? Was it at his dictation?"*[b] [18]*And Baruch answered them, "He*[a] *dictated to me all these words, and I wrote them on the scroll with ink."*[b]

[19]*And the princes*[a] *said to Baruch, "Go, hide, you and Jeremiah, and let no one know where you are."* [20]*And they went to the king, to the court, and they deposited the scroll in the room of Elishama the scribe;*[a] *and they reported all the words*[b] *in the hearing of*[c] *the king.*

[21]*Then the king sent Jehudi to get the scroll, and he took it from the room of Elishama the scribe;*[a] *and Jehudi read it in the hearing of the king, and in the hearing of all the princes who stood beside the king.* [22]*And the king was sitting in the winter house, in the ninth month,*[a] *and there was a fire*[b] *burning*[c] *in the brazier before him.* [23]*And as Jehudi read three or four columns, he*[a] *would tear it off the scroll with a penknife and cast it into the fire which was in the brazier until all the scroll was consumed in the fire which was in the brazier.* [24]*Yet they were not afraid, and they did not tear their garments—neither the king nor any of*[a] *his servants who heard all these words.* [25]*And even when Elnathan and Delaiah*[a] *and Gemariah pleaded with the king not*[b] *to burn the scroll, he would not listen to them.*[c] [26]*And the king commanded Jerahmeel the son of the king, and Seraiah the son of Azriel, and Shelemiah the son of Abdeel*[a] *to take Baruch the scribe*[b] *and Jeremiah the prophet;*[c] *but the LORD hid them.*[d]

[27]*Now the word of the LORD came to Jeremiah after the king's burning of the scroll and the words*[a] *which Baruch had written at Jeremiah's dictation:* [28]*"Take another scroll, and write upon it*[a] *all the former words which were upon the first*[b] *scroll which Jehoiakim the king of Judah*[c] *burned.* [29]*And concerning Jehoiakim the king of Judah,*[a] *say, 'Thus says the LORD, you burned this scroll, saying, "Why did you write upon it that the king of Babylon will surely come and destroy this land, and cut off from it people and animals?"*

[30]*"'Therefore, thus says the LORD concerning Jehoiakim the king of Judah, there will not be for him anyone to sit upon the throne of David, and his corpse will be cast out to the heat by day and to the frost by night.* [31]*And I will punish him and his descendants and his servants because of their iniquity,*[a] *and I will bring upon them and upon the inhabitants of Jerusalem and to the people*[b] *of Judah all the evil which I have pronounced to them, but they would not listen.'"*

[32]*Then Jeremiah*[a] *took another scroll, and he gave it to Baruch the son of Neriah, the scribe,*[b] *who wrote upon it at the dictation of Jeremiah all the words of the scroll which Jehoiakim the king of Judah*[c] *burned in the fire,*[d] *and many similar words were added to them.*

Notes

1.a. LXX has λόγος κυρίου, "the word of the LORD."
1.b. LXX has "to me."

2.a. The phrase מְגִלַּת־סֵפֶר, "book-scroll," occurs only here, v 4, Ps 40:8 (Eng 7), and Ezek 2:9.

2.b. Though many scholars read "Jerusalem" with LXX, MT "Israel" should probably be retained. Bright (179) and Thompson (621–22) point out key arguments for the retention of "Israel." The pattern used by Jeremiah is "Judah and Jerusalem," not the reverse as would be here following LXX. The content of the scroll would also allow for broader concerns than those of Judah and Jerusalem.

2.c. LXX adds "the king of Judah."

4.a. "Baruch" lacking in LXX.

6.a. וּבָאתָ אַתָּה, "So you are to go," lacking in LXX.

6.b. LXX has χαρτίῳ τούτῳ, "this scroll," lacking the longer explanatory phrase אֲשֶׁר־כָּתַבְתָּ מִפִּי אֶת־דִּבְרֵי יְהוָה, "the words of the LORD which you wrote at my dictation."

7.a. LXX lacks אִישׁ, "every one" or "each."

7.b. LXX has "wrath of the LORD."

7.c. LXX lacks יְהוָה, "the LORD"; LXX reads ἐλάλησεν, "*he* has pronounced."

8.a. LXX lacks "son of Neriah."

8.b. LXX lacks "the prophet."

9.a. LXX has τῷ ὀγδόῳ, "the eighth."

9.b. "they" likely refers to the authorities (with Rudolph, 196). The people of Jerusalem and the people from outlying areas could not "proclaim a fast"; that could only be done by the proper authorities.

9.c. LXX has "and the house of Judah" instead of MT "and all the people who came from the cities of Judah to Jerusalem."

12.a. LXX reads Σελεμίου, "Shelemiah."

12.b. Some Gk. MSS propose variously Ιωναθαν, "Jonathan," Ναθαν, "Nathan," or Ελδαθαν, "Eldathan."

13.a. LXX lacks "from the scroll."

14.a. LXX adds "the son of Neriah."

14.b. LXX lacks "the son of Neriah."

14.c. LXX lacks "in his hand."

14.d. LXX has κατέβη = Heb. יָרַד, "he went down."

15.a. LXX adds πάλιν, "again."

15.b. LXX lacks בְּאָזְנֵיהֶם, "to them," lit. "in their hearing."

16.a. LXX lacks "to Baruch."

17.a. LXX has πόθεν, "how?"

17.b. מִפִּיו, "Was it at his dictation?" (lit. "From his mouth?"), lacking in LXX. Interrogative ה lacking by haplogr, so RSV.

18.a. LXX has "*Jeremiah* dictated . . ."

18.b. LXX lacks "with ink."

19.a. LXX lacks הַשָּׂרִים, "the princes."

20.a. LXX lacks "the scribe."

20.b. Some Gk. MSS have "*these* words . . ."

20.c. LXX has τῷ βασιλεῖ, "to the king," rather than the Heb. idiom בְּאָזְנֵי הַמֶּלֶךְ, "in the hearing [lit. the ears] of the king."

21.a. LXX lacks "the scribe."

22.a. "in the ninth month" missing from LXX.

22.b. Reading וְאֵשׁ, "fire," with LXX. MT sign of the direct obj, וְאֵת, is probably in error.

22.c. LXX lacks "burning."

23.a. "he" probably refers to the king.

24.a. LXX lacks וְכֹל, "any of."

25.a. LXX has Γοδολίας, "Gedaliah."

25.b. Some Gk. MSS lack the negative particle, which has the effect of presenting the three princes as pleading with the king to burn the scroll!

25.c. LXX lacks "he would not listen to them."

26.a. "and Shelemiah the son of Abdeel" missing in LXX.

26.b. LXX lacks "the scribe."

26.c. "the prophet" absent in LXX.

26.d. LXX has "they hid themselves" rather than MT "the LORD hid them."

27.a. LXX has "*all* the words . . ."

28.a. LXX lacks "upon it."

28.b. LXX lacks "first."
28.c. LXX lacks "of Judah."
29.a. "Concerning Jehoiakim the king of Judah" lacking in LXX, probably the result of homoioteleuton, the copying error resulting from similarity of phrase endings.
31.a. אֶת־עֲוֹנָם, "their iniquity," not in LXX.
31.b. LXX has γῆν, "land," rather than MT אִישׁ, "people."
32.a. LXX has "Baruch."
32.b. "and he gave it to Baruch the son of Neriah, the scribe" lacking in LXX; see *Note* 32.a.
32.c. LXX lacks "the king of Judah."
32.d. "in the fire" not in LXX.

Form/Structure/Setting

Jer 36 is generally categorized as part of Mowinckel's "Source C" (*Zur Komposition des Buches Jeremia*, 1914), material written in prose very similar to the language of Deuteronomy. Mowinckel's form-critical work on Jeremiah is treated as the standard from which all other such efforts begin (see Introduction of volume 1 of our commentary). Modern interpreters, while offering a number of variations to Mowinckel, do not depart very far from his basic theses (cf. Rudolph, 195, and his additional "book," which isolates so-called oracles of Baruch, and Kessler, *CBQ* 28 [1966] 398, who identifies two major tradition complexes, chaps. 26–36 and 37–45).

Jer 36 has often been treated as a description of the origins of the book of Jeremiah. While there is no way to determine the precise contents of the scroll prepared by Baruch, most scholars have assumed that the present book of Jeremiah represents the core of that scroll as well as additional materials added by later editors and preservers of the Jeremiah tradition.

Attention has tended to focus on the earlier chapters of Jeremiah as the most likely content of the scroll. Duhm (292), while not wishing to be too specific, speculated that portions of chaps. 1–25 could well represent Baruch's scroll. He and others ruled out a larger body of material because of the narrative of Jer 36, which describes three readings of the scroll in a relatively short period of time.

For that same reason, Holladay (*Jeremiah: Spokesman Out of Time*, 155–56) has suggested that Jer 1–6, or elements within those chapters, would represent material comparable to that described in the scroll. Hicks, on the other hand, has argued on the basis of the way leather scrolls were prepared that the material covered in such a scroll could have been more extensive (*VT* 33 [1983] 66). Little imagination is required in order to see the possibility that at least the earlier chapters of Jeremiah could be roughly equivalent to the scroll of Jer 36.

Carroll (665–67) has cautioned against assuming too much about the role of Baruch. His contention is that Jer 36 is likely a literary invention to give legitimacy to the role of scribes in the Jeremiah tradition. Certainly, there is a logical consistency in Carroll's argument, but the same reasoning could apply to the more traditional interpretation. A significant role for Baruch seems to be as much supported by the larger text of Jeremiah as it is called into question by it. Deuteronomistic involvement in the transmission of the Jeremiah tradition is highly likely. It does not necessarily represent the only creative stage of that tradition. Carroll's arguments notwithstanding, the account in Jer 36 gives Baruch a major role and should not be passed over too quickly.

Whether or not it relates to existing Jeremiah texts (and it probably does), this passage gives considerable insight into the process whereby the Jeremiah tradition was preserved. Nowhere else in the biblical record is a description of the actual production of a written oracle provided. Jer 36 gives one the feel of an onlooker to the earliest examples of the recording of "scripture."

Carroll (666) and Nicholson (*Preaching to the Exiles*, 45) provide a needed warning (cf. also Kessler, *CBQ* 28 [1966] 398). Both emphasize what they perceive to be the key issue with regard to this passage. The focus of the text is not upon Jeremiah, or Baruch, or their actions. Instead, the focus is upon the word of the LORD and its encounter with and rejection by the king, personifying the people of Israel. The power of that word dwarfs the role of any individual involved in relating it or being confronted by it.

Parallels between Jer 36 and 2 Kgs 22–23 offer enticing possibilities for the interpreter of this passage. The work of Isbell (*JSOT* 8 [1978] 33–45) is the most precise treatment of those parallels (cf. Kessler, *CBQ* 28 [1966] 396, who also called attention to the parallels and their importance). Isbell's work is quite convincing in pointing out the possibility that 2 Kgs 22–23 provided an intentional foil for the message of Jer 36. The points of contact include important similarities but also provide glaring differences, differences that add power to the message of the prophet.

The similarities include: the rare use of a written scroll to deliver a divine message, the prophetic claim of authority (the "thus says the LORD" oracular introduction), the concern for "evil" (רעה) specifically noted in both passages, and the call for reform (Isbell, *JSOT* 8 [1978] 33–35). The similarities seem too pronounced for mere coincidence.

The crucial distinctions are particularly noteworthy. Both episodes involve "tearing" on the part of the king. Josiah "tears" his garments, the traditional sign of distress and mourning for sin. Jehoiakim, on the other hand, "tears" the sections of the scroll from the whole and casts them into the fire. "Burning" (שרף) is important to both episodes. Josiah burns altars in an attempt at reform; Jehoiakim attempts to invalidate the message by burning the scroll. Josiah "heard" the word of the LORD, while Jehoiakim pointedly does not "hear." Finally, the end result is that God "hears" Josiah, while the outcome for Jehoiakim and Judah is another matter, as Jer 36:30–31 clearly indicates (Isbell, *JSOT* 8 [1978] 35).

Isbell's analysis indicates the use of a special "form" of prophetic activity that, by means of the crucial deviations from type (Josiah being the standard), serves to heighten the impact of Jeremiah's oracle of judgment. That such a background adds weight to the interpretation of Jer 36 goes without saying.

Baumann has added yet further to the structural "mix" of this chapter by means of his treatment of vv 1–12 as a liturgical form employed by the prophet (*ZAW* 80 [1968] 350–73). Jer 4:5–6:26 and Jer 14:1–15:3 are set forth by Baumann as examples of this "form" used by Jeremiah. He identifies the likely liturgy involved in a fast day at the temple. Jeremiah's pattern becomes a conscious attack on that liturgy, involving a contradiction of its central feature, the assurance of Yahweh's positive response to the formal petitions by priests and people. Baumann's conclusions are rather speculative, but the thrust of those conclusions fits well in the setting of Jer 36 as noted above.

The scene is set by v 1 as the fourth year of King Jehoiakim of Judah, 605 B.C. The date given is specific, though not everyone accepts it as the date of the events described. Rudolph (195–97) cites the unlikelihood of such a frivolous response on the part of the king if the Babylonians were already on the scene in the powerful way that would have been the case in 605 B.C. after the crucial battle at Carchemish (cf. Kessler, *ZAW* 81 [1969] 382, who would not agree that Jehoiakim's actions should be seen as "frivolous"). He would, therefore, argue for a time before such a clear picture of Babylonian power had emerged. Rudolph attributes to Jeremiah the prophet's insight, which allowed him to see that which escaped Jehoiakim and his advisors.

There is merit in Rudolph's argument, but it does not necessarily rule out the date as listed. Who is to say that poor judgment on the part of the king would suddenly improve because of external events on the world stage? Persons living in a self-indulgent "cocoon" like that Jeremiah describes of Jehoiakim and Judah could no doubt convince themselves that all was serene, willingly ignoring the implications of Babylonian power upon their own nation. In fact, the incredible blindness of Jehoiakim and Judah is precisely the point of much of Jeremiah's message.

The chapter unfolds as a drama in seven acts. The drama revolves around a variation from the more common oracle formulas used by the prophets. In this case, the oracle is not presented fully but is referred to indirectly as the "words which I have spoken to you." From the events themselves, the substance of the oracle is clear. It is a word of judgment pronounced against the faithlessness of Judah and her leaders, specifically the king.

In microcosm, the drama models the conflict in which the prophet Jeremiah was involved with Judah's leaders for virtually his whole life. This setting of conflict sets the prophet against his bitterest enemy, King Jehoiakim. Burke O. Long has called attention to some of the key issues that should be considered in evaluating the conflict (*Semeia* 21 [1981] 31). Theological agendas generally are given primary significance in any such discussion. Long suggests that societal and political issues ought also to be taken into account.

The possibility of another "setting" for this text should also be recognized. The setting of its use among the exiles provides a sound raison d'être. Jer 36 and its companion texts provide ample explanation for the tragedy of exile. It also serves as an argument for coexistence with the Babylonians (Long, *Semeia* 21 [1981] 31). After all, none other than the great prophet led the way!

Long argues that, while "true religion" is identified with the prophet and his supporters in the text of Jeremiah, there may have been considerable ambiguity present at the time of the conflict. How is "true religion" distinguished from that which is false? The biblical tradition preserves rather than eliminates this tension. When the sphere of activity is the political arena, decisions are made from many perspectives. All who make them can claim to do so on the basis of religious understanding.

Numerous attempts have been made to restructure this chapter, moving verses so as to provide a more "logical" chronology of events. Where relevant, those attempts will be noted in the *Comment* below.

Comment

1–3 The "word of the LORD" comes to the prophet in 605 B.C., a crucial date indeed because of the strategic defeat of the Egyptians at Carchemish by the Babylonians. Hegemony over the whole region seemed fated to belong to the rising power of Babylon. It is difficult to ignore the connection of those events with what transpires in this chapter.

Jeremiah is commanded to prepare a scroll containing the substance of his message from the LORD dating from its earliest forms, supposedly in the last "days of Josiah," and including elements up to the time of the command.

In the introductory words of this message, it seems obvious that the future of Judah is not without hope. The purpose of the recorded message is the potential repentance and pardon of the nation. Hope grows more and more dim as the events of the chapter unfold.

4–8 Baruch is summoned to write the scroll at Jeremiah's direction. Some caution should perhaps be exercised in following the traditional habit of designating Baruch as the "scribe" of Jeremiah (cf. Carroll, 658).

Jeremiah calls attention to his own inability to go to the temple. No specific reason is given for "debarring" (RSV) the prophet. Speculation has ranged from the hostile reaction to earlier words of Jeremiah (chap. 26) by the authorities to a more pragmatic reason, some ceremonial impurity that affected him. Thompson (623) represents the former, Duhm (290) the best-known proponent of the latter.

Whatever the reason for the prohibition against Jeremiah, Baruch is to read the scroll publicly in the temple on a fast day. No specific occasion is noted, rather as if the prophet assumed some such ceremony would be forthcoming. Baumann (*ZAW* 80 [1968] 357) suggested that Jeremiah could well have had some specific fast day in view at the time the scroll was drafted, with two possible occasions uppermost. The most obvious would likely be an impending political crisis caused by Nebuchadrezzar's march into Syria-Palestine. The other option would be a called fast such as that noted in the Mishna (*Ta'an.* 1:5) to be employed whenever the winter rains were delayed.

The reason for the reading is presented as the hope for repentance on the part of Judah. The events that take place later in the chapter demonstrate this to be a futile hope.

9–10 Baruch follows Jeremiah's instructions, though the ordering of vv 8 and 9 appears somewhat awkward in chronology of events. Rudolph (196–97) proposed altering the order of verses, placing v 9 before v 5 (cf. however Baumann's response, *ZAW* 80 [1968] 354, noting the problems created by the alteration, which are no less severe than the original). V 9 gives a specific date for the fast day on which Baruch carries out his responsibility; depending on the way the year is ordered (fall to fall or spring to spring), the date would vary. Most likely it is to be seen as December 604 B.C. (following the Babylonian calendar, spring to spring, since the ninth month would fit with the description of the season found in this passage; cf. v 22).

Baruch reads the scroll to the gathered worshipers from a room in the upper court of the temple. Gemariah apparently was sympathetic to Jeremiah as indicated by the use of his official quarters in the temple.

11–19 A chain reaction ensues that serves to emphasize the importance of the message contained in the scroll and the nature of the crisis that gripped Judah. Micaiah, son of the above-mentioned Gemariah, was so affected by the message he heard from Baruch that he immediately went to a group of high officials who were gathered at the palace. (Was this "meeting" an official part of the fast?) The officials are given a report by Micaiah of the "words" that had been read in the temple.

The officials call for Baruch and get their own reading of the scroll, the second reading. Such a sequence tends to heighten the tension and add dramatic effect. One of the interesting contrasts of Jer 36 is set up in v 15, when Baruch is invited to sit and read the scroll. V 21 provides a very different reception for the words of the scroll.

The officials are obviously very alarmed at what they hear and determine to relay the information to the king. That they are realistic in their perception of Jehoiakim can be seen from the way they proceed. After authenticating the message ("was it at his dictation?"), the officials take the precaution of sending Jeremiah and Baruch into hiding.

20–26 The way in which the officials view Jehoiakim is further underscored by their precautions with the scroll. They leave the scroll in the room of Elishama while they proceed to report its contents to the king.

Jehoiakim is not satisfied with an oral report. Jehudi is sent to fetch the scroll and then is directed to read it for the king. The scene for the reading is carefully set, providing a kind of foreshadowing of the events to follow. The king sits before a brazier in which a fire is burning. Given the importance attached to the words of the scroll by the actions of the officials, what happens next is climactic indeed.

As Jehudi finishes reading "three or four columns" of the scroll, Jehoiakim takes the portions and severs them from the scroll with a penknife (typically used to sharpen the scribe's quill), then casts the severed portion into the fire (cf. Hicks, *VT* 33 [1983] 61, for an interesting hypothesis related to Jehoiakim's actions). Kessler's contention (*ZAW* 81 [1969] 382) is that Jehoiakim intends to act symbolically against the scroll. Since the words of the scroll would be understood to set in motion divine judgment against Judah, by destroying the words, Jehoiakim provides his own kind of symbolic action.

One of the important statements of this passage is found in v 24. The king and his servants are portrayed as unafraid and unremorseful. Such a description serves to seal the doom of the nation and her leaders. When Judah's leaders have no more regard than this for the "word from the LORD," there can be only one outcome.

Jeremiah evidently was not as isolated in his concern for Judah as some portions of the book would indicate. At some risk, three of the officials, those previously identified as concerned at the "words," attempt to dissuade the king from his rash behavior. Their protest falls on deaf ears.

After the scroll is reduced to ashes, Jehoiakim gives orders to arrest Jeremiah and Baruch. In light of past history (the fate of Uriah as described in chap. 26), prospects for Jeremiah and his companion would not appear to be bright. The intent of the king is thwarted by Yahweh himself (note, however, the reading in LXX, "they hid themselves").

27–31 In a passage rich with symbolic action, yet more is to follow. Strikingly similar to the struggle of Jeremiah with Hananiah (Jer 28, during the later reign of Zedekiah), symbolic actions seem to forge a kind of duel between two crucial points of view. With Hananiah, stroke and counterstroke involve a yoke symbolizing captivity and servitude. In the case of Jeremiah and Jehoiakim, it is a more direct struggle related to the power of the "word." As Hananiah later attempts to render the symbolic word of judgment futile by destroying the wooden yoke, so Jehoiakim attempts to destroy the word literally, in the fire. In Jer 28, a yoke of iron is Yahweh's last word. The end of this scene introduces a new scroll, with specific "words" added for Jehoiakim in light of his rejection of the scroll. Jehoiakim cannot thwart the word of the LORD, and to attempt to do so brings inevitable consequences.

Jehoiakim's indictment includes a voiding of the Davidic covenant for Jehoiakim and his descendants. Supposedly, none of his descendants will succeed him upon the throne of David. Since Jehoiakim is succeeded by his son, Jehoiachin, some tension is introduced into the interpretation of this text. One possible approach would be to point out the short-lived nature of Jehoiachin's "reign" and its end in exile.

In many ways, the end of Jer 36 provides a fitting climax to the whole of Jeremiah's message, even to the larger prophetic tradition of Israel. V 31 concludes with the poignant words "they would not listen."

32 The final scene in the drama describes the re-creation of the scroll, with "all the words . . . that Jehoiakim . . . burned" along with many other such words. The second scroll, though its production is described in understated fashion, closes the door forever upon Jehoiakim. Though he is to be followed by other leaders, and though Judah is to survive for a number of years, this incident provides sufficient explanation for ultimate doom.

Explanation

Jer 36 is an exclamation point applied to the biblical understanding of the dynamic nature of the "word of the LORD." Here is a full treatment of the way that word functions. Its intent is first and foremost the salvation of God's people. The possibility of "hearing" and "turning" is inevitably present. Nevertheless, that same possibility introduces the tragic dimensions of the divine word. The failure to hear and turn brings the judgment of God.

The "contest" of Jer 36 presents graphically the dilemma of "power" continually confronting God's people. Jehoiakim represents one aspect of power. He and his advisors see the world in their own way. Any decisions made by them were fraught with peril. The conclusive issue became how such decisions were to be made. What role, if any, was to be played by divine purpose? How could one determine what that purpose might be? Jeremiah sought to influence the arena of power, but, as is so often the case, his "word from the LORD" did not serve the goals or the ambitions of Jehoiakim and his counselors. In the almost inevitable ambiguity of crucial decisions, the royal decision was to follow their own judgments. Secure in their vision of what the "word from the LORD" meant for Judah, they made their choice.

The contrast between Jer 36 and 2 Kgs 22–23 presents one of the more powerful impacts of this message. Whether the reforms of Josiah were superficial or authentic, at least his response to the divine word epitomizes a sincere "hearing" of that word. From the tearing of his garments to the concrete measures he instituted to bring about reform, Josiah gave evidence of "hearing." Jehoiakim, on the other hand, represents the other extreme. Here is a king who has no regard for the divine word. His arrogance is such that he would dare challenge it directly. The conclusions of Jer 36 are clear. Arrogance like that exhibited by Jehoiakim will have its end.

One question that seems to emerge from this scene of intense conflict involves the nature of rebellion against God. Is the arrogance of a Jehoiakim the most bitter enemy of the prophetic word, or are there more subdued enemies no less threatening? The following chapters of Jeremiah introduce a more subdued challenge to the divine word, that offered by Zedekiah. Compared to Jehoiakim, Zedekiah could almost be identified as a positive figure. It might be useful to ponder which of the two patterns of rebellion poses the greatest threat to the "word from the LORD." Whatever form rebellion against divine purpose takes, the words of v 31 echo hauntingly, "they would not listen."

XXIV. The Last Days of Judah and Jerusalem (37:1–44:30[LXX 44:1–51:30])

Bibliography

Holladay, W. L. "A Fresh Look at 'Source B' and 'Source C'." In *A Prophet to the Nations*, ed. L. G. Perdue and B. W. Kovacs. Winona Lake, IN: Eisenbrauns, 1984. 213–28. **Kremers, H.** "Leidensgemeinschaft mit Gott im Alten Testament." *EvT* 13 (1953) 122–40. **McEvenue, S.**"The Composition of Jeremiah 37.1 to 44.30." In *Studies in Wisdom Literature*, ed. W. C. van Wyk. Old Testament Studies, OTWSA 15 & 16. Pretoria: Society for the Study of the OT, 1972. 59–67. **Pohlmann, K.-F.** *Studien zum Jeremiabuch*. Göttingen: Vandenhoeck & Ruprecht, 1978. **Rietzschel, C.** *Das Problem der Urrolle*. Gütersloh: Mohn, 1966. **Seitz, C. R.** *Theology in Conflict*. BZAW 176. Berlin: de Gruyter, 1989. **Wanke, G.** *Untersuchungen zur sogenannten Baruchschrift*. BZAW 122. Berlin: de Gruyter, 1971. 91–133. **Weippert, H.** *Die Prosareden des Jeremiabuches*. BZAW 132. Berlin: de Gruyter, 1973.

Form/Structure/Setting

Eissfeldt, in *The Old Testament: An Introduction* (354–55), summarized the view of traditional scholarship regarding Jer 37–44. He noted that these chapters are typically assigned to Baruch, following "the generally accepted and probable assumption, that the man who is mentioned so closely bound up with the fortunes of Jeremiah, and who appears as his secretary in xxxvi, is likely to have had a share in the book as we have it."

Mowinckel (*Zur Komposition des Buches Jeremia*) classified these chapters as biographical, part of his "Source B," though rejecting the authorship of Baruch. Mowinckel developed the hypothesis concerning the composition of Jeremiah that continues to be widely accepted by most OT scholars. Mowinckel's "Source B" contains material from earlier in the book, but chaps. 37–44 represent a unit that is universally recognized as such within the biographical prose of Jeremiah.

Kremers (*Der leidende Prophet; EvT* 13 [1953] 122–40), in his dissertation and an article developing some ideas further, proposed the label "passion narrative" for this portion of Jeremiah. Kremers suggested Baruch should be joined to the larger company of biblical authors who struggle with the question of innocent suffering. In the course of developing his idea, Kremers identified ten passages that form a single unit within Jer 37–45 (*EvT* 13 [1953] 122–23). Kremers' "divisions," rather than his concerns related to passion story, have led to considerable discussion by other students of Jeremiah.

Wanke (*Untersuchungen*) did not deal with Kremers' focus on Jer 37–44 as passion story but depended heavily on the ten-passage structure that Kremers identified (*EvT* 13 [1953] 122–23). Wanke argued that ten units arranged in five pairs are to be found in Jer 37:11–43:7. He challenged the attribution of Mowinckel's "Source B" to Baruch, while continuing to recognize the biographical characteristics that mark this material. According to Wanke, additions have been made to the ten units to make up the final text, but he contended that the basic outline of each unit, consisting of an introduction, main body, and final observation (*Schlussbemerkung*), can be isolated from these additions (*Untersuchungen*, 94–95). The five "pairs," each of which Wanke divides into the proposed three-part outline, are as follows: (1) 37:11–16 and 37:17–21; (2) 38:1–6 and 38:7–13; (3) 38:14–28a and 38:28b–40:6; (4) 40:13–41:2 and 41:4–9; and (5) 41:10–15 and 41:16–43:7.

In the discussion that follows regarding this section of Jeremiah, Wanke's pairings will not be used as the basis for the structure of Jeremiah under consideration. The pairings will provide a means for addressing some of the issues that are raised by the texts that are divided in less dramatic ways but whose internal shaping raises redactional questions.

Mowinckel's thesis, which identified these passages as biographical in nature, has been widely accepted. Baruch's authorship is accepted by many scholars who do not share Mowinckel's skepticism in that area. As might be expected, any number of theses regarding the redactional shape of this unit in Jeremiah have emerged. Wanke's development of Kremers' structural theories may represent the most productive advance in this area.

Volz, Rudolph, and Weiser essentially accept these chapters as the product of one redactor, with some minor peripheral exceptions (Pohlmann, *Studien*, 48). Duhm and Rietzschel (*Urrolle*), in addition to Wanke, who is referred to above, contend for a much more complicated process of development for Jer 37–44 (Pohlmann, *Studien*, 48). No approach is without complications.

The following treatment of these texts seeks to take into account the issues raised by scholars who have identified serious redactional issues, yet seeks to maintain the essential shape of the unit as found in MT. Mowinckel's category has received warranted support by the world of OT scholars. Nevertheless, there yet remain questions about "biography" as it relates to Jer 37–44. Is such a label sufficient to describe the historiography contained in these chapters? How does one address the absence of the "biographee" in a critical unit such as Jer 40:7–41:18, particularly in light of his supposed presence in Mizpah in the immediately preceding text?

In their interpretative comments upon these texts, various scholars have provided at least some answers to the questions posed above. Carroll, for example, comments upon the crucial importance of the early verses of Jer 37. He notes the tone of dismissal with which Zedekiah is introduced and described. He and his followers are known as those who "would not listen to the word of the LORD." According to Carroll, nothing more need be known about Zedekiah. He is suitably identified (Carroll, 671).

On the other hand, what of the ambiguity to be found in the character portrait of Zedekiah? No such ambiguity is present in 37:1–2, but that is not the case in the larger passage. Duhm (301), Thompson (631), and Rudolph (203) have called attention to the almost tragic figure of Zedekiah in this part of Jeremiah. His longing to maintain contact with Jeremiah, his anxious need for a "word from the LORD," yet his inability to act on the basis of either, all support the tragic pose of the king.

From a simplistic perspective, it is possible to identify these texts as conclusive evidence of Israel's inevitable fall to judgment and the reasons for that judgment. Similarly, they can be seen to drive home a warning for future generations (the exile?) concerning the ongoing danger of such folly for them. These texts, like the Deuteronomistic History, provide both an explanation for the exile and a word of instruction to those in exile.

While it is correct to note the truisms above, more should be added. It would be a mistake to ignore the dynamic nature of the texts themselves. There is present within them more than any single theory about them can exhaust. While they lack some of the majestic power of other biblical stories, there is nevertheless much to be gained from hearing the stories and the manner in which they are told, quite apart from a redactional intent.

In the *Form/Structure/Setting* units of the following chapters, I give attention to specific issues of textual development and to relationships that exist between various texts. As many of the crucial matters of technical relevance as possible are identified. In the *Explanation* units, I will attempt to assess some of the broader issues and the ways more technical matters impinge upon the message of the whole.

No doubt the recitation of Jerusalem's fall and her subsequent trials is the product of persons who lived after Jeremiah. At the same time, the meticulous attention to specific names and events suggests access to eyewitness records. The use of deuteronomistic themes has in no way obscured key issues found in Jeremiah's oracles. Instead, these lengthy narratives seem to interweave the thrust of Jeremiah's oracles and the deuteronomistic themes by means of rather straightforward historiography. The end result is a powerful statement not at all at odds with other "words from the LORD" proclaimed by the prophet.

A. Jeremiah's Imprisonment (37:1–21 [LXX 44:1–21])

Bibliography

Kessler, M. "Jeremiah Chapters 26–45 Reconsidered." *JNES* 27 (1968) 81–88. **Long, B. O.** "Social Dimensions of Prophetic Conflict." *Semeia* 21 (1981) 31–53. **Malamat, A.** "Jeremiah and the Last Two Kings of Judah." *PEQ* 83 (1951) 81–87. **McEvenue, S.** "The Composition of Jeremiah 37.1 to 44.30." In *Studies in Wisdom Literature*, ed. W. C. van Wyk. Old Testament Studies, OTWSA 15 & 16. Pretoria: Society for the Study of the OT, 1972. 59–67.

Translation

[1] *Zedekiah the son of Josiah, whom Nebuchadrezzar the king of Babylon* [a] *made king of the land* [b] *of Judah, reigned* [c] *in the place of Coniah the son of* [d] *Jehoiakim.* [2] *But neither he, nor his servants, nor the people of the land listened to the words of the LORD, which he spoke through Jeremiah the prophet.* [a]

[3] *King Zedekiah sent Jehucal* [a] *the son of Shelemiah and Zephaniah the priest the*

son of Maaseiah to Jeremiah the prophet, [b] *saying: "Pray on our behalf to the LORD our God."* [c] [4]*Now Jeremiah was going in and out* [a] *among the people,* [b] *for they had not yet put him in prison.* [c] [5]*When the army of Pharaoh went out from Egypt, the Chaldeans who were besieging Jerusalem* [a] *heard news of them, and they withdrew from Jerusalem.*

[6]*Then the word of the LORD came to Jeremiah the prophet:* [7]*"Thus says the LORD, the God of Israel,* [a] *thus you shall say* [b] *to the king of Judah, who sent you to me,* [c] *to inquire of me, 'Behold, the army of Pharaoh, which came to help you, will return to its own land, Egypt.* [8]*And the Chaldeans will return and fight against this city, and they will capture it and burn it with fire.'* [a]

[9]*"Thus says the LORD,* [a] *do not deceive yourselves, saying: 'The Chaldeans will surely go away from us,' for they will not go away.* [10]*For even if* [a] *you should defeat all the army of the Chaldeans who are fighting against you, and there remained of them* [b] *only wounded men in their tents,* [c] *they would rise up and burn this city with fire."* [d]

[11]*And when* [a] *the army of the Chaldeans had withdrawn from Jerusalem because of* [b] *the army of Pharaoh,* [12]*Jeremiah left Jerusalem to go to the land* [a] *of Benjamin, to receive his portion there* [b] *among the people.* [13]*When he was at the Benjamin Gate, a captain of the guard there, named* [a] *Irijah,* [b] *the son of Shelemaiah the son of Hananiah, seized Jeremiah the prophet,* [c] *saying: "You are deserting to the Chaldeans."* [14]*And Jeremiah* [a] *said, "A lie! I am not deserting to the Chaldeans." But Irijah* [b] *would not listen to him and seized Jeremiah and brought him to the princes.* [15]*And the princes were enraged at Jeremiah, and they beat* [a] *him, and they imprisoned* [bc] *him in the house of Jonathan the scribe, for they had made it a prison.* [16]*So Jeremiah went* [a] *to the prison, to the cells,* [b] *and Jeremiah* [c] *remained there many days.*

[17]*King* [a] *Zedekiah sent for him and received him,* [b] *and the king asked him secretly in his house* [c] *and said, "Is there a word from the LORD?" And Jeremiah* [d] *said, "There is." Then he said,* [e] *"You will be delivered into the hand of the king of Babylon."* [18]*Jeremiah said to King Zedekiah,* [a] *"How have I wronged you or your servants or this people, that you have put* [b] *me in prison?* [19]*And where* [a] *are your prophets who prophesied to you, saying, 'The king of Babylon will not come against you* [b] *and against this land'?* [20]*And now hear,* [a] *I pray you, my lord the king, let my plea come before you, and do not return me to the house of Jonathan the scribe, lest I die there."* [21]*So King Zedekiah* [a] *gave a command, and they deposited Jeremiah* [b] *in the court of the guard, and they gave him a loaf of bread daily, from the street of the bakers, until all* [c] *the bread of the city was gone. So Jeremiah remained in the court of the guard.*

Notes

1.a. LXX lacks "the king of Babylon."
1.b. LXX lacks "the land of."
1.c. MT מלך־וימלך, "reigned as king," probably defective as a result of dittogr; read simply וימלך, "reigned," with LXX.
1.d. LXX lacks "Coniah the son of," changing the basic thrust of the verse. In LXX, it is Jehoiakim, not his son, whom Nebuchadrezzar displaced.
2.a. LXX lacks "the prophet."
3.a. Vg and Syr read Ιουχαλ, "Jucal"; cf. 38:1.
3.b. LXX lacks "the prophet."
3.c. "our God" lacking in LXX.
4.a. Some MSS read ויצא impf, "and he went," instead of ויצא, ptcp, "and he was going . . . out." The former pattern is followed in LXX.

4.b. LXX has τῆς πόλεως = הָעִיר, "the city," instead of MT הָעָם, "the people."

4.c. Following Q הַכְּלוּא, which with בֵּית, has the meaning of "house of confinement" or "prison." This same Q-K pattern is to be found in 52:31.

5.a. LXX lacks "who were besieging Jerusalem."

7.a. "the God of Israel" not in LXX.

7.b. For MT תֹּאמְרוּ, "you shall say" (pl), LXX has sg.

7.c. LXX has πρὸς σέ, "(to) you," lacking MT אֵלַי, "to me." The result is "sent you to inquire of me" instead of "sent you to me to inquire of me."

8.a. MT וּשְׂרָפָהּ בָּאֵשׁ, "and burn it with fire," is believed by most scholars to be an additional gloss, though retained in the versions. Cf. similar phrasing with variations in 21:10; 34:2.

9.a. LXX begins the verse with ὅτι, "for" or "because," not present in MT.

10.a. LXX has καὶ ἐάν = וְאִם, "and if," rather than MT כִּי אִם, "for if."

10.b. "of them" missing in LXX.

10.c. LXX has ἐν τῷ τόπῳ αὐτοῦ = בִּמְקוֹמוֹ, "in his (their) place(s)," instead of MT בְּאָהֳלוֹ, "in his (their) tent(s)."

10.d. *BHS* suggests "burn it with fire" is a possible gloss, with another option of adding וְלָכְדוּ, "and capture"; cf. v 8.

11.a. *BHS* proposes וַיְהִי, instead of וְהָיָה, because the former represents the more regular narrative pattern; cf. similar problems in 3:9; 38:28; 40:3.

11.b. Lit. "from before."

12.a. Fragment from the Cairo Geniza suggests לְאֶרֶץ, "to the land of," for MT אֶרֶץ, "(to) the land of"; a few MSS have אֶל אֶרֶץ, "into the land of."

12.b. לַחֲלֹק מִשָּׁם, "to receive his portion there," is a problematic phrase, lit. "to divide from there." Gk. versions do not agree, reading variously τοῦ ἀγοράσαι, "to buy," παροικεῖσαι, "to dwell," ἀποδρᾶσαι, "to flee," μερισθῆναι, "to be divided," μερίσασθαι, "to divide"; Vg (with Syr and the targums) does not eliminate the difficulty. See *Comment* below.

13.a. MT has וּשְׁמוֹ, lit. "and his name"; missing in LXX.

13.b. LXX has Σαρουια, "Sarouia"; Syr reads נֵרִיָּה, "Neriah."

13.c. LXX lacks "the prophet."

14.a. LXX lacks "Jeremiah."

14.b. LXX has "Sarouia"; Syr "Neriah"; cf. v 13.

15.a. MT note marks this as *sebir*, that is, an unusual form for which a correction is proposed: וַיַּכּוּ, "and they beat," hiph impf instead of MT וְהִכּוּ, "and they beat," hiph pf.

15.b. Also *sebir*, with the suggestion qal impf יִתְּנוּ, "and they put," instead of MT וְנָתְנוּ, "and they put," qal pf; cf. *Note* 15.a. above.

15.c. MT reads וְנָתְנוּ אֹתוֹ בֵּית הָאֵסוּר, lit. "and they put him in prison"; LXX lacks בֵּית הָאֵסוּר, "prison," thus reading "put him in the house of Jonathan the scribe."

16.a. LXX has καὶ ἦλθεν = וַיָּבֹא, simply "and he went"; MT has in addition the initial כִּי, "so" or "thus."

16.b. LXX reads χερεθ, "Chereth"; Origen's recension has ανιωθ, "Anioth."

16.c. LXX lacks the redundant use of the prophet's name.

17.a. LXX lacks "King."

17.b. LXX reads καὶ ἐκάλεσεν αὐτόν, "and he called him," rather than MT וַיִּקָּחֵהוּ, "and he received him."

17.c. LXX lacks "in his house."

17.d. LXX lacks "Jeremiah."

17.e. LXX lacks "Then he said."

18.a. "Zedekiah" absent in LXX.

18.b. MT has "you [pl] have put me in prison"; LXX and Vg have "you [sg]."

19.a. K וְאַיּוֹ, "and where is he" (?); Q וְאַיֵּה, "and where."

19.b. LXX lacks "against you," probably because of haplogr.

20.a. MT שְׁמַע־נָא, "hear," absent from LXX.

21.a. "Zedekiah" not in LXX.

21.b. LXX has "him" in place of MT "Jeremiah."

21.c. LXX lacks "all."

Form/Structure/Setting

Jer 37 is necessarily treated in many respects with the following chapter. The two represent a collection of similar stories about the prophet, his personal crises at the time of Jerusalem's siege, his encounters with Zedekiah, and, ultimately, his faithfulness and consistency to the task to which he was called.

Theories abound regarding how the "collection" should be viewed. The recorded events are perceived by some to be created amalgams of one basic story (Bright, 233; Skinner, *Prophecy and Religion*, 258), the crisis of Jeremiah brought about by zealous "nationalist" enemies and Jeremiah's rescue by the king (or perhaps by God). Names of individuals and the location of events create difficulties that none has solved with regard to the unitary theory. These "details" are not easily dismissed.

Other features suggest a grouping of disparate traditions about Jeremiah in one account of the siege. Carroll (675) notes the presence of two different versions of Jeremiah's actions during the siege. In one, he is free to move about at will, while in the other, he is confined, though with access to some visitors. Carroll emphasizes the redactional purpose, to relate the complete destruction of Judah by the Babylonians. However the specific events are described, the end result is constant.

The clearest element in Jer 37 is the heading of vv 1–2. In these verses, Zedekiah and all of Judah are summarily damned for their refusal to hear or heed the word from the LORD. (Rudolph, 201, identifies these verses as the "introduction" for all the Zedekiah stories, establishing the pattern that is to be seen throughout.) There follow three distinct events with a common thread. The first is Zedekiah's request for a "word from the LORD." The irony of this passage immediately following vv 1–2 should not be overlooked. The consistency of the prophet's message is underscored by his response to the king in this initial encounter.

The attempt by Jeremiah to leave the city provides the second event of Jer 37. Linkage to Jer 32 is almost inevitable. The encounter describes effectively the hostility to Jeremiah found among some of the Judean leaders.

Whoever was responsible for the final compilation of this section of Jeremiah also made considerable use of what must have been firsthand accounts of events. The use of detail is striking throughout these narratives. Personal names and roles, political divisions and their effects, and even descriptions of the mood of the people indicate more than general theorizing or speculation. Whether Baruch was responsible for the recording of such detail, as is often suggested, or some other source is responsible, these details enrich the telling of the story and the honing of the story's purpose.

The sketch of Zedekiah contained in these stories should also be considered. Apparently, it is intended that some distinction be given to Zedekiah in contrast with the uniformly evil Jehoiakim. Zedekiah becomes more of a "gray" character, neither fully positive nor fully negative, but consistently weak. It may be a more damning characterization, on the whole, than that of Jehoiakim, for here is one portrayed as knowing the truth on many occasions when he refused to act upon it. Mingled with the deuteronomistic rejection of kingship is the perspective of monarchic possibility, occasionally seen in Zedekiah, perhaps a future hope, but never able to erase the more powerful condemnation leveled against kings in general, and these few kings in particular.

The purpose of these lengthy historical narratives has been mentioned above but bears further attention. The form of the narratives is relatively consistent. All bear great resemblance to the narrative accounts of the Deuteronomistic History (Joshua–2 Kings). At the same time, more emerges from these narratives than the summarized theological themes for which the deuteronomistic material is known. Those themes are to be discerned, but there is no contradiction with issues present in the oracular material attributed to the prophet elsewhere in the book of Jeremiah. In many ways, what is presented is a plausible sequence of events, replete with detail, reflecting the prophet's message as it is to be seen in the oracles, but also projecting that message so that it has relevance for those who hear it long after the fall of Jerusalem.

These narratives, then, do far more than relate historical events. They place those events in theological perspective. Eyewitness data are used, well-known features of Jeremiah's oracles are reflected, and the final product emphasizes much the same focus that the prophet used in his oracles: the word of the LORD is ignored at great peril. Further, as Clements has suggested in his commentary (223), these narratives provide the stage for the message of hope contained in Jeremiah and the means by which that hope can become reality.

Clements (216) has rightly observed that the events described in these chapters constitute the center of attention for all of Jeremiah's message, perhaps even for the whole of the OT. The fall of Jerusalem and subsequent happenings are crucial to any future identity or hope for the people of God called Israel.

Thompson (631) contends that these chapters were joined to the book of Jeremiah as a single unit, regardless of their possible independent histories. Carroll (669–70) supports that view by means of his reference to an underlying redactional theme to these chapters, the continual revelation of the divine word, undiminished by the various events and the complex textual issues contained therein. Carroll emphasizes the disparate nature of the individual blocks of text in this section of Jeremiah. At the same time, he notes the consistency of the unfolding divine message given here.

The setting of this chapter (and the more or less chronologically developed narratives of subsequent chapters) involves some of the most crucial events in all of Israel's history and persons whose actions had earth-shattering effects upon future generations. Zedekiah/Mattaniah ruled Judah after the death of Jehoiakim and the forced exile of Jehoiakim's son and successor, Jehoiachin, here referred to as Coniah (37:1). Zedekiah was one of Josiah's sons, brother of Jehoiakim, and uncle of the exiled king (see Malamat for a fuller treatment of Jehoiachin and Zedekiah). The corpus of Jeremiah skips over the reign of Jehoiachin completely. Though it was a brief reign (only three months), it is somewhat surprising that it bears no mention at all. The Septuagint omits any mention of Jehoiachin.

Jehoiachin was in the first group of Judeans taken into exile by the Babylonians. Apparently, he was confined for several years, then later given more lenient treatment under the Babylonian ruler Evil-Merodach (2 Kgs 25:27; Jer 52:31–32). The title of king appears to be attached to both Jehoiachin and Zedekiah during the time of Jehoiachin's exile. No one has been able to determine precisely the roles played by Jehoiachin and Zedekiah respectively. Malamat (81) suggests support from Babylonian records for Jehoiachin's retention of kingship. Regardless of Jehoiachin's official status, Zedekiah functioned as ruler of Judah during these last years of Judah's existence. A dual monarchy of sorts may well have been used by the Babylonians to accomplish their purposes. If, as is likely, groups within Judah saw themselves as more or less loyal to one or the other individual, that circumstance could have been used to advantage by the Babylonian overlords.

At the outset, Zedekiah would have been identified with pro-Babylonian sentiment as a result of the method by which he came to power. The majority pro-Egyptian party in Judah would not have responded well to anyone they perceived to be a Babylonian puppet. The longstanding conflict between those in Judah who saw future hopes through an Egyptian alliance against Babylon and those pragmatists who deemed the Egyptian alliance to be folly is probably to be seen between the lines of much of Jeremiah's narrative in these latter chapters.

The focus on Zedekiah suggests the need to examine the passages that are directly identified with Zedekiah in Jeremiah. Of obvious importance in interpreting Jer 37 are chaps. 21 and 34, both of which emerge from the same approximate time and reflect the same series of events. Some of the same stock phrases appear in all of the Zedekiah material. Particularly significant is the repeated prophecy of the fall of the city and the forecast uttered by Jeremiah that the Babylonians would "burn it with fire." This "promise" is repeated virtually verbatim no fewer than five times in four distinct passages (21:10; 34:2; 34:22; 37:8, 10) and in two other passages with slight variations (32:29; 38:23). Either the prophet repeated his message on several occasions, or, as is more likely, the redactors of Jeremiah perceive a climactic message, which they present as the crux of Judah's predicament and later disaster.

The historical events that establish the setting of this chapter occur following the invasion of Judah by the Babylonians in 589 B.C. and the subsequent siege of Jerusalem. Virtually all of the outlying cities fell quickly to the invaders, leaving only Jerusalem, Lachish, and Azekah (34:7). Chap. 34 describes Jerusalem in the midst of siege and the terror of Jerusalem's inhabitants. The "bargain" with God in 34:10, in which Hebrew slaves were freed, came as a result of the siege.

The specific setting of chap. 37 is a temporary lifting of the siege because of an oncoming Egyptian force. The Babylonians evidently moved to meet the Egyptians and in the process left Jerusalem unguarded.

Comment

1–2 Jer 37:1 refers to the "kingship" of Zedekiah. Zedekiah/Mattaniah was a son of Josiah and brother to Jehoiakim. Jehoiakim's son, Jehoiachin, referred to as Coniah here, succeeded his father upon the throne of Judah but was taken into captivity in 598 B.C. by the Babylonians. Zedekiah was placed in control in his stead.

3–5 This is one of two occasions on which Zedekiah sends emissaries to the prophet, seeking some definitive word from the LORD (cf. 21:1). Zephaniah the priest is included in the similar event described in Jer 21. Zephaniah is also the recipient of a letter of accusation against Jeremiah (29:24–29). Jehucal is one of those who call for Jeremiah's death because of his "treason" against Judah (38:4).

Zedekiah's purpose is to elicit Jeremiah's prayers to the LORD on behalf of Judah. Throughout the various crisis episodes, Zedekiah always seems to pay "secret" attention to the words of Jeremiah. He seems all but convinced of the truth of those words but never has the courage to act on his convictions.

Jeremiah is portrayed as free to move about in the city. The focal event of this passage is the movement of the Egyptian army toward Jerusalem. The presence of an Egyptian army results in a temporary lifting of the siege of the city. The Babylonians move out to meet the Egyptian force.

6–10 The message that Jeremiah gives in response is anything but encouraging. These verses challenge the optimism brought about by the Egyptian relief force. Jeremiah's word from the LORD is that the Egyptian army will soon be returning to Egypt, leaving Judah in the same predicament as before. The message to those who hope for some positive end to the crisis is blunt. No matter how much success, from whatever quarter, Judah has against the Babylonians, the end result is already decided. Should only wounded (or dead?) Babylonian soldiers remain, even they would be sufficient to destroy Jerusalem. Clearly implied is God's role in the destruction of the city.

11–16 During the interlude when the siege is lifted, Jeremiah attempts to leave the city in order to journey to Anathoth on family business. Scholars disagree as to the connection or lack of same between this incident and the purchase of ancestral land described in Jer 32. Jer 37:12 is a difficult verse to translate. Do the events to transpire at Anathoth have something to do with Jeremiah's inheritance (cf. Rudolph, 203; also RSV "to receive his portion")? The Septuagint attempts to resolve the difficulty by rendering MT לַחֲלִק hiphil (< חלק, "to divide, obtain one's share"; hiphil occurs only here in Jeremiah) as "to buy" (ἀγοράσαι). (To illustrate the difficulty, no fewer than four other Greek terms appear in the various manuscripts as attempts to render this Hebrew term appropriately.)

In spite of the difficulties raised by Jeremiah's confinement in Jer 32 and freedom in this chapter, some argue for a connection between the two accounts (Rudolph, Cunliff-Jones, Bright, Thompson). Seitz (*Theology in Conflict*, 241–81, 283) posits a reordering of much of the "scribal" material of Jeremiah, including this passage, into "pre-texts for redactional elaboration" (Seitz, 242). He considers much of Jer 32 and 37 to be linked.

Others deny any link (Carroll, Martens, Nicholson). Carroll (675) suggests that Jer 32 and 37 "are . . . different traditions . . . about Jeremiah's fate during the siege." He alludes to the prophet's freedom of movement in Jer 37, while in Jer 32, Jeremiah has no such liberties. More significant is Carroll's suggestion concerning the purpose of both traditions as intended by the editors of Jeremiah. Everything is to be destroyed by the Babylonians. Of that there can be no mistake.

Despite Jeremiah's protests, he is seized, beaten, and imprisoned. The "princes" who treat the prophet in this manner are obviously not the same as those described in the previous chapter. These "princes" have no concern for Jeremiah's welfare. Quite the contrary, they include him with others whom they deem threats to the nation's security and incarcerate him in a detention facility (the house of Jonathan) set aside for such persons. There Jeremiah remains for "many days" (v 16).

17–21 The ambiguous portrait of Zedekiah is underscored in these verses. The emphasis on secrecy should probably be noted; in such notations some clues may be found regarding Zedekiah's actions. Intense nationalism characterized what was left of Judah. Perhaps even the king dared not challenge such intense feelings. Nevertheless, Zedekiah always seems to value the opinions of Jeremiah. He simply lacked the courage or the will to respond to the message Jeremiah delivered.

The exchange between Jeremiah and Zedekiah is curiously flat. Zedekiah seeks a word from the LORD. Jeremiah delivers a message assuring Zedekiah's doom. Then there is an abrupt shift in focus. Jeremiah completely changes the subject and pleads on his own behalf to the king. His method is to call attention to the clearly false words of the prophets of salvation. These verses assume the resumption of the siege (v 21). The period of optimism had been all too brief. Jeremiah protests his innocence of wrongdoing. All he had done was speak the truth, in contrast to the prophets of salvation. Further, he argues, to return him to the house of Jonathan would be a sentence of death.

Zedekiah heeds Jeremiah's plea and makes arrangements for him to be placed in a more lenient form of custody in the court of the guard. He is assured of food as long as it is available. Zedekiah's positive response to Jeremiah adds to the puzzling picture of this hero/villain of Judah.

Explanation

Following the very negative portrayal of Jehoiakim in Jer 36, the accounts of Zedekiah's reign highlight the intransigence of Judah's rulers. Though some positive qualities may be present in Zedekiah's character, he is still identified as one who refused to hear the "word of the LORD." A tragic sameness seems to afflict Judah from one generation to another. Though circumstances and individual players change, the one constant is the stubborn rebellion of Judah against her God.

Contrasted with Judah's stubborn rebellion is the equally consistent faithfulness of the prophet Jeremiah. Events at times suggest that his message is wrong. The prophet, while no doubt assailed by internal questions, never wavers in his public pronouncements. The prophets of salvation are wrong. Attitudes and actions such as those exemplified by Judah can bring only one result, the judgment of God.

A final poignant note may also be sounded by these verses. In many ways, Zedekiah is a tragic figure. It seems that he is attracted to Jeremiah and his message like iron filings to a magnet, yet he is never able to summon enough resolve to act in response to that message. While such conclusions are speculative, it is possible that Zedekiah presents a paradigm of persons whose rejection of the purposes of God through their weakness of character is every bit as damaging and damning as the aggressive rebellion of Jehoiakim.

B. *Jeremiah in the Cistern* *(38:1–28a* *[LXX 45:1–28a])*

Bibliography

Kessler, M. "Jeremiah Chapters 26–45 Reconsidered." *JNES* 27 (1968) 81–88. **North, R.** "Palestine, Administration of (Judean Officials)." *ABD* 5:87. **Pohlmann, K.-F.** *Studien zum Jeremiahbuch.* Göttingen: Vandenhoeck & Ruprecht, 1978. 69–93. **Pritchard, J. B.,** ed. *ANET.* 322 (line 6). **Vaux, R. de** "Les Ostraka de Lachis." *RB* 48 (1939) 181–206. **Wanke, G.** *Untersuchungen zur sogenannten Baruchschrift.* BZAW 122. Berlin: de Gruyter, 1971. 102–16.

Translation

[1]*Now Shephatiah the son of Mattan, Gedaliah the son of Pashhur, Jucal the son of Shelemiah, and Pashhur the son of Malchiah*[a] *heard the words that Jeremiah was say-ing to all*[b] *the people,* [2]*"Thus says the LORD,*[a] *whoever remains in this city will die by the sword, by famine, and by pestilence,*[b] *but whoever goes out to the Chaldeans will live;*[c] *his life will be for him a prize of war,*[d] *and he will live.* [3]*Thus*[a] *says the LORD, this city will surely be given into the hand of the army of the king of Babylon, and he will capture it."* [4]*And the*[a] *princes*[b] *said to the king, "Let this man be put to death, for he is*[c] *weakening*[d] *the hands of the soldiers who remain in this*[e] *city and the hands of all the people, speaking these words to them, for this man is not seeking peace for this people, but harm."* [5]*King Zedekiah said, "Behold, he is in your hands, for the king can do nothing*[a] *against you."*[b] [6]*So they took Jeremiah,*[a] *and they cast him into the cistern*[b] *of Malchiah the son of the king, which was in the court of the guard, and they let Jeremiah*[c] *down with ropes;*[d] *and there was no water in the cistern, only mud, and Jeremiah*[e] *sank*[f] *in the mud.*

[7]*And Ebed-melech the Ethiopian, an official*[a] *who was in the king's house, heard that they had put Jeremiah into the cistern, and the king was sitting at the Benjamin Gate.* [8]*Ebed-melech*[a] *went from the king's house*[b] *and spoke to the king, saying:* [9]*"My lord the king,*[a] *these men have done evil in all that they have done to Jeremiah the prophet, whom they have cast into the cistern.*[b] *And he will die*[c] *there*[d] *from hunger, for there is no bread left in the city."*[e] [10]*Then the king commanded Ebed-melech the Ethiopian,*[a] *"Take with you from here three*[b] *men and lift Jeremiah the prophet*[c] *from the cistern before he dies."* [11]*So Ebed-melech took the men with him,*[a] *and he went to the king's house, to the wardrobe*[b] *of the storehouse, and he took from there old rags*[c] *and worn-out clothes. He let them down by ropes*[d] *to Jeremiah in the cistern.* [12]*And Ebed-melech the Ethiopian*[a] *said to Jeremiah,*[b] *"Put the worn-out rags and clothes between your armpits*[c] *and the ropes," and Jeremiah did so.* [13]*Then they drew Jeremiah*[a] *up by the ropes and lifted him from the cistern, and Jeremiah remained in the court of the guard.*

[14]*King Zedekiah*[a] *sent and received*[b] *Jeremiah the prophet*[c] *at the third entrance of the house of the LORD, and the king said to Jeremiah, "I am going to ask you something. Do not hide anything from me."* [15]*Jeremiah said to Zedekiah,*[a] *"If I tell you, will you not*

be certain to have me put to death? And if I advise you, you will not listen to me. "[16]*But King Zedekiah*[a] *swore to Jeremiah*[b] *secretly,*[c] *"As the* LORD *lives,*[d] *who gave us this*[e] *life,*[f] *I will not put you to death, nor give you into the hand of these men who seek your life."*[g]

[17]*Then Jeremiah said to Zedekiah,*[a] *"Thus says the* LORD, *the God*[b] *of Hosts, the God of Israel:*[c] *If you will go out*[d] *to the princes of the king of Babylon, then your life will be spared*[e] *and this city will not be burned with fire; you and your household will live.* [18]*But if you will not go out to the princes*[a] *of the king of Babylon,*[b] *this city will be given into the hand of the Chaldeans, and they will burn it with fire, and you will not escape from their hand."*[c]

[19]*King Zedekiah*[a] *said to Jeremiah, "I am afraid of the Judeans who deserted to the Chaldeans, lest they hand me over to them and they deal ruthlessly with me."* [20]*Jeremiah said, "They will not give you up;*[a] *obey now the voice of the* LORD *in what I am saying to you, that it may be well for you and you may live.*[b] [21]*But if you refuse to go out, this is what the* LORD *has shown me.* [22]*Behold, all the women who remain in the household of the king of Judah will be taken out to the princes of the king of Babylon, and will say,*

> *'They have deceived you;*
> *your trusted friends have prevailed over you.*[a]
> *Your feet*[b] *are sunk in the mire;*
> *they have forsaken you.'*

[23]*All*[a] *your wives and your sons will be brought to the Chaldeans, and you will not escape from their hand, for by the hand of the king of Babylon you will be seized and this city will be burned*[b] *with fire."*[c]

[24]*Then Zedekiah said to Jeremiah,*[a] *"Let no one know of these words and you will not die.*[b] [25]*If the princes hear that I have spoken with you, they will come to you and say to you, 'Tell us what you said to the king and what the king said to you.*[a] *Do not hide it from us, and we will not put you to death.'* [26]*Then you say to them, 'I pleaded with*[a] *the king that he not return me to the house of Jonathan to die there.'"*

[27]*All of the princes came to Jeremiah and questioned him, and he told them just as*[a] *the king had instructed.*[b] *They said nothing more,*[c] *for the conversation*[d] *had not been overheard.* [28]*And Jeremiah remained in the court of the guard until the day when Jerusalem was captured.*

Notes

1.a. "Pashhur the son of Malchiah" not found in LXX.

1.b. LXX lacks "all."

2.a. Same wording as 21:9 with the addition of "thus says the LORD."

2.b. ובדבר, "and by pestilence," not in LXX.

2.c. Cf. notes on 21:9; LXX, Syr, and Vg all suggest a more regular form, יִחְיֶה. The same is likely here, with the addition of the conj.

2.d. MT שָׁלָל, "booty, plunder." Probably a stock phrase (Nicholson, 1:177), found in 21:9; 38:2; 39:18; 45:5, with some minor variations. The reference is to a soldier who barely escapes from battle, "my life is my spoil."

3.a. LXX prefixes ὅτι, "For," which is not in MT.

4.a. *BHS* and Rudolph (204) suggest הָאֵלֶּה, "these," has dropped out as a result of haplogr.

4.b. "princes" not in LXX.

4.c. LXX lacks the emphatic particle עַל־כֵן, "surely," not reflected in the *Translation* above.

4.d. Some MSS have different vocalization, מֻרְפָּא.

4.e. LXX lacks "this."

5.a. MT יוּכַל, impf verb; LXX has the ptcp יָכוֹל.

5.b. LXX has "them."

6.a. "So they took Jeremiah" not in LXX.

6.b. *BHS* suggests omitting waw; cf. LXX. See also GKC § 127f.

6.c. LXX lacks "Jeremiah."

6.d. LXX has "into the cistern," not in MT, and LXX lacks "with ropes."

6.e. LXX lacks "Jeremiah."

6.f. LXX lacks "sank" and instead has simply "he was in the mud."

7.a. LXX lacks "an official"; Heb. אִישׁ סָרִיס tr. often as "eunuch." Likely refers to a minor court official, not necessarily a "eunuch" in the sense often assumed. See North, *ABD* 5:87.

8.a. "Ebed-Melech" not in LXX.

8.b. LXX has "went out *to him*," lacking "from the king's house"; MT does not have "to him."

9.a. LXX does not have "my lord the king."

9.b. LXX and MT are completely different here. LXX focuses upon the king, MT upon those who have put Jeremiah in the cistern. Carroll (681) notes that MT appears to ignore vv 4–5 earlier. LXX has Ebed-melech accuse the king, "you have done evil by sentencing this man to die." MT is more a plea for the king's intervention.

9.c. *BHS* suggests alternative vocalization וַיָּמָת, but see also GKC § 111l.

9.d. Lit. "under it."

9.e. *BHS* suggests the last extended phrase, "from hunger, for there is no bread left in the city," is a gloss, perhaps from 37:21, since it makes little sense in context. Jeremiah's predicament is not primarily acute because of lack of bread!

10.a. "the Ethiopian" not in LXX.

10.b. *BHS* and commentators follow minor MSS evidence, changing שְׁלֹשִׁים, "thirty," to שְׁלֹשָׁה, "three." LXX reads "thirty."

10.c. "him" instead of "Jeremiah the prophet" in LXX.

11.a. LXX lacks "with him."

11.b. MT reads lit. "to under the storehouse." *BHS* and commentators suggest מֶלְתָּחָה const, "wardrobe"; LXX has ὑπόγειον, "the underground."

11.c. *BHS* suggests ה is assimilated from v 12. Terms here translated "old rags and worn-out clothes" are parallels, i.e., "worn-out rags and worn-out rags."

11.d. LXX lacks "by ropes." Carroll (682) notes influence of v 6 here. LXX has "threw them," a more logical reading.

12.a. "Ebed-melech the Ethiopian" not in LXX.

12.b. LXX lacks "to Jeremiah."

12.c. With typical brevity, LXX lacks "the worn-out rags and clothes between your armpits," instead reading "put those under the ropes."

13.a. LXX has "him" instead of "Jeremiah."

14.a. "Zedekiah" lacking in LXX.

14.b. LXX lacks "and received."

14.c. LXX has simply "The king sent for him," as usual omitting "Jeremiah the prophet."

15.a. LXX has "to the king" instead of "Zedekiah."

16.a. LXX lacks "Zedekiah" and reads "the king."

16.b. LXX lacks "Jeremiah," instead reading "to him."

16.c. LXX does not have "secretly."

16.d. Q lacks the אֵת (the sign of the direct obj?) that appears in K, a likely scribal error.

16.e. Occurs in K of Eastern MSS as זֶה, "this" (m).

16.f. MT reads lit. "who made for us this life."

16.g. LXX lacks the phrase "who seek your life."

17.a. LXX has "to him."

17.b. Cairo Geniza fragments lack "the God of," yielding "the Lord of Hosts, the God of Israel."

17.c. LXX lacks the expanded phrase "the God of Hosts, the God of Israel."

17.d. Heb. is emphatic.

17.e. Lit. "your life will live."

18.a. Cairo Geniza fragments lack "the princes of."

18.b. LXX lacks the entire phrase "to the princes of the king of Babylon."

18.c. LXX lacks "from their hand."

19.a. LXX lacks "Zedekiah."

20.a. Lit. "they will not give."
20.b. Lit. "that your life may live."
22.a. Cf. poem in Obad 7.
22.b. MT has "your foot," but many MSS have "your feet."
23.a. "All" not in LXX.
23.b. "will be burned" with LXX and other MSS; MT reads lit. "you will burn this city."
23.c. LXX lacks "with fire."
24.a. LXX has "Then the king said to him."
24.b. *BHS* suggests possible connection with 37:21; see also Carroll's comments related in *Form/Structure/Setting* below.
25.a. LXX reverses the order of the questions, "what did the king say to you and what did you say to the king"; MT and Syr follow the order given in the *Translation* above.
26.a. Lit. "presented my supplication before."
27.a. Lit. "according to all these words which."
27.b. Several MSS read צוּהוּ, "they instructed."
27.c. Lit. "they were silent from him," that is, "they ceased speaking to him." LXX lacks "to him."
27.d. Lit. "the word." LXX has "the word of the LORD."

Form/Structure/Setting

The early verses of chap. 38 parallel closely events already described in the preceding chapter. The message proclaimed by the prophet is the consistent message of Jeremiah to his people. The one refrain that never changes is the certainty of destruction. In these chapters (37–38) it is repeated on several different occasions (37:6–10; 37:16–17; 38:1–3; 38:18; 38:22–23). As in 37:15, 38:4 presents the "princes" as Jeremiah's bitter enemies, seeking his death. The "cistern of Malchiah . . . in the court of the guard" becomes Jeremiah's prison, just as the house of Jonathan is in Jer 37. Following the chronology of the passages, Jeremiah's lot worsens as he is taken from the "court of the guard" (37:21) and cast into the cistern within the court of the guard (38:6).

One of the key questions relates to the series of perils and rescues portrayed in Jer 37–38. To what extent are these occurrences repeated? Is repetition used to emphasize the harsh response to the word of the LORD? As with other such questions noted above, no single answer is sufficient. The wealth of detail argues against too quick a dismissal of the accounts as they stand. At the same time, the redactional effectiveness of the telling and retelling of perilous circumstances experienced by the prophet is clear.

Carroll (679) notes the repetition of pattern, but he also notes the differences in detail. His conclusion is to suggest the presence of "doublets" (two more or less parallel accounts) of Jeremiah's fate during the siege (Carroll, 679). One such "doublet," which is striking, is 38:24–28, at least a close parallel of 37:20–21. Carroll suggests these verses would fit better following 37:20, because of the reference to the house of Jonathan (Carroll, 688). There are, however, other such dual references in Jer 37 and 38. Is this one more significant than others? Rearranging the text may be an unnecessary extreme. Perhaps accepting the present state of the text and seeking to understand the significance of such parallels would be a better approach. Varied details allow flexibility in the use of the tradition. Thompson (637) finds it appealing to treat Jer 37 and 38 as different accounts of the same events and refers to the similar occurrence in Jer 7 and 26.

Bright (233–34) mentions the similarities in outline between chaps. 37 and

38. In both chapters, Jeremiah is brought before princes, charged with treason and confined either to a cistern or a cistern house, the house of Jonathan plays a key role, secret interviews with the king occur, Jeremiah requests the king's intervention, and the prophet ends up in the court of the guard. While Bright accepts the possibility that these are consecutive events, he also underscores the repetitiveness clearly present here (Bright, 233).

Carroll alludes to the "art of story-telling" (683) as a possible underlying cause for the many variations, and that may be worth careful consideration. Given the significance of these fateful days in Judah's history, given as well the importance of the role of Jeremiah in any subsequent review of those days, it should not be surprising to find a wealth of "stories" about the prophet's involvement in the climactic events of Judah's demise. It would in fact be more surprising to find a unitary strand of tradition, uncomplicated by contradiction or ambiguity. When the various strands are considered individually, and these "strands" stand out like scenes in a play (37:3–10; 37:11–15; 37:16–21; 38:1–6; 38:7–13; 38:14–28), each has an interesting contribution to make to the larger tradition of the prophet. More important, as Carroll points out (669), each adds emphasis to the importance of the "word from the LORD" and its central role in these events.

Editorial activity is clearly visible at several points (e.g., Pohlmann, *Studien*, 70–72). The transitions between some of the different stories about the prophet are not always smooth, not always consistent. The end product, however, presents a description of persons and events that is consistent with the larger message of Jeremiah, and the larger message is thereby enriched.

Comment

1   Jer 38 begins by introducing an audience of four persons who react strongly to Jeremiah's message. As is often the case, specific information about the persons named is lacking. Jucal the son of Shelemiah is likely the Jehucal of 37:3, though no other information is given about him. Passhur, based on the listing of his paternity, is evidently not the Passhur of Jer 20, who proved to be a bitter enemy of the prophet.

Since Jeremiah's words are heard by "all" the people, it is fair to assume that 38:1 describes events prior to any incarceration of Jeremiah. The perceived threat attached to the message and the reference to audience suggest relative freedom for the prophet.

2–3   Jeremiah's message is the consistent message uttered in the final days of Judah's existence: The end is coming. Survival is possible by means of leaving the city. To remain is to face all but certain death from the various hazards related to the end of a terrible siege. Surrender to the Babylonians offers the hope of narrow escape, life as a prize of war, but better than no escape at all. Jeremiah offers no hope of deliverance; rather, he suggests that the LORD himself is responsible for giving the city "into the hand" of the Babylonians.

4   The "princes" rightly interpret Jeremiah's words as treasonous. That would appear to be beyond question. To call for mass desertions of the city would indeed tend to harm the morale of those defending the city. Whether "treason" at this stage is good or bad for the people of Judah is another matter. The "princes" are of the opinion that Jeremiah's words are not good for the city but lead inevitably to harm. Their response is to call for his execution as a traitor.

5–6 The weakness of Zedekiah is apparent in v 5. With the briefest of reactions to the charges against Jeremiah, Zedekiah opts out of the action. In essence, he tells the officials to do what they will; it is out of his hands.

Less clear is the reason that Jeremiah escapes execution immediately, the outcome one would expect following the previous exchange. Instead, the prophet is taken to a cistern in the court of the guard and lowered into it. Perhaps this was intended as a form of execution. The reaction of Ebed-melech (v 7) would indicate that as a possibility.

7–9 Ebed-melech the Ethiopian enters the picture in v 7 in an exchange with a rather strange twist. The initial scene describes Ebed-melech's alarm at Jeremiah's plight and his attempt to remedy it. The king is at the Benjamin Gate when the Ethiopian finds him. Though it is not certain, Zedekiah may well have been fulfilling his judicial function by sitting "in the gate," rendering decisions in cases of legal dispute.

Ironically, in v 9 Ebed-melech advises the king of Jeremiah's difficulty. It is ironic because Zedekiah is already well aware of that difficulty. The strange twist is the specific concern voiced by the Ethiopian. He fears that Jeremiah will die of hunger! From the language of v 6, hunger would appear to be well down the list of the prophet's problems (cf. Carroll, 682; Thompson, 640). Further, if there is no bread left in the city, Jeremiah would find that situation no better out of the cistern than in it. (*BHS* suggests that the phrase about bread is a possible gloss, see *Notes*.)

10–13 Without acknowledging prior awareness of the prophet's problems, Zedekiah gives the Ethiopian instructions to free Jeremiah. Ebed-melech is told to take three men with him to assist in the task. (MT and LXX have thirty, though no reason is given for so many. Perhaps the idea is some protection from those who would resist the rescue. Manuscript evidence listing "three" is probably to be preferred.)

The rescue is described in elaborate detail. Ebed-melech first finds rags from a storeroom to pad the ropes with which Jeremiah is to be lifted from the cistern. The prophet is instructed to use the padding under his arms and is then pulled from his predicament. He remains confined in the court of the guard (cf. 32:2; 37:21), but the immediate threat to his life is averted.

14–16 Vv 14–16 record another of the encounters between Jeremiah and Zedekiah (cf. 37:16) in which the king seeks counsel from the prophet. Since this is such a repeated theme, it necessarily colors the character portrait of Zedekiah. The repeated counsel of the prophet yields nothing (37:1–2?). Jeremiah seems never to give the counsel that Zedekiah longs to hear, or some hubris prevents him from acting on the advice given.

Jeremiah's response to the king's request for advice fits well in the sequence of events that has unfolded. He fears for his life if he should give the king a bad forecast, as he must to report the "word from the LORD." Zedekiah vows not to harm the prophet, or allow others to do so. The vow is "secret," indicating Zedekiah's tenuous position, a factor underscored by the king's plea in v 24 that Jeremiah tell no one the specifics of their conversation.

17–23 Jeremiah gives counsel to the king. It is not a new word, only a reemphasis of the consistent message delivered by the prophet to king and people. The only hope for the future of Judah is capitulation to the Babylonians. As Carroll (685) has noted, the scenario depicted by Jeremiah is a bit optimistic. It is doubtful that any action on the part of Zedekiah would divert the wrath of the Babylonians. He is a rebellious vassal who has dared to challenge the suzerain. While surrendering the city might save it from destruction and avert much loss of life, Zedekiah himself likely faces a no-win situation. What he seeks is some supernatural intervention (Carroll, 686), a hope that Jeremiah cannot encourage.

Jeremiah presents a grim alternative to surrender. If the city is not surrendered, it will be captured and burned, a key element in the prophet's forecast of doom (21:10; 32:29; 34:2, 22; 37:8, 10; 38:23). The prospects for the king are equally dim.

Zedekiah's professed fear is of Jews who have already fled to the Babylonians. Perhaps he intends to suggest reprisals for poor treatment during the terrible hardships of siege. Jeremiah reassures the king on that count, though it would seem more danger would lie elsewhere (the Babylonians). The prophet's forecast is one of survival for the king if the word from the LORD is heeded, doom otherwise.

Jeremiah uses a poem, portions of which closely resemble a similar refrain in Obad 7, to highlight the dire nature of his warning. In the poem, the women of the king's household, as they are being led away as captives, accuse the king of succumbing to the treachery of "friends," "friends" who quickly turn away at the first signs of trouble. V 23 describes the effects of the wrong decision upon the king's household and upon the king himself. The royal family will be captured, and the city will be "burned with fire."

24–28 The conversation ends with yet another plea from the king for secrecy. He rehearses with Jeremiah the appropriate response should any of the officials question him about the nature of his meeting with the king. The rehearsed answer is a partial truth that obscures the king's wavering and emphasizes Jeremiah's personal concerns. As the king suspected, some of the officials were aware of the meeting and were suspicious about its purpose. Whether or not the rehearsed answer satisfied their curiosity, the chapter ends with Jeremiah in the court of the guard and with nothing else changed.

The last phrase in the chapter (MT) is actually a transition to the account of Jerusalem's fall in Jer 39. Many translators follow versions that omit the transitional phrase. I have chosen to place v 28b at the beginning of the following chapter as an appropriate introduction to the capture of the city of Jerusalem by Babylonian forces.

Explanation

Jer 38 concludes the confusing, yet interesting, amalgam of accounts about the prophet's imprisonment, the king's dilemma, and the various intrigues surrounding the last days of Jerusalem. Whatever the source of the stories about Jeremiah related here, they are used to establish beyond question certain realities about Judah and her people in the final days of the siege.

The central reality is the consistent message of the prophet. There is no hope apart from surrender to the Babylonians. Any other action will result in the destruction of the city and its "burning with fire."

A clear picture is also drawn of a powerful group of anti-Babylonian nationalists who influence even the actions of the king. Jeremiah is a threat to their cause, and they seek to eliminate him. From their perspective, he is a traitor who undermines the patriotic zeal of the city's defenders.

There are those who at one level or another are drawn to the prophet and his message. Key among these is the tragic figure of Zedekiah, the star-crossed king who cannot or will not respond to the message that he nevertheless seeks again and again. His fate and that of the city seem sealed, a fact reflected in the somber tones of 37:1–2. Others, like Ebed-melech, are more openly supportive of Jeremiah but cannot exert enough influence to affect the outcome of events.

Jer 37 and 38 stress the repeated opportunities given to God's people to respond and experience "deliverance." As with the Deuteronomist's historiography, the result is always a stubborn refusal to hear the word of the LORD. Jeremiah is consistently faithful to his task in the face of extreme threat, but to no avail. Hope, if it is to be found at all in this pessimistic description of Jerusalem's last days, must be found in a call to faithfulness like that of the prophet, and perhaps others who stood with him. It is only in that kind of faithful response that the people of God can find hope for their future.

C. The Capture of Jerusalem   (38:28b–39:18 [LXX 45:28b–46:18])

Bibliography

Bewer, J. A. "Nergalsharezer Samgar in Jer. 39:3." *AJSL* 42 (1925/26) 130. **Kessler, M.** "Jeremiah Chapters 26–45 Reconsidered." *JNES* 27 (1968) 81–88. **North, R.** "Palestine, Administration of (Judean Officials)." *ABD* 5:87. **Pohlmann, K.-F.** *Studien zum Jeremiabuch.* Göttingen: Vandenhoeck & Ruprecht, 1978. 69–93. **Wanke, G.** *Untersuchungen zur sogenannten Baruchschrift.* BZAW 122. Berlin: de Gruyter, 1971. 102–16.

Translation

[28b]*This is*[a] *how Jerusalem was captured:*[b]

[39:1]*In the ninth year*[ab] *of Zedekiah the king of Judah, in the tenth month,*[c] *Nebuchadrezzar the king of Babylon and all of his army came against Jerusalem and besieged it.* [2]*In the eleventh year of Zedekiah, in the fourth*[a] *month, on the ninth*[b] *day of the month, the city was breached;* [3]*and*[a] *all of the officers of the king of Babylon came and sat in the middle gate: Nergal-*[b]*sharezer,*[b] [c]*Samgar-nebo, Sar-sechim the Rabsaris,*[d] *Nergal-*[b]*sharezer*[b] *the Rabmag,*[c] *and all of the rest*[e] *of the officers of the king of Babylon.*

^{4a}*When Zedekiah the king of Judah and all the soldiers saw them,*^b *they fled and went out at night from the city by way of the king's garden through the gate between the walls; and they went out*^c *toward the Arabah.* ⁵*But the army of the Chaldeans pursued them and overtook Zedekiah in the plains of Jericho*^a *and took him and brought him to Nebuchadrezzar the king of Babylon at Riblah, in the land of Hamath; and he passed judgment upon him.* ⁶*The king of Babylon slaughtered the sons of Zedekiah at Riblah before his eyes, and the king of Babylon slaughtered all of the nobles of Judah;* ⁷*and he blinded the eyes of Zedekiah and bound him in fetters to take him to Babylon.*^a ⁸*The Chaldeans burned the house of the king and the houses of*^a *the people with fire; and they pulled down the walls of Jerusalem.* ⁹*Then Nebuzaradan the captain of the guard took into exile to Babylon the rest of the people who remained in the city, the ones who had deserted to him and the rest of the people*^a *who remained.*^b ¹⁰*Nebuzaradan the captain of the guard left in the land of Judah some of the poor people who had nothing, and he gave to them vineyards and fields*^a *in that day.* ^{11a}*And Nebuchadrezzar the king of Babylon commanded concerning Jeremiah, by the hand of*^b *Nebuzaradan the captain of the guard, saying:* ¹²*"Take him and look after him and do not do any harm*^a *to him; whatever*^b *he says to you, do with him."*

^{13a}*So*^b*Nebuzaradan the captain of the guard, and*^b *Nebushazban the Rabsaris, and Nergal-*^c*sharezer*^c *the Rabmag, and all the chief officers of the king of Babylon sent*^d ¹⁴*and took Jeremiah from the court of the guard; and they gave him*^a*to Gedaliah the son of Ahikam the son of Shaphan*^a ^b*to take him to the house.*^b *So he remained among the people.*

^{15a}*The word of the LORD came to Jeremiah*^b*while he was shut up*^b *in the court of the guard, saying:* ¹⁶*"Go and say to Ebed-melech the Ethiopian, saying: 'Thus says the LORD of Hosts, the God of Israel, behold I am sending*^a *my words against this city for evil and not for good;* ^b*and they will happen before you in that day.*^b ¹⁷*But I will deliver you in that day, says the LORD, and you will not be given into the hand of the men of whom you are afraid.* ¹⁸*For I will surely deliver you, and you will not fall by the sword; your life will be spared for a spoil because you have trusted in me, says the LORD.'"*

Notes

28.a. A few MSS have ויהי, "and it came to pass" (impf), for MT והיה, "and it came to pass" (pf), tr. above "this is."

28.b. LXX, Syr lack the last phrase, "this is how Jerusalem was captured," which connects Jer 38 and the account of Jerusalem's fall in Jer 39.

39:1.a. *BHS* suggests vv 1–2 may be added from 52:4.

1.b. LXX^B and LXX^S have (ἐν) τῷ μηνί, "in the month."

1.c. "in the tenth month" absent from the MSS noted above in *Note* 1.b.

2.a. Some MSS have החמישי, "fifth."

2.b. Vg has *quinta*, "fifth."

3.a. Many translations shift "when Jerusalem was taken" from 38:28b to here.

3.b-b. Many MSS have שראצר, "Sarezer" (no maqqeph in the second part of the name); several MSS have שראצר, "Sharezer," followed in the *Translation* above. MT has שר־אצר, "Sarezer" (with maqqeph).

3.c-c. שַׂר סַמְגַּר רַב־מָג וּנְבוּשַׁזְבָּן רַב־סָרִיס, "prince (of) Si(n)-magir [principal city Sin-magir] the Rabmag and Nebushazban the Rabsaris," should probably be read here; cf. v 13. The rendering of the names follows the work of Rudolph (208) and Bright (243).

3.d. While no one is certain of what the various names/titles mean, Rabsaris can be read literally as "chief of the officials"; cf. North, *ABD* 5:87.

3.e. *BHS* suggests this probably should be deleted as dittogr; cf. v 13.

4.a. LXX omits vv 4–13 (probably because of homoioteleuton, copyist's error caused by similar endings of different verses [Rudolph, 209]; cf. the end of v 13); vv 4–10 added from 52:7–11, 13–16; and *BHS* suggests moving vv 11–12 before 40:1. Cf. *Note* 13.a.

4.b. *BHS* proposes רָאָה, "saw it."

4.c. Several MSS (θ', Syr, Vg) have וַיֵּצְאוּ, "and they went out"; MT has "he went out"; *Translation* above follows the plural, reading וילכו, "and they went," as with 52:7.

5.a. A few MSS (Syr included) add וכל-חילו נפצו מעליו, "and all his army was scattered from him," with 52:8; 2 Kgs 25:5.

7.a. θ' has expanded text; cf. LXX of 52:11.

8.a. Syr has pl; read בָּתֵּי, "the houses of" (cf. 52:13; 2 Kgs 25:5), or insert יהוה ואת-בתי, "(the house of) Yahweh and the houses of" (cf. the same verses as noted).

9.a. *BHS* suggests reading, with 52:15, הָאָמוֹן, "the artisans."

9.b. *BHS* suggests deleting "who remained"; cf. 52:15; 2 Kgs 25:11.

10.a. MT has וְיגֵבִים, "and fields," but the reading is considered dubious. LXX, θ', Vg have "cisterns" = וְגֵבִים; Jer 52:16 and 2 Kgs 25:12, which are parallel, would support וּלְיֹגְבִים, "and plowmen," or "and husbandmen."

11.a. *BHS* suggests moving this verse before 40:1; cf. *Note* 4.a.

11.b. σ', Syr, Vg lack "by the hand of."

12.a. רָע, "evil, bad," daghesh forte in ר following L; see GKC § 22s.

12.b. Q omits אִם, the Heb. hypothetical particle, which is found in K; the sense is not altered in either case (Rudolph, 209).

13.a. Vv 4–12 added from 52:7–11, 13–16, omitted initially probably as a result of homoioteleuton (scribal error due to similarity in endings of texts) in LXX (Rudolph, 209).

13.b-b. *BHS* suggests that "Nebuzaradan the captain of the guard and" is added from v 11.

13.c-c. Many MSS have שַׂראֶצֶר, "Sarezer."

13.d. The verb וישלח, "and he sent," which begins v 13, is repeated in the pl at the beginning of v 14, חו וישל, "and they sent." The *Translation* omits the redundancy, likely the result of an attempt to harmonize vv 11–12 with vv 3, 14 (Bright, 243–44).

14.a-a. "to Gedaliah the son of Ahikam the son of Shaphan" is considered by *BHS* to be an addition from 40:6.

14.b-b. LXX omits "to the house"; *BHS* suggests reading לְהוֹצִיאוֹ וְלַהֲבִיאוֹ, "to let him go out and come in"; cf. 37:4. If "to the house" is read, a proposal such as that by Thompson (648), to read "house" as the governor's residence, has merit.

15.a. Vv 15–18 are perhaps out of place here. Holladay (2:269) suggests they belong properly after 38:27; Rudolph (212), after 38:13.

15.b-b. Lacking in LXX.

16.a. Read with Q מֵבִיא, "sending"; K has מֵבִי (translation uncertain, though Q probably provides a reasonable option).

16.b-b. Lacking in LXX; *BHS* suggests it is perhaps an addition by dittogr from v 17.

Form/Structure/Setting

The text of Jer 39 presents some problems that are not easily solved. There are several key issues to consider.

The first obvious issue is the segment of the chapter that is missing completely in the Greek text. The LXX does not contain vv 4–13. The missing verses describe the attempt by Zedekiah and other leading citizens of Judah to escape from the doomed city of Jerusalem. There is much in common with Jer 52:7–11, 13–16 as well as 2 Kgs 25:4–12. Most scholars suggest that the parallel is omitted in LXX because of haplography, scribal omission as the result of a copying error (Bright, 245; Carroll, 691; Rudolph, 209; Thompson, 644). Bright (245) suggests vv 4–13 are inserted to make Jeremiah's situation and that of the city clear (Holladay, 2:292, also considers these verses to be a secondary insertion).

Though vv 4–13 may represent an insertion of material originating in a context different from the surrounding material, it provides information useful in narrating the fall of the city. The description of Zedekiah's actions and his fate at the hand of the Babylonians follows logically the accounts of conversations between Jeremiah and Zedekiah in chaps 37 and 38. Zedekiah's tragic end is presented as a consequence of his failure to heed the prophet's advice.

The events related in Jer 39:1–10 parallel very closely the account in 52:4–16 (and 2 Kgs 25:1–12). This is the more logical placement for the description of the city's fall and Zedekiah's fate. Why the events are described again in Jer 52 as a postscript to the book is difficult to ascertain. That issue will be addressed more fully below in discussion of Jer 52.

Another difficulty with this text involves the Babylonian officials named in vv 3, 13. In v 13, the prophet is released by those who are earlier named as "officers" (the translation rendered above) or "princes" of the king of Babylon, with special mention of Nebuzaradan, a figure who is to have great importance in the larger narrative. There is no consensus regarding who these officials are. There is not even certainty about which of these "names" are names and which are titles. The most extensive work in this area is that done by Rudolph and Bright on the basis of Babylonian records roughly contemporary with this period (Bright, 243; Bewer, *AJSL* 42 (1925/26) 130; Rudolph, 208).

Of the officials named in v 3, Nergal-sharezer (a name that is spelled differently in different text traditions, cf. translation notes above) is probably the individual who ascended to the throne of Babylon in 560 B.C. (Holladay, 2:269; Rudolph, 208). "Samgar-nebo" probably should be read as a geographical reference to the district ruled by Nergal-sharezer, Sin-magir (Bewer, *AJSL* 42 (1925/26) 130; Bright, 243; Carroll, 691; Rudolph, 208). "Sar-sechim the Rabsaris" may refer to one of the chief Babylonian officials (see *Note* 3.d. above). Further, while "Nergal-sharezer" appears twice in v 3, it probably refers to only one individual, who is the Nergal-sharezer of v 13 as well.

Nebuzaradan, who is first mentioned in v 9, is described as רב־טבחים, literally "the chief butcher." The intention is apparently to identify him as a principal officer of Nebuchadrezzar by means of an archaic title (Bright, 242; Carroll, 692; Rudolph, 209; Thompson, 648). He is identified in the *Translation* above as "the captain of the guard."

Perhaps the most perplexing problem of structure in this chapter is that of vv 15–18. These verses seem to provide a flashback to earlier events as a kind of afterthought. Jeremiah's rescue at the hands of Ebed-melech (38:7–13) leads to reward for Ebed-melech when the city falls to the enemy. Carroll (696) suggests that the placement of this account serves to join the fates of Jeremiah and his rescuer: both are to survive (see also Thompson, 649). Bright (229–34), on the other hand, rearranges the material so as to place 39:15–18 following 38:28a, nearer to the events that involve Ebed-melech. Rudolph (212–13) calls attention to the contrasting pictures of Zedekiah, the "anointed of Yahweh," and an unimportant foreigner. The "anointed" one does not believe and goes to his ruin. The foreigner believes and is preserved. Placement by content, then, would perhaps indicate another location for these verses, but there is significant reason for their present location.

The setting of 39:1–18 is the culmination of the Babylonian siege of Jerusalem. In the midst of the chaotic events, there is marked contrast in the pathetic flight and tragic end of Zedekiah and the deliberate care for Jeremiah on the part of the Babylonian officials. It is assumed by many, if not most, scholars that this material continues the so-called Baruch scroll, eyewitness accounts of events at the end of Jeremiah's career (Holladay, 2:286; Duhm, xvi; Rudolph, xiv–xv; Bright, lxvii; though note the view of Wanke, *Untersuchungen*, 146).

Comment

1–3 The introductory verses of the chapter summarize the Babylonian siege of Jerusalem and its end result. The siege began in the ninth year of Zedekiah, January 588 B.C., and lasted until July 587 B.C. (Holladay, 2:291; Thompson, 646). The common assumption is that the Babylonian army attacked Jerusalem from the north and eventually breached the northern wall of the city (see Holladay, 2:291).

The list of Babylonian officials raises questions that defy obvious answers. As noted in *Form/Structure/Setting* above, it is not even possible with certainty to distinguish proper names from titles in this list. It seems clear, however, that the actions of the officials served to indicate complete Babylonian power over the city and its inhabitants. To "sit in the gate" indicated authority.

4 Zedekiah's response to the end of the siege was predictable. As the Babylonians broke through the wall to the north, he and many of his retinue attempted to flee to the south. Holladay (2:292) suggests that Zedekiah was attempting to reach the protection of the Ammonite king on the other side of the Jordan.

5 Whatever Zedekiah had intended, his attempted escape is foiled and he is captured. The Judean ruler and those with him are brought to Nebuchadrezzar's headquarters at Riblah, where the Babylonian king passes judgment upon him. Zedekiah has been disloyal to the Babylonian king and is treated accordingly.

6–7 The punishment of Zedekiah is severe. In many ways it is worse than a sentence of death. He is forced to watch the execution of his own sons; then he is blinded by his captors. The last sight he will ever see is the death of his children. The final picture of Zedekiah is that of a pathetic, defeated figure led away to end his days as an exiled prisoner in Babylon.

8 The city itself suffered considerable destruction from the Babylonian army. The royal palace and private homes were burned. The city walls were torn down. According to 2 Kgs 25:8, this destruction occurred a month after the fall of the city and included the destruction of the temple.

9–10 The bulk of the surviving population of Jerusalem is taken away into exile, both those who had deserted to the Babylonians during the siege and those who survived the siege in the city. From the poorest of the people, some are allocated land that they are to cultivate and on which they are to settle. Any visions of grandeur that once might have applied to Judah are replaced by the grimmest of pictures of survival and subsistence in the land.

11–14 The prophet Jeremiah is singled out for special care by the Babylonian authorities. Nebuchadrezzar himself gives orders concerning provisions for

Jeremiah. Jeremiah is given a choice. Apparently his options are to go with the exiles to Babylon, where he no doubt will be well treated, or to remain in the land. Whichever choice Jeremiah makes, he is to be well treated.

Jeremiah had spoken and acted as the messenger of the LORD as the crisis in Judah grew ever more severe, announcing what he understood to be the purpose of God for Judah. The fact that the purpose of God as he understood it was favorable to the Babylonians identified Jeremiah as an ally of Babylon. Consequently, when the Babylonians crushed Zedekiah's rebellion, Jeremiah was afforded treatment suitable to such an ally.

Jeremiah chooses to remain in the land of Judah. He is entrusted into the care of Gedaliah, a member of the royal family loyal to Babylon who was named governor of Judah.

15–18 The final paragraph in chap. 39 refers to Ebed-melech, the Ethiopian who had been responsible for Jeremiah's rescue from the cistern (Jer 38). A word from the LORD came to the prophet prior to his release from the court of the guard. Jeremiah was to inform Ebed-melech of the city's demise and Ebed-melech's deliverance. Ebed-melech was promised that he would not fall by the sword but would survive because of his trust in the LORD. Rudolph's observations regarding this episode are persuasive (213, see *Form/Structure/Setting* above). The chronology of events in vv 1–18 is not as one might expect, but there does seem to be the linking element of contrast between the faithlessness of Zedekiah and the faithfulness of Ebed-melech.

Explanation

That which the prophet Jeremiah had predicted all along finally became a reality for Judah. The prophet had warned against trust in the Egyptian alliance or in any means of security other than Yahweh alone. Jeremiah repeatedly sought to persuade Zedekiah to make the difficult choices that would lead to Judah's survival. Those efforts were never successful. The reader of this section of Jeremiah observes the vacillation of the weak-willed ruler who seems to follow the pressure group of the moment. He is attracted to the advice of the prophet but ultimately succumbs to the pressures of pro-Egyptian forces in Jerusalem. It is perhaps proper to suggest that Zedekiah decided by not deciding. He delayed decision until the decision was no longer his to make.

Jer 39 presents a strong contrast between faithfulness and the lack of faith. Jeremiah and Ebed-melech represent those who are faithful to the LORD and to whom the LORD is faithful in return. Zedekiah represents faithlessness. In some respects, Zedekiah's faithlessness is of the most troublesome sort among people of faith. His faithlessness is not rejection of the LORD but an inability to act in courage when pressures mount. Like the church at Laodicea in Rev 3:15, Zedekiah was neither hot nor cold, and he paid a terrible price for his indecision.

D. *Jeremiah's Release* (40:1–12
[LXX 47:1–12])

Bibliography

Eissfeldt, O. "Baruchs Anteil an Jeremia 38,28b–40,6." In *Kleine Schriften*. Tübingen: Mohr, 1968. 4:176–80. ———. *The Old Testament: An Introduction*, tr. P. R. Ackroyd. New York: Harper and Row, 1965. 346–65. **Morton, W. H.** "Netophah." *IDB* 4:541. ———. "Ramah." *IDB* 4:7–8. **Muilenburg, J.** "Mizpah." *IDB* 3:407–9. **Pohlmann, K.-F.** *Studien zum Jeremiabuch*. Göttingen: Vandenhoeck & Ruprecht, 1978. 93–108. **Vaux, Roland de.** "Mélanges: Le Sceau de Godolias, maître de Palais." *RB* 45 (1936) 96–102.

Translation

[1] *The word* [a] *which came to Jeremiah from the LORD after Nebuzaradan the captain of the guard released him from Ramah, when he had taken him bound* [b] *in chains* [c] *with all* [d] *the captives of Jerusalem and* [e] *Judah who were being exiled to Babylon.* [2] *The captain of the guard took Jeremiah* [ab] *and said to him, "The LORD your God pronounced this evil against this place.* [3] *The LORD brought it about* [a] *and has done just as he said.* [b] *Because you [pl] sinned against the LORD* [c] *and you [pl] did not obey his voice, this thing* [d] *has come upon* [e] *you [pl].* [4] *Now* [a] *behold, I release you today* [b] *from the chains* [c] *which are upon your hands.* [d] *If it seems right to you to come with me to Babylon, come and I will look after you; if it seems wrong to you to come with me to Babylon, do not come.* [e] *See, the whole land is before you; go wherever you please.* [fg] [5] *If you remain, return* [a] *to Gedaliah the son of Ahikam the son of Shaphan, whom the king of Babylon has set over the cities* [b] *of Judah, and dwell with him among the people* [c] *or* [d] *go into any of the remainder of the land where you wish to go." And the captain of the guard gave to him food and* [e] *a gift and sent him away.* [6] *So Jeremiah* [a] *went to Gedaliah the son of Ahikam* [b] *at Mizpah, and he dwelled with him* [c] *among the people who were left in the land.*

[7a] *When all the officers of the forces which were in the field and their men heard that the king of Babylon had made Gedaliah the son of Ahikam* [b] *governor over the land and had set him over men, women, and children, the poorest of the land* [c] *who had not been taken into exile to Babylon,* [8] *they came to Gedaliah at Mizpah, Ishmael the son of Nethaniah, Johanan and Jonathan* [a] *the sons* [b] *of Kareah, Seraiah the son of Tanhumeth, the sons of Ephai* [c] *the Netophathite, and Jezaniah* [d] *the son of the Maacathite, they and their men.* [9] *Gedaliah the son of Ahikam the son of Shaphan* [a] *swore to them and to their men, "Do not be afraid of serving* [b] *the Chaldeans; remain in the land and serve the king of Babylon and it will be well with you.* [10] *As for me, I will dwell* [a] *at Mizpah to stand before the Chaldeans who have come to us; but as for you, gather wine and summer fruit and oil and put them in your vessels, and live in your cities* [b] *which you have captured."* [11] *Also,* [a] *when all the Jews who were in Moab, and among the Ammonites, and in Edom, and in all the lands* [b] *heard that the king of Babylon had left a remnant in Judah and that he had made Gedaliah the son of Ahikam the son of Shaphan* [c] *governor over them,* [12] *then all the Jews returned from all the places where they had been*

banished,[a] *and they came to the land of Judah to Gedaliah*[b] *at Mizpah; and they gathered wine and summer fruit in abundance.*

Notes

1.a. Confusion in the order of the text is indicated by the formal introduction to a prophetic oracle with no oracle following; *BHS* suggests reordering the text: 39:11–12, 40:2a, 1b, 1aβ moved to follow 6a, with 1aα deleted, that is, removing the formal oracular introduction while combining segments related to Jeremiah's encounter with Nebuzaradan.

1.b. "bound" not in LXX.

1.c. *BHS* follows Q בָּאזִקִּים, "in chains," rather than K בָּאֶזְקִים (meaning uncertain).

1.d. LXX lacks "all."

1.e. LXX lacks "Jerusalem and."

2.a. *BHS* questions the preposition לְ, attached to "Jeremiah"; Carroll (698) suggests it is an Aramaism.

2.b. LXX has "took him."

3.a. "brought it about" not in LXX.

3.b. LXX lacks "just as he said."

3.c. LXX has "against him."

3.d. The article should be included, as with Q.

3.e. *BHS* proposes וַיְהִי, "has come" (cf. 37:11).

4.a. "Now" lacking in LXX.

4.b. LXX does not have "today."

4.c. Variation in spelling; see *Note* 1.c.

4.d. Following the many MSS that have a dual form, "your hands," rather than MT "your hand."

4.e. "if it seems wrong to you . . . do not come . . . go wherever you please" is missing in LXX. See *Notes* on v 5 below.

4.f. Lit. "to the good and to the right in your eyes to go, go there"; *BHS* proposes אִם־טוֹב, "where it is good," the particle אִם giving the sense "where it is good and right . . ." in place of the preposition לְ, "*to* the good . . ."

4.g. *BHS* suggests that "to the right in your eyes to go, go there" is an addition from v 5 (tr. above by the phrase "go wherever you please"). See *Notes* on v 5 below.

5.a. Heb. is obscure, likely corrupt (LXX is likewise obscure, following the Heb.); MT reads lit. "but he was still not turning, and turning." *BHS* proposes "if it seems right in your eyes to return, return"; cf. *Note* 4.f.

5.b. LXX has "over the land" instead of "over the cities."

5.c. LXX adds "in the land of Judah."

5.d. "or" not explicit in LXX.

5.e. LXX lacks "food and."

6.a. "Jeremiah" not in LXX; LXX reads "so he went . . ."

6.b. LXX lacks "the son of Ahikam."

6.c. LXX lacks "with him."

7.a. For vv 7–9, cf. 2 Kgs 25:22–24.

7.b. LXX lacks "the son of Ahikam."

7.c. LXX has "men and their wives who had not been taken into exile," lacking "and children, the poorest of the land" in MT.

8.a. LXX, Tg lack "and Jonathan," probably as a result of haplogr; cf. 2 Kgs 25:23.

8.b. LXX, Tg have "son of," consistent with absence of "and Jonathan" noted above; cf. 2 Kgs 25:23.

8.c. Syr, Tg follow Q עֵיפַי, "Ephai"; LXX, Vg follow K עוֹפַי, "Ophay."

8.d. A few MSS, 2 Kgs have וְיַאֲזַנְיָהוּ, "Jaazaniah."

9.a. LXX lacks "the son of Ahikam the son of Shaphan."

9.b. LXX has παίδων, "servants of"; cf. 2 Kgs 25:24 מֵעַבְדֵי, "servants of."

10.a. LXX adds "before you."

10.b. LXX has "in the cities."

11.a. LXX lacks "also."

11.b. LXX has sg "land."

11.c. LXX lacks "the son of Shaphan."

12.a. LXX lacks "all the Jews returned from all the places where they had been banished."

12.b. LXX has different order, "to Gedaliah in the land of Judah," rather than MT "to the land of Judah to Gedaliah."

Form/Structure/Setting

This chapter begins with a formal oracular introduction without the oracle it introduces. Various options have been proposed to provide an explanation for the passage as it stands or to emend it so as to give a sensible alternative, among them the simple removal of the introduction as not belonging in its present location (Rudolph, 211). Bright (244) and Carroll (698) suggest the possibility that vv 2–3 may represent what remains of the oracle.

The parallel account of these events in 2 Kgs 25, while not providing answers to all the questions posed, probably does provide the content source from which this chapter of Jeremiah emerged. At some points the wording is virtually identical, and some problems can be tentatively resolved based on a comparative reading of 2 Kgs 25 (e.g., Johanan and Jonathan in v 8).

One of the key issues to be resolved related to this text is the accommodation of what appear to be two stories of Jeremiah's release from imprisonment. Jer 39:11–12 describes the simple release of Jeremiah and his subsequent association with Gedaliah. Jer 40:1–6 seems to present an entirely different and more complicated picture. Jeremiah is released in this story, too, but only after time spent among those rounded up for deportation.

Bright (245–46), Clements (229), and Thompson (651–52) find the two stories to be compatible if not essentially in accord with one another. Carroll (699) considers the two accounts to be very different and contradictory. He refers to the "absurd picture of the preacher going into exile and being made the recipient of a sermon preached to him by the pagan military commander Nebuzaradan" (Carroll, 699). Carroll does note the similar manner in which the Babylonians view Jeremiah in both strands of escape stories.

Pohlmann (*Studien*, 99) insists that v 1 must be viewed as the product of redactional arrangement and did not originally belong with the verses which follow. He argues for a rather complex redactional development of this text, in which v 1 is altered because of the insertion of 39:15–18 between an earlier, more understandable linkage of 39:1–14 to 40:2–6. Pohlmann (*Studien*, 99) goes into great detail in an attempt to describe various redactional stages leading to the textual difficulties apparent in vv 1–6. He posits an original linkage between 39:1–14 and 40:2–6, with a later insertion of 39:15–18 and the necessitated alteration of 40:1 to make the unit intelligible. The procedures Pohlmann describes, in his view, account for the difficulties in the present text.

Whatever one chooses to do in order to resolve the problems this text presents, it seems clear that the initial verse of Jer 40 remains problematic. One cannot but expect an actual oracle to follow the introduction this verse provides. Yet, there is no oracle, unless the oracle from the LORD is that which is given by means of the Babylonian officer. While that explanation is no more certain than any other proposed, the words of the Babylonian do reflect the tone and content of other oracles that Jeremiah delivered to the nation of Judah.

The stylized prophetic speech is all but ludicrous in the mouth of a Babylonian army officer, but that, too, may be worthy of some attention. What is the purpose of presenting the pagan soldier as the spokesperson for the LORD? Is this any more unusual than depicting Nebuchadrezzar as the LORD's servant (Jer 27:6)? There may be more intentional structure than careless editing involved in the present form of this text.

40:7–12 represents an expanded version of what is described in 2 Kgs 25:23–24. Where the descriptions are parallel, the wording is almost identical. One feature of the expansion is almost propagandalike as the text describes an "abundance" of various foodstuffs and what appears to be a rather comfortable life for those who join Gedaliah (vv 10–12). The propaganda flavor is heightened by the mention of the return of many Jews who had taken refuge earlier in Ammon, Moab, Edom, and "other lands." It seems possible that such touches serve to heighten the tragic nature of the crisis that begins to threaten Gedaliah and the hopeful remnant of Judah.

The setting for the events described in this chapter is Mizpah, the location of which is the subject of considerable debate. Tell en-Nasbeh, a site about eight miles north of Jerusalem, is suggested by some (Bright, 244; Thompson, 653), but Holladay (2:294–95) argues persuasively against it and in favor of Nebi Samwil, an elevated site five miles north of Jerusalem that, in his view, more consistently fits the events of the narrative.

Jeremiah is notably missing from the narrative. What unfolds in this passage, however, is of considerable significance to the larger message of the book of Jeremiah, and the narration of it is consistent in context (see Eissfeldt, *Introduction*, 365).

Comment

1 Jer 40 begins with a formulaic introduction announcing a "word from the LORD." This "word" comes to Jeremiah after his release from custody by Nebuzaradan, the Babylonian official. The reference to Jeremiah's release seems redundant in light of 39:11–14 and perhaps even contradictory to that account. In this case, it seems that Jeremiah was brought from Jerusalem along with numbers of other survivors of the siege and released at Ramah. Ramah, some five miles north of Jerusalem, was apparently a staging area for the exiles who were bound for Babylon (see Morton, *IDB* 4:8).

2–3 The absence of any declared word from Jeremiah has been noted by most interpreters of this passage, and some have proposed reconstructions of the text in order to resolve what is seen to be a problem with the text (see *Form/Structure/Setting* above). There is, however, another way to perceive the "word from the LORD."

It seems particularly consistent to the book of Jeremiah, if not the prophetic tradition in general, to have a word from the LORD delivered by a Babylonian official. This is precisely the jarring note that prophets occasionally use to indicate the radical nature of Yahweh's dealings with Israel/Judah. Nebuchadrezzar, the savage tyrant king of Babylon, can freely be identified by Jeremiah as the servant of the LORD (Jer 27:6). The inability or refusal to hear the word from the LORD on the part of Judah and her leaders is underscored by the ludicrous picture of the pagan soldier speaking as Yahweh's messenger. The two elements seem to fit well into a pattern that itself communicates part of Jeremiah's message.

The content of the oracle, if Nebuzaradan's words can be so described, is consistent with Yahweh's words concerning Judah previously delivered. The terrible disaster that came upon Jerusalem was no chance event but the act of God's judgment. A Babylonian soldier was able to identify the sins of Judah as cause for Jerusalem's destruction. To note the irony of these verses is to restate the obvious. This ironic twist is typical of the way harsh truth is sometimes conveyed by the prophets.

4–5   Jeremiah is given the choice by Nebuzaradan of journeying to Babylon, where he will be afforded Nebuzaradan's good offices, or of remaining in Judah at a place of his own choosing. He is urged, however, to join Gedaliah and those who were with him at Mizpah. Gedaliah's base of operations probably represented a more secure haven than would have existed elsewhere in the chaotic turmoil of the defeated nation. Nebuzaradan presents Jeremiah with provisions of food and a gift and then sends him on his way.

6   Jeremiah accepts the advice and settles at Mizpah with Gedaliah. The description of v 6 suggests that many of the surviving inhabitants of Judah gathered around this more stable location. Further comments later in the chapter regarding those who returned from distant locales to Mizpah serve to support this idea.

7–8   When news of Gedaliah's appointment as governor becomes known, the remnants of Judean military forces gather to him at Mizpah. Two of the officers named, Ishmael and Johanan, are crucial to the events that unfold subsequently. It is impossible to determine with certainty how these remnants survived the Babylonian onslaught, though it is quite likely they represented groups overlooked or ignored in the larger victory by Babylonian forces.

9   Gedaliah announces a clear policy of accommodation to Babylonian rule. In all likelihood, he had been a realist with regard to Judah's relationship to Babylon during the crisis years. Otherwise, he would not have been selected by the Babylonians to serve as their governor. Such realism was the focus of many of Jeremiah's arguments with Zedekiah.

10–12   Gedaliah appeals for calm and industry. He urges the people to gather produce from the fields and vineyards and to resume normal life in the region. Gedaliah offers a covenantal promise to "stand before the Chaldeans." His will be the official presence between the Babylonian occupiers and the people who remain in the land. This language suggests both an oath of loyalty to the Babylonians and a promise to act as mediator on behalf of the remnant Jewish community.

Vv 10–12 suggest that as the news of a surviving community reached pockets of Jews in the surrounding territories, many responded by joining the emerging group at Mizpah under Gedaliah's leadership. The picture is very different from the one generally assumed of life in Judah after Jerusalem's fall. There is an apparent abundance of foodstuffs to care for the needs of the community. As noted in *Form/Structure/Setting*, the positive tone of the passage sounds almost like propaganda.

There is no way to establish a precise date for these events. Were sufficient fields and vineyards left undamaged to make this scene possible soon after

Jerusalem's destruction or had sufficient time elapsed to allow the restoration of parts of the land? Holladay suggests a date of September/October 587 for the assassination of Gedaliah (2:287), which would place the events of Jer 40 some-time in the late summer of 587. Other scholars note the mention of a third deportation c. 582 (Jer 52:30), which may represent an aftershock to Gedaliah's assassination (see Bright, 253–54; Thompson, 657). Such a view would allow for a greater lapse of time between the fall of Jerusalem and the events of Jer 40–41.

Explanation

The story of Jeremiah's release to Gedaliah in Jer 40:1–6 begins with a dra-matic example of the prophetic understanding of the word from the LORD as universal word. The prophetic oracle is announced, but not delivered by the prophet. Instead, the word from the LORD comes from an unexpected source. Nebuzaradan, a Babylonian soldier, pronounces in grave tones the judgment of Yahweh upon Jerusalem. The intent is less historical than theological. No one should mistake the impact of the fall of Jerusalem. The blindness of Judean lead-ership is emphasized by the clarity of vision of a Babylonian conqueror. Even a godless pagan could see what Yahweh was doing.

The release of Jeremiah is an expected reward for one who had expressed clear sympathies toward Babylon during the crisis years. It mattered not that the prophet's motives had nothing to do with self-interest or political loyalty.

It is significant that Jeremiah chose to remain in Judah within the remnant community. Does the optimistic picture of vv 10–12 reflect Baruch's (and Jeremiah's) sense of hope? If so, it was a hope soon to be dashed by the lingering fires of nationalist passion.

The elevation of Gedaliah to governor, first noted in Jer 39, presented an op-portunity for Judah to minimize the trauma of defeat. The "poorest of the land" may have been the largest segment of the remnant community, but this chapter suggests they were not the only segment. Elements of the military had survived the conquest by Babylon and formed part of the emerging community. Jer 40:12 also indicates that a number of Jews who had fled the crisis returned when stabil-ity was regained under Gedaliah.

Jer 40 gives a glimpse of hope in the form of a revived community of survivors. Gedaliah was a realist with a pragmatic philosophy for addressing life under Babylonian rule. The way in which the theme of prosperity is developed in this chapter indicates the possibilities such pragmatism presents for a new Judah. The bright picture may be intentionally misleading, however. It is almost as if the theme of prosperity has been exaggerated for a purpose, to set the stage for the darker themes of tragedy to return in force. For all of Gedaliah's pragmatic wis-dom and abilities to mediate affairs between conquerors and conquered, subsequent passages indicate the kind of fatal flaws that seem pervasive among the leaders of Israel and Judah throughout their history.

Zedekiah personifies flawed character. His successor, appointed by the Babylonians, gifted in many respects with rare potential for leadership in a diffi-cult time, nevertheless soon exhibits his own flaws. The narrative, by means of two very different individuals who represent very different perspectives, tends to emphasize the kind of hubris with which Israel seemed to be afflicted through-out her history.

E. The Plot against Gedaliah (40:13–41:15 [LXX 47:13–48:15])

Bibliography

Ackroyd, P. R. *Exile and Restoration: A Study of Hebrew Thought of the Sixth Century* B.C. London: SCM, 1968. 25–28. **Dalglish, E. R.** "Chimham." *IDB* 1:561. **Herr, L. G.** "The Servant of Baalis." *BA* 48 (1985) 169–72. **Holladay, W. L.** "A Fresh Look at 'Source B' and 'Source C' in Jeremiah." In *A Prophet to the Nations: Essays in Jeremiah Studies*, ed. L. G. Perdue and B. W. Kovacs. Winona Lake, IN: Eisenbrauns, 1984. 213–28. **Jones, D. R.** "The Cessation of Sacrifice after the Destruction of the Temple in 586 B.C." *JTS* 14 (1963) 14–16. **McCown, C. C.**, ed. *Tell en Nasbeh I: Archeological and Historical Results*. Berkeley: Pacific School of Religion; New Haven: American Schools of Oriental Research, 1947. **Noth, M.** "The Jerusalem Catastrophe of 587 B.C. and Its Significance for Israel." In *The Laws in the Pentateuch and Other Studies*. Philadelphia: Fortress, 1967. 264. **Pohlmann, K.-F.** *Studien zum Jeremiabuch.* Göttingen: Vandenhoeck & Ruprecht, 1978. 108–22. **Pritchard, J. B.** "Gibeon." *IDB* 2:392–93. ———. "Gibeon's History." *SVT* 7 (1960) 1–12. ———. "The Water System at Gibeon." *BA* 19/4 (1956) 66–75. **Wampler, J. C.** *Excavations at Tell en-Nasbeh: 2. The Pottery.* Berkeley/New Haven: The Palestinian Institute of Pacific Schools of Religion and the American Schools of Oriental Research, 1947.

Translation

[13]*Johanan, the son of Kareah, and all the officers of the forces which were in the fields, came to Gedaliah at Mizpah,* [14]*and they said to him, "Do you know that Baalis, the king of the Ammonites, has sent*[a] *Ishmael the son of Nethaniah*[b] *to take your life?" But Gedaliah the son of Ahikam*[c] *would not believe them.* [15]*Then Johanan the son of Kareah*[a] *said to Gedaliah secretly at Mizpah, "Let me go and kill Ishmael the son of Nethaniah,*[b] *and no one will know; why should he take your life and all of Judah be scattered who have been gathered about you, and the remnant of Judah perish?"* [16]*But Gedaliah the son of Ahikam*[a] *said to Johanan the son of Kareah,*[b] *"Do not do*[c] *this thing, for you are speaking falsely about Ishmael."*

[41:1a]*In the seventh month, Ishmael the son of Nethaniah the son of Elishama*[b] *of the royal family,* [c]*who had been one of the chief officers of the king,*[c] *came with ten men to Gedaliah the son of Ahikam*[d] *at Mizpah. While they ate bread together there in Mizpah,*[e] [2]*Ishmael the son of Nethaniah*[a] *and the ten men who were with him arose and struck down Gedaliah* [b]*the son of Ahikam the son of Shaphan with the sword and killed*[c] *him,*[b] *whom the king of Babylon had made overseer in the land.* [3a]*Ishmael also struck down*[a] *all the Jews who were* [b]*with Gedaliah*[b] *in Mizpah*[c] *and the Chaldean soldiers*[d] *who were found there.*

⁴*On the day after the murder of Gedaliah,* ᵃ*when no one knew of it,* ᵃ ⁵*eighty men came from Shechem, from Shiloh,* ᵃ *and from Samaria, with their beards shaved and their garments torn and cutting themselves, with a grain offering and incense in their hands to bring to the house of the LORD.* ⁶*And Ishmael the son of Nethaniah* ᵃ *went out to meet them from Mizpah,* ᵇ ᶜ*weeping* ᵈ *as he went,* ᶜ ᵉ*and when he met them,* ᵉ *he said to them,* ᶠ "*Come in to Gedaliah the son of Ahikam.* "ᵍ

⁷*When they came into the middle of the city, Ishmael the son of Nethaniah* ᵃ *slaughtered them (and threw them)* ᵇ *in the middle* ᶜ *of the cistern,* ᵈ*he and the men who were with him.* ᵈ ⁸*But ten men were found among them* ᵃ *who said to Ishmael, "Do not kill us, for we have hidden treasures in the field: wheat, barley, oil, and honey"; so he stopped, and he did not kill them with their brothers.* ⁹*The cistern where Ishmael cast there all* ᵃ*the corpses of the men* ᵃ *whom he struck down,* ᵇ*a great cistern,* ᵇ *that which King Asa had made against Baasha the king of Israel, Ishmael the son of Nethaniah* ᶜ *filled it with the slain.* ¹⁰*And Ishmael took back* ᵃ *all the rest of the people who were in Mizpah,* ᵇ*the* ᶜ *daughters of the king,* ᵈ*and all the remaining people in Mizpah* ᵇᵈ *whom Nebuzaradan* ᵉ *the captain of the guard had entrusted to Gedaliah the son of Ahikam;* ᶠ*and Ishmael the son of Nethaniah captured* ᵍ *them,* ᶠ *and he went to cross over to the Ammonites.*

¹¹*When Johanan the son of Kareah and all the officers of the army who were with him heard all the evil which Ishmael the son of Nethaniah* ᵃ *had done,* ¹²*they took all the men* ᵃ *and went out to do battle with Ishmael the son of Nethaniah;* ᵇ *and they found him at the great pool which is in Gibeon.* ᶜ ¹³*When all the people who were with Ishmael saw Johanan the son of Kareah* ᵃ *and all* ᵇ *the officers of the army who were with him, they rejoiced.* ᶜ ¹⁴ᵃ*And all the people whom Ishmael had captured from Mizpah turned aside;* ᵃ *and they returned and went* ᵇ *to Johanan the son of Kareah.* ᶜ ¹⁵*But Ishmael the son of Nethaniah* ᵃ *slipped away from Johanan* ᵇ *with eight men and went to the Ammonites.*

Notes

14.a. LXX adds "to you."
14.b. LXX lacks "the son of Nethaniah."
14.c. LXX lacks "the son of Ahikam."
15.a. LXX lacks "the son of Kareah."
15.b. LXX lacks "the son of Nethaniah."
16.a. LXX lacks "the son of Ahikam."
16.b. LXX lacks "the son of Kareah."
16.c. K תעשׂה; Q תעשׂה, "do (not) do." GKC (§ 75hh) suggests the variation is related to pronunciation rather than an alteration in meaning.
41:1.a. Cf. 2 Kgs 25:25; this passage expands the account in 2 Kgs 25.
1.b. LXX has Ελεασα = אֶלְעָשָׂה, "Eleasah"; three codices of the Syr have "Ishmael."
1.c-c. Lacking in LXX and in 2 Kgs 25:25.
1.d. "the son of Ahikam" not present in LXX.
1.e. Second reference "in Mizpah" lacking in LXX.
2.a. LXX lacks "the son of Nethaniah."
2.b-b. This phrase does not appear in LXX.
2.c. Gk. recensions of Lucian and Origen, Syr, Tg, and Vg have pl form here; MT has sg.
3.a-a. Absent in LXX.
3.b-b. LXX lacks "with Gedaliah"; MT has lit. "with him, (that is) with Gedaliah."
3.c. *BHS* proposes reading "at the feast" (Rudolph, 214).
3.d. LXX lacks "soldiers," lit. "those who were soldiers."
4.a-a. Lacking in Syr.
5.a. LXX has καὶ ἀπὸ Σαλημ, "and from Salem"; LXXᴬ, α´, σ´, have Σαλωμ, "Salom."
6.a. LXX lacks "the son of Nethaniah."

6.b. "from Mizpah" not in LXX.

6.c-c. *BHS* suggests OG has αὐτοὶ ἐπορεύοντο καὶ ἔκλαιον, "he rushed at them and called (to them)."

6.d. Several MSS have וּבָכֹה, "weeping," qal inf abs, instead of MT וּבָכֹה, "weeping," qal act ptcp; see GKC § 113u; cf. 2 Sam 3:16.

6.e-e. Absent in LXX.

6.f. LXX lacks "to them."

6.g. "son of Ahikam" not in LXX.

7.a. "Ishmael the son of Nethaniah" is missing in LXX.

7.b. Syr, LXX^V, LXX^L add the equivalent of וַיַּשְׁלִיכֵם, "and he cast them"; cf. v 9.

7.c. אֶל־תּוֹךְ, "in the middle of," is lacking in LXX, but see *Note* 7.a.

7.d-d. "he and the men who were with him" not in LXX.

8.a. LXX has ἐκεῖ = שָׁם, "there," instead of "among them."

9.a-a. "the corpses of the men" not present in LXX.

9.b-b. MT has "by the hand of Gedaliah"; read instead, with LXX, φρέαρ μέγα = בּוֹר גָּדוֹל, "great cistern"; cf. 1 Macc 7:19.

9.c. "the son of Nethaniah" not in LXX.

10.a. Read with LXX καὶ ἀπέστρεψεν = וַיָּשֶׁב, "and took (them) back."

10.b-b. Syr lacks the entire phrase "the daughters of the king, and all the remaining people in Mizpah"; cf. *Note* 10.d-d. below.

10.c. *BHS* suggests reading with many MSS (LXX and some Tg MSS) וְאֵת, "*and* (the daughters of the king)."

10.d-d. LXX lacks "and all the remaining people in Mizpah."

10.e. "Nebuzaradan" absent in LXX.

10.f-f. LXX lacks "and Ishmael the son of Nethaniah captured them."

10.g. A few MSS have וַיַּשְׁכֵּם, "and he rose early," rather than וַיִּשְׁבֵּם, "and he captured them."

11.a. LXX lacks "the son of Nethaniah."

12.a. LXX has τὸ στρατόπεδον αὐτῶν, "their army."

12.b. Instead of "with Ishmael the son of Nethaniah," LXX has "with him."

12.c. *BHS* proposes בְּגֶבַע, "in Gibeah."

13.a. LXX lacks "the son of Kareah."

13.b. "all" absent in LXX.

13.c. LXX lacks "they rejoiced."

14.a-a. Absent in LXX.

14.b. "and went" lacking in LXX.

14.c. LXX lacks "the son of Kareah."

15.a. LXX lacks "the son of Nethaniah."

15.b. LXX lacks "from Johanan."

Form/Structure/Setting

The final section of Jer 40 and the bulk of Jer 41 focus upon the plot by Ishmael, one of the members of the royal family, to assassinate Gedaliah. The manner in which the plot is revealed and ultimately carried out suggests the possibility that more is at work in the larger narrative than simply the description of events. At least three major characters within the framework of Jer 37–44 exhibit flawed judgment. Their decisions and actions serve to underscore the tragic nature of Judah's overall history. When faced with choices that may result in good or ill for the people, inevitably the choices result in disastrous consequences for the individual involved, for the people, or for both.

40:13–16 introduces Ishmael's plot against Gedaliah. Johanan and other military officers attempt to warn Gedaliah of the danger he faces from Ishmael, but to no avail. The pattern of ignored warnings began with Zedekiah at the beginning of Jer 37. Gedaliah becomes the second key figure to ignore warnings that have grave implications for the future of the remnant community. Johanan will complete the pattern in Jer 43.

The conspiracy of Ishmael is important in its own right in the larger message of Jeremiah but may be of greatest significance as it signals a consistent pattern of poor judgment and, in the cases of Zedekiah and Johanan, direct disobedience to divine word. Is this an indirect means of shifting all arenas of hope to the exilic community in Babylon? The effect is clearly to discredit any claims for future hope based in Judah. The glowing portrait of prosperity in Jer 40:1–12 takes on an ironic quality in the face of subsequent events.

41:1–3 describes the actual assassination of Gedaliah by Ishmael and his cohorts. Though Pohlmann (*Studien*, 115–16) would not concur, the description of events seems consistent with what has been introduced in the preceding chapter.

The timing of Ishmael's dastardly act is assumed by most interpreters to be relatively soon after the fall of Jerusalem and the establishment of Gedaliah as governor. September/October 587 B.C., only a few short months after the siege ended, is the date of choice for a number of scholars (Holladay, 2:296; Rudolph, 215). Others (Bright, 254; Thompson, 657) note that much has happened in the recorded narrative since the account of the fall of Jerusalem, perhaps more than would be likely in such a short period of time. All of these scholars noted consider the early date to be most consistent with a straightforward reading of the text. Hyatt (5:778, 1087) considers a third deportation by the Babylonians in 582 B.C. to be in retaliation for the assassination of Gedaliah. He therefore assumes a five-year period in which Gedaliah served as governor. As indicated, the text would seem to support the former views rather than the latter.

The pilgrim episode of vv 4–7 provides near sensory overload with the vivid description of Ishmael's vile murder of innocent worshipers who happen to be in the wrong place at the wrong time. Pohlmann (116) suggests that the pilgrim episode may originally have been separate from the reference to the ten men of v 8. Hidden foodstores could relate to persons already living in the vicinity of Mizpah rather than to persons new to the region. On the other hand, the stores could just as well be goods hidden by the pilgrims prior to approaching Mizpah (Holladay, 2:297–98), or the reference could be to goods still in the possession of family members in the north, available as a ransom for those whom Ishmael held captive (Bright, 254).

It seems clear that the eighty men referred to in v 5 were on their way to Jerusalem as part of some kind of vow—hence their appearance and the offerings of cereal grains and incense. There is no obvious discontinuity between the description of Ishmael's murderous actions and the pleas of the ten men in v 8. In fact, such a scene would be quite consistent with the larger context. In any case, the murder of pilgrims serves to emphasize the brutality of Ishmael and is a fitting inclusion within the larger story of intrigue.

Vv 9–10 are almost an aside. Specific information is provided about the cistern where Ishmael disposed of the bodies of his victims. It was the cistern built by King Asa of Judah as described in 1 Kgs 15:16–22.

The members of the larger party forced to travel with Ishmael are also noted. Jeremiah should be a part of the group gathered at Mizpah with Gedaliah; yet no specific reference is made to him in this account. Only in 42:2 is Jeremiah again mentioned, when he is called upon to provide a word from the LORD for the group headed for Egypt. This passage is one of the key texts involved in the broader discussion of Mowinckel's Source B and Source C in Jeremiah (see Holladay, "A Fresh Look," 213–16.).

The simplest explanation for the absence of any mention of Jeremiah in this passage is to suggest the incorporation into the larger narrative of historical information that originally had no connection with Jeremiah. These are obviously key events, and their inclusion at this point in the Jeremiah corpus is helpful in providing a fuller picture of the crisis at hand. Jer 41 expands considerably the brief description of 2 Kgs 25:25 related to the same incident. 2 Kings also neglects any mention of the prophet. It would not be at all unexpected to have originally unconnected references to similar events brought together in the manner found in Jer 40–42. The alternative explanation, that Jeremiah was away from Mizpah at the time (Thompson, 661, notes this as one option), has no more concrete evidence to support it.

The reference to the "king's daughters" (v 10) is something of a puzzle. The most obvious explanation is to assume that the reference is to daughters of Zedekiah, though Holladay (2:298) notes the oddity of such potentially important captives being left behind by the Babylonians, particularly in light of the treatment predicted for Zedekiah's wives before the fall of Jerusalem (38:23).

The final episode is the account of Ishmael's pursuit by Johanan and forces loyal to the assassinated governor. A group of captives (referred to in v 10) is forced to go with Ishmael and his companions on their flight to Ammon. One of the puzzling aspects of the flight of Ishmael is its route. The MT indicates Ishmael went initally to Gibeon, to the southwest of Mizpah and in the opposite direction from Ammon. *BHS* proposes an alternative reading, "Gibeah," which would seem more logical in that the proposed location of Gibeah is more on a direct route between Mizpah and Ammon. On the other hand, references to the "great pool" (v 12) seem to fit what is known of the pool at Gibeon (see Pritchard, *BA* 19/4 (1956) 66–75). Some unstated reason might have existed for Ishmael to go first to Gibeon. The puzzle is not capable of simple solution. Holladay's (2:294) alternative site for Mizpah (Nebi Samwil; see *Form/Structure/Setting* for Jer 40) could perhaps afford a more direct route to Ammon through Gibeon, but the evidence is inconclusive.

The last sequence of verses describes the flight of Ishmael along with eight of his followers to safety among the Ammonites. The Ammonite king, Baalis, has been named in preceding texts as a sponsor for Ishmael's deeds, so Ishmael flees to Ammon when the pursuing forces led by Johanan overtake him. The Ammonite role in the events is not altogether clear, though Rudolph (215) suggests that the Ammonite king used to his own advantage the jealous response of Ishmael to the appointment of Gedaliah as governor. What advantage the Ammonites would gain by means of this intrigue is difficult to determine, but such international treachery was not (and is not) uncommon.

Comment

13–14 Johanan and others among the Judean officers make Gedaliah aware of a plot against him devised by Ishmael. The tone of this verse (v 14) suggests that no great mystery surrounded the plot. Gedaliah is not willing to heed the warning.

There are reasonable explanations for Gedaliah's response. He had no doubt functioned as a government official at a time when Ishmael was a prince in the royal household. As Carroll (707) notes, his reluctance may also indicate a leader intent on preventing factional discord, refusing to accept what he deems baseless rumors.

The plot itself is also understandable, given the emotional intensity with which many in Judah had experienced the events related to Jerusalem's fall. The plots against Jeremiah recorded earlier in the book serve to highlight that intensity. The Babylonians were the clear enemy: they had destroyed the beloved city and the temple; they had been the architects of a terrible siege. Furthermore, there were apparently still external elements that encouraged action against Babylon, as illustrated by the references to the Ammonite king, Baalis (40:14). Gedaliah would have been seen by diehard groups in Judah as a Babylonian puppet and a traitor. The mystery may be in the unwillingness of Gedaliah to recognize the peril at hand.

15–16 In a later secret meeting, Johanan continues to urge Gedaliah to take the danger from Ishmael seriously. He even proposes a drastic measure to counter the plot, the assassination of Ishmael, as a means of preserving what was beginning to emerge as a renewed community in Judah. He rightly observes that any action like the rumored plot of Ishmael will prove fatal not only to Gedaliah but to the entire community.

In spite of the repeated warnings by Johanan and others, Gedaliah will not believe the rumors about Ishmael. He refuses to allow any action against Ishmael by Johanan.

41:1–3 Jer 41 quickly provides justification for the fears of Johanan expressed in the previous passage, in an incident described as occurring "in the seventh month." Unresolved is whether this was September/October 587 B.C. or the same time of year in a later year (see *Form/Structure/Setting* above). Ishmael, identified as a member of the royal family, comes to Mizpah to meet with Gedaliah. Ishmael was named in 40:8 as one of the officers remaining in Judah after the fall of Jerusalem to whom Gedaliah made an appeal for loyalty to the Babylonians. The events of Jer 41 suggest that Ishmael considered Gedaliah's attempt at harmony to be foolish at best, treasonous at worst.

In the course of a meal with Gedaliah, Ishmael and the ten who are with him assassinate the governor. The choice of setting adds to the sense of treachery. It is hard to imagine a more horrid breach of proper conduct than this bloodthirsty response to Gedaliah's hospitality.

V 3 describes the slaughter of "all the Jews who were with Gedaliah" along with the hapless Babylonian soldiers who had been left with him at Mizpah. No further explanation is given for "all the Jews." V 10 indicates that a number of people were left alive in Mizpah, so "all the Jews" may be intended as some sort of special label. Another alternative is to classify this as one of the many "inconsistencies" common to this set of narratives.

Consistent with the rest of this chapter, no mention is made of the prophet Jeremiah. One would assume from earlier narratives that Jeremiah was with Gedaliah. If so, he somehow escaped the swords of the assassins, though his espoused policy of appeasement with the Babylonians would seem to make him a likely target of persons like Ishmael.

4–8   Vv 4–8 describe the arrival in Mizpah of a group of northern pilgrims unaware of the assassination of Gedaliah. From their description, these are religious pilgrims bringing offerings to the temple in Jerusalem. They bear the marks of fasting (torn clothing, gashed bodies) and apparently stop to make a courtesy call upon the governor of the territory.

Ishmael meets them at the gate, weeping, and invites them into the city. The tears of Ishmael are obviously portrayed as a form of subterfuge, but their precise intent is not given. The incident with the pilgrims boldly underscores the terrible nature of Ishmael's actions. He is pictured as one who will stop at nothing in carrying out his vendetta against all who have willing contact with Babylon.

Once in the city, the pilgrims are brutally murdered by Ishmael and his followers. Ten of the eighty pilgrims are able to barter hidden foodstores in exchange for their lives. The bodies of the other seventy are tossed into a cistern (about which further details are furnished in v 9).

9–10   The word picture of v 9 continues to build the horror of the larger scene. An apparently empty cistern is filled with the corpses of the slain pilgrims. Reference to the cistern's connection to King Asa reflects a time of earlier tension between the two Israels. The reference may be intended as no more than a concrete historical contact for the slaughter by Ishmael. A more speculative reading could possibly note a linkage between two times of disorder, characteristic of the hubris that had afflicted Israel throughout her history, though such a proposal is indeed only speculation.

Those left alive in Mizpah are forced to leave the city with Ishmael as he sets out with them toward Ammon. V 10 continues the theme of Ammonite involvement, but with no further clarity regarding its nature or purpose.

11–12   News of the slaughter at Mizpah brings immediate reaction from Johanan and the other Judean military leaders. Ishmael is pursued and overtaken at the pool of Gibeon. It is somewhat curious that Ishmael went to Gibeon if his ultimate destination was Ammon, since Gibeon is in the opposite direction, southwest of Mizpah (if traditional locales are accepted). Ammon was to the east or northeast. Was he after the foodstuffs referred to by the spared pilgrims? This is yet another of the puzzles found in the larger narrative scheme. One resolution of the puzzle is possible by accepting the emendation suggested by *BHS* which reads "Gibeah" instead of "Gibeon." Gibeah would more nearly fall along the normal route from Mizpah to Ammon.

Pritchard (*BA* 19/4 (1956) 66–75) provides rather substantial verification for the location of Gibeon. The expedition he describes in his article found a very large pool with access by a stepped tunnel near the modern village of el-Jib, some eight miles north of Jerusalem. Pottery at the site was marked with the name Gibeon and dated from the time of the events described in Jer 41 and earlier. The issue is whether one reads "Gibeon" or "Gibeah" in v 12. Details regarding the pool fit with "Gibeon" but indicate a seemingly illogical course of travel by Ishmael.

13–15   When pressed by Johanan and other pursuers, Ishmael and eight of his companions abandon their captives and escape to Ammon. Clearly, Johanan's forces would have outnumbered the small group led by Ishmael. The Mizpah captives welcome Johanan and his accompanying force with rejoicing. These verses suggest that Johanan became de facto leader of the survivors from Mizpah.

Explanation

The brutal murders of Gedaliah and many of those with him illustrate the tragic nature of Israel's larger history. As the book of Jeremiah tells the story, it becomes much like a classical tragedy. There are many opportunities for change that would yield a positive future, but some flawed decision or flawed character always stands in the way.

Jer 40:13–41:15 provides two such flaws. (1) Gedaliah rejects clear warnings about Ishmael's intentions. Had the governor been more willing to listen to the counsel of the other military officers, the tragedy might have been avoided. (2) Ishmael's flaw seems to be his blind hatred of anything Babylonian and of those who do not share his opinion about Babylon. The two ingredients provide the recipe for disaster at Mizpah.

There appears to be some hope for the future under the leadership of Gedaliah and the more lenient policies that the Babylonians impose through him. With his death, all of that changes dramatically. Though Jeremiah would argue strongly against the decision to flee to Egypt, his seems to be a lonely voice very much in the minority. Once the dread scenes of Jer 41 are played out, hope for the future moves from the immediate to the distant future. Hope becomes a casualty of flawed character, flawed choices, and too fragile faith.

F. The Flight to Egypt (41:16–42:22 [LXX 48:16–49:22])

Bibliography

Berridge, J. M. *Prophet, People and the Word of Yahweh: An Examination of Form and Content in the Proclamation of the Prophet Jeremiah.* Basel Studies of Theology 4. Zurich: EVZ, 1970. 202–7. **Reventlow, H. G. von.** *Liturgie und prophetisches Ich bei Jeremia.* Gütersloh: Gütersloher (Mohn), 1966. 143–49. **Kremers, H.** "Leidensgemeinschaft mit Gott im Alten Testament." *EvT* 13 (1953) 122–40. **North, R.** "Palestine, Administration of (Judean Officials)." *ABD* 5:87. **Pohlmann, K.-F.** *Studien zum Jeremiabuch.* Göttingen: Vandenhoeck & Ruprecht, 1978. 123–45. **Stulman, L.** *The Other Text of Jeremiah.* Lanham, MD: UP of America, 1985. 150–56. **Wanke, G.** *Untersuchungen zur sogenannten Baruchschrift.* BZAW 122. Berlin: de Gruyter, 1971. 116–33.

Translation

[16]*Then Johanan the son of Kareah*[a] *and all of the officers of the army who were with him took all the rest of the people whom Ishmael* [b]*the son of Nethaniah* [c]*had brought from*[c] *Mizpah after he had struck down Gedaliah the son of Ahikam,*[b] *men,*[d] *women, children,*[e] *and officials*[f] *whom he had brought from Gibeon.*[g] [17]*And they went and*

dwelled at Geruth[a] *Chimham,*[b] *which is near Bethlehem, intending to go to Egypt,* [18]*away from the Chaldeans because they were afraid of them, because Ishmael the son of Nethaniah*[a] *had struck down Gedaliah the son of Ahikam*[b] *whom the king of Babylon had made overseer over the land.*

[42:1]*Then all of the officers of the army, and Johanan the son of Kareah,*[a] *and Jezaniah*[b] *the son of Hoshaiah,*[c] *and all the people, from the least to the greatest, drew near;* [2]*and they said to Jeremiah the prophet, "Let our supplications fall before you and intercede on our behalf*[a] *to the LORD your God,* [b]*on behalf of all of this remnant,*[b] *because we are left, only a few from the multitude, just as you see us.*[c] [3]*Let the LORD your God*[a] *tell us the way we should go and what we should do."* [4]*Jeremiah the prophet*[a] *said to them, "I have heard; behold, I will pray to the LORD your God*[b] *according to your words, and whatever*[c] *the LORD shall respond to you,* [d] *I will tell you; I will not hold back anything from you."* [5]*Then they said to Jeremiah, "May the LORD be a true and faithful witness against us if we do not do everything which the LORD your God*[a] *sends you for us.* [6]*Whether it is good or evil, we will obey the voice of the LORD our God to whom we*[a] *are sending you, so that it may be well with us, for we will obey the voice of the LORD our God."*

[7]*At the end of ten days the word of the LORD came to Jeremiah.* [8]*Then he called Johanan the son of Kareah,*[a] *and all*[b] *of the officers of the army who were with him,*[c] *and all of the people, from the least to the greatest.* [9]*He said to them, "Thus says the LORD,* [a]*the God of Israel, to whom you sent me to let your supplications fall before him.*[a] [10]*'If you return*[a] *and abide in this land, then I will build you up, and I will not tear down, and I will plant you, and I will not pluck up, for I repent concerning the evil which I did to you.* [11]*Do not be afraid of the king of Babylon, whom you now fear; do not be afraid of him,'*[a] *says the LORD, 'because I am with you to deliver you and to snatch you away from his hand.* [12]*I will be merciful*[a] *to you, so that he will be merciful to you and bring you back*[bc] *to your land.* [13]*But if you say "we will not remain in this land" and if you do not obey the voice of the LORD your God,*[a] [14]*saying, "No,*[a] *for we will go to the land of Egypt where we will not see war nor hear the sound of the trumpet nor be hungry for bread, and we will live there,"* [15]*. . . therefore, hear the word of the LORD, O remnant of Judah,*[a] *thus says the LORD of Hosts, the God of Israel,*[b] *if you indeed*[c] *set your face to go*[d] *to Egypt and go to dwell there,* [16]*then the sword which you fear will overtake you there*[a] *in the land of*[b] *Egypt, and the famine about which you are anxious will cling to you there*[c] *in Egypt,*[d] *and there you will die.* [17]*All of the men*[a] *who set their faces to go*[b] *to Egypt*[c] *to dwell there will die by the sword, by famine, or by plague,*[d] *and there will not be for them a survivor*[e] *or a fugitive from the disaster which I am bringing upon them.'*

[18]*"For thus says the LORD of Hosts, the God of Israel,*[a] *'just as my anger and*[b] *my rage were poured out upon the inhabitants of Jerusalem, so will my rage be poured out upon you when you go to Egypt; and you will become an oath, a waste, a curse, and a reproach, and you will not see this place again.'*[c] [19]*The LORD spoke*[a] *to you, O remnant of Judah, 'Do not go to Egypt.' Know*[b] *for a certainty that I have warned you today*[c] [20]*that you have erred*[a] *at the cost of your souls, for*[b] *you sent me to the LORD your God,*[c] *saying, 'pray on our behalf to the LORD our God,*[d] *and everything which the LORD our God*[d] *shall say, thus you shall tell us*[e] *and we will do it.'* [21]*And I told you today,*[a] *and you did not obey the voice of the LORD your God for anything*[bc] *which he sent me to (tell) you.* [22]*And now you will know for a certainty that*[a] *you will die by the sword, by famine, and by pestilence*[b] *in the place where you desire to go to sojourn."*

Notes

16.a. LXX lacks "the son of Kareah."

16.b-b. The entire phrase "the son of Nethaniah (had brought) from Mizpah after he had struck down Gedaliah the son of Ahikam" is missing in LXX.

16.c-c. *BHS* suggests reading שָׁבָה אֹתָם, "he had taken (them) captive" for MT הֵשִׁיב מֵאֵת, "he had brought back"; cf. v 14. See also Holladay (2:273) and Rudolph (216), among others.

16.d. MT has גְּבָרִים, "men"; the connotation is strength. A few MSS have גִּבּוֹרִים, "strong"; cf. LXX, Tg, and Vg. אַנְשֵׁי הַמִּלְחָמָה, "warriors," is considered by most scholars to be added to the earlier text; *Translation* above omits it; cf. Stulman (*Other Text*, 150), Rudolph (216), Bright (255), and Thompson (659).

16.e. LXX has καὶ τὰ λοιπά, "and the rest"; cf. 43:6.

16.f. Heb. סָרִסִים, is often translated as "eunuchs," but in this setting "officials" is to be preferred. See North, *ABD* 5:87; also cf. *Notes* on Jer 38:7.

16.g. *BHS* proposes בְּגֶבַע, "from Gibeah"; cf. v 12. *Translation* above retains "Gibeon."

17.a. While this word is treated as a place name above, *BHS* proposes a meaning "in a lodging place"; various MSS choose different options here: σ΄, Tg, Vg follow essentially what *BHS* proposes; LXX, θ΄ have a proper noun, "Gaberoth"; α΄ has "in the walls"; Syr, "in the threshing floor."

17.b. כְּמוֹהֶם, "Chimoham," in K is not clear; Q suggests כְּמָהּ, "Chimham," a place name near Bethlehem, location unknown, but associated with a son of Barzillai in 2 Sam 19:38 (cf. Thompson [662], Holladay [2:273]); *Translation* above follows Q.

18.a. "the son of Nethaniah" not in LXX.

18.b. LXX lacks "the son of Ahikam."

42:1.a. LXX lacks "the son of Kareah."

1.b. *BHS* suggests reading וַעֲזַרְיָה, "Azariah," with LXX; cf. 43:2.

1.c. LXX has Μαασαίου, "Maaseiah," here and at 43:2; MT has "Hoshaiah" in both places. There is no way to determine the better reading; cf. Bright (250) and Holladay (2:273).

2.a. "on our behalf" absent in LXX; LXX has "to him."

2.b-b. Syr lacks "on behalf of all of this remnant."

2.c. LXX lacks "us."

3.a. A few MSS have "our God" here.

4.a. "the prophet" not in LXX.

4.b. LXX has *our* God.

4.c. MT has lit. "every word"; LXX lacks כל, "every." *Translation* above renders this phrase "whatever."

4.d. MT has אֶתְכֶם, "you"; LXX lacks "you"; *BHS* proposes the possible reading "your God" instead of "you" here.

5.a. LXX lacks "your God."

6.a. Q has אֲנַחְנוּ, "we," the normal Heb. form; K has the postbiblical form אָנוּ, "we," the only occurrence in biblical Heb. (Holladay, 2:274).

8.a. "son of Kareah" absent in LXX.

8.b. LXX lacks "all."

8.c. LXX lacks "who were with him."

9.a-a. This entire phrase is absent in LXX.

10.a. LXX, Vg, Tg change to the inf abs of יָשַׁב, "stay," to match the finite verb that immediately follows, but Holladay (2:274) suggests MT can be properly read as is with the same grammatical force.

11.a. LXX lacks "of him."

12.a. MT reads וְאֶתֵּן לָכֶם רַחֲמִים, lit. "and I will give you mercies." LXX, Syr, Vg have sg "mercy."

12.b. LXX reads "I will restore you to your land" in place of the MT "(he will) bring you back (restore you) to your land."

12.c. α΄, Syr, Vg have καὶ καθίσω ὑμᾶς, "and I will make you sit" = Heb. יָשַׁב. Thompson (666) suggests reading both רחם, "show mercy," and הֵשִׁיב, "make return," as inf abs, retaining the first person pattern noted in the LXX and other versions with Yahweh as subj.

13.a. LXX lacks "your God."

14.a. לֵאמֹר לֹא, "saying, No," does not appear in LXX.

15.a. "O remnant of Judah" not present in LXX.

15.b. LXX lacks the expanded title "of Hosts, the God of Israel."

15.c. The emphatic construction in MT of inf abs followed by finite verb, tr. above "indeed set," does not appear in LXX.

15.d. "to go" lacking in LXX.

16.a. "there" not in LXX.

16.b. LXX does not have "the land of."

16.c. LXX lacks "there."

16.d. Read with LXX "in Egypt"; MT lacks the prep.

17.a. LXX adds "and all the strangers."

17.b. LXX lacks "to go."

17.c. LXX expands "to Egypt" (MT) to "to the land of Egypt."

17.d. "or by plague" absent in LXX.

17.e. LXX lacks שָׂרִיד, "a survivor."

18.a. LXX lacks "of Hosts, the God of Israel."

18.b. LXX lacks "my anger and."

18.c. *BHS* suggests the transposition of 42:19–22 and 43:1–3; vv 19–22 assume a rejection of Jeremiah's word (Holladay, 2:275), which is explicit in 43:1–3. If the verses are transposed, וַיֹּאמֶר יִרְמְיָהוּ, "and Jeremiah said," should be inserted at the beginning of v 19.

19.a. *BHS* suggests the alternative "This is the word of the LORD" for "The LORD spoke," though see *Note* 18.c.

19.b. LXX precedes the emphatic construction "know" by the words "and now."

19.c. LXX lacks the end of the verse in MT, "that I have warned you today."

20.a. K reading is not clear; read with Q, הִתְעֵיתֶם, "you have erred." *BHS* proposes, with MS support, הֲרֵעֹתֶם, "you have done evil."

20.b. "For" lacking in LXX.

20.c. LXX does not have "to the LORD your God."

20.d. "our God" absent in LXX.

20.e. LXX lacks "thus you shall tell us."

21.a. "And I told you today" not in LXX.

21.b. LXX lacks "your God for anything."

21.c. *BHS* proposes, with MSS support, reading לְכֹל, "for anything," instead of וּלְכֹל, "and for anything." The LXX reading is clearer here: "But you have not obeyed the voice of the LORD who sent me to you." *Translation* above follows *BHS* suggestion.

22.a. "you will know for a certainty that" lacking in LXX.

22.b. LXX lacks "and by pestilence."

Form/Structure/Setting

The passage that begins in Jer 41:16 and ends in 43:7 provides what Carroll (714) describes as the "last stage of the story of the fate of Gedaliah's community." In this episode, Jeremiah once again assumes a pivotal role after his unexplained absence in the preceding passages (40:7–41:15). Jer 42 provides an inclusio with Jer 37 in the larger unit of Jer 37–44. Just as Zedekiah is presented as one who would not listen to the words of the LORD (37:2), so Johanan and those who are with him ultimately reject the word from the LORD, though they have specifically requested such a word.

The request made by Johanan and company (42:2) uses almost the same wording as that of Zedekiah in 37:3. In both cases, those making the request for a word from the LORD are presented as unwilling to abide by that word (37:2; 42:21). Such similarity in form suggests similarity in circumstance, with the end of any hope for the future vested in the Judean survivors.

The impact of this request pattern and its outcome is exaggerated by other structural features in the chapter. Thompson (664) points out the strong language used by the people. Yahweh is referred to as a "true and faithful" witness rather than merely a witness. The strong pledge of the people at the time of their request adds emphasis to their disobedience when the word from the LORD is disregarded. Holladay (2:299) refers to this pattern as "rhetorical overkill." The exaggerated rhetoric accompanies a clear implication that the decision to go to Egypt has already been made (41:17). The ten-day waiting period is yet another element in the structure that emphasizes the disobedience of the people. The result is a rather strange picture of a people who essentially call a curse upon themselves by their knowing rejection of a divine word.

Considerable discussion has transpired regarding the final section of Jer 42. As indicated in *Notes* above (see *Note* 18.c.), a number of scholars (Rudolph, 218–19; Bright, 258; Holladay, 2:285) have suggested that Jer 42:19–22 and 43:1–3 should be transposed. 42:19–22 seems to assume a negative response to the requested word from the LORD, a response that is explicitly given in 43:1–3. Shifting the placement of the verses indicated provides a very clear reading, but as Carroll (719) and Thompson (667) indicate, it is not necessary. The very strong warning of 42:15–17 seems to imply that a negative response is expected by Jeremiah, as does the stated intention of 41:17.

Comment

16–18 Once the immediate crisis regarding the Mizpah captives was resolved, an even more serious dilemma had to be addressed. What would happen when the Babylonian authorities learned of the carnage at Mizpah?

Johanan (v 16) summarily lists those who were included among Ishmael's captives: soldiers, women, children, and officials. One question that has been asked of this verse in relation to the larger episode involves the "soldiers." Why would "soldiers" be powerless against a small force like that of Ishmael's (see Carroll, 713)? It would seem that some reasonable effort to thwart Ishmael would have been attempted. These soldiers are treated as powerless in their contact with Ishmael.

When Johanan rescues the captives from Mizpah, the entire party moves to an intermediate stop near Bethlehem, apparently to consider their options. The choice is made to leave for Egypt in order to escape the repercussions expected from Babylon. Such trepidation was probably warranted, given the way powers like Babylon tended to respond to any act deemed rebellious on the part of a conquered people. Nevertheless, Jeremiah insists (42:11) that no repercussion need be feared.

42:1–3 The initial verses of Jer 42 reintroduce Jeremiah to the narrative. The passage uses descriptive language to indicate a wholesale appeal to the prophet for a definitive word from the LORD. "All the commanders," three of whom are named, as well as "all the people from the least to the greatest," bring their request to Jeremiah.

As Holladay has noted (2:285), the request made to Jeremiah by Johanan and others in the group of survivors balances the similar pattern of request for divine guidance involving Zedekiah in Jer 37. It seems likely that the use of similar "request" forms is intended to communicate powerfully the theological significance of the events that next unfold. It is not just the form of the request made to the prophet that is similar. There is also a similarity in outcomes.

Emphasis is given in v 2 to the "remnant" that the group under Johanan represents. Only these few are left of what was once the nation of Judah. Jeremiah is assured that once the word from the LORD is given, it will be heeded. Holladay (2:299) suggests that Jeremiah knows of the intentions of Johanan to go to Egypt, in spite of the interest expressed in hearing the word from the LORD. Jer 41:17 indicates precisely such intentions.

Why would the request be made of Jeremiah if there was no intent to act on the prophet's words? This question is not easy to answer, but the pattern indicated is a recurring one for Judah.

An issue that also may relate to this request is the instruction given to the prophet Jeremiah in Jer 11:14 not to intercede on the people's behalf. Johanan is asking Jeremiah to do precisely that. Is the instruction of 11:14 still operative? Does the prophet have the option of "interceding" for this people? It can be argued that the events surrounding the fall of Jerusalem have created a new environment of possibility. Even Jeremiah considers hope for the future to be possible under certain conditions.

4 Jeremiah takes them at their word and promises to do as they have requested. As is true of the passage describing the request given to Jeremiah, this verse also contains some points of exceptional emphasis. Vv 1–3 stress the inclusive desire of "all" to hear a word from the LORD. Jeremiah, in v 4, stresses his intention to deliver "all" of that word to the people. "I will not hold back anything from you" (42:4).

5–6 The emphatic exchange continues in vv 5–6. Johanan and those with him vow to act in response to the word from the LORD, "whether it is good or evil." A key may be found in the final phrase of v 6, where the supplicants insist that they will obey the word that Jeremiah brings from the LORD, "whether it is good or evil."

The dramatic pledge to obey sets the stage for an equally dramatic word of judgment when the pledge is ignored. As noted earlier in comments related to Jer 36, it is difficult to determine which act of rebellion is most egregious, that of the openly defiant Jehoiakim or that of persons who pledge obedience with no intention of fulfilling their pledge.

7–8 V 7 provides for a significant passage of time. There is a delay of ten days while the prophet waits for a word from the LORD. At the end of ten days, the word of the LORD comes to Jeremiah, and he calls together Johanan and the entire assembly to announce that word. In keeping with the rhetorical pattern established earlier (v 1), "all the people, from the least to the greatest," are called to hear Jeremiah's announcement.

One of the fascinating elements in this episode involves the delay by Jeremiah to await the word from the LORD. It seems very clear from the outset that the intention of the group is already firm; they intend to go to Egypt (see Holladay, 2:299). Jeremiah appears to be fully aware of the group's plans. Even so, the word from the LORD is diligently sought by the prophet. Jeremiah does not predetermine either what Yahweh will do or what the people will do. The prophetic calling as mediator is taken with utmost seriousness, allowing full freedom both to God and to the people.

Carroll (717) comments on the passivity of Jeremiah in this episode. Carroll suggests that Jeremiah moves from an activist figure in Jer 1–25 to become increasingly passive, until in Jer 37–45 he is "almost inert." Carroll proposes (669) that Jeremiah's role is of less significance than the centrality of the "word" from the LORD that emerges in these chapters of the book.

The contents of Jer 37–45 do not contradict Carroll's proposal. Indeed, the prophet's absence in a significant portion of this section underscores his lesser role. Of greatest importance is the final description of faithlessness on the part of the Judean survivors.

9–12 Jeremiah announces the LORD's response to the "supplications" of the Judean community. The response is consistent with the convictions the prophet repeatedly professed during the years of political crisis; hope for the future continues to exist only in submission to Babylonian suzerainty. "Return" is used with potential double meaning. Actual physical return to Mizpah is an obvious surface meaning of the instruction that Jeremiah brings from Yahweh, but "return" is also the key term for repentance. It is not yet too late for that kind of "turning" on the part of the survivors. The bounty explicitly described in 40:12 can be the reward for faithfulness.

The divine response reported by Jeremiah follows the classic pattern of covenant promise/warning. Yahweh is ever in dynamic relationship with Judah/Israel, "repenting," changing judgment into forgiveness in response to the "turning" of Judah/Israel in repentance. The use of the covenant formula in this way makes the refusal of the audience to hear an even more radical act of disobedience.

There is hope for a future in Judah if the word from the LORD is heeded. The structure of this chapter, perhaps even the structure of the entire section of Jer 37–44, seems to suggest that such hope will go unclaimed because of a refusal to hear. In the present text, those who have explicitly requested a word from the LORD will ultimately reject it.

The message of the text seems less directed to its contextual audience than to later audiences. The way in which the events are described leaves little hope for a positive outcome; Johanan and those with him are determined to go to Egypt. Subsequent events will demonstrate the folly of such a choice. When this message is shared with future generations, the appeal is given even greater force by the structure in which it is placed.

V 12 underscores the sovereignty of Judah's God, one who is more in control than is the king of Babylon. For that reason, the king of Babylon need not be feared. Covenant is with one far greater than he. If that assurance will not be heard by Johanan and his followers, perhaps someone will hear it.

13–17 Covenant language is often set in the tone of promise/warning. Vv 13–17 provide the warning to those who refuse to hear and heed Yahweh's word. Not to remain in the land is to disobey the voice of the LORD (v 13).

The reason the surviving remnant intends to go to Egypt is noted in v 14. They say no to Yahweh because they believe that in Egypt famine and warfare can be avoided. The LORD's sovereignty is once again emphasized in v 15. Just as Yahweh's sovereignty can insure the safety of the faithful against repercussions from the king of Babylon, so will the judgment of Yahweh reach even to Egypt. The feared outcome that Johanan and company seek to avoid by fleeing to Egypt will follow them there. The language of v 17 emphasizes the horrors of war and its effects on a population. Sword, famine, and plague will come to Egypt. Those who seek to survive by disobeying and disregarding the word from the LORD will find that disregarding that word will in fact rob them of any survivors, a fate worse than that which they might imagine if they remained in the land and experienced the worst at the hands of the king of Babylon.

It is Yahweh who both plants and plucks up. Throughout the message of Jeremiah, that truth has been repeatedly emphasized. Whether it is Judah/Israel or some other nation, planting and plucking up are within Yahweh's domain. Within the larger prophetic tradition, it seems that Judah/Israel is willing to hear and accept the "planting" role of Yahweh when it applies to them. They are seldom if ever willing to hear the "plucking up" role of Yahweh directed toward them. It is perhaps for that reason that the latter seems almost to be the thematic word for the prophetic tradition.

18–22 The final section is Jeremiah's dismissal of his "unhearing" audience. In fairly typical fashion for oracular language, there is a merging of Jeremiah's word and Yahweh's word delivered in response to this disobedient people.

V 18 reviews the terrible end of Jerusalem and her inhabitants. Their fate is described as a consequence of Yahweh's wrath. Implied is the disobedience of Jerusalem and the similarity of that disobedience to the actions of Johanan and his followers. Their fate will also be similar. They are warned explicitly (v 19), "Do not go to Egypt." Failure to heed the warning will bring inevitable consequences of disaster.

V 20 repeats the earlier request for a word from the LORD as a way of emphasizing the radical disobedience of this people. Since the supplicants have not only disobeyed but have done "nothing" that Yahweh commanded (v 21), the certainty of judgment is assured. Johanan and those with him will go to Egypt and will die there as a consequence of the very disasters they are fleeing (v 22).

Explanation

The episode in Jer 41:16–42:22 provides a significant thematic element for the larger unit of Jer 37–44, which establishes once and for all the loss of hope for any future vested in the surviving Judean community in Judah. Paradoxically, this message is communicated by means of a word from the LORD that offers the potential of just such a hope.

When Johanan and company reject the clear word from the LORD, which they had explicitly requested, the outcome is assured to be one of judgment upon a disobedient people. As noted above in *Form/Structure/Setting* and *Comment*, there are structural and formulaic patterns that make these events even more dramatic than they might otherwise be. This final representative group of survivors parallels by their actions the actions of significant figures from earlier in the book. Jehoiakim refused to hear the word of the LORD in aggressive fashion. Zedekiah provides an even closer parallel in that he, too, overtly requests a word from the LORD, which he refuses to heed (Jer 37). It is this episode, however, that emphasizes in the strongest way the disobedient pattern characteristic of Judah/Israel's relationship with Yahweh. Key phrases are repeated in which the supplicants insist that any word from the LORD will be obeyed. The actions in the end refute those promises.

While the specific rejection of Yahweh's word does not come until 43:1–7, the outcome appears to be clear to the prophet at the end of Jer 42. It is not necessary to reorder the end of Jer 42 and the beginning of Jer 43 in order to assume a negative response to the prophet's/Yahweh's word.

Two chapters yet remain in the unit Jer 37–44, but the word of judgment in Jer 42 essentially seals the fate of the survivors from Judah. Persistent disobedience to the "words" of Yahweh throughout the history of Judah/Israel has led to a climactic moment of judgment. Hope on one level is at an end. Any hope for the future will require a redefinition of what hope means for this people, and it will shift to the remnant who alone can be the recipients of that hope, the exiles in Babylon.

G. The Flight to Egypt Continued (43:1–13 [LXX 50:1–13])

Bibliography

Ackroyd, P. R. "Historians and Prophets." *SEÅ* 33 (1968) 18–54. **Doorslaer, J. V.** "Sicut Amicitur Pastor Pallio Suo . . . [Jer. 43:12]." *CBQ* 13 (1951) 314–25. **Horowitz, W. J.** "Audience Reaction to Jeremiah." *CBQ* 32 (1970) 555–64. **Kessler, M.** "Jeremiah Chapters 26–45 Reconsidered." *JNES* 25 (1968) 81–88. **Lambdin, T. O.** "Heliopolis." *IDB* 2:579. **Lemke, W. E.** "Nebuchadrezzar, My Servant [Jer. 25:9, 27:6, 43:10]." *CBQ* 28 (1966) 45–50. **Lorcher, H.** "Das Verhältnis der Prosereden zu den Erzählungen im Jeremiabuch." *TLZ* 102 (1977) 395–96. **Pritchard, J. B.,** ed. *ANET.* 308. **Seitz, C.** "The Crisis of Interpretation over the Meaning and Purpose of the Exile." *VT* 35 (1985) 78–97. **Tov, E.** "Some Aspects of the Textual and Literary History of the Book of Jeremiah." In *Le Livre de Jérémie, le prophète et son milieu, les oracles et leur transmission,* ed. P.-M. Bogaert. BETL 54. Leuven: Leuven UP, 1981. 146–67.

Translation

[1a]*And when Jeremiah had finished speaking to all[b] the people all of the words of the LORD their God,[c] which the LORD their God,[c] sent him to them, all these words,* [2]*Azariah the son of Hoshaiah,[a] and Johanan the son of Kareah, and all of the insolent[b] men said[cd] to Jeremiah, "You are speaking[e] a lie; the LORD our God[f] did not send you, saying, 'you should not go to Egypt to sojourn there,'* [3]*but Baruch the son of Neriah has incited you against us, in order to give us into the hand of the Chaldeans, to kill us or to take us away into exile to Babylon."* [4]*Johanan the son of Kareah,[a] and all of the officers of the army, and all of the people would not obey the voice of the LORD to remain in the land of Judah.* [5]*Johanan the son of Kareah[a] and all of the officers of the army took all the remnant of Judah who had returned to sojourn in the land of Judah[b] from all of the nations where[c] they had been banished,* [6]*men,[a] women, children,[b] the daughters of the king and all[c] the people whom Nebuzaradan the captain of the guard[d] had left behind with Gedaliah the son of Ahikam the son of Shaphan;[e] also Jeremiah the prophet and Baruch the son of Neriah.* [7]*They went to the land of[a] Egypt, for they did not obey the voice of the LORD; they went to Tahpanhes.*

⁸ *Then the word of the LORD came to Jeremiah in Tahpanhes, saying:* ⁹ *"Take in your hand large stones and bury them in the mortar*ᵃ *in the quadrangle*ᵇ *which is*ᶜ *in the entrance of the house of Pharaoh in Tahpanhes, in the sight of the men of Judah,* ¹⁰ *and say to them,* ᵃ *'Thus says the LORD of Hosts, the God of Israel,*ᵇ *behold, I am sending and I will take Nebuchadrezzar the king of Babylon, my servant,*ᶜ *and I will set*ᵈ *his throne over these stones which I have buried,*ᵉ *and he will spread his royal canopy*ᶠ *over them.* ¹¹ *He will come*ᵃ *and smite the land of Egypt, those (marked)*ᵇ *for death to death, those (marked) for captivity to captivity, and those (marked) for the sword to the sword.*ᶜ ¹² *I will kindle a fire*ᵃ *in the houses of the gods of Egypt,*ᵇ *and he will burn them and take them captive; and he will pick clean*ᶜ *the land of Egypt as the shepherd would pick clean*ᵈ *his garment, and he will depart from there*ᵉ *in peace.* ¹³ *He will break in pieces the pillars of Heliopolis, which is in the land of Egypt,*ᵃ *and the houses of the gods of Egypt*ᵇ *he will burn with fire.'"*

Notes

1.a. *BHS* proposes inserting 43:1–3 after 42:18; see *Note* 42:18.c.
1.b. "all" lacking in LXX.
1.c. LXX does not have "their God."
2.a. LXX reads Μαασαιου, "Maaseiah."
2.b. LXX lacks "insolent."
2.c. MT אמרים, lit. "ones saying," is problematic without the article; *BHS*, following Cornill, Bright, Rudolph, suggests the emendation והמרים, "the contentious ones"; cf. Holladay, 2:275.
2.d. LXX adds λέγοντες = Heb. לאמר, "saying."
2.e. "You are speaking" absent in LXX.
2.f. LXX has πρὸς ἡμᾶς = Heb. אלינו, "to us."
4.a. "son of Kareah" not in LXX.
5.a. "son of Kareah" not in LXX.
5.b. LXX has only "in the land," lacking "of Judah"; Holladay (2:276) suggests reading "in the land of Egypt" as fitting the context of the departure led by Johanan, but this seems unnecessary in light of possible readings of the MT as it stands.
5.c. LXX lacks "from all of the nations where."
6.a. LXX has τοὺς δυνατούς = Heb. גבורים, "the strong men" or "warriors" (see Holladay, 2:276); cf. 41:16 for a similar occurrence.
6.b. Lit. "ones taking quick little steps"; cf. 41:16.
6.c. "all" not in LXX.
6.d. LXX lacks "the captain of the guard."
6.e. LXX lacks "the son of Shaphan."
7.a. LXX lacks "the land of."
9.a. α′, θ′ have ἐν τῷ κρυφίῳ = Heb. בלט, "in secrecy, secretly."
9.b. *BHS* suggests that "in the quadrangle," a problematic reading, is a likely scribal addition resulting from dittogr, the mistaken repetition of a word in copying.
9.c. LXX lacks the entire phrase "in the mortar in the quadrangle which is."
10.a. LXX lacks "to them."
10.b. LXX lacks "of Hosts, the God of Israel."
10.c. "my servant" not in LXX.
10.d. LXX has καὶ θήσει τόν, "and he will set."
10.e. LXX has "you have buried," 2ms (instead of 1cs of MT).
10.f. "his royal canopy" an uncertain reading; Q has שפרירו, which does not change the reading.
11.a. "He will come," with Q ובא.
11.b. "marked" used here following Holladay, 2:277.
11.c. *BHS* suggests "and those (marked) for the sword to the sword" as a likely expansion of the text.
12.a. LXX, Syr, Vg read 3ms הצית, "he will set on fire."

12.b. LXX has "of their gods" rather than "of the gods of Egypt."
12.c. LXX has φθειριεῖ, "delouse."
12.d. LXX has φθειρίζει, "delouse."
12.e. LXX lacks "from there."
13.a. "of Egypt" not present in LXX.
13.b. LXX has "their houses" rather than "the houses of the gods of Egypt."

Form/Structure/Setting

Jer 43 provides the response from Johanan and the other Judean leaders to the requested word from the LORD that Jeremiah has provided. The intent to go to Egypt is suggested earlier but is explicitly stated in the early verses of this chapter. The journey itself is also described in the first half of the chapter. The final section of the chapter represents the prophet's response to the rejection of Yahweh's word by the Judean survivors, a response that is announced after the arrival of the group in Tahpanhes in Egypt.

The early verses of Jer 43 (vv 1–3) are the object of considerable discussion by interpreters of Jeremiah. A number of interpreters assume that these verses are out of place as they now stand, belonging instead at the end of the episode narrated in Jer 42 (following 42:18; e.g., Bright, 258; Holladay, 2:283; Rudolph, 218–21). With that rearrangement, the clear rejection of the word from the LORD renders the final verses of judgment in 42:18–22 more consistent with the larger context.

It has been argued above that rearranging the verses is not necessary. As it stands in MT, Jer 42–43 can be read as a straightforward treatment of events, modified by the prophet's early impressions, culminating in an explicit rejection of Yahweh's word by the Judean leaders. That the prophet would suspect an outcome in advance of its occurrence does not require clairvoyance on Jeremiah's part. Nicholson (2:147) and Carroll (720) point out the tendency at many points in the book to anticipate a disobedient response on the part of the populace to the word from Yahweh (see also Thompson, 668).

Baruch's presence in v 3 is also worthy of comment. Baruch is not mentioned in chaps. 37–42. His reappearance in 43:3 is quite sudden. Johanan, Azariah, and "all of the insolent men" accuse Baruch of betraying the group of survivors to the Babylonians. The charge deflects some attention from Jeremiah and seems to implicate Baruch as the individual they suspect to harbor the strongest pro-Babylonian sentiments. It is not altogether clear what this charge accomplishes. Jeremiah has acted on earlier occasions in ways that would certainly color him as pro-Babylonian, without the necessity of Baruch's involvement as he is accused by Johanan and company.

Carroll (722) contends that the reintroduction of Baruch is consistent with the passive portrayal of Jeremiah throughout Part IV of the book (Jer 37–45, Carroll's division). Carroll also alludes to the ironic treatment of Jeremiah as passive, when the prophet has acted forcefully on many and varied occasions prior to this portion of the book. The passive portrait would serve to protect Jeremiah from repercussions on the part of the Babylonians, in contrast to the harsh treatment that would likely face Johanan and Azariah (Carroll, 722).

Quite apart from this specific episode, Carroll suggests that Baruch here and elsewhere serves as little more than a literary device, an invented companion for

Jeremiah to fill key roles at various points in the Jeremiah corpus (723). Carroll refers to Baruch as an "aleatory" figure in the book, defined as a "contingency" figure.

There is reason to note the passive character of Jeremiah in this section of the book, though there may not be sufficient warrant to project as much from this as Carroll does. The characterization of Baruch likewise has some merit, though other explanations, including the secondary nature of all characters to the larger message of the book, might explain Baruch's appearances and disappearances.

Vv 8–13 describe a final word from the LORD through Jeremiah, which came to the prophet while he was a part of the exilic community in Tahpanhes, in the Nile Delta region of Egypt. The sign-act that Jeremiah is instructed to perform raises some questions.

Jeremiah is told to bury large stones in the courtyard before the palace of Pharaoh. The Egyptian pharaoh had no palace as such in Tahpanhes, so the reference should probably be understood to refer to an official government building that would symbolize the authority of the Egyptian ruler.

Whether such an event ever transpired is open to question. Bright (265) is convinced that the incident described is authentic; that is, Jeremiah carried out the sign-act, and the fulfillment of it should be seen in the invasion of 568 B.C. referred to in *ANET*, 308b. Bright points out that the end result of the Babylonian incursion was not conquest but a brief punitive expedition, since the pharaoh of the period (Amasis) retained his throne and maintained amicable relationships with Babylon (265; see also Thompson, 671–72; Holladay, 2:302; Carroll, 727). Nicholson suggests that the lack of historical evidence of the kind of wholesale destruction described in Jeremiah's oracle supports the authenticity of the oracle.

V 13 makes reference to the "pillars" of Heliopolis, or "Beth-shemesh," "house of (the) sun." The city was once an important cult site from which the symbol of the sun-god Atum-Re originated (Lambdin, "Heliopolis," 579; Holladay, 2:302). The worship symbols and centers of Egypt are designated for destruction, a universalizing of the judgment word previously announced against Judah for failure to recognize and obey Yahweh. No evidence exists that such wholesale destruction of the temples occurred, but the intent of the prophet seems clear regardless. Jeremiah's sign-act expresses more concern with the impact on Judah, or what remains of Judah (the survivors in Tahpanhes), than on the effect upon the Egyptians.

Comment

1–3 Jer 43 begins with the reaction of the survivors of the Mizpah massacre to Jeremiah's warning from the LORD not to go to Egypt. Johanan, Azariah, and the "insolent men" accuse Jeremiah of lying and blame Baruch for instigating a conspiracy to betray the group to the Babylonians. As Johanan and Azariah see it, the only possible outcome will be exile or death. In the case of the group's leaders, death is all but certain.

Whether the accusation assumes some plot by Jeremiah and Baruch to profit by the scheme described (Carroll, 722) is not clear. In keeping with the consistent patterns of the message of the book, the story emphasizes disobedience. Even at this last moment of opportunity, those who represent the remnant of Judah continue to reject the word from the LORD.

4–7 Instead of following Jeremiah's counsel, Johanan and company flee to Egypt, apparently as they had always intended to do. V 4 specifies that they are disobeying Yahweh's instruction to remain in the land.

Vv 5–6 describe the company who journeyed to Egypt. All of those who had returned to Judah from surrounding territories to which they had fled from the terrors of war in response to the good report of Gedaliah's governorship, as well as others related to the Mizpah episodes, are included. Jeremiah and Baruch are also part of the group. In all likelihood they did not enter Egypt voluntarily. Their presence, however, enables the oft-repeated message to continue even in Egypt.

V 7 stresses yet again that in fleeing to Egypt the Judeans disobey the voice of the LORD. Disobedience cannot be missed as the dominant theme portrayed in Jer 43. The final comment of the verse places the company in Tahpanhes, on the Nile Delta, where there may already have been a Jewish community (Holladay, 2:301).

8–9 Vv 8–9 underscore a prominent theme in the larger prophetic tradition, the theme of Yahweh's universal sovereignty. That theme is introduced by means of a new word from the LORD to Jeremiah in the exile community of Tahpanhes in the Nile Delta.

The specific "word" from the LORD instructs Jeremiah to perform a sign-act very similar to those performed by the prophet Ezekiel (Ezek 4:1–12; 5:1–4; 12:3b–6, 18; 37:15–17) and to actions described of Jeremiah in 13:4–7, 19:1–13, and 27:1–28:16. This sign-act is to underscore the certainty of judgment upon the survivors of Judah even in their supposed place of safety in Egypt.

Jeremiah is to take large stones and hide them in the pavement at the entrance to Pharaoh's Tahpanhes palace. These stones are to serve as the base for a temporary throne, which the king of Babylon will erect when he exercises his power over Egypt. (See Holladay, 2:301–2, regarding the "mortar" or paving stones of the quadrangle and their soft clay as insufficient to support Nebuchadrezzar's throne.) The point is that no escape is possible from the judgment that Yahweh has pronounced.

10–13 The sign Jeremiah enacts is to be made clear to the Judean exilic community in Egypt. The prophet is instructed to explain the meaning behind what he has done. Nebuchadrezzar, Yahweh's "servant," will successfully exercise power over Egypt and her pharaoh and will be Yahweh's instrument of judgment upon those who thought to find safety there against the counsel of Yahweh and Yahweh's prophet.

V 12 is reminiscent of the oracle against Moab in Amos 1:14. In both texts, Yahweh "kindles a fire" as a means of judgment. V 12 begins in first person, "I will kindle," though it shifts to third person in the latter part of the verse. Rather than indicating an awkward reading, as variant texts suggest (see *Notes* above), this shift may well be intentional and related to the idea noted in Amos 1:14 if not to that particular event. Yahweh kindles the fire, even though Nebuchadrezzar is the conqueror.

Information in the Babylonian historical record is too sparse to allow definitive conclusions relative to any event that would correspond to Jeremiah's prediction. In any case, the emphasis of Jer 43 is more focused on the crucial theological assertion that the sovereignty of Yahweh is universal; the judgment of Yahweh cannot be escaped.

The latter portion of v 12 describes Nebuchadrezzar engaged in a "delousing" of Egypt, with a probable reference to the Judean exiles. The shepherd is pictured as "picking clean" his cloak, or removing the vermin that would infest it. Are the Judean refugees the "vermin" that are to be removed?

The end of v 12 and v 13 describe a successful campaign by Nebuchadrezzar against this region of Egypt and all who dwell in it. He will depart unscathed, leaving behind the destruction of Egypt's places of worship as well as the implied destruction of the Judean exile community.

Explanation

Jer 43 emphasizes yet again the stubborn refusal of the people of Judah to hear and respond to the word of the LORD. The very structure of Jer 42–43 adds to that emphasis. Their refusal to hear is entirely predictable and is consistent with the history of Israel/Judah's relationship with Yahweh from the beginning. The atmosphere created in the early verses of Jer 43 suggests that the leaders of the Mizpah survivors never had any intention of remaining in the land but simply sought divine sanction for their planned flight. The message of Jeremiah repeatedly rejects the call for a popular response from Yahweh to a "people of God" whose actions make a mockery of the relationship they believe to be intact.

Vv 8–13 trumpet the universal scope of Yahweh's power. The attempt to flee to Egypt might bring temporary respite from Babylonian pressures, but the foe threatening this rebellious people is not Babylon but Yahweh. Yahweh will accomplish the word proclaimed by Jeremiah in Egypt as easily as in Judah. The impact of the LORD's judgment upon the Egyptians and their worship sites and symbols serves to reiterate the sovereignty of the LORD whom the Judeans have chosen to ignore. While it is not altogether certain that Jeremiah intends to portray the Judean exile community as the "vermin" of 43:12, such a reading is fitting in light of the larger message of this section of Jeremiah.

If any question remained to this point about the possible hope to be vested in Judah, the judgment of the LORD pronounced and carried out against the stubborn remnant in Tahpanhes settles the matter rather conclusively. Hope is not necessarily at an end for Israel/Judah, but any future hope must look beyond Judah, and Egypt, to find expression. Consistent with other strands of the larger prophetic tradition (notably Ezekiel), Jeremiah by implication leaves open a door of hope only for Israel/Judah as found in the Babylonian exile.

H. The Word of the LORD to the Judeans in Egypt (44:1–30[*LXX* 51:1–30])

Bibliography

Cowley, A. *Aramaic Papyri of the Fifth Century* B.C. Oxford: Clarendon Press, 1923. 4–6. **Kraeling, E. G.** "Elephantine." *IDB* 2:83–85. **Lambdin, T. O.** "Memphis." *IDB* 3:346–47. ———. "Migdol." *IDB* 3:377. ———. "Pathros." *IDB* 3:676. ———. "Tahpanhes." *IDB* 4:510. **Oren, E. D.** "Migdol: A New Fortress on the Edge of the Eastern Nile Delta." *BASOR* 256 (1984) 7–44. **Pritchard, J. B.**, ed. *ANET.* 308. **Selms, Adrian van.** "Telescoped Discussions as a Literary Device in Jeremiah." *VT* 26 (1976) 99–112. **Wilson, J. A.** "Hophra." *IDB* 2:643–44.

Translation

[1] *The word which came to Jeremiah to all the Judeans who were living in the land of* [a] *Egypt, the ones living in Migdol, in Tahpanhes, in Memphis,* [b] *and in the land of Pathros, saying:* [2] *"Thus says the LORD of Hosts,* [a] *the God of Israel: You saw all the evil which I brought upon Jerusalem and upon all* [b] *the cities of Judah; behold, they are a desolation this day* [c] *and there is no one living in them,* [d] [3] *because of their wickedness which they have done to provoke me to anger, by going to burn incense and by serving* [a] *other gods whom they did not know, neither they, nor you, nor your fathers.* [b] [4] *Yet I sent persistently to you all* [a] *my servants the prophets, rising early and sending, saying: 'Do not do this abominable thing which I hate!'* [5] *But they did not listen;* [a] *they did not incline their ears to turn from their evil, not to burn incense to other gods.* [6] *My burning rage and my anger were poured out and kindled in the cities of Judah and in the streets of Jerusalem; and they became a waste and a desolation* [a] *as at this day.*

[7] *"Now, thus says the LORD, the God* [a] *of Hosts, the God of Israel:* [b] *Why are you continuing to do great evil to yourselves, to cut off for you man and woman, child and infant, from the midst of Judah, so that there is not left for you a remnant?* [8] *Why do you provoke me to anger by the deeds* [a] *of your hands, by burning incense to other gods in the land of Egypt where you came* [b] *to sojourn there,* [c] *so that you are cut off* [d] *and* [c] *become a curse and a reproach among all* [e] *the nations of the earth?* [9] *Have you forgotten the wickedness of your fathers, the wickedness of the kings of Judah, the wickedness of their wives,* [a] *your wickedness* [b] *and the wickedness of your wives,* [c] *which they did in the land of Judah and in the streets of Jerusalem?* [10] *They have not been contrite* [a] *to this day, they did not fear,* [b] *and they have not walked in my law and in my statutes* [c] *which I set before you and before* [d] *your* [e] *fathers.*

[11] *"Therefore, thus says the LORD of Hosts, the God of Israel: behold, I will set my face against you for evil, to cut off all Judah.* [a] [12] *I will take* [a] *the remnant of Judah* [b] *who have set their faces to go to the land of Egypt to sojourn there,* [c] *and they will all be consumed, they will fall in the land of* [d] *Egypt, they will be consumed by the sword and* [e] *by famine; from the least to the greatest, they will die by the sword and by famine;* [f] *and they will become an execration,* [g] *a horror, a curse, and a reproach.* [13] *I will punish* [a]

those who dwell in the land of Egypt just as I punished[a] *Jerusalem, with the sword, with famine, and with pestilence.*[b] [14]*There will not be a fugitive or a survivor for the remnant of Judah who went to sojourn there* [a] *in the land of Egypt, to return*[b] *to the land of Judah where they desire*[c] *to return to dwell*[d] *there, for they will not return except as fugitives."* [e]

[15]*Then all of the men who knew that their wives were making sacrifices to other gods and all of the women standing by,*[a] *a great assembly,* [b] *and all of the people who dwelled in the land of Egypt, in Pathros,*[cd] *answered Jeremiah:* [16]*"As for the word which you spoke to us in the name of the LORD, we will not listen to you.* [17]*For we will do everything which went forth from our mouths, to burn incense to the queen*[a] *of heaven, and pouring out*[b] *to her drink offerings just as we have always done, we and our fathers, our kings and our princes, in the cities of Judah and in the streets of Jerusalem; then we had excess of food, we prospered, and we saw no evil.* [18]*But since we ceased to burn incense to the queen*[a] *of heaven and pour out to her drink offerings,* [b] *we have lacked everything and we have been consumed by the sword and by famine."* [19]*And the women said,* [a] *"When we burned incense to the queen*[b] *of heaven and poured out to her drink offerings, was it apart from our husbands we made for her cakes to form her image*[c] *and poured out to her drink offerings?"*

[20]*Then Jeremiah said to all the people, to the men and to the women, and to all the people who had answered him:* [21]*"The incense which you burned in the cities of Judah and in the streets of Jerusalem, you and your fathers, your kings and your princes and the people of the land, has not the LORD remembered them*[a]*? Has it not come to his mind?* [22]*The LORD can no longer bear the evil of your deeds, the abominations which you do; therefore your land has become a desolation, a waste, and a curse, without inhabitant,* [a] *as it is this day.* [23]*Because you burned incense and you sinned against the LORD, you did not obey the voice of the LORD, and you did not walk in his commandments, his statutes, and his testimonies; therefore, this evil has befallen you, as it is this day."*[a]

[24]*Then Jeremiah said to all*[a] *the people, and to all*[a] *the women, "Hear the word of the LORD, all of Judah who are in the land of Egypt,* [b] [25]*Thus says the LORD of Hosts,*[a] *the God of Israel,* [b] *You women*[c] *have spoken with your mouths and fulfilled with your hands, saying, 'We will surely perform our vows which we vowed, to make sacrifices to the queen of heaven and to pour out for her drink offerings'; then carry out*[d] *your vows and perform your vows!*[ef]

[26]*"Therefore, hear the word of the LORD, all of Judah who dwell in the land of Egypt, behold I have sworn by my great name, says the LORD, that my name will not again be called*[a] *by the mouth of any one*[b] *from Judah in all the land of Egypt who says 'As the Lord GOD*[c] *lives.'* [27]*Behold, I am watching over them for evil and not for good, and every one*[a] *from Judah who is in*[b] *the land of Egypt will be destroyed by the sword or by famine until they are at an end.* [28]*Those who escape the sword will return from the land of Egypt*[a] *to the land of Judah few in number, and all*[b] *the remnant of Judah who went to the land of Egypt to sojourn there*[c] *will know whose word will stand, mine or theirs.* [d]
[29] *This will be the sign to you, says the LORD,* [a] *that I will punish you in this place, in order that you may know that my words will indeed stand against you*[b] *for evil:*

[30]*"Thus says the LORD, I will give Pharaoh*[a] *Hophra, the king of Egypt, into the hand of his enemies and into the hand of those who seek his life, just as I gave Zedekiah, the king of Judah, into the hand of Nebuchadrezzar, the king of Babylon, his enemy and the one who sought his life."*

Notes

1.a. LXX lacks "the land of."

1.b. "in Memphis" not in LXX.

2.a. LXX lacks "of Hosts."

2.b. LXX lacks "all."

2.c. "this day" absent in LXX.

2.d. LXX lacks "in them."

3.a. "to serve" not in LXX.

3.b. LXX has only οὐκ ἔγνωτε = Heb. לֹא יְדַעְתֶּם, "you did not know," lacking the final phrase in MT, "neither they nor you nor your fathers."

4.a. LXX lacks "all."

5.a. LXX has "listen *to me*."

6.a. Several MSS add the conj, i.e., וּלְשַׁמָּה, "*and* (for) a desolation."

7.a. LXX lacks "the God."

7.b. LXX lacks "the God of Israel."

8.a. Many MSS, including Syr, have בְּמַעֲשֵׂה, instead of בְּמַעֲשֵׂי; the tr. "the deeds of" is unaffected either way.

8.b. MT has בָּאִים, lit. "are coming"; probably בָּאת, "you came" is a clearer reading.

8.c-c. *BHS* suggests the phrase is a likely addition in light of the wording of v 7.

8.d. Heb. reads lit. "so that there is cut off for you"; LXX lacks "for you" in the literal reading.

8.e. "all" absent in LXX.

9.a. MT lit. "of his wives"; LXX has τῶν ἀρχόντων ὑμῶν, "of your rulers"; *BHS* proposes reading נְשֵׁיהֶם, "of their wives," on the basis of the Syr text, the option chosen in the *Translation* above.

9.b. "your wickedness" lacking in LXX.

9.c. Syr lacks "and the wickedness of your wives."

10.a. LXX has ἐπαύσαντο, lit. "they have (not) stopped themselves," which *BHS* suggests is equivalent to נִכְלְאוּ, "they have (not) restrained"; *BHS* proposes נִכְאוּ, "they have (not) been afraid"; the *Translation* reflects the unaltered MT reading.

10.b. LXX lacks "they did not fear."

10.c. LXX has τῶν προσταγμάτων μου = Heb. בְּחֻקֹּתִי, "in my ordinances (statutes)."

10.d. LXX does not have "before you."

10.e. LXX, Syr have "before *their* fathers."

11.a. LXX has the briefer "Therefore, thus says the LORD, behold, I will set my face."

12.a. "I will take" absent in LXX.

12.b. LXX lacks "of Judah."

12.c. The phrase "set their faces to go to the land of Egypt to sojourn there" is missing in LXX.

12.d. LXX lacks "the land of."

12.e. Read "by the sword *and* by famine" with many MS witnesses.

12.f. LXX lacks "they will be destroyed by the sword and by famine."

12.g. LXX has only three parts of the fourfold designation of MT; "an execration" is lacking.

13.a. Lit. "visit upon."

13.b. LXX has "with death."

14.a. LXX lacks "there."

14.b. MT lit. "and to return"; read with LXX "to return."

14.c. Lit. "lift up their souls."

14.d. "to dwell" not in LXX or Syr.

14.e. "except as fugitives" considered a gloss by most scholars (Holladay, 2:278; Rudolph, 222), since it seems to contradict what is said at the very beginning of the verse.

15.a. הָעֹמְדוֹת, "standing by," not in LXX.

15.b. *BHS* proposes קוֹל, "voice," for קְהַל, "assembly," i.e., "with a loud voice" rather than "a great assembly." Unaltered MT is followed above.

15.c. *BHS* suggests reading "*and* in Pathros," following Syr.

15.d. The phrase "and all of the people who dwelled in the land of Egypt, in Pathros" is considered a probable addition by *BHS*.

17.a. Many MSS read לִמְלֶאכֶת, "to the service of," rather than reading לִמְלֶכֶת, as "queen"; cf. LXX, Vg, also Jer 7:18.

17.b. *BHS* proposes the alternative וּלְהַסִּיךְ, "and to pour out," which would be consistent with the preceding verb, "to burn incense."

18.a. See *Note* 17.a. above.

18.b. LXX lacks "and pour out to her drink offerings."

19.a. "And the women said" not in MT; proposed here following LXX[L], Syr.

19.b. See *Note* 17.a. above.

19.c. לְהַעֲצִבָה, "to form, shape, fashion," lacking in LXX, Syr; BDB (781) proposes the reading לְהַעֲצִבָה, "to form her (image)," as in the above *Translation*.

21.a. Absent in LXX; *BHS* suggests אֹתָהּ, "it," corresponding to the verb וְתַעֲלֶה, "and has it (not) [lit. gone up] come."

22.a. LXX lacks "without inhabitant."

23.a. "as it is this day" lacking in LXX.

24.a. LXX lacks "all"; *BHS* suggests these are additions influenced by v 20.

24.b. LXX lacks the final phrase, "all of Judah who are in the land of Egypt"; *BHS* suggests this is an addition influenced by v 26.

25.a. LXX lacks "of Hosts."

25.b. MT introduces the divine utterance by לֵאמֹר, "saying"; LXX lacks it.

25.c. Read with LXX "you women," consistent with the fem verb that follows, instead of MT אַתֶּם וּנְשֵׁיכֶם, "you and your wives."

25.d. GKC § 72k suggests that תְּקִימְנָה represents an erroneous transposition of יָ and should be rendered תְּקַמֵּנָה, "you will carry out," which this *Translation* assumes.

25.e. *BHS* proposes דִּבְרֵיכֶם, "your deeds"; a few MSS read נִסְכֵּיכֶם, "your drink offerings."

25.f. LXX lacks "your vows."

26.a. LXX lacks "called," reading simply "be *in* the mouth," which does not change the sense of the verse.

26.b. LXX lacks אִישׁ, lit. "man," tr. above "one."

26.c. MT reads אֲדֹנָי יְהוִה, here translated Lord GOD, lit. "Lord, LORD"; LXX in one recension has only "Lord," in the majority text, "Lord, Lord."

27.a. LXX lacks אִישׁ, lit. "man," tr. above "one."

27.b. LXX adds "who dwells."

28.a. "from the land of Egypt" not in LXX.

28.b. LXX lacks "all."

28.c. *BHS* treats "who went to the land of Egypt to sojourn there" as an addition to the text.

28.d. LXX lacks "mine or theirs."

29.a. LXX lacks "says the LORD."

29.b. LXX is missing the extensive phrase "in this place, in order that you may know that my words will indeed stand against you." This is likely a scribal omission resulting from confusion over the same word that appears twice in this verse: עֲלֵיכֶם, "against you." The scribe's eye probably skipped erroneously from one form to the next, omitting the phrase noted.

30.a. "Pharaoh" is absent in LXX.

Form/Structure/Setting

Jer 44 concludes Jer 37–44 with a self-standing oracle directed against Judean exiles settled in a number of places throughout the land of Egypt. Four communities are mentioned specifically: Migdol, Tahpanhes, Pathros, and Memphis.

These communities represented concentrations of Judeans who over a period of time had established a significant presence in Egypt. Migdol, meaning "tower" or "fortress," has been tentatively located some twenty-five miles east-northeast of Tahpanhes (see Oren, *BASOR* 256 [1984] 7–44; Lambdin, *IDB* 3:377). Tahpanhes itself is usually identified with modern Tell Defneh, located in the northern delta region of Egypt. It is now a desert area near Lake Menzaleh (Lambdin, *IDB* 4:510). Pathros designates the region of Egypt also referred to as Upper Egypt, which was above Memphis (Lambdin, *IDB* 3:676). Memphis was located about fourteen miles south of modern Cairo on the western bank of the Nile (Lambdin, *IDB* 3:346–47).

An oddity of this passage is that it appears to address Jews gathered in virtually all of Egypt, not just those who happen to be in the vicinity of Jeremiah and/or Baruch. The word not only is said to come to Jeremiah "concerning" the larger group, but then it is declared in oracular form with the larger group as the intended hearers.

Not clear from the text itself is how much time has passed between Jer 43 and Jer 44, though clearly the oracle of Jer 44 assumes the passage of time. Carroll (731) has pointed out the edited nature of the chapter and its function as an edited passage as opposed to any relationship to historical events. Key elements internal to the chapter that indicate its distance from historical concerns include the assumed audience of "all" the Judeans of the Egyptian diaspora as Jeremiah presents one sermon and the reported responses in dialogue form that take place between prophet and people.

The redactional purpose seems to be an attempt to discredit the Judean community in Egypt as a community judged to be unfaithful. Whether this purpose presumes a Second Temple period context (Carroll, 731) or some other, in any case it discounts the possibility of a faithful people of God in Egypt. The portrait of the Judean community in Egypt presented in this chapter is dramatically negative. In fact, few other texts portray the stark rejection of Yahweh described in Jer 44. The persons so described clearly cannot be considered a part of Yahweh's future for Israel.

Ezekiel provides a rationale that supports the Babylonian community of Judeans as the only proper reservoir of hope for the future of the people of God. The disenfranchisement of the people who remain in the land of Judah following the Babylonian invasion is accomplished in Ezekiel by means of very damaging descriptions of a corrupt religious system, notably in Ezek 8. It may well be that Jer 44 functions in much the same way to establish what is not so graphically indicated elsewhere in Jeremiah. The word of judgment is pronounced upon the Judean remnant, but in this case, its scattered elements who had fled to Egypt are similarly damned.

The following is an outline of the chapter:

    I. Announcement of an oracle to the Judeans living in Egypt (vv 1–6)
        A. Specific identification of four communities of Jewish exiles: Migdol, Tahpanhes, Memphis, Pathros (v 1)
        B. Reminder of the effects of Yahweh's judgment in Judah (v 2)
        C. Reasons for judgment (vv 3–6)
           1. Sin of false worship (v 3)
           2. Refusal to heed warnings from the prophets of Yahweh (vv 4–5)
           3. Inevitable consequences (v 6)
    II. Shift of attention to the Jews in Egypt (vv 7–10)
        A. Why is there such a bent toward self-destruction? Why is there no willingness to learn from the past? (v 7)
        B. Why provoke Yahweh by continued false worship? (v 8)
        C. Have you learned nothing from the sins of the past and Yahweh's judgment? (v 9)
        D. Focus on stubborn refusal to change as much as on the sins themselves (v 10)

III. Word of judgment against the Judean community in Egypt (vv 11–14)
    A. Destruction of the Egyptian remnant (vv 11–13)
    B. Total destruction, with any possible survivors described as fugitives (v 14)
IV. Stubborn rejection of Yahweh's word as given by Jeremiah (vv 15–19)
    A. Assumed response from a gathered audience (v 15)
        1. Men whose wives are implied to be primary participants in false worship
        2. The women present
        3. The total Jewish population in Egypt apparently assumed
    B. Blatant refusal to heed (vv 16–19)
        1. Direct reference to past practices in Judah (v 17)
        2. Cessation of previous blessings when worship of the queen of heaven stopped
        (v 18)
        3. Clear reference to inclusive guilt; the statement of the women indicating the
        implicit support of their husbands in the acts of worship (v 19)
 V. Repeated word of judgment (vv 20–23)
    A. Description of the sins of false worship (v 21)
    B. Sins as cause of the trouble experienced rather than the cessation of the wor-
    ship of the queen of heaven (vv 22–23)
VI. Final word of judgment against false worship (vv 24–29)
    A. Jeremiah's echo of the determined intent of the women to worship the queen
    of heaven (vv 24–25)
    B. Resulting oracle of judgment (vv 26–29)
        1. Yahweh's oath by "my name" that no one from the Judean community in
        Egypt will again vow by Yahweh (v 26)
        2. Forecast of destruction (v 27)
        3. Few survivors, who will know the truth of Yahweh's word of judgment (vv
        28–29)
VI. Judgment against the Egyptian pharaoh (v 30)
    A. Hophra to experience the same fate as Zedekiah
    B. Events in Egypt to mirror those that occurred in Judah as a result of Yahweh's
    judgment

Comment

1 V 1 introduces an oracle from the LORD that came to Jeremiah regarding the Jews dwelling at four named sites, one of which (Pathros) may refer more to a larger region than to a specific community.

2–6 These verses initiate the actual oracle, beginning with a rehearsal of the past history of faithlessness that has brought judgment upon Judah. The destruction wrought upon Jerusalem and the other cities of Judah is mentioned as evidence of God's judgment, witnessed by those in Egypt.

In clearly hyperbolic language, Jeremiah describes the cities as desolate and without inhabitant. Such was not the actual reality, but Jeremiah's hyperbole serves to highlight the terrible finality of the destruction that Babylon brought upon Judah, destruction that came as Yahweh's judgment upon a stubborn and rebellious people.

The cause of Judah's destruction is the apostasy that is one of Jeremiah's central themes. Jerusalem and Judah were guilty of the evil of burning incense to other gods, false worship made more perverse because of Yahweh's persistent efforts to warn against false worship by means of the prophets.

Failure to heed the repeated warnings of God's messengers ultimately called forth the "anger" of God, which is portrayed as "kindled" in the streets, burning the cities with the fire of judgment. All that survives the fiery ordeal is waste and desolation.

7–10 Jeremiah's attention turns in v 7 to the Jews in Egypt. In light of what happened in Judah, why have these surviving members of the Judean community not learned anything? The prophet accuses them of "cutting off" from Judah "man and woman, infant and child." Practices of false worship had been all too common in Judah, and such practices have continued among the Jews who fled to Egypt.

In calling attention to several illustrations of persons and groups guilty of false worship (v 9), Jeremiah may be alluding not only to the worship practices themselves but to the consequences that came upon those who were participants in Judah. In a characteristic summation, the prophet identifies arrogance as the fundamental reason for the stubborn sins of these people. They repeatedly resist any call to right living: they have not "walked in my law and my statutes."

V 9 introduces the role of "the wives" as one of special significance in the false worship that is condemned. This is a likely reference to worship practices devoted to the "queen of heaven," mentioned specifically in vv 17–19, which seem to be particularly attractive to women. Worship of the queen of heaven began in Judah and had continued to be practiced by those who fled to Egypt.

11–14 Because of the flagrant sins of false worship and the people's stubborn refusal to acknowledge their allegiance to Yahweh, the pronouncement of judgment is particularly harsh. Yahweh "sets his face" against the Judean survivors in Egypt. The image is one of unyielding judgment. All Judah is to be "cut off." Even the remnant that has escaped to Egypt will be consumed in the judgment of Yahweh (v 12). The entire population will experience the horrors of judgment, whether they are among the powerful or the poorest people of the land. Warfare (the sword), famine, and disease will decimate the remnant of Judah to the point that they will become symbolic illustrations of what it means to be cursed (v 12).

The punishment to come upon those in Egypt is of exactly the same sort, with the same force, as that which initially fell upon Judah. V 14 erases one of the key biblical promises that on occasion had been emphasized as the reality beyond the trauma of judgment by Yahweh. With all of the horror and destruction, there was still the hope for a future vested in those who would one day return to Judah. The loftier promises of the exilic prophets even portray Yahweh originating a second exodus back to Judah. That hope is denied the Egyptian survivor community. Only a handful of "fugitives" will ever again see Judah. All the rest will perish in Egypt.

It is interesting to note that Jer 29:18–19 presents almost exactly the same picture of Yahweh's judgment, but in a context that nevertheless holds out hope for the future. The same can be said for Jer 32:29–35, with the added dimension in Jer 32:29 of virtually the same sins against Yahweh as those committed by the Jews who fled to Egypt. Jer 32 concludes with a glowing word of hope and promise on the other side of terrible judgment. In striking contrast, no hope at all is offered to the recipients of the judgment oracle of Jer 44. The Egyptian community seems to carry with it a special level of guilt that annuls any such hope.

15–19 Vv 15–19 represent an emphatic example of the resistance to Jeremiah's words. The defiant attitude confirms the circumstances Jeremiah has described. Unlike the response so often encountered in the prophetic literature when accusation has been made by a prophet, this passage offers no defense. Instead, those responding are determined to continue in the worship practices Jeremiah condemned.

V 15 introduces the respondents. The men are those whose wives have been active participants in the false worship patterns. They are joined by an assembled group of women. The gathering is described as "all of the people . . . in Pathros," the region above Memphis (see *Form/Structure/Setting*).

The specific answer they give to the prophet acknowledges that the word from Jeremiah was presented as "from the LORD." Nevertheless, the respondents say they will not listen to Jeremiah. They intend to continue doing exactly the same things they have always done (v 17), with particular attention to the worship of the queen of heaven.

The rationale offered is quite pragmatic. When these people engaged in the worship of the queen of heaven in Judah, there was plenty of food and life was untroubled. In their view, it was when the worship of the queen of heaven was interrupted that trouble came to Judah. There could hardly be a clearer challenge to the ultimate sovereignty of Yahweh than this response.

The Egyptian refugees do not associate their problems with Yahweh's judgment but with a failure to "protect" themselves by means of adequate offerings to the queen of heaven. Trouble became intense when such offerings stopped, and they are not about to make that mistake again.

In v 19, the women make it clear that the worship practices involve more than just women worshipers. The husbands are specifically included as participants in all of the activities directed toward the queen of heaven.

Excursus: The Queen of Heaven

Bibliography

Ackerman, S. "'And the Women Knead Dough': The Worship of the Queen of Heaven in Sixth-Century Judah." In *Gender and Difference in Ancient Israel*, ed. P. L. Day. Minneapolis: Fortress, 1989. 109–24. **Dahood, M.** "La Regina del Cielo in Geremia." *RivB* 8 (1960) 166–68. **Gray, J.** "Queen of Heaven." *IDB* 3:975. **King, P. J.** *Jeremiah: An Archaeological Companion*. Louisville: John Knox, 1993. 102–7. **Malamat, A.** "Mari." *BA* 34 (1971) 21. **Olyan, S. M.** "Some Obervations concerning the Identity of the Queen of Heaven." *UF* 17 (1987) 161–74. **Rast, W. E.** "Cakes for the Queen of Heaven." In *Scripture in History and Theology.* FS J. Coert Rylaarsdam, ed. A. L. Merrill and T. W. Overholt. PTMS 17. Pittsburgh: Pickwick, 1977. 167–80. **Smith, M. S.** *The Early History of God: Yahweh and the Other Deities in Ancient Israel.* San Francisco: Harper, 1990. 145, 155. **Smith, M.** "The Veracity of Ezekiel, the Sins of Manasseh and Jeremiah 44:18." *ZAW* 87 (1975) 11–16. **Weinfeld, M.** "The Worship of Molech and the Queen of Heaven and Its Background." *UF* 4 (1972) 148–54.

The queen of heaven is an enigmatic figure in the prophetic tradition. (See *Comment* on Jer 7:18.) Several different identities have been proposed for the queen of heaven. She has been identified as Anat, the Canaanite fertility goddess (Albright made this determination based on evidence he found in the Ras Shamra tablets; see Olyan, *UF* 17 [1987] 161), whereas other scholars for various reasons have identified the queen of heaven with Astarte or Ishtar (see M. S. Smith, *The Early History of God*, 145). An Egyptian inscription from the Nineteenth Dynasty found at Beth-shan refers to the Canaanite fertility goddess Anat as "queen of heaven." The functions elsewhere associated with Anat are ascribed in Palestine to the goddess Ashtoreth, who is mentioned on several occasions (Judg 2:13, 10:6; 1 Sam 7:4, 12:10; 1 Kgs 11:5, 33; 2 Kgs 23:13) in connection with Israel's apostate worship practices (J. Gray, *IDB* 3:975). Olyan (171) concludes that the evidence supporting the identification with Ashtoreth is insubstantial compared to other options available.

Attempts have also been made to identify the "queen of heaven" in Jer 7 and 44 with the east Semitic goddess Ishtar. Susan Ackerman ("The Worship of the Queen of Heaven," 109–18) suggests that the figure of the queen of heaven noted in Jer 44 is a composite figure exhibiting qualities associated with both Astarte (Ashtoreth) and Ishtar. Such a composite provides the full pattern associated with the queen of heaven in Jer 44. There is the clear fertility function embodied by both goddesses. War imagery (inferred of the queen of heaven in Jeremiah through the references to security) also applies to both. Astral associations can be found for both Astarte and Ishtar. Only Ishtar is connected with the baking of cakes as part of worship ritual. What appear to be baking molds in the shape of a female fertility figure were found at Mari and have been tentatively connected with the practices described in Jer 7 and 44 (A. Malamat, *BA* 34 [1971] 21).

Weinfeld (*UF* 4 [1972] 149–54) presents a case for identifying the queen of heaven with Ishtar, the Assyrian-Aramean goddess of fertility. Weinfeld links the worship of Ishtar to the lengthy period of Assyrian influence in the region, with the peak of such practices during the reign of Manasseh. He considers it likely that Canaanite and Aramean cults existed side by side in Palestine, though host-of-heaven worship should be associated primarily with the Assyrian cult. The Assyrian texts provide evidence of practices such as those noted in Jer 7 and 44: the offering of incense, pouring out of libations, and mixing of cakes. All such practices are dedicated to Adad and Ishtar.

While Olyan (*UF* 17 [1987] 173) accepts the possibility that a case can be made for identifying the queen of heaven with Ishtar, he is not ultimately convinced. Instead, Olyan argues that the strongest evidence by far identifies the queen of heaven with the Canaanite goddess Astarte. The lack of evidence for the use of cakes in a worship ritual connected with Astarte he attributes to the general lack of information available about such worship practices. The local Canaanite goddess provides, in his view, the best application for the title "queen of heaven." (Olyan also rejects the idea of a fusion of patterns as proposed by Ackerman and others; *UF* 17 [1987] 174.)

Ackerman's proposal is connected with an attempt to determine what can be known regarding women's worship in ancient Israel. Her thesis is that normative worship patterns practiced by women are submerged in the dominant patriarchal culture of Israel, especially as remembered from the perspective that considered such practices to be apostate. The intention is to offer a new reading of the OT patterns of worship with a sensitivity to feminist issues. As Ackerman notes, however, to seek to recover these practices as a positive aspect of Israelite worship is to do so in the face of fierce attack from the message of Jeremiah. Jer 44 represents perhaps the strongest word of denunciation in the entire prophetic tradition, and it is reserved for those who worship the queen of heaven and persist in that worship despite repeated warnings of its apostate character. To attempt to "redeem" the worship of the queen of heaven as a positive aspect of

Israelite worship requires setting aside the biblical tradition, something few are likely to be willing to do.

20–23 In the manner of an ongoing disputation, Jeremiah turns the focus back upon the worship practices as sinful actions, which Yahweh "remembered" (v 21). Jeremiah argues that the disaster that has befallen Judah is Yahweh's judgment. The "evil" is not the result of a failure to make an offering to the queen of heaven but is the inevitable consequence of such false worship.

24–25 The prophet accepts the refusal of the people to change. In an oracular formula, Jeremiah repeats the intention of the people to perform vows to the queen of heaven. In essence, Jeremiah urges them to do exactly as they have stated they would do. Even before the tone shifts directly to a warning of judgment, the urging of the prophet seems to imply that such actions will have inevitable results.

26–29 Beginning with the characteristic "therefore," Jeremiah announces the judgment of the LORD against this obstinate people. Yahweh swears by "my great name" to silence the mention of that name by the Judeans who dwell in Egypt. Yahweh's taking such an oath adds force to the word of judgment. Yahweh vows that no longer will anyone in Egypt "vow" by means of the name of Yahweh (v 26). In light of the movement from the "vows" of the women in v 25 to the reference to the "vow" in v 26, is it possible that the women were making vows to the queen of heaven in the name of Yahweh? While there is no way to resolve the question, it offers an intriguing possibility regarding the level and nature of syncretistic worship that may have occurred among the Israelites and could possibly explain much of the denunciation of false worship by the prophets, which is not perceived to be false by the worshipers themselves.

Jeremiah forecasts the complete destruction of the Judean community in Egypt. Only a few will escape the devastation of sword and famine that is coming. The implication seems to be that some may survive so as to give evidence of whose word was true in this instance. V 29 is almost stated as a challenge. If the massive destruction predicted comes to pass, then it will offer definitive proof that Yahweh's word, not that of the adherents of the queen of heaven, is the authentic word.

30 Whereas prior comments had focused exclusively on the Judean community residing in Egypt, the final verse of the chapter refers to the Egyptian pharaoh. This concluding sentence connects the actions of the LORD with a more universal purpose, for it is not just in the affairs of Judah that Yahweh plays a role. The fate of Egypt's pharaoh is just as much dependent on Yahweh's actions as that of Zedekiah, the king of Judah, whose disastrous end was all too familiar.

The pharaoh named is Hophra, who ruled over the Twenty-sixth Dynasty in Egypt from 588 to 569 B.C. (see J. A. Wilson, *IDB* 2:633–34). He was likely instrumental in Zedekiah's ill-fated revolt against the Babylonians, which is perhaps one reason for the inclusion of this radical word of judgment against the pharaoh. Hophra was killed in an internal Egyptian power struggle in 566 B.C., consistent with the fate Jeremiah forecast for him.

This message undermined those who believed that Egypt offered protection from outside threats. The rivalry of opinion that had simmered for so long in Judah between those who believed future hope to be gained by accepting Babylonian sovereignty and those who saw that hope fulfilled by Egyptian alliance was highlighted and answered. Those who had hoped in Egypt had hoped in vain.

Explanation

In one of the strongest examples of direct defiance against Yahweh by Israel/Judah portrayed in the Hebrew Bible, Jer 44 underscores the inevitable judgment that will fall upon the Judean survivors in Egypt. The concluding passage in Jer 37–44 seals forever the fate of the Judean community that sought safety in Egypt.

At various points in the narrative events of Jer 37–44, glimmers of hope regarding the future seem to appear, most prominently in the glowing reports associated with Gedaliah's gathered community at Mizpah. In some respects, that apparent hope leads to an even bleaker picture than might have existed otherwise. The contrast between what seems so possible under Gedaliah's leadership at Mizpah and the despair that follows Gedaliah's murder is stark.

At the end of Jer 44, there can be no doubt regarding the conclusions drawn by the message of Jeremiah concerning the future. Any hope for the future is vested by implication and by a process of elimination in the exiled community in Babylon. While the prophets Jeremiah and Ezekiel reach their conclusions in somewhat different fashion, and Jeremiah's conclusion does not become obvious until this point in the message, the factors that eliminate other options are remarkably similar and the conclusions drawn are identical.

XXV. A Word for Baruch   (45:1–5 [LXX 51:31–35])

Bibliography

Gunneweg, A. H. "Konfession oder Interpretation im Jeremiabuch." *ZTK* 67 (1970) 395–416. **Lundbom, J. R.** "Baruch, Seraiah, and Expanded Colophons in the Book of Jeremiah." *JSOT* 36 (1986) 89–114. **Mowinckel, S.** *Prophecy and Tradition.* Oslo: Dybwad, 1946. 61–62. **Muilenburg, J.** "Baruch the Scribe." In *Proclamation and Presence.* FS G. Henton Davies, ed. J. I. Durham and J. R. Porter. Richmond: John Knox, 1970. 215–38. **Schulte, H.** "Baruch and Abedmelech: Personaliche Heilsorakel im Jeremiabuch." *BZ* 32 (1988) 256–65. **Selms, A. van.** "Telescoped Discussion as a Literary Device in Jeremiah." *VT* 26 (1976) 99–112. **Skinner, J.** *Prophecy and Religion.* Cambridge: Cambridge UP, 1922. 346. **Taylor, M. A.** "Jeremiah 45: The Problem of Placement." *JSOT* 37 (1987) 79–98. **Weiser, A.** "Das Gotteswort für Baruch: Jer. 45 und die sogenannte Baruchbiographie." In *Glaube und Geschichte im Alten Testament.* Göttingen: Vandenhoeck & Ruprecht, 1961.

Translation

[1] *The word which Jeremiah the prophet spoke to Baruch the son of Neriah when he wrote these words* [a] *in a book at the dictation of Jeremiah in the fourth year of Jehoiakim the son of Josiah the king of Judah, saying:* [b] [2] *"Thus says the LORD, the God of Israel,* [a] *to you Baruch,* [3] [a]*you said, 'Woe is me,* [b] *for the LORD has added grief upon my pain; I am weary with my groaning and I find no rest.'* [4] *Thus* [a] *say to him, thus says the LORD, behold, what I have built I am tearing down, and what I planted I am plucking up, and* [b]*that is the whole land.* [b] [5] *And you seek great things for yourself? Do not seek them; for I am bringing evil upon all flesh, says the LORD, but I will give to you your life for a spoil wherever you may go."*

Notes

1.a. The "words" referred to do not seem to be those of Jer 44 (see Carroll, 744; Thompson, 683; contra Duhm, 334–36). As Carroll suggests, the events of Jer 36 may be the more likely point of reference (see also Lundbom, *JSOT* 36 (1986) 100–101).

1.b. LXX lacks "saying."

2.a. LXX lacks "the God of Israel."

3.a. LXX has ὅτι, "for"; MT missing כִּי, "for," because of haplogr (Thompson, 683; Rudolph, 226; Carroll, 744).

3.b. LXX repeats οἴμμοι, "woe is me," probably as a result of dittogr, erroneous repetition.

4.a. "Thus" absent in LXX; *BHS* considers "thus say to him" an addition to the text.

4.b-b. Many MSS have "the whole land is mine [lit. to me]" rather than "that is the whole land." *BHS* suggests reading "I will smite the whole land," based on the Syr version. LXX missing "and that is the whole land."

Form/Structure/Setting

The context for Jer 45 appears to shift from that of the preceding chapters. No reference is made to events that transpire in Jer 44; the Egyptian community does not seem to be at all connected with this text. The more likely context is the time just after the burning of the scroll in Jer 36 and the scroll's reproduction (Carroll, 744; Thompson, 683). As Rudolph notes (227), vv 4–5 indicate that the destruction of the land is yet to be accomplished, virtually ruling out the context of Jer 44.

Some scholars refer to the position of the oracle in the book and the nature of its contents as a farewell oracle of sorts (Skinner, *Prophecy and Religion*, 346) and argue on that basis that it fits better at the end of Jeremiah's (and Baruch's) career. Hyatt (1101–2) brings yet another factor into play when he suggests the altering and placement of this material by a deuteronomic editor. He concludes that the dating of v 1 ("the fourth year of Jehoiakim") is the most obvious indication of the work of the editor.

Holladay (2:308–9) follows the majority in suggesting the context of Jer 45 to be as noted in v 1. This text functions as colophon at the close of the Jeremiah corpus (see also van Selms, *VT* 26 (1976) 99–103; Lundbom, *JSOT* 36 (1986) 89–114). As such, it may have appeared at different placements at various times during the life of the larger manuscript, but any time the manuscript itself was enlarged, the colophon would have been shifted to the end (Holladay, 2:309; Holladay assumes that the proper placement for Jer 46–51 is in the middle of Jer 25, as in LXX). Lundbom (100–101) calls attention to the ambiguity of "these words" in v 1 and the possibility (noted by Mowinckel, *Prophecy and Tradition*, 61–62) that the context likely shifted at various times in the history of the text, with the present context clearly larger than the events (or words) of Jer 36.

The form of the text is that of an oracle by Jeremiah in response to a lament of Baruch, a lament not that different from those attributed to the prophet earlier in the book. The shifting of person in these verses poses some problems for the interpreter in that it suggests a constantly shifting immediate setting with different speakers alternating, from the narrator to Jeremiah to Baruch to Yahweh to Jeremiah. Van Selms proposes a solution to such problems by positing a series of exchanges in the background of the text that are assumed in the explicit dialogue (*VT* 26 (1976) 99–103). Van Selms reconstructs the production of the scroll of Jer 36 and the traumatic impact that project had on Baruch. He speculates that Baruch had experienced a sleepless night with no answer from Jeremiah to ease the emotional burden Baruch bears because of the extremely negative nature of the message contained in the scroll. According to van Selms, Jeremiah is in turn overwhelmed by the despair of Baruch and presents Baruch's complaint to God, whereupon the divine answer is offered, an answer that then is used to close the book. The major problem with van Selms' proposal is that it tends to assume a psychological and emotional experience that is based on little more than the commentator's own imagination.

Bright (184–86) not only identifies Jer 45 with the events of Jer 36 but reorders the text accordingly. He, like van Selms, identifies the text as an emotional response of Baruch to the terrible word of judgment that the prophet has pronounced in Jer 36. While Bright's proposal is not so elaborate as that of van Selms, it, too, is based on his own speculative reconstruction of Baruch's emotional turmoil and depends on no more evidence than that of van Selms.

Taylor seeks to offer an alternative to the interpretive attempts that have tended to focus exclusively upon the historical issues related to the placement of this chapter in the book of Jeremiah. She calls for a contextual reading of the chapter that is more concerned with literary than historical issues (*JSOT* 37 [1987] 86–87) and that focuses upon the function of the chapter within the MT.

The superscription must connect Jer 45 to Jer 36 in Taylor's view. There is too much intentionality to that effect to be ignored. On the other hand, the placement following Jer 44 makes yet another kind of statement. The impact of the passage is to seal the doom of Judah, reinforcing the finality of Yahweh's judgment. As was noted in connection with Jer 44, at least one possible outgrowth is a shift in focus for any possible hope for the future. It certainly is not to be found in Judah (or in Egypt). Babylon offers the only remaining option.

The following is an outline of the chapter:

    I. The superscription introduces the oracle and connects Jer 45 with other key texts in the book of Jeremiah (v 1).

    II. Jeremiah reports Yahweh's word to Baruch in answer to the scribe's complaint (vv 2–3). The complaint is repeated, obviously in the same form as the laments of both Jeremiah and those commonly found in psalms of lament.

    III. Yahweh's instructions indicate that his larger purposes outweigh the personal issues of any individual, even one dedicated to serving Yahweh (vv 4–5).

The theme of building and planting, tearing down and plucking up, is repeated in a way that emphasizes the negative elements in the theme. The only word of hope for Baruch is the possibility his own life will be spared, described in language that appears to be stereotypical of persons who have barely escaped some terrible threat. He will have his life as a spoil of war.

Comment

1 The initial verse in the chapter serves as superscription. The date given is the fourth year of Jehoiakim, a date that links Jer 45 with Jer 36 and the events revolving around the scroll and its destruction by Jehoiakim. Taylor (*JSOT* 37 [1987] 88) calls attention to the fateful nature of this particular year. In addition to the internal importance for the book of Jeremiah of the scroll incident, this was also the year of Carchemish, the decisive defeat by Nebuchadrezzar of the Egyptians. Perhaps of equal importance was the fact that it was the year when Jeremiah renewed his proclamation of judgment against Judah and the nations (Jer 25, 36, 46). Is this date, as Taylor argues (88), a code for judgment?

Do the "words," which are written in a book, refer to the scroll of Jer 36 or to its reproduction after Jehoiakim burned the first copy? Taylor suggests that it may not be necessary to select one or the other, but it may be more appropriate to allow the ambiguity to remain as intentional, even to include the words of the immediately preceding chapter (*JSOT* 37 [1987] 88).

2–3 The initial word is uttered by Yahweh through Jeremiah to Baruch. The convoluted nature of the exchange has led to a number of different theories related to the compositional history of this text. In fact, the thrust of the sentences is not that difficult to follow. While the identification of various speakers is awkward, it is nevertheless clear in terms of what is communicated and to whom.

The word from Yahweh echoes Baruch's words of complaint, remarkably similar to the laments of the prophet (the so-called confessions) and to elements in common lament psalms. Rather than attempting to dissect the emotional state of Baruch, as with van Selms and Bright, there may be another possible approach. The connection with Jeremiah's similar words may be more than coincidental. It may, in fact, offer the key interpretive clue to the role of the chapter in the larger message (as Taylor, *JSOT* 37 [1987] 88–89).

4–5 The prophet is instructed to deliver a strong word to Baruch in response to the scribe's complaint. Interestingly, the word begins with a reiteration of an important thematic element of the larger message of Jeremiah. Yahweh as the one who builds and plants and breaks down and plucks up reprises the very beginning of the book and the prophet's own commission (1:10). References to this chapter as colophon are certainly supported by the way these terms function as book ends for the prophet's career (Lundbom refers to the inclusio created by the repetition of these key terms, *JSOT* 37 [1986] 101). That is not likely to be the only purpose for this reference, however.

As the terms appear in Jer 45, the emphasis is upon destruction. 1:10 concludes with the positive images of building and planting. 45:4 concludes with breaking down and plucking up. There is a note of finality. Where once hope was possible, it is so no longer, at least in the prophet's (and the scribe's) immediate context. In that regard, connection exists directly with the awful scenes of Jer 44.

In v 5, the chapter ends with a reminder of the priority of the divine economy. The experience of Baruch, like that of Jeremiah, is secondary to the larger purposes of Yahweh. It is Yahweh who acts to fulfill what he has determined. Even those who function as agents of Yahweh's purpose, even the righteous sufferers, are swept up in the greater events of Yahweh's purpose. All they can hope for is the possibility of their lives as "spoil" from the carnage (see 21:9; 38:2; 39:18).

Explanation

As the people of Judah experience the climactic events of Yahweh's judgment, the overwhelming nature of that judgment is evidenced even in the lives of Yahweh's faithful servants. Baruch appears sporadically throughout the book of Jeremiah as the prophet's companion. This chapter seems to indicate that Baruch shared more than a series of life events with Jeremiah.

As noted above, the complaint of Baruch in Jer 45 shares key features with the similar, more extended complaints of Jeremiah and other examples of the complaint genre in the Hebrew scriptures. It seems likely that this chapter functions as a concluding word, a final "book end" to the stories of Jeremiah and Judah. The chapter is the last mention of the prophet as part of the "story."

Baruch is at once reassured and reprimanded. While it may seem odd to hear the seemingly harsh words with which Yahweh responds to Baruch, the response provides a crucial reminder related to the larger message of the book. When God's judgment comes, its sweep is broad indeed. It is the rare exception when provision is made to spare the innocent (Ezek 8). Far more often, the consequences of faithlessness on the part of the majority impact all of society.

If any reinforcement was needed to the message that hope is ended for Judah and her survivors, this word to Baruch provides it. The end is announced clearly and with finality, perhaps making the LXX placement of Jer 45 even more appropriate than that of MT. All Baruch can anticipate is perhaps the possibility that his own life will be spared.

XXVI. Oracles concerning the Nations (46:1–51:64[LXX 25:14–31:44])

Bibliography

Barré, M. L. "The Meaning of *lᵓ ᵓšybnw* in Amos 1:3–2:6." *JBL* 105 (1986) 611–31. **Hayes, J. H.** "The Oracles against the Nations in the Old Testament: Their Usage and Theological Importance." Diss., Princeton, 1964. **Hillers, D. R.** *Treaty Curses and the Old Testament Prophets.* BibOr 16. Rome: Biblical Institute Press, 1964. **Overholt, T. W.** "King Nebuchadnezzar in the Jeremiah Tradition." *CBQ* 30 (1968) 39–48. **Watts, J. W.** "Text and Redaction in Jeremiah's Oracles against the Nations." *CBQ* 54 (1992) 432–47.

Oracles against foreign nations (OAN) appear in every prophetic book except Hosea. Collections of OAN are found in Amos 1–2, Isa 13–23, Ezek 25–32, Zeph 2:2–15, and Jer 46–51 (MT).

The origin of the OAN tradition is to be found among the earliest practices of the Israelite people. The earliest of the OAN was the war oracle, summoning the people to battle, pronouncing disaster for the enemy, and often including a taunt against the enemy. Characteristic of the war oracle was the imagery of the LORD (Yahweh) as divine warrior. With the establishment of the Davidic empire, the war oracle was institutionalized in the cult. Royal psalms were used to proclaim the sovereignty of the monarch under the divine suzerain in order to keep the empire intact. The war oracle was placed within the context of the international treaty. The empire was viewed as Yahweh's imperium, the constituent parties of which were related to Yahweh's rule by treaty stipulations. The idea of Yahweh's imperium is the most important factor in the consideration of the OAN in the prophetic books. The concepts of Yahweh's universal sovereignty, of Yahweh's utilization of foreign powers to achieve divine purposes with reference to Israel, and of Yahweh's right to judge foreign nations existed at least as early as the eighth-century prophets. In the prophetic books, foreign nations are most often condemned for pride, military aggression, and idolatry. The OAN had three main purposes: (1) to pronounce doom on a foreign nation, sometimes for mistreatment of Israel; (2) to serve as a salvation oracle or oracle of encouragement for Israel; (3) to warn Israel about depending on foreign alliances for their security (for the best survey of the development of the OAN, see J. H. Hayes, "The Oracles against the Nations in the Old Testament").

The collection of OAN in Jeremiah appears in LXX immediately after 25:13, with 25:15–38 following (in LXX: 32:15–38), while in MT the collection appears in 46–51. In addition, the order of the oracles differs in the two text traditions. The differences in location and in order require comment.

Jer 25:30–33 presents the announcement of the LORD's lawsuit against the nations. The language of the announcement is formulaic. 25:30a recalls Amos 1:2, the frontispiece for that collection of OAN. 25:30b, like Isa 16:9–10, the oracle against Moab, uses the language of the vineyard. 25:30c, 31b echo the language of the announcement of a lawsuit against Israel in Hosea 4:1. 25:31c recalls Joel 4:2(Eng 3:2) in the phrase "to enter into judgment with" (שׁפט in niphal). As in Amos 1–2, the underlying idea is the suzerainty of Yahweh. While in Amos 1–2 the imperium of Yahweh reflects David's empire, in Jer 25 suzerainty is expanded over all the earth. In the context of 25:30–33, 25:15–29, the cup-of-wrath passage, the list of nations to experience Yahweh's wrath is given, a list that covers all the Fertile Crescent, but beginning with Jerusalem. MT adds Uz, Arabia, Zimri, and Babylon, while both LXX and MT omit Damascus.

In the LXX *Vorlage,* the OAN were placed between 25:13 and 25:15 (LXX 32:15), apparently in no particular order. This is the most logical location for the OAN, and most commentators agree it was the original or earliest location. But with the insertion of the collection of OAN at this point, 25:1–11, 13 was now in a new context, so ways were devised to allow this text, which had originally concerned only Judah, to become a part of the scene of universal judgment. To 25:9 were added the words "all the nations round about" in order to lead up to the inclusion of the OAN (see Holladay, 1:663). 25:12 was added to include the punishing nation, the "tribes of the north" sent to bring judgment against Judah, with the result that "that land" in 25:13, which originally designated Judah, now came to signify that punishing nation. This redaction of Jer 25 evidenced in the text tradition reflected in the LXX does not name Babylon as the foe from the north, the punishing nation. In summary, the LXX *Vorlage* included the OAN in the context of the announcement of the LORD's lawsuit against the nations and redacted 25:1–11, 13 so that those verses now fit the total context of the chapter. It is assumed in this view about redaction that the OAN formed a pre-existing collection that was placed within Jer 25 so that (1) its connection with the preaching of Jeremiah could be affirmed and (2) it could present the LORD as the sovereign of the nations who announced judgment for all nations.

The MT edition of 25:1–14 represents another redaction. MT exhibits several expansions, most of which emphasize the role of Nebuchadrezzar, king of Babylon, the servant of the LORD (vv 1, 9, 11, 12–14), and one of which identifies Babylon as the "tribes of the north" (v 9), which would receive retribution from the LORD in the course of time. The cup of wrath passage, 25:15–29, is also expansionistic in MT. Notable is the addition of the sentence "and after them the king of Sheshak [Babylon] will drink" in v 26. MT in Jer 25 is clearly preoccupied with Babylon's international role and her eventual ruin. While the MT rendition of 25:1–14 provides a suitable introduction for the OAN, the oracles themselves were shifted to the end of the book (46–51), and the order of the oracles was rearranged in a generally chronological order, thus placing the Babylon oracle at the end. The shift in location required a new introduction to, or title for, the OAN collection (46:1; see J. W. Watts, *CBQ* 54 [1992] 432–47, for the most recent treatment of the redaction of the OAN).

The MT redaction is probably to be explained on the basis of historical events resulting in a shift of emphasis. It may be suggested that the events surrounding the conference in Jerusalem related in Jer 27 (594) were crucial. By this time Jeremiah had clearly identified Babylon as the "the foe from the north," and MT added vv 7, 13–14ab to emphasize this fact. Three of the five foreign nations that received a warning from Jeremiah were Edom, Ammon, and Moab. Not only were these nations to expect judgment from the LORD for opposing Babylon, but also

Judah was being warned not to trust in an alliance with them (cf. Holladay, 2:23–24; T. W. Overholt, *CBQ* 30 [1968] 44).

While in some OAN in the prophetic books foreign nations are condemned for their mistreatment of Israel and Judah, it is remarkable that, with the exception of the Babylon oracle (for the special problems relating to Jer 50–51 (see *Form/Structure/Setting*), none of the foreign nations in the OAN in Jeremiah is to be judged for such mistreatment. The oracles are not clearly nationalistically motivated, and thus it cannot be shown that they functioned primarily, if at all, as salvation oracles for Judah. In six of the oracles in Jer 46–49, no reasons are given for judgment. The language about destruction is not strident; it gives no hint of xenophobic hatred. In view of this, why would a prophet concern himself with the nations?

Michael Barré has demonstrated convincingly that the OAN in Amos 1–2 are to be understood in the context of the international treaty. All of the nations, foreign and domestic, were a part of the LORD's imperium. With respect to the foreign nations, they are condemned for treaty violations, specifically for unauthorized aggression against a fellow vassal. They are not judged because they attacked Israel specifically or because they violated laws of human decency or some general law of Near Eastern morality (M. Barré, *JBL* 105 [1986] 611–31).

It is suggested here that the OAN in Jeremiah, especially those in Jer 47–49, be interpreted in the context of the treaty. Those nations formed a part of the Babylonian empire, and since Jeremiah declared Nebuchadrezzar to be the LORD's servant under the LORD's suzerainty, the prophet could be expected to deliver oracles against those nations for covenant violations or as a warning against violations. The oracles provide data that suggest that they were viewed in a treaty context. First, the oracles contain judgment statements that are similar to the curses characteristic of international treaties, especially the Aramaic treaties of Sefire and the Esarhaddon treaties (D. R. Hillers, *Treaty Curses*, 41–79). Second, the cup-of-wrath concept may reflect the treaty and the manner in which it was imposed (see *Excursus: The Cup of Wrath*). Third, there are references to military aggression against fellow vassals that point to treaty violations (48:1–2, 45; 49:1–2).

The conclusion reached is that the OAN in Jer 47–49 reflect the context of the international treaty, providing the prophet a metaphor for expressing his understanding of the relationship of the LORD to the nations. The oracles, whether or not they were all intended to be heard by the nations, served first of all to affirm the sovereignty of the LORD over all the world, and second, they served as a warning to Judah, to refrain from trusting in alliances with, or in dependence upon, nations that stood under divine judgment.

Excursus: The Cup of Wrath

Bibliography

Brongers, H. A. "Der Zornesbecher." *OTS* 15 (1969) 177–92. **Gressmann, H.** "Der Festbecher." In *Sellin Festschrift: Beiträge zur Religionsgeschichte und Archäologie Palästinas.* Leipzig: A Deichertsche Verlagsbuchhandlung, 1927. 55–62. ———. *Der Ursprung der* *israelitisch-jüdischen Eschatologie.* FRLANT 6. Göttingen: Vandenhoeck & Ruprecht, 1905. **McKane, W.** "Poison, Trial by Ordeal and the Cup of Wrath." *VT* 30 (1980) 474–92. **Ringgren, H.** "Vredens kalk." *SEÅ* 18 (1953) 19–30. **Schmidt, H.** *Die Psalmen.* HAT 15. Tübingen: Mohr, 1934. **Veenhof, K. R.** Review of *Salbung als Rechtsakt im Alten Testament und im Alten Orient,* by E. Kutsch. *BO* 23 (1966) 308–13. **Volz, P.** *Der Prophet Jeremia.* KAT 10. Leipzig: Deichert, 1928. **Wiseman, D. J.** "The Vassal-Treaties of Esarhaddon." *Iraq* 20 (1958) 29–80.

The cup of the wrath of the LORD is a well-attested metaphor in the Hebrew Bible and plays a particularly important role in the book of Jeremiah. The key verses in Jeremiah are 25:15–16, 27–29, where the prophet is commanded to take the cup of wrath from the LORD's hand and to cause all the nations to drink it, including Judah. The result of the drinking would be the downfall of every nation, expressed in terms of drunkenness, staggering, lunacy, and vomiting. In the collection of oracles concerning the nations, Moab (48:26), Edom (49:12–13), and Babylon (51:39, 57) were to be made drunk, resulting in their defeat. 51:7 reveals that Babylon had been a golden cup in the LORD's hand, causing all the earth to be drunk and to go mad. The figure of the cup of wrath or judgment is found also in Ezek 23:31–35; Lam 4:21; Isa 51:17–23; Hab 2:15–17; Pss 11:6; 60:5; 75:9; Obad 15–16; Zech 12:2.

The origin of the metaphor and a possible setting in life have been sought in several directions. Was the image based on an Israelite practice, on a non-Israelite practice, or on a practice common in international relations? Was the setting in life cultic, juridical, or divinatory?

H. Gressman proposed that the metaphor arose from an Israelite cultic meal held in a sanctuary, a meal in which the LORD gave joy and delight, and that in the course of time the prophets distorted the meaning of the ceremony in line with their view that the day of the LORD was a day of judgment (*Die Ursprung,* 131–35). Similarly H. Ringgren sought a setting in the Babylonian cult. He referred to the *Enuma elish* 3:1–10, which relates a meal consumed by the divine assembly, replete with wine and beer, in the context of which they determined the destiny of Marduk. Thus, Ringgren emphasized the connection of the meal and the drinking of the cup with the allotment of fate (*SEÅ* 18 [1953] 19–30).

P. Volz suggested divination as the source for the cup metaphor. Referring to the diviner's cup possessed by Joseph (Gen 44:5), Volz regarded the use of the cup as a means to predict the future and as a means of determining destiny (*Der Prophet Jeremia,* 392–93). H. Schmidt sought to interpret Ps 75:9 in light of the ordeal in Num 11: the cup of the ordeal became a cup of poisoned wine (*Die Psalmen,* 144).

Mesopotamian glyptic art has been resorted to for the origin of the cup metaphor. H. Gressmann drew attention to a dedicatory cup of Gudea that portrayed a goddess holding two cups in her hands. He interpreted this representation as evidence that the goddess held the cups of destiny, in one cup the water of life and in the other the water of death, and he related this directly to Jer 25:15–17 ("Der Festbecher," 61). Brongers has cited two other glyptic representations from Assyria. On the obelisk of Shalmaneser III, the king is portrayed in one panel holding a cup in his right hand, grasping the hilt of his sword with his left hand, while Jehu, king of Israel, bows in obeisance. From a later time, Esarhaddon is portrayed on one of his stelas holding a cup in his right hand, a club in his left, while two prisoners grovel before him. Although the combination of cup and prisoners or vassals is striking, Brongers nevertheless rejects these artistic portrayals as the origin for the cup metaphor because there is no evidence that the defeated had to drink the cup (*OTS* 15 [1969] 188–89; for the stelas, see *ANEP* 120, 154).

Brongers surveyed all these attempts to solve the questions of origin and setting in life for the cup metaphor and offered balanced criticisms of each. His conclusion was that the metaphor was wholly Israelite in origin, that it should be viewed only as a symbol, and that it was unnecessary to seek a setting in life outside the poetic power of the writer (*OTS* 15 [1969] 189–92).

W. McKane has turned to the "trial by ordeal" model. He relied heavily on the Targum's renderings of the key passages in Jeremiah, renderings that used Num 5 as the basis for interpretation. Nevertheless, McKane denied that the "trial by ordeal" model by itself was sufficient to explain the cup-of-wrath passages, and consequently he added the banquet-of-death theme, "the gruesome reversal of the benevolent host and wholesome hospitality" (*VT* 30 [1980] 491).

One other possibility, which comes from the sphere of the treaty, remains to be explored. The Esarhaddon treaties mention several rites by which treaties or agreements could be made. In lines 153–56 persons swear by the laden table, by drinking from the cup, by the glow of fire, by water and oil, and by touching one another's breast (the critical edition of the text is provided by Wiseman, *Iraq* 20 [1958] 29–80). Far too little is known about such treaty-making rites to draw firm conclusions about how they actually functioned in the process, but it is clear that "these are the symbolic means by which the people swore the treaty" (Wiseman, *Iraq* 20 [1958] 84). The oath was the necessary act that established a treaty, and the cultic rites seem to have confirmed it. But as the treaties show, the oath sworn by the vassal was a self-curse, and in the case of treaty violation all the curses would take effect. It is interesting to speculate whether the rites that accompanied the oath were subject to reversal. The rites seem to point to well-being and amicable accord, but in the case of treaty violation and renunciation of the oath, one wonders whether the benefits referred to in the rites could be taken away. If so, the laden table would turn into famine (see the curses in lines 440–52, 479–81). The blessings of fire would exist as long as the treaty was kept, but the curse said, "May Girra burn your offspring and descendants" (lines 524–25). K. R. Veenhof understood that the rite with water and oil involved the drinking of water and smearing the body with oil. He related the drinking of the water to the water of curses in Num 5:19 and the oil to the curse in the Esarhaddon treaties: "Just as this oil enters your flesh, so may they make this oath enter your flesh . . ." (lines 622–25). Veenhof was of the opinion that the curses were conveyed to the water and oil and that the one receiving the water and oil received the potential curses (*BO* 23 [1966] 313). If this line of reasoning has merit, one is left to wonder whether the drinking of the cup as a treaty rite could also have contained the curse that would have turned it into a cup of staggering and madness.

A. Concerning Egypt   (46:1–28[LXX 26:1–28])

Bibliography

Bach, R. *Die Aufforderungen zur Flucht und zum Kampf im alttestamentlichen Prophetenspruch.* WMANT 9. Neukirchen: Neukirchener, 1962. **Barthélemy, D.** *Critique textuelle de l'Ancien Testament.* OBO 50/2. Göttingen: Vandenhoeck & Ruprecht, 1986. **Christensen, D. L.** *Transformations of the War Oracle in Old Testament Prophecy: Studies in the Oracles against the Nations.* Missoula: Scholars, 1975. **Donner, H.,** and **W. Röllig.** KAI 2:318. **Doorslaer, J. van.** "No Amon." *CBQ* 11 (1949) 280–95. **Eissfeldt, O.** "Jeremias Drohorakel gegen Ägypten und gegen Babel." In *Verbannung und Heimkehr*, ed. A. Kuschke. Tübingen: Mohr, 1951. 31–37. **Galling, K.** "Goliath und seine Rüstung." In *Volume du Congrès*. VTSup 15. Leiden: Brill, 1966. **Harrison, R. K.** "Balm." *IDB* 1:344. **Höffken, P.** "Zu den Heilsätzen in der Völkerorakelsammlung des Jeremiabuches." *VT* 27 (1977) 398–412. **Holladay, W. L.** "The Covenant with the Patriarchs Overturned: Jeremiah's Intention in 'Terror on Every Side' (Jer 20:1–6)." *JBL* 91 (1972) 305–20. **Honeyman, A. M.** "Māgôr Misābîb and Jeremiah's Pun." *VT* 4 (1954) 424–26. **Janzen, J. G.** *Studies in the Text of Jeremiah.* HSM 6. Cambridge: Harvard UP, 1973. **Jong, C. de.** "Deux oracles contre les Nations." In *Le Livre de Jérémie,* ed. P.-M. Bogaert. Leuven: Leuven UP, 1981. 369–79. **Lambdin, T. O.** "Put." *IDB* 3:971. ————. "Migdol." *IDB* 3:377. **Lundbom, J. R.** *Jeremiah: A Study in Ancient Hebrew Rhetoric.* SBLDS 18. Missoula: Scholars, 1975. **May, H. G.** "Some Cosmic Connotations of *Mayim Rabbim*, 'Many Waters'." *JBL* 74 (1955) 9–21. **Mellink, M. J.** "Lud, Ludim." *IDB* 3:178–79. **Mendenhall, G. E.** *The Tenth Generation: The Origins of the Biblical Tradition.* Baltimore: Johns Hopkins UP, 1973. **Snaith, J. G.** "Literary Criticism and Historical Investigation in Jeremiah Chapter XLVI." *JSS* 16 (1971) 15–32. **Soderlund, S.** *The Greek Text of Jeremiah: A Revised Hypothesis.* JSOTSup 47. Sheffield: The University of Sheffield, 1985. **Watson, W. G. E.** *Classical Hebrew Poetry: A Guide to Its Techniques.* JSOTSup 26. Sheffield: JSOT Press, 1984. **Weippert, H.** "Schild." In *Biblisches Reallexikon,* ed. K. Galling. Tübingen: Mohr, 1977. 279–80. ————. "Panzer." In *Biblisches Reallexikon,* ed. K. Galling. Tübingen: Mohr, 1977. 248–49. **Westermann, C.** *Isaiah 40–66.* Philadelphia: Westminster, 1969. **Wiseman, D. J.** *Chronicles of Chaldean Kings (626–556 B.C.) in the British Museum.* London: The Trustees of the British Museum, 1956. **Yadin, Y.** *The Art of Warfare in Biblical Lands.* New York: McGraw-Hill, 1963.

Translation

The Superscription

1 [a]*The word of the LORD which came to Jeremiah the prophet*[b] *concerning the nations.*[c]

The First Oracle concerning Egypt (2–12)

2*About Egypt: concerning the army of Pharaoh Neco,*[a] *king of Egypt, which was by the river Euphrates at Carchemish, which Nebuchadrezzar, king of Babylon, smote in the fourth year of Jehoiakim son of Joash, king of Judah.*

3 *Prepare buckler and shield!*	(3)
Advance for battle!	(2)
4 *Harness the horses!*	(2)
Mount the stallions!	(2)
Take your stand[a] *with your helmets!*	(2)
[b]*Polish lances!*[b]	(2)
Put on coats of mail!	(2)
5 *Why have I seen (this)?*[a]	(2)
They are terrified,	(2)
they turn back,	(2)
their warriors are crushed,	(2)
they flee in haste,[b]	(2)
they do not look back;	(2)
terror on every side—oracle of the LORD.	(2+2)

6   ^a*The swift cannot flee,* (2)
     the warrior cannot escape;^a (2)
     in the north,^b *beside the river*^c *Euphrates* (3)
     they stumble and fall. (2)

7   *Who is this who rises*^a *like the Nile,*^b (3+3)
     like rivers whose waters surge?
8   *Egypt*^a *rises like the Nile;*^b (3+3)
     ^c*like rivers its waters*^d *surge.*^c
     He said: I will rise and cover the earth, (4+4)
     I will destroy cities^e *and their inhabitants.*
9   *Get up, horses!* (2+2)
     Drive madly,^a *chariots!*
     March,^b *warriors,* (2+4+4)
     men of Cush and Put handling the shield,
     men of Lud handling^c *and stringing the bow.*^c
10   *That day belongs to the*^a*Lord GOD of Hosts,*^a (5+4)
     a day of vindication to vindicate himself against his enemies;^b
     The sword has devoured and is sated (3+2)
     and has drunk its fill from their blood;
For the LORD, God of Hosts, held a sacrifice^c *in the land of the north at the river Euphrates.*

11   *Go up to Gilead and take balm,* (4+2)
     ^a*O virgin daughter Egypt!*^a
     In vain you multiply healings; (3+3)
     there is no healing^b *for you.*
12   *The nations have heard of your shame,*^a (3+3)
     and the earth is full of your cry.
     For warrior has stumbled against warrior; (3+3)
     both of them have fallen^b *together.*^c

The Second Oracle concerning Egypt (13–24)

¹³*The word*^a *which the LORD spoke to*^b *Jeremiah the prophet*^c *concerning*^d*the coming of Nebuchadrezzar,*^d *king of Babylon, to smite the land of Egypt.*
14   ^a*Announce in Egypt,*^a *and declare in Migdol,* (4+3)
     declare in Memphis^b*and in Tahpanhes;*^b
     say: ^c*Take your stand and prepare yourself,*^c (4+3)
     for the sword will devour round about you.^d
15   *Why has Apis fled?*^a (3+3)
     (Why) did your bull^b *not stand?*^c
     Because the LORD thrust him away;^d (3+2+3)
16   *he multiplied the ones stumbling;*^a
     indeed, each has fallen against his neighbor,
     And they say: Arise,^b *and let us return to our people,* (4+2+3)
     to the land of our birth,

away from the sword of the oppressor.[c]

[17] *Call the name of Pharaoh,*[a] *king of Egypt,* [b] *"Noise"; he lets the appointed time go by.* [b]

[18]   *As I live, oracle of the King,*[a] *the LORD* [b]*of Hosts is his name:*[b]   (5+3+2+1)
         for as Tabor is among the mountains, [c]
         and as Carmel is by the sea,
         one will come. [d]

[19]   *Baggage for exile make for yourself,* [a]*inhabitant of Egypt,* [a]   (6+3+3)
         for Memphis will become a ruin;
         she will be desolated[b] *without inhabitant.*

[20]   *A beautiful*[a] *heifer*[b] *is Egypt;*   (4)
         a fly[c] *from the north has come against her.* [d]   (4)

[21]   *Even her mercenaries in her midst are like fatted calves.*[a]   (4)
         For they also turned and fled together,   (5+2)
            they did not stand;
         for their day of disaster[b] *has come upon them,*   (5+2)
            the time of their punishment.

[22]   *The sound*[a] *of her is like a serpent going.*[b]   (3)
         For they come with an army;[c]   (2+3+2)
            they come with axes against her,
            like those who fell trees.

[23]   *They will cut down*[a] *her forest—oracle of the LORD,*   (4+3)
            for it is impenetrable.
         For they are more numerous than locusts;   (3+3)
            they cannot be counted. [b]

[24]   *Daughter*[a] *Egypt will be put to shame;*   (3+4)
         she will be given into the hand of the people of the north.

A Prose Oracle concerning Egypt (25–26)

[25a] *The LORD of Hosts, the God of Israel, said: "Behold, I am bringing punishment upon Amon of Thebes,* [b] *and upon Pharaoh, and upon Egypt, her gods and her kings, and upon Pharaoh and those trusting in him.* [26a] *And I will give them into the hand*[b] *of ones seeking their life, and into the hand of Nebuchadrezzar, king of Babylon, and into the hand of his servants; and afterward she will be inhabited like the days of yore"— oracle of the LORD.*

An Oracle of Salvation for Jacob (27–28)

[27]   *And as for you, do not fear, my servant Jacob,*   (4+2)
         do not be dismayed, Israel.
         For, behold, I will save you from afar,   (4+3)
            and your seed from the land of their captivity,
         and Jacob will return and be quiet and at ease, [a]   (3+3)
            and none will make him afraid. [b]

[28]   *As for you, do not fear, my servant Jacob—oracle of the LORD—*   (4[2]+3+8)
         for I am with you,[a]
         for I will make an end of all the nations to which I have driven you,

^b*But of you I will not make an end;*^b   (3+2+3)
I will discipline you justly,
but I will not at all leave you unpunished.

Notes

1.a. This same kind of introduction to an oracle (beginning with אֲשֶׁר, "which") may be observed in 14:1; 47:1; 49:34.

1.b. Syr adds *dntnb*', "to prophesy."

1.c. Verse is lacking in LXX.

2.a. For Neco, Syr and Tg read *hgyr*' and חֲגִירָא, respectively, meaning "the lame one," apparently reading נְכֹו as נָכֶה, "lame."

4.a. For הִתְיַצְּבוּ, Syr has *symw*, "put on."

4.b-b. LXX has προσβάλετε τὰ δόρατα, "attack with spears."

5.a. Instead of the question, Syr has the statement *mtwl dhzyt dhnwn*, "for I have seen them." To the question, Tg adds תְּבִרִין, "broken," i.e., "why do I see them broken?"

5.b. Reading נָסוּ נֹוס, understanding mem of מָנוֹס as enclitic mem on the preceding verb and deleting the preceding waw as dittogr (cf. Bright, 301, n. a-a.).

6.a-a. LXX and Vg reflect the juss, not as a strong negative (GKC § 107p).

6.b. Syr lacks "north."

6.c. LXX lacks "river."

7.a. Tg adds בְּמַשְׁרִיתֵיהּ, "with his army."

7.b. LXX, Vg, Syr have "river" for Nile. Tg changes the figure entirely: כַעֲנָנָא דְּסָלִיק וְחָפֵי יָת אַרְעָא, "like the cloud that goes up and covers the earth."

8.a. LXX has ὕδατα Αἰγύπτου, "the waters of Egypt," taking the final word of v 7 as the first word of v 8. Tg, Syr read "king" of Egypt.

8.b. The versions show the same readings noted above in *Note* 7.b.

8.c-c. LXX lacks.

8.d. Reading מֵימָיו, "his waters"; suff lost through haplogr.

8.e. The sg noun is taken as a collective. LXX lacks "cities and."

9.a. Vg *exultate in curribus*, "glory in chariots"; Syr *'štbhw bmrkbt*', "sing in the chariots." Both understood הלל in its sense of "praise, exult."

9.b. Reading impv צְאוּ with LXX.

9.c-c. Tg reads וּמָחַן בְּקַשְׁתָּא, "and who smite with the bow."

10.a-a. LXX has Κυρίῳ τῷ θεῷ ἡμῶν, "to the LORD, our God."

10.b. For מִצָּרָיו, Tg reads מַסְנַאֵי עַמֵּיהּ, "enemies of his people," an important theological interpretation.

10.c. Tg קְטָלָא, "a slaughter."

11.a-a. In place of this phrase, Tg has מַלְכוּת כְּנִשְׁתָּא דְמִצְרַיִם, "kingdom of the assembly of Egypt"; cf. 46:19, 24.

11.b. The rendering of the difficult תַּעֲלָה by "healing" is supported by the versions: LXX has ὠφέλεια, "help"; Vg has *sanitas*, "health"; Syr reads *'wdrn*', "help."

12.a. LXX has φωνήν σου, "your voice," understanding קֹולֵךְ instead of קְלֹונֵךְ, "your shame." Although the LXX reading is more suitable for the parallelism with the following "cry," the idea that defeated nations are "put to shame" is such a prominent feature of oracles against the nations that MT is to be preferred.

12.b. Tg: אִתְקְטַלּוּ, "have been killed."

12.c. Syr adds *bhrb*', "by the sword."

13.a. Tg adds נְבוּאָה, "of prophecy."

13.b. LXX: ἐν χειρί, "by the hand of."

13.c. Lacking in LXX.

13.d-d. Tg renders the phrase with לְמֵיתֵי נְבוּכַדְנֶצַּר, "so that Nebuchadnezzar should come."

14.a-a. Lacking in LXX.

14.b-b. Lacking in LXX.

14.c-c. הִתְיַצֵּב and הָכֵן should be taken as inf abs rather than impv because Egypt is fem in the rest of the section (so Rudolph, 250). For הִתְיַצֵּב, Tg has אִזְדְּרַז, "arm yourself."

14.d. Point סְבִיבָיִךְ, *BHS*. LXX has τὴν σμίλακά σου, "your yew tree," apparently for סֻבְּכֵךְ, "your thicket." Christensen (*Transformations*, 218–19) follows LXX, citing 21:14 where סביביה (emended to סֻבְּכָה) and יערה, "her forest," appear in parallel. However, he points the word with a masc suffix: סֻבְּכֵךְ. The appropriateness of "thicket" as a metaphor for Egypt is confirmed by vv 22–23. Tg renders the last line קְטֵילַת חַרְבָּא סַחֲרָנֵךְ , "the sword has killed your neighbors."

15.a. MT has מַדּוּעַ נִסְחַף אַבִּירֶיךָ, "why has your bull been swept away?" Vg and Syr generally follow MT, except that Vg has *fortis tuus*, "your strong one," and Syr has ʿšynyky, "your strong ones." Tg has מָדֵין אִתְּבַרוּ גִיבָּרַךְ, "why have your mighty men been broken?" LXX has διὰ τί ἔφυγεν ὁ Ἆπις, "why did Apis flee?" reading נסחף as two words, נס חף. Apis (Eg. *Ḥpw*) was worshiped in Egypt in the form of a bull. For the spelling חף in Aramaic and Phoenician, see Donner and Röllig, *KAI* 2:318.

15.b. Point אַבִּירְךָ with many MSS. LXX has ὁ μόσχος ὁ ἐκλεκτός σου, "your choice calf."

15.c. Giesebrecht also understood the first two strophes as parallel (231). Tg lacks the entire second strophe.

15.d. For MT הֲדָפוֹ, LXX has παρέλυσεν αὐτόν, "he paralyzed him."

16.a. So MT. LXX has καὶ τὸ πλῆθός σου ἠσθένησεν καὶ ἔπεσεν, "your multitude has fainted and fallen." Vg has *multiplicavit ruentes*, "he has multiplied them that fall." Syr reads swgʾhwn ʾshpw, "multitudes of them are overthrown." Tg has אַסְגִּיאוּ מַתְקְלֵיהוֹן, "they increased their stumblings." Christensen (*Transformations*, 218) emends the text to read [ ] שָׁל >רָבָא| [ ] כָ< , "your champion has stumbled." Rudolph (250) emends to רַהַב הֹרֶב, "mighty Rahab"; for "Rahab" as a name for Egypt, see Isa 30:7; 51:9; Ps 87:4. Rudolph renders the strophe "mighty Rahab has stumbled and fallen" and suggests that a following line introducing the mercenaries has fallen out.

16.b. LXX has ἀναστῶμεν, "let us arise," to agree in number and person with the following verb. Similarly, Syr reads qwmw, "arise" (pl impv).

16.c. For MT חֶרֶב הַיּוֹנָה, LXX reads μαχαίρας Ἑλληνικῆς, "the Greek sword." After "oppressing sword," Tg adds סַנְאָה דְּהִיא כַחֲמַר מַרְוֵיא, "(sword) of the enemy that is like wine making men drunk," thus connecting the sword and the cup of wrath as in 25:27.

17.a. MT: קָרְאוּ שָׁם פַּרְעֹה, "they call there Pharaoh." The translation offered here follows the LXX: καλέσατε τὸ ὄνομα Φαραω, "call [impv] the name of Pharaoh." LXX adds the name Neco, thus dating the oracle to c. 601 B.C. rather than later in the time of Hophra.

17.b-b. LXX merely transliterates these words. Syr reads the verb הֶעֱבִיר, as mʿbr (ptcp), "the one passing (time)."

18.a. LXX has λέγει κύριος ὁ θεός, "says the Lord GOD."

18.b-b. Lacking in LXX. After שְׁמוֹ, Syr adds ʾlʾnpl prʿwn, "surely Pharaoh will fall."

18.c. Syr ʾyk tbrʾ dṭwrʾ, "like the shattering of the mountain," confusing תָּבוֹר and tbr, "to shatter." Rudolph (270) inserts גָּבֹר after כִּי in v 18b and אוֹיֵב after יָבוֹא (גָּבֹר lacking as a result of haplogr and אוֹיֵב lacking as a result of homoioteleuton) and renders: "*gewaltig wie der Tabor unter den Bergen und wie der Karmel am Meer rückt der Feind heran*," "mighty as Tabor among the mountains and as Carmel by the sea, the enemy draws near."

18.d. Tg has כֵּן יֵיתֵי תַּבְרֵיהּ, "so will his destruction come."

19.a-a. Syr has btwltʾ brt mṣryn, "virgin daughter Egypt." Christensen (*Transformations*, 219–20) suggests בַּת(לַת) for בַּת for metrical balance and cites 46:11.

19.b. LXX has καὶ κληθήσεται οὐαί, "and she will be called Woe," perhaps understanding a form of צְוָה, "cry aloud" (cf. Duhm, 340).

20.a. For MT יְפֵה־פִיָּה, read with many MSS יְפֵיפִיָּה; cf. GKC § 84b n.

20.b. For עֶגְלָה, Tg reads מַלְכוּ, "kingdom."

20.c. Translation of the *hap. leg.* is conjectural; cf. Isa 7:18. The versions do not help. LXX renders קֶרֶץ as ἀπόσπασμα, "destruction," lit. "what is torn off," reflecting the root קרץ, "nip off"; cf. Akk. *karāṣu*, "nip off, break off." Vg has *stimulus*, "sting." Syr has ḥylʾ, "army." Tg reads עַמְמִין קְטוֹלִין, "nations, killing."

20.d. MT has בָּא בָא, "has come, has come." The versions (LXX, Vg, Syr, Tg) all understood בָּא בָהּ, "has come against her." The pronunciation of the two phrases in Heb. are identical. D. Barthélemy (*Critique textuelle* 2:768) suggests that a good case can be made for retaining MT since the repetition of the verb may indicate the incessant return of the gadfly.

21.a. LXX has in addition τρεφόμενοι ἐν αὐτῇ, "fed in her."

21.b. Vg: *interfectionis eorum*, "their slaughter"; Syr tbrhwn, "their defeat."

22.a. For MT קוֹלָהּ, "her sound," LXX reads φωνή, "voice (sound)." Syr has qlh dḥylʾ, "the sound of her army," but it is unclear which army is meant. Tg has קָל נִיקוּשׁ גֵינְהוֹן, "the sound of the rattling of their weapons." Christensen (*Transformations*, 219–20) emends to קַלָּה, "quickly."

22.b. LXX reads ὡς ὄφεως συρίζοντος, "like a hissing serpent." Vg has *quasi aeris sonabit*, "will sound like brass," reflecting נחשת, "copper." Christensen (*Transformations*, 220) suggests זחל, "glide," for ילך, "going," and cites the parallel of נחש and זחלי in Mic 7:17. Barthélemy (*Critique textuelle* 2:769) retains MT ילך and refers to the collocation of נחש and תלך in Gen 3:14. He suggests that the serpent may be a reference to the uraeus, the erect serpent with darting tongue that formed a part of the pharaoh's headdress.

22.c. For MT בחיל, LXX has ἐν ἄμμῳ, "on the sand" (בָּחוֹל).

23.a. For MT כָּרְתוּ, Syr reads *pswqw*, "cut down," understanding כִּרְתוּ (impv). LXX translates as a future. Tg has שיצו רברבהא, "her great men have been destroyed."

23.b. Barthélemy (*Critique textuelle* 2:770) understands the last two strophes as referring to trees, not to the attacking army. Thus לא יחקר, "cannot be counted," would refer to all the trees of the forest mentioned in v 22 and throughout v 23. The meaning would be that, even though the trees are numerous and the forest may be impenetrable, they can still be cut down.

24.a. Christensen (*Transformations*, 219–20) emends to בת(לח), "virgin"; cf. v 19.

25.a. LXX has a shorter text: ἰδοὺ ἐγὼ ἐκδικῶ τὸν Αμων τὸν υἱὸν αὐτῆς ἐπὶ Φαραω καὶ ἐπὶ τοὺς πεποιθότας ἐπ᾽ αὐτῷ, "behold I will avenge Amon his son upon Pharaoh and upon the ones trusting in him." Rudolph (*BHS*) suggests that the LXX text results from homoioteleuton, while Bright (305) regards MT as expansionistic.

25.b. The name of Thebes, נא, seems to have caused ancient translators difficulty. For מנא, "of Thebes," LXX read בְּנָהּ, "her son." Syr has *ᵓmwn dmyᵓ*, "Amon of the waters." Vg, Tg understood אמון as המון, "noise," and נא as "Alexandria." For a defense of the interpretation of Vg, see J. van Doorslaer, *CBQ* 11(1949) 280–95.

26.a. The verse is lacking in LXX.

26.b. Syr inserts *bᶜldbbyhwn*, "of their enemies."

27.a. LXX has ὑπνώσει, "he will sleep" (יישׁן), for MT שָׁאן, "at ease." Vg translates it *prosperabitum*, "he will prosper."

27.b. Syr has *lyt mn dmhr lh*, "and there will be none to harm him."

28.a. Tg renders this clause מימרי ארי אעביד, "my Memra will be at your assistance."

28.b-b. Tg has ושיצאה לא אשיצינך, "I will certainly not destroy you."

Form/Structure/Setting

46:1 functions as the superscription to the collection of oracles against the nations in MT (46–51). The superscription to the collection in the LXX occurs at the end of 25:13: "which Jeremiah prophesied against the nations." The odd word order of this announcement of the divine word to the prophet in MT (the relative "which," verb "was, came," subject, and prepositional phrase), found also in 14:1; 47:1; 49:34, leaves the impression that a preceding noun or clause is now missing. Janzen (*Studies*, 113), in line with his theory of the composition of the book, has proposed that the phrase at the end of 25:13, "which Jeremiah prophesied against all the nations," was the original superscription for the collection in MT and that when the oracles came to be placed at the end of the book, the original superscription was expanded secondarily and placed appropriately at MT 46:1. The LXX does regard 25:13b as a superscription to the collection of oracles. However, as Soderlund has pointed out (*The Greek Text of Jeremiah*, 209), MT 25:13b "is not a title at all but a relative clause syntactically connected to the previous construction . . ." In any case, the explanation of the unusual "which" formula remains unavailable.

The historical context of the first oracle concerning Egypt (46:2–12) is the battle at Carchemish in 605, as indicated by 46:2. This crucial battle settled the question of what nation would inherit international supremacy from the Assyrians. In 609 the Egyptian army marched to the aid of the remnant of the Assyrian army at Haran, but Babylon shattered the Assyrians and pushed Neco's army beyond the Euphrates, leaving Egypt temporarily in command of Syria-Palestine. In 605 Egypt was encamped at Carchemish, and it was there that Nebuchadrezzar decisively defeated Neco. A second battle was fought near Hamath, and the rout of the Egyptian forces was complete. These campaigns of 605 effectively ended Egyptian control of Syria-Palestine.

Although the oracle in 46:3–12 functioned on one level as a taunt against Egypt, its real purpose seems to have been to deter Jehoiakim and the pro-Egyptian party in Judah from rejecting Babylonian overlordship in favor of an alliance with Egypt, in light of the Egyptian debacle at Carchemish. 46:25–26, a prose addition to the first two oracles, suggests the key to understanding the purpose of the oracles: the LORD would bring punishment upon Amon of Thebes, upon Pharaoh, and upon "all those who trust in him" (v 25) (cf. Ezek 29:6–8, 16). According to Jeremiah, safety for Judah lay in submission to Babylon, and, indeed, in his view the LORD was using Babylon to achieve divine purposes. In this way Jeremiah incorporated international events into the domain of Judah's religious and political affairs (Carroll, 764). However, Jeremiah was not successful in his attempt to dissuade Jehoiakim from revolt against Babylon (2 Kgs 24:1).

The first oracle may be outlined as follows (following the suggestions of de Jong, "Deux oracles," 369–74; for suggestions of a different structure, see Christensen, *Transformations*, 217, and Watson, *Classical Hebrew Poetry*, 383):

I. Call to arms and reversal (I)
  A. Command to attack (3–4)
  B. The transition (5a)
  C. The reversal (5b–6)
II. Interlude: a satirical antiphon (7–8a)
III. Call to arms and reversal (II)
  A. Pharaoh's purpose (8b)
  B. Call to arms (9)
  C. The transition: the LORD's purpose (10a)
  D. The reversal (10b–d)
IV. The taunt (11)
V. Conclusion: the judgment (12)

This outline of the oracle emphasizes dramatic reversal. The first division (vv 3–6) presents the bare facts of the event: the confident call to arms issued to the Egyptian forces and the subsequent debacle. Terms in vv 5b–6 reverse terms in vv 3-4: "they turn back" versus "advance"; "they flee in haste" versus "take your stand"; "they stumble and fall" versus "go up" (mount up). V 5a provides the transition of (feigned?) surprise. After the antiphonal interlude of vv 7–8a, the pattern of call to arms and the dramatic reversal is repeated with expansions (vv 8b–d, 10c) in order to explain the event in vv 3–6. V 9 is a reprise of vv 3–4, the call to attack; v 10 announces the reversal with a reprise of v 6c. V 12 gives the concluding announcement of judgment with a reprise of v 6d. The structure of the poem highlights the one central point: the success of the LORD's purpose over the purpose of Pharaoh.

Watson (*Classical Hebrew Poetry*, 379–83) has called attention to rhetorical features that highlight the literary qualities of the poem. Three key words are repeated throughout the poem: the root עלה, "go up" (vv 4b, 7a, 8a, 8c, 9a, 11a,

11e), גִּבּוֹר, "warrior" (vv 5d, 6b, 9c, 12c twice), and אֶרֶץ, "earth, country" (vv 8c, 10f, 12b). Wordplay may be recognized in the uses of the root עלה: the imperatives "go up," "attack" in vv 4b, 7a are to be contrasted with the ironic "go up to Gilead" in v 11a and תַּעֲלָה, "healing," in v 11e. The "foes" (מְצָרָיו) of v 10b forms a wordplay with "Egypt" (מִצְרַיִם) in v 11b. And within v 11 צֳרִי, "balm," and מִצְרַיִם, "Egypt," form a wordplay. The staccato beat (2:2) of vv 3–4, 9 and the assonance of the -*u*- sound on the verb forms evoke the rhythm of attack. The antiphonal interlude of vv 7–8b shows the use of simile, the twice-repeated "like the Nile," "like rivers," while v 10 employs the metaphor of the sword of the LORD, characteristic of Holy War imagery. Merismus is seen in v 12ab, where totality is expressed in abbreviated form.

The poem evidences the use of stereotyped features characteristic of judgment oracles/oracles against the nations. The imagery of attack in vv 3–4, 9 is paralleled in 6:23–24. The association of Egypt with waters in vv 7–8 is found also in Ezek 29:3–5, 9–10; 32:2, 13; Isa 19:5–8. The language of v 8c–d appears in 8:16 and 47:2. The mention of the Egyptian allies recurs in Nah 3:9 and Ezek 30:5. The Day of the LORD as a day of vindication for the LORD in v 10 is paralleled in Isa 34:8. The designation of defeat for the enemy as a "sacrifice" for the LORD is found also in Zeph 1:7–8; Ezek 39:17–20. The metaphor of the sword drinking its fill appears in Isa 34:5–6; for the "mouth of the sword," see Num 21:24; Judg 3:16; 1 Sam 15:8. Such traditional or stereotypical features indicate the fund of poetic materials available to composers of oracles concerning the nations.

Neither the redactional introduction (v 13) nor the internal data permit one to determine the historical context for the second oracle concerning Egypt (46:13–24). The introduction mentions that Jeremiah delivered the oracle in the context of an attack against Egypt by Nebuchadrezzar. Four dates come into view as possibilities: 604, 601, 588, and 568. Most commentators have related v 13 to v 2 and have viewed the aftermath of the Egyptian defeat at Carchemish as the most likely setting for the oracle (e.g., Bright, 308; Rudolph, 250; Thompson, 691, although on 692 he refers to the events of 588). Nebuchadrezzar pursued the Egyptian forces from Carchemish and devastated their remnant at Hamath. For four successive years Nebuchadrezzar campaigned in Ḥatti (Syria), destroying Ashkelon in 604 and marching about victoriously in the land (cf. Wiseman, *Chronicles of Chaldean Kings*, 67–71). It must have seemed to any informed observer like Jeremiah that Babylon would be likely to invade Egypt at any time.

In 601 Babylon and Egypt fought a battle near the border of Egypt in which neither side could prevail. The high cost of the conflict is indicated by Nebuchadrezzar's decision to stay at home the following year to refurbish his army. It is possible that the oracle in vv 14–24 was delivered in the context of the events of 601 in anticipation of a Babylonian victory.

In 588 Hophra became king of Egypt at the very time that Nebuchadrezzar was besieging Jerusalem. Hophra made a move to relieve the pressure on Jerusalem (37:6–7; 34:21), a decision that would have encouraged the pro-Egyptian party in Jerusalem. Nebuchadrezzaar lifted the siege temporarily in order to repel Hophra. An imminent invasion of Egypt was possible in such circumstances. The proposed wordplay on the name Hophra (Apries) in v 17 (see *Comment*) would lend support to the view that the events of 588 provided the setting for this oracle. Cornill (451) accepted the wordplay as decisive for dating the oracle in the reign of Hophra, but only after Jeremiah had taken up residence in Egypt (in 582 or after). Eissfeldt ("Jeremias Drohorakel," 32–34) similarly placed the oracle in the setting of 43:8–13. Most recently Holladay posits the events of 588 as the proper setting (2:328).

The fourth possible date is 568, when Nebuchadrezzar invaded the Nile Delta (see Bright, *A History of Israel*, 352), although nothing is known of the extent of the hostilities. Those who place the beginning of Jeremiah's ministry in 627 would argue that it would be unlikely that the prophet was still alive in 568 (Bright, 308).

It is difficult to decide whether the poem should be taken as an anticipation of events or as a description of them. If it is dated to 604 or 601, the poem would anticipate invasion, for in neither campaign did the events referred to in the poem occur. If it is dated to 588, the poem could be a description of the poor showing of Hophra with a warning to homeland Egypt that invasion was imminent (Holladay, 2:327–28), with v 19 taken as anticipatory. Weiser (384) thought that v 19 proved that the whole oracle was a future oracle. If 568 is the date of the poem, the poem would be viewed as anticipatory.

As in vv 3–12, the purpose of the judgment oracle is to juxtapose the power of the LORD to that of the king of Egypt. The unidentified people of the north appear again as the tool of the LORD to humble Egypt. With sarcasm, wordplay, simile, and metaphor, the helplessness of Egypt before the invader is detailed.

Several key words demonstrate the unity of the poem. The word עמד, "stand," in vv 15, 21 is to be contrasted with the command to "take your stand" in v 14. The "name" of Pharaoh in v 17 is counterposed to the "name" of the LORD of Hosts in v 18, along with the word "king." In v 19 appear "dwellers of Egypt" and the "lack of a dweller" (יושב: "one who sits on the throne"[?]; cf. Amos 2:5, 8). The "heifer" in v 20 and the "fatted calves" in v 21 both recall the "bull" in v 15, none of whom could make a stand. The verbal root בוא, "come," in vv 20, 21, 22 recalls the יבוא, "he will come," in v 18.

There are several significant similarities to the poem in vv 3–12: "the day" as a day of calamity in v 21 (cf. v 10); "take a stand" in v 14 (cf. v 4); the surprised question in v 15 (cf. v 5); the parallel pair of words "stumble and fall" in v 16 (cf. vv 6, 12); "the people of the north" in v 24 (cf. vv 6, 10); and the shame of defeat in v 24 (cf. v 12).

The poem is composed of three strophes or stanzas:

    I. Disaster (I): vv 14–27
    II. The cause of the disaster: vv 18–19
    III. Disaster (II): vv 20–24

The first stanza begins with a summons to war uttered by messengers, this time to prepare for a defensive engagement. The failure of the Apis bull, the symbol of power, to stand firm and the consequent disintegration of the mercenary force are the source of the ridicule of the Pharaoh.

The second stanza picks up on the theme of v 15c and identifies the LORD as the real king of the world. The words "name" and "king" in v 17 provide the transition to the second stanza. The concept of name, indicative of one's nature or essence, is the key to the central idea of the poem: "the" king, whose name is the LORD of Hosts, reverses any pretension of supremacy by the king of Egypt, whose name is "Big Noise, who frittered away his chance."

The third stanza presents disaster revisited, the figure of the heifer Egypt playing on the reference to Apis, the sacred bull in stanza 1, and the reference to the mercenaries as "fatted calves" recalling their panic in v 16. Thus stanzas 1 and 3 form a kind of inclusio, with the second strophe highlighting the LORD standing at the midpoint and explaining all.

For whom was the oracle intended? Although the poem is a judgment oracle against Egypt, most likely it was intended for the benefit of Judah. During the reigns of both Jehoiakim and Zedekiah, a powerful segment of Judean leadership advocated rebellion against Babylon and alliance with Egypt. Like the oracle in vv 3–12, this oracle, if delivered at some point in the events of 604–588, would have served to discourage government leaders from placing unwarranted reliance upon the failed power of the Pharaoh.

The judgment oracle in vv 25–26, which has its own introductory formula in MT, supplies, together with v 2, the redactional interpretative frame for the two preceding oracles. It provides a detailed explanation (Weiser, 387) or a prosaic commentary (Rudolph, 252) on v 24, with v 25 enlarging on v 24a and v 26a giving the details of v 24b. It is not possible to date these verses. The identification of Nebuchadrezzar and his officers as the foe from the north does not require a date as late as 568. The shift of emphasis from Memphis and the Nile Delta to Thebes could reflect, however, some aspect of Nebuchadrezzar's campaign in 568 about which no information is available. V 26b is probably an even later insertion that seems to present an additional redactional viewpoint.

V 25 in LXX has only "Behold, I will avenge Ammon her son, upon Pharaoh, and upon those who trust in him." Bright (304–5) follows LXX, regarding MT as expansionistic, while Rudolph (*BHS*) suggested that the shorter LXX text resulted from homoioteleuton. V 26 is lacking in the LXX.

Most commentators regard vv 25–26 (MT) as prose (e.g. Bright, 308; Rudolph, 252). Thompson (694; cf. NEB) altered the text of MT in v 25 by omitting the first "and against Pharaoh" and scanned the lines of both verses as poetic. If one adopts the LXX rendering of v 25, the verse easily scans as poetic.

The consolation or salvation oracle, which appears again in 30:10–11 (MT only) with minor variations, calls on Jacob, the LORD's servant, to have no fear because of the assurance of the LORD's presence with him, the LORD's promise to return the exiles, and the LORD's explanation of the original judgment against him.

Although Cornill (457) thought that these verses had their original setting here in Jer 46 (he emphasized the importance of the beginning "and you" as a contrast to Egypt in the preceding verse), most scholars have been of the opinion that they had their original context in Jer 30 (Carroll, Thompson, Weiser, Rudolph). The verses can be taken as a genuine continuation of 30:5–7 (Rudolph, 173).

The discussion of the function of vv 27–28 must be undertaken in the light of the two text traditions (MT and LXX). In LXX vv 27–28 stand between the Egypt oracles and the Babylon oracles. As Carroll (773) has indicated, the verses function as a frontispiece to the Babylon oracles in LXX. In the MT tradition the order of the foreign nation oracles is different, with the result that vv 27–28 stand between the Egypt oracles and the oracle concerning the Philistines, but with no discernible relationship to the latter. Thus in MT the verses can only be seen as a postscript to the Egypt oracles, in which case their appropriateness comes into question when "I will make a full end of the nations" (v 28) is compared to the promise of repopulation for Egypt in v 26b (so Carroll, 773). Rudolph (253) regarded vv 27–28 as an addition to v 26b that served as a protest against the promise of v 26b, indicating that the promise would have only a temporary force.

In form, vv 27–28 constitute a salvation oracle that strongly resembles several passages in Deutero-Isaiah: 41:8–13, 14–16; 43:1–7; 44:2–5. Westermann (*Isaiah 40–66*, 68–73) found the oracle's original setting in the cult and considered it to be the priestly oracle of salvation given in response to an individual's lament. Thus the prophet made use of a liturgical form, just as prophets adopted and adapted forms from legal and wisdom settings. Jer 30:10–11 (= 46:27–28), in Carroll's view (578), stems from the prophetic circles that produced Deutero-Isaiah; the passage functions in Jer 30 in the same way that the similar passages function in Deutero-Isaiah, with the function being less clear for 46:27–28.

Comment

2 The heading "about Egypt" is identical in form to the headings in 48:1; 49:1; 49:7; 49:23; 49:28 and serves as the title for both oracles concerning Egypt in the chapter. The rest of v 2 functions as the introduction to the first oracle. This redactional statement is found in all the versions and is generally accepted as providing the historical context for the oracle that follows. Although Egypt's foe in the north is not named in the oracle itself, and only the phrase "in the north by the river Euphrates" (vv 6, 10) has any historical value, the battle of Carchemish in 605 provides the only likely setting for the circumstances described in the oracle.

3–4 The summons to war is an often-used literary form, both within and outside the oracles concerning the nations, which stemmed ultimately from the Holy War tradition (Bach, *Die Aufforderungen*, 51–91). The brief, staccato commands convey urgency and the excitement of impending battle. The dominant stress in these verses is 2:2.

צנה and מגן are "large shield" and "small shield," respectively. Although the etymologies of these two words are not known (Galling, "Goliath," 157 n. 3), the relative sizes of the shields can be deduced from 1 Kgs 10:16, where 600 shekels of gold were used for the large ornamental shields and 150 shekels of gold for the smaller shields. The smaller shield is elsewhere described as being made of leather (on a wooden frame), oiled (2 Sam 1:21; Isa 21:5), and sometimes carried in a cover (Isa 22:6). For a survey of information on shields in the ancient Middle East provided by excavations and art work, see H. Weippert, "Schild," 279–80.

The coat of mail (סריון, related to Akk. *siriam, širiam*) was a leather coat reinforced with overlapping metal pieces or scales made for soldiers, horses, and chariots (see Weippert, "Panzer," 248).

Opinion is divided about who gave the command to attack and to whom. Carroll (764) and Thompson (688) take the view that Jeremiah reported the command as it would have been issued by an Egyptian officer. Christensen (*Transformations*, 217) suggests that the command to attack was given to the forces assembled against Egypt. De Jong ("Deux oracles," 373) regards the command as issued by the LORD in order to lead the Egyptian troops to their defeat. Holladay (2:316, 318) suggests that vv 3–8 are addressed to the Babylonians and vv 9–12 to the Egyptians. The first opinion is to be preferred in light of v 9.

5 The satirical question "Why have I seen (this)?" (literally: "why do I see?") provides the transition from attack undertaken in all confidence to complete defeat. If the oracle was addressed to Jehoiakim and the pro-Egyptian party in Jerusalem, this question would alert the hearers to Jeremiah's intention to disabuse them of trust in an alliance with Egypt.

The remainder of v 5 consists of six cola, all with the same two-beat rhythm of vv 3–4, which has the effect of stressing the rapid and chaotic course of defeat. The subject of the first five verbs, "their warriors," is located at the midpoint of the series. The concluding colon, "terror on every side," characteristic of Jeremiah's preaching (cf. 6:25; 20:3, 4, 10; 49:29), may be a proverbial curse formula (Thompson, 688). Bach (*Die Aufforderungen*, 51–52 n. 3) translates מגור as "ambush," while Honeyman (*VT* 4 [1954] 424–26) opts for "destruction." For a study of the phrase in all of its nuances, see Holladay, *JBL* 91 (1972) 305–20.

6 For the use of the negative אל to express the conviction that something cannot happen, see GKC § 107p. For similar language in a judgment oracle, see Amos 2:14–15.

7–8a These lines are best taken as a satirical antiphonal interlude. The question "who is this?" in v 7a is answered in v 8a: "it is Egypt." The effect is to ridicule Egypt, which thought its power was as irresistible as the flooding Nile. May (*JBL* 74 [1955] 9–21) has suggested that the symbolism of the insurgent waters may reflect passages such as Isa 17:12–14, in which the "many waters" that surge and roar are the nations that oppose the LORD. Just as the LORD subdued the waters of chaos at the creation, so the LORD continued to battle chaos, symbolized by the many waters.

8b The symbolism of the rising Nile is continued as an expression of Pharaoh's hubris. In the oracles against the nations, the sin of overweening pride, along with idolatry and aggression, is condemned consistently.

9 Pharaoh's summons to war is repeated in terms similar to vv 3–4, except that the forces of Egypt's allies are mentioned. Cush was Ethiopia, independent of Egypt since about 1000 B.C., but now either allied with Egypt or a source of mercenaries. The identity of Put is uncertain, but it is probably Libya (Lambdin, *IDB* 3:971; cf. Bright, 306, who favored Punt on the east coast of Africa). Lud probably refers to the Lydians of Asia Minor, whose king, Gyges, had sent troops to help the Egyptians in their struggle against Assurbanipal in the reign of Psammetichus I (663–609 B.C.) (Mellink, *IDB* 3:178–79; cf. Bright, 306, who discounts Lydians in favor of an African people suggested by Gen 10:13).

The second חפשי, "handlers of," is awkward and may be a scribal addition. Cornill (449) deleted it for grammatical and rhetorical reasons. "To tread the bow" means to use the knee or foot to bend the bow for stringing.

10 The entire verse employs the imagery of Holy War ("day of vindication," "devouring sword," "sacrifice"). The root נקם, usually translated "vengeance," should be translated "vindication" (Mendenhall, *The Tenth Generation*, 69–104).

This sudden outburst of Holy War prophecy contrasts the failure of Pharaoh's war with the success of the LORD's Holy War (Snaith, *JSS* 16 [1971] 25–26).

C. de Jong ("Deux oracles," 375–76) has emphasized the ambiguity of the term צָרָיו, "his enemies." On the one hand, the Egyptians are clearly meant, and the wordplay with מִצְרַיִם, "Egypt," reinforces this identification. On the other hand, the partisans of Josiah, the anti-Egyptian party in Judah, who would have understood Egypt's defeat as judgment for the death of Josiah, would have included Jehoiakim and his supporters as the LORD's enemies.

11–12 The association of balm with the region of Gilead is well attested in the Bible (Gen 37:25; 43:11; Ezek 27:17; Jer 51:8). The identification of the plant producing balm has not been determined, nor do biblical references establish that balm trees grew in Gilead (Harrison, *IDB* 1:344). More likely is the view that the association of balm with Gilead results from the location of Gilead on the trade route that brought aromatic resins from the east.

The command "to go up to Gilead" is ironical. Just as the Egyptian command to attack (עלה) resulted in defeat, so the command to go up (עלה) to Gilead would have the same lack of success. The wordplay of עלה, "go up," with תְּעָלָה, "healing," indicates Egypt's total failure.

Snaith (*JSS* 16 [1971] 17) has called attention to the political importance of Gilead for Egypt, a territory prized for commerce and as a defensive barrier. Between 609 and 605, Egypt again gained control over Gilead along with the rest of Syria-Palestine. But the defeat at Carchemish severed Egypt's hold on Gilead, and thus the taunt of v 11 becomes sharper: no Gilead meant no territorial expansion and no healing for her grievous wound.

C. de Jong ("Deux oracles," 376–77) sees in v 11cd a reference to Assurbanipal's conquest of Egypt in 663 and Egypt's attempt to rebound from that defeat with the forceful new policies of Neco. But Egypt's new dreams proved illusory. All the world had heard of Egypt's defeat, but would Jehoiakim listen and draw the lesson?

13 For the discussion of this verse, see *Form/Structure/Setting*.

14 The first four verb forms are plural imperatives. Who are the messengers commissioned to warn Egypt of attack?

Migdol and Tahpanhes were located in the Nile Delta, while Memphis was situated near the point where the Nile branches to form the delta. Migdol ("tower") is consistently located in biblical tradition in northern Egypt (Exod 14:2; Num 33:7; Jer 44:1; Ezek 29:10; 30:6), perhaps to be identified with Tell el-Her (Lambdin, *IDB* 3:377). Tahpanhes was a frontier city of eastern Egypt, the modern Tell Defneh. Memphis, an early capital of Egypt and at all times an important cult center, Migdol, and Tahpanhes are mentioned in 44:1, along with the land of Pathros ("the land of the south") as centers of Jewish population after 582. Whether the mention of these particular cities in 46:14 is happenstance or the oracle in 46:14–24 was at one point directed against those who had fled to Egypt for safety after the murder of Gedaliah is impossible to determine.

15 Apis, the sacred bull and symbol of fertility, was the representation of an aspect of the god Ptah of Memphis. In Hellenistic and Roman times, Apis was identified with Osiris, god of the realm of the dead, to form the god Serapis. The figure of the mighty bull running away in panic is, of course, incongruous, and the question of astonishment recalls 46:5. The word for bull, אַבִּיר, "mighty one," is also used for the LORD (Gen 49:24; Isa 1:24; 49:26; 60:16; Ps 132:2, 5) and is commonly translated as the "Mighty One." In this oracle it is deity against deity, bull against bull, king against king. Duhm (339) pointed to the parallel in Isa 19:1: "the idols of Egypt will tremble at the approach of the LORD."

16 The verse offers another example of the literary form "summons to flight," not listed, however, by Bach, *Aufforderungen*, 15–20.

The words "stumble" and "fall," a parallel pair in vv 3–12, appear again here. See *Notes* for the textual variants and some suggestions for the emendation of הרבה. Giesebrecht (229) emended הרבה to עֵרְבְּךָ, "your foreign folk" (or "troops") (cf. 25:20; 50:37), whereas Duhm (339–40) and Rudolph (251) understood the ones stumbling and falling to be foreign traders.

17 שָׁאוֹן, "Noisy One" or "Big Noise." Rudolph (251) and Weiser (385) placed the derisive name on the lips of the mutinous mercenaries.

The possible wordplay הֶעֱבִיר, "he let pass by," and Apries (Hophra) has occasioned every kind of comment. Duhm (340) recognized the possible wordplay, but he rejected v 17 as a marginal gloss on the basis that a joke hardly fits in the context of serious statements. Rudolph (251) cautioned against overemphasizing the force of the wordplay because it is over-subtle. Thompson (692) and Holladay (2:330) accept the wordplay without serious question, while Cornill (451) made the wordplay decisive for dating the oracle. What is known of Hophra would support the impression left by the wordplay; he was a young, impetuous king whose every military venture failed or showed only brief success (*ABD* 3:286–87).

18 "As I live" is an oath formula; cf. Exod 6:8; Ezek 17:16; 20:5; Isa 62:8; Zeph 2:9. The purpose of the oath was to certify that one told the truth. In Isa 62:8 the LORD swore by his right, strong arm; in Ezek 17:16 and in Zeph 2:9 he swore by his own life. Here the oath serves to emphasize the victory of the LORD's purpose in the strongest possible terms. The following phrase, "whose name is the LORD of Hosts," sets the honorific title of the LORD in contrast to the derisive name of Pharaoh with a liturgical, hymnic ring (Weiser, 385).

Mount Tabor and Mount Carmel, imposing and dominating topographical features in their settings, provide a fitting analogy for the might of the invader from the north (so Bright, 306, and Thompson, 692). Or does the area of one notable victory (Judg 4–5) serve as analogy for another? The LORD declares that "he will come"; the lack of identity of the invader has an ominous tone.

19 "Prepare baggage for exile" may be conventional language used in the context of defeat, although if the oracle is dated to 588 or later, the poet may have had in mind the recent experience of the deportation of citizens of Jerusalem to Babylon (so Thompson, 693). The inhabitants of Egypt would have a new habitation, leaving behind a ruined land and a vacant throne.

20 Egypt as a beautiful heifer is a symbol both of a fruitful land and of a helpless beast, perhaps recalling the incompetent bull of v 15. She is afflicted by a gadfly (horsefly?). The *hap.leg.* קֶרֶץ may be related to Akk. *karāsu*, "nip off clay," but also "stampede" (cf. the noun *karrisu*, "one who speaks calumny"). The metaphor of the gadfly was intended to depict more than just a worrisome insect, for it was sufficient to put the soldiers to flight (v 21). The phrase "has come upon her" recalls the ominous "he will come" of v 18; cf. also v 21. Lundbom regards vv 20–21 as an example of inclusio, with the verb בוא, "come," marking the inclusio (*Jeremiah: A Study in Ancient Hebrew Rhetoric*, 59).

21 The mercenaries are likened to fatted calves of the stall, either pampered and useless in a crisis or fattened for slaughter (so Thompson, 693). The language describing their route recalls the parallel passage in v 5.

22–23 Duhm (340) noted that the heifer of Egypt has become a snake and a forest, and the gadfly has become a band of woodcutters as numerous as locusts (note the wordplay רבו מארבה). The reason for the choice of these symbols is not clear, but Cornill (455) referred to the uraeus serpent, the symbol of supreme power on the crown of the Pharaoh. Just as the Apis bull could not stand, so the serpent slinks away at the sound of the approaching woodcutters. The might of Egypt stands helpless and discredited.

The metaphor of the forest for a people or a country is found also in Isa 10:33–34. In Jer 21:14; 22:7 the metaphor refers to the palace of the king in Jerusalem (cf. 1 Kgs 7:2, "the House of the Forest of Lebanon"). Weiser (386) interpreted the forest as an image of the thick population of the Nile Delta, or perhaps of the numerous army. As an alternative to taking the forest as metaphor, reference may be made to the practice of cutting trees in time of siege to build a containment wall around a city (cf. Yadin, *The Art of Warfare in Biblical Lands* 2:346; in a scene at the mortuary temple at Medinet Habu, Egyptian soldiers are portrayed cutting down trees during a siege). Deut 20:19–20 lays down strictures against cutting down fruit trees to use in siege works.

24 As in v 12, Egypt "will be put to shame," either a general term for being discredited before the nations or a reference to the violation of captive women by conquering troops (so Thompson, 693; Carroll, 771). The verse is a concluding summary for the oracle (Weiser, 387).

25 Carroll (772) identified "those who trust in him" as the Egyptians themselves. However, the threat may go beyond the political realities that characterized the relationship of Egypt and Babylon and focus on the religious and political threat to Judeans posed by Egypt. "Those who trust in him" may refer to the Judeans who fled to Egypt in 582 to escape the expected wrath of Babylon for the crimes at Mizpah (Jer 40; Cornill, 456; Weiser, 387); since they placed their confidence in Egypt, they would suffer the same fate as that of the Egyptians. Alternatively, "those who trust in him" may refer to the remnant of the pro-Egyptian party in Jerusalem, which had consistently advocated alliance with Egypt. Political alliance often entailed religious syncretism, whether or not it was decreed by the stronger power. In any case those who trusted in him (Amon or Pharaoh) had not trusted in the LORD; worshiper and worshiped alike were subject to divine punishment.

26 The tool of the LORD's punishment is identified as Nebuchadrezzar and his officers, thus identifying the "foe from the north" alluded to in the two previous oracles. For the language "I deliver them into the hand of those seeking their life," cf. 21:7; 44:30.

The promise of a future repopulation of Egypt comes as something of a surprise in view of the unrelieved doom and disaster proclaimed against her in the preceding oracles. Carroll (772) points out that the promise probably reflects a more positive view of Egypt than is found in the rest of the book of Jeremiah (cf. Isa 19:18–25). Rudolph (252) suggested that the promise was not intended to negate Jeremiah's oracles of judgment but to indicate that they were temporally limited. Other commentators, such as Duhm (342) and Weiser (387), considered v 26b to simply reflect the historical reality following 568; Egypt was not depopulated and retained her sovereignty.

A different understanding of v 26b can be achieved if it is studied in connection with the similar passages in 48:47; 49:6; 49:39. In these latter passages a reversal of fortunes is promised to Moab, Ammon, and Elam. Why were these four nations singled out for special consideration? Höffken (*VT* 27 [1977] 398–412) has argued that these four "salvation" statements serve a redactional purpose in relation to an ideal conception of the land of Israel. Egypt and Elam were never Israelite territories, and therefore nothing stood in the way of their future restoration. Of course Israel never claimed Babylonian territory, either, but in the Babylon oracles, the great Chaldean kingdom already assumed something of the status of the great "world power" inimical to the purpose of the LORD (404). Consequently, no salvation statement could be made about Babylon. The lands of Philistia, Edom, and Kedar were areas claimed for Israel in all the descriptions of the ideal land. The question of Moab and Ammon is more complex, because on the one hand both areas were included in David's empire, while on the other hand the concept of the ideal land of Israel in the post-exilic era proposed by the deuteronomic literary circle adopted the Jordan River as the eastern boundary and thus excluded them (Ezek 47). Höffken concluded that the statements about the restoration of Moab (48:47) and of Ammon (49:6) reflect a redactional viewpoint representative of the deuteronomic circles. The question of Damascus is still more difficult because, in addition to the ideal boundaries of the Davidic empire, which included Syria, the northern boundary of Israel was viewed differently in several passages (Num 33 and Ezek 47). Even if the latter concept of the ideal boundaries of the land was in the mind of the redactor, Höffken concluded that Israel could not entertain thoughts of restoration for Damascus because of the historical threat from that quarter due to adjoining boundaries (403).

The promise of restoration for Egypt must still be seen in a broader context: the similar passages in Isa 19:18–25 and Ezek 29:13–16. In the latter passage Egypt was to be restored and exiles returned, but the new Egypt was to be so small and weak that never again could she be a reliance for the people of Israel.

27–28 This salvation oracle resembles most closely the oracle in Isa 41:8–13, both in form and in content. V 27 begins with the address "but you" (cf. Isa 41:8), the call "fear not" (cf. Isa 41:10), noun clauses in v 27b (cf. Isa 41:10) substantiating the call, followed by verbs in perfect (cf. Isa 41:8–9) constituting the assurance of salvation. V 28b continues with verbs in imperfect (cf. Isa 41:11–12) pointing to a future reality (cf. Westermann, *Isaiah 40–66*, 69–73). Both oracles promise return from exile and annihilation of foes.

The correspondences between Jer 46:27–28(30:10–11) and Isa 41:8–13 are clear. What is not so clear is whether Jeremiah or his circle influenced the circles that produced Deutero-Isaiah, or vice versa. While Carroll (578) is of the opinion that Jer 46:27–28 originated in the Deutero-Isaiah circles, Thompson (557) noted that v 28(30:11) contains expressions found elsewhere in the book of Jeremiah: (1) "I will not make a full end of you" (4:27; 5:10, 18; 30:11); (2) "nations among whom I have driven you" (9:16); (3) "I will punish you in just measure" (10:24); (4) "I am with you to save you" (1:8; 15:20).

Explanation

The precipitous decline of Assyria and the rapid rise of Babylon to power on the international scene toward the end of the seventh century brought turmoil to the whole Middle East. Egypt was the only nation in the area strong enough militarily to challenge Babylon. The small nations situated between them had to try to divine what the future held in store for them. Since independence was hardly possible for them, they had to decide which power to submit to, Egypt or Babylon. Wherein lay the greatest advantage, and under the rule of which emperor would they fare the best?

Since the lands of Judah and Egypt were contiguous, and since the land of Canaan throughout most of its history had known Egyptian sovereignty, the political, social, and economic problems facing the nation of Judah after 609 were severe. It is apparent that political parties arose to advocate policies that they hoped would avoid tragedy for the nation. The two most important parties, the pro-Egyptian and pro-Babylonian parties, were active from the time of Josiah until after the end of the kingdom. Josiah favored support for Babylon, and he lost his life in a vain attempt to bar Egypt's northward course to fight Babylonian forces. The "people of the land" who had placed Josiah on the throne in 640 also enthroned Jehoahaz, his successor, only to see him removed summarily by Neco and replaced by his brother, Jehoiakim. Jehoiakim was forced to swear allegiance to Babylon after Egypt's disastrous defeat in 605 at Carchemish by the Babylonians. But by 601, probably in light of the indecisive battle fought by Egypt and Babylon on Egypt's frontier, Jehoiakim rebelled against Babylonian rule. Jehoiakim died before he could see the outcome of his decision, but his brother, Jehoiachin, suffered defeat and exile to Babylon. Jerusalem was captured on 16 March 597, and Zedekiah was appointed by Babylon to rule in Judah. By that time political intrigue ruled, and weak Zedekiah surrendered to the pressure and rebelled against Babylon. The decision was disastrous, for in 587 Judah was devastated and the nation ceased to exist as a national entity.

These events provided the setting for most of Jeremiah's ministry. Whether he was an active member of the pro-Babylonian party is unknown, but he consistently counseled kings to serve the king of Babylon. The prophet saw Nebuchadrezzar as the LORD's servant, appointed to achieve the LORD's plan, meaning that rebellion against Babylon was rebellion against the LORD. For Jeremiah the most important question was not that of national power, prestige, or independence but rather that of national survival. Egypt was a weak reed, and those who trusted in the Pharaoh for support were destined to perish with him.

These events provide the settings for these judgment oracles concerning Egypt. It is important to note that nowhere in these oracles is there the suggestion that Egypt faced disaster because of her mistreatment of Israel/Judah. There is no expression of hatred or vengeance against Egypt, although satire, irony, and the taunt are fully in evidence. Egypt is judged for pride and aggression as is typical in other oracles concerning the nations. In fact it is doubtful that these oracles were intended for Egyptian ears. Rather the purpose of the oracles was to lead the kings of Judah away from dependence on Egypt and toward the acceptance of vassalage to Babylon so that the nation might live.

The LORD is the chief actor in these oracles. The oracles are structured to contrast the plan of Pharaoh with that of the LORD. Pharaoh's claim to sovereignty over the world had not reckoned with the reality of the LORD's plan. The mocking name given to Pharaoh expressed his true character and incompetence, while the power of the name of the God of Israel, the LORD of Hosts, is demonstrated by the LORD's ability to effect the divine word. Human beings may propose; God disposes.

B. Concerning the Philistines (47:1–7 [LXX 29:1–7])

Bibliography

Fitzmyer, J. A. "The Aramaic Letter of King Adon to the Egyptian Pharaoh." *Bib* 46 (1965) 41–55. **Katzenstein, H. J.** "'Before Pharaoh conquered Gaza' (Jeremiah xlvii 1)." *VT* 33 (1983) 249–51. **Kutsch, E.** "'. . . denn Yahwe vernichtet die Philister': Erwägungen zu Jer 47, 1–7." In *Die Botschaft und die Boten. FS* H. W. Wolff, ed. J. Jeremias and L. Perlitt. Neukirchen: Neukirchener, 1981. 257–67. **Malamat, A.** "The Historical Setting of Two Biblical Prophecies on the Nations." *IEJ* 1 (1950–51) 154–59. **Soderlund, S.** *The Greek Text of Jeremiah: A Revised Hypothesis.* JSOTSup 47. Sheffield: JSOT Press, 1985.

Translation

1a *The word*[b] *of the LORD which came to Jeremiah the prophet concerning the Philistines, before Pharaoh smote Gaza:*[c]
2 *"Thus says the LORD,*

Behold, [a]*waters are rising*[a] *from the north,*	(4+3+3+3)
and they will become a flooding torrent,	
and they will overflow[b] *the land and its fullness,*	
the city and those dwelling in it.	
And people will cry out,	(2+4)
and every inhabitant of the land will wail.	
3 *At the sound of* [a]*the stamping of the hooves of his stallions,*[a]	(4+2+2)
at the rattling of his chariots,	
the noise of his wheels,	
fathers do not look back for children	(3+2)
on account of the weakness of their[b] *hands,*	
4 *because of the day that is coming to destroy all the Philistines,*	(5+6)
[a]*to cut off for Tyre and Sidon every surviving helper,*[a]	
for Yahweh is destroying[b] *the Philistines,*[c]	(3+3)
the remnant of the [d]*coastland of Caphtor.*[d]	
5 *Baldness*[a] *has come upon Gaza;*	(3+2+2+2)

> Ashkelon has been silenced,[b]
> the remnant of the Anakim.[c]
> "'How long will you gash yourself?'"[d] (2)
>
> 6 'Ah, sword of the LORD, how long will you not be quiet?[a] (6+2+2)
> Gather yourself into your sheath,
> rest and be silent.'[b]
>
> 7 'How can it be quiet?[a] (2+2+5)
> The LORD has ordered it against Ashkelon,
> and against the shore of the sea, there[b] he has appointed it.'"[c]

Notes

1.a. The introduction of an oracle with אשר may be noted in 14:1, 46:1, 49:34.

1.b. Tg adds נבואה, "of prophecy."

1.c. For this verse LXX has only ἐπὶ τοὺς ἀλλοφύλους, "against the foreigners." Carroll (774) suggests that in light of 46:2b; 48:1; 49:1, 7, 23, 28, LXX may have preserved the original title for the oracle.

2.a-a. Syr has instead mytʾ ʾnʾ ʿlymʾ, "I am bringing young men." For "waters," Tg has עממיא, "peoples."

2.b. Tg has ויבזון, "they will plunder." Cf. below on 47:4.

3.a-a. Vg has pompae armorum et bellatorum ejus, "of the marching of arms and of his soldiers." Tg renders אביריו, "his stallions," as גיברוהי, "his mighty men."

3.b. LXX and Syr supply "their."

4.a-a. For להכרית, "to cut off," 2QJer has הכרתי, "I will cut off." The parallelism of the first two lines suggests that Philistia was the "surviving helper," or ally, of Tyre and Sidon. For the mention of Tyre and Sidon in league with other states against Babylon, see 27:3. All the versions present a different viewpoint about the fate of Tyre and Sidon. The LXX is representative: καὶ ἀφανιῶ τὴν Τύρον, καὶ τὴν Σιδῶνα, καὶ πάντας τοὺς καταλοίπους τῆς βοηθείας αὐτῶν, "and I will destroy Tyre and Sidon and all the rest of their allies."

4.b. Syr, Tg translate "to plunder."

4.c. LXX lacks "the Philistines."

4.d-d. LXX has τῶν νήσων, "the islands." Vg, Syr, Tg have "Cappadocia" for "Caphtor."

5.a. For "baldness," Syr has mhwtʾ, "sore, wound." Tg has פורענותא, "punishment."

5.b. For MT נדמתה, LXX has ἀπερρίφη, "is cast away," reflecting נרמתה (BHS). Syr, Tg both use the root חבר, "to break," in the pass.

5.c. MT עמקם, "their valley, plain"; cf. also Vg. Bright (310) suggests the meaning "strength" as attested in Ug. He also cites 49:4, where his suggestion may carry more weight. Tg supports this view with תוקפהון, "their strength." The tr. adopted here follows the LXX Ενακιμ, "Anakim," and presupposes a confusion of nun and mem. This reading recalls Josh 11:22; an enclave of the Anakim survived (נשארו) in Philistia. For a thorough review of the problem of translating עמקם, see Barthélemy (Critique textuelle, 771–72).

5.d. MT תתגודדי, "gash yourself." 2QJer has תתגוררי, "whirl about"; it is unclear whether Philistia or the sword is meant. LXX has ἕως τίνος κόψεις ἡ μάχαιρα τοῦ κυρίου, "how long will you smite, sword of the LORD?" Since ritual cutting of the body in time of mourning is so well attested (Deut 14:1; Jer 16:6; 48:37), MT is to be preferred.

6.a. Syr adds wlʾ ttnyhyn mn dlmhrb, "and not cease from destruction?"

6.b. LXX ἐπάρθητι, "be elated."

7.a. Translation follows LXX πῶς ἡσυχάσει, "how shall it be quiet?" Note that the rest of the verse in MT refers to the sword with 3fs suff. Barthélemy (Critique textuelle, 773–74) accepts MT תשקטי (2fs), because it is the more difficult reading, and thus treats the last part of the verse as an aside.

7.b. 2QJer has שמה for שם.

7.c. LXX has ἐπεγερθῆναι, "to awaken."

Form/Structure/Setting

This brief chapter contains an oracle of doom against all of Philistia. The oracle describes an imminent, all-consuming catastrophe with the most frightful results: the wailing of the stricken, panic that produces an unreasoning lack of paternal care, mourning rites, and the anguished cry. The oracle begins with the typical messenger-speech formula, "thus says the LORD," and vv 4, 6, 7 confirm that, whoever the foe from the north may be, the LORD is the warrior. In its present form, the poem employs four images for the source of the disaster, the first three of which have been met already in the first oracle against Egypt: the rising waters overflowing the land (46:7–8; cf. Isa 8:7–8), the tumult of war (46:3–4, 9), the appointment of a day of the LORD against the foe (46:10, 21), and the sword of the LORD (cf. Jer 50:35–38).

The poem is a unified whole composed of two sections: the oracle of doom (vv 2–5) and the song about the sword (vv 6–7). Vv 2–3 are parallel in theme: the descriptions of the threat and the responses to the threat. V 4 describes the threat in terms of "the day that is coming," and for the first time in the poem the Philistines are named as the ones threatened. V 5 lists mourning practices appropriate for disaster. V 6 furnishes a lament about the LORD's sword, while v 7 supplies the prophet's reply to the lament.

V 2 comprises a tetracolon and a bicolon, v 3 a tricolon and a bicolon, v 4 a tricolon and a bicolon, v 5 a tetracolon, v 6 a bicolon, and v 7 two bicola. Christensen (*Transformations,* 212) and Holladay (2:335) read v 5b with v 6 so that v 5b is a part of the song of the sword (see *Notes*).

Why was this oracle of doom delivered against the Philistines? No accusations are mentioned. There is no hint of hatred or recrimination against the Philistines for attacks against Judah; indeed, the announcement of doom is matter of fact. Two possibilities may be hazarded here. First, Philistia formed a part of David's empire, or at least had been brought within the orbit of David's control. It may be surmised that David was content to let Philistia have some measure of independent action for economic reasons. However, in succeeding centuries Philistine cities were often at war with Judah and may be viewed as being in violation either of treaty obligations, of which we know nothing, or of the *pax Davidica.* Second, if the oracle is from Jeremiah, it could reflect his conviction that any state that resisted Babylonian power was in violation of the LORD's will. Since the time of Adad-nirari III (810–783), Philistine cities had paid tribute to Assyria. But with the fall of the Assyrian state, Egypt and Babylonia competed for domination of the Syro-Palestinian parts of the Assyrian empire. Already Psammetichus I (664– 610) had spent twenty-nine years besieging Ashdod (Azotus). Neco (610–594) exerted power over Philistia and Palestine, and apparently Philistine cities owed allegiance to Egypt prior to the rise of Nebuchadrezzar. The letter of Adon, the ruler of one of the Philistine cities, represents a plea for Egyptian help against an imminent invasion by the king of Babylon (605–604) (cf. J. A. Fitzmyer, *Bib* 46 [1965] 41–55). Therefore Philistia could deserve judgment from the viewpoint of Jeremiah's theology.

The date of this oracle continues to elude interpreters. The superscription (v 1b) includes a temporal clause, "before Pharaoh smote Gaza," which may imply that a pharaoh was responsible for the catastrophe described in the oracle and that the attack may have come from the south. The oracle itself (v 2) describes "waters rising from the north." The figure of the foe from the north is used throughout the book of Jeremiah, presumably of the Babylonians.

Three typical approaches to the problem may be summarized here. First, there have been attempts to harmonize v 1b and the oracle itself. Before the publication of the remainder of the Chronicles of the Chaldean Kings by Wiseman in 1956, some scholars held that the superscription was explained by the statement of Herodotus (*Hist.* 2:159) that Neco defeated the Syrians at Magdolus and then captured Cadytis (Gaza) from the north, Magdolus being taken as Megiddo and the battles dated 609 (A. Malamat, *IEJ* 1 [1950–51] 154–55). More recently Magdolus has been understood as Migdol near the northeastern frontier of Egypt, and the battle referred to by Herodotus has been taken to be the successful repulse of the Babylonians by Egypt in the winter of 601/600 followed by the seizing of Gaza (Katzenstein, *VT* 33 [1983] 249–51; Thompson, 696). In this view Herodotus' Syrians would be the Babylonians or their Syro-Palestinian allies, and the capture of Gaza would reflect a follow-up campaign (from the north?) after Neco had pursued the retreating Babylonian forces.

A second approach focuses on the poem itself, which highlights Ashkelon (47:5, 7). The Chronicles of the Chaldean Kings (Wiseman, *Chronicles*, 68–69) report that Ashkelon was taken by Nebuchadrezzar in his first regnal year, 604. Relating the oracle to this context would retain the image of the foe from the north, and it would not rule out an Egyptian attack on Gaza in 601/600.

A third approach is based on a literary-critical analysis. E. Kutsch (". . . denn Yahwe vernichtet die Philister," 253–67) has suggested the following solution: (1) vv 2, 3b, 4a*a* contain the original oracle about an imminent attack from the north against Philistia; (2) vv 6–7 are an expansion, which provides the fulfillment of the original oracle and probably reflects the destruction of Ashkelon by Nebuchadrezzar in 604; (3) vv 1b, 3a, 4a*βγ* suggest an Egyptian invasion of Philistia from the south, reflecting the events of the campaign of Apries against Tyre and Sidon (Herodotus, *Hist.* 2:161), which he dates 568/7.

The problem of the date of the oracle remains unsolved like so much else in the oracles concerning the nations. Of the three approaches described above, the second has the most to offer.

Comment

1 The form of the superscription is identical with that in 14:1; 46:1; 49:34 (see *Comment* at 46:1 for a discussion of the unusual אשר formula). LXX has only "concerning the Philistines" and is generally taken to be the original introduction. Kutsch (". . . denn Yahwe vernichtet die Philister," 265) suggests the following redactional development: (1) "concerning the Philistines" was the original superscription; (2) the remainder of v 1a was added probably when the oracle was included in the book of Jeremiah; (3) the temporal phrase in v 1b was a later supplement added in the time of Pharaoh Apries. For a discussion of the problems surrounding the temporal clause in v 1b, see *Form/Structure/Setting.*

2 The use of the figure of overflowing waters for an imminent military invasion is found also in 46:7–8 and in Isa 8:6–8. The waters overflow "from the north," recalling the foe from the north mentioned throughout the book. Some older commentators saw here a description of an eschatological-apocalyptic event. B. Duhm (343) believed that the author regarded the fate of the Philistines as a part of a worldwide catastrophe described in eschatological colors. Giesebrecht (231) interpreted אֶרֶץ, "earth," as "world" and הָאָדָם, "humankind," as the world population and concluded that the Philistines were to perish under a general overflowing. Cornill (459) regarded v 2c as a later addition because of its supposed eschatological-apocalyptic character. However, אֶרֶץ can mean simply "land," and the figure of the overflowing waters does not have here a clearly apocalyptic coloring any more than does Isa 8:6–8. Rudolph (255) is certainly correct to point to the Palestinian coloring of the description of the flood. The language of the verse seems to expand logically the catastrophe: waters rising from the north, overflowing the wadis, and flooding the whole land.

According to the present versification, v 2c describes the panic and anguish of the population resulting from the overflowing waters. However, Rudolph (252), apparently following the phrasing of LXX, linked v 2c with v 3a and v 4 with v 3b.

3 As Weiser pointed out (389), the image of overflowing waters changes to military reality (cf. 46:7–9). The language of v 3a is vivid and staccato (Thompson, 697), using only nominal phrases. The *hap. leg.* שַׁעֲטַת (construct) is easily interpreted by context as "stamping" or the like.

4 For the coming day of destruction, a day of the LORD, see 46:10.

The Philistines are viewed here as allies of Tyre and Sidon, a circumstance about which nothing more is known. Jer 27:3 refers to cooperative efforts, if not treaty alliances, of Tyre and Sidon with Transjordanian kingdoms, so a Philistine-Phoenician alliance would not be surprising. For whatever reason, the translators of LXX found the verse troubling and translated "and I will utterly destroy Tyre and Sidon and all the rest of their allies."

5 Because of the catastophe, the Philistines practice mourning rites: the shaving of the head, silence, and the ritual cutting of the body (cf. Deut 14:1; Jer 16:6; 41:5; 48:37). For the textual problems, see *Notes;* see also S. Soderlund (*The Greek Text of Jeremiah,* 220) for the retention of תִּתְגּוֹדָדִי in v 5.

The translation of עִמְקָם as "their plain" makes good sense, but the emendation to "Anakim" has been met with approval by most interpreters and has been followed here. For more discussion, see *Notes.* Cornill (461) suggested "Ekron" instead, because he expected a third city, and Weiser (390) read "Ekron" through homoioarchton. Rudolph (252) wanted to add "Ashdod" after "Ashkelon" (as in Josh 11:22). Cornill (461) wanted to replace "Ashkelon" with "Ashdod" and see a wordplay on שָׁדַד, "to destroy," in v 4.

6–7 The symbol of destruction now passes from overflowing waters and military invasion to the sword of the LORD (cf. 25:27; 50:35–38). The lament was placed in the mouths of the Philistines (Rudolph, 255).

The reply of the prophet is given in v 7. The emendation of תִּשְׁקֹטִי, "(how) can you be quiet?" to תִּשְׁקֹט, "(how) can it be quiet?" makes for a smoother translation (see *Notes*), although a change in person in a verse is met with often enough to occasion no real difficulty. In any case the prophet could have addressed the sword in v 7aα and the Philistines about the sword (third person feminine singular suffix) in the remainder of the verse.

Explanation

This oracle concerning the Philistines shows no close relationship to other oracles about Philistia in the other prophetic books (Amos 1:6–8; Isa 14:29–32; Zeph 2:4–7; Ezek 25:15–17), although several terms are shared: "remnant," "inhabitants," "city," "from the north," and "seacoast." The oracle is typical of oracles against the nations generally, and apart from the historical datum in v 1, nothing in its content suggests a date for it.

The poem leaves no doubt that it is Yahweh the warrior who moves against the Philistines. But the reason for the oracle remains unclear. As already indicated, no accusations are mentioned, nor is there any hint of Philistine aggression against Judah. However, v 4 suggests that Tyre and Sidon were allies of the Philistines at the time reflected by this poem. As Jer 27:3 indicates, in 594 representatives of Tyre, Sidon, Edom, Moab, and Ammon met in Jerusalem to discuss rebellion against the Babylonians. Although the Philistines are not mentioned in Jer 27:3, and although a date for this oracle cannot be determined with accuracy, the alliance with Tyre and Sidon reflected in v 4 may indicate a situation in which the Philistines along with allies would be contemplating an attempt to throw off the Babylonian yoke. This view of the situation, though tenuous and based on no firm historical data, would explain Jeremiah's inclusion of the Philistines in his oracles against the nations. Jeremiah remained convinced that opposition to Nebuchadrezzar was opposition to the LORD's plan (27:6–7).

C. Concerning Moab   (48:1–47[LXX 31:1–44])

Bibliography

Bardtke, H. "Jeremia der Fremdvölkerprophet." *ZAW* 54 (1936) 240–49. **Blau, J.** "Über Homonyme und angeblich homonyme Wurzeln." *VT* 6 (1956) 242–48. **Clark, D. J.** "Wine on the lees (Zeph 1.12 and Jer 48.11)." *BT* 32 (1981) 241–43. **Couroyer, B.** "Corne et arc." *RB* 73 (1966) 510–21. **Dearman, A.** "Historical Reconstruction and the Mesha Inscription." In *Studies in the Mesha Inscription and Moab*, ed. A. Dearman. Atlanta: Scholars, 1989. 155–210. ———, ed. *Studies in the Mesha Inscription and Moab*. Atlanta: Scholars, 1989. **Driver, G. R.** "Reflections on Recent Articles." *JBL* 73 (1954) 125–36. **Gevirtz, S.** "Jericho and Shechem: A Religio-Literary Aspect of City Destruction." *VT* 13 (1963) 52–62. **Grohman, E. D.** "Elealeh." *IDB* 2:75. ———. "Kir-hareseth." *IDB* 3:36. ———. "Moab." *IDB* 3:409–19. ———. "Sibmah." *IDB* 4:342. **Hyatt, J. P.** "The Deity Bethel and the Old Testament." *JAOS* 59 (1939) 81–98. **Kegler, J.** "Das Leid des Nachbarvolkes: Beobachtungen zu den Fremdvölkersprüchen Jeremias." In *Werden und Wirken des Alten Testaments*. FS Claus Westermann, ed. R. Albertz et al. Göttingen: Vandenhoeck & Ruprecht, 1980. 271–87. **Kuschke, A.** "Jeremia 48:1–8: Zugleich ein Beitrag zur historischen Topographie Moabs." In *Verbannung und Heimkehr: Beiträge zur Geschichte und Theologie Israels im 6. und 5. Jahrhundert v. Chr.* FS W. Rudolph, ed. A. Kuschke. Tübingen: Mohr, 1961. 181–96. **Lambert, W. G.** "Kammuš." *RLA* 5:335. **Landes, G. M.** "The Fountain at Jazer." *BASOR* 144

(December 1956) 30–37. **Luckenbill, D. D.** *Ancient Records of Assyria and Babylonia.* Vol. 2. New York: Greenwood, 1968. **Matthiae, P.** *Ebla: An Empire Rediscovered.* Garden City: Doubleday, 1981. **Mattingly, G.** "Moabite Religion and the Mesha Inscription." In *Studies in the Mesha Inscription and Moab,* ed. A. Dearman. Atlanta: Scholars, 1989. 216–27. **Mendenhall, G.** *The Tenth Generation: The Origins of the Biblical Tradition.* Baltimore: Johns Hopkins UP, 1973. **Mittmann, S.** "The Ascent of Luhith." In *Studies in the History and Archaeology of Jordan,* I, ed. A. Hadidi. Amman: Department of Antiquities, 1982. 175–80. **Moran, W. L.** "Ugaritic *sîsûma* and Hebrew *sîs* (Eccles 43:19; Jer 48:9)." *Bib* 39 (1958) 69–71. **Piccirillo, M.** "The Mosaics at Um er-Rasas in Jordan." *BA* 51 (1988) 208–13, 227–31. **Rendtorff, R.** "Zur Lage von Jaser." *ZDPV* 76 (1960) 124–35. **Schottroff, W.** "Horonaim, Nimrim, Luhith und der Westrand des 'Landes Ataroth': Ein Beitrag zur historischen Topographie des Landes Moab." *ZDPV* 82 (1966) 163–208. **Simons, J.** *The Geographical and Topographical Texts of the Old Testament.* Leiden: Brill, 1959. **Trever, J. C.** "Juniper." *IDB* 2:1027. **Worschech, U.,** and **Knauf, E. A.** "Alte Strassen in der nordwestlichen *Ard el-Kerak*: Ein Vorbericht." *ZDPV* 101 (1985) 128–33. **Yadin, Y.** "Expedition D." *IEJ* 12 (1962) 227–57. **Zyl, A. H. van.** *The Moabites.* Leiden: Brill, 1960.

Translation

[1]*For Moab: thus says the LORD* [a]*of Hosts, God of Israel,* [a]
   Alas for Nebo, for it is devastated. [b]   (4+3+3+4)
      Kiriathaim is shamed, [c] *is captured,* [d]
      the fortress [e] *is shamed, is shattered;*
[2]   *the glory* [a] *of Moab is no more.*
   In Heshbon they planned calamity against her: (4+3+6)
      "*Come,* [b] *and let us cut her off* [c] *from being a nation.*"
      Also Dimon, [d] *wail aloud,* [e] *after you the sword will go.*
[3]   *Hark, a cry from Horonaim,*   (3+3+2)
      "*Destruction and great shattering!*
[4]   *Moab is shattered!*"
   A cry is heard as far as Zoar. [a]   (3)
[5] *For at the ascent of Luhith* [a]   (3+3)
      they go up with weeping; [b]
   For at the descent of Horonaim   (3+4)
      they hear a cry of shattering. [c]
[6] *Flee, save your lives!*   (3)
   You will be [a] *like a juniper bush* [b] *in the desert.*   (4)
[7] *For on account of your trusting in your works* [a]   (4+1)
   and in your treasures,
   also you [b] *will be captured;*   (2)
   Chemosh will go into exile,   (3+3)
      his priests [c] *and his officials together.* [d]
[8] *And the destroyer* [a] *will come unto every city,*   (3+3+2+2)
      and no city will escape,
      and the valley will perish,
      and the plateau will be destroyed,
      [b]*says the LORD.*
[9] *Give salt* [a] *for Moab, for* [b]*she will surely surrender,* [b]   (6+6)
   her cities will become a desolation, [c]*without inhabitant in them.* [c]

[10] *Cursed is the one who does the work of the LORD with slackness, and cursed is the one who holds back his sword from bloodshed.*

[11]	Moab has been at ease from his youth,	(3+3)
	ᵃkeeping quiet upon his lees;ᵃ	
	he has not been emptiedᵇ from vessel to vessel,	(3+3)
	he has not gone into exile;	
	therefore his taste remains in him,	(4+3)
	his scent is not changed.	
[12]	Therefore, behold the days are coming, says the LORD,	
	I will send to him ᵃcellar-men who will tilt him,ᵃ	(3+2+2)
	and they will emptyᵇ his vessels,ᶜ	
	and hisᵈ jars they will shatter.	

[13] *And Moab will be ashamed of Chemosh just as the house of Israel were ashamed of Bethel,ᵃ their confidence.*

[14]	How can you say,	(2+2+3)
	"We are heroes,	
	mighty men of war?"	
[15]	The destroyerᵃ of Moab and of her cities has come up,ᵇ	(4+4+5)
	and the choicest of his young men go down to slaughter,	
	ᶜsays the King, whose name is LORD of Hosts.ᶜ	
[16]	The disasterᵃ of Moab is drawing near,	(4+3)
	and his calamity hastens speedily.	
[17]	ᵃBemoan him, all who are round about him,ᵃ	(3+3)
	all who know his name;	
	say: "How the powerful scepter is shattered,	(4+2)
	the glorious staff."	
[18]	Descend from (your) glory and sitᵃ on the dry ground,ᵇ	(4+3)
	O inhabitant of Dibon.ᶜ	
	For the destroyer of Moab has come against you;	(4+2)
	he has destroyed your strongholds.	
[19]	Stand by the road and look, O inhabitant of Aroer;ᵃ	(5+3+3)
	ask him who flees and her who is escaping,	
	say "What has happened?"	
[20]	"Moab is shamed because it is shattered.ᵃ	(3+2+2+3)
	ᵇWail and cry out!ᵇ	
	Tell it at the Arnon:	
	'Moab is destroyed.'"	

[21] *Judgment has come to the tableland, to Holon, Jahzah, and Mephath,* [22] *against Dibon, Nebo, Beth-diblathaim,* [23] *Qiryathaim, Beth-gamul, Beth-meon,* [24] *Qerioth, Bozrah, and all the cities of the land of Moab, far and near.* [25] *The horn of Moab is cut off,ᵃ and his arm is shattered, says the LORD.*

[26] *Make him drunk,ᵃ for against the LORD he has magnified himself;ᵇ Moab ᶜwill dash his hand in his vomit;ᶜ even he will become a source of derision.* [27] *Wasᵃ not Israel a derision to you? Was he foundᵇ among thieves?ᶜ For ᵈas often as you spoke of him,ᵈ you shook your head.ᵉ*

[28]	Leaveᵃ the citiesᵇ	(2+2+2)
	and dwellᵃ in the rock,	
	O inhabitantsᶜ of Moab.	

Be[a] like a dove; (2+3)
   she builds a nest in the sides[d] of the gorge.
29 We have heard[a] of the pride of Moab,[b] (3+2)
   overweening pride—
his haughtiness,[c] his pride,[d] his arrogance, (3+2)
   the haughtiness of his heart.
30 I know, [a]says the LORD,[a] his arrogance;[b] (4+3+3)
   [c]his boasts are false,[c]
   they have not accomplished[d] anything.
31 Therefore I wail[a] over Moab; (3+3+4)
   for Moab, all of it, I cry out,
   for the men[b] of Qir-heres[c] I moan.[d]
32 More than[a] the weeping for Jazer I weep for you, O vine[b] of Sibmah.
   Your branches passed over the sea, (3+4)
   they reached as far as[c] Jazer;
upon your summer fruit and your vintage[d] the destroyer[e] has fallen.
33 Gladness and rejoicing have been taken away from the orchard,[a] (4+2)
   from the land of Moab,
and I have stopped[b] the wine from the presses. (3)
(The treader) does not tread with a shout; (2+3)
   there is no shout.
34 The cry[a] of Heshbon (is heard) as far as Elealeh; as far as Jahaz[b] they utter their voice, from Zoar as far as Horonaim and[c] Eglath-shelishah; indeed even the waters of Nimrim are desolated. 35 I will bring to an end for Moab,[a] says the LORD, the one who goes up to the high places,[b] the one sacrificing to his gods. 36 Therefore my heart moans for Moab like flutes, my heart moans for the men of Qir-heres like flutes; therefore, [a]the abundance they have gained[a] will perish. 37 For every head is bald,[a] and every beard cut off;[b] upon all hands are gashes, and upon loins sackcloth.

38 Upon all roofs of Moab and in her squares,[a] all is mourning,[a] for I have shattered Moab like an unwanted vessel, says the LORD. 39 How it is shattered![a] (How) they wail![b] How Moab has turned[c] the neck in shame! Moab will become a derision, a horror to all round about him!

40 For thus says the LORD:
   [a]Behold, like an eagle one will fly swiftly (3+3)
   and will spread his wings against Moab.[a]
41 The cities will be captured; (2+2)
   the strongholds will be seized,[a]
[b]and the heart of the heroes of Moab on that day will be like the heart of a woman in labor.[b]
42 Moab will be destroyed as a people[a] (3+3)
   because he magnified himself over the LORD.
43 Terror, pit, and trap
   are upon you, O ruler of Moab, (3+3+2)
   [a]says the LORD.[a]
44 The one who flees from the terror (3+2)
   will fall into the pit,
and the one getting out of the pit (2+2)
   will be captured in the trap.

> For I will bring these things[a] against Moab, (3+2+2)
> the year of their punishment,
> [b]says the LORD.[b]
> 45a In the shadow of Heshbon fugitives stand without strength,[a] (3+3)
> for a fire goes forth[b] from Heshbon,
> a flame from the house[c] of Sihon. (3+3)
> It consumes the forehead of Moab,
> the head of the sons of tumult.
> 46 Woe to you, O Moab! (2)
> The people of Chemosh perish,[a] (3+3+2)
> for your sons have been taken into captivity,
> your daughters into captivity.

47 And I will restore the fortunes of Moab in the latter days, says the LORD. Thus far is the judgment of Moab.

Notes

1.a-a. Lacking in LXX.

1.b. For שְׁדָדָה, Syr and Tg have ʾtbzzt and אתבזזת, "despoiled," respectively. The root בז is used often in these chapters by Syr and Tg to translate שדד and derivatives.

1.c. LXX lacks הבישה.

1.d. For נלכדה, Syr has ʾhprt, "is confounded."

1.e. MT understood המשׂגב to be a place name, and thus the verb forms are fem. If משׂגב, "fortress," is understood, as here, the final ה on the verb forms should be dropped; cf. BHS. For משׂגב, Syr has ʿwshnh, "its strength."

2.a. For תהלה, "renown," LXX has ἰατρεία, "healing," understanding תעלה (cf. 46:11) and reads תהלה with the following "Heshbon" (cf. Vg).

2.b. LXX lacks "come."

2.c. LXX has ἐκόψαμεν, "we have cut her off."

2.d. For מדמן תדמם, LXX has παῦσιν παύσεται, "she will be completely still," apparently reading inf abs of דמם for מדמן. Similarly, Syr has ʾpn mštq ʾn tštqyn, "even if you keep your peace." מדמן may reflect מי דימון of Isa 15:9; see comments by J. Simons, The Geographical and Topographical Texts of the Old Testament, 436–37. Rudolph was of the opinion "Dibon" was meant (254).

2.e. Christensen (Transformations, 234) and Kuschke ("Jeremia 48:1–8," 185) read for the accompanying verb a root דמם, "to wail," attested in Akk. and Ug.

4.a. LXX has ἀναγγείλατε εἰς Ζογορα, "proclaim (it) to Zogora [Zoar?]," understanding הַשְׁמִיעוּ as impv along with some Heb. MSS. Christensen (Transformations, 236, 238) reads צערה, "as far as Zoar," with LXX and the parallel passage in Isa 15:5. Tg renders צעוריה, "her little ones," with שלטוניהון, "her rulers." K צעריה, Q צעוריה; also 14:3.

5.a. Reading Q הלחית, "Luhith"; cf. Isa 15:5 הלוחית. LXX has ὅτι ἐπλήσθη Αλαωθ ἐν κλαυθμῷ, "for Aloth is filled with weeping," and phrases the verse differently: "one shall go up with weeping by the way of Oronaim" (cf. Isa 15:15). MT phrasing is to be retained so that the ascent of Luhith is balanced by the descent of Horonaim.

5.b. MT's בְּכִי results from dittogr; read בו as in Isa 15:5.

5.c. LXX lacks צרי, "distresses of"; Vg understood צרי as "enemies" and as subj of "have heard."

6.a. The difficult ותהיינה (fem pl) has been explained as 2m pl with energic ending by D. N. Freedman in Bright, 314 n. e-e, and is followed here. Holladay (2:341) retains MT by understanding "your lives" as pl (cf. LXX).

6.b. Vg quasi myricae, "like the tamarisk," and Syr ʾykʿqrʾ, "like a plant," both suggest כערער, "like a tamarisk" (17:6; cf. Duhm, 346). LXX has ὥσπερ ὄνος ἄγριος, "like a wild ass" (ערוד).

7.a. For מעשׂיך, "your works," LXX has ὀχυρώμασίν σου, "your strongholds," perhaps a misreading of במצדותיך, "your treasures."

7.b. For את, f sg, 2QJer has אתה, masc.

7.c. For כהניו, "his priests," Tg has פלחוהי, "his worshipers"; cf. 49:3.

7.d. יחד is to be read with Q יחדו (haplogr).

8.a. LXX has ὄλεθρος, "destruction," for שׁדד, "destroyer," and lacks the second עיר, "city."

8.b. אשׁר is to be deleted because of an error of dittogr (Rudolph, *BHS*).

9.a. Reading with W. L. Moran, *Bib* 39 (1958) 69–71. The versions reflect the uncertainty over ציץ: LXX has σημεῖα, "signs" (ציון); Vg has *florem*, "flower," the usual meaning of ציץ; Syr has *klyl*ʾ, "crown," as does Tg.

9.b-b. With Moran, *Bib* 39 (1958) 71, reading תצא יצא (cf. 38:17). The versions reflect the root נצה, "fall into ruins" (Syr), or the root יצת, "to be set on fire" (LXX).

9.c-c. LXX has a question: πόθεν ἔνοικος αὐτῇ, "from where will there be an inhabitant for her?"

11.a-a. LXX has καὶ πεποιθὼς ἦν ἐπὶ τῇ δόξῃ αὐτοῦ, "and trusted in his glory."

11.b. LXX has act verb: ἐνέχεεν, "he has (not) poured."

12.a-a. LXX has κλίνοντας καὶ κλινοῦσιν αὐτόν, "deceivers who will lead him astray." Syr, Tg have "plunderers."

12.b. LXX has λεπτυνοῦσιν, "will break in pieces" (= ידקו).

12.c. LXX has κέρατα, "horns"; cf. κεράμιον, "earthenware vessel."

12.d. Read with LXX "his jars."

13.a. LXX adds ἐλπίδος αὐτῶν, "their hope."

15.a. Read שׁדד for שׁדד; cf. v 18b. The versions all reflect שׁדד; cf. v 20b.

15.b. LXX lacks עלה. Vg has *civitates illius succiderunt*, "they have cast down her cities."

15.c-c. Lacking in LXX.

16.a. LXX has ἡμέρα, "day."

17.a-a. Syr has ʾtdlhw wzʿw kl dhdrwhy, "all who are around him are troubled and agitated."

18.a. Reading Q וּשְׁבִי.

18.b. LXX has ὑγρασίᾳ, "wet place;" Vg *in siti*, "in thirst;" Syr *bsʿr*, "in contempt." Rudolph (*BHS*) suggests בצאה, "in vomit" or "in dung," suggested by Syr.

18.c. Syr has *Rybwn*, "Ribon"; cf. v 22.

19.a. Syr has ʿdwʿr, "Adoer."

20.a. Read חח for חתה, final ה resulting from dittogr (*BHS*).

20.b-b. Q has pl impvs in agreement with the following הגידו. LXX makes all the impv forms sg.

25.a. LXX has κατεάχθη, "is broken."

26.a. Syr has dwʾwhy, "make him wretched."

26.b. 2QJer reads הגדילה (3fs).

26.c-c. Vg: *allidet manum Moab in vomitu suo*, "Moab will dash his hand in his own vomit." LXX has ἐν χειρὶ αὐτοῦ, "with his hand," for בקיאו.

27.a. 2QJer inserts היאה before [יתה]ה.

27.b. Reading Q נמצא.

27.c. LXX ἐν κλοπαῖς σου, "among your thefts."

27.d-d. Lacking in LXX and Syr. Vg *propter verba ergo tua, quae adversum illum locutus eo*, "because of your words, therefore, which you spoke against him." For דבריך read דברך (*BHS*).

27.e. LXX has ἐπολέμεις αὐτόν, "you fought against him" (cf. Syr).

28.a. LXX took the three impvs as finite verbs. 2QJer has שׁכוני for שׁכנו.

28.b. 2QJer has ערך [ער], "your cities."

28.c. 2QJer has the sg ישׁבת.

28.d. LXX has ἐν πέτραις, "in the rocks."

29.a. 2QJer has שׁמעו נא (pl impv). LXX has ἤκουσα, "I have heard."

29.b. Syr has rwrbnʾ dmwʾb, "princes of Moab" (cf. also Tg).

29.c. Lacking in LXX and in 2QJer.

29.d. 2QJer adds [ו]ואיננו, "and he is no more."

30.a-a. Lacking in LXX.

30.b. LXX has ἔργα αὐτοῦ, "his works"; Syr ʿbdyhwn, "their works."

30.c-c. LXX has οὐχὶ τὸ ἱκανὸν αὐτοῦ, "is it not enough for him?" (= דיו). For "boasts" Syr reads qswmwhy, "his diviners"; cf. Isa 44:25, where בדים and קסמים, "diviners," are in parallel, and Jer 50:36.

30.d. 2QJer has עשׂתה, "she has done," for עשׂו, "they have done."

31.a. LXX has ὀλολύζετε, "howl ye."

31.b. Isa 16:7 has אשׁישׁי, "raisin cakes of."

31.c. LXX has Κιραδάς [= קיר חדשׁ?] αὐχμοῦ. Vg has *ad viros muri fictilis*, "for the men of the brick wall" (חרשׂ = clay). 2QJer has קיר] חרשׂת[.

31.d. Q^Or = אהגה.

32.a. LXX has ὡς, "as," and understood כבכי for מבכי. Isa 16:9 has בבכי. Rudolph (*BHS*) proposed מִבְּכִי, "sources" (Ug. *mbk*, *npk*), but in his commentary he rejected the proposal.

32.b. 2QJer lacks the definite article.

32.c. Deleting יָם, "sea," with Isa 16:8.

32.d. Isa 16:9 reads קְצִירֵךְ, "your harvest," for בְּצִירֵךְ.

32.e. Isa 16:9 reads הֵידָד, "battle shout," for שֹׁדֵד.

33.a. Lacking in LXX.

33.b. Syr has *nbtl*, "will cease." LXX has πρωί, "in the morning" (= הַשְׁכֵּם). Rudolph (*BHS*) proposed הָשְׁבַּת, "was stopped."

34.a. Delete initial mem, or regard it as enclitic on preceding הֵידָד (Christensen, *Transformations*, 239).

34.b. LXX has αἱ πόλεις, "their cities" (עָרִים).

34.c. Adding waw with LXX.

35.a. LXX has καὶ ἀπολῶ τὸν Μωαβ, "and I will destroy Moab."

35.b. Vg inserts קוּרבָּן, "offering," before "high place."

36.a-a. Vg reads *plus fecit quam potuit*, "he has done more than he could." For יִתְרָה read either יִתְרָה (Isa 15:7) or pl יִתְרֹת. Syr has *byšp*, "evil."

37.a. LXX adds ἐν παντὶ τόπῳ, "in every place."

37.b. 2QJer has impf תגר[ע].

38.a-a. Lacking in LXX.

39.a. LXX has πῶς κατήλλαξεν, "how he has changed."

39.b. Lacking in LXX.

39.c. 2QJer has הפנו (pl).

40.a-a. Lacking in LXX.

41.a. Q^Or points as pl.

41.b-b. Lacking in LXX.

42.a. LXX has ἀπὸ ὄχλου, "from a multitude."

43.a-a. Lacking in LXX.

44.a. Reading אֵלֶּה, "these things," with LXX and Syr. Holladay (2:345) reads אָלָה, "curse."

44.b-b. Lacking in LXX.

45.a-a. Lacking in Syr. For מכֹּח, "without strength," θ′ reads ἀπὸ παγίδος, "from the trap" (cf. Vg). Vv 45–47 are lacking in LXX.

45.b. יָצָא in the parallel in Num 21:28.

45.c. Reading מִבֵּית with some MSS. Num 21:28 has מִקִּרְית, "from the city of."

46.a. θ′, Vg, Tg: "you have perished," along with Num 21:29.

Form/Structure/Setting

Jer 48 is a mosaic of poetic and prose materials concerning Moab. Other oracles concerning Moab are found in Isa 15–16; Amos 2:1–3; Zeph 2:8–11; Ezek 25:8–11. The collection in Jer 48 is distinguished by its length; only the collection of materials concerning Babylon (Jer 50–51) is longer. The collection reflects an extensive knowledge of Moab and its characteristic life: culture (viniculture), trust in its military might, and especially its topography.

Several characteristic literary forms are used in the chapter: the woe oracle (vv 1b–5), the summons to flight (vv 6–8, 28), the summons to lament (vv 17, 20), the lament itself (vv 31–32), and the oracle of doom (vv 11–16, 40–44). Several prose passages (vv 10, 12–13, 21–25, 26–27, 34–39) are interspersed among the poetic pieces, complicating the questions of structure and of the literary history of the chapter.

No unanimity of opinion exists on how the chapter is to be divided into its component parts. H. Bardtke identified three basic units: vv 1–13, 14–27, 28–47 (*ZAW* 54 [1936] 240–49). J. Bright divided the chapter into five parts: vv 1–10, 11–17, 18–28, 29–39, 40–47 (311–19). Rudolph differed from Bright only in that he subdivided vv 40–47 into two parts: vv 40–42 and vv 43–46, omitting v 47 (257–63). A. Weiser provided a more minute analysis: vv 1–2, 3–6, 7–9 (10), 11–13, 14–17, 18–25, 26–27, 28, 29–39, 40–42, 43–46, 47 (396–402). D. Christensen divided the chapter into two major divisions: vv 1–28, 29–44 (omitting vv 45–47 with LXX). Based on his identification of literary forms, he subdivided the first major section into seven parts, vv 1–5, 6–8, 9–10, 11–16, 17–19, 20–27, 28, and the second section into three parts, vv 29–36, 37–39, 40–44 (*Transformations,* 240–41).

W. Holladay has offered an analysis that purports to distinguish authentic material from secondary material. For Holladay the prime determinant for recognizing authentic material in the chapter is the recognition of the characteristic diction of Jeremiah (Holladay, 2:347–49). Therefore, he has identified as authentic material vv 1–4; 6–9; 11–12; 14–17; 18–20, 25; 28 + 38b; 39, 41a, 42; 43–44a + 45a + 44b. The secondary material consists of either prose material that intrudes on the continuity of the text (vv 10, 13, 21–24, 26–27) or poetic and prose materials that are adapted from Isa 15–16; Jer 49:22; Num 21:24 (vv 29–38a; 40aβb, 41b; 45–46) and that do not contain Jeremiah's characteristic diction (Holladay, 2:346–48, 352–53).

Much more intriguing is Holladay's attempt to suggest plausible settings for the authentic material. He concluded that Jeremiah delivered three oracles. The first oracle was composed of vv 1–4, 6–9, 11–12; the second of vv 14–17, 18–20 + 25, 28 + 38b; and the third of vv 39–40aα + 41a + 42, 43–44a + 45a + 44b. Holladay dates these oracles to the years 605, 599/598, and 594, respectively, dates when the prophet could be expected to pronounce oracles concerning Moabite activities. Nebuchadrezzar's victory at Carchemish in 605 was decisive for demonstrating his ability to impose his imperial designs on Syria-Palestine, including Transjordan. In 599/598 Moab pressured Judah (2 Kgs 24:2), and in 594 Moab joined Judah, Ammon, Edom, Tyre, and Sidon to consider organized opposition to Babylon (27:3), which Jeremiah opposed. Referring again to passages in Jeremiah's poetry elsewhere in the book that parallel these three oracles, Holladay shows that the first poem has the most parallels to material already dated to 605, the second poem is predominately paralleled by material dated to 599/598, and the third poem has the most parallels to material dated to 594 (2:353–54).

Holladay's attractive analysis, while it is the most complete to date, is not without its difficulties. A close reading of his effort to determine authentic material in Jer 48 by reference to parallels to poetic diction elsewhere in the book shows the paucity of the evidence, consisting as it does of a few isolated words and phrases. His dating of the sections containing the poetic parallels is dependent on his theory of the literary development of the book, which, while plausible, is nevertheless unproved (2:15–24). In sum, Holladay's attempt to determine authentic material and to date it to certain periods of Jeremiah's ministry is not thoroughly convincing.

Another view of the delimitation of the constituent parts of Jer 48 is offered here: vv 1–5, 6–9, 11–12, 14–17, 18–20, 21–25, 26–27, 28–33, 34–39, 40–44, 45–47, with vv 10, 13 as editorial comments. This tentative analysis is offered partly on the basis of form analysis and partly on the basis of the internal coherence of several passages. The chapter contains a mixture of genres, along with poetic and prose sections that cannot be characterized confidently as to genre. Changes in the number of speaker and person of the addressees render analysis difficult. While most, if not all, of the material may be credited to Jeremiah, any attempt to provide settings for the material is unconvincing.

Several verses in Jer 48 show marked similarities to, or perhaps literary dependence on, several other OT passages:

48:5 = Isa 15:5b
48:7b = 49:3d; Amos 1:15
48:29, 31–33 = Isa 16:6–10
48:31b = Isa 15:5a
48:34ab = Isa 15:4a, 5a
48:34c = Isa 15:6a
48:35 = Isa 16:12
48:36 = Isa 16:11
48:37–38 = Isa 15:2c–3
48:40–41 = Deut 28:49, 52; Jer 49:22
48:43–44 = Isa 24:17–18ab
48:45b = Num 21:28a
48:45c = Num 24:17c
48:46 = Num 21:29

In some cases it seems to be a matter of using traditional materials for standard similes (Deut 28:49, 52; Jer 49:22) and metaphors (Isa 24:17–18ab), or for stereotyped judgments (Jer 49:3d; Amos 1:15). However, in Jer 48:45–46 the poet has reprised a part of perhaps the earliest of the oracles against the nations, this one also against Moab (Num 21:27–30).

The relationship of Jer 48 to the oracle concerning Moab in Isa 15–16 calls for special comment. Isa 15–16 constitutes more a lament over Moab than an oracle of judgment and, therefore, should be distinguished from Jer 48 form-critically. The poet in Jer 48 has quarried lament materials from Isa 15–16 and has adapted them for the purpose of announcing judgment (Wildberger, 2:605–6). Wildberger has argued convincingly for the primacy of Isa 15–16 (2:605–6). It seems gratuitous to deny to Jeremiah any of the material shared with Isa 15–16 because the material shows none of the characteristics of Jeremiah's poetry (Holladay, 2: 347–48); one would hardly expect such correspondences.

Comment

1   The traditional limits of the Moabite kingdom were defined by the Arnon River (Wadi Mujib) on the north, the Zered River (Wadi Hasa) on the south, and the Dead Sea and desert on the west and east, respectively. During certain periods the Moabite territory was extended to include the Mishor, the plateau or tableland north of the Arnon as far as Heshbon, and including the "plains of Moab" north of the Dead Sea, a state of affairs clearly reflected in this extensive series of oracles.

The origin of the people called Moabites is obscure. Standard reference works have little to offer on the topic. A. H. van Zyl, whose monograph is still standard in many respects, offered the opinion that the Moabites came from nomadic tribes in the Syrian-Arabian desert who found it easy to enter Moab from the east and who eventually became the dominant group (van Zyl, *The Moabites* 109–11). Recently G. Mendenhall has offered considerable historical, cultural, and onomastic evidence that the Moabites and related Transjordanian peoples, in whole or in part, migrated from Anatolia and northern Syria at the close of the Late Bronze Age primarily because of the political/economic disruption and endemic plague (G. Mendenhall, *The Tenth Generation,* 105–21, 142–73).

Nebo is probably to be identified with Kh. al Muḥaiyat just south of Mount Nebo, where Iron Age tombs have been excavated (A. Dearman, "Historical Reconstruction and the Mesha Inscription," 180). The Mesha Inscription records the capture of Nebo from the Israelites. The best candidate for Qiryathaim seems to be al Qureiye (A. Dearman, "Historical Reconstruction and the Mesha Inscription," 176). מִשְׂגָּב, *Misgab,* "fortress or citadel," is probably a common noun rather than a place name, even though the feminine verbs would suggest a town. Everywhere else the term is best rendered "fortress." It is used as an epithet for the LORD in 2 Sam 22:3 and regularly in the Psalms (9:10; 18:3; 46:8, 12; passim). As viewed from Judah, the western edge of the Mishor looks like a fortress, forbidding and difficult of access, and may be seen as a symbol of the pride of Moab (v 29).

2   Heshbon is the modern Tel Hesbān and formed the northernmost boundary of Moab during periods of expansion. Earlier it had been in the possession of Reuben (Josh 13:17) or Gad (Josh 13:26). Note the wordplay חֶשְׁבּוֹן, "Heshbon," and חָשַׁב, "to think, devise." The planning of the ruination of Moab at Heshbon raises the question whether Heshbon was in possession of Moab when this oracle was issued. In Jer 49:3 Heshbon is included in the territory of Ammon. Was the calamity against Moab perpetrated by the Ammonites? Or is Heshbon simply the logical starting point for an invasion of Moab by any enemy (Babylon?).

If "Madmen" is a place name, it is mentioned only here. The renderings of LXX and Syr reflect infinite absolute דָּמֹם, thus "she will be completely silenced" (see *Notes*). Another possibility is to see a wordplay on a city Madmen (מַדְמֵן) and מַדְמֵנָה, "dung-pit" (Isa 25:10b: "Moab shall be trodden down in his place, as straw is trodden down in a dung-pit"). Or מדמן may reflect מֵי דִימוֹן, "the waters of Dimon," in Isa 15:9, thus showing a wordplay with the following root דמם. Since a place name is probably to be sought here, rather than an infinite absolute, the last possibility is preferred, especially in light of the fact that Dimon is an alternative form of Dibon (Holladay, 2:356).

It is possible to translate the root דמם either as "to be silent, be destroyed" or as "to weep" (see *Notes*). The usual rendering is "to be silent, be still," and that is the sense required in such passages as 25:37; 47:6; 49:26; 50:30; 51:6. In Akkadian and Ugaritic the root means "to weep, to wail" (cf. *KTU* 1.16.1.25–26, where *ʾl tdm* parallels *ʾl tbkn,* "do not weep"). Such a meaning is especially appropriate for דֹּמּוּ in Isa 23:2 because it parallels הֵילִילוּ, "wail," in 23:1. Holladay (2:291) favors this rendering for Jer 8:14 as well. J. Blau (*VT* 6 (1956) 242–48) has viewed these two meanings of דמם as evidence of two homonymous roots that over the course of time devolved into each other.

3–5   These verses shift attention to the southern part of Moab. The cry of calamity is raised at Horonaim and is heard as far as Zoar, and the panicked inhabitants flee up the ascent of Luhith to the plateau. If vv 1–5 compose one oracle, the land of Moab was caught in a pincers movement, attacked from north and south, the population eventually to be forced out into the desert (v 6).

Zoar is known as one of the cities of the plain (Gen 13:12) and is most likely located in the Gor aṣ-Ṣafi at Kh. aš-Šeh-ʿIsā (S. Mittmann, "The Ascent of Luhith," 175). Horonaim, Luhith, and the waters of Nimrim are associated in Isa 15:5–6. The most likely identification of Luhith presented so far is with Kathrabba (S. Mittmann, "The Ascent of Luhith," 179). The waters of Nimrim then would be identified with the Wadi en-Numera (A. Dearman, "Historical Reconstruction and the Mesha Inscription," 188). Although Horonaim is presented as being in the vicinity of Luhith, its precise location is made problematic by whether Horonaim and Luhith are viewed as being on two different roads or connected by one road. W. Schottroff (*ZDPV* 82 [1966] 200) pointed to the parallelism of Horonaim and Luhith in Isa 15:5 and thought the sites were connected by one road. U. Worshech and E. A. Knauf thought that the sites were located on two parallel roads and suggested a site further north, ed Deir, as the location of Horonaim (*ZDPV* 101 [1985] 132). In any case, the sites of Horonaim, Luhith, and the waters of Nimrim are to be sought in southwestern Moab rather than in northwestern Moab, as Kuschke thought ("Jeremia 48:1–8," 188–90).

Holladay regards v 5 as having originally been a part of v 34 (other parts of Isa 15:4–6 are in v 34) and perhaps "represents an omission written in the margin and incorporated by error into the preceding column of text" (Holladay, 2:346). But it is just as likely that the prophet has seen fit to use traditional or borrowed material and to insert it in a perfectly logical place, as here.

6 The oracle in vv 6–9 is form-critically a summons to flight. Its characteristic form is the summons itself followed by the reason for flight introduced by כִּי, "for" (R. Bach, *Die Aufforderungen*, 20–22).

MT has כַּעֲרוֹעֵר, "like Aroer," the city located on the northern bank of the Arnon commanding the ford. But Aroer is not located in the desert. LXX has ὥσπερ ὄνος ἄγριος, "like a wild ass" (עָרוֹד). Aquila and the Vulgate translated the word as tamarisk (עֲרָעָר; cf. 17:6), and this is preferred. This low shrub is *Juniperus phoenicia*, called ʿrʿr in Arabic (J. C. Trever, *IDB* 2:1027). The image is an apt one for a displaced people condemned to seek a rudimentary, marginal existence.

7 This verse, along with v 8, provides the reason for the summons to flee: improper or misplaced trust. One wonders whether the charge of trusting in one's own works and treasures is tantamount to a charge of lack of trust (rebellion) in the suzerain (Nebuchadrezzar, 27:1–7).

Bach (*Die Aufforderungen*, 16) denied originality to v 7, but none of his arguments is convincing, especially the argument that points to change in address to second person singular from the second person plural in v 6.

Although Chemosh was the major deity in Moab according to the Bible and the Mesha Inscription, this god had been venerated in northern Syria and in Mesopotamia at least since the third millenium (for the best collection of references to Chemosh, see G. Mattingly, "Moabite Religion and the Mesha Inscription," 216–27). A god Kamish (ᵈKa-mi-iš) is mentioned in the Ebla texts (P. Matthiae, *Ebla: An Empire Rediscovered*, 187; note that Jer 48:7 has this spelling, as does the city name Carchemish (*Kar-kamiš*, "quay of Kamish") on the upper Euphrates in northwestern Mesopotamia. At Ugarit appears the binomial *ṯṯ-w-kmṯ*, "clay-and-Kemosh," which apparently associates Chemosh with the underworld (RS 24.244, line 36; RS 24:251, obv line 16; it appears as *ʿt-w-kmt*, "bird of prey and Kemosh," in RS 24.271, obv line 5). Chemosh is a name of Nergal, the infernal god in Mesopotamia, attested in a Middle Assyrian and in a Late Babylonian god list (W. G. Lambert, "Kammuš," *RLA* 5:335). These references to Chemosh from north Syria and Mesopotamian sources strengthen the supposition that the Moabites may have originated in the far north. In the Mesha Inscription the compound divine name Ashtar-Kemosh appears (line 17). Ashtar (Athtar) was the planet Venus, and the compound name Ashtar-Kemosh apparently reflects a late, local religious development. In Judg 11:24 Chemosh is referred to as the god of the Ammonites. Either the Ammonites also revered Chemosh or, as Boling suggests, the reference indicates that the Ammonites were in possession of territory formerly controlled by the Moabites (R. G. Boling, *Judges*, AB 7 [Garden City, NY: Doubleday, 1975] 202). The worship of Chemosh was introduced into Israel by Solomon (1 Kgs 11:17, 33) and persisted until the reform of Josiah (2 Kgs 23:13).

The deportation of the images of gods after military defeat is a well-known practice in the ancient Middle East (see D. D. Luckenbill, *Ancient Records of Assyria* 2:207, 209, 210, 307, 308) and is mentioned elsewhere in the Bible (Amos 5:25; Isa 46:1–2; Jer 49:3).

8 Because of the place names mentioned in Josh 13:27, "the valley" (העמק) is to be recognized as a reference to Moabite holdings in the Jordan valley north of the Dead Sea and east of the Jordan River that had formerly been a part of the Amorite kingdom of Sihon. The tableland or plateau, the Mishor, refers to the region from Aroer on the Arnon River northward to Heshbon (Josh 13:15–17).

9 The first colon is difficult. The meaning of ציץ is uncertain, and therefore the understanding of נצא תהא is obscured (see *Notes*). Most interpreters, ancient and modern, have rendered ציץ as "wings" (see Barthélemy, *Critique textuelle*, 783–85 for a listing), but the proposal finds its main support in the Targums. More recently Moran (*Bib* 39 [1958] 69–71) has suggested the meaning "salt" for ציץ on the basis of Akkadian texts from Ugarit in which "fields of salt" (*eqil ṣabti*) is glossed by *ṣisuma* and *ṣi-e-ṣi-ma*, "salt marshes." These valuable salt deposits were listed along with other properties, such as vineyards, olive groves, and villages, which were distributed to favored persons and on which a *pilku* (feudal tax) could be levied (although in the extant examples the *pilku* is forgiven). Moran concluded that "salt marsh" could have the more general meaning "salt(s)." However, additional texts in alphabetic cuneiform (*PRU* 5:96, 97) list the amounts of salt produced by the salt marshes (singular *ṣṣ*) of several owners, and the word for salt as product of the salt marshes is *mlḥt*. Thus, it cannot be established that the Ugaritic *ṣṣ* means anything other than salt marshes. Still, to make Moab into a salt marsh would be an apt metaphor, although it would mean a reversal from a valuable economic resource, as at Ugarit, to a land made unproductive (compare the agriculturally infertile salt pans of the nearby Dead Sea). Compare the oracle against Moab and Ammon in Zeph 2:8–11, which includes in v 9 the oath of the LORD to make them a district of chickpeas and a saltpit.

The association of ציץ with salt calls to mind Judg 9:45, where it is related that Abimelech sowed Shechem with salt. This act has most often been understood as a means to make a destroyed site infertile or as a declaration of defeat. S. Gevirtz (*VT* 13 [1963] 52–62) has argued, on the basis of parallels from Hittite, Akkadian, and Greek sources, that the sowing of a destroyed city with salt and other spices was correlative with cursing anyone who would rebuild it and was in fact a part of the act of purification of the site so that it could be presented to the victorious deity.

The troublesome נצא תצא has been treated in a variety of ways. LXX apparently understood the root יצת, "to be set on fire." Some translators identified a root נצא, "to fly," to agree with their rendering of "wings" for ציץ, but without clear support (Barthélemy, Critique textuelle, 784). Others accepted a root נצה, "to fall into ruins," thus repointing תֵּצֵא to תִּצֶּה (BHS). It seems best to retain תֵּצֵא, "she shall go forth," and to explain נָצֹא either as infinitive absolute of נצה, which would be an example of the connection of two homonymous roots (Barthélemy, Critique textuelle, 784) or, since initial Y/W roots often have a counterpart in initial N roots, as an alternative infinitive absolute of the root יצא, "to go forth" (see Gevirtz, VT 13 [1963] 62).

The resulting sense of the colon would be either "to make Moab into an infertile salt field, for she will certainly go forth in surrender" or "to purify Moab with salt as a possession of the conquering deity, for she will certainly go forth in surrender."

The verse ends with the phrase מאין יושב בהן, "without inhabitant in them." An alternative is to take יושב as a shortened form of יושב על־כסא, "the one who sits on the throne" (Isa 6:1; Deut 17:18; 1 Kgs 1:10, 27, 46; 2:12). In another oracle against a foreign nation, Damascus, in Amos 1:5, 8, the יושב is parallel with תומך שבט, "the one who wields the scepter." Since the priests and princes were condemned to exile along with their god, Chemosh, in v 7, it would not be unexpected for the oracle to contain a reference to the ruler.

10 Most commentators bracket this verse because it is in prose and does not fit the context (e.g., Rudolph, 258; Holladay, 2:346–47). However, the origin and form of such a verse remain of interest. R. Bach raised the question whether the verse may not be a vestige of Israelite Holy War. In form the verse is identical to the curses in Deut 27:15–26, although those curses are not related to war. Especially interesting is the mention of the "work of Yahweh" here in v 10 and the commands in Deut 7:16 not to pity or fear the enemy in military campaigns (R. Bach, Die Aufforderungen, 88–89). If this verse was inserted by a glossator to incite Judean vengeance against the Moabites, as suggested by Carroll (783), it is out of keeping with the rest of the oracles concerning the nations in Jeremiah, except for the Babylonian oracles, which evidence remarkably little hatred for the nations.

11–12 The center of viticulture in Moab is identified in Jer 48:32 and Isa 16:8–9 as the town of Sibmah, one of the towns mentioned as being built by the Reubenites in the northern Mishor in the vicinity of Heshbon (Num 32:37). The reference to "its shoots passing over the sea" in Jer 48:32 and Isa 16:8 may indicate the ability of Moab to engage in international trade with this valuable commodity by managing to by-pass the strictures of foreign suzerains (cf. *Comments* on vv 32–33).

Although Moab was most often in vassalage, first to David and later to Omri and to the Assyrians, and experienced independence only under Mesha, she had never experienced exile. No more fitting figure for a complacent nation could be chosen than uncasked wine maturing on its lees with its aroma intact. The coming judgment on Moab is described in terms of foreign "tilters" who would decant the wine, prepare it for dispersal (exile), and destroy the casks (jars).

An alternative approach has been taken by D. J. Clark who, noting the ambiguity of the language in v 11c and emphasizing the danger to wine left too long on its lees, suggests rendering v 11c "Its flavor remains weak and its taste never develops well" (*BT* 32 [1981] 240–41). This view is strengthened by the fact that newly fermented wine should be racked within one or two weeks after the completion of fermentation because off-odors may form as a result of the autolyzation of the yeasts in the lees (*Encyclopaedia Britannica*, 15th ed., s.v. "winemaking," 19:880).

13 This prosaic conclusion to the oracle predicts or announces the disillusionment (so Thompson, 705) of the Moabites with their god, Chemosh, who would prove incapable of avoiding the catastrophe. The comparison is drawn with the disillusionment of the Israelites in their source of confidence, Bethel (for this deity see J. P. Hyatt, *JAOS* 59 [1939] 81–98).

15 Since Moab in vv 14–20 is masculine, עריה, "her cities," is suspect. But note that in this chapter masculine and feminine alternate for Moab (vv 2, 4), and in any case the desire for complete agreement in gender of suffixes or in the person and number of contiguous verb forms is no reason to insist on emendation.

Although it is tempting to preserve the Masoretic pointing שֻׁדַּד מוֹאָב, "Moab is destroyed," and to recognize an envelope construction with v 20, it is preferable to read שָׁדַד here as in v 18 in order to preserve the contrast: "the enemy has come up . . . the choicest young men have gone down" (note the same wordplay in v 18 in reverse order).

17 The reference to the מטה עז, "mighty scepter," is reminiscent of Ezek 19:10–14, where the history of Judah 598–587 is related in allegorical fashion. After the mother was transplanted like a vine (= the king of Judah and his court were exiled), the מטה עז, "the strong stem" (Zedekiah), sprang up and flourished until the east wind (Nebuchadrezzar) dried it up and transplanted (exiled) it so that no מטה עז, "mighty scepter," remained.

V 17b supplies the words of the lament, apparently intended as a taunt (cf. Isa 14:4; Mic 2:4 where the lament is clearly called a מָשָׁל, "taunt"). Other occurrences of the same phenomenon are Isa 14:13; Jer 48:39; 50:23; 51:41; Ezek 26:7; Obad 5, 6; Zeph 2:15. Also see *Comments* below on vv 31–32.

18–19 Dibon is the modern Dhiban, less than two miles north of the Arnon River. Aroer is the modern Kh. ʿAraʿir on the north bank of the Arnon River. Since the focus in this oracle is on Dibon, the defeat of its king and the destruction of its fortifications, the stream of refugees must be from Dibon fleeing past Aroer to cross the Arnon. However, if vv 3–5 refer to an actual event rather than to a threat, and if the events in vv 14–20 coincide with those in vv 3–5, the refugees from Dibon, rather than finding safety in the south, would only meet a similar group fleeing from the south.

21–24 These verses furnish a devastating litany of towns in the Mishor taken by the invader, although the list makes no claim to be complete (cf. v 24b). The location of Holon is unknown. Dearman makes a strong case for the identification of Jahzah (Jahaz, v 34) with Kh. Medeiniyeh on the Wadi eth Themed (Dearman, "Historical Reconstruction and the Mesha Inscription," 181–84). This

imposing site would have been a fortified outpost along the eastern border of
the kingdom. Um er Rasas is the leading candidate for the site of Mephaath.
Excavations have uncovered mosaics from the seventh century A.D. that identify
the site as "camp Mephaa" (M. Piccirillo, *BA* 51 [1988] 230–31). Um er Rasas is
located on the eastern frontier directly south of Kh. Medeiniyeh and directly east
of Dhiban. For the location of Dibon, see the *Comment* on v 18. For Nebo, see
Comment on v 1. The location of Beth Diblathaim is uncertain; for a discussion of
problems and opinions, see A. Dearman, "Historical Reconstruction and the
Mesha Inscription," 187. For Kiryathaim, see *Comment* on v 1. Beth Gamul may be
Kh. Jemeil, about one mile southwest of Um er Rasas. Beth-meon is identified by
most scholars with Maʿin, about five miles southwest of Medeba on the edge of
the Mishor (Dearman, "Historical Reconstruction and the Mesha Inscription,"
175–76). In the Bible Beth-meon is also called Baal-meon (Num 32:38) and Beth-
baal-meon (Josh 13:17). If Kerioth is a place name and not the plural word for
cities, it should be identified with the קריית of the Mesha Inscription, line 13. קרית
was a worship center for Chemosh; Mesha claimed to have transported the אראל
(altar hearth?) from Ataroth to קרית before Chemosh. For the most recent discussion of the problems with the location of Kerioth, see Dearman, "Historical
Reconstruction and the Mesha Inscription," 178–79. Bozrah, not the Edomite
Bozrah, is also of uncertain location (Dearman, "Historical Reconstruction and
the Mesha Inscription," 186). OT Bezer (Josh 20:8; 21:36) was a levitical city located on the Mishor near the eastern desert in the tribal holdings of Reuben.
    Of these towns the following are mentioned in the Mesha Inscription: Jahaz,
Dibon, Nebo, Beth Diblathaim, Qiryathaim, Beth-meon, Qiryat, and Bozrah. The
importance of these sites in Mesha's time is indicated by the references to his
building (fortifying) them or performing acts that indicated they were cult sites
(Nebo, Kerioth).
    25 "Horn" and "arm" are standard metaphors for strength in the OT (for
"horn," cf. Lam 2:3; for "arm," Ps 44:4). B. Couroyer (*RB* 73 [1966] 510–21) has
suggested that "horn" may also be understood as "bow."
    26–27 The judgment upon Moab is put in terms of making Moab drunk.
One is reminded of Jer 25:15–17, 27–29, which focuses on the cup of Yahweh's
wrath that the prophet is commanded to take to all the nations and make them
drink (note here in 48:26 that the verb form is imperative plural). The metaphor
of the cup of wrath, which produces drunkenness, staggering, insanity, and vomiting, is well-attested in the Bible (Ezek 23:31–35; Lam 4:21; Isa 51:17–23; Hab
2:15–17; Zech 12:2; Obad 15–16; Pss 11:6; 60:5; 75:9) and plays a significant role
in Jeremiah in the context of the oracles concerning the nations (Jer 25:15–17,
27–29; 49:12–13; 51:6–10; 51:39; 51:57). The search for some cultic, ritual, or
juridical act that may have given rise to the metaphor of the cup of wrath/drunk-
enness continues (see *Excursus*). In any case, the cup of wrath always indicates
the certainty of divine judgment.
    The reason for the judgment is twofold: exalting himself against the LORD and
treating Israel with derision. The first reason is repeated in v 42 without the accompanying derision of Israel. The significance of Moab's exalting himself against
the LORD is difficult to fathom unless it is seen in a political context. The most
likely event is that referred to in Jer 27 when the kings of Edom, Moab, Ammon,
Tyre, and Sidon conspired with Zedekiah to oppose Nebuchadrezzar and throw

off their yokes of vassalage. Jeremiah was convinced that Nebuchadrezzar was the LORD's servant and that rebellion against the LORD would incur divine wrath.

The gravity of the charge that Moab had held Israel in derision may be clarified by Zeph 2:8–11, where the taunts of Moab and Ammon against Israel are combined with their threats of territorial aggression.

28 Again there is a summons to flee to a remote place where normal life would not be possible, literally in the rock, in the sides of the mouth of the pit (cf. 4:29). The reputed silliness of the dove with its rickety nests is proverbial.

29–30 These verses are an adaptation of, and an enlargement on, Isa 16:6 (for a treatment of the relationship of Jer 48 with Isa 15–16, see *Form/Structure/ Setting*). Holladay, already having decided that vv 29–34 are secondary material, suggested that the adaptation evidenced in vv 29–30 was carried out by an editor after Jeremiah's death (2:354) and possibly reflects a campaign of Nebuchadrezzar against Moab and Ammon mentioned by Josephus (*Ant.* 10.9.7). However, if Moab's pride is understood in terms of political opposition to an overlord, the meeting of foreign ministers in 594 mentioned in Jer 27:3 may be appealed to as justification for the charge (see *Comment* on vv 26–27).

31–32 The language of lamentation is prominent in the oracles concerning the foreign nations (see Isa 13:6–8; 14:31; 15:2–5, 8; 16:7, 9–11; 19:8–10; 21:3; 22:4; 23:1, 5–6; Ezek 26:16–18; 27:28–36; 28:12–19; 30:2–4; 32:18). As in several passages just listed, here in Jer 48 the Moabites are described as wailing (48:3–5, 34, 38–39); they are called to wail (48:20) concerning their fate, and surrounding peoples are summoned to bemoan the Moabites (48:17), perhaps because the calamity of Moab presages their own (cf. Ezek 32:9–10). Most striking, however, are the references in Jer 48 to wailing and mourning in the first person (the LORD or prophet?) (48:31–32, 36; cf. Isa 15:5; 16:9, 11). Are these references to be taken as taunt, as hypocritical delight in the misfortunes of another, as genuine expressions of compassion or pity, or in some other way? Rudolph, while admitting that the parallels in Isa 15–16 show sincere compassion, argued that vv 31–32 are openly derisive. For support he pointed to the indictment of the context provided by vv 29–30, to the change to the first person singular in v 31 (third person masculine singular in Isa 16:7), and to the mention of Moab's becoming a derision (שְׂחֹק) in v 39, and he included Judah among the neighbors summoned in v 17 to offer a "lament" for Moab. Rudolph concluded that the ironic use of the lament language of vv 31–32, 36a is an example of taking delight in the calamity of a neighbor (Rudolph, 261). In a similar vein Weiser's view was that the satisfaction over the disaster for Moab in vv 31–32 clearly shines through the words of compassion borrowed from Isa 16 (Weiser, 400).

More recently J. Kegler, pointing to the communal nature of the "I" in the psalms of lament as well as to other evidence, concluded that 48:31–32, 36, together with other similar passages from the oracles concerning the nations, reflects the genuinely humanitarian attitude of certain circles in Judah before and during the exile (J. Kegler, "Das Leid des Nachbarvolkes," 271–87). However, Kegler's treatments of several key passages are so questionable as to render his conclusion unconvincing. For example, Kegler assumes, rather than proves, that the lament and request in 47:6 come from Israelites rather than Philistines (Kegler, "Das Leid des Nachbarvolkes," 278–79). He ignores the adaptations of Isa 15–16 that characterize Jer 48 and that effectively change the pity of Isa 15–16

into its opposite (Kegler, "Das Leid des Nachbarvolkes," 284–86). He misunder-
stands fundamentally Isa 16:2–4, making these words come from compassionate
Israelite circles rather than recognizing them as words proper to people from a
devastated neighbor state, pledging fealty and requesting the benefits of a vassal
(Kegler, "Das Leid des Nachbarvolkes," 285–86).

Decisive for vv 31–32, 36 is the context of the whole chapter: the final, catastrophic end for Moab is in view as divine judgment for pride. The language of
lament and dirge is employed as a way to announce, in other terms, the reality of
destruction (cf. Amos 5:1–3). However, it is too much to say that these verses are
a taunt or an example of malicious joy.

Kir-heres, or Kir-hareseth (Isa 16:7; 2 Kgs 3:25), is commonly identified with
the modern Kerak, about seventeen miles south of the Arnon (E. D. Grohman,
"Kir-hareseth," *IDB* 3:36). Kir-heres, "city or wall of potsherds," may be a dispar-
aging corruption of קיר חדש, "new city," as suggested by the LXX in Isa 16:11: καὶ
τὰ ἐντός μου ὡσεὶ τεῖχος ὃ ἐνεκαίνισας, "and my inner parts you have reno-
vated like a wall."

The locations of Jazer and Sibmah are unknown. According to Num 21:32;
32:33–35, Jazer was earlier an Amorite city that was occupied and rebuilt by the
Gadites. In Josh 21:39 it is mentioned as a levitical city. There is no indication
that it was ever under the rule of Moab, despite its prominence in Isa 16 and Jer
48. Num 21:24 (LXX) indicates that Jazer was a city on the Ammonite border.
Eusebius mentions a Jazer located eight or ten Roman miles west of Philadelphia
(Rabbath-Ammon) and fifteen Roman miles from Heshbon (G. M. Landes,
BASOR 144 [December 1956] 31). 2 Sam 24:5 places Jazer at the southern end of
Gilead. While its general location seems clear, its precise identification with the
ruins of a site is not. Three plausible sites are Khirbet Djazzir, fifteen miles west
of Amman (R. G. Boling and G. E. Wright, *Joshua*, AB 6 [Garden City, NY:
Doubleday, 1982] 344), Tall ʿarayma, northwest of Naʿur (R. Rendtorff, *ZDPV* 76
[1960] 124–35), and Khirbet es-Sireh, a site that best suits the data supplied by
Eusebius (G. M. Landes, *BASOR* 144 [December 1956] 37).

Sibmah, like Jazer, was originally an Amorite site that was occupied by the
Reubenites (Num 32:3, 38; Josh 13:19). It appears in Isa 16 and Jer 48 as the
center of the Moabite wine industry. A plausible suggestion for its location is Qurn
el-Kibsh, between Heshbon and Nebo (E. D. Grohman, *IDB* 4:342).

32–33 These verses are an adaptation of Isa 16:8b–10. As in Jer 48:11–12, the
description of the calamity of Moab is centered on its wine industry. The sea in
the phrase "your branches passed over the sea" (cf. Isa 16:8) is commonly taken
to refer to the Dead Sea (Holladay, 2:362; Wildberger, 628), although the significance of this interpretation is not clear. Landes, reading מבך, "fountain," for מבכי,
"more than the weeping," of Jazer, thought that the sea referred to this small
source of water at Jazer (Landes, *BASOR* 144 [December 1956] 33). It must be
asked, however, whether the sea may not refer more logically to the Mediterra-
nean Sea, and whether the "branches passing over the sea" may not refer to
Moab's international trade. Other than grain, the most highly valued of Moab's
exports would have been its wine. In Ezekiel's oracle on Tyre is a description of
Tyre as a trading center receiving goods from the Greeks and other Mediterra-
nean peoples from the west and from the east handling the goods from Edom,
Judah, Israel, Damascus, Arabia, and Sheba (Ezek 27:12–22). Although Moab is

not mentioned in this connection, its neighbors are, and it is logical to assume that historically Moab had had its place among them. No more appropriate lament for Moab's calamity could have been made than the lament over the cessation of the joys of the grape harvest and its promise for the benefits provided by international trade.

34 The verse is a composite of the parallels in Isa 15:4a, 5b, 6a. On the location of Heshbon, see the *Comment* on v 2. Elealah is identified with el-ʿAl northeast of Heshbon (Grohman, *IDB* 2:75). For Jahaz, see the *Comment* on vv 21–24; for Zoar, Horonaim, and the waters of Nimrim, see the *Comment* on vv 3–5. The identification of Eglath-shelishiyah, "the third Eglath," remains uncertain. Its collocation here with other sites in the south of Moab provides a general location. Of some help is the reference to ʿAgaltain, "the double Eglah" or the "second Eglah," in one of the deeds from the Naḥal Ḥeber from the time of Bar Kochba. Two of the contracting parties, then resident in Ein-Gedi, were originally from Luhith in the district of ʿAgaltain (see Y. Yadin, *IEJ* 12 [1962] 249–51). The association in Jer 48:34 and Isa 15:5 of Eglath-shelishiyah with Zoar and Horonaim point to the area east-southeast of the Dead Sea (see also W. Schottroff, *ZDPV* 82 [1966] 196–97).

35–36 For v 35 compare Isa 16:12, and for v 36 compare Isa 16:11. Cult would cease along with commerce and all organized life (cf. 48:7). Note that in Isa 16:11 the lament comes as a result of the loss of the wine trade, whereas here the lament follows the cessation of organized cult.

37 The shaving of facial and head hair, the gashing of the body, and the donning of sackcloth are included among traditional mourning rites (cf. 4:8; 16:6; 41:5; Mic 1:16; Amos 8:10). Such activity was forbidden to Israel by laws in Leviticus (19:27; 21:5) and in Deuteronomy (14:1), apparently because of its association with foreign cults. Such rites were apotropaic (magic to avert evil) in origin. In the Baal cycle from Ugarit, El, upon receiving word that Baal was dead, put the dust of mourning on his head, girded himself in a loincloth, shaved off his beard, and ritually incised his arm, chest, and back (*KTU* 1.5.6.15–22). Ritual incision was a part of the rain dance by the prophets of Baal on Mount Carmel (1 Kgs 18:28).

38–39 The utter ruin of Moab is graphically likened to the breaking of an unwanted pot that cannot be repaired (cf. Jer 22:28). There would be universal lamentation in once-proud Moab, with the only reward being shame and derision. The mention of lamentation on the housetops suggests carefully structured, ritual lamentation, for it was on housetops that people in Judah had offered incense and libations to foreign deities (Jer 19:12; 32:29).

40 The swiftly advancing enemy is likened to a נֶשֶׁר, "eagle" or "vulture" (cf. Jer 49:22; Ezek 17:3–5, 7–8, referring to Nebuchadrezzar and Psammetichus II), which "soars" (דָּאָה) menacingly and spreads its wings to grasp its prey.

41 The incapacitation of the Moabite military is likened to that of a woman giving birth, a standard metaphor for helplessness (cf. Jer 6:24).

42 The scheme of the enemy to cut Moab off from being a nation (v 2) is paralleled here. For an interpretation of "magnifying himself against the LORD," see *Comment* on vv 26–27.

43–44 These verses are almost identical with Isa 24:17–18ab, the most significant difference being the substitution of "inhabitant of Moab" in v 43 for "inhabitant of the earth" in Isa 24:17. For the use of traditional or stereotyped materials, see *Form/Structure/Setting*. The wordplay or assonance of פַחַד, "terror," פַחַת, "pit," and פָּח, "trap," is impressive. Similar language or imagery is found in Jer 50:24 and in Ezek 17:15–21.

The phrase יוֹשֵׁב מוֹאָב is taken by most interpreters in the sense of "inhabitant(s) of Moab." Holladay understands the phrase to mean "enthroned Moab" (Holladay, 1:578; 2:364), the sense being that Moab had assumed a position of prominence that belonged only to the LORD. To be preferred here is "the (throne-)sitter of Moab," that is, the king as the symbol and sum of his people (see the *Comment* on v 9). In the context of the parallel in Isa 24:17–18, the יוֹשֵׁב הָאָרֶץ who would fall into the pit and trap is associated with the kings of the earth who would be gathered into a pit (בּוֹר) and be closed up in prison (Isa 24:21–22).

45–46 Vv 45–47 are not found in LXX and are usually regarded as a later addition since current opinion is disposed to regard the LXX as a witness to a Hebrew text earlier than MT.

Vv 45–46 are an adaptation of Num 21:28–29; 24:17, another example of the use of traditional materials. A more fitting conclusion to this ensemble of oracles concerning Moab in Jer 48 could hardly be imagined. In Num 21:26 there is a reference to the successful campaign of Sihon, king of the Amorites, against Moab. Sihon occupied all the Moabite territory as far south as the Arnon. Consequently, the ballad singers sang a song of victory (Num 21:27–30), describing the start of the campaign from Heshbon (cf. Jer 48:2), the capital of Sihon, and the issuing of the call to rebuild Heshbon. This most ancient exemplar of an oracle against a foreign nation in the Bible entered the Jeremiah tradition as a fitting climax for Jer 48. Here again the invasion was to start from Heshbon. The references to fire and flame in v 45 point again to the use of traditional motifs, as evidenced in the references to fire coming against the strongholds of foreign nations in Amos 1:4, 7, 10, 12, 14; 2:2.

47 Similar statements are made for Ammon (49:6) and for Elam (49:39). For a discussion of these passages, see the *Comment* on 46:26.

Explanation

Other than the oracle against Babylon (Jer 50–51), this oracle is the most extensive in the collection of OAN. Why this should be the case, or why this oracle should show such extensive knowledge of Moab's topography and way of life, is not clear. There is nothing in the oracle to suggest that Moab was judged because of its treatment of Israel or Judah. Moab comes under judgment for hubris against the LORD (48:26, 42), for complacency (48:11–12), and for pride in its sense of self-sufficiency (48:14, 29–30).

What is clear is that the oracle presents the LORD as the divine warrior who directs the judgment against Moab. Moab is described as being in direct opposition to the LORD. Without trying to date all the material in the oracle, it is suggested here that the best historical setting for an oracle concerning Moab is supplied by the conference of foreign ministers that convened in Jerusalem in 594 (Jer 27) to plot rebellion against Babylon and to urge Judah's leaders to join in the rebellion. Jeremiah warned Moab, Ammon, and Edom that they were plotting against the LORD's plan being effected by Nebuchadrezzar, the LORD's servant. The effect of the chapter, as in all the OAN in Jeremiah, is to affirm the LORD's sovereignty over the nations.

D. Concerning the Ammonites (49:1–6 [LXX 30:17–21])

Bibliography

Barré, M. "The Meaning of *l*² *²šybnw.*" *JBL* 105 (1986) 611–31. **Dahood, M.** "The Value of Ugaritic for Textual Criticism." *Bib* 40 (1959) 164–68. **Jackson, K. P.** *The Ammonite Language of the Iron Age.* HSM 27. Chico: Scholars, 1983. **Landes, G. M.** "Ammon, Ammonites." *IDB* 1:112. ———. "The Material Civilization of the Ammonites." *BA* 21 (1961) 66–86. **North, F.** "The Oracle against the Ammonites in Jeremiah 49:1–6." *JBL* 65 (1946) 37–43.

Translation

¹*Concerning the Ammonites.*
Thus says the Lord:

Has Israel no sons? (3+3)
Has he no heir?

*Why has Milcom*ᵃ *dispossessed Gad,* (4+3)
*(why) has his people settled in its cities?*ᵇ

²*Therefore, behold, the days are coming* (4+2)
—oracle of the Lord—

I will make the blast of war heard (3+2)
*against Rabbath of the Ammonites,*ᵃ

*and it will become*ᵇ *a desolated tell;* (3+3)
*her villages*ᶜ *will burn with fire,*

and Israel will dispossess his dispossessor, (3+2)
ᵈ*says the Lord.*ᵈ

³*Howl, O Heshbon, for Ai*ᵃ *is destroyed.* (4+3)
Cry out, villages of Rabbah.

Gird yourselves in sackcloth, mourn, (3+2)
ᵇ*run about with gashes,*ᵇ

*for Milcom*ᶜ *will go into exile,* (4+3)
his priests and his officials together.

⁴*Why do you boast of your plains?*ᵃ (2)
*Your strength*ᵇ *flows away,* (2+2+2)
ᶜ*O faithless daughter,*ᶜ
the one trusting in her treasures:
"Who will come against me?" (3)

5   *Behold me bringing against you terror*   (4+3+2)
         —ᵃ*oracle of the Lord, God of Hosts*ᵃ—
    from all the ones around you.
    And you will be driven out, single file,   (3+3)
         and there will be none to gather the ᵇ*fugitive.* ᵇ
6   *Afterward I will restore the fortunes of the Ammonites*   (4+2)
         —*oracle of the Lord.*ᵃ

Notes

1.a. MT has מַלְכָּם, "their king," as does Tg. Reading מִלְכֹּם with LXX, Syr, Vg.
1.b. LXX reads "their cities."
2.a. LXX lacks "sons of Ammon."
2.b. LXX has ἔσονται, "they will become."
2.c. Tg reads כפרנהא, "her villages," as does Syr; cf. also v 3. LXX reads βωμοί, "altars."
2.d-d. Lacking in LXX.
3.a. The versions all understood "Ai" as a place name.
3.b-b. MT is to be rendered "run about on the walls." The phrase is lacking in the LXX. Tg translates it "make a loud noise with troops" (בגדות). Syr rendered it "fight against one another." *BHS*'s emendation, accepted here, reads בִּגְדֻדוֹת, "with gashes," since gashing one's body was a sign of mourning; cf. 48:37.
3.c. See *Note* 1.a.
4.a. LXX reads ἐν τοῖς πεδίοις Ενακειμ, "plains of the Enakim."
4.b. עמק can mean "valley" or "plain" as in the preceding clause, but it can also mean "strength," as in Job 39:21 and in Ug. (M. Dahood, *Bib* 40 [1959] 166–67).
4.c-c. MT is retained because it expresses the treaty violations that may underlie the oracle. LXX reads "haughty daughter"; Tg has "O stupid kingdom"; Syr reads "O beloved daughter"; Vg has "delicate daughter."
5.a-a. LXX has only "says the LORD."
5.b-b. Lacking in LXX.
6.a. The verse is lacking in LXX.

Form/Structure/Setting

The oracle concerning Ammon contains typical themes of oracles concerning the nations: condemnation of aggression, the announcement of the coming of a destroyer, destruction by fire and resulting desolation, the defeat and exile of deity and officials, the denunciation of pride and false trust, and the sovereignty of the LORD. The disaster is centered on Rabbah, the Ammonite capital. Although Israel had suffered from Ammonite aggression, there is neither anger against Ammon nor gloating over Ammon's fate. For other oracles concerning Ammon, see Amos 1:13–15; Zeph 2:8–11; Ezek 21:20, 28–32; 25:1–7.

Form-critically, this is a judgment oracle, with the several questions serving as definitions of the indictment. The structure of the passage has been variously described. Christensen (*Transformations*, 226) saw the passage as a unified poem of three strophes, with the summons to mourn (v 3) intervening between two oracles of judgment, vv 1–2 and vv 4–5. Holladay recognized two judgment oracles, vv 1–2 and vv 3–5, each with form-critical integrity, the first possibly dating to 587 and the second dating possibly to 598 (2:367).

Poetic analysis is determined in large measure by text-critical analysis. F. North (*JBL* 65 [1946] 37–43) produced a radically reduced text for the oracle based on text-criticism, historical considerations, and his opinion of what was poetically superfluous. Despite the problems caused for metrical analysis, it seems better to take a maximalist approach, including for metrical analysis all material justified by careful text-criticism. With the exception of the superscription and the announcement of divine speech, v 1 is a tetracolon with מדוע, "why?" doing double duty for the fourth colon. V 2 is also a tetracolon. Rudolph (267) excised the last colon of v 2 because it seemed to be a wishful dream of later Judaism. For a defense of its authenticity, see the *Comment* on v 2. V 3 begins and ends with bicola, with a tricolon intervening. V 4 is best taken as a tetracolon. V 5 is a tricolon.

The oracle itself supplies no sure indicator for a setting. The only information about a historical event has to do with Ammonite aggression against the territory of Gad. H. Bardtke ("Jeremia der Fremdvölkerprophet," *ZAW* 54 [1936] 250) dated the oracle to the last years of Josiah, and he was followed in this by Christensen (*Transformations*, 227) and by Landes (*IDB* 1:112). Holladay, as noted above, suggested the events of 587 as the setting for vv 1–2 and 598 as a plausible setting for vv 3–5. Carroll cautioned that the stereotypical elements in the poem divorce it from a specific situation (800).

Comment

1 Biblical tradition preserves the memory of a kindred relationship between Ammon and Israel (Gen 19:18). The kingdom of Ammon seems to have been established in Iron I with its capital at Rabbah (modern Amman). In terms of land area, its size was smaller than most of the contiguous or neighboring states. Beginning in Iron I the Ammonites constructed a north-south chain of forts or strongholds to the west of Rabbah, thus giving the small kingdom a definitive western boundary (G. M. Landes, *BA* 24 [1961] 68–70). Judg 11:4–33 provides the first data on an Ammonite attempt at expansion. Later, in Saul's time, an Ammonite invasion provided the occasion for Saul's first military campaign (1 Sam 11:1–11). After a period of good relations with David, Ammon broke the accord and summoned help from the Syrians, and war began. After a protracted military campaign, David incorporated Ammon into his empire (2 Sam 10). During subsequent history Ammon touched the life of Israel often, usually in connection with Ammonite attempts at expansion. On one occasion Ammon contemplated an alliance with Judah, Edom, Moab, Tyre, and Sidon to try to win independence from Babylon (Jer 27:3). Ammon continued to exist after Jerusalem was destroyed, giving sanctuary and aid to Ishmael (Jer 41).

The population of Ammon, like most of its neighbors, was heterogeneous. Ammonite personal names in the Bible and the data from the few surviving Ammonite inscriptions point to a basic Semitic stock. The Ammonite lexicon, onomastics, and morphology of the inscriptions establish Ammonite as a Canaanite language, with a distinctive orthography (K. P. Jackson, *The Ammonite Language of the Iron Age*, 93–109).

The word for "heir," יורש, from the root that means "to possess," prepares the way for the charge that Ammon (dis-)possessed Gad of its territory. The two opening questions imply that the territory of Gad had not been abandoned by the Gadites and that the Ammonite action was unjustified aggression for territorial gain. For a discussion of possible settings for this aggression, see *Form/Structure/ Setting.* A similar situation occurred in Jephthah's time when Ammon campaigned to take possession of Gilead (Judg 11:4–33), and Jephthah's reply to the Ammonites used the same root ירשׁ in both its senses: possess and dispossess (Judg 11:24).

For the reading "Milcom" rather than "their king" (MT), see *Notes.* Milcom was the chief god of Ammon. The name occurs in two Ammonite inscriptions in its consonantal form: מלכם (Jackson, *The Ammonite Language,* 10, 74). The only basis for its customary vocalization is MT. Both Milcom and Molech, who was associated with Milcom in 1 Kgs 11:7, are related to the word מלך, "king," and it is most likely that they are not names but a title, King, in the same way that the LORD bore that title. For a treatment of the possibility that Milcom was identical with Chemosh, the god of the Moabites, see the *Comment* on 48:7.

2 The judgment against Ammon was centered on Rabbah, the capital, and its "daughters," i.e., the villages that together with the capital, composed the city-state. The war shout, desolation, and the burning of cities are a part of the traditional store of terminology for oracles against the nations. As a result of the coming military attack and Ammonite defeat, Israel would regain its lost territory.

3 The summons to the defeated to wail, to mourn, and to put on sackcloth is a common feature of the oracles against the nations (cf. 48:37–38). Ritual gashing of the body was also a typical mourning rite (see the *Comment* on 48:37).

In *Translation* and *Notes,* עַי has been rendered "Ai," a place name, mainly on the basis of versional evidence. However, Ai in the vicinity of Bethel cannot be meant, and no Ai is known in Ammon. The term means "ruin," but it makes no sense to translate here "the ruin is destroyed." P. Volz offered the emendation שֹׁדֵד עָלָה, "the destroyer has come up" (cf. 48:18). The emendation makes sense and solves the problem of the text but is without any textual support.

For "Heshbon," see the *Comments* on 48:2, 34, 45. Heshbon was a border town between Ammon and Moab, and apparently the town changed hands on several occasions. Here in 49:3 Heshbon is considered to be Ammonite. In Jer 48 the situation is ambiguous. In 48:2, 45 Heshbon was the initial point of danger for the Moabites, while in 48:34 Heshbon cried out in alarm and thus at times was a Moabite town. Ostraca written in Ammonite script that were excavated at Heshbon date from the seventh to the sixth centuries and witness to an Ammonite presence there (Jackson, *The Ammonite Language,* 51–55).

4 As is common in oracles against the nations, the nation to be judged is accused of pride (Jer 46:8; 48:7, 29–30, 42; 49:16; 50:29, 31–32; Isa 13:11; 14:11; 16:6; 23:9; Ezek 28:2, 5, 17; 32:12). Ammon is accused of placing unwise confidence in its strength and treasures (cf. 48:7), in such a way as to believe itself capable of initiating hostilities. The wordplay on עמק, "plain" or "strength," is significant. Whether the plains refer to fortified plains/valleys or to well-cultivated plains is hard to say.

Ammon is labeled הבת השׁובבה, "faithless daughter, apostate daughter" (cf. 31:22). The ancient versions (see the *Notes*) and most modern commentators have been suspicious of the phrase. Duhm emended השׁובבה to השׁאננה, "at ease," on the basis that it was unknown against whom Ammon could have been unfaithful (B. Duhm, 353). But השׁובבה may have political implications after all. M. Barré has shown that the Hebrew word שׁוב, "turn," and its semantic equivalents in Akkadian, *târu* and *saḫāru*, often denoted a change of allegiance, usually with reference to an action of a vassal state (M. Barré, *JBL* 105 [1986] 611–31, esp. 626–31). It is plausible to understand that Ammon was a vassal of Babylon at the time of this oracle and that Ammon threw off the yoke of servitude and attacked the territory of another vassal without the permission of the suzerain. Thus "faithless daughter" would be an apt and an accurate designation of Ammon. If this approach is followed, then Israel's repossession of its territory mentioned in v 2 would not be a reverse aggression but a return to the previous legal situation.

5 Another aspect of the judgment against Ammon was the initiation of terror from every side, or perhaps from all its neighbors.

The clause "you will be driven out single file" suggests the departure of prisoners of war, through the breaches of the destroyed city, for exile. For fuller expressions of the same reality, see Mic 2:13; Amos 4:3.

6 See the *Comment* on 46:26.

Explanation

The oracle concerning Ammon emphasizes Ammon's military aggression (49:1) and unwarranted, prideful trust in geographical location and in treasures. Military aggression would suggest treaty violation (see Introduction to Oracles concerning the Nations [46:1–51:64]). As in the other OAN, the LORD as divine warrior moves against Ammon, bringing destruction, terror, and exile.

While the oracle itself provides no sure date, it seems probable that the conference in Jerusalem in 594 (Jer 27), including ministers from Tyre, Sidon, Ammon, Moab, Edom, and Judah, provides the setting for an oracle concerning Ammon. Not only was Ammon intended to hear such an oracle, but also Judah was to understand an implicit warning about joining a coalition against Babylon. During the conference Jeremiah declared the LORD's plan and Babylon's place in that plan. Consequently, any opposition to Babylon was opposition to the LORD.

E. Concerning Edom (49:7–22[LXX 30:1–16])

Bibliography

Bartlett, J. R. *Edom and the Edomites.* JSOTSup 77. Sheffield: JSOT Press, 1989. **Bekel, H.** "Ein vorexilisches Orakel über Edom in Klageliederstrophe—die gemeinsame Quelle von Obadja, 1–9 und Jeremia 49, 7–22." *TSK* 80 (1907) 315–43. **Bennett, C.-M.** "Excavations at Buseirah (Biblical Bozrah)." In *Midian, Moab and Edom: The History* and *Archaeology of Late Bronze and Iron Age Jordan and North-West Arabia,* ed. J. F. A. Sawyer and D. J. A. Clines. JSOTSup 24. Sheffield: JSOT Press, 1983. **Cohen, S.** "Dedan." *IDB* 1:812. **Ephʿal, I.** *The*

Ancient Arabs: Nomads on the Borders of the Fertile Crescent 9th–5th Centuries B.C. Leiden: Brill, 1982. **Glueck, N.** "Explorations in Eastern Palestine, II." AASOR 15. New Haven: University of Pennsylvania Press, 1935. **Kselman, J. S.** "A Note on Jer 49,20 and Zeph 2,6–7." *CBQ* 32 (1970) 579–81. **Pope, M.** "Job, Book of." *IDB* 2:911–25. **Sauer, J.** "Transjordan in the Late Bronze and Iron Ages: A Critique of Glueck's Synthesis." *BASOR* 263 (1986) 1–26. **Scott, R. B. Y.** *Proverbs, Ecclesiastes.* AB. Garden City: Doubleday, 1965. **Stuart, D.** *Hosea-Jonah.* WBC 31. Waco: Word Books, 1987. **Wolff, H. W.** *Obadja und Jona.* BKAT 14/3. Neukirchen: Neukirchener, 1977.

Translation

7 *Concerning Edom.*
Thus says the LORD *of Hosts:* [a]
   [b] *Wisdom is in Teman no more;*   (4+3+2)
      counsel has perished from the prudent, [c]
      their wisdom has been corrupted.
8 [a] *Flee, turn away,* [a]   (2+2+2)
      descend to dwell (at home),
      O inhabitants of Dedan. [b]
   For the calamity of Esau I bring against him,   (5+2)
      the time when I punish him.
9 *If grape gatherers came to you,*   (3+3)
      they would not leave gleanings.
   If thieves by night,   (3+2)
      [a] *they would destroy* [b] *only enough for themselves.* [a]
10 *For I have stripped Esau bare;*   (3+2)
      I have uncovered his hiding places,
   He is not able to hide himself; [a]   (3+3)
      [b] *destroyed are his seed and his brothers.* [b]
   And there is no neighbor [c] *of his (to say),*   (2+2+2+3)
11   *"Leave your orphans,*
      I will keep them alive;
      your widows can rely on me."
12 *For thus says the* LORD: *If those who did not receive the sentence to drink the cup have to drink it, will you be cleared from punishment? You will not be cleared, you will surely drink it.* 13 *For I have sworn by myself—oracle of the* LORD—*that Bozrah* [a] *will become a desolation, a reproach, a waste,* [b] *and a curse, and all her cities will become ruins forever.*
14 *I have heard a report from the* LORD;   (4+3)
      a messenger has been sent [a] *among the nations:*
   "Gather yourselves and come against her,   (3+2)
      rise up for war."
15 *For* [a] *behold, I will make you small among the nations,*   (4+2)
      despised [b] *by humankind.* [b]
16 *Your horror has deceived you,* [a]   (3+2)
      the pride of your heart,
   O dweller [b] *in the clefts of Sela,*   (3+3)
      the one holding [b] *the height of the hill.*
   Though [c] *you make high your nest like the eagle,*   (3+2)

> *from there I will bring you down,*
> *says the LORD.*

¹⁷*Edom will become a desolation; everyone passing by her* ^a*will be appalled*^a *and will hiss* ^b*because of all her blows.*^b ¹⁸*Like the overthrow of Sodom and Gomorrah and its neighbors, says the LORD.*

A man will not live there,	(3+3)
a human will not sojourn in her.	

¹⁹*Behold, like a lion goes up from the jungle of the Jordan to the pasture well watered,*

so I will in a moment ^a*run away her sucklings;*^a	(4+4)
I will single out ^b*the choicest of her rams.* ^b	
For who is like me?	(3+2+5)
Who can summon me?	
Who is that shepherd who can stand before me?	

²⁰*Therefore, hear the plan of the LORD, which he has planned concerning Edom, his purposes, which he has devised concerning the residents of Teman:*

Surely the little ones of the flocks will be dragged away; ^a	(4+4)
their pasture will appall their sucklings. ^b	
²¹ *At the sound of their fall the earth will shake,*	(4+4)
a cry will be heard at the Red Sea. ^a	
²² *Behold, one rises*^a *and soars*^b *like an eagle*	(4+3)
and spreads his wings over Bozrah,	
and the heart of the warriors of Edom will be on that day	(6+3)
like the heart of a woman in labor.	

Notes

7.a. LXX lacks "Hosts."

7.b. Omitting interrogative ה with LXX and Syr.

7.c. MT has, בנים, "sons"; Tg, Vg. LXX, Syr understood the root בין, "to understand," which is followed here.

8.a-a. For MT הָפְנוּ (hoph), "be turned back," read הִפְנוּ (hiph) (*BHS*). For "flee, turn away," LXX reads ἠπατήθη ὁ τόπος αὐτῶν, "their place has been deceived."

8.b. LXX has, in addition, ὅτι δύσκολα ἐποίησεν, "for he has done grievously."

9.a-a. LXX reads ἐπιθήσουσιν χεῖρα αὐτῶν, "they will lay their hand," understanding ישׁיתו ידם.

9.b. Reading impf for pf.

10.a. With LXX read niph inf abs of the root חבא (חבה), "to hide."

10.b-b. LXX reads ὤλοντο διὰ χεῖρα ἀδελφοῦ αὐτοῦ, "destroyed each by the hand of his brother," understanding זרוע for זרעו.

10.c. Reading as a sg noun with LXX.

13.a. For בצרה, "Bozrah," LXX reads ἐν μέσῳ αὐτῆς = בתוכה, "in her midst."

13.b. LXX lacks "a waste."

14.a. Reading שָׁלַח with the parallel in Obad 1. LXX has "he has sent."

15.a. Obad 2 lacks "for."

15.b-b. Obad 2 has מאד אתה, "you utterly."

16.a. Reading a fem verb: הִשִׁיאַתְךָ; cf. Obad 3. LXX reads ἐνεχείρησέν σοι, "has taken you in hand."

16.b. *Ḥireq compaginis;* GCK § 90k, l. LXX has κατέλυσεν, "has destroyed."

16.c. Obad 4 has אם, "if," for כי.

17.a-a. Lacking in LXX.

17.b-b. Lacking in LXX.

19.a-a. Reading with Holladay אָרִיצָה עָלֶיהָ.

19.b-b. Reading with Holladay, Rudolph, and Bright וּמֵחַר אֵילֶיהָ.

20.a. Pointing and reading as niph.

20.b. Reading עֲלֵיהֶם; cf. J. S. Kselman, *CBQ* 32 (1970) 579–80, who translates the colon "surely the nurslings of their pasture shall be appalled."

21.a. Omitting קוֹלָהּ with LXX.

22.a. Lacking in LXX.

22.b. LXX has ὄψεται, "he looks," reading the root ראה, "to see," for דאה, "to soar."

Form/Structure/Setting

Other oracles concerning Edom are found in Amos 1:11–12; Isa 21:11–12; 34:5–15; 63:1–6; Ezek 25:12–14; 35:1–15; Obad; Mal 1:2–5. In addition, there are passages that express either enmity against Edom or the threat of judgment: Isa 11:14; Lam 4:21–22; Ezek 32:29; Joel 4:19; Ps 60:10–11; 137:7–9. A remarkable feature of the oracle in Jer 49:7–22 and of the other oracles listed above, with the exceptions of Ezek 25:12–14; 35:1–15; Obadiah, is the lack of hatred or of nationalistic rancor.

V 7 is a tricolon, v 8 has two bicola, v 9, a variant of Obad 5, has two bicola, and v 11 is a tricolon. Vv 12–13 are in prose. Vv 14–16, a variant of Obad 1–4, form a clear unit. V 14 has two bicola, v 15 is a bicolon, and v 16 contains three bicola. Vv 17–18 belong together, v 17 is prose, and v 18 can be scanned as poetic. Vv 19–22 can be regarded as a unit. V 19 contains two bicola and a tricolon, v 20 has two bicola, v 21 is a bicolon, and v 22 contains two bicola.

The appearances in Jer 49:7–22 of prose passages (vv 12–13, 17, 18?) and of poetic material found also in other prophetic passages have encouraged most commentators to try to define the original Jeremiah oracle. H. Bardtke identified vv 7–8, 22a, 10–11 as original (Bardtke, *ZAW* 54 [1936] 254); Rudolph, vv 7–8, 10–11, 22 (Rudolph, 268–69); Weiser, with caution, vv 7–8, 10b–11, and perhaps other verses (Weiser, 407); Christensen, vv 7–11 (Christensen, *Transformations*, 233); and Holladay 7aβ–8, 10–11, 18–22, on the basis that they reflect Jeremiah's diction and compose a form-critical unit (Holladay, 2:372).

Still unsolved is the relationship between Jer 49:9, 14–16 and Obad 1–5. The situation is analogous to that of Isa 2:1–5 and Mic 4:1–4. Which variant is original? Or are both passages dependent on an already existing traditional text? H. Bekel argued for a common source, which he tried to reconstruct from the two variants (H. Bekel, *TSK* 80 [1907] 315–38). H. W. Wolff argued that the variants were dependent on the same text, transmitted orally (H. W. Wolff, *Obadja und Jona*, 21–22). More recently Stuart, after doing a comparative analysis, concluded that the two passages are probably independent compositions using commonly known materials (D. Stuart, *Hosea-Jonah*, 415–16). Clearly the uses made of such a common text in Jeremiah and Obadiah are quite different: Obadiah condemned Edom for its hostile attitude toward Judah, while Jeremiah lacks such a perspective. In any case there seems no good reason to deny vv 9, 14–16 to Jeremiah, especially since the oracles concerning the nations in the book of Jeremiah show consistent use of traditional materials in passages assigned almost universally to Jeremiah. V 9 is separated from vv 14–16 in the same way Obad 5 is separated from Obad 1–4, by the rubric "says the LORD." V 9, far from being an intrusive element that destroys the connection between v 8 and v 10, provides a perfect lead-in for v 10 (cf. 6:9 for a picking that leaves no gleanings). Also, vv 14–16 continue the "I" of vv 7–11 and vv 19–21.

Vv 12–13 are usually bracketed as secondary or as a later insertion on the basis that they are prose and on the assumption that those who did not deserve to drink the cup were the Judeans. Rudolph saw v 12 as an expression of Jewish conceit and a wrong concept of election, an attitude not in accord with Jeremiah's preaching (Rudolph, 269; cf. Weiser, 408). The only other possible identification for those who did not deserve to drink the cup, the Dedanites of v 8, seems unlikely in light of Jer 25:23.

Vv 17–18 may be an elaboration on the poetic sections that use traditional or standardized language of judgment (for v 17, cf. 18:16, 19:8; for v 18, cf. 33b; 50:40; Isa 13:19; 34:10).

It seems possible, therefore, to identify three poetic passages in the Edom oracle that have form-critical integrity. The first poem, vv 7–11, is a judgment oracle promising a complete destruction of Edom. The second poem, vv 14–16, beginning with an audition report and a summons to the enemy to prepare for battle, condemns Edom for unwarranted trust in its deity and its pride and concludes with the sentence of complete abasement. The third poem, vv 19–22, uses the metaphors of the attacking lion and the swooping eagle to describe the judgment of the LORD against Edom.

Since the Edom oracle contains no hint that judgment would be sent because of Edom's hostile attitude or actions against Judah, a setting of 587 or shortly thereafter seems unlikely. A more likely setting would be the conference of foreign ministers held in Jerusalem in 594 (Jer 27:3), when Edom and other neighboring states met to contemplate an independence movement against Babylon. Since Jeremiah's position was that any opposition to Nebuchadrezzar was opposition to the LORD's plan, any action taken to violate a treaty or to declare independence from Babylon would be sufficient reason to occasion an oracle of judgment from the LORD.

Comment

7 The territory of Edom was centered in the mountainous region south of the Wadi el-Ḥesa and bordering the Wadi Arabah to the west. The exact boundaries for Edom for any period cannot now be determined, because the boundaries shrank or expanded in view of shifting economic and political realities. In the Neo-Assyrian period the southern boundary extended to the Gulf of Aqabah. The ruins of most Edomite sites lie on the plateau between the Wadi el-Ḥesa and the scarp of Naqb esh-Shtar (for a description of the land of Edom in light of literary data and archaeology, see J. R. Bartlett, *Edom and the Edomites*, 33–54).

N. Glueck thought that Teman was to be identified with Ṭawīlān near Petra (Glueck, "Explorations," 82–83). In Jer 49:20 Edom and Teman are in parallel. In Obad 8–9 both Edom and Teman are in parallel with Mount Esau. In Hab 3:3 Teman is in parallel with Mount Paran. Most scholars conclude that Teman is an alternate name for Edom or the name for a region in Edom (Bartlett, *Edom and the Edomites*, 40).

The wisdom of Edom is well known in biblical tradition. The wise men of Edom are mentioned in 1 Kgs 5:11 and in Obad 8. The book of Job is commonly held to be of Edomite origin (M. Pope, *IDB* 2:912) as are Prov 30:1–4 and 31:1–8 (R. B. Y. Scott, *Proverbs, Ecclesiastes*, xlii). Edom's vaunted wisdom has failed, along with its pride, to avert catastrophe.

8 Here is found another summons to flee, a common feature in the oracles concerning the nations (48:6–8; 48:28; 49:30; 50:8–10; 51:6, 45; cf. R. Bach, *Die Aufforderungen*, 15–50). Those counseled to flee for safety are the Dedanites. Dedan was an Arabian city to the southeast of Edom, el ʿUla. For the various interpretations of העמיקו לשבת, "make deep to dwell," see Holladay, 2:375. Holladay took the expression as a warning to the Dedanites to remain in the lower elevations and not travel the caravan routes through Edom. However, Cohen's suggestion that this reference to Dedanites may indicate a settlement of theirs in Edom (S. Cohen, *IDB* 1:812) seems reasonable in light of Edom's location astride the caravan routes in its region and its dependence on international trade for economic prosperity. Consequently, it seems preferable to take the expression "make deep to dwell" to mean something like "descend from your present location in Edom and return home to Dedan." For a treatment of the Arab tribes, their caravan routes, and the literary sources that provide the basis of our knowledge of them, see I. Ephʿal, *The Ancient Arabs*.

For a parallel to the last two cola, see Jer 48:44b.

9 The image of picking the grapevines clean is found also in Jer 6:9. There are two significant differences between this verse and its parallel in Obad 5. In Obad 5 the thieves are mentioned before the grape gatherers, and both apodoses begin with interrogative ה plus לוא.

10 V 10a is parallel to Obad 6 in content if not in language (note חשׂף in v 10; חפשׂ in Obad 5). If v 9 is bracketed because it is simply a variant of Obad 6 and shows none of Jeremiah's diction, it is difficult to see why v 10 is retained as authentic (Holladay, 2:372–73). In addition, the remainder of v 10, with its references to "brothers" and "neighbors," is a free adaptation of Obad 7, or a variant of a common text, in order to make a different point. In any case, v 9 fits so well with v 10 that it can hardly be bracketed (see *Form/Structure/Setting*).

11 Most commentators have understood this verse to mean that the LORD would protect the Edomite orphans and widows. Accepted here is the view of Bright (328), Rudolph (266), and Holladay (2: 376) that v 11 is a quotation of Edom's brothers (treaty partners?) and neighbors. Contrary to their willingness to help, however, they would be in no position to do so, for they would suffer the same fate as Edom's posterity in v 10.

12 The image of drinking the cup of judgment is common in the oracles concerning the nations. See the *Comment* on 48:26 and *Form/Structure/Setting* in this chapter.

13 Bozrah (modern Buseirah) appears prominent enough in the Edomite references in the Bible to be taken as Edom's capital. C.-M. Bennett's excavations at Buseirah, thirteen miles south of Tafileh, revealed a well-fortified and imposing site dating from about the beginning of the eighth century and lasting until sometime in the sixth century (Bennett, "Excavations at Buseirah [Biblical Bozrah]," 9–17; for a list of preliminary excavation reports on Bozrah, see J. Sauer, *BASOR* 263 [1986] 19–20).

14—15 These verses are paralleled in Obad 1–2. The speaker has heard a report from the LORD, and a messenger (from the divine assembly?) has carried the report to the nations calling on them to prepare for war. The summons to battle is a frequent feature of the oracles concerning the nations (for Jeremiah alone, see

46:3–6, 9; 49:28, 31; 50:14, 16, 21, 26–27, 29; 51:3, 11, 16, 27–28). For a form-critical analysis of this prophetic genre, see R. Bach, *Die Aufforderungen,* 51–91. The fate of Edom was to suffer decimation and dishonor (Stuart, *Hosea-Jonah,* 416–17).

16 The word תפלצתך, translated here as "your horror," is lacking in the parallel in Obad 3. It appears to be a by-form of מפלצת (1 Kgs 15:13), some kind of image or symbol sacred to Asherah, which Asa burned at the Wadi Kidron. The word is derived from the root פלץ, "to shudder, be horrified." If this interpretation is correct, Edom was chided for placing undue trust in their deity and for their pride. But what deity? Holladay has pointed out that there was a god called Edom, as the name Obed-edom would indicate (Holladay, 2:376), just as Asshur was both a divine name and the name of the country Assyria. Several figurines representing Astarte or some other fertility goddess have been found in Edomite territory. The Edomites also revered a god named Qos. This deity is not mentioned in the Bible, and most of the evidence for the veneration of Qos is late. The earliest reference to Qos, the theophoric element in a personal name, dates to the time of Tiglath-pileser III (for a discussion of Edomite religion and of Qos, see Bartlett, *Edom and the Edomites,* 187–207).

Whether Sela is to be understood as a city name or simply as "rock" is not clarified by biblical passages. The problem is illustrated by the account of Azariah's campaign in Edom. In the version in 1 Kgs 14, Amaziah took Sela by storm, whereas in the parallel in 1 Chr 25, the men of Judah captured 10,000 Edomites, took them to the top of the rock, and threw them down from the top of the rock. Some have identified Sela with Umm el-Biyara at Petra, others with Khirbet SilꜤ, but neither identification has been upheld by excavations. For a discussion of the problem and the proposed identification of Sela, see Bartlett, *Edom and the Edomites,* 51–52.

17 Cf. Jer 18:16 and 19:8. Hissing, or better, whistling, while walking past a ruined site may have been a defense against the demons of destruction (KB 1011).

18 The overthrow of the cities of the plain (Gen 14) had long since become proverbial and is here used as the pattern of complete destruction for Edom. For Jer 49:18b, see 49:33b.

19–21 Vv 19–21 are a variant of 50:44–46. The interpretation offered here is based on the repointing of two words and on a different word division in another case (see *Translation* and *Notes*). The new readings carry forward the imagery of the attack of the lion on the flock and recall Isa 34:5–7.

The three questions in v 19 highlight the incomparability of the LORD: no deity can so summon nature and nations to accomplish the divine purposes, and no foe can thwart the plan of the LORD.

22 For the figure of the soaring eagle as a sign of military attack, see the *Comment* on 48:40 and the references there.

Explanation

The oracle concerning Edom emphasizes Edom's trust in the deceptive guidance of its deity, its pride, and its dependence for security on its reputedly inaccessible heights. There is no hint that Edom was to be destroyed for any of its depredations of Israel or Judah. The incomparable LORD, the divine warrior, is described as effecting complete devastation on the kingdom of Edom.

As suggested in *Form/Structure/Setting*, the meeting of foreign ministers in Jerusalem in 594, including the minister from Edom, provides an appropriate setting for an oracle against Edom. The oracle stresses the sovereignty of the LORD over every part of the divine imperium, and any violation by any member of the imperium brought disaster.

F. Concerning Damascus   (49:23–27 [LXX 30:29–33])

Bibliography

Astour, M. "Arpad." *IDBSup* 55. **Nötscher, F.** "Zum emphatischen Lamed." *VT* 3 (1953) 372–80. **Pfeiffer, R. H.** *Introduction to the Old Testament.* Rev. ed. New York: Harper and Brothers, 1948. 508. **Talbert, R. M.** "Ben-Hadad." *IDBSup* 95.

Translation

23 *Concerning Damascus.*
    Confounded are Hamath and Arpad,   (3+3)
      for they have heard a report of calamity;
    they are agitated by worry like the sea,[a]   (3+3)
      which cannot be still.
24   *Damascus has become weak;*   (2+2+2)
      she has turned to flee,
      panic has seized her,[a]
    [b]*Distress and pains have seized her*   (3+1)
      like a woman giving birth.[b]
25   *"How it is forsaken,*[a] *the famous*[b] *city,*   (4+2)
      the city of my joy."
26   *Therefore her young men will fall in her squares,*   (4+5+3)
      and all the men of war will be silenced[a]*on that day*[a]
         —oracle of the LORD of Hosts.[b]
27   *And I will kindle a fire in the wall of Damascus,*   (4+3)
      and it will devour the strongholds of Ben-Hadad.

Notes

23.a. Reading כים for בים; LXX lacks בים. Cf. Isa 57:20.
24.a. Reading mappiq in final ה with LXX, Tg, and Vg.
24.b-b. Lacking in LXX.
25.a. Omitting לא, "not," with Vg, or perhaps read as emphatic lamedh (see *Comment*).
25.b. Q has תהלת.

26.a-a. Lacking in LXX.
26.b. "Hosts" is lacking in LXX.

Form/Structure/Setting

This oracle, the shortest of the oracles concerning the nations in the collection in Jeremiah, seems to be composed almost entirely of traditional materials characteristic of the genre. Other than the references to the place names and the dynastic name Ben-Hadad, there is nothing that would help to identify it as an oracle concerning Damascus or Syria. In contrast to the other oracles, nothing is contained in it about Syria's geography or topography, its characteristic culture, or its gods or religious life. Conspicuous by its absence is any reason for judgment.

Anxiety over impending calamity begins in Hamath and Arpad, capitals of earlier significant Aramean states to the north of Syria. Their panic has been explained as resulting from the news of the fate of Damascus (H. Bardtke, *ZAW* 54 [1936] 254; Rudolph, 271; Carroll, 808). In light of the common theme in Jeremiah of the "foe from the north," however, it seems reasonable to expect that those cities would be among the first to hear the unsettling news of an army on the move. The bad news then reaches Damascus, causing panic (v 24) and a lament over the abandoned city (v 25). The word of judgment announces military defeat and the burning of the city.

V 23 contains two bicola. V 24 is a tricolon followed by a colon of double length. Vv 25–26 each have two bicola. V 27 is a bicolon. Only the superscription in v 23a and the oracular rubric in v 26 fall outside the prosodic analysis.

Bardtke, followed by Rudolph, set the limits of the original oracle as follows: vv 23–24a, v 25 (Bardtke, *ZAW* 54 [1936] 254). Holladay saw v 26 as essential, omitting only v 24b and v 27 (Holladay, 2:379). Christensen (*Transformations*, 246) omitted only v 24b, because LXX lacked it. Since the oracle seems to be composed of traditional materials throughout, it is questionable whether v 27 should be excluded, and Christensen's analysis is followed here.

Most commentators have dated the oracle late and thus have denied it to Jeremiah. Pfeiffer regarded the oracle as a deliberate attempt at archaizing in the fifth century, drawing on a knowledge of Assyrian campaigns in the second half of the eighth century when the Aramean states were strong (Pfeiffer, *Introduction*, 508). Rudolph gave five arguments against ascribing the oracle to Jeremiah, only one of which has much weight: Damascus is missing from the list of nations in Jer 25 (Rudolph, 271).

The oracle itself offers no data to determine a setting. Christensen suggested the possibility that the original setting may have been Josiah's program of political expansion to reinstitute David's empire, the imperium of the LORD (Christensen, *Transformations*, 248). The only other reason for placing the oracle within the context of Jeremiah's ministry is the mention in 2 Kgs 24:2 of Aramean hostility against Judah during the period 601–598. The lack of a reason for judgment in the oracle against Damascus, however, renders this supposition questionable. In addition, no information is available regarding any hostile stance of Damascus against Babylonia or of any Babylonian campaign against Damascus after 604.

Comment

23 Damascus was the capital of a strong Aramean kingdom from the end of the second millenium. Situated in a fertile, well-watered plain east of the Anti-Lebanon mountains, it was able to control the caravan routes that ran north to Haran or northeast, by way of Palmyra, to the Euphrates. Its incessant hostilities with Israel and Judah are covered extensively in the books of Samuel and Kings. The Assyrians, beginning with the campaigns of Tiglath-pileser III, finally put an end to Damascus as a regional power.

Hamath, the modern Nahr el-ʿAsi, was located on the Orontes River in northern Syria. Arpad, modern Tell Rifʿat, was situated some twenty miles north of Aleppo (Astour, *IDBSup* 55). During the Neo-Assyrian period, both cities suffered extensively at the hands of the Assyrians. The mention of these states suffering anxiety over unsettling news prior to the description of the abandonment of Damascus may indicate the advance of an enemy from the north, although no enemy is mentioned explicitly in the oracle.

25 The cry of lament is understood here to be uttered by the inhabitants of Damascus itself. It is possible, however, to understand it as a taunt; cf. the *Comment* on 48:17.

MT has the negative לֹא, "not," before the verb "forsaken." Vg deleted the negative and has been followed by most modern translators. Another possibility is to take the lamedh as the asseverative particle "surely" (so Christensen, *Transformations*, 246; F. Nötscher, *VT* 3 [1953] 372–80, who dealt with passages in which asseverative לֹא may be concealed by לֹא, chose to leave this verse outside his consideration).

The final yodh on "joy" may be either the first person singular "my" or an archaic genitive ending.

27 This verse uses traditional materials; cf. Amos 1:4, 7, 10, 12, 14; 2:2.

There were several kings of Damascus named Ben-Hadad, perhaps as many as four (cf. R. M. Talbert, *IDBSup* 95 for a discussion of the problems.) If there was a king Ben-Hadad IV, he would be dated at the end of the ninth century.

Explanation

No reason for judgment is given in this oracle. Although 2 Kgs 24:2 mentions Aramean hostility against Judah in the period 601–598, there is nothing in the oracle itself to suggest that this was the reason for the judgment. Nor do we know of any move by Damascus to oppose Babylon's program for hegemony.

Damascus is simply included among the nations under judgment by the LORD, almost as though any concept of an imperium of the LORD omitting Damascus would be inconceivable. In any case, the LORD is presented here, as typically in OAN, as the divine warrior who brings judgment.

G. *Concerning Qedar   (49:28–33*
[LXX 30:23–28])

Bibliography

Dumbrell, W. J. "Jeremiah 49.28–33: An Oracle against a Proud Desert People." *AJBA* 21 (1972) 99–109. **Eph^cal, I.** *The Ancient Arabs: Nomads on the Borders of the Fertile Crescent 9th– 5th Centuries B.C.* Leiden: Brill, 1982. **Hamp, V.** "חָצֵר *ḥāṣēr*." *TDOT* 5:131–39. **Orlinsky, H.** "*Ḥāṣēr* in the Old Testament." *JAOS* 59 (1939) 22–37.

Translation

[28] *Concerning Qedar and the* [a]*kingdoms of settlement(s)* [a] *which Nebuchadrezzar, king of Babylon, smote:*

Thus the LORD said:

Arise, go up against Qedar;	(3+3)
devastate the children of the East.	

[29] *Their tents and their flocks they will take,* (3+3+3)
their curtains [a] *and all their utensils;*
their camels will carry (them) for them,
and they will call out [b] *on them,* (2+2)
"Terror on every side!"

[30] *Flee,* [a]*wander far away;* [a] (3+3+2)
dwell down below in the settlement(s) [b]
—[c]*oracle of the LORD*[f]—
for Nebuchadrezzar, [d] *king of Babylon, has counseled against you a counsel* (5+3)
and has devised against them [e] *a plan.*

[31] *Arise, go up against a nation at ease,* (4+2+2)
one dwelling securely
—[a]*oracle of the LORD.* [a]
It has no doors and no bar; (3+2)
they dwell alone.

[32] *Their camels will be for spoil,* (3+3)
the multitude of their cattle for booty,
and I will scatter them to every wind, (3+2)
the ones whose temples are clipped,
and from every side I will bring their calamity (3+2)
—*oracle of the LORD.*

[33] *And the settlement will become a dwelling for jackals,* (4+2)
a destruction forever.
No man will dwell there; (3+3)
no human will sojourn in it.

Notes

28.a-a. LXX has βασίλισσῃ τῆς αὐλῆς, "queen of the court."
29.a. LXX reads ἱμάτια, "garments."
29.b. LXX has impv: "call out!"
30.a-a. Lacking in LXX.
30.b. Omitting "dwellers" before חצור.
30.c-c. Lacking in LXX.
30.d. Lacking in LXX.
30.e. Q has עליכם, "against you," to agree with the previous עליכם; so also LXX. Syr has "against them" in both cases; Vg has "against you" in both cases.
31.a-a. Lacking in LXX.

Form/Structure/Setting

The structural analyses of the oracle concerning the Qedarites have differed considerably. Bardtke included vv 28 (except for the mention of Nebuchadrezzar), 29, 31, 32, with no justification given for the omission of v 30 (*ZAW* 54 [1936] 255). Rudolph (272) accepted vv 28a, 30–32, with no explanation for the deletion of vv 28b–29). Thompson (726–27) and Christensen (*Transformations*, 210–11) include all of vv 28–33 in the oracle, and only Christensen, among those mentioned, analyzed the oracle as consisting of two divisions.

Holladay's analysis has greater merit. After the redactional introduction in v 28a, Holladay has recognized that the oracle consists of two stanzas, vv 28b–30 and vv 31–32, with ten cola in each stanza; only v 33 stands outside the structure of the poem (2:384). The structures of the two stanzas are remarkably parallel, with the contents of the first ten cola generally matching those of the second ten cola. This schema will illustrate the parallels:

Stanza 1 (vv 28b–30)	*Stanza 2 (vv 30–32)*
Cola 1–2: call to attack	Cola 1–2: call to attack
Cola 3–4: manner of life	Cola 3–4: manner of life
Cola 5–6: camels, commotion	Cola 5–6: camels, commotion
Cola 7–8: flight from disaster	Cola 7–8: scattering of people
Cola 9–10: a plan for devastation	Cola 9–10: calamity

V 33 falls outside the structure of the poem and may be a later summary statement using the phraseology of Jer 9:10 and Jer 49:18 (Carroll, 810; Rudolph, 272).

Although the two stanzas are generally parallel in form and content, they do not refer to exactly the same set of circumstances. The view adopted here, following Holladay, is that the two stanzas refer to two consecutive scenarios, the first reflecting an attack on nomadic Qedarites, the second reflecting a subsequent attack on more settled Qedarites to whom the first group are warned to flee for help. The irony is that the second group was to suffer the same fate as the first.

The following may be said in defense of this interpretation. In the first place, v 30b provides a transition from the first stanza to the second. MT provides the alternation "against you" and "against them": "he has counseled against you a counsel and has devised against them a plan." Qere corrects "against them" to "against you." LXX, Vg, and Tg have "against you" in both cases, whereas Syr has "against them" in both cases. The Kethib is the more difficult reading and is to be preferred. The transition between the two stanzas is thus preserved: calamity is to be visited on both groups of people referred to in the two stanzas.

In the second place, v 29 is most easily understood to refer to a group of Qedarites different from those referred to in vv 31–32. Admittedly, the verse is easily susceptible of two interpretations. Virtually all commentators have taken the verse as a description of what the invaders will do to the Qedarites: their tents, sheep, curtains, and utensils will be taken from them, their camels will be borne away (RSV), and the attackers will cry out to them, "terror on every side." However, as Holladay has pointed out, the verse is somewhat ambiguous and permits another interpretation: the Qedarites themselves will take their possessions and load them on their camels while crying out from the backs of the camels the distress call "terror on every side." However, the ambiguity is not so great, and the second interpretation requires no emendations, i.e., taking יקחו, "they will take," and ישאו, "they will carry," as passives or imperatives. The Qedarites, then, are described as packing up their belongings and preparing to flee.

In the third place, the phrase in v 30, העמיקו לשבת, "dwell down below," must be considered. The phrase occurs in Jer 49:8, where the Dedanites are cautioned to flee Edom and return to Dedan (see the *Comment* on Jer 49:8). In the same way, it may be supposed that the Qedarites are warned to flee and to descend from their mountainous dwellings (not from the backs of their camels, Holladay, 2:383) and dwell with their brothers in the settled encampments below.

In the fourth place, there is the question of how to understand the term חצור (vv 28, 30, 33). Most translations, ancient and modern, have taken it as a place name, "Hazor," although LXX rendered it with the term αὐλή, "court." While several places in Israel were named Hazor, no such place is known in the areas where the Qedarites dwelled. αὐλή seems to presuppose the word חצר. Extensive analyses of this term חצר in the Hebrew Bible and in cognate literatures have been provided by Orlinsky (*JAOS* 59 [1939] 22–37) and by Hamp (*TDOT* 5:131–39). Whether חצר represents the assimilation of two similar roots that are still distinguished in Arabic, it is clear that in the Bible it can mean, in context, either "court" or "settlement." Passages that provide data for the latter meaning are Lev 25:31, which describes חצרים as having no wall around them, and Isa 42:11, which refers to the חצרים that Qedar inhabits (cf. Jer 49:32, "which has no gates or bars"). These would be permanent settlements as distinct from the movable camps of nomads. In sum, the term חצור is taken here not as a place name but as the replacement for an original חצר, "settlement." Holladay (2:383) has summarized it: "the Hebrew חצור then refers to Arabs who had settled by water sources, particularly at oases, and it thus stands in opposition to the nomads or Bedouin, who are referred to here by the term 'Kedar'."

In summary, the view taken here is that the two stanzas or strophes of the oracle represent two phases of a military action, the first directed against nomadic Qedarites and the second directed against settled Qedarites to whom the nomads were warned to flee for help. Since vv 28a and 33 are redactional and appear to have understood חצור as a place name, it is possible that an original חצר or חצרים in v 30 may have been changed to bring it in line with the redactor's viewpoint.

The superscription in v 28a suggests the setting of the oracle: a military campaign by Nebuchadrezzar. The entry in the Babylonian Chronicle for Nebuchadrezzar's sixth year reads: "In the sixth year in the month of Kislev the king of Akkad mustered his army and marched to the Ḫatti-land. From the Ḫatti-land he sent out his companies, and scouring the desert they took much plunder from the Arabs, their possessions, animals and gods. In the month of Adar the king returned to his own land" (Wiseman, *Chronicles of Chaldean Kings*, 71). From 606 to 601 Nebuchadrezzar had conducted consecutive campaigns in the Ḫatti-land. In the campaign of 601 he sought a decisive engagement against Egypt, but his hopes were thwarted. Both armies suffered enormous losses, and Nebuchadrezzar spent the year 600 rebuilding his army. With Babylon absent and her power at a low ebb, Jehoiakim declared his independence in Jerusalem. But in 599 Nebuchadrezzar conducted his campaign against the Arabian tribes, and the following year he seized Jerusalem.

Comment

28   Our knowledge of the Qedarites during the biblical period comes from two main sources, the Bible and cuneiform literature from Assyria and Babylonia. The Bible provides mostly social and cultural data. The Israelites knew the Qedarites as a desert people, dwelling in tents and in unwalled settlements (Isa 42:11; Jer 49:28; Ps 120:5; Cant. 1:5), defended by famous archers (Isa 21:16–17), a source of lambs, rams, and goats for Israel (Ezek. 27:21), and using the camel as beast of burden (Jer 49:29, 32). In addition to the term "Qedar," they are referred to as "the kingdoms of Hazor" (see *Form/Structure/Setting* on "Hazor"), "the people of the East," and "the ones whose temples are clipped" (Jer 49:28, 32). Gen 25:12–18 preserves a tradition that includes Qedar as one of the twelve descendants of Ishmael who dwell from Havilah to Shur. The biblical information is thus of a general nature, with little hint of close contacts between Israel and Qedar and certainly no indication of a hostile relationship.

The conflict of Arabian tribes with Assyria began in the reign of Shalmaneser III. They are listed on the Monolith Inscription as members of the anti-Assyrian confederation in the battle of Qarqar in 853. The Qedarites are mentioned for the first time in inscriptions from the reign of Tiglath-pileser III. From that time until near the end of the Assyrian empire, Assyria's policy was to exercise economic and political control over the Arabian tribes, including the Qedarites. There were two main reasons for Assyrian concern. First, these mobile peoples could and did make regular incursions into Syrian and Babylonian territory. Second, the Arabian tribes lived along the trade routes leading from south Arabia and participated in the spice trade. There is little doubt that during most periods Assyria's main concern was economic advantage.

In turn, the Babylonians had to concern themselves with these tribes, as tablets from the times of both Nebuchadrezzar and Nabonidus indicate. The Babylonian Chronicle mentions a raid by Nebuchadrezzar against the Arabs in 599 (see the comments in *Form/Structure/Setting*). Documents from the reign of Nabonidus (556–539) describe his campaigns to pacify the Temaᵓ region. (For a critical analysis of biblical and cuneiform evidence relating to the Arabian tribes, see I. Ephᶜal, *The Ancient Arabs*. For translations of Assyrian documents and inscriptions relating Assyrian contacts with the Arabs, see D. Luckenbill, *Ancient Records*, vol. 2, §§ 17, 18, 55, *passim*.)

The reference to the ממלכות, "kingdoms," is not without warrant. Ephᶜal has shown that the rather extensive distribution of the Qedarites reflected in the cuneiform literature indicates that they were a confederation of tribes (*The Ancient Arabs*, 226). In fact, the inscriptions of Assurbanipal mention two Qedarite leaders, Yautaᶜ and Ammuladi, contemporary with each other, and both were designated "king of the Qedarites" (Ephᶜal, *The Ancient Arabs*, 151–52, 226; Luckenbill, *Ancient Records*, vol. 2, §§ 314, 337). LXX's rendering of ממלכות as מַלְכַּת, "queen," is not as strange as it may seem because the Assyrian records mention several queens of the Arabs who apparently were the heads of their respective tribes or states, or at least figure prominently in the accounts. Included are Adiya, Samsi, and Teʾelḫuna (see Ephᶜal, *The Ancient Arabs*, 152–53 and citations in the index, 249).

The term "people of the East" is a summary term for the peoples inhabiting the desert east of Syria and Transjordan (1 Kgs 5:10; Isa 11:14; Jer 49:28; Ezek 25:4, 10; Job 1:3; see S. Cohen, "East, the People of the," *IDB* 2:4).

29 For the interpretation of this verse, see *Form/Structure/Setting*.

The Arabian tribes, including the Qedarites, kept sheep, goats, and camels (Ezek 27:21; Jer 49:29, 32). The camel had long since become the chief beast of burden for desert dwellers and indispensable for the extensive caravan trade on the Arabian peninsula. In the Assyrian royal inscriptions, camels are mentioned consistently as tribute paid by the Arabs and/or as spoil taken by the Assyrians, along with gold, silver, and spices. The Assyrians themselves found the camel indispensable for their military campaigns across desert regions. Esarhaddon employed a large force of camels supplied by kings of Arabia to transport materiel and water across the Sinai during his campaign against Egypt (Luckenbill, *Ancient Records*, vol. 2, § 558). The camel was also used as a part of the fighting force; Gindibuʾ, an Arabian participant in the coalition against Shalmaneser III at the battle of Qarqar in 853, brought a force of 1000 camels (Luckenbill, *Ancient Records*, vol. 1, § 611). Ephᶜal (*The Ancient Arabs*, 76–77) suggests that so large a contingent of camels implies their use as a fighting force and not simply as pack animals (cf. Pritchard, *ANEP* #63: armed Arabs fighting from the backs of their camels).

30 "Nebuchadrezzar" is lacking in LXX and may be a later addition. LXX does have "king of Babylon." Rudolph deleted "king of Babylon" for metrical purposes (270), while Christensen deleted all reference to Nebuchadrezzar, king of Babylon, thus implying that the LORD is the one devising the plan (*Transformations*, 209, 211).

32 ומכל עבריו is difficult. The third person masculine singular suffix is questionable because the other suffixes in the verse are third person masculine plural. Rudolph replaced waw with mem (270), while Christensen added mem to עברי and retained the waw as emphatic waw with the following verb (*Transformations*, 209). Holladay suggested extensive emendation, including metathesis: לְכָל־מַלְכֵי־עֲרָב, "to all the kings of the Arabs" (2:382, 386). The emendation is excessive and without any textual support. The parallelism of "wind" and "side" is decisive for retaining עבר, "side," and Christensen's suggestion of emphatic waw results in the least amount of emendation, the addition of mem.

33   The oracle closes with the rubric "oracle of the LORD" at the end of v 32. V 33 falls outside the structure of the original poem. The verse is an addition, completely appropriate, composed of phrases from Jer 9:10 and Jer 49:18.

Explanation

The inclusion of this oracle concerning Qedar among the oracles concerning the nations in the book of Jeremiah may seem strange. Israel knew about the Arab tribes and their way of life, but there is little evidence of sustained close contact with them of a political nature. This is not a hate oracle; there is no cry for vengeance because Qedar has harmed Israel.

The presence of this oracle may be seen to be appropriate when it is put in the context of the position reflected in Jeremiah that the LORD had a world-changing plan in motion that involved Babylon. Jeremiah preached consistently that those who opposed Nebuchadrezzar were opposing the LORD. The nations included in Jer 46–49 are addressed with oracles of calamity and devastation, not because they have harmed Israel but because they have opposed, or threaten to oppose, the power of Babylon. There is in place here an inclusive view of the LORD's power over the world that includes a plan in which Israel is simply included as another nation to be judged (Jer 25).

This oracle once again focuses on the power of the LORD to act decisively in an international arena. However one may decide the redactional question of v 30 (whether "Nebuchadrezzar" and/or "king of Babylon" are redactor's additions), v 32 makes it clear that all power is in the hands of the LORD and that the plan to be executed is the LORD's plan.

H. Concerning Elam   (49:34–39
[LXX 25:14–20])

Bibliography

Dresden, M. J. "Elam (Country)." *IDB* 2:70–71. **Malamat, A.** "The Last Kings of Judah and Fall of Jerusalem: An Historical-Chronological Study." *IEJ* 18 (1968) 137–56. **Weinfeld, M.** *Deuteronomy and the Deuteronomic School.* Oxford: Clarendon, 1972. **Wiseman, D. J.** *Nebuchadrezzar and Babylon.* Oxford: Oxford UP, 1985.

Translation

> [34a] *What came as the word of the LORD to Jeremiah the prophet concerning Elam, at the beginning of the reign of Zedekiah, king of Judah, saying:* [a]
> [35] *Thus says the LORD* [a]*of Hosts:* [a]

> *Behold* ᵇ*me shattering*ᵇ *the bow of Elam,* (4+2)
> *the chief (weapon) of their power.*

³⁶*And I will bring against Elam the four winds from the four corners of the heavens, and I will scatter them to all these winds, and there will not be a nation to which the refugees of Elam will not come.*

> ³⁷ *And* ᵃ*I will fill Elam with terror*ᵃ *before their enemies,* (4+3)
> *before*ᵇ *the ones seeking their life,*
> *and I will bring against them calamity,* (3+2+2)
> *my fierce wrath*
> ——ᶜ*oracle of the* LORD.ᶜ
> *And I will send after them the sword* (3+3)
> *until I have put an end to them.*
> ³⁸ *And I will put my throne in Elam,* (3+4+2)
> *and I will make perish from there king and princes*
> ——ᵃ*oracle of the* LORD. ᵃ
> ³⁹ *And it will come to pass in the latter days* (3+2+2)
> *I will restore the fortunes of Elam*
> ——*oracle of the* LORD.

Notes

34.a-a. The superscription in LXX reads only "the things which Jeremiah prophesied concerning the nations: Elam." V 34b is placed in LXX at the end of v 39.

35.a-a. Lacking in LXX.

35.b-b. LXX has a pass verb, making the action impersonal.

37.a-a. LXX lacks "Elam" and reflects perhaps the 3m pl suff on the verb.

37.b. Prep is lacking in LXX.

37.c-c. Lacking in LXX.

38.a-a. Lacking in LXX.

Form/Structure/Setting

The oracle concerning Elam is contained in vv 35–38, with rubrics for divine speech at beginning and end. The superscription in v 34 received different treatments in the two text traditions, MT and LXX (see *Notes*). V 39 is a redactional statement in the same vein as Jer 46:26b; 48:47; 49:6 (see *Comment* on those passages).

The determination of the structure of the poem hinges on the identification of prose elements. Duhm deleted vv 36b, 37c because they derived from Jer 9:15 (359). Cornill thought that vv 36, 37ab, and 38a were secondary (489–91). Surprisingly, Bardtke retained essentially all of vv 35–38 because he thought they were Jeremianic in content (*ZAW* 54 [1936] 257–58). Rudolph viewed v 36aγ as stemming from v 32 and as both metrically disturbing and premature in light of vv 37–38; vv 36b, 37a he saw as borrowed from Jer 9:15 (273). Christensen (*Transformations*, 221–22) regarded only v 36b as secondary, while Holladay accepted the judgment of Rudolph (2:387).

It is suggested here that only the phrase "there will not be a nation to which one (they) will not go" in v 36 is clearly prose. 37c may be scanned as poetry (perhaps delete עַד, "until"), even though in Jer 9:15 it seems to be prose. The rest of the language and usages in the oracle are found elsewhere in Jeremiah and are not necessarily borrowed or added secondarily from those other locations (for a survey of language in the passage found elsewhere in Jeremiah, see Holladay, 2:388). The poem may then be seen as consisting of seven bicola, each beginning with a first-person verb form. The third bicolon in v 36b is to be read "I will scatter them to all the winds [omit הָאֵלֶּה, "these"], the refugees of Elam." The poem is compact and spare, piling up the language of judgment and unrelieved disaster in a series of different images (cf. Bardtke, ZAW 54 [1936] 257).

This oracle is unique among the oracles concerning the nations in Jeremiah in that it consists almost entirely of statements of threat and judgment. No characteristic element of Elamite life or culture is mentioned except for the use of the bow (cf. Isa 22:6), and the Elamites were no more noted for their use of the bow than other peoples (cf. Isa 21:17; Jer 50:29; 51:3). There are no calls to attack, no summons to flight, no description of Elamite reactions, and no expressions of sorrow or mourning.

From beginning to end the only actor is the LORD, although the LORD was envisioned using and commanding the winds of heaven and attacking enemies. In contrast to the other oracles concerning the nations in Jeremiah, human agency recedes drastically. The sovereignty of the LORD over the affairs of all nations is accented by the announcement that the LORD would place his throne in Elam and destroy its gods (king and princes). Although some have viewed this statement as being eschatological in nature, it must be pointed out that this view of the LORD's kingship over the nations appears at least as early as the eighth-century prophets.

The superscription in v 34 places the oracle at the beginning of the reign of Zedekiah. According to the Babylonian Chronicle, Jerusalem surrendered to the forces of Nebuchadrezzar on the second day of the month of Adar in Nebuchadrezzar's seventh year (16 March 597; Wiseman, *Chronicles of Chaldean Kings*, 73). Jehoiachin, who had reigned for only three months and ten days, was deposed and exiled to Babylon, and Zedekiah was installed as king by Nebuchadrezzar (2 Kgs 24:17). If one reckons Zedekiah's first official year as beginning in the month of Tishri 597, it would overlap the second half of Nebuchadrezzar's eighth year and the first half of his ninth year (Malamat, *IEJ* 18 [1968] 147). The entry in the Babylonian Chronicle for Nebuchadrezzar's ninth year is a fragmentary account of his campaign along the bank of the Tigris River. Nebuchadrezzar pitched his camp alongside the Tigris, and while there was still a day's march separating the opposed forces, fear seized the enemy, and, panic-stricken, he returned to his own land (Wiseman, *Chronicles of Chaldean Kings*, 73). In both places in the Babylonian Chronicle where the opponent was named, the text is broken. Wiseman at first thought that the remaining signs may have indicated an unnamed king of Elam (the facsimile has *[Š]àr^{mat}NI[ ]*; Wiseman, *Chronicles of Chaldean Kings*, 36), but later he expressed doubt about the proposed restoration (*Nebuchadrezzar and Babylon*, 34). Elam is usually written *^{uru}NIM.MA.KI*. The hand copy shows what may be the first part of the *NIM* sign, and after the break a verticle wedge that could be the last part of the *MA* sign. The case remains open.

So little is known about Babylonian-Elamite political relations from the time of

Nabopolassar (in 625 he returned Elam's gods) until the time of Nabonidus almost a century later that a campaign against Elam in 596 cannot be established by other means. The Medes under Cyaxares assumed control of Elam after the fall of Nineveh in 612 (M. J. Dresden, *IDB* 2:71). Although the Medes and Babylonians had joined forces against their common enemy, Assyria, one must wonder if these two young powers did not jostle one another in succeeding years, seeking to test weak points and to gain advantage. The campaign in Nebuchadrezzar's ninth year could conceivably reflect such an event, and a hostile movement by Elam would be reasonable. But speculation cannot solve the problem.

Comment

34 For the differences in the two text traditions represented by MT and LXX, see *Notes*. In Jer 25 MT, Elam appears, along with Media, as the last of the nations condemned to drink the cup of wrath (25:25), while in LXX, Elam heads the list. For the peculiar form of the announcement of the divine word, see Jer 46:1, *Form/ Structure/Setting*.

35 For the expression "to break the bow," see 1 Sam 2:4; Hos 1:5. For extrabiblical references, consult M. Weinfeld, *Deuteronomy*, 136.

36 The four winds of heaven refer to the four points of the compass. For additional references of scattering to all the winds as a sign of judgment or defeat, see Ezek 5:10, 12; 12:14; 17:21; Jer 49:32. *Enuma elish* mentions the four winds and the storm wind (*imḥullu*) as divine weapons (*Enuma elish* 1:105–7; 4:96, 98–99). By contrast, Ezek 37:9 refers to the four winds bringing the breath of life to the dry bones.

37 For the contracted form הַחְתְּתִי, "I will terrify (them)," see GKC § 67aa.

38 The idea of the LORD establishing the divine throne in a foreign nation is without strict parallel in the OT. Rudolph (273) thought that, based on the parallel with Jer 43:10, the phrase affirmed the LORD's intention to establish the rulership of Elam's new lord, Nebuchadrezzar, over Elam. However, Nebuchadrezzar's name does not appear in the oracle, and indeed human agency in the oracle recedes. It is sufficient to see in the statement an assertion of the LORD's sovereignty to the ends of the world. In fact, the idea is not far from the concept found in Jer 23:24.

39 For this verse, see the *Comments* on the parallel passages in Jer 46:26b; 48:47; 49:6.

Explanation

This compact, tightly structured oracle piles up the language of horror and devastation. All the verbs are in the first person singular, and all refer to the activity of the divine warrior bringing both cosmic and terrestrial forces against Elam.

As with all the oracles concerning the nations in Jeremiah, here the main idea is the LORD's uncontested sway over the affairs of nations near and far. But again the question arises: why would an Israelite prophet be concerned with Elam, a nation that lay at the farthest bounds of its world sphere? Apart from the tradition of a king of Elam's attack against the cities of the plain in which Abram's nephew was captured (Gen 14), there is no extant reference to hostilities between Israel and Elam. The oracle itself offers no reason for the devastation of

Elam. The language of catastrophe is staccatolike but without emotion. Unless Nebuchadrezzar did in fact attack Elamite forces near the Tigris (see *Form/Structure/Setting*), it is not possible to determine the reason for Elam's inclusion among the nations to drink the cup of wrath.

I. Concerning Babylon   (50:1–51:64 [LXX 27:1–28:64])

Bibliography

Aitken, K. T. "The Oracles against Babylon in Jeremiah 50–51: Structures and Perspectives." *TynBul* 35 (1984) 25–63. **Bach. R.** *Die Aufforderungen zur Flucht und zum Kampf im alttestamentlichen Prophetenspruch.* WMANT 9. Neukirchen: Neukirchener, 1962. **Bardtke, H.** "Jeremia der Fremdvölkerprophet." *ZAW* 54 (1936) 240–62. **Barthélemy, D.** *Critique textuelle de l'Ancien Testament.* Vol. 2. OBO 50/2. Göttingen: Vandenhoeck & Ruprecht, 1986. **Budde, K.** "Über die Capitel 50 und 51 des Buches Jeremia." *JDT* 23/3 (1878) 428—70. **Christensen, D.** *Transformations of the War Oracle in Old Testament Prophecy.* Missoula: Scholars, 1975. **Eissfeldt, O.** "Jeremias Drohorakel gegen Ägypten und gegen Babel." In *Verbannung und Heimkehr,* ed. A. Kuschke. Tübingen: Mohr (Siebeck), 1961. 31–37. **Fohrer, G.** "Vollmacht über Völker und Königreiche." In *Wort, Lied und Gottesspruch: Beiträge zu Psalmen und Propheten,* ed. J. Schreiner. Würzburg: Echter, 1972. 145–53. **Jacobsen, T.** "Pekod." *IDB* 3:709. **Kessler, M.** "Rhetoric in Jeremiah 50 and 51." *Semitics* 3 (1973) 18–35. **Lundbom, J. R.** *Jeremiah: A Study in Ancient Hebrew Poetry.* SBLDS 18. Missoula: Scholars, 1975. **May, H. G.** "Some Cosmic Connotations of *Mayim Rabbîm,* 'Many Waters'." *JBL* 74 (1955) 9–21. **Mellink, M. J.** "Ararat." *IDB* 1:194–95. **Muilenburg, J.** "Merathaim." *IDB* 3:351. **Roberts, B. J.** "Athbash." *IDB* 1:306–7. **Roberts, J. J. M.** *Nahum, Habakkuk, and Zephaniah: A Commentary.* OTL. Louisville: Westminster/John Knox, 1991. **Robinson, T. H.** "The Structures of Jeremiah l, li." *JTS* 19 (1917/18) 251–65. **Shiloh, Y.,** and **Tarler, D.** "Bullae from the City of David: A Hoard of Seal Impressions from the Israelite Period." *BA* 49 (1986) 196–209. **Sommerfeld, W.** "Marduk." *RLA* 7:366–67. **Steuernagel, C.** *Lehrbuch der Einleitung in das Alten Testament.* Tübingen: Mohr (Siebeck), 1912. **Voightlander, E. N. von.** "A Survey of Neo-Babylonian History." Diss., University of Michigan, 1963. **Waltke, B. K.,** and **O'Connor, M.** *An Introduction to Biblical Hebrew Syntax.* Winona Lake, IN: Eisenbrauns, 1990.

Translation

[1a] *The word which the LORD spoke*[a] *concerning Babylon,* [b]*concerning the land of the Chaldeans, by Jeremiah the prophet.*[b]

[2]   *Declare among the nations and announce,*   (3+3+2)
           [a]*lift up a standard, announce,*[a]
       do not conceal it, say:
           Babylon is captured,   (2+2+2)
           Bel[b] *is put to shame,*[c]

Marduk^d is shattered,
^eher images are put to shame,
    her idols are shattered.^e   (2+2)

3   For a nation from the north has gone up against her;   (5+4 +3+4)
    it is the one which will make her land a desolation,
    and there will be no inhabitant in her;
    both humans and beasts ^awill flee. ^a

First Movement: 50:4–20

4   In those days and at that time   (4+2)
          —^aoracle of the LORD ^a—
The children of Israel will come,   (3+4)
    They and the children of Judah together;
They will walk, weeping as they walk;   (3+3)
    the LORD their God they will seek.
5   They will ask for Zion;   (2+3)
    The way^a thither is before them. ^b
They will come^c and join themselves^d to the LORD:^e   (3+4)
    the eternal covenant will not be forgotten.
6   My people were^a a perishing flock;   (3+3+2)
    their shepherds ^bled them astray, ^b
    they led them away^c (to) the mountains.
From mountain to hill they went;   (3+2)
    they forgot their fold.
7   All who found them ate them,   (3+4)
    and their enemies said, "We are not guilty, ^a
because they sinned against the LORD, the true pasture,   (5+3)
    the hope^b of their fathers."^c
8   Flee from the midst of Babylon;   (3+3+3)
    exit^a from the land of the Chaldeans
    and be like he-goats^b before the flock.

⁹For behold, I am stirring up ^aand bringing up^a against Babylon a ^bcompany of great nations;^b from the land of the north they will array themselves against her, from there she will be captured; his arrows are like a bereaving^c warrior who does not return empty-handed.

¹⁰ And Chaldea will become spoil,   (3+3+2)
    and all those plundering her will have their fill
          —^aoracle of the LORD. ^a
¹¹ Although you rejoice, ^a   (2+2+2)
    although you exult,
    O plunderers of my heritage,
although you paw the ground like a heifer at pasture,   (4+2)
    and ^bneigh like stallions, ^b
¹² your mother is utterly shamed;   (3+2)
    the one who bore you^a is abashed.
Behold, (she is) ^b the last of the nations,   (3+3)
    ^ca dry wilderness and a desert. ^c

13   *On account of the wrath of the* Lord,   (3+2+3)
         she will not be inhabited;
         all of her will be a desolation.
         Everyone who passes by Babylon will be appalled   (4+3)
         and will hiss because of all her wounds.
14   *Array yourselves against Babylon all around,*   (3+3)
         all you who bend the bow.
         Shoot[a] *at her;*   (2+2+3)
         spare no arrow,
         [b]*for she has sinned against the* Lord.[b]
15   *Raise a shout*[a] *against her all around;*[b]   (3+2)
         she has given her hand.[c]
         Her towers[d] *have fallen;*   (2+2+4)
         Her walls are overthrown,
         for that is the retribution of the Lord.
         Take retributions against her,   (2+3)
         as she has done, do to her.
16   *Cut off the sower*[a] *from Babylon,*   (3+4)
         and the one who wields the sickle at harvest time.
         From the presence of the [b]*sword of the oppressor,*[b]   (3+3+3)
         let each turn to his own people;
         let each flee to his own land.

[17]*Israel is a hunted sheep (which) lions have driven away; the first one, the king of Assyria, consumed him, and this last one, Nebuchadrezzar,*[a] *king of Babylon, gnawed*[b] *his bones.* [18]*Therefore, thus says the* Lord [a]*of Hosts, God of Israel:*[a] *Behold, I am punishing the king of Babylon and his land just as I punished the king of Assyria.* [19]*But I will restore Israel to his pasture, and he will feed on Carmel* [a]*and in Bashan,*[a] *and on Mount Ephraim and Gilead he will sate himself.*

20   *In those days and at that time*   (3+2)
         —[a]*oracle of the* Lord[a]—
         one will seek for the iniquity of Israel,   (3+1)
         and there will be none,
         for the sins of Judah,   (3+2)
         and they will not be found,
         for I will pardon those whom I have spared.[b]   (4)

Second Movement: 50:21–32

21   *Against*[a] *the land of Merathaim,*[a]   (2+2)
         go up against it,
         against the inhabitants of [b]*Peqod;*   (2+3+2)
         slaughter[b] *and devote to destruction* [c]*after them*[c]
         —*oracle of the* Lord—
         and do according to all I command you.   (4)
22   *The sound of war is in the land,*   (3+2)
         and great shattering.[a]
23   *How the hammer*[a] *of all the earth is cut down and shattered!*   (5+5)
         How Babylon has become a desolation among the nations!

²⁴ *I set a trap for you,* ^a *and you were taken, O Babylon,*   (5+3)
    but you did not know it.
    You were found and seized,   (2+3)
    because you strove against the LORD.
²⁵ *The* LORD *has opened his storehouses*   (3+3)
    and has brought out his weapons of wrath,
    for there is work for the Lord GOD ^a*of Hosts,* ^a   (5+2)
    in the land of the Chaldeans.
²⁶ ^a*Come to her from every side,* ^a   (3+2+3+1+2)
    open her granaries, ^b
    ^c*pile her up like heaps,* ^c
    devote her to destruction,
    let there not be a remnant to her.
²⁷ ^a*Slay all her bulls,* ^a   (2+2)
    let them descend to the slaughter.
    Woe to them, for their day has come,   (4+2)
    The time of their punishment.
²⁸*The voice of those fleeing and escaping from the land of Babylon, to announce in Zion the retribution of the* LORD, *our God,* ^a*retribution for his temple!*^a
²⁹ *Summon archers*^a *against Babylon,*   (3+2)
    all those who bend the bow,
    encamp against her round about,   (3+3)
    let there be no escape ^b*for her,* ^b
    repay her according to her deed,   (3+4)
    do to her as she has done,
    for she has acted with insolence against the LORD,   (3+3)
    against the holy one of Israel.
³⁰ ^a*Therefore her young men will fall in her squares,*   (4+5+2)
    and all her men of war will be destroyed ^b*on that day*^b
    —*oracle of the* LORD. ^a
³¹ *Behold, I am against you, O insolent one,*   (3+4)
    ^a*says the Lord* GOD *of Hosts,* ^a
    for your day has come,   (3+2)
    the time when I will punish you.
³² *The insolent one will stumble and fall,*   (3+3)
    and there will be none to raise him;
    I will kindle a fire in his cities, ^a   (3+3)
    and it will consume everything around him.

Third Movement: 50:33–46

³³*Thus says the* LORD ^a*of Hosts:*^a *The children of Israel together with the children of Judah are oppressed, all their captors have seized them,*
    they refuse to let them go.   (2)
³⁴ *The one redeeming them is strong,*   (2+3)
    the LORD *of Hosts is his name.*
    ^a*He will by all means plead their case,*   (3+3+3)
    so that he may give rest to the earth^a

[b]*and give disquiet to the inhabitants of Babylon.* [b]

35 *A sword on the Chaldeans*   (2+2+2+2)
                    —[a]*oracle of the LORD*[a]—
         and on the inhabitants of Babylon,
         and on her princes and her wise men;

36 [a]*a sword on the diviners*[b] *that they may act foolishly,* [a]   (3+3)
         a sword on her soldiers that they might be destroyed;

37 *a sword on* [a]*his horses and his chariots,* [a]   (3+3+2)
         and on all[b] *the mixed company in her midst*
         that they may become women;
         a sword on her treasuries that they may be plundered;   (3)

38 *a drouth*[a] *on her waters that* [b]*they might dry up,* [b]   (3+4+2)
         for it is a land of images,
         [c]*and they act madly over frightful things.* [c]

39 *Therefore* [a]*demons will dwell with the jackals,*[a]   (4+4)
         ostriches will dwell in her,
         and she will not be inhabited any more forever,   (3+4)
         [b]*and she will not dwell for all generations.* [b]

40 *Like God's overthrow of Sodom and Gomorrah and her neighbors*   (5+2)
                    —*oracle of the LORD*—
         a man will not dwell there,   (3+3)
         a human will not sojourn in her.

41 *Behold, a people comes from the north,*   (4+2)
         a great nation,
         and many kings are aroused   (3+2)
         from the far reaches of the earth.

42 *They take hold of bow and spear,*   (3+4)
         cruel are they and without mercy;
         their sound moans like the sea,   (3+3)
         they ride upon horses,
         arranged as a man for war, [a]   (3+2)
         against you, O daughter Babylon.

43 *The king of Babylon heard the report of them,*   (3+2)
         and his hands grew weak;
         distress seized him,   (2+2)
         pain like a woman in childbirth.

44 *Behold, like a lion goes up from the jungle of the Jordan to the well-watered plain,*
         so I will in a moment [a]*run away her sucklings;*   (4+4)
         I will single out the choicest of her rams. [a]
         For who is like me,   (3+2+5)
         and who will summon me,
         and who is the shepherd who can stand before me?

45 *Therefore, hear the plan of the LORD which he has planned against Babylon, and*
his purposes which he has devised against the land of the Chaldeans:
         Surely the little ones of the flock will be dragged away, [a]   (4+4)
         surely the pasture will appall their sucklings. [b]

46 *At the cry "Babylon has been seized,"*   (3+2+3)

> the earth will tremble,
> an outcry^a will be heard among the nations.

Fourth Movement: 51:1–33

^{51:1}*Thus says the* LORD:

> Behold me stirring up against Babylon   (3+3+2)
>   and against the inhabitants of Chaldea^a
> a destroying wind,
> ² and I will dispatch winnowers^a to Babylon,   (3+1+2)
>   and they will winnow her,
>   and they will empty her land,
> when they are against her on every side   (3+2)
>   on the day of calamity.
> ³ ^aLet not the archer bend his bow,^a   (3+2)
>   and let him not^b lift himself up in his coat of mail;
> do not spare her young men,
>   devote to destruction her whole army.
> ⁴ The slain will fall in the land of the Chaldeans,   (4+2)
>   and the wounded in her streets,

⁵*For Israel [and Judah]*^a *has not become a widower of his God, of the* LORD *of Hosts,* ^b*for their land is full of guilt against the holy one of Israel.* ^b

> ⁶ Flee from the midst of Babylon,   (3+3+2)
>   and escape, each one for his life;
>   do not be destroyed in her punishment,
> for the time of retribution is this for the LORD,   (5+4)
>   the recompense he is paying her.
> ⁷ A golden cup was Babylon in the hand of the LORD,   (5+2)
>   making all the earth drunk.
> From her wine the nations drank;   (3+3)
>   therefore the nations^a went mad.
> ⁸ Suddenly Babylon has fallen and is shattered;   (4+2)
>   wail for her.
> Take balm for her pain;   (3+2)
>   perhaps she can be healed.
> ⁹ We applied healing to Babylon,   (2+2)
>   but she was not healed.
> Leave her^a and let us go, each to his own land,   (4+4+2)
>   for her judgment has reached the heavens
>   and is lifted up to the skies.
> ¹⁰ The LORD has brought forth our victory;^a   (3+3+3)
>   come and let us relate in Zion
>   the work of the LORD our God.
> ¹¹ Sharpen the arrows;   (2+2)
>   fill the bow-cases.^a

The LORD *has stirred up the spirit of the kings*^b *of the Medes, for his purpose concerning Babylon is to destroy it;*

for that is the retribution of the LORD,	(3+2)
the retribution of his temple. ^c	

¹² *Against the walls of Babylon raise a standard,* (3+2+2+2)
   ^a*strengthen the watch,*^a
   put watchmen in place,
   ^b*prepare the ambushers,*^b
for the LORD has both planned and done what he spoke concerning the inhabitants of Babylon.

¹³ *You who dwell*^a *by many waters,* (3+2)
   rich in treasures;
   your end has come, (2+2)
   the limit of your thread.

¹⁴ *The LORD of Hosts has sworn* ^a*by himself:*^a (4)
   Surely I filled you with people like locusts, (4+3)
   and they will respond against you with a shout.

¹⁵ ^a*He is the one*^a *who made earth by his power,* (3+3+3)
   the one who established the world by his wisdom,
   and by his understanding he stretched out the heavens.

¹⁶ ^a*When he utters his voice,*^a (2+3)
   (there is) a roar of waters in the heavens,
   and he makes mists rise from the end of the earth; (4+3+3)
   he has made lightning bolts for the rain,
   and he brings forth wind from his storehouses.

¹⁷ *Every human is too stupid to know;* (3+3)
   every smith is put to shame by his idol,
   for his molten image is fake, (3+3)
   and there is no breath in them.

¹⁸ *They are a puff of wind,* (2+2)
   the work of mockers;
   at the time of their punishment they will perish. (3)

¹⁹ *Not like these is the portion of Jacob,* (3+3)
   for he is one who formed everything,
   and Israel^a *is the tribe*^b *of his inheritance,* (2+3)
   the LORD of Hosts is his name.

²⁰ ^a*You are a war-club to me,* (3+2)
   a weapon of war,^a
   and I will smash nations with you, (3+3)
   I will destroy^b *kingdoms with you,*

²¹ *I will smash horse and rider with you,* (4+4)
   I will smash chariot and its rider with you,

²² *I will smash husband and wife with you,* (4+4+4)
   ^a*I will smash the old man and the youth with you,*^a
   I will smash the youth and the maiden with you,

²³ *I will smash the shepherd and his flock with you,* (4+4+4)
   I will smash the farmer and his team with you,
   I will smash officials and commanders with you.

²⁴*And I will pay back Babylon and all the inhabitants of Chaldea all their evil which they have done in Zion before your eyes—oracle of the LORD.*

25   *Behold, I am against you, O destroying*ᵃ *mountain*   (4+2)
                —oracle of the LORD—
    the destroyer of all the earth,   (2)
    and I will stretch out my hand against you,   (3+2+3)
       and I will roll you down from the crags,
       and I will make you a burned mountain.
26   *They will not get from you a stone for a corner,*   (4+2)
       or a stone for foundations,
    for you will be a desolation forever   (3+2)
               —oracle of the LORD.
27   *Lift up a standard in the land,*   (3+3)
      blow the trumpet among the nations,
    dedicate nations against her,   (3+3)
      summon kingdoms against her:
    *Ararat, Minni,*ᵃ *and Ashkenaz;*   (3)
    appoint a recruiter (scribe) against her,   (3+4)
      bring up horses like bristling locusts.
28   *Dedicate nations against her,*   (3+2+2+3)
      *The kings*ᵃ *of the Medes,*
    ᵇ*her officials and all her commanders,*ᵇ
    *and every land*ᶜ *of his dominion.*
29   *The earth will quake and writhe,*   (3+5)
      *for the plan*ᵃ *of the* LORD *has arisen against Babylon,*
    to make the land of Babylon   (3+3)
      a desolation without inhabitant.
30   *The warriors*ᵃ *of Babylon have ceased fighting,*   (4+2)
      they sit in the strongholds;
    their strength is dried up,   (2+2)
      they have become women;
    *her dwellings are burned up,*ᵇ   (2 +2)
      her bars are shattered.
31   *Runner runs to meet runner,*   (4+3)
      messenger to meet messenger,
    to tell the king of Babylon   (3+4)
      that his city is captured on every side;
32   *the fords have been seized,*   (2+3+3)
      *the reed-pools*ᵃ *have been burned with fire,*
      and the men of war are terrified.
33*For thus says the* LORD ᵃ*of Hosts, the God of Israel:*ᵃ
    *Daughter*ᵇ *Babylon is like a threshing floor*   (3+2)
      at the time when one treads it;
    yet a little while   (2+3)
      *and the time*ᶜ *of harvest will come to her.*ᵈ

Fifth Movement: 51:34–44

34   *Nebuchadrezzar, king of Babylon,*   (3)
  ᵃ*has devoured me,*   (1)

has disturbed me,	(1)
has made me an empty vessel,	(3)
has swallowed me like a monster,	(2)
has filled his belly with my delicacies, [b]	(3)
has expelled me. [ac]	(1)

35   "The violence and desolation[a] done to me (be) upon Babylon,"   (3+3)
      let the inhabitant of Zion say;
      "and my blood (be) upon the inhabitants of Chaldea,"   (3+2)
      let Jerusalem say.

36 Therefore, thus says the LORD:
      Behold, I will hear your case,[a]   (3+2)
      and I will bring about retribution for you;
      I will dry up her sea,   (2+2)
      and I will dry up her source,

37   and Babylon will become heaps of stones, [a]   (3+2+2+2)
      a lair of jackals, [a]
      a desolation and a hissing,[a]
      without inhabitant.

38   They will be fierce[a] like lions;   (2+3)
      They will be aroused[b] like lions' cubs.

39   When they are heated[a] I will set out their feast,   (3+3)
      and I will make them drunk so that they swoon away,[b]
      and they will sleep an everlasting sleep,   (3+2+2)
      and they will not wake up
           —oracle of the LORD.

40   I will bring them down like lambs for the slaughter,   (3+2)
      like rams with he-goats.

41   How Babylon[a] is captured!   (3+3+5)
      (How) seized is the praise of all the earth!
      How Babylon has become a desolation among the nations!

42   The sea has come up against Babylon;   (3+3)
      she is covered with the tumult of its waves.

43   Her cities have become a desolation, [a]   (3+3)
      a dry land and a desert;
      [b]no person will dwell in them,   (4+3)
      and no human will pass through them.

44   And I will punish Bel[a] in Babylon;   (3+3)
      I will take out from his mouth what he has swallowed.
      The nations will not flow to him any more;   (4+3)
      [b]indeed, the wall of Babylon has fallen. [b]

Sixth Movement: 51:45–53

45   Exit from her midst, my people!   (3+3+3)
      Escape, each for his life
      from the burning wrath of the LORD!

46   Let not your heart be faint,   (2+1)
      nor be fearful

at the report being heard in the land, (3+3+3)
  when a report comes^a in one year
  and after it (another) report in (the next) year:
"Violence is in the land, (2+2)
  and ruler against ruler!"
⁴⁷ Therefore, behold, the days are coming (4+3)
  when I will punish the images of Babylon,
and all her land will be humiliated, (3+3)
  and all her slain will fall in the midst of her.

⁴⁸And heaven and earth and all which is in them will sing for joy about Babylon, for out of the north the destroyers will come^a against her—oracle of the LORD.

⁴⁹ Babylon will surely fall, O slain of Israel, (4+4)
  just as all the slain of the earth have fallen for Babylon.
⁵⁰ You who escape ^afrom her sword, go,^a (3+1)
  do not stand still!
Remember the LORD from afar, (3+3)
  and let Jerusalem come into your mind.
⁵¹ We are shamed, for we have heard reproach, (3+3)
  dishonor has covered our face,
for strangers have come against ^a the sanctuary, ^a (4+2)
  the house of the LORD.
⁵² Therefore, behold, the days are coming (3+2)
      —oracle of the LORD—
when I will punish her idols, (2+3)
  and in all her land the slain will groan.
⁵³ Though Babylon should mount up to heaven, (3+4)
  and though she should fortify her strong-point in the heights,
destroyers will come from me against her (4+2)
      —oracle of the LORD—
⁵⁴ The sound of an outcry from Babylon, (3+4)
  and great shattering from the land of Chaldea!
⁵⁵ For the LORD is devastating Babylon, (3+4)
  and he will extinguish from her (that) great cry.
Their waves will roar like many waters; (4+3)
  the roar of their sound is raised,
⁵⁶ for a destroyer has come ^aagainst her,^a against Babylon, (5+2+2)
  her warriors are captured,
  ^btheir bow is shattered,^b
for the LORD is a God of recompense; (4+2)
  he will surely pay back.

⁵⁷And I will make drunk her princes, her wise men, her officials, her commanders, and her soldiers, ^aand they will sleep an everlasting sleep and not awaken,^a says the king, whose name is the LORD of Hosts.

⁵⁸Thus says the LORD ^aof Hosts:^a

The broad wall^b of Babylon will surely be demolished, (3+2)
  her high gates will be kindled with fire;
the peoples labor for nought, (2+2)
  the nations weary themselves (only) for fire.

⁵⁹*The word which* ^a*Jeremiah the prophet commanded Seraiah*^a *the son of Neriah son of Mahseiah, when he went from*^b *Zedekiah, king of Judah, to Babylon in the fourth year of his reign. Seriah was the officer in charge of the tribute.* ^{c 60}*Jeremiah wrote all the calamity which should come against Babylon in one book, all these words written against Babylon.* ⁶¹*And Jeremiah said to Seraiah, "When you enter Babylon, see and read all these words,* ⁶²*and say, 'LORD, you have spoken against this place to cut it off so that there will not be in it an inhabitant, neither human being nor beast, for it will be a desolation forever.'* ⁶³*And when you have finished reading this book, you are to tie a stone to it and cast it into the midst of the Euphrates,* ⁶⁴*and you will say, 'Thus Babylon will sink and will not arise because of the calamity which I am bringing against her.'"*^a *Thus far are the words of Jeremiah.*

Notes

1.a-a. LXX reads "The word of the LORD which he spoke." Syr begins the superscription with the rubric "concerning Babylon."

1.b-b. Lacking in LXX.

2.a-a. Lacking in LXX.

2.b. For "Bel," LXX reads ἡ ἀπτόητος, "the fearless." Holladay suggests that LXX read בֵּל חַת as בַּל חַת, "not panicked."

2.c. Syr has "has fallen."

2.d. LXX has ἡ τρυφερά, "the luxurious one."

2.e-e. Lacking in LXX.

3.a-a. Verb lacking in LXX.

4.a-a. Lacking in LXX.

5.a. LXX joins "the way" to the preceding colon.

5.b. LXX reads "hither will they set their face," understanding the Heb. idiom נתן פנים.

5.c. Reading בָּאוּ with LXX, pf instead of impv.

5.d. LXX has "will flee for refuge."

5.e. LXX adds "God."

6.a. Reading Q הָיוּ.

6.b-b. LXX has ἐξῶσαν, "thrust them out."

6.c. Reading Q.

7.a. LXX has μὴ ἀνῶμεν, "let us not set upon them." Syr reads "we will not spare them."

7.b. LXX has τῷ συναγαγόντι, "the one gathering (their fathers)," understanding קוה II, "to collect."

7.c. יהוה at the end of the verse is lacking in LXX and was probably originally הוי, which would have begun v 8.

8.a. Reading with Q, impv instead of impf, with all the versions.

8.b. LXX has "serpents."

9.a-a. Lacking in LXX.

9.b-b. LXX has "companies of nations."

9.c. LXX and Syr read מַשְׂכִּיל, "skilled."

10.a-a. Lacking in LXX.

11.a. All four verbs are to be read with Q as pls.

11.b-b. LXX reads "and pushed with the horn as bulls."

12.a. LXX adds "for good."

12.b. *BHS* proposes הִיא, "she," for הִנֵּה, "behold."

12.c-c. LXX has only ἔρημος, "desert."

14.a. Reading ירו for MT יָדוּ.

14.b-b. Lacking in LXX but not in Syr.

15.a. LXX has "subdue her."

15.b. Lacking in LXX.

15.c. LXX has "her hands are weakened," understanding not only a different verb but also a pass form (perhaps נִתְּנָה for נָתְנָה).

15.d. Reading the Q. Syr has "foundations."

16.a. LXX has "seed," reading זֶרַע for זֹרְעַ.

16.b-b. LXX has "the Grecian sword," reading יָוָן for MT הַיּוֹנָה; cf. 46:16.

17.a. Lacking in LXX.

17.b. Verb is lacking in LXX.

18.a-a. Lacking in LXX.

19.a-a. Lacking in LXX.

20.a-a. Lacking in LXX except for A.

20.b. LXX adds the two following words in the next verse to this one, "on the land," and adds "says the LORD."

21.a. LXX has πικρῶς, "harshly," understanding the noun adverbially.

21.b-b. LXX read "Peqod" as an impv "avenge" and חָרֹב, "slay," as חֶרֶב, "sword." Cf. Syr "awake the sword."

21.c-c. LXX lacks "after them."

22.a. LXX has, in addition, "in the land of the Chaldeans."

23.a. Syr has "the mighty one."

24.a-a. Rudolph in *BHS* reads the form as the archaic 2fs (cf. 2:19, 20, 33). LXX reflects a 3m pl of another verb. Syr has "has stumbled."

25.a-a. Lacking in LXX.

26.a-a. LXX has "her times have come," taking קֵץ as "the end."

26.b. Syr has "her gates."

26.c-c. LXX has "search her as a cave," understanding ערמים as מְעָרָה. Syr has "leave her as a naked woman," understanding עֶרְמָה.

27.a-a. LXX has "dry up all her fruits," a rendering that the consonants will allow but without sense in the context. Syr also reads "her fruit" or "offspring" and makes it subj of the following verb.

28.a-a. Lacking in LXX.

29.a. Reading רֹבִים for רַבִּים, "many."

29.b-b. Reading with Q אַל־יְהִי־לָהּ.

30.a-a. The verse is identical to 49:26.

30.b-b. Lacking in LXX.

31.a-a. LXX has "says the LORD."

32.a. LXX has "her forests," for יַעַר, "forests," instead of the MT עָרֶיהָ, "its cities."

33.a-a. Lacking in LXX.

34.a-a. LXX understood that the case to be taken up by the LORD was the case against Babylon: "he will enter into judgment with his adversaries that he may destroy the earth." However, it is clearly Israel's case that is to be entertained by the LORD with a good verdict for them and a bad one for Babylon.

34.b-b. Lacking in LXX.

35.a-a. Lacking in LXX.

36.a-a. Lacking in LXX.

36.b. Reading בַּדֶּיהָ.

37.a-a. The 3ms suffs are out of step with the rest of the suffixes in the sword oracle. The clause may stem from 51:21.

37.b-b. Lacking in LXX.

38.a. Lacking in LXX.

38.b-b. LXX reads "they will be ashamed," understanding the root בוש instead of יבש.

38.c-c. LXX has "and in the islands where they boasted," understanding הלל II for the verb and אִיִּים (cf. v 39) for אֵימִים.

39.a-a. LXX has "idols will dwell in the islands"; see preceding *Note*.

39.b-b. Lacking in LXX and probably an addition.

42.a. LXX adds "like fire."

44.a-a. See the *Notes* on 49:19.

45.a. Point as niph.

45.b. Reading עֲלֵיהֶם; see the *Note* on 49:20.

46.a. Rudolph in *BHS* proposed to read 3fs suff "her outcry," here and at 49:21.

51:1.a. לֵב קָמָי is an *atbash* cipher for *Chasdim*, "the Chaldeans"; cf. 25:26, שֵׁשַׁךְ for בבל, "Babylon." LXX did not employ the cipher here. Syr understood the reference to indicate what the LORD was stirring up along with the wind, a man of proud heart. (For explanation of *atbash*, see Drinkard's discussion in *Jeremiah 1–25*, 371; see also *IDB* 1:306–7.)

2.a. Reading זֵדִים with Rudolph, *BHS*.

3.a-a. Deleting with Syr, Vg, Tg the second יִדְרֹךְ and pointing עַל as אַל, "not"; cf. אַל in v 3b. The references in v 3a are to Babylonian soldiers.

3.b. Pointing עַל as אַל.

5.a. Delete for metrical and syntactical reasons.

5.b-b. Logically v 5b precedes v 5a and originally stood there; see the note by Holladay.

7.a. Lacking in LXX.

9.a. LXX, Syr, Vg have a 1 pl verb.

10.a. LXX reads "his judgment." MT has "our victories"; reading צִדְקָתֵנוּ with Syr.

11.a. שֶׁלֶט, always in pl in MT, means "shields" in all other occurrences (2 Sam 8:7; 2 Kgs 11:10; Ezek 27:11; Cant 4:4; 1 Chr 18:7; 2 Chr 23:9). The verb "fill" directs attention elsewhere; cf. *AHW* 1151, which offers *šalṭu*, "bow cases."

11.b. Sg in LXX, Syr.

11.c. LXX reads "his people."

12.a-a. LXX reads "prepare the quivers."

12.b-b. Syr reads "and drown her in waters" and omits the preceding clause.

13.a. 2fs pf in K with archaic ending; fem act ptcp in Q.

14.a-a. LXX reads "by his arm."

15.a-a. LXX, Syr read "the LORD" and take the ptcp עָשָׂה as pf verb.

16.a-a. LXX reads εἰς φωνὴν ἔθετο, "at a voice he put or placed"; cf. 10:13.

19.a. Add here from 10:16.

19.b. Lacking in LXX.

20.a-a. LXX reads "you scatter for me the weapons of war," taking מֵפֵץ as a verb form.

20.b. Reading כְּלִי for כְּלֵי.

22.a-a. Lacking in LXX; LXX also reverses the order of 22a and 22c.

25.a. LXX reads τὸ διεφθαρμένον, "ruined" = הַמָּשְׁחָת, hoph ptcp. Holladay proposes הַמִּשְׁחָה, "anointing oil," with reference to 2 Kgs 23:13 and the Mount of Olives.

27.a. LXX reads "by me" and lacks the preceding "Ararat."

28.a. Reading sg with LXX; cf 51:11.

28.b-b. LXX, Syr have 3ms suffs.

28.c. LXX places this phrase after "king of the Medes." The last clause is lacking in Syr.

29.a. Reading the const מַחֲשֶׁבֶת with LXX, Syr.

30.a. Sg in LXX.

30.b. Reading pass הָצְּתוּ in agreement with LXX.

32.a. אֲגָם means "a pool filled with reeds." The strange image of burning a pool is apt since reedy places could provide hiding places. KB proposes to emend to הַגְּמָאִים (metathesis).

33.a-a. Lacking in LXX.

33.b. LXX reads "houses of," בָּתֵּי; for בַּת.

33.c. Lacking in LXX.

33.d. Lacking in LXX.

34.a-a. All six verbs have 1 pl suffs in the K, 1cs suffs in the Q (the versions also).

34.b. Pointing מְעַרְדְנִי with Rudolph (*BHS*).

34.c. LXX carries the verb over to the next verse and reads "my troubles and my distresses have driven me out into Babylon."

35.a. Reading either וְשָׁאתִי with Rudolph (*BHS*) or וְשׁוֹדִי with Holladay.

36.a. LXX reads τὴν ἀντίδικόν σου, "your adversary."

37.a. LXX lacks all three terms, retaining only "desolation."

38.a. Reading with Holladay יָחֹדוּ in line with Hab 1:8 but with the meaning "to be fierce."

38.b. Reading נָעֲרוּ (*BHS*) as reflected in LXX ἐξηγέρθησαν, "arouse." But note the Akk. cognate *naʾāru*, "to roar," which is perhaps an Aram. loanword.

39.a. Syr has "with venom."

39.b. Reading יַעֲלֹפוּ with LXX; cf. Rudolph (*BHS*). MT may be retained if "rejoice" is understood as irony (Barthélemy, *Critique textuelle* 2:850).

41.a. שֵׁשַׁךְ is an *atbash* cipher for Babylon; cf. *Note* on 51:1.

43.a. The word is lacking in LXX.

43.b. The line in MT begins with אֶרֶץ, "land"; delete with LXX.

44.a. Lacking in LXX.

44.b-b. Lacking in LXX, together with vv 45–49a.

46.a. Reading an inf with Rudolph (*BHS*); בָּא does not agree in gender with הַשְׁמוּעָה.

48.a. Cf. v 53: יָבֹאוּ.

50.a-a. LXX reads "go out of the land" = מֵחָרְבָּה. Accepted here is מֵחַרְבָּה לְכוּ.

51.a-a. Deleting the yodh. MT has "sanctuaries of the house of the LORD." But the pl "sanctuaries" is nowhere else used in reference to the house of the LORD, and its occurrence here is questionable. Vg, Syr, Tg have sg "sanctuary" without suff. LXX reads "our sanctuaries."

56.a-a. Lacking in LXX, Syr, and omitted here.

56.b-b. Reading חִתָּה קַשְׁתָּם. MT has קַשְׁתוֹתָם, "their bows," along with a sg verb form. LXX, Vg read "their bow."

57.a-a. Lacking in LXX.

58.a-a. Lacking in LXX.

58.b. Reading חוֹמַת, for MT הֹמוֹת, "walls."

59.a-a. LXX has a longer text, which impacts form-critical analysis: "the word which the LORD commanded Jeremiah the prophet to say to Seraiah."

59.b. Reading מֵאֵת, "from with," for אֶת, "with"; cf. LXX παρά.

59.c. Reading מִנְחָה for מְנוּחָה, "resting place"; cf. LXX δώρων.

64.a. Deleting MT וְיָעֵפוּ, "and they will weary themselves." See *Comment.*

Form/Structure/Setting

The oracles concerning Babylon in 50:1–51:58 compose almost half of the material in the collection of oracles concerning the nations in Jer 46–51 (104 verses as compared to 121 verses for 46–49). Two main themes run throughout: (1) the coming judgment of the LORD on Babylon and (2) the restoration of the exiled people of Judah and Israel to their homeland by the intervention of the LORD. These two themes are reprised repeatedly in a variety of literary forms. Readers have been impressed either with the monotony of the material (cf. K. Budde, *JDTh* 23/3 [1878] 459, who thought that the prophecy could have been closed at any point once the motifs had been exhausted) or with the richness and variety of the literary forms, which invite an attempt to fathom its structure (cf. K. T. Aitken, *TynBul* 35 [1984] 25–63).

Several problems vex the interpreter. The oracles concerning Babylon are located in the LXX in third position, following those concerning Edom and Egypt. There is the question of authenticity: how much of the material in Jer 50–51 can be attributed to Jeremiah? There is the question of coherence or consistency: if some, most, or all of the oracles can be attributed to Jeremiah, how can the oracles of judgment against Babylon be seen as consistent with Jeremiah's preaching that Nebuchadrezzar was the LORD's servant and that all opposition to him was opposition to the LORD's plan? If "all these words that are written concerning Babylon" (51:60), which Seraiah was ordered in 594 to carry to Babylon and to sink in the Euphrates, are taken to be the collection of oracles in 50:1–51:58, then how can one maintain Jeremiah's consistency of viewpoint when in the same year he preached against rebellion by vassal states, including Judah (27:1–15)? Finally, there are the literary questions concerning delimitation of pericopes and the determination or explanation of a structure for the ensemble.

A brief survey of the work of key commentators over the last century will illustrate the widely differing opinions about the authenticity of Jer 50–51. B. Duhm (360) regarded the chapters as a product of literary art characteristic of later Judaism, which met the need for edifying and entertaining literature. C. H.

Cornill, although accepting 51:59–64 as authentic, rejected 50:1–51:58 for a variety of stylistic, historical and theological reasons (491–96). C. Steuernagel denied authenticity to most of chaps. 50–51, especially to those passages that portrayed the judgment against Babylon as an imminent event or that emphasized the judgment as the LORD's vengeance against Babylon for its treatment of Judah. However, he did believe that Jeremiah occasionally delivered judgment oracles against Babylon that would be fulfilled only after a long time. Consequently, he concluded that in 50:1–10, 17–20, 30–35; 51:25–32, 41–44a, 49b, 50, 52–53 it was possible to recognize a basic stock of Jeremianic material (563–64). P. Volz attributed 50:1–52:64, along with 46–49, to a "Deutero-Jeremiah," who wrote soon after the death of Nebuchadrezzar in 561 (378–443). H. Bardtke's view was that Jeremiah delivered oracles against the nations only as a young prophet, prior to 617, subsequently preaching to his own people. Although he thought that Jeremiah must have preached judgment also against Babylon, he did not accept chaps. 50–51 as authentic and did not even make an analysis of these chapters (ZAW 54 [1936] 258–59). A. Condamin (353–57) listed many of the objections to the authenticity of chaps. 50–51, but he sought to defend Jeremianic authorship by criticizing the objections rather than by making a careful analysis of the material. A. Weiser (426–27) did not accept the authenticity of the chapters, citing the usual reasons, and concluded that the chapters stemmed from a later time from Jerusalem (50:5; 51:34–37). W. Rudolph rejected authenticity for chaps. 50–51 except for 51:59–64, which he took to be part of the original Baruch materials and which belonged chronologically between Jer 29 and Jer 34:2–7 (274–75, 295). G. Fohrer concluded that Jer 50–51 differed so widely in style and content from clearly authentic Jeremianic material that they had to stem, at least for the most part, from later authors. As for Jer 51, he identified at least three layers of redactions, each with its own special emphasis ("Vollmacht über Völker und Königreiche," 145–53). O. Eissfeldt, while agreeing with Steuernagel that chaps. 50–51 contain passages that can be attributed to Jeremiah (50:17–20 he thought could not be denied authenticity), concluded that most of the material could not be authentic because it was borrowed from other sources and because it evinces a malicious spirit not in harmony with Jeremiah ("Jeremias Drohorakel," 31–37).

More recently D. Christensen argued for the authenticity of most of the material in Jer. 50–51. Following his prosodic analysis (Transformations, 249–57, 263–69), Christensen argued that chaps. 50–51 represent a nucleus of oracles against Babylon from Jeremiah himself that underwent subsequent expansion. He attributed 51:25–40 confidently to Jeremiah prior to 590 (Transformations, 276, 278–79), and he thought it possible that 51:1–14 could be assigned to the following decade. Although he assigned the oracle in Jer 50 to a later period (Transformations, 263, 279), he was reluctant to deny the nucleus to Jeremiah on the basis that the poem was thoroughly Jeremianic in its language and literary forms. His recognition of inauthentic material, which is kept at a minimum, is determined on the basis of its absence in LXX or because it represents, in his opinion, secondary expansion. Christensen discounted the apparent inconsistency in Jeremiah's preaching about Babylon by viewing Jeremiah's pro-Babylon policy, in Jer 27 for example, as historical necessity for the moment, relating to Judah's foreign policy. Even in 594 Jeremiah declared a seventy-year limit to Babylon's suzerainty, after which Judah would be restored (27:7; 29:10–14). In

Christensen's view, the purpose of the oracles against Babylon was to encourage the people of Judah, especially those in exile, to maintain hope for their future deliverance (*Transformations*, 260, 262–63, 277). Fohrer solved the problem of apparent contradiction by regarding the reason given for Babylon's judgment to be redactional ("Vollmacht über Völker und Königreiche," 150).

Holladay has made the most extensive attempt to identify the authentic material in Jer 50–51 (2:402–8). Most interpreters have made their decisions on the basis of a priori theological, historical, or literary convictions. Holladay's method focused on the identification in these chapters of Jeremiah's characteristic diction as well as on the reuse or adaptation of poems generally regarded as Jeremianic. He concluded that 82 of the 104 verses in Jer 50–51 are authentic to Jeremiah. The verses or sections deemed inauthentic are 50:1, 17b–18, 29cd, 30, 39–46; 51:11b, 15–19, 24b, 28, 45–48.

While Holladay's analysis offers nothing like proof for authenticity, it remains the most objective method because of its emphasis on what the text itself supplies. However, questions may be raised about his treatments of particular passages. For example, he judges 50:39–40, 41–43, and 51:15–19 to be inauthentic because they echo or reproduce 49:18, 6:22–24, and 10:12–16, respectively. These judgments are almost a betrayal of his method of comparative analysis, and one wonders why Jeremiah could not have used the latter passages again for similar or different purposes in other locations. Also, to decide in addition that 51:15–19 is secondary because idolatry does not loom large in these chapters is to ignore that OAN in prophetic literature generally condemn aggression, pride, and idolatry. Nevertheless, Holladay's conclusion that most of Jer 50–51 represents authentic Jeremianic material is followed here.

Any attempt to describe the structure of Jer 50–51 must take into consideration the delimitation of pericopes, the analysis of genres, and the identification of authentic materials, matters on which full agreement has not been reached. Because analyses of structure have differed so widely, it is helpful to summarize the most important attempts. Some interpreters have deemed it impossible to recognize or construct a coherent structure for this sprawling collection of oracles (Duhm, 360; Cornill, 491; Rudolph, 274; Weiser, 427; Bright, 359). Others have suggested structures that are not structures at all but merely outlines of material. T. H. Robinson identified approximately fifty oracles in the collection, a true fragment hypothesis, on the basis of his metrical analysis and assuming throughout the superiority of the LXX for determining the meter (*JTS* 19 [1917/18] 251–65). Fohrer ("Vollmacht über Völker und Königreiche," 50–51) recognized twenty or twenty-one oracles in the two chapters. In chap. 50 he identified ten speeches in an alternating Babylon/Israel pattern, concluding with an addition (50:39–46), while in chap. 51 he isolated ten or eleven oracles with extensive redactional elements. Neither Robinson nor Fohrer hinted at an overall structure for the chapters.

Most recent commentators have focused on the structural analysis of pericopes or units. Kessler (*Semitics* 3 [1973] 3–32), dealing only with chap. 50, identified three themes: war against Babylon (A), Judah's departure from Babylon (B), and historical reminiscence (C). His analysis resulted in the following sequential pattern, which he argued showed structural coherence: A B C B A B C A B A B A C A. Christensen recognized a lack of consensus about the literary structure of Jer

50–51 and the need for a new methodology (*Transformations*, 249). On the basis of his prosodic-textual analysis and the grouping of strophes into larger units, he identified thirteen coherent units, five in chap. 50 (2–5, 6–10, 11–32, 33–40, 41–46) and eight in chap. 51 (1–14, 15–19, 20–24, 25–40, 41–43, 44b–49a, 49b–57, 58; *Transformations*, 257–59, 269–72). It appears that, in most cases, he determined the limits of these larger units on the basis of form-critical considerations. His comments on structure are confined to the analysis of individual units. He analyzed 50:11–32, for example, as a war oracle of seven strophes, every other one being a summons to battle, and strophes 1 and 7 forming an inclusio. His analyses of individual units do not eventuate in a description of a structure for Jer 50–51 as a whole.

Holladay confines his consideration of structure to the passages he identifies as authentic material. For this and other reasons, his delimitation of units differs widely from that by Christensen and others. He delineated ten units that are roughly comparable in length: 50:2–13; 50:14–24; 50:25–32; 50:33–38; 51:1–6; 51:7–14; 51:20–26; 51:27–33; 51:34–44; 51:49–58. Although he draws attention to structures and symmetries both within and among the units, he concludes that there are no obvious symmetries that would enable one to see any overall pattern for chap. 50–51 (2:411–14).

Carroll offers an analysis designed to illustrate the structural coherence of the final form of the text by stressing key words, themes, and motifs (818–54). He identifies 50:2–3 and 51:54–58 as the framework for the ensemble of oracles. 50:4–20 forms the first section, with vv 4 and 20 forming a closure with similarity of terms and theme. The first section is made up of six units: 4–5, 6–7, 8–10, 11–13, 14–16, 17–20. 50:21–40 forms the second section, with the theme of "utter destruction" providing closure. The second section is composed of at least seven units: 21–27, 28, 29–30, 31–32, 32–34, 35–38a, 39–40. 50:41–46 forms the third section, composed of two units of conventional material: 41–43, 44–46, with v 46 forming a closure with v 2 and providing the midpoint for the whole ensemble of the oracles against Babylon. The fourth section is composed of 51:1–33, made up of eight units: 1–5, 6–10, 11–14, 15–19, 20–23, 24, 25–26, 27–33, with the threshing floor and harvest motifs in v 1 and v 33 providing closure. The fifth section is 51:34–44, composed of five units: 34–35, 36–37, 38–40, 41–43, 44, with the key word "swallow" in v 34 and v 44 providing closure. The final section, 51:45–53, is composed of exhortations in vv 45, 46, 50, a confession in v 51, two variant oracles on Babylon's destruction, vv 47–48, 52–53, and an explanation of the reason for Babylon's judgment, v 49, providing a kind of compendium of major themes throughout chaps. 50–51.

Finally, K. T. Aitken attempts to elucidate the rhetorical and semantic coherence of chaps. 50–51 in their final form by identifying a well-ordered complex of materials that are structurally related (*TynBul* 35 [1984] 25–63). First, he divides the composition into six movements (50:4–20; 50:21–32; 50:33–46; 51:1–33; 51:34–44; 51:45–53, with 50:2–3 and 51:54–58 as the framework). Second, he divides each movement into thematic sections and determines how they are structurally related rhetorically. Third, he restates the rhetorical pattern in terms of a thematic deeper structure: situation, intervention, and outcome. He concludes that each movement is composed of at least one basic pairing of these components. Fourth, he returns to the surface structure in order to restate the abstract, deeper structure in specific terms. Fifth, he relates the movements and their structures to each other to arrive at an integrated structure of the whole of chaps. 50–51. While his rhetorical analysis of each movement and its segments is the most convincing part of his treatment, the cumulative weight of the evidence for his view of the structure of the composition as a whole is only slightly less so. He concludes that the structure of chaps. 50–51, as he identifies it, is "to assure the exiled people of their return to their homeland in days future, and to encourage faith in the LORD's power and lively expectation of their return to Jerusalem in days present" (*TynBul* 35 [1984] 62–63). Although one may differ with Aitken in particulars, he has demonstrated successfully that Jer 50–51 is not a shapeless mass, but at some point in its formulation (final redaction?) it was consciously structured literarily in order to convey a particular message. Accordingly, Aitken's analysis will form the basis of the following treatment.

Each of the structural analyses by Christensen, Aitken, Carroll, and Holladay offers reasonable ways to delimit pericopes, while those of Aitken and Carroll suggest satisfactory ways to view the structure of the entire ensemble of oracles against Babylon. Carroll's analysis follows a kind of minimalist approach that focuses on macro-structures, while Aitken's essay, which will be followed here, emphasizes both macro- and micro-structures.

50:2–3, 46; 51:54–58 form the framework for the collection. Several key words and synonyms shared by these verses help set the tone and present the main theme of destruction for Babylon: the roots לכד, "to capture," and חתת, "to be dismayed, shattered," in 50:2 and 51:56; the correspondences "destroyer" in 51:56 and "nation from the north" in 50:3. 50:46 shares with 50:2 the root שמע, "to hear," the phrase "among the nations," and the synonyms "is taken" in v 2 and "is captured" in v 46. 50:46 shares with 51:54 the words קול, "voice," and זעקה, "outcry" (Aitken, *TynBul* 35 [1984] 30–31).

The first section in Jer 50 is composed of vv 4–20. Vv 4–5 are balanced by vv 19–20, expressing the theme of Israel's return and restoration, while vv 6–7 are balanced by vv 17–18, which narrate Israel's past experience. Units 2 (vv 8–10) and 3 (vv 14–16) are balanced by use of the themes of the appearance of the foe and flight from Babylon, while unit 3 (vv 11–13) provides the central pivot with the theme of Babylon's doom (Aitken, *TynBul* 35 [1984] 31–36).

The second section in Jer 50 is vv 21–32, composed of three units (vv 21–25, 26–28, 29–32) with a common structure: a summons to battle followed by a description of disaster. In addition, the three units are closely linked by means of four roots: חרב, "slay," in v 21 and v 27, חרם, "complete destruction," in v 21 and v 26, פלט, "escape," in vv 28 and 29, פתח, "open," in vv 25 and 26 and by the synonyms שארית and פלט, "remnant," in vv 26 and 28–29 (Aitken, *TynBul* 35 [1984] 36–40).

The third section of Jer 50 is formed by vv 33–46, divided into five units: vv 33–34, 35–38, 39–40, 41–43, 44–46. Unit 5 balances unit 1 with the theme of the LORD's intention to carry out the divine plan against Babylon and with the use of the root רגע, "give disquiet," in v 34 and v 44. Unit 4 balances unit 2 with the idea of the agents of destruction (sword in unit 2 and people from the north in unit 4). Unit 3 provides the pivot point with the theme of total doom for Babylon (Aitken, *TynBul* 35 [1984] 40–44).

The first section in Jer 51 is composed of vv 1–33, divided into six units: 1–2,

3–5, 6–10, 11–19, 20–26, 27–33. V 33 balances v 1 with the ideas of threshing floor and harvest. Units 1 and 5 share the key words שחת, "destroy," and רעה, "calamity." Units 2, 3, and 4 have the same structure: a summons, either to battle or to flee, followed by a saying about Israel's deliverance. Unit 6 begins also with a summons to battle and concludes with a summary statement about Babylon's imminent demise (Aitken, *TynBul* 35 [1984] 44–50).

The second section in Jer 51 is made up of vv 34–44, divided into five units: vv 34–35, 36–37, 38–40, 41–43, 44. The key word בלע, "swallow," in vv 34 and 44 provides the closure for the section. Units 2 and 4 are balanced thematically by means of the key words ים, "sea," in vv 36 and 42, שמה, "horror," in vv 37 and 41, 43, and גלים, "heaps of ruins, waves," in vv 37 and 42 and by means of the correspondence "without inhabitant" in v 37 and "no one dwells" in v 43 (Aitken, *TynBul* 35 [1984] 5–53).

The third section in Jer 51, the last before the framework in vv 54–58, is composed of vv 45–53, divided into five units: vv 45–46, 47–48, 49, 50–51, 52–53. The first two and last two units have the same pattern: summons to flight, exhortation, and an announcement of judgment. In addition, units 1 and 4 are balanced by means of the synonyms מלט, "save," and פלט, "escape," in vv 45 and 50 and the expression לבבכם, "your heart," in vv 46 and 50, while units 2 and 5 show a balance by sharing the word חלל, "slain, wounded," in vv 47 and 52, the expressions "behold, the days are coming," "all the land," and "the destroyers will come," and the theme of judgment against idols. The third unit is the pivot point for the section, the judgment of Babylon (Aitken, *TynBul* 35 [1984] 53–56).

Form-critical analysis of the collection of oracles against Babylon has identified eight genres or forms: (1) a summons to messengers, 50:2–3, (2) the oracle of salvation or restoration, 50:4–5, 19–20, 33–34, (3) the summons to flee, 50:8–10; 51:6–10, 45–46, (4) the summons to battle, 50:14–16, 21, 26–27, 29–30; 51:3–5, 11, 12–14, 27, (5) the song or apostrophe, 50:35–38; 51:20–24a; (6) a hymn, 51:15–19, (7) a lament with answering oracle, 51:34–44 and (8) oracles of judgment, represented by virtually all of the remaining passages.

Any attempt to determine a setting for Jer 50–51 must consider the following: (1) the question of authenticity of the oracles, (2) the significance of 51:59–64, (3) the question of coherence in Jeremiah's preaching concerning Nebuchadrezzar's place in the LORD's plan, and (4) the significance of 51:11, 27–28. The first three of these topics must be considered together.

In both MT and LXX, Jer 51:59–64 (LXX 28:59–64) has the effect of pointing to the oracles against Babylon in Jer 50–51 as the ones Seraiah was to read from the scroll while standing on Babylonian soil. Since Jer 51:62 reflects 50:3 and 51:26, Holladay (2:414) held forth the possibility that the whole collection of oracles against Babylon was taken to Babylon by Seraiah. This accords with his judgment, reached on other grounds, that the Babylon oracles are, for the most part, authentic to Jeremiah.

The embassy of Seraiah to Babylon is dated 594, the fourth year of Zedekiah. Also in 594 (Jer 27), Jeremiah donned yoke-bars and confronted the envoys from Edom, Moab, Ammon, Tyre, and Sidon, who had arrived in Jerusalem to plot with Zedekiah against Babylon. His message was direct: the LORD, the creator, had given all those lands into the hand of Nebuchadrezzar, his servant, and rebellion against Nebuchadrezzar was rebellion against the LORD. Still in 594 (for the date see Holladay, 2:140), Jeremiah sent a letter to the exiles in Babylon informing them that their exile would be long, that they should resume normal lives as much as possible, and that they were to seek the welfare of the city of their exile, for in its welfare was their welfare (Jer 29). These passages accord well with Jeremiah's consistent theme: the foe from the north was being summoned by the LORD to bring well-deserved catastrophe to Judah.

The fact that Jer 27 and Jer 29 are pro-Babylon in stance, or at least show no hostility to Babylon, while Jer 50–51 announces a violent end for Babylon because of her violence to Judah and other nations, raises the question of consistency in Jeremiah's preaching if all or most of the passages are to be attributed to him. Rudolph denied authenticity to 50:1–51:58, even though the two main themes of Judah's restoration and the end of Babylon's rule were a part of Jeremiah's preaching program (cf. 3:14; 24:6; 27:7; 29:10, 32). His main reasons are as follows: (1) Jeremiah proclaimed the end of Babylon only after a long time (27:7; 29:10), whereas 50:1–51:58 speaks of an imminent end for Babylon (51:13, 33; 51:24). (2) A prophecy of Babylon's imminent demise in 594 would have been useless to a people who would not live to see it fulfilled, and it would endanger the LORD's intention to effect the conversion of the people through the catastrophe produced by Nebuchadrezzar. (3) Nowhere outside the Babylon oracles did Jeremiah suggest that Nebuchadrezzar had overstepped the LORD's commission or had resisted the LORD, whereas in the oracles themselves Nebuchadrezzar is depicted as insatiable, guilty of atrocities (51:34–35), and guilty of insolence against the LORD (50:24, 29, 31). (4) The two passages 50:41–43 and 51:15–19, which repeat 6:22–24 and 10:12–16, respectively, were used out of the desire to speak in Jeremiah's name. Since 50:1–51:58 was inauthentic, Rudolph concluded that 51:59–64 originally stood in the Baruch scroll between Jer 29 and 34:2–7 and had no connection with the Babylon oracles. The scroll sent by Seraiah was not for publication; it was to be heard neither by the Babylonians nor by the exiles. It was Jeremiah's conviction that Babylon's end would finally come, but it was not imminent (Rudolph, 293–95).

The contrasting viewpoints with respect to Babylon evidenced in Jer 27–29, 39–40 and in the oracles against Babylon have led Carroll to consider them as irreconcilable (815–16, 824, 831, 842–43). Carroll's approach is to see the contradictory elements in the tradition as a major feature of the editing of the book (816).

Jer 51:11, 27–28 are usually taken to be glosses. Rudolph argued that the prose statement in 51:11, which mentions the LORD stirring up the Medes to destroy Babylon because of Babylon's actions against the temple in Jerusalem, interrupts the poetic flow and was probably a marginal gloss, which subsequently found its way into the text. He insisted that the prophet spoke consistently and anonymously of the "foe from the north" (285). Similarly, Rudolph bracketed the mention of Ararat, Minni, and Ashkenaz in 51:27 as metrically superfluous, as well as 51:28, which mentions the Medes (286–87). Holladay took the same position on these passages for essentially the same reasons (2:397, 398, 423, 426–27).

However, it may be that one of the strongest evidences for the authenticity of 51:11, 27–28, and perhaps of the longer passages of which they are a part, is the mention of Ararat, Minni, Ashkenaz, and Media. The Urartians (Ararat) fell to attacks by the Medes in the early sixth century and ceased to be an autonomous state (M. J. Mellink, *IDB* 1:194–95). I. M. Diakonov (cited by E. N. von

Voightlander, "A Survey of Neo-Babylonian History," 115; Diakonov's work, in Russian, was unavailable to the writer) dated the reference to the three peoples in 51:27 to 593 and concluded that the assimilation of the Mannai (Minni) and Ašguzai (Ashkenaz) by the Medes was complete by 590. Since Media began a series of attacks against Lydia in Asia Minor in 590, and since Media would hardly have begun a campaign against Lydia without securing nearby territory, Diakonov argued that the collocation of Urartu, Mannai, Ašguzai, and Media would make little sense after 590 (von Voightlander, "A Survey of Neo-Babylonian History," 135 n. 26). In this case, 51:28 could be a simple parallel to 51:27, with "every land under their dominion" in 51:28 referring to the three nations listed in 51:27. In any case, the mention of the three nations in 51:27 does not mar the poetic structure of the verse, nor does 51:28 have to be scanned as prose. Moreover, the vengeance of the LORD for the temple in Jerusalem does not have to assume that the temple had been destroyed, only violated (cf. 51:35, 50b–51), thus preserving a setting in 594.

As for the apparent contradiction in the Jeremiah tradition regarding Babylon, room must be left for Jeremiah's view of the sovereignty or imperium of the LORD. It was commonplace in the ancient Near East for deities to summon or co-opt foreign rulers to initiate change in their own realms. The LORD used both Assyria and Persia to achieve divine purposes (Isa 7:20; 8:7–8; 44:28; 45:1–6). Jeremiah was convinced that the LORD had a work to do in Jerusalem and Judah and that the king of Babylon was summoned to perform it.

It should also be kept in mind that in Jeremiah's lifetime there were competing political parties in Judah. There was a pro-Egyptian party, a pro-Babylonian party, a party espousing autonomy at any cost, and perhaps more. The competing claims of these parties caused stresses that Zedekiah finally could not withstand. It was not so much that Jeremiah was pro-Babylonian as that he was for the surest means to preserve life and nationhood for Judah. To espouse his policy meant that he had to engage in the political turmoil, thus making enemies for himself of almost every segment of society. He was focused on the LORD's plan and thus was not wedded to the platform of any political party, no matter how he may have been perceived by others. He advocated submission to Babylon for the short term, while at the same time setting a limit on Babylon's sovereignty (29:10) and declaring the ultimate return of the exiles and the restoration of the national life (29:11–14; 32:15, 42–44). It is, therefore, possible to find room in Jeremiah's preaching for both submission to Babylon according to the LORD's plan for Judah in the short term and for providing encouragement to the exiles through the oracles against Babylon.

Comment

1 The superscriptions to the oracles concerning the nations in Jer 46–51 assume three basic forms: (1) "the word of the LORD which came unto" (Jer 46:1; 49:34); (2) "concerning GN" (49:1; 49:7; 49:23; 49:28); and (3) "the word which the LORD spoke to" (Jer 46:13, 50:1). The exceptional feature in 50:1 is the use of בְּיַד, "by the hand of, by means of," the prophet, which stresses the mediating role of the prophet in communicating the divine word (cf. Hag 1:1, 3; 2:1; Mal 1:1; see Rudolph, *Jeremia*, 276–77).

2 Marduk was the national god of Babylon, who enjoyed his highest point of veneration during the time of the neo-Babylonian kingdom, especially during the reign of Nebuchadrezzar II (604–562; W. Sommerfeld, "Marduk," *RLA* 7:366–67). Already in the middle-Babylonian era Marduk's rise to prominence was celebrated in *Enuma elish*. Over time the title Bel (lord), which had been used to refer to a number of gods, came to be applied exclusively to Marduk (W. Sommerfeld, *RLA* 7:361).

3 Elsewhere in the book the "enemy from the north" is taken to be Babylon. Now Babylon itself would be attacked by "a nation from the north." Holladay suggests that this "nation from the north" may be the exiles of Israel (2:415; see his treatment of the "mace" in 51:20 as Israel in 2:405–7). Elsewhere in this oracle, however, "the nation from the north" is referred to as "a company of great nations" (50:9), "a people from the north, a mighty nation and many kings, from the farthest parts of the earth" (50:41), and "the destroyers from the north" (51:48, 53). In Jer 51:11, 27–28 the enemy is specified as the Medes. It seems preferable to understand the "nation from the north" here as a general designation in order to express the great reversal: Babylon, the great enemy from the north, would experience the same fate she had meted out to others.

4 Some kind of communal, cultic activity is suggested by the phrase "seek [בקשׁ] the LORD" (cf. Hos 3:5; 5:6; Zeph 1:6; 2:3; and its synonym דרשׁ in Amos 5:4, 6, 14). Jer 29:13 stresses seeking the LORD with the whole heart, which may or may not imply cultic activity. Note that Israel and Judah will come together to seek the LORD, weeping as they come (cf. 31:1–9). The relationship of the "everlasting covenant" here with the "new covenant" in 31:31–34 is problematic. Although the emphases differ in the two passages, the fact that they occur in contexts that speak of restoration may suggest they are alternate ways to describe the same reality.

6 For the figure of deceptive shepherds who destroyed and scattered the flock, see 23:1–4. The references to mountains and hills as the places to which the flock had been led astray recall Hos 4:13 and Deut 12:2, passages that mention mountains, hills, and the trees upon them, as sites of fertility worship (cf. also Jer 3:3). The word שׁכח, "to forget," was one of Jeremiah's favorite words to characterize the nature of Judah's unfaithfulness (2:32).

7 At the beginning of the covenant relationship, in the context of covenant fidelity, all who consumed Israel would be held guilty (Jer 2:3). But now the enemy had not only devoured them but had also disclaimed guilt because it had been Israel who had sinned. Jer 30:16 held out the promise that, although Israel was guilty, all who devoured them would in turn be devoured.

8–10 Although the summons to flight is usually addressed to the citizens of doomed cities or countries in Jer 46–51 (48:6; 49:28; 49:30), here the summons is most likely addressed to foreign residents in Babylon, the Judean exiles in particular (see also the treatment in the *Comment* on Jer 49:8). The metaphor of the flock is continued from the preceding verses. When the sheepfold was opened, the rams would lead the way. The summons was for the exiles to flee the coming catastrophe to be brought by a coalition of great nations from the north.

11–13 Those who plundered (50:10) shall now be plundered, their victory shouts being turned into disgrace. Babylon is here personified as "mother" (cf. Hos 2:4, 7; 10:14; Isa 50:1). The mother ("land") will become a desert, unable to give and sustain life (cf. Hos 2:5). She will become the "last of the nations" (cf. Amos 6:1, where the prideful citizens of Samaria boasted that their nation was the "first of the nations"). Babylon was to fall because she was the "plunderer of my heritage." As Carroll (824) points out, this is a different theological perspective on the exile than that evidenced in the earlier chapters in Jeremiah. The language of hissing or whistling at a defeated nation is stock language for derision (cf. Jer 49:17, 33).

14–16 Here is another summons to battle issued to Babylon's enemy (cf. the summonses in 46:3–4, 9; 46:14; 49:28, 31; see R. Bach, *Die Aufforderungen*, 51–91, for a critical treatment of this genre).

15 The phrase "she has given her hand" is usually taken to mean "she has surrendered" (so NRSV, ASV, NAB, NASB, NEB). LXX reads παρελύθησαν αἱ χεῖρες αὐτῆς, "her hands are weakened" (cf. 50:43, where MT has ורפו ידיו, "his hands are weakened"). However, the phrase may refer rather to the making/breaking of a treaty or covenant. Compare 2 Kgs 10:15, where Jehonadab "gave his hand" and joined Jehu in his campaign against the house of Omri. Also, in Ezek 17:11–21 Zedekiah is condemned for breaking his treaty with Babylon, going to Egypt for military support against Babylon. Ezek 17:18 describes this rebellion in these terms: "he despised the oath, he broke the covenant, he gave his hand." What is clearly in view here is treaty violation by concluding a treaty with another party. In 1 Chr 29:24 the leaders, the mighty men, and the sons of David "gave the hand to [literally 'under'] Solomon. They did not surrender; rather they pledged their allegiance to him. In 2 Chr 30:1–9 is the account of Hezekiah circulating a letter to all Israel and Judah to celebrate the passover in Jerusalem. He warned them not to be rebellious as their fathers had been but rather "to give the hand to the LORD," i.e., to be faithful, in a right relationship. In EA 298.26, Iapaḫi of Gazri reported that his younger brother had become his enemy and "had given his two hands" to the Ḫabiru; i.e., he had joined himself to Iapaḫi's enemies. In view of these references, Lam 5:6, "we gave the hand to Egypt, and to Assyria, to get enough bread," may stress entering into treaty relations rather than simply surrender. Thus, when Babylon is described here as "having given the hand," it may indicate that although Babylon had made an alliance to stave off destruction, the effort would be fruitless. Nabonidus in fact did make a treaty with Cyrus, the very ruler who later captured Babylon (VA 2536.1.27–33).

The *hap. leg.* אָשִׁיָה is rendered "tower" on the basis of its Akkadian cognate *asātu*, "tower as part of a city wall" (*CAD* 1.2.332–33).

16 Captive peoples in Babylon are urged to flee (the verbs may be jussives) from the sword of Babylon's oppressor, which would cause famine in the land (cf. Isa 13:14). Compare the stated intention of mercenaries to flee Egypt "because of the sword of the oppressor" in Jer 46:16 and the summons issued to the Dedanites to flee or to avoid entering Edom in view of Edom's imminent calamity (Jer 49:8).

17–20 This passage contains both historical recollection and the promise of restoration. Assyria and Babylon are characterized as lions chasing a sheep (cf. Isa 5:29 for Assyria and Jer 4:7 for Babylon). The king of Assyria consumed Israel, and Nebuchadrezzar gnawed the remains. But just as Assyria fell under God's judgment, so Babylon's was impending. Vv 17a, 19–20 are poetic, while v 18 is prose.

19 The image of the sheep in v 17 is retained in the pastoral language. The restored Israel/sheep would pasture on those most fruitful areas of the land, denied to them by Assyria (Rudolph, 279).

20 Compare Jer 31:34.

21–27 Vv 21, 27a constitute another summons to battle. The invader is described as a part of the LORD's armory in v 25 at the command of the LORD (v 21d). V 23 is an ironic dirge against Babylon.

21 Holladay appeals to the masculine singular imperatives as his basis for understanding the addressee as Israel (Holladay, 2:418). But the imperatives in vv 26–27, referring apparently to the same attacker, are masculine plural.

Merathaim ("double rebellion") and *Peqod* ("punishment") may be understood on one level as wordplays on the roots מרה and פקד, respectively (cf. Cushan-rishatayim in Judg 3:8). On the historical level, "Merathaim" may reflect *nār mārratu*, "bitter, brackish river," in southern Babylonia (J. Muilenburg, *IDB* 3:351). Sometimes the "bitter river" referred to any body of salt water and at other times to the Persian Gulf (*CAD* 10.1.286). Also, on the map of the world placing Babylon at the center of the world, the "bitter river" is placed at the outer edges of the sphere of earth (CT 22, 48). It would be a masterful use of irony or satire if the oracle here means to suggest that the center of the world is to be placed at its outer edges. "Peqod" may reflect *Puqûdu*, an Aramean tribe located on the lower Tigris (T. Jacobsen, *IDB* 3:709). Ezek 23:23 mentions Peqod in the sequence "Babylonians, Chaldeans, Peqod, Shoa, and Koa."

Note that the words חרב, "slay," חרם, "devote to destruction," and פקד, "punish, "Peqod," recur in vv 26—27, thus forming an inclusio and suggesting the limits of this unit.

23 This verse is a mocking or ironic dirge (cf. 49:25). The hammer פטיש, referring to Babylon, is called מפץ in 51:20. See *Comment* on 50:25.

25 The idea of the LORD's armory containing the weapons of divine wrath (foreign nations to accomplish the LORD's purpose) is known from Isa 13:5. Babylon had been the LORD's hammer (50:23; 51:20–23) but now will suffer the fate of those whom she had pounded into submission. Included in the LORD's armory on occasion had been Assyria as the flooding river sweeping all before it (Isa 8:7–8), as the rod of the LORD's anger (Isa 10:5), and as the LORD's axe. And much earlier the poet had waxed eloquent in declaring that from heaven the stars in their circuits had fought against Sisera (Judg 5:20). Jer 51:1 mentions the destroying wind aroused by the LORD to winnow Babylon.

26–27 מקץ, "from the end," is to be rendered "from all sides," "from every extremity" (cf. 51:31, מקצה). Total destruction is in view here: the destruction or removal of every staff of life. The "bulls" may be understood literally, or, perhaps better, figuratively for soldiers or leaders of the nation (cf. Isa 34:6–7).

28 The unit consisting of vv 21–27 is capped with this climactic verse, which declares the accomplishment of the LORD's vindication for the temple.

29–32 These verses may be taken as a unit, with the root סבב, "to surround," in vv 29 and 32 indicating the inclusio. Vv 29–30 are taken here as poetic. The unit is composed of typical features of oracles concerning the nations found elsewhere. V 29 is another summons to battle, with terminology met already in 50:14. V 29b repeats v 15d. V 30 repeats 49:26, v 31a is similar to 51:25, v 31b parallels v

27b, and v 32bc recalls 21:14bc and Amos 1:4, 7, 10, 12, 14; 2:2, 5. Also, one of the three reasons for judgment against foreign nations is mentioned in v 31: pride. Indeed, Babylon is pride personified. Thus the entire unit is composed of standard, stereotypical features of the genre oracle concerning the nations.

33–34 The language of this oracle of salvation recalls the deliverance in the Exodus from Egypt. The oppressed of Israel and Judah whom Babylon refused to set free (cf. Exod 7:14) are to be rescued by the Redeemer (גֹּאֵל; cf. Exod 6:6; 15:13), who will take up their legal case (cf. Exod 2:23–25; 3:7–8). The passage is replete with wordplays: הֶחֱזִיקוּ בָם, "they held them strongly," and גֹּאֲלָם חָזָק, "their redeemer is strong"; הִרְגִּיעַ, "he will give rest," and הִרְגִּיעַ, "he will give unrest"; and שֹׁבֵיהֶם, "their captors," and יֹשְׁבֵי בָבֶל, "the inhabitants of Babylon."

35–38 This poem is similar in style and structure to 4:23–26, 5:17, and 51:20–23. The key word חֶרֶב, "sword," occurs five times, with חֹרֶב, "drought," appearing in v 38. V 35 is a tricolon, with the word "sword" appearing once. Vv 36–37ab are a tetracolon; vv 37d–38 are a bicolon. Comprehensive destruction is in view for Babylon, from its general population to the essential constituent parts of its society: leaders, diviners, military, treasury, even its waters essential for normal life.

הַבַּדִּים (read בַּדֶּיהָ) is rendered here as "her diviners" (cf. Isa 44:25 where בַּדִּים parallels קֹסְמִים, "diviners"). Some interpreters have suggested reading בָּרִים (cf. Akkadian *bārû*, "diviner"). The *bārû* prophets were regularly connected with the army and marched in front of the army to ensure the safety of the march (see the references in *CAD* 2.123–124; cf. also Ezek 21:18–23). An attempt to explain בדים on the basis of the term *baddum*, referring to some kind of military leader at Mari (*CAD* 2:27), is hazardous because the term occurs only at Mari and in only one letter.

39–40 This oracle is paralleled more fully in the oracle against Babylon in Isa 13:19–22, which includes all the key words and themes of Jer 50:39–40, including the reference to the overthrow of Sodom and Gomorrah.

41–43 These verses reproduce 6:22–24, the greatest change being that the one hearing the report of invasion is now the king of Babylon instead of Judah (see *Comment* on 6:22–26). In this ironic reversal, Babylon, which turned out to be "the foe from the north" against Judah, is terrorized by news of a people from the north reported in almost identical terms.

44–46 These verses are an application of 49:19–21 to Babylon (see *Comment* on 49:19–21).

51:1 A destroying wind must be added as a weapon to the LORD's armory (see *Comment* on 50:25).

לֵב קָמָי is an *atbash* for כַּשְׂדִּים; see the *Note* on 51:1. In 51:41 שֵׁשַׁךְ is an *atbash* for בָּבֶל (see B. J. Roberts, *IDB* 1.306–7).

2 זָרִים, "foreigners," may be retained as a wordplay on זֵרוּהָ, "they will winnow her," but it is preferable to point it זֹרִים, "winnowers." The destroying wind would not just blow away the chaff so that the grain could be saved, but would lay waste (בקק) the land.

3 The first two occurrences of אֶל in this verse are to be read as אַל, the negative used with the jussive. Thus, the archers and those wearing mail are the Babylonians. LXX does not read אַל as a negative and thus understands the archers and those wearing mail as the enemy of the Babylonians. In any case, the following "spare not" is a command addressed to the attackers.

5   For אשם, "guilt," compare the denial of guilt by the enemies of Israel in 50:7.

אַלְמָן is the masculine form of אַלְמָנָה and occurs only here. The meaning is clear enough: Israel has not been forsaken by the LORD, although technically Israel should, if forsaken by the LORD, be called a widow.

6–10   These verses constitute a summons to the exiles to flee the LORD's requital against Babylon so as not to be caught up in the devastation.

7   The image of Babylon as the golden cup in the LORD's hand recalls 25:15–16. (See *Excursus: The Cup of Wrath* following the Introduction to 46:1–51:64.)

8–10   These verses may be understood as a quotation of those who are summoned to flee the doomed land. The golden cup has been broken. V 8cd may be taken as an ironical taunt, although the exact intention of v 9a is not clear. The time draws near to return to Zion and to give witness to the LORD's great act of bringing forth "our victory."

11–14   That vv 11–14 form a unit is indicated not only by their content but also by the inclusio supplied by the occurrences of the root מלא, "to fill," in vv 11 and 14 (see J. R. Lundbom, *Jeremiah: A Study in Ancient Hebrew Poetry*, 50–51).

11   This verse, along with v 12, is a summons to battle, with plural imperatives used throughout. The word שלטים, usually rendered "shields," is to be taken as "bow cases" (cf. *AHW* 3:1151, where *šalṭu* is understood as "bow case," an Aramaic loanword into Akkadian). Re-curved bows were carried unstrung in bow cases in order to retain the shape, and consequently the verb מִלְאוּ, "fill," may be retained.

For the designation of the Medes as the expected invaders of Babylon, see the comments by von Voightlander and Diakonov mentioned in *Form/Structure/ Setting*.

12   For the phrase "raise a standard," see 4:6; 50:2; 51:27. Setting in place guards and ambushers implies a complete siege of Babylon.

13   Babylon was situated, of course, among "many waters," between the Euphrates and Tigris rivers in territory criss-crossed by canals to facilitate agriculture and commerce. But the phrase מִים רבים, "many waters," occurs in other passages where "many waters" refers to the primeval deep, the waters of chaos (see H. G. May, *JBL* 74 [1955] 9–21). Perhaps the intent of this passage is not only to locate Babylon among many water sources but also to suggest that she was sitting above the chaotic waters which would erupt and bring about her end.

אמת בצעך means literally "the cubit (limit) of your being cut off," thus "the limit of your thread." The noun בֶּצַע also means "profit," so that she who was rich in treasures would lose all.

15–19   This section repeats 10:12–16; see the treatment of that section in volume 1 (*Jeremiah 1–25*, WBC 26).

20–23   For a detailed analysis of the chiastic structure of this poem, see J. R. Lundbom, *Jeremiah: A Study in Ancient Hebrew Rhetoric*, 91–92. Nine times the phrase ונפצתי בך, "and I break in pieces with you," occurs in staccato fashion suggesting the sound of the striking hammer. The series is broken only in the fourth colon of v 20 where there occurs והשחתי בך, "and I destroy with you." The poem is a true work of art, with the words "old man" and "youth" in v 22 forming the pivot point for the chiastic structure. "Old man" points back to the "man" and "woman," while the "youth" points forward to the "young man" and the "maiden."

"Nations" and "kingdoms" in v 20 are balanced in v 23 by their officials, the governors and the commanders. Thus, comprehensive destruction is indicated as much by literary structure as by the contents of the poem.

מַפֵּץ, "hammer," or better, "mace," is derived from the root נפץ, "to shatter." Compare also Ezek 9:2, כְּלִי מַפָּץ, and possibly also Prov 25:18.

Who is the "hammer"? Lundbom thought that the hammer was the prophet himself, who shattered with both words and rhetoric (Lundbom, *Jeremiah: A Study in Ancient Hebrew Rhetoric*, 91). Holladay has identified the hammer as Israel, pointing to the different words for hammer in 50:23 (Babylon) and in 51:20 (Holladay, 2:405–7). Rudolph emphasized the perfect forms of the verbs as pointing to a previous or existing state of affairs and thus identified the hammer as Babylon, although Babylon was not to be a hammer for long (Rudolph, 287). Rudolph's view is followed here.

24 This prose interpretation of vv 20–23 presents the great reversal. Although Nebuchadrezzar had been the "servant of the LORD" (27:6), and Babylon had been the hammer of the whole earth (50:23), the LORD would repay Babylon for her evil in much the same way that Isaiah said the LORD would punish the king of Assyria, the rod of his wrath, for his pride (Isa 10:12–16).

25–26 While the general sense of these verses is clear enough, an interpretation that encompasses all its terms remains lacking. Especially troublesome is the phrase "I will roll you from the rocks." Since Babylon was situated in a flat plain, some have taken the reference to the mountain as symbolic language (Rudolph, 287; Weiser, 435). The "mountain" may reflect the ziggurat, or temple-tower, of Babylon, *E-temen-an-ki*, which underlies the idea of pride in the Tower of Babel passage in Gen 11. Babylon was the destroyer, as the figures of hammer (50:23) and mace (51:20) suggest. The figure of Babylon as the mountain of the destroyer or the destroying mountain is a fitting one. But the phrase "I will roll you from the rocks" is puzzling, for any rocks had to be shipped into Babylon, and the word used for rocks (סלעים) usually refers to the lofty crags of mountains. In any case, the destroying mountain was to become a burned mountain. The destruction was to be so complete that rebuilders would be unable to salvage foundation stones. Holladay (2:425–26) suggested that הַר הַמַּשְׁחִית here and in 2 Kgs 23:13 was originally הַר הַמִּשְׁחָה, "mount of oil," and that after 587 the expression was changed to "mountain of destruction." Perhaps it is enough to suggest that the language of 51:25 is stock or formulaic language akin to the description of the anticipated destruction of Mount Seir in Ezek 35:3–4, and that the author/editor was not making an attempt either to relate the passage to the ziggurat or to make a play on words.

27–33 This unit concludes the first section of the chapter, the language of harvest in v 33 reflecting that of v 1. Vv 27–28 furnish another summons to battle, employing plural imperatives (cf. 51:12). As is often the case with this genre, the effect of the anticipated battle is described: the land trembles; the defenders lose heart and panic because all the news is calamitous.

27–28 For the possibility of using these verses as a dating device for at least this part of the oracles against Babylon, see above the comments by von Voightlander and Diakonov mentioned in *Form/Structure/Setting*.

The term מִפְסָר, usually translated "marshal" or the like, is to be related to Akkadian *ṭupšarru*, "scribe." There is no evidence that a scribe was also a "marshal." Rather, the appointment of a scribe against Babylon probably refers to the scribe(s) who accompanied armies to record the booty taken in a victory.

34–44 That these verses form a unit is indicated by the chiastic structure: the root בלע, "swallow," in v 44 recalls the same root in v 34 (Aitken, *TynBul* 35 [1984] 50–53; Lundbom, *Jeremiah: A Study in Ancient Hebrew Rhetoric*, 93–94), with v 44 reversing the sense of v 34. Indeed the unit suggests a service of lamentation.

34 There is a mixture of metaphors to describe the rapacity of the king of Babylon: the king of Babylon is like a sea monster that has swallowed up Jerusalem and filled its belly with her delicacies; he has discomfited her; and she is like an empty vessel that has been rinsed out (or perhaps "expelled"). It seems pointless to try to make the metaphors cohere. For similar language, see 50:17.

35 The attributions of Babylon's guilt are voiced in liturgical style (cf. Ps 129:1–3). Completely absent here is any sentiment that Judah suffered its terrible fate because of its own faults. For the formula "let the blood of X be upon Y," see Lev 20:9, 11–13, 16, 27.

36 The LORD responds with the assurance of taking up Jerusalem's case and winning vindication for her. The LORD's promised victory over "her sea" and "her fountain" recalls the LORD's victory over sea at creation and in the Exodus (Exod 15:8; Pss 74:13–14; 89:9–10; Isa 27:1). The reference to "sea" recalls v 34 and anticipates v 42.

37 For similar language of total destruction, see 49:18; 49:33; 50:39–40.

38–40 The ravening lions (Babylon) will become like sheep for slaughter when they have drunk the cup (cf. Jer 25). In contrast to 50:17 and 51:34, where the king of Babylon gorged on Israel, here they will be provided a feast that will lead to their death.

41 The verse is an ironical or taunting lament. ששך is an *atbash* cipher for "Babylon" (cf. 26:26; 51:1).

42 The sea refers to the forces of the invader (cf. 46:7; 47:2). In this unit, the king of Babylon was likened to a sea monster that swallowed the people of Zion (v 34), but the LORD would dry up the sea. And now the swelling tide of invasion would inundate Babylon. The sea is reminiscent of the "many waters" of 51:13.

43 The verse replays v 37 and helps to show the chiastic structure of the entire unit.

44 For Bel, "lord," as a title of Marduk, the chief god of Babylon, see 50:2 and the *Comment* there. The chiastic structure of vv 34–44 is indicated here by the reversal of v 34. The root נהר, "flow," reminds one of Isa 2:2; Mic 4:1, where the nations "flow" as a river to Zion because Zion was to become the center of the world. In this verse, nations would no longer view Babylon as the center, or as we would say, all roads would no longer lead there, for the wall of Babylon will have fallen.

45–46 This is yet another summons to flight, which characterizes the oracles concerning nations (R. Bach, *Die Aufforderungen*, 15–50). The Judean exiles are summoned to flee before the wrath of the LORD should befall Babylon and they be caught up in the destruction. They are warned against becoming confused because of conflicting reports and rumors about conditions.

49 Just as all the slain of the earth fell for Babylon, now Babylon was to fall, specifically for the slain of Israel. A ל has probably dropped before חללי, "slain," of the first colon because of haplography, and the lamedh may be vocative

(Holladay, 2:430). It is possible that the lamedh on לִנְפֹּל may be asseverative lamedh, thus "Babylon will surely fall," although Babylon is consistently construed as feminine. More likely is the view that the infinitive with lamedh conveys an imminent sense: "about to fall" (Waltke and O'Connor, 36.2.3g).

50–51   Here is yet another summons to flee. Those who manage to avoid the coming onslaught are commanded to go, to leave Babylon, and to recall the disgrace of Babylonian victory over Jerusalem. To "remember" the LORD may be seen as a call to the many who had adopted Babylonian religion while in exile to readopt their former religion in light of the LORD's impending deliverance.

52–53   The verses are essentially another version of vv 47–49. Idolatry, along with military aggression and pride, appears consistently in the various collections of oracles against nations as a major reason for the LORD's judgment. V 53ab recalls the language of the Tower of Babel narrative in Gen 11: its top was to reach heaven, and nothing was to be inaccessible to (RSV: "impossible for") them. But even more pertinent is the oracle against Babylon in Isa 14:4b–20, especially vv 13–14: "I will ascend to heaven," and "I will ascend above the heights of the clouds."

54–58   50:2–3, 46; 51:54–58 form the framework for the extended oracle against Babylon. See the treatment in *Form/Structure/Setting*. In these verses, 51:54–58, key terms are shared with 50:2–3, 46, providing an inclusio for the whole series of oracles.

54–55   The key term of these verses is קוֹל, "sound, voice, cry." Babylon's cry in the face of attack (v 54a) will be stilled by the LORD (v 55) by means of the sound of the "many waters" (cf. *Comments* on 51:36, 42).

57   Cf. 51:39.

58   No more fitting, comprehensive conclusion to the oracles against Babylon could be devised. With economy of language, all that has been said in two chapters is summed up here.

V 58cd essentially repeats Hab 2:13bd, with the two verbs being pointed differently and the terms "nought" and "fire" being reversed. It is likely that this passage predates the parallel in Hab 2:13 since Hab 2:13 appears to be a gloss that permits Hab 2:13bd to function as a condemnation of Babylon for harsh treatment of nations. Here, v 58cd functions to pass sentence on the nations for their willing cooperation in keeping Babylon strong (cf. 51:44; thus Roberts, *Nahum, Habakkuk, and Zephaniah*, 123).

59–64   For a discussion of the relationship of these verses to the oracles against Babylon, see *Form/Structure/Setting*.

59   LXX has a longer version of the first part of this verse: "the word which the LORD commanded Jeremiah to say to Seraiah." This reading seems plausible since it is usually the LORD who "commands" (צוה; cf. 13:5; 26:8). Nowhere else in the book of Jeremiah does Jeremiah "command." However, in Jer 35:6, 14, 18 reference is made to Jonadab ben Rechab, who commanded (צוה) his followers to abstain from wine and to follow a nonagricultural lifestyle. Whether Jeremiah had the authority to command the brother of his secretary, Baruch, is unknown.

Did King Zedekiah make a trip to Babylon? MT suggests that he did: "when he [Seraiah] went with [אֶת] Zedekiah." Such a journey is not inconceivable, but there is nothing in the account in the book of Kings to suggest that he did. The LXX understood "from Zedekiah" (מֵאֵת) and is followed here.

The fourth year of Zedekiah's reign was 594.

Seraiah, the brother of Baruch (32:12), was an official of the Judean administration. According to MT, Seraiah was שַׂר מְנוּחָה, "officer of the resting place [bivouac]" (RSV: "quartermaster"), an office nowhere else mentioned. The Syriac version rendered the phrase "commander of an army (camp)" (= Hebrew מַחֲנֶה). LXX has ἄρχων δώρων, "officer over the gifts (tribute)" (= Hebrew מִנְחוֹת). A seal-stamp impression has turned up in excavations in Jerusalem with the inscription "belonging to Seraiah (son of) Neriah" (see Shiloh and Tarler, *BA* 49 [1986] 204).

60 "All these words that are written concerning Babylon" implies a lengthy document and may very well have included most, if not all, of the material in chaps. 50–51.

61 The symbolic action to be performed by Seraiah begins with the public reading of the document describing the calamity for Babylon. Perhaps, with the release of the words in public reading, it was thought that the realization of the words could be initiated.

63–64 The symbolic action is concluded with the throwing of the rock-weighted scroll into the Euphrates, thus signaling the sinking of Babylon.

The appearance of וְיָעֵפוּ, "and they will weary themselves," before the words "thus far the words of Jeremiah" suggests that MT may give witness of an earlier redactional stage in which the final words of v 64 followed immediately on v 58 (Barthélemy, *Critique textuelle*, 853).

Explanation

It is altogether fitting that in the MT the oracles against Babylon conclude the collection of the OAN. In the other OAN, destruction is announced against the various nations in light of their opposition to Nebuchadrezzar, king of Babylon, the LORD's servant. This oracle against Babylon recalls Babylon's role in the LORD's plan by referring to her as the cup in the LORD's hand (51:7) and as the hammer used to smash the nations (51:20–23; cf. also 50:23). Ultimately, however, even Babylon had to experience her own invasion by "a foe from the north" and had to drink her own cup of wrath down to the dregs. Foreign nations could be used, unwittingly or wittingly, by the LORD to further the divine plan, but they too in time came under judgment for their deeds. Babylon is condemned for pride (50:31–32, 51:25–26), for idolatry (50:38, 51:17–18), and for sinning against the LORD (50:14, 24, 29; 51:5). The full extent of Babylon's sin against the LORD, other than pride and idolatry, is not clear, although it may be that Babylon's action against Judah, even though sanctioned by the LORD, may have exceeded in severity anything that the LORD had intended (cf. 50:33). In any case, for the first time in the collection of OAN in Jeremiah is a nation judged for its treatment of the people of God.

The central idea in the OAN is that the LORD reigns supreme over all nations and peoples and that the LORD's purposes cannot be thwarted ultimately. No nation can vaunt itself over other nations without finally having done to it as it has done to others (50:15, 29).

XXVII. The Capture of Jerusalem Revisited: A Concluding Word (52:1–34[LXX 52:1–34] = 2 Kings 24:18–25:30)

Bibliography

Ackroyd, P. R. "Historians and Prophets." *SEÅ* 33 (1968) 18–54. **Begg, C. T.** "The Significance of Jehoiachin's Release: A New Proposal." *JSOT* 36 (1986) 49–56. **Green, A. R.** "The Chronology of the Last Days of Judah: Two Apparent Discrepancies." *JBL* 101 (1982) 57–73. **Henton Davies, G.** "Threshold." *IDB* 4:636. **Hobbs, T. R.** *2 Kings.* WBC 13. Waco: Word Books, 1985. 345–69. **Levenson, J. D.** "The Last Four Verses in Kings." *JBL* 103 (1984) 353–61. **MacLean, H. B.** "Zedekiah." *IDB* 4:948–9. **Montgomery, J. A.** *A Critical and Exegetical Commentary on the Books of Kings.* ICC. Edinburgh: T. & T. Clark, 1951. 554–69. **Noth, M.** *The Deuteronomistic History.* JSOT 15. Sheffield: JSOT, 1981. 74, 98. **Pritchard, J. B.,** ed. *ANET.* 308. **Rad, G. von.** *"Deuteronomium-Studien.* FRLANT 58. Göttingen: Vandenhoeck & Ruprecht, 1947. 64. **Zenger, E.** *"Die deuteronmistische Interpretation der Rehabilitierung Jojachins."* *BZ* n.s. 12 (1968) 16–30.

Translation

[1] *Zedekiah was twenty-one years old when he began to reign, and he reigned for eleven years in Jerusalem. His mother's name was Hamital[a] daughter of Jeremiah of Libnah.* [2][a]*He did what was evil in Yahweh's eyes, as Jehoiakim had done.* [3]*Indeed, because the anger of Yahweh was against Jerusalem and Judah,[a] he cast them out of his presence. Yet Zedekiah rebelled against the king of Babylon.* [4]*It was the ninth year of his reign, in the tenth month and on the tenth day of the month that Nebuchadrezzar[a] king of Babylon came, he and all his army, against Jerusalem. They encamped against it and erected siegeworks round about against it.* [5]*The city came under siege until the eleventh year of King Zedekiah.* [6][a]*By the fourth month,[a] the ninth day of the month, the famine was so severe in the city that there was no bread for the people of the land.* [7]*Then the city was broken into, and all the soldiers [a]fled[b] and went from the city by night by the road between the two walls near the king's garden. While the Chaldeans surrounded the city, they[a] fled along the Arabah road.* [8]*A Chaldean force pursued the king and caught up with Zedekiah[a] at the Jericho Flats; then all his men[b] deserted him.* [9]*The Chaldeans captured the king and brought him up to the king of Babylon at Riblah [a]in the land of Hamath,[a] and he passed sentence[b] upon him.* [10]*The king of Babylon[a] butchered the sons of Zedekiah before his eyes [b]and also butchered all the princes of Judah at Riblah.[b]* [11]*The king of Babylon blinded Zedekiah, bound him in chains, brought him to Babylon, and put him in prison[a] until the day of his death.*
[12]*In the fifth month, on the tenth[a] day of the month—[b]it was the nineteenth year of*

King Nebuchadrezzar king of Babylon[b]— *Nebuzaradan the captain of the guard came into*[c] *Jerusalem as an* [d]*attendant before*[de] *the king of Babylon.* [13]*And he burned the house of the LORD and the house of the king and all the houses of Jerusalem;* [a]*every great*[b] *house he burned*[a] *with fire.* [14]*And all*[a] *the army of the Chaldeans who were with the captain of the guard pulled down all*[b] *the walls around Jerusalem.* [15ab]*Some of the poor people,*[b] *the remnant of the people who remained in the city, those who had deserted to the king of Babylon, and the remnant of the artisans, Nebuzaradan the captain of the guard sent into exile.* [16a]*Some of the poor*[b] *of the land*[a] *Nebuzaradan*[c] *the captain of the guard left for vinedressers and plowmen.*[d]

[17]*The bronze pillars which were in*[a] *the house of the LORD and the stands and the bronze sea which were in the house of the LORD the Chaldeans broke in pieces, and they took away all*[b] *their bronze to Babylon.* [18a]*They took the pots and the shovels and the snuffers and the bowls and the incense pans and all the bronze utensils which they used in the temple service;* [19]*the basins*[a] *and the firepans and the bowls*[b] *and the pots and the lampstands and the vessels and the sacrificial bowls the captain of the guard took away, what was gold as gold, what was silver as silver;* [20]*as for the two pillars, the one sea,*[a] [b]*and the twelve bronze bulls which were under the sea*[bc] *and the ten*[d] *stands which King Solomon had made for the house of the LORD, there was no weighing the bronze*[ef]*(of) all these articles.*[f] [21]*As for the pillars,*[a] *eighteen*[b] *cubits was the height*[c] *of the one pillar,* [d]*its circumference was twelve cubits, and its thickness was four fingers, (and it was) hollow.*[de] [22]*Upon it was a capital of bronze; the height of the one*[a] *capital was five*[b] *cubits, and lattice work and pomegranates were all around the capital, all of bronze, and the second pillar likewise,* [c]*with pomegranates.*[c] [23a]*There were ninety-six pomegranates on the sides;*[b] *all the pomegranates were a hundred upon the lattice work round about.*

[24]*The captain of the guard took Seraiah*[a] *the chief priest and Zephaniah*[a] *the second priest and the three keepers of the threshold,*[b] [25a]*and he took from the city*[a] *one official who was*[b] *an overseer over the soldiers, and seven*[c] *men of the king's advisors who were found*[d] *in the city, and the scribe of the army commander*[e] *who mustered the people of the land, and sixty men from the people of the land who were found in the midst of the city.* [26]*Nebuzaradan the captain of the guard took them and sent them to the king of Babylon at Riblah.* [27]*The king of Babylon smote*[a] *them and killed them*[b] *at Riblah in the land of Hamath,* [c]*and Judah went into exile from its land.*[c]

[28a]*This is (the number of) the people whom Nebuchadrezzar sent into exile: in the seventh year,*[b] *three thousand twenty-three Jews;* [29]*in the eighteenth year of Nebuchadrezzar,*[a] *from Jerusalem, eight hundred thirty-two persons;* [30]*in the twenty-third year of Nebuchadrezzar, Nebuzaradan the captain of the guard sent into exile, of Jews, seven hundred forty-five persons; all of the persons were four thousand six hundred.*

[31]*In the thirty-seventh year of the exile of Jehoiachin*[a] *the king of Judah, in the twelfth month, on the twenty-fifth*[b] *day of the month, Evil-merodach, the king of Babylon, in the year he became king,*[c] *lifted up the head of Jehoiachin*[a] *the king of Judah,*[d] *and he brought him out of prison.*[e] [32]*He spoke kindly with him and gave him a seat above the seat of the kings*[a] *who were with him in Babylon.* [33]*So he changed his prison garments, and he ate bread before him regularly all the days of his life.* [34]*As for his allowance, a regular allowance was given to him from the* [a]*king of Babylon*[a] *daily* [b]*until the day of his death,* [b] [c]*all the days of his life.*[c]

Notes

1.a. Q = "Hamutal."

2.a. LXX lacks vv 2–3.

3.a. Many MSS and 2 Kgs 24:20 have "and against Judah."

4.a. 2 Kgs 25:1, LXX have the spelling "Nebuchadnezzar."

6.a-a. Lacking in LXX; also lacking in 2 Kgs 25:3.

7.a-a. 2 Kgs 25:4 lacks these words and has the soldiers (of Babylon) breaking into the city "by night by the road between the two walls near the king's garden."

7.b. "fled" lacking in LXX.

8.a. 2 Kgs 25:5 has "caught up with *him.*"

8.b. LXX reads "his servants."

9.a-a. Absent in LXX and in 2 Kgs 25:6.

9.b. MT has pl for "passed sentence," lit. "pronounced judgments"; LXX and 2 Kgs have sg "judgment."

10.a. 2 Kgs 25:7 has "*they* butchered."

10.b-b. Lacking in 2 Kgs 25:7, where the action in Jer 52:10–11 is compressed into a single verse with some omissions. 2 Kgs 25:7 reads "They butchered the sons of Zedekiah before his eyes; then they blinded Zedekiah, bound him in chains, and brought him to Babylon."

11.a. LXX reads "millhouse"; slaves were sometimes condemned to work the mill (see LSJ, 522).

12.a. 2 Kgs 25:8 has "seventh."

12.b-b. Lacking in LXX.

12.c. 2 Kgs 25:8 lacks the prep before Jerusalem.

12.d-d. Instead of the phrase עמד לפני, lit. "he stood before," translated above "attendant before," 2 Kgs 25:8 has עבד, "servant of."

12.e. LXX treats עמד, "he stood," as a ptcp, "standing," which supports the reading adopted above.

13.a-a. *BHS* suggests this phrase is a possible addition.

13.b. Read "every great house" with LXX and 2 Kgs 25:9, instead of "every house of significant person(s)" as in MT; the difference is determined by the presence of the definite article in MT.

14.a. Lacking in LXX.

14.b. "all" lacking in 2 Kgs 25:10; Jer 39:8.

15.a. LXX lacks v 15.

15.b-b. Lacking in 2 Kgs 25:11; Jer 39:9. There is also the oddity of the pl spelling of "poor," since this word is typically understood as a collective noun (see Holladay, 2:437).

16.a-a. LXX has "the remnant of the people" for MT "some of the poor of the land."

16.b. 2 Kgs 25:12 has a sg form; here it is pl. Holladay (2:437) notes the puzzle created by the pl form, since the noun for "poor" is understood collectively. He suggests the possibility that it refers to poor women.

16.c. "Nebuzaradan" lacking in LXX and 2 Kgs 25:12.

16.d. Heb. uncertain; LXX has καὶ εἰς γεωργούς, "and for husbandmen"; cf. 39:10.

17.a. Read "in" with LXX and a few MSS; MT has "belonging to." Prep is lacking entirely in the first phrase in 2 Kgs 25:13; ב, "in," in the second phrase.

17.b. LXX and 2 Kgs 25:13 lack "all."

18.a. The various items used in temple worship that are listed as plunder taken by the Babylonians pose many textual problems. MT and LXX differ in the items listed. Further, the comparable text of 2 Kgs 25:14–15, while briefer than the Jeremiah text, includes still other items. Holladay (2:437) attempts to unravel the difficulties he perceives to be the result of a conflate text.

19.a. LXX has τὰ σαφφωθ; *BHS* suggests it be read as הַסִּפּוֹת, "the basins." Both masc and fem endings appear for this word.

19.b. LXX has τὰ μασμαρωθ, which *BHS* indicates may be equivalent to הַמְזַמְּרוֹת, "the snuffers," of v 18. *BHS* also suggests the possibility of a corruption of the MT form in its Gk. transliteration.

20.a. Read "*the* one sea" as in 2 Kgs 25:16.

20.b-b. 2 Kgs 25:16 lacks any reference to the twelve bulls, consistent with Ahaz's actions described in 2 Kgs 16:8, 17.

20.c. Insert "sea" as in LXX, probably dropped out in MT by haplogr.

20.d. Add "ten" consistent with the other numbers in the passage; cf. 1 Kgs 7:27.

20.e. MT has "their" bronze; *Translation* above as in 2 Kgs 25:16.

20.f-f. LXX lacks "all these articles."

21.a. 2 Kgs 25:17 lacks "the pillar."

21.b. LXX has "thirty-five cubits" as in 2 Chr 3:15.

21.c. *Translation* above follows Q and 2 Kgs; K has "its height."

21.d-d. Lacking in 2 Kgs 25:17.

21.e. LXX has "round about" instead of "hollow."

22.a. 2 Kgs 25:17 lacks "one."

22.b. 2 Kgs 25:17 reads "three cubits."

22.c-c. The phrase "with pomegranates" seems out of place. 2 Kgs 25:17 has "with lattice work"; LXX offers a much clearer option, "eight pomegranates to the cubit for the twelve cubits."

23.a. This verse does not appear in 2 Kgs 25.

23.b. The versions translate this word in various ways; Syr omits it entirely.

24.a. LXX does not include the names of the priests.

24.b. LXX has "keepers of the way."

25.a-a. Lacking in LXX.

25.b. 2 Kgs 25:19 has אוה, "he," instead of היה, "was"; the sense of the verse is unaffected.

25.c. 2 Kgs 25:19 has "five."

25.d. Syr has "who were left."

25.e. LXX lacks "commander."

27.a. 2 Kgs 25:21 has ויך, "and (he) smote"; both forms are found in MT as hiph impf 3ms of נכה.

27.b. LXX lacks "and killed them."

27.c-c. Lacking in LXX.

28.a. LXX and 2 Kgs 25 do not have vv 28–30.

28.b. Syr adds "of his reign."

29.a. Some MSS add "he sent into exile."

31.a. LXX has *Ιωακιμ*, "Joakim," perhaps referring to Jehoiakim, the Judean king who preceded Jehoiachin on the throne. 2 Chr 36:6 describes Nebuchadrezzar "binding" Jehoiakim in fetters to take him to Babylon. There may be a connection between that account and the LXX use of "Joiakim." "Jehoiachin" is the more appropriate reference.

31.b. LXX reads "twenty-fourth"; 2 Kgs 25:27 has "twenty-seventh."

31.c. Reading with LXX and 2 Kgs 25 instead of MT "in the year of his reign."

31.d. LXX[B] adds "and shaved him."

31.e. Lit. "house of confinement"; cf. 37:4. In both verses the spelling of the word is uncertain.

32.a. Including the article as do Q, LXX, 2 Kgs 25:28.

34.a-a. 2 Kgs 25:30 has "the king."

34.b-b. Lacking in a few MSS and 2 Kgs 25:30.

34.c-c. Lacking in LXX.

Form/Structure/Setting

The final chapter of the book of Jeremiah presents a number of dilemmas for the interpreter. First, the content of the chapter is virtually a repetition of material in 2 Kgs 25, some of which appears as well in Jer 39. Why does the book end in this manner? In particular, why the use of what seems obviously to be borrowed material rather than a summarized version that could have been freshly written?

A second dilemma is related to the structural distinctions between the Greek and Hebrew texts of Jeremiah. Following the Greek order of the book, Jer 52 immediately follows the word to Baruch in Jer 45 of the MT. MT itself has the oracles against the nations dividing the narrative material that relates the fall of Jerusalem and associated events from the final chapter. Is there any interpretive significance in the respective ordering of material?

A third matter is the absence of any reference to the prophet Jeremiah in the chapter. This, however, is not the first such instance. There are notable sections of the narrative material in chaps. 37–44 that make no mention of the prophet.

It is possible that this concluding chapter serves a purpose similar to that of the earlier passages.

In response to the first dilemma noted above, the use of narrative material from the Deuteronomistic History is not limited to Jeremiah. The book of Isaiah also contains a large block of material "lifted" from 2 Kings (18:13–20:19). What is distinct about the use of material from Kings in Jeremiah is that the prophet Jeremiah is not referred to in that material. Isaiah is a prominent actor in the material from 2 Kings that is repeated in Isa 36–39.

It has been argued that the use of historical material to close a prophetic scroll is a pattern within the prophetic tradition (see Holladay, 2:439). That seems to be a rather tenuous conclusion to defend since the two texts mentioned are the only examples of the pattern. The more persuasive argument seems to be the editorial effectiveness of the historical summary of Jerusalem's fall as an indication of the fulfillment of Jeremiah's message. Further, the final section of Jer 52 provides a word of hope that may also be significant as part of the larger Jeremianic message. While it is no more than conjecture, the choice of borrowing an existing account of Jerusalem's fall may well provide more "convincing" evidence of prophetic fulfillment than that produced by an editorial summary.

The structural distinctions between the Hebrew and Greek text traditions resist any simple explanation. Perhaps the most cogent explanation addresses the entire text of the book of Jeremiah. The explanation that this is an entirely different text tradition seems to make sense. There are no obvious interpretive objectives that are served better or worse by one order or the other.

Jeremiah's absence in Jer 52 may be somewhat curious in an appendix to the book of Jeremiah, but no more so than the absence of the prophet in other contexts of the book where his presence would be even more expected (the slaughter at Mizpah, for example, described in Jer 41). The use of information from sources independent of the book of Jeremiah provides one obvious explanation. While Jeremiah is not a character in the events described, the inclusion of the material in Jer 52 as well as that in 40:7–41:18 reinforces the validity of the prophet's word. In the case of Jer 52, the final passage of the book adds a dimension of hope for the exiled community to the complete lack of hope for the community in Judah. On more than one occasion, this dual emphasis appears to be an important aspect of Jeremiah's message.

Comment

1 When Jehoiachin was exiled to Babylon, Zedekiah began to reign in Jerusalem in his stead. Zedekiah was the throne name for Mattaniah and means literally "Yahweh is my righteousness." There is some difficulty in deciphering kinship relation as indicated by various Hebrew terms. Zedekiah is traditionally assumed to be Jehoiachin's uncle, a younger brother to Jehoiakim, though he is referred to in 2 Chr 36:10 as Jehoiachin's brother. The Hebrew term in 2 Chr 36 may be understood in the broader sense of kinsman.

There is some ambiguity in the role of Zedekiah. This verse would indicate that he became king in Judah. On the other hand, Jehoiachin is referred to as king in 2 Kgs 25:27. It may well have served the purposes of the Babylonians to use the ambiguity of two "kings" to their own advantage. In any case, the royal person in Jerusalem was Zedekiah.

2 The common negative judgment by the Deuteronomist against the monarchs of Judah and Israel is assigned to Zedekiah. (See the discussion of Zedekiah in the commentary material on Jer 37–39.) The litmus test applied allows for little margin of error. A king was either good or bad. That is illustrated here in the linkage made between the evil of Zedekiah and that of Jehoiakim. Clearly, Zedekiah was far more open to the words and actions of Jeremiah than Jehoiakim had been. That does not alter the evaluation of his reign as "evil." It is also consistent with the negative judgment upon the Judean community.

3 The judgment against Zedekiah also provides a foundation for the destruction of Jerusalem and Judah by the Babylonian forces. Zedekiah's rebellion against Babylon is interpreted in v 3 as an act that exacerbated what was already a time of trouble. The sin of Jerusalem and Judah had resulted in the "anger" of Yahweh being directed against them. Instead of providing a remedy, Zedekiah further sealed the fate of his people by his rebellion. It was not just a rebellion against Babylon but a rebellion against Yahweh as well.

4 The siege of Jerusalem began approximately early January 588 B.C., though the dating of key events during the last stages of Judah's existence is notoriously difficult (see A. R. Green, *JBL* 101 [1982] 57–73]. The precise nature of the "siegeworks" referred to cannot be determined with any certainty. Holladay (2:440) suggests the term used indicates some form of rampart built against the walls of the city (see also Thompson's reference to Assyrian reliefs for some idea of what may have been involved, 774). Carroll (859–60) points out that Nebuchadrezzar himself likely never physically participated in the siege but remained in his headquarters at Riblah (see v 9).

5–6 The duration of the siege was a little over eighteen months. By that time, food supplies were exhausted and the circumstances of the populace, which had no doubt already been desperate, became even more so. A siege of the sort described here brought incredible suffering upon the besieged population. Death from disease and starvation in many cases would involve greater numbers than casualties from any military action. Ezekiel's vision of the siege of Jerusalem in Ezek 5 includes a reference to cannibalism, probably not uncommon in a time of siege when all sources of food are exhausted. "People of the land" is understood here as the general population of the city, including any persons who may have entered the city for protection at the time of the Babylonian incursion. At times, this phrase refers to those in the lower stratum of society. While that is possible here, the fact that the lack of food noted led to the dramatic end of the siege suggests the scarcity affected the entire city and not just the poorest segment (see Holladay, 2:440; Rudolph, 276).

7 The different readings in Jeremiah and 2 Kings may be of some importance in this verse. 2 Kgs 25:4 seems to present a breach from the outside by the Babylonian soldiers, while the verse in Jeremiah indicates the breach may well have been caused by those fleeing the city. The location at which the Judean soldiers fled the city does not correspond with any known gate (see Thompson, 774–75; Carroll, 860), though the reference to Zedekiah's attempted escape in Jer 39:4 refers specifically to a gate.

Once outside the city, Zedekiah and those fleeing with him headed in the direction of the Arabah, in this case a plain west of the Jordan near Jericho (note that v 8 describes the capture of Zedekiah at this location, translated in v 8 above as the Jericho Flats, following T. R. Hobbs [2 Kings, 357]). How Zedekiah and the others were able to elude the Babylonian forces besieging (and by now attacking) Jerusalem is not clear, though Thompson (775) suggests that local knowledge such as that which Zedekiah would have possessed would make such an escape feasible.

8–9 The Babylonian forces pursued Zedekiah and those with him, eventually overtaking them near Jericho. With the arrival of the Babylonians, those with Zedekiah deserted him. Zedekiah was taken to Nebuchadrezzar at his headquarters in Riblah, where his fate was decided by the Babylonian king.

10–11 Nebuchadrezzar meted out severe punishment to the Judean rebels. Zedekiah was forced to watch the "butchering" of his own sons as well as a similar fate assigned to the princes of Judah. In these actions, Nebuchadrezzar was following a rather standard pattern exercised by suzerains against those who chose to challenge authority: dramatic reprisal that served to dissuade other vassals from similar actions.

The final act of Nebuchadrezzar was against Zedekiah personally. The Judean king was blinded and sent away to Babylon where he was to remain a prisoner until his death. This passage describes the haunting picture of Zedekiah witnessing the execution of his sons—his last visual image before his blinding.

12–14 Approximately a month after the entrance of Babylonian forces into Jerusalem, Nebuzaradan, one of Nebuchadrezzar's commanders, supervised the systematic destruction of key parts of the city. The people of Judah had been guilty of the unthinkable, rebellion against their Babylonian suzerain, and thus suffered the consequences of their foolishness.

All of the major structures of Jerusalem were destroyed. The temple was burned along with the royal palace. In addition, the walls of the city were pulled down by Babylonian troops. The city was left in ruins.

15–16 Of the survivors in the city, a significant number were sent into exile in Babylon. The group included some of the poor, artisans who had not been included in the earlier deportation (597 B.C.), and those who had deserted to the Babylonians during the siege. Some agricultural labor (the vinedressers and plowmen are explicitly named) was left behind, perhaps to care for the needs of the occupying Babylonian forces, though Holladay (2:441) suggests the possibility of agricultural products for export, products that would be produced by the efforts of the laborers mentioned here.

17–23 Vv 17–23 describe the systematic pillage of the temple. Portions of the description raise questions in light of the earlier looting of the temple in 597. Jer 27:16 alludes to the temple vessels, which had been taken into Babylon at the time of the first deportation (see also 2 Kgs 24:13). This would mean that either the vessels had been replaced (as Thompson, 778) or that the looting of 597 was less than complete.

Holladay (2:441) notes that Nebuchadrezzar would not have left much of value in the temple following the Babylonian victory in 597. Carroll (866) chooses not to dwell on the historical dilemma involved in the explanation of the vessels. Instead, he properly emphasizes the theological focus on the judgment of Yahweh that the loss of such vessels implied.

Vv 17–19 seem to imply that at least some of the sacred articles were melted down for their value as precious metal. It is not clear whether this was done for most of the items or for only some of them. The phrase at the end of v 19, "what was gold as gold, what was silver as silver," suggests more concern with the value of the metal than with the value of the objects themselves. Careful description of the designs of the capitals of the pillars (vv 22–23) may mean that the artistic value of those items was noted, though this is only a speculative conclusion.

24–27 Key officials who remained in the city after its capture were treated in the same harsh manner as those who tried to escape with Zedekiah. Temple officials were obviously judged to be part of the rebellion. Seraiah, the chief priest, is presumably the individual referred to in 1 Chr 6:14, a grandson of Hilkiah. The "keepers of the threshold" apparently referred to priests assigned special responsibility over particular temple entrances (see G. Henton Davies, *IDB* 4:636).

V 25 includes a number of military and civic officials in the round-up supervised by Nebuzaradan. In addition to key advisors and a military overseer, sixty men identified with the "people of the land" were taken. It is very doubtful that harsh action would have been taken against the poorest segment of Jerusalem society; thus this is likely a different use of the phrase. Carroll suggests that "landed gentry" may be the best understanding of "people of the land" here, though he notes the ambiguity of the phrase (Carroll, 867; also Holladay, 2:443). "Landed gentry" may be as good a description as any in light of the context (see also *Comment* on v 6 above).

Vv 26 and 27 matter-of-factly describe the execution of this group of officials at Riblah. Nebuchadrezzar brutally punished those he deemed part of Judah's rebellion. Many who escaped death by execution faced the hardship of exile to Babylon. The final portion of v 27 may be intended as a parallel to v 15, or it may include additional persons who became part of the exiled populace. (The possible redundancy of this part of v 27 is supported by its absence in the LXX.)

28–30 These verses provide the numbers of persons exiled by Nebuchadrezzar from Judah in three different deportations. These verses do not appear in 2 Kgs 25. Likewise, 2 Kgs 25:22–26 is not paralleled in Jer 52. The absence of 2 Kgs 25:22–26 may be explained by the detailed account of Gedaliah's actions and his fate provided in a form much expanded from 2 Kgs 25 in Jer 40–41. Jer 40:7–9 is a very close parallel to 2 Kgs 25:23–24; 41:1–3 closely parallels 2 Kgs 25:25. The remaining material in Jer 40–41 represents an expansion of the account of events surrounding Gedaliah as recorded in 2 Kgs 25 (see the commentary on Jer 40 and 41 above).

As noted above (*Comment* on v 4), specific dates for specific events are difficult to determine. The same may be said for the use of numbers such as those listed in these verses to indicate the total of deportees. There is a discrepancy between the report of numbers in 2 Kgs 24:14, 16 and here for the deportees of the first exile. Montgomery (*Kings*, 555–56) argues that the two accounts differ because Jer 52 gives numbers of men only, while 2 Kgs 24:14, 16 includes women and children. This explanation is challenged by Holladay (2:443), who attributes the difference in number to inflation by later redactors. Carroll (869) offers what is probably the best response to the discrepancy; that is, it is to be accepted as is without an attempt to harmonize the different numbers (contra Rudolph, 281).

The first two deportations noted refer to two well-known episodes in Judah's history. The specific dates may be elusive, but extensive information surrounding the events themselves is to be found in the Bible. The third deportation is not so easily explained.

The traditional explanation identifies the third deportation of Jer 52:30 with the assassination of Gedaliah and Babylon's response to it. The key issue has to do with the time lag between the fall of Jerusalem and the assassination. Was Gedaliah assassinated shortly after the fall of the city (as Holladay, 2:296, 443), or did some years pass before he was killed by Ishmael? The context of Jer 40 would seem to indicate a short span of time between Jerusalem's fall and Gedaliah's death. On the other hand, agricultural prosperity is described in Jer 40:10, which would not seem likely soon after a major invasion with its accompanying destruction. If one assumes, as does Carroll (705), that the picture of prosperity in Jer 40 is more theologically than historically oriented, it becomes less a consideration in dating the assassination of Gedaliah.

One of the more novel attempts at addressing the complexity involved with the deportations referred to in vv 28–30 is that of Green (*JBL* 101 [1982] 66). He suggests that the deportations listed in Jer 52 should be treated as distinct from the general deportations that followed military action against Jerusalem in 597 and 587 B.C. If these are understood as relatively minor deportations (as opposed to much larger numbers that would be assumed of forced exile immediately following a catastrophic defeat), then the dating discrepancies can be resolved.

The summary statement of v 30 would seem to raise problems for Green's hypothesis. The more obvious reason for the mention of the numbers noted in vv 28–30 would be to summarize the effects of exile upon the inhabitants of Judah. While the numbers are smaller than would perhaps be anticipated, that does not necessarily support Green's conclusions any more than other options.

The effect of vv 28–30 is to focus attention on the various deportations endured by the inhabitants of Judah (including the third deportation, for which there is no other evidence). This passage also prepares the way for the final passage in the book of Jeremiah, a passage that provides hope from an unexpected quarter.

31–34 V 31 records the release of the exiled Judean king Jehoiachin from prison in approximately 560 B.C. Vv 31–34 are almost a verbatim repetition of 2 Kgs 25:27–30.

No extrabiblical evidence exists to confirm the release of Jehoiachin. The only reference that provides what could be interpreted as a positive word about Jehoiachin's treatment in Babylon is that in Babylonian cuneiform tablets indicating provisions made for Jehoiachin and his sons during their captivity (*ANET*, 308; note the reference to provisions in v 34).

Evil-merodach is Akkadian Amel-Marduk (562–560 B.C.), "son of Marduk," the son of Nebuchadrezzar who succeeded him on the throne. Josephus cites Berosus concerning Amel-Marduk as one who "governed public affairs after an illegal and impure manner" (Jos., *Ag. Ap.* 1.20). Amel-Marduk was assassinated by Nergal-shar-uṣur (Nergal-sharezer of Jer 39:3?) after a reign of only two years.

Carroll (871) calls attention to the symmetry between the references to Zedekiah and Jehoiachin in the final chapter of Jeremiah. One could hardly imagine more harsh treatment than that received by Zedekiah and his sons from the Babylonians. Jehoiachin, by contrast, is portrayed as well treated, along with his sons. The result is a word of hope for the future, if somewhat muted.

According to these final verses of the book of Jeremiah, Jehoiachin and his sons were well treated "all the days of his life." Context suggests that the reference refers to all the days of Jehoiachin's life, though, if applied to Amel-Marduk, the meaning is much more enigmatic (see Rudolph, 282; Holladay, 2:443).

The portion of this final passage that may offer the greatest sense of hope is the elevation of Jehoiachin to a "seat" or "throne" higher than that of other subordinate kings in the Babylonian domain. This action on Jehoiachin's behalf may be the strongest argument supporting the classification of these verses as a word of hope (see Levenson, *JBL* 103 [1984] 353–61).

Explanation

The book of Jeremiah concludes in such a way as to provide a puzzle for readers that may not be easily solved. Why does the book end with what amounts to a repetition of the final chapter of 2 Kings (with only minor alterations)?

The only other example of a text from the Deuteronomistic History used in a prophetic book occurs in Isa 36–39. Do the two texts serve a similar purpose for Isaiah and Jeremiah?

The proposal offered here is that there may indeed be a common purpose for the borrowed texts in Isaiah and Jeremiah, though the evidence is too scant to draw ironclad conclusions. One common purpose that would apply to both Isaiah and Jeremiah would be the confirmation offered by an account that comes from a source other than the prophet. The historiography utilized confirms the message of the prophet already presented in the book. That applies to both texts. Jeremiah's message concerning the judgment to come upon Jerusalem and Judah is certainly supported by the description of Jerusalem's capture and the horrendous circumstances that accompanied the fall of the city. The inclusion of material from 2 Kgs 18–20 serves much the same purpose for Isaiah.

Whether a word of hope can be perceived for both Isaiah and Jeremiah is more problematic. It is not difficult to perceive the end of Jeremiah as a word of hope because of the improved status of Jehoiachin. Isaiah 39, however, portends calamity, even the exile to Babylon. The one potential positive is the response of Hezekiah himself, that peace and security would last all his days.

Jer 52 combines devastation with a glimmer of hope for the future. The description of Jerusalem's destruction and of the fate of her citizens leaves no doubt about the finality of Jeremiah's message. All hope vested in Judah and her citizens is demonstrated to be false hope. Consistent with texts such as Jer 44, any vision of hope for Judah must be directed away from the geographic locale of Judah. As with Ezekiel, the remaining hope for the restoration of the Jewish nation lay with that remnant people residing in Babylon.

The glimmer of hope represented by the leniency shown Jehoiachin preserves that hope still associated with monarchy. As with the reference to Amel-Marduk, this idea also offers some indication of the date of at least one stage of the shaping of Jeremiah. Hope in Jeremiah is not yet completely divorced from kingship. The time does come in the post-exilic period when that is no longer true. Jer 52, though, like Haggai and Zechariah, leaves open the possibility of God at work through a king.

Index of Authors Cited

Index of Principal Subjects

Index of Biblical Texts

A. Old Testament

Reference	Pages
31:28	27
32:6	114
32:8–9	113
32:10	122
34:8	115
34:10	180

Joshua

Reference	Pages
1:13	108
1:15	108
6:24	77
7:7	148
7:19	21
7:25	6
9:25	25
11:22	298, 301
12:7	153
13–19	89
13:15–17	313
13:17	311, 316
13:19	318
13:26	311
13:27	313
15:1–12	128
15:8	138
18–19	17
18–22	15
18:1	17, 18, 22
18:25	117
19:51	16, 17, 18
20:8	316
21:1–3	153
21:36	316
21:39	318
22	17
22:4	108
22:12	17
22:19	17
22:29	17
24:13	71
24:17	188
24:25	188
LXX 24:1	17
LXX 25	17

Judges

Reference	Pages
1:7	74
2:13	267
3:8	367
3:16	287
4–5	293
5:20	367
6:8	188
9:45	313
10:6	267
11:4–33	322, 324
11:24	313, 324
11:34	109
11:35	148
11:37–38	109
18:30–31	17
19:23–24	78
20:1	22
20:6	78
20:10	78
21	15
21:5	20
21:19–21	17

Ruth

Reference	Pages
1:11	120
4	88, 153
4:1–4	155
4:1–12	23
4:9	27
4:11	27, 109

1 Samuel

Reference	Pages
1–4	15
1:3	17
1:9	18
1:24	18
2	18
2:4	343
2:12–17	17
2:27–36	18
2:28	17
3:3	17, 18
3:11–14	18
3:15–18	13
3:17–18	27
4:21	17, 18
5:3	27
6:19	74
6:21–7:2	30
7:4	267
10:2	119
10:9	160
10:25	103
11:1–11	323
12:10	267
14:15	93
14:24–46	20, 21
14:26–46	30
14:43	21
14:44	6
14:45	25
15:8	287
15:29	14
15:35	14
16:12	93
18:6	109
21:15	78
22:6	119
22:6–19	20, 21
22:13	21
22:18–19	31
23:3	174
27:7	43
27:12	50

2 Samuel

Reference	Pages
1:21	290
2:8–11	49
3:16	240
3:28–29	26
4:8	30
5:5	113
5:8	113
6	30
7:6	18
7:11–16	173
7:12	104, 120
7:14	114
7:22–24	148
8:2	356
8:7	322
10	21
12:9	26
12:13	20
12:14	78
13:12	30
14:7	30
14:14	20
14:32	30
15:2	23
19:24	26
19:38	247
20:14	22
20:19	30
21:1	26
22:3	311
23:1–7	173
23:8–9	30
23:38	138
24:5	318
24:12	179
24:15	74
24:16	3
24:24	154

1 Kings

Reference	Pages
1:10	314
1:27	314
1:36	54
1:46	314
1:51	31
2:4	174
2:8	31
2:12	314
2:26	30
2:36–46	20, 21
2:43	21
3:9	160
3:12	160
5	49
5:10	339
5:11	329
6:11	12
6:38	104
7:12	12
7:13–14	53
7:13–47	49, 53
7:2	294
7:23	126
7:27	42, 376
7:51	49
8:2	3, 22
8:23–53	148
8:25	174
8:29–30	158
9:5	174
10:9	174
10:16	290
10:24	160
11	17
11:5	267
11:7	324
11:29–31	54
11:40	30, 31
12:4	51
12:6	27
12:8	27
12:13	27
13:30	92
14	331
14:8	49
14:27–28	23
15:1	12
15:9	12
15:13	138, 331
15:16–22	241
15:33	12
18:3–4	9
18:13	9
18:28	319

B. New Testament

C. Apocrypha

D. Rabbinic and Mishnaic Materials

Index of Key Hebrew Words